NOTES ON THE GREEK TEXT OF EXODUS

SOCIETY OF BIBLICAL LITERATURE
SEPTUAGINT AND COGNATE STUDIES SERIES

Edited by
Claude E. Cox

Editorial Advisory Committee

N. Fernández Marcos, Madrid
M. Mulder, Leiden
I. Soisalon - Soininen, Helsinki
E. Tov, Jerusalem

Number 30

NOTES ON THE GREEK TEXT OF EXODUS

John William Wevers

NOTES ON THE GREEK TEXT OF EXODUS

John William Wevers

Scholars Press
Atlanta, Georgia

NOTES ON THE GREEK TEXT OF EXODUS

John William Wevers

Library of Congress Cataloging-in-Publication Data

Wevers, John William
    Notes on the Greek text of Exodus / John William Wevers.
    p. cm. -- (Septuagint and cognate studies series / Society of
    Biblical Literature ; no. 30)
    Includes bibliographical references.
    ISBN 1-55540-453-7 (alk. paper). -- ISBN 1-55540-454-5 (pbk. :
    alk. paper)
    1. Bible. OT. Exodus. Greek--Versions--Septuagint. 2. Bible.
O.T. Exodus--Translating. I. Title. II. Series.: Septuagint and
cognate studies series. : no. 30.
BS1244.G7W48 1990
                                             90-32274
                                           CIP

Printed in the United States of America
on acid-free paper

This book is dedicated to ROBERT HANHART, loyal friend, learned colleague, and dedicated scholar, for a quarter century of close friendship, for his genuine scholarship, and for an intimately shared colleageal devotion to the Göttingen Septuaginta, on the occasion of his formal retirement as Leiter des Septuaginta-Unternehmens in Göttingen, July, 1990.

INTRODUCTORY STATEMENT

In the course of preparing the Göttingen edition of Exodus a voluminous body of notes on the text and its interpretation of the Hebrew was accumulated. With the completion of the Exodus volumes (edition as well as The Text History) the Pentateuch is finished. In casting about for a further project I felt constrained to reorder the notes I had made, and once again go through the text and write up in a systematic way some of these notes. It was suggested to me by one of my students that others might find some of my analyses helpful, and the volume here presented is the result.

1. The most obvious characteristic of Exod is that it is a translation document. I have written elsewhere on the difficulties faced by translators confronted with the problem of rendering Hebrew into Greek,[1] but it would not be amiss to recapitulate some of these.

As a translation document the LXX cannot present a one to one correspondence to its parent text. Hebrew as a Semitic language has a quite different coding system from the Indo-European Greek. This is obvious at all levels of language.

1.1. At the graphemic level Hebrew uses 22 signs to represent consonantal phonemes, but even this it did imperfectly. Thus it could not distinguish between šin and śin, or between ᶜain and ġain or between ḥeth and Ḥeth. Vowels were not indicated at all except for the sporadic use of the vowel letters, waw, yodh and final hē. Hellenistic Greek used 24 signs of which only 17 represented consonants, and seven, vowels. Greek differed considerably from the Hebrew phonemic system. Greek had no laryngeals and only two sibilants, whereas Hebrew had four laryngeals and five sibilants. Accordingly when the translator had to transcribe a Hebrew word such as a proper noun the result was perforce inexact.

1.2. This inexact correspondence becomes even more obvious at the morphological level. In both systems the two word classes, nouns and verbs,

---

1. The Use of Versions for Text Criticism: The Septuagint, La Septuaginta en la Investigacion Contemporanea (V Congreso de la IOSCS), editado por Natalio Fernández Marcos (Madrid, 1985.), pp.15ff.

constitute the major unlimited classes, but their inflections mark quite different distinctions.

1.2.1. The nominal system. Hebrew has two classes of nouns usually designated as masculine and feminine. These two classes inflect for 1) number: singular and plural. Hebrew also retains a dual but its use is limited in the main to common units of time (hours, days, months, and years), and parts of the body (eyes, ears, nostrils, lips, etc.). 2) definiteness. This can be marked by the presence of a prefixed article. Indefiniteness can only be inferred from its absence. 3) state: bound versus free forms.

1.2.2. Greek on the other hand inflects for three genders: masculine, feminine and neuter. It also uses both a definite and an indefinite article inflected for number, gender and case. Greek also inflects for five cases (nominative, genitive, dative, accusative, vocative). Pronouns also inflect for three genders, two numbers and five cases.

1.2.3.1. Greek recoding of the Hebrew categories was handled in various ways. Gender had to be disregarded altogether, since there simply is no correspondence; in fact even biological gender did not fit. There is no way in which a two gender system of Hebrew can be represented in the three gender system of Greek. The two are wholly different, and no conclusions can be drawn here whatsoever.

1.2.3.2. Number is on the face of it the easiest category to deal with since both systems have singular and plural. The Greek of LXX no longer used the dual, and the few duals that Hebrew does use were changed into the plural; when duality was important the translator would add the word for "two." Nonetheless LXX did not unthinkingly equate its categories with those of the parent text. Both languages use collective nouns, but the two have different collectives. E.g. the Hebrew words for heart, לבב, לב, can be collective or individual, but are almost always collective in MT. In fact, the plural form occurs only seven times (though an eighth problematic one does exist), whereas the singular occurs 781 times. In other words in Hebrew people have a heart, but in Greek they have hearts. The translators commonly adapt to the sense rather than to the form.

But even when Hebrew has a concrete noun LXX does not necessarily render the number of the Hebrew in a literal way. Thus the word פתח only occurs in the singular in Exodus, but Exod disregards this; sometimes the singular, but sometimes the plural, is used.

1.2.3.3. Definiteness differs in the systems as well. Both have definite articles, but Greek also has an indefinite article, which is, however, only rarely used in LXX. Both systems thus can show lack of definiteness by an unarticulated noun. Theoretically then Greek should be able to reproduce the system of the Hebrew, but this is not the case. The use of the article is highly idiomatic for both languages, and the presence or absence of the article in Greek by no means automatically indicates this for its parent Hebrew. Articulation as learners of English as a Second Language soon discover to their consternation is extremely complicated and differs from language to language. In fact only when articulation in the target language seems to be unnatural may this be cited as evidence for a parent Hebrew text. Patterns of usage may also differ from translator to translator, and these must be studied carefully for each translator's work.

1.2.3.4.*State.* A bound phrase in Hebrew must be ordered as possessed - possessor with the first word always unarticulated; furthermore the phrase has a single phrase accent, the first word being vocalized as lacking a primary word accent. Thus "God's word" becomes דבר האלהים in Hebrew. Only the free element, "God," can take the article, whereas the bound element, "word of," is unarticulated. Greek would normally render the possessor by a genitive, i.e. τοῦ θεοῦ. So Hebrew has "word-of the God," but Greek inflects both nouns for case with the second one in the genitive, and both nouns articulated, i.e. "the word of the God." When a translator imitates the parent text by leaving the first word unarticulated the result is unidiomatic, Hebraic, uncouth Greek.

1.2.3.5. In fact, Greek must inflect for case over against Hebrew which has no case inflection at all. At times this means that Greek must make distinctions which are not present in Hebrew. Suppose the Hebrew text has the phrase על השלחן. The translator would probably use the preposition ἐπί for על, but is then faced with the fact that this preposition can govern the genitive, dative or accusative, and he must make a choice. If he chooses the genitive it answers the question of "where" or "whither"; with the dative it strictly denotes location, and with the accusative some motion is necessarily implied such as in the sense of "he placed it on the table."

1.3.1. The verbal system of the two codes also differs substantially. Hebrew has two inflections, a suffixal inflection called the perfect, and a prefixal one called imperfect. These terms are traditional and are often misleading. Suffice it to say that the suffixed form in isolation is usually past tense, whereas in context, i.e. with a coordinating conjunction prefixed, it is often future; on the other hand, the prefixal inflections operate in the opposite manner.

In other words if one wanted to say "and he arose and went and did," one would use the prefixal inflection throughout, but if one wanted to say "he will arise and go and do," one would start with the isolate prefixal form and continue with the suffixal forms since these are now contextual.

Actually the inflectional system is much more complex than the skeletal outline given here. In fact, Hebrew can, though it seldom does, express a potential mood in the prefixal inflection as well.

1.3.1.1. The Hebrew verb inflects for singular and plural number, for three persons (1st, 2nd and 3rd), and inflects for gender in 2nd and 3rd persons only.

1.3.1.2. A Hebrew verbal root can be inflected in seven stems. These more or less resp. reflect a simple active, a simple medio-passive, a D (for duplicative) active, a D reflexive, a D passive, a causative active, and a causative medio-passive.

1.3.1.2.1. These stems also inflect for an imperative mood in the singular and plural as well as for masculine versus feminine. They also inflect for two infinitives and a participle.

1.3.2.1. Greek inflects for seven aspects or tenses. These are present, imperfect (a past continuous), future, aorist, perfect, pluperfect and future perfect.

1.3.2.2. Greek also has three voices: active, middle (or reflexive) and passive. It can distinguish four moods: indicative, subjunctive, optative and imperative. It also has an infinitive and a participle.

1.3.2.3. The Greek verb does not inflect for gender, but it does distinguish number as singular versus plural as well as among three persons:

1st, 2nd and 3rd.

1.4.1. Comparison of the two verbal systems shows them to be incongruent at many points. They are congruent in the finite inflections for number and person but not for gender. If one wanted to contrast "and he said" with "and she said" Hebrew would simply use ויאמר and ותאמר resp. In English this is done by means of a pronoun "he" vs "she," which theoretically would also be possible in Greek but not overly idiomatic. The translators normally have used a neat device by using the inflected nominative singular definite article, i.e. ὁ δὲ εἶπεν vs ἡ δὲ εἶπεν. Greek would then use the neuter article τὸ δὲ εἶπεν if the antecedent were a neuter noun as e.g. τὸ παιδίον "child."

1.4.2. For the seven stems of a Hebrew root the three types: simple, duplicative and causative, can only be distinguished lexically. Greek does have three voices, and can inflect for the active, middle as well as passive. For some tenses the last two coalesce into a medio-passive inflection.

1.4.3. Hebrew has very little in the way of potential moods but is basically paratactic, i.e. it tends to string along clauses by means of coordinating conjunctions. It does have a few subordinating particles but it uses them sparingly. Such relations as result, purpose, concession, temporality, etc. are commonly strung along with indicatives all at the same level of discourse.

Greek can do this as well, and the LXX translators often do, but parataxis in ordinary Greek means something quite different. So when Greek chooses a paratactic indicative construction, it does not opt for the potential or subordinate constructions, and thereby also conveys a message, a message of its Hebrew background.

1.4.4. *Aspect/tense.* Hebrew's two inflections must be distributed among seven aspects in Greek. The past of narration is most commonly rendered by the aorist, but an imperfect may obtain if a process is indicated; it could also be translated by one of the three perfect tenses, though admittedly the future perfect is rare indeed. Exod often shows keen exegetical insight in its use of tenses, making distinctions which Hebrew cannot make, but which show shrewd understanding of what the Hebrew probably intended.

On the other hand the isolate imperfect of Hebrew is usually translated by the future, or possibly the future perfect, and sometimes even the present.

1.4.5. The Greek imperative can to a great extent render the Hebrew imperative adequately, even though it cannot make gender distinctions. Usually the context leaves no doubt as to the addressee. Greek also has a singular and plural 3rd person imperative which LXX uses occasionally to render a prefix verb in parataxis so as to show desired action.

1.4.6. The Hebrew participle is often used as a predicate in a nominal clause, particularly with pronominal subjects, as e.g. אֲנִי אוֹמֵר. This pattern is normally rendered in Exod by pronoun + present tense verb, i.e. ἐγὼ λέγω, "as for me, I say."

1.4.7.1. Hebrew throughout has two infinitives, one bound and one free. The bound infinitive, as its name implies, cannot occur as an isolate. It often occurs either as a purposive or a complementary infinitive usually with the marker "to" prefixed, e.g. לִקְרֹא "to call." Greek easily translates this literally by an infinitive either with or without articulation.

The bound infinitive is characteristically also used as the nucleus of a prepositional phrase such as לְשׁוּבוֹ, i.e. a preposition + infinitive + pronominal suffix, "in his returning," or more idiomatically "when he returns/ returned/shall return." Since infinitives are tenseless only the context can determine how such a phrase should be translated.

In Greek temporal clauses of various types obtain; these would state tense as well as mood exactly; thus the translator would have to make an exegetical decision. But LXX often avoids this by imitating the Hebrew exactly by an ἐν τῷ ἐπιστρεφεῖν αὐτόν construction, which is much better Hebrew than Greek; the construction is not impossible Greek, but it is not overly idiomatic, and temporal clauses make for much better Greek.

1.4.7.2. The free infinitive has no counterpart in Greek whatsoever. It is a free form in distinction from the bound one which is always bound to some other morph, preposition, and/or subject pronominal suffix, or a verb. The free infinitive has no such restrictions and merely sets forth the verbal idea.

The free infinitive can have one of four contexts. 1) It can appear by itself as an isolate form: זכור את יום השבת, i.e. one puts out the verbal idea: "remember!" This is as in English equal to an imperative: "remember the Sabbath day." It is then quite correctly rendered in Exod 20 by μνήσθητι, a singular, 2nd person imperative. 2) contextually, i.e. with *waw* before it. The free infinitive cannot inflect; it has no number, person, aspect/ tense or mood, all of which must be taken from the context. All the inflections of the contextual verb are then transferred as well to the infinitive. E.g. were וזכור preceded by a 3rd masculine singular perfect verb such as דבר, it would mean "he spoke and he remembered." In other words the infinitive would also be understood as 3rd masculine singular perfect. 3) The infinitive may follow its cognate finite verb. This usage occurs only infrequently but it serves to stress the continuity of the verbal idea: e.g. "you will keep on returning." 4) Most commonly the infinitive occurs immediately before its cognate finite verb. Thus one finds מות תמות which serves to intensify the verbal idea: "You will really die."

Greek had a great deal of trouble with this common pattern. Since it seemed rather tautological Greek could omit the infinitive, simply saying "you will die." But more often it would attempt to render the infinitive in one of four other ways: a) by a cognate participle: "dying you will die." b) By a cognate noun in the dative: "by death you will die." c) by a noncognate but semantically related participle: "by perishing you will die." d) by a noncognate but related dative noun: "by demise you will die." Exod uses all five of these alternatives and the Notes will point these out.

1.4.8. It should be said that the above sketch is no more than a suggestive outline of some of the major characteristics of the nominal and verbal systems of the two systems. It would be pointless to try and compare some of the other classes, especially the limited classes of the two languages. But this should suffice to clarify how one can observe the LXX's manipulation of the target language to bring out what the source language is thought by the translator to intend, and this is what makes the books of the LXX so fascinating.

1.5. Already at 1.4.3. some statements were made concerning clause structure. It is precisely at the syntactic level that Hebrew syntax has exerted a major influence on the syntax of Exod as the Notes abundantly show. Its syntax is far more Hebraic than ordinary Greek composition would be, and the stringing along of clauses in paratactic fashion also characterizes many structures in Exod.

1.6. At the lexical level translation also encounters difficulties. Some Hebrew words simply had no counterpart in Greek, and such words as שבת "sabbath," שלמים "peace offerings," שקל "shekel," or הין "hin" forced the translator to be inventive with σάββατα, θυσία σωτηρίου, σίκλος and ἵν.

But even where Greek counterparts abound the semantic fields between corresponding lexemes of the two systems seldom have the same boundaries, and Exod uses various words to render individual Hebrew lexemes. The Notes will often give the reader such information.

2.0. I began these Notes with at least four presuppositions, ones that have evolved in the course of decades of working in LXX, more particularly with the text of the Pentateuch.

2.1. The first presupposition is that the translators were at work on a canonical text.[2] Theirs was a holy task, something not to be taken lightly. They were after all interpreting God's Torah, written in a language imperfectly understood by many Jews of the Alexandrian community, and rendered it into their common speech, the Hellenistic Greek spoken and understood in Alexandria. This meant that translation was not just a casual kind of work, but was a studied procedure. It meant that the translators pondered their task, tried to give their work an inner consistency. This can be seen again and again in their product. E.g., Exod 24 and 34 show mutual influence, and the translator of Exod B carefully examined Exod A, whereas the translator of chh.25--28 knew the Hebrew B account of chh.36--40 and was influenced by it. And as the Notes make clear, at times other books of the Pentateuch have left traces of their influence in Exod as well.

The translators realized that their product was itself God's word; it was declared canonical,[3] and presumably served as the synagogal Scriptures

2. A thesis which I illustrated from Exod in Transl.
3. According to Aristeas 308--311 the priests, elders and leaders of the Jewish community when they had heard the Greek Pentateuch read to them stated that it had been translated both καλῶς καὶ ὁσίως as well as throughout accurately - ἠκριβωμένως. Then they ordered accursed εἴ τις διασκευάσει προστιθεὶς ἢ μεταφέρων τι τὸ σύνολον τῶν γεγραμμένων ἢ ποιούμενος ἀφαίρεσιν, with which one might well compare the NT

in Alexandria.

2.2. The Notes are also based on the presupposition that the canonical text being translated was in the main much like the consonantal text of MT; in other words the extant textual tradition must be taken in deadly seriousness. The age of rampant retroversion, of wild emendations, is past. This is not to be disrespectful of the great scholars of yesteryears, of the nineteenth and early twentieth centuries, but rather to be distrustful of texts which are extant only in the minds of scholars eminent though they be.

This is not to suggest that the parent text which Exod had was in every respect the consonantal text of BHS, but rather that text criticism should be solidly based on evidence. We do have Qumran fragments of Exodus, as well as other ancient witnesses which must be carefully compared throughout, and there will be passages where the translator either had a different reading or misread his parent text, but it is suggested that one must begin with a prejudice towards the text that we actually have.

Furthermore it makes sense to suggest that the Hebrew text which the Jewish community of Alexandria had in the third century B.C. could not have been wildly different from MT. After all, it was canonical, it was divine law, God's instruction; it was special, and one approached it with reverence. Admittedly canon had not yet taken on its later coloration in which the form as well as the contents was inviolable, but it seems only fair to begin with the consonantal text of MT, and to accept change only after all other avenues of understanding have been explored.

2.3. A third presupposition is that the product of the Alexandrian translators was throughout sensible. Their translation may not have been perfect, but it made sense to them; they did not create nonsense, and when the modern reader is puzzled the fault must lie with him or her, not with the translator. It means that the student of LXX must try to understand what the translators meant rather than stand in arrogant judgment over their product. This means that one must at least try to explain difficulties, seeming contradictions and problems of language from their point of view rather than from our own rationalistic sense of logic and consistency.

---

affirmation in Apoc 22:18--19.

This is essentially what the modern reader of any ancient writing faces; one must bridge in our case over two millenia of time, transport ourselves to the Jewish community of the third B.C. century in Alexandria, i.e. to people who spoke Hellenistic Greek, a language which they knew much better than we do, to a culture quite foreign to our twentieth century western world. They did share our humanity, but not our culture, our way of thinking, or even our demand for logical consistency. On the other hand, they feared God above all else, were Jews of the diaspora, and so removed from the immediacy of Temple worship and priesthood as well as from the volatile politics of Palestine.

And so the Notes try to explain Exod from their point of view rather than ours; this brings us to the fourth and last presupposition.

2.4. The Greek Pentateuch is a humanistic document of great value for its own sake; this means that Exod is of real interest by itself even without reference to a parent text. It represents what Alexandrian Jewry of the third B.C. century thought their Hebrew Bible meant.

This Greek text, and not the Targums or the Mishnah, is the earliest exegetical source that we have for understanding the Pentateuch. As such it surely must be the first document to which one turns when trying to understand the Torah. The LXX may interpret its text incorrectly; it is not a perfect document, but it is far and away the earliest, the closest in time to the original authors.

A new appreciation for the LXX is long overdue. For far too long scholars have treated the LXX as a grabbag for emendations. Unfortunately only too many have treated the note *lege cum Graece* found again and again in the various editions of "the Kittel Bible," and by no means wholly absent from BHS either, as sacred lore, almost as a divine injunction to emend the text, i.e. as superior to the text itself. It is time to stop this nonsense, to go back to the LXX and read it for what it is, a humanistic document which should be pondered both for its own sake and for understanding the Hebrew text.

2.5. These then are the prejudices with which I began composing these Notes. They are precisely the ones which were confirmed by the time I finished them as well.

3.0. These Notes are intended primarily for the serious student of the Torah, rather than for the professional LXX scholar. They are meant to help those individuals who would like to make use of the Greek text in an intelligent way, but may feel at a loss how to proceed or how to understand the LXX over against MT. If at times what is said may seem elementary or overly tedious I can only apologize for it.

To that end the Notes deal principally with an analysis of the text itself rather than with a review of scholarly opinions; for this I do not apologize since it always seems better to go back to the text itself than to read about it. The text is far more important than what scholars say about it, and that is certainly true of these Notes as well.

The text commented on is not the text of Rahlfs but that of the Göttingen LXX. Rahlfs never thought of his text as anything but an interim offering, whereas the critical editions do yield the state of the art, and in the nature of the case are as complete in their review of the textual evidence as possible. The critical text is based on all the available help, the textual witnesses, and the usage of contemporary papyri; in short it constitutes a text as close to the original translation as possible as far as the editor's abilities extend. Unfortunately at the time of writing the volume has not yet appeared; it is at the compositors, but getting such volumes through press is a major task, and the difficult proof must be read and corrected a number of times.

4.0. Primary stress has been placed on the Greek text of Exodus, on how it was put together, and how the translator approached his task. His problem was how to put the message of the Hebrew parent text into a Greek mode which his synagogal readers and hearers would understand. To realize how he did this is to see how the Greek text is constructed, how the Greek code actually worked. The stress is thus placed throughout on the morphological, syntactic and lexical levels of discourse.

4.0.1. But Exod is a translation document; this means that a comparison must be made at every point between the Hebrew and the Greek. The Hebrew text compared is of course MT, for which see the discussion under 2.2. above. We do have some fragmentary Qumran texts for which see the edition; these were consulted as well. Other ancient texts which were compared at every step were Sam (the Samaritan Hebrew), the Tar (i.e. Onkelos as representing the Babylonian, and Neophyti as representing the Jerusalem Targumic traditions), as well as the Syriac Peshiṭta and the Latin Vulgata. These then along with LXX and MT constitute the ancient witnesses.

4.0.2. The emphasis in the Notes lies on what the translator did, not on how later users interpreted the text. Herein lies a major difference between these Notes and the Exodus volume in the series: La Bible d'Alexandrie.[4] These splendid volumes are ably researched but the stress is put not so much on the work of the translators as on the early exegesis of the Greek text. Much emphasis is placed on Philo, Josephus and the Church Fathers of the first five centuries, and their interpretations. I make no such references at all.

Nor do I offer a running translation of Exod, except for difficult passages, or where a contrast with MT is pointed out, i.e. where it seemed relevant to some point being made. The volume arrived after the Notes had been written, midway in the course of revising the manuscript, somewhat too late to make extensive use of its suggestions. It is a fine and learned work, and the serious student is urged to make use of it along with these Notes.

4.0.3. Another major difference between these Notes and the volume of my French colleagues is my use of the tradition. By tradition is meant the development of the text from the autographon as it left the translator (which at least in theory the critical text of Exod approximates) up to the time of Gutenberg in the fifteenth century. This tradition is presented in summary fashion in the large, or first apparatus of the Göttingen editions.

4.1. Attention to this tradition is indeed warranted, because that tradition constitutes the textual history of the LXX; it is part and parcel of LXX. That text underwent a complicated history of revisions which is reflected in the texts of the text families; it is then a living text which is summarized in the large apparatus of the edition. When the Fathers commented on the LXX it was part of that living tradition, and it seems to

---

4. La Bible d'Alexandrie. 2.L'Exode, par A. Le Boulluec et P. Sandevoir. Paris, 1989. I am most grateful to M. Sandevoir for sending me a copy of their work as soon as it appeared.

me important to view LXX from a double focus: the text as it was translated, and the text as a living organism which served as canon throughout the long history of Biblical interpretation. After all those who read and pondered the LXX did not have the autographon; they had copies, in fact, had copies of copies. It was the mss which readers had, not the original text. And these mss represent later developments of the text; all these mss constituted eclectic texts, based on a complicated and often untraceable textual genealogy. Many of these represent in their variant readings conscious revisions based on the Hebrew, especially the hex(aplaric) recension of Origen; others grew out of copyist errors. Reference is then made in the Notes to many such readings, variants subjectively chosen for their interest in showing a different understanding of the text or demonstrating how variant readings have developed, or simply for their popular support.

4.1.1. It would have made the Notes quite unusable had all the evidence for such variant traditions been recorded. The interested reader will find that information given in the first apparatus of the Göttingen edition. To identify such variant readings I have arbitrarily adopted a system of abbreviations which should suffice to identify the reading in the large apparatus if one so desires. I have largely disregarded scattered support and concentrated on support by textual families.

4.1.2. The following table details these families with their members; the numbers follow the Rahlfs catalogue.[5]

Textual witnesses as used in this work

O: G-58-72-376-426(to 20:1)-767 Arab Arm Syh
oI: 64-381-618-708
oII: 15-29-82-135-707

5. A. Rahlfs, Verzeichnis der griechischen Handschriften des Alten Testaments, für das Septuaginta-Unternehmen aufgestellt, MSU 2. Berlin, 1915. The Verzeichnis is being kept up-to-date by the Unternehmen and there are active plans for a revised edition.

C: 14-16-25-52-54(to 40:13)-57-73-77-78-126(to 25:5)-131-313-413-
   414-422-500-550-551-552-615-739-761

b: 19-108-118-314-537

d: 44-106-107-125-610

f:53-56-129-246-664

n: 54(from 40:13)-75-127(from 6:27)-458-628(to 13:1)

s: 30-85-127(to 6:26)-130(from 16:29)-321-343-344-346-730

t: 46(to 13:9)-74-76(from 28:39b)-84-134-370

x: 71-527(from 28:8)-619

y: 121-318-392-527(to 28:7)

z: 68-120-122-126(from 25:6)-128-407-628(from 13:2)-630

Uncial mss: A B F M

Unclassifiable Codices: 18 46(from 13:9) 55 59 76(to 28:39a) 130(to
   18:28) 319 416 424 426(from 20:1 508 509 646 799

Translations: Arab(ic), Arm(enian), Eth(iopic), Co(ptic) which
   includes Ach(mimic) Bo(hairic) Fa(yyumic) and Sa(hidic),
   La(= Vetus Latina). Pal(estinian-syriac), and Syh(=Syro-
   hexaplar)

4.1.3. A variant may be identified as a one, two or three family
variant. Thus a *b f s* reading means that the reading is supported by all or
most mss of the *b f* and *s* families; it may also have scattered support from

other mss or from the versions, but that is disregarded. When such readings are identified as e.g. a *b* reading this means that the reading has been judged to be a *b* family reading. But should more than three families support a reading it is simply called a popular reading, whereas if the support includes over half of all witnesses, i.e. of mss and versions, it is called a very popular or a majority reading.

4.1.4. Since the uncial texts, A B F M, constitute on the whole the oldest Greek ms witnesses I have often listed them as well, e.g. A F *b f s*. Except for the later F^a and F^b readings uncial support is only listed if it is unclouded; thus "corrector" readings of uncial mss are usually not cited.

Occasionally the + sign is used to signal ms support; it is to be understood as "along with scattered support." Thus the designation B + means that a reading is found in cod B as well as in scattered ms(s) not identifiable as constituting a textual family or families.

4.1.5. From the table in 4.1.2. it appears that a large number of mss constitute the *C* text. The edition subdivides these witnesses into a main group, *C*, and two subordinate groups, *cI* and *cII*. Since most readers will probably not be interested in Catena criticism these have all been subsumed under the siglum *C*.

4.1.6. Frequent reference is also made to a Byzantine text. The term applies to the family readings which characterize the text of the Byzantine lectionaries. A Byzantine textual reading means a reading supported by all or a majority of *d n t*.

5.0. Certain information has been almost routinely relegated to footnotes, not because it is unimportant but rather since it is not central to the Notes.

5.1. The Notes do not detail reasons for choosing the readings of Exod in favor of variant readings. Such arguments concerning the originality of the text are fully discussed in THGE Chapter VII entitled "The Critical Text," and such matters are all referred to in the footnotes where the relevant section of THGE VII is given. The user who is not interested in such matters can simply disregard these references.

5.2. Materials gleaned from the second apparatus of the Göttingen edition are also routinely placed in footnotes. Readings from The Three,

Aq, Sym and Theod, as well as occasionally from Samariticon, are given, usually without comment. This relegation does not constitute a judgement on the value of this evidence, but is due to the fact that the Notes deal with the LXX text, whereas hexaplaric readings are in essence extra-Septuagintal materials usually gleaned from the margins of LXX texts. Such readings have in the long course of LXX tradition history often influenced that tradition, sometimes actively invading it, especially through Origen's hexapla. Their origins lie in the Hebrew tradition, and their interests were revisional. They are thus of importance in understanding the text history rather than the text of LXX, and so should be carefully distinguished from LXX itself.

5.3. A number of abbreviations of items often cited are used throughout the volume, principally, though not exclusively, in the footnotes. The following table of Sigla explains them.

Sigla

AASF = Annales Academiae Scientiarum Fennicae

Aejmelaeus = Aejmelaeus, Anneli, Parataxis in the Septuagint: A Study of the Renderings of the Hebrew Coordinate Clauses in the Greek Pentateuch. AASF: Dissertationes Humanarum Litterarum 31. Helsinki, 1982.

Aejmelaeus ZAW = idem, What Can We Know about the Hebrew *Vorlage* of the *Septuagint?*, Zeitschrift für die Alttestamentliche Wissenschaft IC (1987), 58-89

Aq = Aquila

Aristeas = Aristeas to Philocrates (Letter of Aristeas), edited and translated by M. Hadas. New York, 1973

Bauer = Arndt, W.P. and Gingrich, F.W., A Greek-English Lexicon of the New Testament and Other Early Christian Literature, transl. and adapt. from W. Bauer, Griechisch-Deutsches Wörterbuch zu den Schriften des Neuen Testaments und der übrigen urchristlichen Literatur, 4te Aufl., 1952. Chicago, 1957; 2nd ed. revised and augmented by F.W.Gingrich and F.W.Danker from the 5te Aufl.

BHS = Biblia Hebraica Stuttgartensia, ed. K.Elliger et W.Rudolph. Stuttgart, 1977

Bl-Debr = Blass, F., Debrunner, A. u. Rehkopf, Fr., Grammatik des neutestamentlichen Griechisch, 14te völlig neubearb. Aufl. Göttingen, 1975

Boisacq = E. Boisacq, Dictionaire étymologique de la langue grecque. Paris, 1938

Cox, VI Congress = Cox, Claude, ed., VI Congress of the International Organization for Septuagint and Cognate Studies: Jerusalem 1986, SBL: Septuagint and Cognate Studies Series 23, Altanta, 1986

Crönert = W. Crönert, Memoria Graeca Herculanensis, Lipsiae, 1903

Daniel = Daniel, S., Recherches sur le vocabulaire du culte dans la Septante. Études et Commentaires 61. Paris, 1966

Dillmann = A. Dillmann, Die Bücher Exodus und Leviticus für die zweite Aufl. nach A.Knobel. Leipzig, 1880

Exod = The text of SEPTUAGINTA Vetus Testamentum Auctoritate Academiae Scientiarum Gottingensis editum. II,1 Exodus edidit John William Wevers (in press)

Field = Field, Fr., Origenis Hexaplorum quae supersunt. Oxonii, 1867-1875

GK = Gesenius' Hebrew Grammar as edited and enlarged by the late E.Kautzsch. Second English edition revised by A.E.Cowley. Oxford, 1910

Helbing = Helbing, R., Die Kasussyntax der Verba bei den Septuaginta. Göttingen, 1928

Helbing, Gramm. = Helbing, R., Grammatik der LXX: Laut- und Wortlehre. Göttingen, 1907

HR = Hatch, E. & Redpath, H.A., A Concordance to the Septuagint and the other Greek Versions of the O.T. I-II, Suppl. Oxford, 1897-1906

Johannessohn, Gebrauch = Johannessohn, M., Der Gebrauch der Präpositionen in der Septuaginta. MSU 3,3. Berlin, 1926

Lampe = Lampe, G.W.H., A Patristic Greek Lexicon, Oxford, 1961

Later Revisers = οἱ λοιποί or οἱ λ'

Lee = Lee, J.A.L., A Lexical Study of the Septuagint Version of the Pentateuch. Chico, 1983

LS = Liddell, H.G., Scott, R., & Jones, H.S., A Greek-English Lexicon, 9th ed., Oxford, 1940

Mayser = Mayser, E., Grammatik der griechischen Papyri aus der Ptolemäerzeit. I., Leipzig, 1906. II 1, Berlin, 1926. II 2, 1933/34. II 3, 1934. 2 Aufl. I 1, 1970. I 2, 1938. I 3, 1936

MSU = Mitteilungen des Septuaingta-Unternehmens d. Akademie d. Wissenschaften zu Göttingen

MT = Masoretic Text as found in BHS

Pesh = Peshiṭta. The O.T. in Syriac according to the Peshiṭta Version. Part I, fasc 1. Exodus by M.D.Koster. Leiden, 1977

Prijs = Prijs, L., Jüdische Tradition in der Septuaginta. Leiden, 1948

Ra = Rahlfs, A., Septuaginta, Stuttgart,1935

Sam = Samaritan Pentateuch. Der hebräische Pentateuch der Samaritaner, herausg. von A. von Gall. Giessen, 1918

Schl = Schleusner, J.F.,Novus Thesaurus philologico-criticus, sive Lexicon in LXX et reliquos interpretes Graecos ac Scriptores Apocryphos V.T. Lipsiae, 1820-1821

Sollamo = Sollamo, R., Renderings of Hebrew Semiprepositions in the Septuagint, AASF: Dissertationes Humanarum Litterarum 19. Helsinki, 1979

SS = Soisalon-Soininen, I., Studien zur Septuaginta-Syntax, AASF 237. Helsinki, 1987

SS Inf = idem, Die Infinitive in der Septuaginta. AASF 132, 1. Helsinki, 1965

Suidas = (Suda). Suidae Lexicon, Graece & Latine ... Aemilii Porti. Cantabrigiae, 1705

Syh = The Syrohexaplar

Sym = Symmachus

Targ = The Targums Onkelos and Neophiti

Tar^O = Targum Onkelos. Sperber, A., The Bible in Aramaic based
on Old Manuscripts and Printed Texts. Vol.I. The Pentateuch
according to Targum Onkelos. Leiden, 1959

Tar^P = The Palestinian Targum. A. Díez Macho, NEOPHYTI 1:
Targum Palestinense ms de la Biblioteca Vaticana. Tomo II
Exodo. Madrid, 1970

Thack = Thackeray, H.St.J., A Grammar of the Old Testament in
Greek according to the Septuagint: I. Introduction,
Orthography and Accidence. Cambridge, 1909

The Others = οἱ λοιποί or οἱ λ'

The Three = οἱ γ'

Theod = Theodotion

THGD = Wevers, J.W. Text History of the Greek Deuteronomy,
MSU 13, Göttingen, 1978

THGE = idem, Text History of the Greek Exodus, (in press)

THGG = idem, Text History of the Greek Genesis, MSU 11.
Göttingen, 1974

THGL = idem, Text History of the Greek Leviticus, MSU 19.
Göttingen, 1986

THGN = idem, Text History of the Greek Numbers, MSU 16.
Göttingen, 1982

Transl. = idem, Translation and Canonicity: A Study in the
Narrative Portions of the Greek Exodus, Scripta signa vocis:
Studies about Scripts, Scriptures, Scribes and Languages in
the Near East, offered to J.H. Hospers by his pupils,
colleagues and friends. (Groningen, 1986), 295-302

VT = Vetus Testamentum

Vulg = The Vulgate. Biblia Sacra: Vulgatae Editionis Sixti V Pont.
Max. iussu recognita et Clementis VIII auctoritate edita.
Romae, 1965

Walters = Walters, P., The Text of the Septuagint, edited by
D.W.Gooding. Cambridge, 1973

6.0. Throughout the Notes the reader will note that central stress is placed on understanding how the translators interpreted the text. Exod is an exegetical document, and its exegesis can be understood by close attention to the linguistic mode which Exod used to translate the parent Hebrew. This can often be seen when the Greek makes some nice point of clarification or seems to deviate from the received meaning of the parent text. Whenever Exod deviates from the obvious intent of the Hebrew it is noted, and I have often speculated on the possible reason for such deviation. When differences between the two obtain a different parent is not automatically presupposed, but other explanations are first proposed and investigated. Through such details a picture of the attitudes, theological prejudices, even of the cultural environment of these Jewish translators gradually emerges. These Notes are presented in the hope that readers will uncover such a picture.

7.0. It may be noted that no bibliography (except for a sigla table) has been included in this work, under the egoistic illusion that readers by taking this volume in hand might be more interested in using these Notes as a help to understanding Exod than in checking on the state of the art. Readers can always consult the detailed Bibliography that appeared in 1973.[6] For a special bibliography particularly applicable to Exodus the excellent and extensive one in the L'Exode volume referred to in Note 4 above might be consulted. I could hardly have presented a better one.

8.0. Finally it remains to recognize a few special individuals for their help and encouragement. I owe a special debt of thanks to Detlef Fraenkel of Göttingen for the many detailed discussions, criticisms and arguments on the Tabernacle Accounts we had through the Post. Only he will recognize how much I am endebted to him. In a similar vein I should like to recognize the substantial help given more indirectly by Udo Quast of Göttingen. Through his painstaking editorial work both on the edition and on the Text History he is largely responsible for the accuracy of myriads of details. And then I should also like to thank Claude Cox, the editor of the series in which this work appears. He urged me to place these efforts in the series, thereby

6. A Classified Bibliography of the Septuagint, compiled by S.P. Brock, C.T. Fritsch, S. Jellicoe. Leiden, 1973.

making them more readily available to students at an affordable price, an aim to which I gladly subscribe.

9.0. This work has been produced by the author as camera ready copy using the Nota Bene plus Special Language Supplement computer program, and copied on a HP Laser Jet Plus/Series II printer. The Greek Index was also extracted through the above computer program.

NOTES

1:1 Since the opening sentence begins the book the Greek does not render MT's anomalous conjunction. Exodus constitutes a new work; it has its own title, its own translator, and it is not tied by a conjunction to the end of Genesis. Exod (the critical text of the Greek Exodus or its translator) interprets the articulated participle הבאים by a perfect participle. From the narrator's point of view the sons of Israel (Exod here uses τῶν υἱῶν ᾽Ισ-ραήλ in the literal sense, not as otherwise to indicate the Israelites) not only had entered Egypt but were still there. A popular variant voids this nicety by changing the participle to the present stem. The variant is closer to MT, and it may have been created under Hebrew influence.

Exod makes clear that υἱῶν ᾽Ισραήλ is to be taken literally by identifying Jacob as τῷ πατρὶ αὐτῶν. Later on (v.7) the phrase "sons of Israel" takes on its more usual sense of "Israelites."

A grammatical incongruity emphasizes this same fact. The phrase איש וביתו is rendered by ἕκαστος πανοικίᾳ αὐτῶν; the use of the plural αὐτῶν against MT is part of this same patterr of interpretation. The popular B text has the adverb πανοικι by haplography.

The verbal clause with which the verse concludes has the classical aorist form εἰσῆλθον.[1] The clause is interruptive since the nominal sentence ταῦτα τὰ ὀνόματα... continues with vv.2-4.

1:2-4 Textually the list equals MT except for ᾽Ιούδας where the Hebrew has ויהודה. The failure to render the conjunction of the Hebrew is probably palaeographically conditioned. The preceding word is לוי. In some Hebrew scripts the *waw* and *yodh* are difficult to distinguish and the difference between Exod and MT is due to haplography/dittography; it is impossible to determine which is the earlier.

1. For its originality rather than the popular hellenistic εισηλθοσαν supported by A and B cf THGE VII.M.9; cf also Thack 213f..

Except for the above-mentioned ' Ιούδας Exod uses conjunctions exactly as MT and Tar do; only Sam differs in having all the names in vv.2-3 joined by conjunctions.

The text tradition on the names of Jacob's sons shows significant variation only for two names. As might be expected ' Ιούδας is "corrected" to ιουδα in a number of witnesses including cod. A. Since the variant is closer to the Hebrew this could be a recensional correction. The form ' Ιούδας with the Hellenistic -ς ending is used by Exod only here, thereby carefully distinguishing it from the φυλῆς ' Ιούδα of 31:2 35:30 and 37:20. The clan father is thus *Youdas*, not *Youda*.

The other name concerns Naphthali. The name occurs 16 times in the Pentateuch, and in each case the popular tradition adds a *mu* to the end of the word, as though the name were a plural gentilic. Why such a pseudo form should be popular with copyists is not clear; it has no basis in Hebrew, since Naphthalites are always called בני נפתלי.

1:5 Exod continues with the statement that Joseph was in Egypt, which hex places at the end of the verse so as to conform to MT. The remainder of the verse states that "all persons out of Jacob were 75." This contrasts with MT's count of 70. Neither number fits the count exactly. MT's 70 does not fit the details from Gen 46:26 which states that "all the people belonging to Jacob who entered Egypt, who were his offspring" were 66 people in total. To this were to be added Joseph and his two sons as well as the patriarch himself for a grand total of 70 (v.27). The Greek's 75 is simply based on the Greek of Gen 46:26f. which Exod must have known. There v.27 states with little rationale that the descendents of Joseph who were born to him in Egypt were nine people. This added to the 66 of v.26 makes up the 75. But the source for the "nine" is puzzling. The offspring of Joseph is given in Num 26:32-41 (Vv 28-37 in MT). Manasseh had one son, one grandson and six great-grandsons which does make nine. But Ephraim had two sons (three in MT) and one grandson, for a grand total of 13(14). The NT has also taken over the tradition of 75 in Stephen's speech (Acts 7:14).

Exod renders יצאי ירך simply by ἐξ, which hex corrected by adding ἐξελθόντων before it. Presumably the *f* tradition αι εξελθουσαι is an attempt to put the hex reading into better Greek, i.e. as a modifier of πᾶσαι ψυχάι. A popular reading articulates ψυχάι which is probably simply a dittograph after πᾶσαι. Origen also added ψυχαι at the end of the verse on the basis of the Hebrew.

1:6 As in v.5 and at the opening clause of v.7 the conjunction used to render the *waw* of MT is not καί as designating coordination of two equal units, but δέ showing change of subject. This distinction is not consistently drawn (cf v.9 e.g.) but Exod does not use these conjunctions completely arbitrarily.

1:7 The multiplication of the Israelite populace is described by four coordinate verbal constructions, the first three as aorists, "increased, became many, became common," and the last as imperfect since it was meant to show the process of becoming powerful. The order in MT is a bit different: פרו וישרצו וירבו ויעצמו, i.e. 1:3:2:4. The verb שרץ also occurs at 8:3 where it is rendered literally by ἐξερεύξεται "the river will swarm with frogs." Here Exod understood the word metaphorically as χυδαῖοι ἐγένοντο "became common, vulgar."[2] The *O* tradition has changed the word order of the clauses to fit MT.

The imperfect κατίσχυον has also been levelled by the popular tradition to an aorist form κατισχυσαν under the influence of the coordinate aorists.

The final clause uses the transitive verb ἐπλήθυνεν with an accusative αὐτούς as though the verb were Hiphil, probably because of the Hebrew's אתם. Note the attempt of mss. 53' to improve the sense by their επληθυνθη αυτοις.[3]

1:8 Nowhere else does LXX render חדש by ἕτερος (in the phrase "another king") but this gives the sense of "new king" exactly.[4] For "did not know

---

2. Aq rendered the word literally in the sense of "swarm" (ἐξήρποσαν) as did Sym with ἐξῆρξαν.
3. The clause is more exactly rendered by Aq and Sym with καὶ ἐπληρώθη ἡ γῆ ἀπ᾽ αὐτῶν.
4. The Later Revisers naturally translated it by καινός.

Joseph" Tar^O has "did not recognize, confirm the law of Joseph," whereas Tar^P adds "and did not walk in his law."

1:9 In contrast to MT Exod distinguishes between Pharaoh's own people, ἔθνει, and the foreign people, γένος, of the Israelites. The *b* tradition turns these around, whereas the majority A tradition by changing γένος to εθνος imitates the Hebrew and is probably an early recensional change. -- Ms 458 has των εβραιων as a doublet for τῶν υἱῶν ' Ισραήλ, which the Catena tradition changes to ισραηλιτων, a later Hellenized designation not found in LXX except adjectivally and that only rarely.

Exod strengthens the Hebrew רב by μέγα πλῆθος as well as by the present tense ἰσχύει[5] for the passive participle עצום.[6]

1:10 The use of the postpositive particle οὖν is particularly apt here since this verse is the action logically following the statement of v.9. Exod fluctuates between the collective singular and the plural: "let us outsmart *them*, lest *it* (the nation) multiply ... *they* (οὗτοι) join the enemy...," whereas MT followed by Vulg has the singular throughout, while Tar Pesh consistently use the plural. The text tradition in *O* and the Byzantine group levels this by changing πληθυνθῇ to πληθυνθωσιν. Presumably Exod uses the singular πληθύνθη intentionally; individuals do not become numerous, but a people can, and as individuals they can join themselves to the ranks of the enemy, engage in war and leave the country.

Exod (and Sam Tar^O Pesh Vulg) understands תקראנה as having a first plural suffix (i.e. with נו-) contrary to MT, but it makes better sense than with the energic nun ending. In the *b* tradition Pharaoh refers to the land as γης ημων instead of simply γῆς.

1:11 It is Pharaoh, not the people as in MT, who appoints works supervisors, over the Israelites. Vulg shares this interpretation. The F + tradition has corrected the verb to the plural, probably on the basis of MT.

5. Cf SS 146.
6. Aq more literally renders the latter by the adjective ὀστέϊνον.

The Israelites (αὐτοῖς) are still referred to in the singular in MT to agree with the antecedent עַם, a nicety that all the versions reject.

For the unique plural מִסִּים Exod uses a neutral translation, τῶν ἔργων; the plural of MT is probably intended to show various kinds of forced labors.[7] TarO interprets as מבאשי. Exod makes no distinction between מסים and סבלתם -- τοῖς ἔργοις, even to the extent of disregarding the suffix which is anomalous in MT since עַם is throughout referred to by a singular pronoun.[8] The former term occurs only here in Exodus (though in the Pentateuch also in Gen 49:15 Deut 20:11), whereas the latter occurs also at 5:4,5 where Exod renders likewise, and at 2:11 as τὸν πόνον, at 6:6 as δυναστείας and at 6:7 as καταδυναστείας.[9]

The common LXX phrase πόλεις ὀχυράς first occurs here. In LXX the adjective ὀχυράς almost always modifies πόλεις, though occasionally it does modify τεῖχος or πύργος, thus always as a term meaning strong for defence. But MT has מסכנת, i.e. "storage"; cf also 2 Chr 8:4,6 17:12 where LXX adopted the Exod interpretation ὀχυρός. In fact. LXX never understood the word to mean "storage." Incidentally Vulg thought of משכנות as its *tabernaculorum* shows.[10]

Three cities are named as Pithom, Ramesse and On, the last-named being identified as Heliopolis, over against MT which has only the first two, Pithom and Raamses. The addition of "and On, which is Heliopolis" seems to show acquaintance with Gen 46:28, 29. In v.28 καθ᾽ Ἡρώων πόλιν (for גשנה) is said to be εἰς γῆν Ῥαμεσσή. In both verses Bo has *Pethom* for Ἡρώων πόλιν. The rendering by LXX of און as Heliopolis is clear from Gen 41:50.

The text tradition had difficulty with Πιθώμ. Some witnesses aspirated the first consonant, i.e. φιθωμ, but most difficulty appeared with the final consonant which obtains as φ, θ, ν, or ρ, but more commonly was omitted. Ramesse often occurs among the witnesses with one *sigma* but MT guarantees two as correct; on the basis of MT the article was added by hex.

7. Sym uses a compound ἐργοδιώκτας for rendering שרי מסים.
8. Cf SS 95.
9. Aq and Sym translate it here by βαστάγμασι.
10. Cf also the σκηνωμάτων of Aq.

The third name, Ὤν, appears as ωρ in b. The entire reference to a third city is omitted by most of f which may well have been the result of Hebrew influence.[11]

1:12 The pattern καθοτι...τοσούτῳ + comparative is idiomatic: "As much as ... by so much the more," and represents MT's pattern כ ... כאשר. Exod does not render the coordinate second כ since it is rhetorically otiose. The use of the Greek imperfects is excellent for bringing out the imperfect aspect of the Hebrew, though the latter probably emphasizes the potential somewhat more. The tradition has changed the τοσούτῳ to the neuter accusative adverbial τοσουτον in a number of mixed witnesses, but this means the same. A minor variant to ἐγίνοντο is the aorist εγενοντο, probably rooted in a careless scribal error. The context makes the aorist clearly secondary. A majority variant has added σφοδρα σφοδρα (or simply σφοδρα by haplography) to ἴσχυον, based on v.7 where it is original.[12]

Exod clarifies the change in subject for the last clause by adding οἱ Αἰγύπτιοι. An *O n s* variant improves the Hebraism of ἀπὸ τῶν υἱῶν Ἰσραήλ by changing the phrase to an accusative as direct modifier of ἐβδελύσσοντο.[13]

1:13 Exod tends to distinguish between מצרים as people and as land or nation. The Masoretes consistently render the last syllable of מצרים in Exodus as -rayim, but Exod presupposes -rim whenever it fits as here. Exod's use of the imperfect here and in the following verse emphasizes the continuity of the enslavement of the people. Exod's choice of the verb "oppress" is more graphic than MT's Hi of עבד. The transposition of οἱ Αἰγύπτιοι after Ἰσραήλ is also found in Vulg.[14]

11. For Hebrew influence on f more particularly on 53' cf THGG 120-124.
12. See THGE VII.O.
13. See Helbing 24f. Aq has a different verb, ἐσικχαίνοντο, "were loathing," in the imperfect, which fits the context nicely.
14. The Later Revisers seemed to have trouble with בפרך which Exod had adequately translated by βίᾳ. Theod made it ἐν ἐμπαιγμῷ "with mockery," and Sym translated freely by means of a participle modifying "the Egyptians," ἐντρυφῶντες, emphasizing the delight which they experienced in oppressing the Israelites.

1:14 The unusual choice of the rare compound κατοδυνᾶν "cause hurt, pain" to render the root מרר Pi may have been stylistically determined, i.e. a succession of κατα compounds: κατεδυνάσευον, κατωδύνων and κατεδουλοῦντο. The variant of the Byzantine group, κατωδυνουν, presupposes an -εω stem formation. The F[b] reading, παρεπικρανον, undoubtedly represents an Aquilanic correction.

Hex naturally corrected the word order of αὐτῶν τὴν ζωήν to conform to the Hebrew; the addition of αυτων after ἔργα later in the verse is also a hex tradition.[15]

Exod rightly understood עבדה (occurring three times in the verse) as a collective and renders by the plural "works." These hard labors are specified as being with clay, with brickmaking and with field labors. The phrase ἔργαἔργον» ὧν κατεδουλοῦντο αὐτούς interprets MT as though the verbal form עבדו were transitive. For this unusual use of עבד ב cf also Lev 25:39. Exod varies the verbs: in v.13 κατεδυνάστευον was used. Exod's love of variation is also well illustrated by μετὰ βίας instead of the βίᾳ of v.13 for בפרך. -- The Byzantine text simplifies the genitive pronoun construction by specifying the relationship to its antecedent as one of means, εν οις.

1:15 Exod not only renders מצרים by τῶν Αἰγυπτίων but also renders the adjectival העברית by τῶν ' Εβραίων as well, i.e. balancing "king of the Egyptians" with "midwives of the Hebrews." The word מצרים occurs 176 times in Exodus and is always vocalized as "Egypt" by the Masoretes. Exod disregards the vocalic tradition in 66 cases where he uses "Egyptians" and in 106 cases correctly uses Αἴγυπτος, with four instances being omitted. On the other hand, Exod has two instances of Αἰγύπτιοι as a plus (cf v.12 supra), and four of Αἴγυπτος, for a total of 178 occurrences. The only generalizations which can be made are that "land of Egypt" is usually "Egypt" but with "hand of," "eyes of," "heart of," "camps of" it is always the "Egyptians." In other words, when the reference is geographic (note also

15. Cf SS 95.

"border of," "waters of," "midst of") Exod uses "Egypt," but when the term refers to peoples he uses "Egyptians."

The omission of the relative pronoun ᾗ by *C s* + in the tradition is the result of simplification of the syntagm; by means of the omission τῇ-- Σεπφωρά is made syntactically coordinate to καί 2°--fin. The Exod syntagm is difficult because of his insistence on including an equivalent for אשר.

Σεπφωρά, the first midwife, is given the same name by Exod as that of Moses' wife; cf 2:21 4:25 18:2, though MT has שפרה over against צפרה. In the edition they have been differentiated by giving Moses' wife a penultimate accent (since the -α is treated by Exod in 2:21 18:2 as a first declensional ending). Vulg follows Exod in giving the same name to both, also declining the second name. Since שפרה occurs only here the distinction in accent is arbitrary though useful.

1:16 Exod understood the difficult phrase יראיתן על האבנים correctly and renders καὶ ὦσιν τῷ τίκτειν as did Vulg by its simple *et partus tempus advenerit*; cf also Pesh: "and you see (them) when they are bowing over (i.e. to give birth)."[16] In the μέν ... δέ construction, the tenses of the imperatives are sensitively used: the aorist for the act of killing, but the present tense for "preserve (it)." The change to the aorist περιποιησασθε in *b f* + is probably due to the influence of ἀποκτείνατε. Other changes in the tradition are the epexegetical *b f* addition of αυτοις after εἶπεν, as in Pesh, the change from the root μαιόομαι to the synonym μαιεύομαι in *z*, and the popular change in case of the articular infinitive. That τῷ should become το in the tradition was almost inevitable; not only are the two homophonous in Byzantine times but the dative is gradually losing out to the accusative to such an extent that after πρός the accusative became almost universal. Here the dative is especially appropriate since what is being emphasized is the proximity of the act of bearing, and the change to the accusative is a thoughtless error. Exod interprets the final verb חיה as a transitive verb and thus added an object αὐτό.

16. But see the interesting suggestion of Aejmelaeus, ZAW, 78--79.

1:17 Exod does not usually render דבר in a כאשׁר clause by συντάσσω; in fact, only at 9:12 and 12:35 does this also occur. Such דבר clauses occur 22 times in Exodus, of which six are rendered by εἴπω and 12 by λαλέω (and one is omitted).

Instead of continuing with the περιποιέομαι of v.16 Exod uses ἐζωογό-νουν in the later sense of "preserve alive,"[17] again in the imperfect. The change in lexeme probably reflects the Hebrew change to the Piel stem.

1:18 Change in subject is throughout the section vv.17--22 reflected by δέ structures; here the king is subject. Exod retains the paratactic construction of MT by which "do this thing" is coordinate with "preserved alive the males," since sensibly the latter identifies τὸ πρᾶγμα τοῦτο.[18]

1:19 Exod uses the Hellenistic εἶπαν rather than the classical ειπον of the Byzantine variant.[19] -- Αἰγύπτου, rather than the adjectival form of the hex correction αι αιγυπτιαι, is used by Exod to modify γυναῖκαι; comp. the note at v.15.

Exod disregarded the causal particle כי with which the words of the midwives begin and simply makes the nominal statement: "Not like the women of Egypt are the Hebrew women," with the explanation in a γάρ clause following. The Greek statement is somewhat ambiguous, however, due to the Hebraic καί ἔτικτον at the end of the verse. The πρὶν ἥ construction must modify τίκτουσιν, i.e. "they give birth before the midwives (not singular as MT) arrive." The καὶ ἔτικτον is coordinate with the entire τίκτουσιν clause, but logically reflects as an afterthought on the arrival of the midwives, i.e. "they were already giving birth." MT's text is somewhat simpler since חיות הנה "they are healthy" has a disjunctive accent[20] and the בטרם clause goes with the וילדו which follows.[21]

17. See Bauer s.v.
18. The word ἄρσενα for ילדים was too free for Aq and Theod who have παιδάρια.
19. Cf THGE VII.M.9 where all the evidence is given.
20. But see SS 81.
21. Both Sym and Theod understood the Hebrew syntax although they did mistranslate חיות, Sym as μαίαι (γάρ εἰσι), and Theod as (ὅτι) ζωογονοῦσιν (αὗται), but they did break after it. Sym continues with καί πρίν and Theod with διότι πρίν. Aq rendered the word by λοχαῖαι,

In the tradition *d s* + have the simplex ελθειν for εἰσελθεῖν. The error need not be taken seriously because it probably originated in auditory confusion since η εισελθειν was heard as /i iselθin/. A popular M reading has προ του instead of πρὶν ἤ, but this means the same.

1:20 The three verbs are all in the imperfect since to Exod progressive verbal action was involved, i.e. was doing, was multiplying, was becoming strong. The odd change in number to the plural for the last verb ויעצמו is not followed by Exod, since ὁ λαός is subject both of ἐπλήθυνεν and ἴσχυσεν. This kind of leveling also occurred in Sam Tar[P] which, however, level to the plural for both verbs. The Catena text changed ἴσχυεν to the plural, a change which must be based on MT.[22]

1:21 For Exod's dealing with ויהי see note at 2:11. Exod has the same subject (the people) for the verbs in both clauses, making a statement of conventional wisdom: "the fear of God produces offspring." That Exod fully intended the plural verb is clear from its use of the reflexive pronoun ἑαυταῖς. This contrasts with MT and all other ancient witnesses in which God is the subject of the second verb; i.e. God provided the midwives with offspring because they feared him. It should be noted that MT as well as Sam Tar has the pronominal reference in the masculine להם; there is no actual masculine plural anaphoric referent in the context, but the העם of v.20 must be intended. Only Pesh corrects to the feminine (the Vulg has "eis" with common gender).

The Catena tradition has επει δε for ἐπειδή resulting from auditory confusion. Hex added και before ἐποίησαν to conform to MT, but in accordance with hex practice did not change the number of the verb.

1:22 Exod sensibly interprets הבן and הבת as ἄρσεν and θῆλυ resp.; the male offspring alone were to be destroyed. Exod, though faithful to the

---

associating the Hebrew word with childbirth.
22. Theod tried to improve on εὖ ἐποίει by revising it to ἠγάθυνεν, but retaining an imperfect.

meaning of the Hebrew, is not bound to it literally.[23]

Exod adds τοῖς ' Ἐβραίοις ad sensum to τεχθῇ (which *x* changes to the feminine ταις εβραιαις with unimaginative biological exactitude). In good style Exod does not render the recapitulative pronoun after ῥίψατε, but then as though in penance adds αὐτό after ζωογονεῖτε against MT. For the last-named verb *b* substitutes περιποιησασθε under the influence of v.16. Puzzling is the change of the preposition εἰς to επι in *f* which is unexpected after ῥίπτω.

23. For ἄν rather than the variant εαν in a relative clause see THGE VII.B.

Chapter 2

2:1 The Greek is a free rendering of MT. ἦν ... ὅς ἔλαβεν is a stylistic improvement over MT's "went and took." Instead of בני Exod has φυλῆς vulß» which is what בית here intends. So too the use of the partitive genitive: "(one) of the daughters" clarifies את בת, and finally the addition of καὶ ἔσχεν αὐτήν is of course the point of the exercise. Variants in the tradition show attempts to improve the text. The change of ὅς to και in *b* La seems based on the Hebrew, whereas the omission in B of καὶ ἔσχεν αὐτήν though equalling MT was probably due to homoiot. The popular tradition of εκ added before the partitive genitive[1] is a matter of simplification, making the implicit explicit.

2:2 Exod does not render האשה as subject for the first two verbs, since it is obvious. In the tradition *x* makes this explicit by substituting the relative pronoun η for the opening καί. As in ch.1 Exod uses ἄρσεν for בן; after all, it was the fact that the child was male that is the point of the story. MT tells the story throughout with the mother as the subject, but the translator changes the subject to the plural as does Pesh, i.e., both the Levite and his wife are persuaded by the winsomeness of the baby to protect it rather than to allow it to be thrown into the river. Presumably to Exod such an exercise could hardly have been effected solely by the mother.

The use of ἀστεῖον is idiomatic.[2] Vulg's *elegantem* appears influenced either by Exod or by Sym rather than by MT. The tradition offers little of interest. The addition by *f* + of ον after ἀστεῖον has really nothing to do with MT; it is simply a dittograph. And the transposition of μῆνας τρεῖς by ms 426 is a hex correction.

1. Cf SS 165.
2. Aq used his usual literal rendering of טוב ἀγαθός, and Sym had καλός.

2:3 Exod continues with the plural for the opening ἐπεί clause, but then changes over to the singular with ἔλαβεν. This forced him to designate the subject as ἡ μήτηρ αὐτοῦ as does Sam; this remains the subject for the remaining verbs in the verse. Within the temporal clause the A b f tradition through auditory confusion has επειδη for ἐπεί because of the δέ following it.[3] A popular A F M hex variant placed αὐτό after κρύπτειν to equal MT. Similarly hex in origin is the popular B F addition of αυτω after ἔλαβεν as the asterisk in Syh proves (though the addition in Syh is placed before the verb). Note also the reordering τὸ παιδίον after εἰς αὐτήν later in the verse.

Exod does not designate the basket's (θῖβιν[4]) material as MT גמא תבה does, which deficiency Origen made up in hex by adding παπυρου.[5]

Exod uses the rare dvandva compound ἀσφαλτοπίσσῃ[6] to render the pair חמר and זפת; that it is rare is clear from its popular separation into two words ασφαλτω πισση in the tradition (in some witnesses even joined by και).

The translator appropriately varies the translation for the two occurrences of ותשם, using καὶ ἐνέβαλεν for putting (the child into it), and καὶ ἔθηκεν for setting (it among the reeds by the river).

2:4 Exod properly uses the imperfect aspect to designate the sister's watching at a distance. This distinction is voided by a popular tradition which changes the verb to the aorist κατεσκοπευσεν. The use of the compound strengthens the notion of watching as "watching carefully." The notion is of course the intent of MT's "setting herself, standing."

Exod's μαθεῖν for לדעה is unusual (the only other occurrence according to HR is at Est 4:5 for לדעה), but it is fitting as "get to know, learn." The variant ιδειν in the tradition is due to the influence of the idiom "to see (what would happen)."

3. For εδυναντο as variant with classical ending cf Thack 198.
4 . See Lee 115, as well as Thack 34.
5. Probably from Theod who had κιβωτὸν παπύρου. The attribution to Aq as well in some mss is probably an error of transmission, especially in view of Aq having ἐν τῷ παπυρεῶνι (for בסוף) later in the verse.
6. An instrumental dative; cf SS 122.

Exod makes an excellent idiomatic translation of לו יעשה מה by τί τὸ ἀποβησόμενον αὐτῷ, i.e. what would happen to him; cf Vulg *eventum rei*.

2:5 With change of subject δέ is used. Ambiguous in the opening clause is the prepositional phrase ἐπὶ τὸν ποταμόν; since it follows λούσασθαι it might be thought to modify it but this is unlikely because ἐπί with the accusative is not locative. In fact, it must modify κατέβη and means "to the river."

The second clause is interruptive with its reference to the ἅβραι, a word borrowed from Semitic; cf חברה in the sense of "company." The word is usually used of companions to a lady in high society; cf especially Judith passim and Est 2;9 4:4,16.[7]

With ἰδοῦσα the subject reverts to Pharaoh's daughter for the remainder of the verse. Since τὴν ἅβραν, this time as rendering for אמתה (the hex tradition adds an αυτης so as to correspond to the Hebrew suffix), intervenes, possible ambiguity as to the subject of ἀνετείλατο obtains, but the story line makes it clear. In the tradition a popular variant has the classical second aorist ανειλετο. Since the classica ἀνειλόμην occurs in v.10 the Hellenistic form might seem questionable but its support in the tradition is too strong to make the classical form plausible.

2:6 The first half of the verse is rendered freely and Origen indicated this by adding το before παιδίον and και ην το παιδιον after it as well as placing ἐν τῇ θίβει and ἡ θυγάτηρ Φαραώ under the obelus to indicate that these had no equivalents in the Hebrew. Origen's plusses are, however, quite unnecessary. The Hebraism of "saw the child and behold a child weeping" is simplified by "saw a child weeping." The addition of ἐν τῇ θίβει locates the child, and is plausible as further explication of ἀνοίξασα.

The addition of an expressed subject for ἐφείσατο[8] ... ἔφη gives balance to the story as a contrast to v.7 where ἡ ἀδελφὴ αὐτοῦ is the expressed subject. Then v.8 again balances the daughter of Pharaoh over against "the

7. Schl defines ἅβρα as *ancilla herae domestica ac honoratior, quali matronae ditiores ad honestiora ministeria utuntur.* Since the Hebrew has נערה Aq has παιδίσκαι and Sym has κοράσια.
8. Cf Helbing 161.

girl," and in v.9 over against "the woman." Furthermore the addition removes any possible ambiguity which the lack of expressed subject for ἀνετείλατο in v.5 might have introduced. The preposition ἀπό is used here as partitive.[9] The *f n* tradition of ειπον for ἔφη is due to the pressure of εἶπεν occurring again and again in LXX and φημί but rarely (only here in Exod).

2:7 Instead of הַאֵלֵךְ "shall I go" Exod idiomatically has θέλεις (as does Vulg). Exod also uses two different roots to render מֵינֶקֶת and תֵינִק of MT, viz. τροφεύουσαν "wet nurse" and θηλάσει "she shall suckle," a typical variation for Exod whereby the richness of the narrative style is enhanced. The change of καὶ εἶπεν to a δε construction in a *b n x+* variant is quite unnecessary in view of the expressed subject ἡ ἀδελφή, but may be due to the influence of the context; cf vv.8-10.

2:8 The elimination of the initial ἡ either through ειπον δε or και ειπεν in the tradition is a case of hypercorrection in view of the named articulated subject ἡ θυγάτηρ. What Exod says is "She said...," i.e. the daughter." V.9 has the more usual εἶπεν δέ ... ἡ θυγάτηρ. A *d* tradition omits both referents in the dialogue, i.e. simply "She said Go." The Byzantine text's substitution of the compound απελθουσα for the simplex may be an exegetical pedantry; the girl after all now leaves the story entirely. The simplex is the livelier for the narrative, and more exactly reproduces the sense of the parent וַתֵּלֶךְ; it is clearly original.

2:9 Exod interprets הֵילִיכִי as διατήρησόν μοι "keep for me." The Hebrew word is unique and is usually emended to הוֹלִיכִי, but Pesh already read the *yodh* as its "lo to you," i.e. הִי לְכִי demonstrates. Vulg has *accipe*. In other words none of the early translations support הוֹלִיכִי. The Exod interpretation fits the narrative line perfectly: "keep for me this child and suckle it for me."

9. See SS 158.

The careful use of δέ to indicate change of subject might be noted. First the subject is Pharaoh's daughter; then the imperatives are directed to the mother. The pronoun ἐγώ refers once more to the daughter, and finally the subject changes to ἡ γυνή for ἔλαβεν ... ἐθήλαζεν. The addition of σου after μισθόν later in the verse is probably a hex plus.

2:10 The verse begins with a genitive absolute construction "when the lad grew up (she brought him)." In the tradition ανδρυνθεντος has become a very popular variant for ἀδρυνθέντος with which it is easily confused; lexically they are synonyms, but only ἀδρύνω occurs in LXX.

The form ἐγενήθη, the aorist passive, occurs eight times in Exod, whereas ἐγένετο occurs 25 times, plus six times in the plural. The passive was much in use in Egypt during the third century B.C.[10] The two forms seem to be almost indistinguishable lexically, and occur in proximity to one another, e.g. here and in v.11. With εἰς the verb in the sense of "become" is especially frequent in the LXX and NT but is also well-attested elsewhere.

The second δέ makes it clear that Pharaoh's daughter did the naming of the boy. The name Μωυσῆς occurs here for the first time but in the accusative, with a popular A F M variant in the genitive, presumably in apposition with αὐτοῦ occurring immediately before it. The stem is regularly corrected to μωσ- to agree with the MT משה in some O mss and in n. The Greek name with its -ωυ- was probably due to the Egyptian pronunciation for various proper names.[11]

Two hex variants are the gloss of οτι after λέγουσα, and the reordering of αὐτὸν ἀνείλομεν at the end of the verse.

2:11 ἐγένετο δέ (ἐν) is the usual rendering for ויהי when designating time or place[12] (though 2:23 has μετά plus accusative), whereas when ויהי introduces a preposition with infinitive or an אם , כי or כאשר clause the verb in ויהי is not rendered in Exod; cf 1:21 4:8 6:28 13:15,17 16:10 32:19

10. Cf Mayser II,2,157.
11. The recurrence of this diphthong is apparently limited to proper names, as Ιναρῶυτος, Πετῶυς, Χεσθώυθης, Ἀρθώυτου, Θαῶυτος, et al: cf Mayser I 1,117.
12. Cf SS 109.

34:29. Exod also adds ταῖς πολλαῖς to modify "in those days" probably to indicate the passing of many years, i.e. from babyhood to adulthood. For ויגדל Exod has μέγας γενόμενος here but ἁδρυνθέντος in v.10. The variation makes for a livelier style. Similarly within the verse itself MT has וירא in successive clauses but Exod has κατανοήσαςέω» δέ ... ὁρᾷ "as he was observing ... he saw." What he observed was "their toil," singular for the plural סבלתם, elsewhere rendered by ἔργοι 1:11 5:4,5, δυναστείας 6:6, καταδυναστείας in 6:7.

Exod identifies "his brothers"[13] as "the Israelites" so that there may be no confusion as to where Moses' loyalties are. MT takes this for granted. At the end of the verse τῶν ἑαυτοῦ ἀδελφῶν is again identified as τῶν υἱῶν ' Ισραήλ (as in Pesh); again the identification is not in MT. The use of the reflexive pronoun stresses this fact as well; the τινα ' Εβραῖον is one of his own brothers.

Within the text tradition ἑαυτοῦ is changed to αυτου and it follows ἀδελφῶν in the popular A F M hex tradition to conform to MT. Note also the change of ἄνθρωπον Αἰγύπτιον to τινα αιγυπτιον ανδρα in the C tradition, thereby distinguishing between ἄνθρωπος "homo" and ἀνηρ "vir," a pedantic correction indeed.

2:12 Exod uses a balanced construction; both halves of the verse have an aorist participle in the nominative plus an aorist finite verb as the central unit of the clause. By means of the balanced clauses Exod maintains the serial character of the Hebrew parataxis in narration. The four verbal ideas are temporally ordered: 1. περιβλεψάμενος Moses looks about; 2. ὁρᾷ he saw no one; 3. πατάξας he kills the Egyptian, and 4. ἔκρυψεν he hid him in the sand.

2:13 Exod again uses the construction: aorist nominative participle plus aorist finite verb, although the parent Hebrew has a הנה marker for a nominal clause for the latter. The marker is well rendered, however, by

13. As rendering for a partitive מן; cf SS 165.

18

ὁρᾷ.[14] The two Hebrew men are contending, wrangling with each other - διαπληκτιζομένους (to which x adds, lest it be misunderstood, πρὸς ἀλλήλους).[15]

καὶ λέγει for ויאמר is unusual for Exod, but occasionally he does use the present in narration. In fact, it occurs 20 times in Exod, of which nine are found in chh.32-33, where MT always has (ו)ויאמר. Over against this εἶπεν/εἶπαν occurs 158 times. There seems to be no particular reason for the translator's occasional lapse into the historical present.

A B f y z variant adds σου before τύπτεις.[16] -- Exod normally does not use a genitive pronoun to render a suffix of רע, except for the ninth and tenth commandments and at 32:27 where the context makes it necessary. When the referent in πλήσιον is obvious from the context as it is here Exod usually omits it.[17] The hex tradition naturally adds the σου.

2:14 The new speaker is the ἀδικοῦντι of v.13 as the δέ structure shows. Exod idiomatically rendered לאיש שר by ἄρχοντα. The hex tradition (from Aq Sym) placed εἰς ανδρα before it to indicate the MT text.

The second question is introduced by the particle μή, i.e. it is a question expecting a negative answer; Vulg follows Exod with its *nun*. A popular variant[18] (supported inter alia by A F M) has the neutral interrogative particle η; this more exactly renders the Hebrew ה. The pattern: personal pronoun + present tense (of θέλεις[19] as Vulg: *tu vis*) is regular in Exod for rendering the Hebrew pattern: personal pronoun + participle.[20] Exod rendered להרג and הרגת by ἀνελείν ... ἀνεῖλες resp.[21]

14. Pesh seems to have a doublet, i.e. both "he saw" (missing in 5b1 7a1) as well as "and behold." In my opinion the doublet is not original text.
15. (Aq? and) Sym render נצים somewhat more literally as διαμαχομένους; cf also Exod's μάχωνται at 21:22.
16. For its secondary character cf THGE VII G.2. The pattern: pronoun + present tense verb is usually reserved for rendering a participial construction in MT.
17. Cf SS 94.
18. From Theod.
19. θέλεις is "corrected" by The Three to λέγεις so as to correspond to MT's אמר.
20. Cf THGE VII.G.2 sub 2:13; cf SS 82.
21. Which Theod retained; Aq and Sym, however, change to ἀποκτείναι ... ἀπέκτεινας in order to reproduce the Hebrew more literally.

Exod has epexegetically added ἔχθες in the ὃν τρόπον clause as did both Pesh and Vulg.It reflects on the fact that the question is asked on τῇ ἡμέρᾳ τῇ δευτέρᾳ (v.13). Its position is not fully certain since the popular A F M variant has the word after τὸν Αἰγύπτιον.

Moses' reaction was one of fear and surprise. What Moses said (to himself) is put in question form "has this matter become so public?," whereas MT uses אכן which also expresses surprise but not in question form. Origen correctly placed τοῦτο under the obelus since it is not in the Hebrew.

2:15 The use of tenses detailing Pharaoh's reaction is exact: he heard (aorist) about it and so he was seeking (imperfect) to kill Moses. Vulg similarly has *audivit* and *quaerebat.* A popular hex variant has added τον before Μωυσῆν so as to represent את משה. Some Byzantine witnesses in turn have added an αυτον before τον by partial dittography.

In verse b Exod uses the mild ἀνεχώρησεν, i.e. "Moses retired from the presence of Pharaoh." MT uses ויברח. Moses was the great hero of the Israelites and he could hardly be described in terms of a precipitous flight. Leaving Egypt for Midian is but a withdrawal.

MT has וישב in two successive clauses but with a difference in meaning;[22] cf Vulg *moratus est* and *sedit.* Exod solved the problem, not only by using κατῴκισεν[23] and ἐκάθισεν resp., but also by making them part of different patterns. The former "and he dwelt in the land of Madian" contrasts with Moses' withdrawal from Egypt. The last clause "(and) he sat down besides a well" needed an introduction which Exod gave it by ἐλθὼν δὲ εἰς γῆν Μαδιάν, i.e. "when he came into the land of Madian, he sat down ...," a tradition adopted by Pesh which, however, used it as a substitute for "and he dwelt in the land of Midian."

A hex plus of και before ἐκάθισεν does equal MT, but makes bad Greek after the ἐλθών clause. The *n* variant of εκαθητο for ἐκάθισεν has

22. But cf Aejmelaus, ZAW 80.
23. For κατῴκισεν over against the B *f n z* simplex variant cf THGE VII N.

practically the same lexical value, though it may emphasize the notion of quiet repose, of sitting still.

2:16 The dative plus ἦσαν simply means possession, i.e. the priest of Madian had seven daughters. MT has no equivalent for ἦσαν, but hex reordered it after θυγατέρες and placed it (according to Syh) under the asterisk. Either this is an error for the obelus or his Hebrew text had something like היו; in any event Pesh also supports the hex text.

In Hebrew the daughters immediately proceed to go and draw water. To make the transition Exod adds ποιμαίνουσαι τὸ πατρὸς αὐτῶν "who were pasturing the sheep of their father" (under the obelus in Syh). The story now brings the seven daughters to Moses at the well, where they began to draw water (n.b. the sensitive use of the imperfect tense). The ἕως clause uses the aorist ἔπλησον; in other words the daughters intended to keep on drawing until they had filled the recepticles, or more literally drinking troughs - ποτίστρας, as a variant marginal reading has it. A popular tradition identifies both instances of πατρὸς αὐτῶν as "Jethro."[24]

2:17 Here the pattern of the opening clause is aorist participle + verb, a pattern repeated in the next clause as well. The aorist is employed here since the story refers only to the one occasion when Moses was present. The widespread B M tradition of reading the imperfect ἐξέβαλλον would make this the common practice, but the narrative is only concerned to introduce Moses again serving as an instrument of fair play; he stood up and rescued them, to which an *f* variant with singular lack of imagination adds in explanation και τα προβατα αυτων απο των ποιμενων.

Furthermore Moses courteously took over their duties. Though MT simply has "and he watered their sheep," Exod adds a prior "and he drew water for them," probably added to make the story consistent with v.19. The gloss is lacking in a strongly supported A F variant. This could have been revisional but is probably simply an error due to homoiot. A curious *oI s* variant makes Moses draw the water but the shepherdesses watering the

24. For the secondary nature of the popular tradition see THGE VII.O.

flock. And an *f s* variant introduces του πατρος after πρόβατα probably due to the preceding verse where "their father's sheep" occurs twice.

2:18 The spelling of ῾ Ραγουήλ presupposes a root with ghain;[25] obviously the phonetic distinction between ayin and ghain was still alive at the time of the translator. Except for Num 10:29 he is always called Yothor, and a popular A tradition has voided the difficulty by substituting Yothor here as well. The αὐταῖς after εἶπεν is epexegetical, and its removal by the Byzantine text may be a revision to equal MT. The B + variant δια τι for τί ὅτι is stylistic and does not change the meaning. The removal of the marker before the infinitive παραγενέσθαι by *O* is clearly secondary. Exod often articulates the infinitive in the genitive, dative or accusative, whether it be a complementary infinitive or after a preposition. Here it is a complementary infinitive modifying ἐταχύνατε.

2:19 Since Greek has no gender distinction in the verbal inflection, the plural feminine subject of εἶπαν is indicated by an initial αἱ δέ. The Attic ειπον is again a popular variant in the tradition; cf note at 1:19. Exod uses ἐρρύσατο again as in v.17 though the verb in MT is now הציל instead of ישע. Exod has tied the two verses together: ἐρρύσατο ... ἤντλησεν ... ἐπότισεν. That this is quite intentional is clear from the sacrifice of the intensive element in וגם דלה דלה לנו "and he even drew water for us" in καὶ ἤντλησεν. The hex recension has fixed this up by adding αυτλων before the verb as an equivalent for the Hebrew free infinitive. A popular B M variant has added ημων after πρόβατα, probably under the influence of ἡμῖν in the preceding clause.[26]

2:20 The conjunction καί before ποῦ ἐστιν is as unexpected in Greek as it is in Hebrew. A well-supported A F M variant omits it as an improvement in style. Both questions are initiated by καί and the Exod text must be interpreted as a balanced construction: "And where ... and why." MT has a conjunction only before the first question, i.e. it begins the father's

25. Cf J.Blau, On Polyphony in Biblical Hebrew (Jerusalem, 1982), 35.
26. Cf THGE VII.G.2.

statement, where since it follows בנתיו it might have been the result of dittography. The z tradition supplies ο ανος as subject of ἐστιν which is of course a correct interpretation, but quite unnecessary. The omission of καί 2° by O witnesses may represent an early recensional change.

οὕτως represents Exod's attempt to render זה adverbially, whereas it is simply a long variant form added to question words like למה. In the context οὕτως may best be translated: "in such a way, manner." The verb καταλελοίπατε is aptly in the perfect since Moses remains at the well. The z tradition having added ο ανος earlier in the verse here uses αυτον instead of τὸν ἄνθρωπον, but then substitutes τον ανθρωπον for αὐτόν; none of these changes improves the narrative. Exod adds οὖν as an inferential particle to the imperatival clause.

2:21 Exod has κατῳκίσθη for ויואל לשבת, i.e. does not translate the first verb.[27] Vulg has *iuravit* (... *habitaret*)[28]; a midrash compares 1Sam 14:24 where the Hebrew verb means "to swear"; cf אלה.[29]

The rendering καὶ ἐξέδοτο...γυναῖκα "he gave as wife" correctly interprets MT's ויתן, but see Sam which reasonably added לאשה. The absolute use of נתן in the sense of "give as wife" is unexpected in Hebrew, but it does occur, e.g. Gen 34:16 38:26 Jdg 15:2. The popular addition of αυτω to the verb is otiose in view of Μωυσῇ later in the verse. On Σεπφώραν see note at 1:15.

2:22 MT begins abruptly "and she bore a son;" Exod adds before it with fine biological logic ἐν γαστρὶ δὲ λαβοῦσα ἡ γυνή. Exod also adds Μωυσῆς as named subject for ἐπωνόμασεν, so as to represent the masculine inflection ויקרא, since Greek does not distinguish gender in verbal inflections. The deletion of Moses in an A F tradition misrepresents MT, even though it equals it quantitatively.

27. Theod fills in the deficiency by ἤρξατο (κατοικεῖν) which adequately renders the Hebrew.
28. Probably from Sym's ὥρκισε (οἰκεῖν).
29. Dillmann citing A. Geiger speaks of a Jewish midrash underlying the translation, but this is unknown to me.

The name Γηρσάμ has an "a" vowel in the second syllable rather than the "o" of MT, which the popular etymology גר + שם "a sojouner there" seems to justify.

Exod by changing the word order of כי אמר to λέγων ὅτι makes the causal particle ὅτι/כי part of the quoted speech. גר is translated by πάροικος as in Gen 15:13 23:4 and Exod 18:3. The word occurs frequently in Exodus to Deuteronomy and is almost always translated by προσήλυτος.[30] The latter is a technical term for resident alien, and πάροικος was considered appropriate for the etymology here and 18:3. Exod uses εἰμι to render הייתי which is more exact than the "I have been" of RSV.

Moses localizes his state in a land ἀλλοτρίᾳ.[31] -- A majority F M tradition adds the naming of Moses' second son (from 18:3) to the end of the verse, as do Pesh and Vulg. For comment see note on 18:3.

2:23 For the rendering of ויהי with designation for time cf note at v.11. Vulg similarly has *post multum vero temporis*. The reference to the death of the Egyptian king introduces a new narrative, viz., the call to Moses to return to Egypt to lead out the people from the house of bondage.

ἀπὸ τῶν ἔργων "because of the labors" occurs twice for מן העבדה - as reason for their groaning and for their cry ascending to God. The first instance is defined by an *f* tradition as being των σκληρων, a gloss which Pesh also supports. This Jewish tradition is also represented by Tar[O] which defines the פולחנא as רהורה קשי עליהון.

2:24 The *n* variant reorders the first clause as verb + object + subject, and also places the object in the genitive which is good classical usage after εἰσακούω. Approximately a quarter of the Greek mss has the genitive plural των στεναγμων, a sensible reading whose origin is rooted in its homophony with τὸν στεναγμόν.[32]

30. As Aq does here.
31. Since Aq reserves ἀλλότριος as a translation for זר, he uses ξένη, his usual equivalent for the root נכר.
32. Aq and Syn render by τῆς οἰμωγῆς "wailing."

24

Exod adds an article after the genitive διαθήκης αὐτοῦ, which serves as a relative pronoun; it is unnecessary for the sense but was probably added because of the intervening αὐτοῦ. The predicate of the relative construction is then πρός -- fin, whereas in MT the phrases directly modify בריתו. In MT God remembered his covenant "with Abraham, with Isaak and with Jacob," but in Exod the covenant is that "which is to Abraham and Isaak and Jacob." The prepositions are not repeated and a conjunction is added between the first two members. But more significantly the preposition is πρός. The divine covenant is not "with" Abraham (as in Gen 17:4), but is (set) towards, or (given) to him. The direction is from God to the patriarchs; cf also 6:5. The interpretation is not original with Exod. The same reinterpretation of את (a divine covenant) is given for Noah at Gen 6:18 and for Isaac at Gen 17:19,21.

2:25 Exod interprets the first part of the verse as parallel to and explicative of the preceding verse. The rather neutral וירא "and he saw (the Israelites)"[33] is interpreted as ἐπεῖδεν "and God looked upon," i.e. in recognition, compassion.[34] A popular A F M variant has εισειδεν, a compound alien to the LXX. Tar had trouble with God's seeing the Israelites and changed the object to "oppression of the Israelites" which makes excellent sense in the context.

The second part of MT is difficult since the verb "and he knew" has no object and "God" is repeated as subject. Tar interpret "and יוי ("he" in TarP) decided to save them." Vulg apparently reread אלהים as אליהם. i.e. it has eos. Exod seems to have done the same; at least it does not have ὁ θεός but αὐτοῖς. Exod by its "and he became known to them" sets the stage for the narratives to follow, first God's revelation of himself to Moses in ch.3 and then through him to the despairing Israelites (3:15ff). The x tradition εμνησθη αυτων is due to the influence of v.24.

33. Rendered literally by Aq and Theod as εἶδεν.
34. Cf Helbing 288.

Chapter 3

3:1 The paratactic shape of this verse is borrowed from the Hebrew as is the use of ἦν + participle to indicate customary action; it is an equivalent for היה רעה. The name ᾽Ιοθόρ is constant as Exod's transcription of יתרו, presupposing a tradition transposing the last two consonants. Yothor is identified as the γαμβροῦ of Moses. The variant tradition of πενθεροῦ which more exactly identiies the relationship as the wife's father, has solidly invaded the text tradition,[1] particularly *d x*, and cf *b*; γαμβρός simply indicates some male in-law.[2]

In the second clause Exod intentionally uses an aorist verb ἤγαγεν since he describes a particular occasion, not the popular A F M imperfect variant ηγεν, which would have carried on the aspectual notion of the first clause.[3] Unusual is Exod's choice of the preposition ὑπό to modify ἤγαγεν. MT has אחר, i.e. behind (the desert); thus if one's orientation is towards the east, it would refer to the western part of the desert. What Exod is saying is that Moses brought the sheep way down below, i.e. into the far reaches of, the desert where Horeb lay. The *f* variant εις simplifies the relation.

Over against MT's (they came to) the mountain of God, Horeb, Exod simply has "mount Horeb." A popular hex tradition has inserted του θεου. The shorter text is fitting, since God has not yet appeared to Moses; it is premature to designate it as mountain of God, whereas later, 4:27 18:5 19:3 24:13, the term is fully in order.

3:2 The opening clause has its word order "corrected" by the hex tradition in two instances: αὐτῷ (pronouns modifying the verb are usually placed next to the verb in Exod) is reordered to follow κυρίου and the phrase ἐν πυρὶ φλογός "in a fire of flame" is changed into the simpler and more common

1. From Sym.
2. Nor is Aq's νυμφευτοῦ specifically father-in-law. For the identification as Aq compare 18:5 and 1Kgdm 18:21.
3. For ינהג Aq uses ἤλασεν, the aorist of ἐλαύνω, rather than ἤγαγεν which he uses only for the Hiphil of בוא.

phrase ἐν φλογὶ πυρος by a popular variant. The latter may actually be a preOrigenian change since the phrase πυρὶ φλογός is unusual and copyists could hardly resist changing it to the common idiom.

The fire of flame is said to be ἐκ τοῦ βάτου. Since MT has מתוך hex has inserted μεσου after the preposition. The gender of βάτος can be either feminine or masculine. There is some disagreement as to which is classical and which is hellenistic,[4] but since both are attested as early as the fifth Century B.C. one can only follow the pattern of support. Here and in the following verses the masculine is clearly preferable, whereas in Deut 33:16 the feminine article seems original.

As at 2:6 Exod simplifies MT by his "he saw that" for the Hebrew "he saw and behold." The ambiguity of MT in failing to indicate change in subject from "angel" to "Moses" is reproduced by Exod, though the context shows that it must be the latter.

Exod introduces a word play in the narrative by contrasting a simplex καίεται with a compound κατεκαίετο. MT has different roots here: בער as active participle Qal vs אכל vocalized as ea passive; cf also Vulg arderet vs combureretur. What Exod is saying is: the bush burns with fire, but the bush was not burning up.[5]

3:3 Exod uses a favored construction of participle + finite verb to render a paratactic Hebrew construction. The נא particle of entreaty attached to אסרה is not rendered. It occurs nine times in Exodus, and three times (3:18 11:2 33:13) Exod has οὖν in its place; otherwise it is not rendered. Hex added δη after παρελθών which makes little sense. -- Exod does not use the cognate οψιν but ὅραμα as object of ὄψομαι to translate the cognate construction of MT.[6]

As in 2:18 מדוע is rendered by τί ὅτι. A popular B variant omits τί, thereby subordinating the clause to ὅραμα rather than modifying ὄψομαι. The choice of verb in the τί ὅτι clause is intentionally different from MT. MT uses יבער as in v.2, but there it was affirmed that it was indeed בער,

4. Cf Bl-Debr 49 and Walters 323f, as well as Thack 145.
5. For Aq and Sym only the rendering for בער is extant: Aq has ἀναπτόμενος "kindled," whereas Sym has ἐφλέγετο "was blazing, flaming."
6. Sym uses the synonym θέαμα.

but here Moses is surprised that it is *not* יבער. V.2 states that the problem was why it was not אכל, and so Exod uses the second verb of v.2, viz., the compound κατακαίεται. The problem is solved in the same way in Tar[P] Pesh and Vulg. A *d x* variant wrongly inflects the verb in the imperfect as in v.2; here only the present tense can be correct since the burning of the bush is a present reality to the inquisitive Moses.

3:4 Exod rightly interprets the first clause of the Hebrew as a subordinate condition, with the ἐκάλεσεν clause as the apodosis. The object clause for εἶδεν appropriately has a main verb προσάγει which like Vulg *pergerat* fits the context, correctly interpreting MT's סר; cf v.3 where παρελθών is used to render the same verb to introduce the root ראה. Exod along with Tar differs from MT in repeating κύριος as subject for ἐκάλεσεν whereas Sam has אלהים in both clauses; MT has אלהים in the second clause but יהוה in the first. Exod probably simply harmonized the text.

    The hex tradition has amplified ἐκ by μεσου in order to represent the חוך in מתוך. -- For the gender of βάτου see note at v.2. -- Moses' idiomatic reply τί ἐστιν is for the Hebrew הנני.[7]

3:5 A possible ambiguity obtains in the verse since no change in speakers is indicated; of course good sense demands that what is said is not from Moses but from God. The simplest "correction" is that of the B *b f z* text which changed καί to δε. Other texts add κ̅ς̅ and still others add an indirect object αυτω or προς αυτον (as Pesh). The context is, however, perfectly clear.

    The middle λῦσαι is idiomatic in the sense of "loose to one's own advantage"; the *b z* variant with the active imperative is no real improvement in sense.[8]

    Exod, along with numerous Hebrew mss, Tar[O] and Vulg, has the singular τὸ ὑπόδημα, since no foot has more than one sandal. Others including MT Sam Tar[P] Pesh have the plural since "feet" (though Tar[P] has

7. This was too free for Aq and Theod, who came up with the Hebraic ἰδοῦ ἐγώ.
8. Aq has ἔκσπασον, attested only here; Sym has the compound ὑπολῦσαι. Either adequately renders נשל.

28

foot!) have sandals. Nor does Exod represent the suffix of MT;[9] it would be otiose in view of the σου after ποδῶν. It is, of course, added in the hex tradition.

The ἐν ᾧ construction appears as εφ ω in Acts 7:33 and ms 130, and betrays the influence of Jos 5:15 where the same sentiment occurs but with ἐφ' ᾧ. Similarly Jos 5:15 has influenced an ƒ reading of αγιος for γῆ ἀγία. -- Hex has added επ αυτου after ἕστηκας to equal MT.

3:6 The ms pair 53' introduces the verse with "And Moses said: Who are you," an exegetical nicety to introduce God's self-identification. -- A B + tradition omits αὐτῷ which does equal MT, but this is secondary as the obelus in Syh shows. -- Exod literally translates the Hebrew with its "I am the God of your father," though three fathers are then listed. A few witnesses in the tradition have "fathers" possibly under the influence of the NT (Acts 7:32), though Sam also has the plural אבתיך. The transposition of τοῦ πατρός σου after ' Ἀβραάμ in the s tradition is another attempt at solving the possible incongruity of Exod.

Exod has καί before "God of Isaac" in contrast to MT, which may have a textual basis.[10] The repetitive θεός has created a number of variations in the tradition.[11] Some witnesses have omitted them as unnecessary, but this does make the singular τοῦ πατρός a real problem.

For ויסתר Exod has the free though adequate rendering ἀπέστρεψεν δέ, i.e. as though his text had read ויסר, but "turning aside the face" does hide the face.[12] εὐλαβεῖτο is an adequate rendering for ירא;[13] The popular variant with augment is the classical form.

Exod's choice of κατεμβλέψαι ἐνώπιον for הביט אל removes the harshness of "to look at (God);" after all, no man can see God and live, and Exod uses a verb to be taken in its literal sense of "to look down." Similarly the choice of ἐνώπιον enhances the avoidance of directly looking at God: "to look down before God." The C ƒ z text καταβλεψαι strengthens this un-

9. Cf SS 94.
10. Some Hebrew mss as well as Sam have ואלהי here.
11. For its articulation cf THGE VII, D.4.
12. Aq renders by ἀπέκρυψεν as might be expected.
13. Cf Helbing 25f.

derstanding by which Exod carefully avoids a literal rendering into Greek, which would itself constitute a misinterpretation.

3:7 As in v.6 the addressee is indicated by πρὸς Μωυσῆν over against MT. This is the third case of εἶπεν without change of speaker, and so Exod has clarified this by adding αὐτῷ in the second instance, and here by πρὸς Μωυσῆν.

The cognate participle ἰδών occurs here, occasioned by the cognate free infinitive in MT. It serves to intensify the verbal notion, i.e. "I really have seen (and mean to do something about it)."

The ἀπό phrase modifies κραυγῆς and describes cause or occasion; it is the taskmasters who are responsible for the outcry. Hex added αυτων after ἐργοδιωκτῶν to represent נגשׂיו, consistent with (ὀδύνην) αὐτῶν later in the verse. MT is inconsistent in the number of its suffixes: מכאביו צעקתם, נגשׂיו,, whereas Tar Pesh make all the suffixes plural.

The use of γάρ in the last clause is occasioned by the כי of the Hebrew, but it can best be understood here as a strengthening particle rather than a causal one: "I do know their pain."

3:8 Exod continues with plural pronouns referring to λαοῦ of v.7 as do Tar (over against MT Sam Pesh Vulg). -- For Αἰγυπτίων instead of "Egypt" cf note at 1:13. Exod's usage is shared by Tar Pesh Vulg.

In the tradition the first infinitive, ἐξέλεσθαι, is articulated by the Byzantine text, but not the second or the third.

Exod amplifies the text by interpreting the Hebrew infinitive להעלתו "to bring up" as consisting of two actions, both a bringing out, ἐξαγαγεῖν (from that land), and a bringing in, εἰσαγαγεῖν (to a good and spacious land); this is revised by the A F M *O C s* text to equal MT by omitting καὶ εἰσαγαγεῖν αὐτούς.

This good land is also designated as γῆν ῥέουσαν γάλα καὶ μέλι, a phrase found in exactly the same form in v.17, 13:5 and 33:3, and becoming a set idiom throughout the LXX. The land is also designated as the home (τόπου - place) where seven nations dwell; cf also v.17, 13:5 23:23 34:11 as well as 33:2. In each case the Gergeshite(s) is included in the list although always absent in MT. Exod knew the fuller tradition of Deut 7:1 Jos 3:10 24:11 where seven tribes are listed as constituting the preIsraelite populace of Canaan, though since Sam includes the Gergashites throughout Exodus it was probably in its parent text. A further difference between Exod and MT concerns articulation. In Exod only the first in the list, τῶν Χαναναίων, has the article; in MT each one is articulated.[14] Exod quite correctly does interpret the singular gentilic nouns as collective and places each one in the plural.

3:9 The adverb ἰδού (for הנה of MT) often occurs as a narrative particle used to highlight something in the story, here that the cry of the Israelites has reached heaven. -- The articulation of κραυγή in the F f tradition is stylistic; Exod leaves it unarticulated as in the Hebrew bound phrase. -- The word וגם is always rendered simply by καί throughout Exod.[15] The addition of ἐγώ to introduce a finite verb in first person is a favored construction in Exod;[16] in fact it occurs 38 times in chh. 1-34 and it is a simple variant to a finite verb occurring by itself, i.e. it does not imply emphasis in any way.[17]

The nominal τὸν θλιμμόν with its cognate verb θλίβουσιν well reproduces את הלחץ and לחצים.[18] In the text tradition the b group changed the simplex verb to εκθλιβουσιν with no real change in meaning.-- The curious and ill-fitting addition of και αποστειλον αυτους by the x text is unique in Exod and is reminisent of ἐξαπόστειλον τὸν λαόν μου which occurs eight times in chh. 4-10.

3:10 The aorist subjunctive ἀποστείλω barely differs in meaning from the future and can be rendered by "I will send." -- The C variant εις for the

14. For a comparative analysis see the discussion in THGE VII.D.5. Nor is the placement of καὶ Γεργεσαίων secure in the tradition; cf the discussion of its order at THGE VII.F.4.
15. The rendering καίγε is naturally found in Aq, but not by Sym and Theod who follow Exod.
16. See also SS 74.
17. For crasis of καὶ ἐγώ in the B f z variant see THGE VII.B.
18. Aq used the απο compound for these and also rendered את by σύν. Sym only changed τὸν θλιμμόν to another cognate τὴν θλίψιν. Theod retained the Exod text.

preposition πρός does not change the meaning.[19]

Exod freely identifies Pharaoh as βασιλέα Αἰγύπτου. This serves as balance to another amplification, i.e. of γῆς before Αἰγύπτου 2° (also found in Tar[O]). Moses is sent to the *king of Egypt* and he is to bring the Israelites out of the *land of Egypt*. -- καὶ ἐξάξεις as a simple future detailing what Moses will do simplifies the structure of והוציא, as does Sam;[20] this simplifies MT, and also harmonizes with the following verse, where Moses refers to his bringing the Israelites out of Egypt. Vulg clarifies by means of a purposive clause *ut educas*, a solution which renders explicit what is implicit in Exod.

3:11 Exod added βασιλέα Αἰγύπτου and γῆς (Αἰγύπτου) against MT as in v.10. -- In v.6 אנכי had been rendered by ἐγώ εἰμι, but here the verb alone obtains. This was not satisfactory to Origen since אנכי is a pronoun, so ἐγω was added in his hexapla, though its position over against εἰμι is uncertain.[21]

3:12 The use of ὅτι after λέγων is a Hebraism, not to be taken causally but rather as a doublet of λέγων, i.e. it introduces direct speech; comp Gen 21:30. MT is almost cryptically brief at this point simply having כי ויאמר. Exod explains who and to whom by adding ὁ θεὸς Μωυσῇ λέγων, the last word simply to remind readers that direct speech follows, though ὅτι already does this at this point. An A F + text omits the words added by Exod, so as to conform to the Hebrew. A *b* variant in the tradition emphasizes the response nature of the speech by changing εἶπεν to απεκριθη; *b s* also change ὁ θεός to κ̄ς̄; fluctuation between "God" and "Lord" seldom need be taken seriously throughout Exod.

The anaphoric referent in τοῦτο is by no means clear. Grammatically it could be the preceding clause ἔσομαι μετὰ σοῦ, i.e. God's constant presence remains signal proof of the divine origin of Moses' commission. Another possible interpretation makes the τοῦτο refer to ἐν 1° -- fin, but it

19. See LS sub εἰς I.b.
20. The Hebrew free infinitive in context takes on that context and continues the first person future of the previous verb, as in Tar[O] and Pesh.
21. According to Syh Aq and Theod had ἐγώ before εἰμι.

is difficult to make a future happening serve as σημεῖον for a present assurance, and it is probably best not to take it in this way.

The tradition shows great variety in dealing with ἀποστέλλω. It appears as future in *d*, and popularly as εξαποστελλω, and as εξαποστελω in B *n*. None of these variant traditions reflects Hebrew influence since MT has שלחתי which would suggest an aorist inflection. Exod, however, uses the present tense since the commission is not an action but a process. Moses is being sent and will remain a sent one.

The use of ἐν τῷ with an infinitive occurs only eight times in Exod (also at 16:7,8 27:7 28:31 29:36 30:15 34:29) and except for 30:15 where ἐν τῷ διδόναι renders לתת, it always represent ב + infinitive in Hebrew. The construction is a literalism taken over from the parent text.[22] The omission of μου in the phrase τὸν λαόν μου by A^txt M + could be a recensional change based on the Hebrew; MT has את העם, and Exod has added the pronoun thereby stressing the relationship σε ... μου: "*you* bring out *my* people."

The apodosis is introduced by καί even though there is no conjunction in MT; this Hebraic construction is hardly expected, and oddly enough is not changed in the tradition. The verb λατρεύσετε represents a change to the plural; i.e. Moses and the people are to worship at this mountain. Two variant texts react to the inconsistency in number: the *n* text changes the verb to an imperative singular, λατρευσαι, and the *x* tradition changes it to the third plural, i.e. as referring only to the people.

3:13 Moses' first objection to God's commission is introduced by ἰδού by which Exod points out something new in the story. It introduces a set of circumstances to which Moses reacts. The objection is laconically placed in the future tense throughout: ἐλεύσομαι ... ἐρῶ ... ἐρωτήσουσίν ... ἐρῶ, not in a potential mood as might be expected, though that is the clear intent. This contrasts with MT where the objection begins with a nominal clause: pronoun + participle, and only the apodosis contains a clear future ᵓōmar, i.e. an imperfect inflection.

22. Cf SS Inf. 80-82. Sym prefers a recognizable temporal clause structure and has ὅταν with a subjunctive verb.

What Moses will then say to the Israelites is that "that the God of your fathers has sent me to you"; by "fathers" is meant Abraham, Isaac and Jacob. An *f n* reading identifies this God as κυριος (as does Pesh), which changes the point of the objection; the question "what is his name?" in this tradition must mean What does that name, κυριος, mean? A popular B variant changes ὑμῶν to its homynym ημων; the resultant text identifies Moses with the people. This God is not just "of your fathers," but I too, am an Israelite, and he is "of our fathers."

The third verb is coordinated with the preceding clause in MT, but Exod makes it (ἐρωτήσουσίν) a conclusion, i.e. "when I shall go and say ... then they will ask." This is "corrected" by the hex tradition which added και to introduce the verb. The verb itself correctly interprets the Hebrew which simply says ואמרו "and they say." A *b x* tradition makes the conditional nature of the clause explicit by reading εαν ερωτησωσιν. The potential question asks for an ὄνομα for the God of the Fathers, which a *d f x* variant articulates in an attempt to improve the style. Exod uses the dative of possession αὐτῷ, i.e. "what name does he have"? An *O n* variant changes this to αὐτοῦ "What is his name," which is closer to MT.

3:14 Change of subject is emphasized in a *b n* + variant by its change of καὶ εἶπεν to a δε construction. The Catena tradition omits the καί and identifies the subject ὁ θεός as κυριος ο θεος, thereby making sure that the reader will realize that the explanation which follows refers to the κύριος which ὁ θεός here interprets. Exod in translating the reply אהיה אשׁר אהיה is faced with making sense out a sentence which would be a tautology if rendered literally.[23] Furthermore Moses is commanded to tell the Israelites 'אהיה has sent me." Exod realizes that the verb can be rendered by εἰμί or γίνομαι; only the first would be applicable to God, But a first person verb as the subject of ἀπέσταλκέν would be a grammatical absurdity. So Exod is driven to a participial form ὁ ὤν "the one who is." Jerome faced the same problem and Vulg renders *qui est misit ad vos*. Now returning to the <u>idem per idem</u> of MT, one can make sense. The first אהיה

23. Notice how Aq followed by Theod rendered it: ἔσομαι ὃς ἔσομαι! A Greek reader would find this an absurd tautology.

can be translated by ἐγώ εἰμι and the relative clause אשׁר אֿהיֿה becomes ὁ
ὤν. Exod thus has "I am the one who is." It is only in v.15 that it becomes
clear that this is the explanation of κύριος; κύριος is the one who is. Exod
thus explains יֿהוֿה as based on the root היֿה. It is doubtful whether one
should understand ὁ ὤν as anything more than this straightforward attempt
to make an acceptable Greek version of the Hebrew; it is not a philosophic
statement; it is rather a religious affirmation.

3:15 The verse begins with a third καὶ εἶπεν in a row without change of
speaker, made clear by πάλιν, which a popular hex variant reorders
according to the Hebrew word order.

The repetition of the formula of v.14 "Thus shall you say to the Israelites: x has sent me to you" makes clear that ὁ ὤν is κύριος identified as the ὁ
θεὸς τῶν πατέρων ὑμῶν of v.13 in turn explained as "God of Abraham and
God of Isaac and God of Jacob." The revelation of the name and its ex-
planation/identification is now complete.

Within the tradition some changes have been made. The Catena Text
has made the speaker κυριος ο θεος as in v.14, which see. -- For confusion
of ὑμῶν/ημων cf note in v.13. -- A popular text articulates the three cases
of unarticulated θεος.[24] The *d* tradition in characteristic fashion shortens
the text to "God of Abraham, Isaac and Jacob." The καί before θεὸς ᾿Ισαάκ
contrasts with MT, but equals Sam, and as in v.6 and 4:5 may have a textual
basis.

The second part of the verse reflects the question posed in v.13 as to
the ὄνομα. God assures the people (this is still part of what Moses is to
transmit to the Israelites) "This is my eternal name and memorial to all
generations." Exod has μού ἐστιν ὄνομα for שׁמי, which Hex reorders to
conform to MT. A *C n* variant changes the pronoun to μοι possibly under
pressure of the τί ὄνομα αὐτῷ of v.13.

Exod uses an adjective to render the idiom לעולם thereby correctly
reproducing the sense of the original. Exod has changed MT's coordinate
nominal clause ending the verse into a coordinate nominal predicate simply
by using καί for וֿזֿה, thereby creating a common Semitic pattern of a + a',

24. See THGE VII.D.4.

a joining of two synonyms to reinforce what is being said. Thus "my name" is called a μνημοσύνην.[25] The pattern: b + b' also obtains with αἰώνιον finding its parallel in γενεῶν γενεαῖς; the latter is transposed in a (hex.?) tradition which suggests MT's לדר דר. The Hebrew repetition of the noun simply means "every," and presumably the Exod phrase can best be translated by "to all generations." The phrase occurs only here in Exod. The repeated דר also occurs at 17:16 as מדר דר but there Exod has ἀπὸ γενεῶν εἰς γενεάς.[26]

3:16 Exod begins with ἐλθὼν οὖν συνάγαγε "so go and collect"; the οὖν is a particle indicating logical consequence in the narrative. A popular A F M variant omits it; the omission is palaeographically conditioned by συν immediately following it. The x variant ἀπελθων for ἐλθών can only be a careless mistake.

Exod, along with Sam Pesh, speaks of the elders of the Israelites rather than of Israel. The Byzantine text group omits τῶν υἱῶν, thereby equalling MT. The term γερουσία is in Exod fully synonymous with πρεσβύτεροι; they are used interchangeably for which compare e.g. 24:1,14 with 24:9. As elders of Israel γερουσία occurs also at 3:18 4:29 12:21 24:9, whereas πρεσβυτέρους occurs at 17:5 18:12 19:7 24:1,14.[27] -- For the variant ημων cf note at v.13.

Divine self-revelation is shown by the passive perfect since the Lord's appearance to Moses results in a present communication. And as in v.15 the God of the Fathers is identified as being God of Abraham and God of Isaac and God of Jacob in exactly the same text form as in the preceding verse though MT has a shorter text.[28]

The choice of the root επισκοπε- to render פקד is common in LXX

25. For which Sym uses ἀνάμνησίς μου -- the noun is synonym.
26. The Hebrew phrase seems to have produced various reactions. Sam has לדר ודר which is similar to Tar[O]: לכל דר ודר. Tar[P] uses a bound phrase but in the plural לדרי דריך. Vulg also coordinates: *in generationem et generationem.*
27. Aq has πρεσβυτέρους; he never uses γερουσία for זקן, though at Isa 37:2 he does have γέροντας.
28. For articulation of θεός in the tradition cf THGE VII.D.4.

and is here used in its root meaning "look upon, observe."[29] The Lord states that he has indeed observed them and the things that have happened. The *b* variant future misses the point of the statement; God is not promising to take a look at their difficulties, but rather has already done so.[30]

3:17 For εἶπα the majority of text witnesses have the classical form ειπον which in turn through uncial confusion of ο-ε led to the widespread B reading ειπεν. The use of εἶπα followed by a future verb suggests divine intention; this is particularly clear from the *O s* text reading a complementary infinitive αναβιβασαι instead of the future. The αναβιβω of the *n* text is the Attic future. -- For τῶν Αἰγυπτίων cf note at 1:13. -- The *b* tradition introduces εἰς τὴν γῆν by και εισαξω υμας thus ridding the text of the zeugmatic ἀναβιβάσω ... εἰς; cf note on להעלתו in v.8. -- For τῶν 2° to the end of the verse cf notes on v.8.

3:18 The first clause constitutes the response of the Israelites to what God says. In these first instructions to Moses Israel's γερουσία is to go with him to Pharaoh and make their demands for release. Once Aaron is introduced into the scene he replaces the eldership in the actual carrying out of the instructions. -- Exod uses the full title "Pharaoh king of Egypt" here and in v.19 (as at vv.10,11), though MT lacks "Pharaoh" in both verses. Usually both MT and Exod have "Pharaoh" alone as MT does at vv.10, 11. Exod consistently gives the full title throughout this ch., and later uses it only in 6:11,13,29 14:8 (in agreement with MT). In the tradition a very popular F M variant omits the word, possible a revision under Hebrew influence. -- Over against MT Exod (and Vulg) continues with the singular ἐρεῖς. It is Moses, not Moses and the elders, who is to address Pharaoh.

As in 5:3 "the God of the Hebrews" as well as "our God" is not identified as "Lord" in Exod. A very popular F M variant has added κυριος and κυρω resp., thereby conforming to MT. -- Exod along with Sam Tar Pesh

29.   For the use of a cognate noun before a finite verb to translate a free infinitive + cognate verb cf Thack 47-50.
30. Vulg first translates the verb פקד in the sense of "to visit," i.e. *visitans visitari (vos)* but since this does not fit for *omnia quae acciderunt* repeats it in the second sense: *et vidi omnia,* etc.

Vulg has understood נִקְרָה as a derivative of קָרָא "call" and that in an active sense of "summoned"; cf 5:3 where MT has נִקְרָא. -- What Moses is to say to Pharaoh is placed in the subjunctive πορευσώμεθα, not in the future indicative as at 5:3 8:27. In the first instance it is still potential: "We would go." The demand becomes much more insistent in the actual encounter with Pharaoh when the future tense is employed. A popular variant possibly under the influence of 5:3 has the future indicative spelling here, a simple scribal error.

3:19 The use of a first or second person pronoun with a corresponding past tense verb, often to indicate contrast of person, occurs 15 times in Exod and is always inspired by a parent text having the pronoun except at 31:11: ἐγὼ ἐνετειλάμην σοι for צִוִּיתִךָ. The verbs are often perfect inflection but where the present reality is in the foreground as here (ἕστηκας v.5; ἑωρά-κατε 20:22; οἴδατε 23:9; δέδωκα 31:6; οἶδας 32:22; ἡμαρτήκατε 32:30). Twice such verbs render a Hebrew participle (ἕστηκα 17:6,9), and once an imperfect (οἴδαμεν 10:26). All others occur with an aorist verb (6:5 10:1 33:12 twice). -- The omission of Φαραώ by *oI C b* probably is a recensional correction to conform to MT.

Exod ends the verse with an ἐὰν μή phrase (as Vulg: *nisi*). This proves nothing with respect to the difficult וְלֹא of MT since Exod as Jerome was simply making good sense. Only a strong might, a brute force, would compel Pharaoh to let the people go as subsequent events proved only too clearly.[31]

3:20 The anthropomorphic description of the display of divine power as a "stretching out of the hand" is taken over by Exod from the Hebrew. Since the subordinate participle modifies the subject of πατάξω no μου is added after χεῖρα, which a popular hex tradition does add. -- For τοὺς Αἰγυπτίους cf note at 1:15.

Only here are the plagues called θαυμασίοις "wonders"; usually they are called σημεῖα "signs," or sometimes τέρατα. Oddly enough only once is a plague called πληγή (11:1). These usages are all due to the parent text.

31. For the unusual μετά construction see SS 119f.

The relative pronoun is in the dative by attraction to the case of its antecedent. The prepositional phrase ἐν αὐτοῖς renders בקרבו idiomatically.[32] -- The idiom μετὰ ταῦτα is used adverbially in the sense of "later on, afterwards." Here it renders אחרי כ as at 11:1,8 34:32, but it is also used for מחר at 13:14.

3:21 The Byzantine text changes the intent of the first clause by reading (καὶ δώσω) τοῦτο (before the Egyptians) instead of χάριν τῷ λαῷ τούτῳ. This then becomes a kind of proleptic statement, the anaphoric referent of τοῦτο being the conditional sentence ὅταν -- fin, whereas Exod makes the straightforward promise "I will extend favor to this people (i.e. the Israelites) before the Egyptians." -- In the tradition ἐναντίον is changed to ενωπιον in a popular F M variant with no change in meaning.[33]

Temporal and conditional clauses in Hebrew are often marked by an introductory ויהי or והיה. In Greek such a marker would be otiose. Exod does omit the marker at times as here (also at 1:21 4:8 12:25 13:14,15 22:27), but may represent it as at 4:9 12:26 καὶ ἔσται ἐάν; 13:5 καὶ ἔσται ἡνίκα ἄν, and 3:11 καὶ ἔσται ὡς ἄν. These latter are all Hebraisms due to the parent text.

Exod's love for variation is well-illustrated within the verse. In MT the same verbal form is found in the protasis and the apodosis: לא תלכו - תלכו. Exod chose two different verbs, the present subjunctive ἀποτρέχητε for the protasis and the future indicative ἀπελεύσεσθε for the apodosis, with no lexical distinction intended.

3:22 This is the positive counterpart to the negative statement of v.21b; this is clear from the adversative ἀλλά, here equivalent to the German *sondern*.[34]

Ms 58 and Sam have an initial "and a man shall ask from his neighbour" on the analogy of Exod's opening "and a woman shall ask from

32. Aq translates in Hebraic fashion as ἐν ἐγκάτῳ αὐτοῦ.
33. For the general pattern of ἐναντίον/ἔναντι/ἐνώπιον in Exod see THGE VII.L.3., and for a full statement see Sollamo.

34. For the sparsely supported A B + variant omitting the word see THGE VII.P.

(her) neighbour"; a stemmatic connection between ms 58 and Sam is, however, most unlikely. -- Exod does not represent the third feminine singular suffix on מִשְׁכֶנְתָּה since αὐτῆς occurs after συσκήνου,[35] and it can be taken as modifying the coordinate noun phrase.

A C b variant has reordered ἀργυρᾶ καὶ χρυσᾶ to the more usual one of "gold and silver." The hex tradition has added σκευη before χρυσᾶ (as before ἀργυρᾶ) thereby conforming to MT. Exod quite correctly used the collective ἱματισμόν to render the plural שְׂמָלֹת, since it is clothing in general rather than specific garments which were taken from the Egyptians.

The verb σκυλεύσετε "you shall despoil" is undoubtedly the text of Exod, though the tradition had much trouble with it. A unique B variant reads an aorist imperative which merely exaccerbated the theological difficulty of God ordering the despoiling of the Egyptians. The majority of witnesses changed it to some form of συ(ν)σκευαζω (either aorist imperative or future indicative) or with double prepositional element (επισυσκ.), but this is no great improvement, since this more or less means "deceive, cheat.[36] Exod, however, had no difficulty in accepting the notion of God's advice to plunder the Egyptians in contrast to later theologians.

35. For which Sym has σταθμούχου "landlord."
36. Sym adopted the Exod reading, whereas Aq translated נִצַּלְתֶּם by συλήσατε which is a synonym of σκυλεύω "strip off" especially of arms, and so in general, "pillage, plunder." The reading of ὁ συρ' according to Procop was ἐκτινάξατε "shake off" which is an exact equivalent of the reading of Pesh.

Chapter 4

4:1 The δέ structures both here in v.2 show change of speaker. Exod understood the particle הן as Aramaic and so made a question instead of a statement. Then to make sense out of the question an apodosis taken from 3:13 τί ἐρῶ πρὸς αὐτούς is added.[1] The translator adds οὖν to ἐάν in order to intensify the question: "But should they"; it is omitted in B C z, probably due to homoiot.

The γάρ clause is unusual and is of course based on the Hebrew כי. Once הן is understood as ἐάν the כי clause no longer fits well, and it can only be taken as an interruptive statement. What Exod presumably means is that the Israelites saying God did not reveal himself to you is proof for the ἐάν clause, viz. that the people do not believe in Moses nor pay attention to what he is saying.

Exod substitutes ὁ θεός for the tetragrammaton, by which it is clear that the revelation of the divine name "Lord" to Moses has not been accepted or believed by the Israelites. -- ὅτι is here used to introduce direct speech; comp note on ὅτι at 3:12.

4:2 The word κύριος as rendering for יהוה is seldom articulated. In the nominative the article occurs at 9:27 where Pharaoh says ὁ κύριος δίκαιος, and where the γάρ particle occurs, i.e. as ὁ γὰρ κύριος, in 14:25 16:29 34:14. In the accusative it occurs only once, 9:30, in οὐδέπω πεφόβησθε τὸν κύριον. Similarly in the genitive it occurs only once in Aaron's statement at 32:5 ἑορτὴ τοῦ κυρίου. As might be expected τῷ κυρίῳ occurs more often (13:12 twice 13:15 15:1,21 16:25 24:1 30:12 31:15) but always for ליהוה except at 24:1 where it has no equivalent in MT. So the articulation in the *b* *n* variant is clearly secondary.

The question in Exod is somewhat wordier than MT which simply has מזה בידך. The τοῦτο is undoubtedly conditioned by the זה of מזה;

1. Aejmelaeus, ZAW 80--81 considers it textually based.

nonetheless it makes for a perfectly intelligible question: "what is this, namely, the thing in your hand?" Variant texts have attempted to simplify the question by various omissions, but none changes the sense of the question.

4:3--4 The narrative continues with καὶ εἶπεν with no indication of change of subject; in the tradition only ms 619 adds κ̅ς̅ to indicate this (as does Vulg).

Exod does not translate the suffixes in the Lord's command to Moses, since it is obvious that Moses stretches out *his* hand and take hold of *its* (the snake's) tail. Hex supplies σου or αυτου wherever they are lacking throughout v.4 to equal MT.

The account of Moses' carrying out the divine order again uses the particle οὖν in the sense of logical sequence. It was popularly replaced by και which equals MT and may constitute an early recensional intrusion into the tradition.

Exod carefully reproduces the pattern of v.3 in Moses' execution of God's command but in past tense. Thus ῥῖψον ῥῖπτω» αὐτὴν ἐπὶ τὴν γῆν becomes ἔρριψεν αὐτὴν ἐπὶ τὴν γῆν and ἔκτεινον τὴν χεῖρα becomes ἐκτείνας (οὖν) τὴν χεῖρα, and ἐπιλαβοῦ τῆς κέρκου becomes ἐπιλάβετο τῆς κέρκου (even though MT has different verbs and modifiers in the last pair). This same parallel occurs with the resultant signal action καὶ ἐγένετο ὄψις and καὶ ἐγένετο ῥάβδος.

4:5 Grammatically this verse does not fit well into its context either in Exod or MT, since it is a purpose clause without a main clause. Presumably the purpose clause depends on the divine orders and their fulfillment given in vv.3 and 4; in other words the sign of Moses' staff becoming a snake and then returning to its original form is enacted ἵνα the people may believe in Moses' commission by the Lord. The awkwardness of the construction was felt in the tradition. Accordingly a popular plus added και ειπεν κ̅ς̅ (or αυτω) at the beginning. (Note Vulg's *inquit* after *ut credant*).

Exod adds σοι after πιστεύσωσίν as in v.1; the Byzantine text omits it, thereby agreeing with MT. -- The subject of ὦπταί is in the same terms as

42

in 3:15 except for the necessary third (for second) pronoun adjustment. B omits κύριος but the identification of κύριος as the God of their fathers" is important to the narrative.[2] For the καί before ' Ισαάκ see note at 3:6.

4:6 The second sign to the people. As usual Exod places the indirect pronominal object of the verb as close to the verb as possible, which hex reorders after κύριος to correspond to MT. The B 843 + text has a first aorist inflection instead of εἰσένεγκε. Both are possible but the B text here and in v.7 is weakly supported (the imperative forms occurs only here in Exod), and the second aorist is probably Exod. In both cases a well-supported A variant spells the -γκε ending as -γκαι which is a spelling rooted in homonymy.

Unusual for Exod is the recurrence of the genitive pronouns σου and αὐτοῦ; the only one missing is after χεῖρα 2°, but αυτου has been supplied in a popular hex tradition.

A popular gloss has added a divine command to introduce verse b: "And he said: Remove your hand from your bosom," probably to correspond to verse a.-- Instead of ויוצאה Exod has an expanded text: "and he brought out his hand out of his bosom." The prepositional phrase has support in some Hebrew mss and Sam, and so may well have a textual basis. A popular F M reading has substituted αυτην as object of the verb, probably as a prehexaplaric correction based on MT.

In the last clause ἐγενήθη is used rather than ἐγένετο. The passive occurs only eight times in Exod (also at 2:10 10:13 11:3 12:29,30 14:24 39:4), whereas the middle ἐγένετο occurs 25 times (as well as six times in the plural) with no distinction in meaning as far as I can see.[3] ἐγένετο is often used in the sense of "it happened" + a time indicator, but the passive also obtains in that sense at 12:29 14:24. Both occur in the sense of "become" (compare 2:10 4:6 with 4:3 7:10), and both are used as past tense of εἶναι (compare 12:30 with 9:26 10:22). As might be expected εγενετο obtains as a popular variant here as well. MT has a הנה construction, which Aq and Theod represented by ἰδού.

2. For the popular articulation of the three unarticulated instances of θεός see THGE VII D.4.
3. The distinction referred to in Thack 238f. can not be seen in Exod.

The Hebrew text insists that Moses' hand became leprous like snow; in Exod his hand simply becomes "like snow," i.e. it became white losing the color of healthy flesh. One variant in the tradition actually adds λευκη as an epexegetical explanation of the simile.[4]

4:7 Once again εἶπεν occurs without subject or object indicated, though an *n* variant does add αυτω. -- πάλιν 1° is introduced rather ambiguously by Exod. It is not clear whether it modifies εἶπεν, i.e. "again he said," or as taken in the critical text, εἰσένεγκε; a *d* variant clarifies this by reordering it after the verb. It has no basis in MT and some witnesses omit it.

Except for the final clause, the language of vv. 6 and 7 is almost word for word the same except for τὴν χεῖρα αὐτοῦ in v.6 which becomes αὐτήν in v.7 (as in MT). A *d* tradition shortens the text considerably to εισενεγκε παλιν αυτην και εισηνεγκεν και εξηνεγκεν ταυτην for the three clauses. Since αὐτήν differs from its parallel in v.6 the urge to conformity created variant texts substituting either την χειρα (F *b x*) or the full την χειρα αυτου (*n s t*) for αὐτήν.

Exod has throughout vv.6 and 7 disregarded the differentiated pattern of MT to impose its own rhetorical form. MT changed from a pattern with Hiphil of בוא in two clauses, then the Hiphil of יצא, and in the final clause of v.6 a nominal pattern with הנה, then the Hiphil of שוב in two clauses, the Hiphil of יצא in the next one, and a final שוב Qal clause. Exod does not follow these changes but repeats the patterns almost exactly. Nor does he follow the pattern in the last clause but interprets the rather cryptic Hebrew "And behold it (i.e.his hand) returned as its flesh (had been)," translating freely: "And again it was restored (from the verb ἀποκαθίστημι) to the color of his flesh," which is probably what MT intended.[5] The tradition had difficulty with Exod's ἀπεκατέστη, some witnesses omitting the augment before κατ-, others having the aorist passive with or without the augment before κατ-. The variants do not change the sense of the

4. Aq and Theod add λεπρῶσα which hex adopted so as to correspond to MT; Sym represents MT by καὶ ἐφάνη ἡ χεὶρ αὐτοῦ λελεπρωμένη.
5. Aq of course used ἀπεστράφη to translate שוב since ἀποστρέφω and ἐπιστρέφω are his usual equivalents for this root.

44

passage. -- The *n* text adds the subject η χειρ αυτου, making explicit what is already implicit.

Exod's τὴν χρόαν τῆς σαρκός is made necessary by his failure to render מצרעת "leprous" in v.6. The "like snow" of v.6 is now made clear; it referred to color, since now the "color of his flesh" is restored. A B *f z* variant changes the "his" (i.e. of flesh) to αυτης, i.e. referring to "hand."

4:8 For Exod's disregard of the marker והיה (in contrast to v.9) see note at 3:21. The protasis of the conditional sentence distinguishes between believing in you and hearing the voice, in conformity to MT. By "the voice of" is meant "pay attention to the message of (the first sign)"; a *d s t* text has σου before τῆς φωνῆς, which leaves the following genitive construction at loose ends; probably it is to be taken as explicative of σου, i.e. "(hear) you, (in) the voice of the first sign."

The conditional sentence is a future more vivid one. A popular A M tradition has an aorist subjunctive instead of πιστεύσουσίν; this would be mixed condition, but the variant may be sensible as expressing doubt in view of v.9 which envisions the possibility of not believing either sign.

The second sign is called τοῦ σημείου τοῦ ἐσχάτου as in MT. But other signs are to follow and an extremely popular F M variant changes ἐσχάτου to δευτερου.[6] The apodosis in MT coalesces the compound protasis into a single zeugmatic structure "believe the voice," which Exod partially clarifies by adding σοι after the verb. Further exegetical clarification is afforded by an *n* variant which adds δια before the genitive, i.e. believe in you through the last sign. The zeugma of MT was neatly solved by Vulg which distinguishes between לקל 1° and 2° in the verse: the first one becomes *sermonem* modifying *audierint*, but the second after *credent* is *verbo*.

4:9 The first verb in the protasis, πιστεύσωσίν, is curiously modified by two datives, one of person σοι, and one of thing τοῖς δυσὶν σημείοις τούτοις for which I can find no parallel; it must mean "believe you in the matter of these two signs." An M C tradition omits σοι, not necessarily due to the

6. Sym has ἐπομένου, i.e. the following sign.

Hebrew since it could be a stylistic change. A *d* variant has simplified it by changing it to σου, i.e. "believe in these your two signs."

The apodosis details instructions to Moses as to what he is to do should the Israelites not accept him even after he has performed these signs. He is to take some water from the river (note the partitive use of the preposition ἀπό[7]) and pour (it) on the dry ground. The first ἐπί modifying a verb of action takes the accusative, whereas ἐπί with the genitive at the end of the verse modifies the verb ἔσται.

The final statement is clearer in Exod than in MT. Exod makes a single clause out of MT's two clauses: "and there shall be water which you will take from the river" and "and it will become blood on the dry ground" by eliminating the peculiar and unnecessary second והיו of MT. The hex tradition inserts και εσται before αἷμα which illustrates the kind of mechanical "fixing up" of the text which Origen did in the hexapla.

4:10 Moses' objects that he is not a speaker. The address δέομαι κύριε also occurs at v.13 and 32:31; it is an entreaty form to begin an urgent request from God for which comp note at v.13. His statement οὐχ ἱκανός εἰμι "I am incapable," or more colloquially "I simply can't," is even more graphic than MT's (אנכי) לא איש דברים, which is rendered literally by Aq as οὐκ ῥημάτων. A popular F M[txt] variant has ουκ ευλογος "not reasonable," in other words I cannot make a reasonable or logical presentation. Much closer to MT is an ευλαλος variant in a number of witnesses, a reading originating in Sym; compare also the semantically closely related ευγλωσσος found in a few mss.

The temporal designation πρὸ τῆς ἐχθὲς οὐδὲ πρὸ τῆς τρίτης ἡμέρας also occurs at 21:36 and without ἡμέρας at 21:29 (compare also מתמל שלשם with כ at 5:7,14), meaning "hitherto, up to now," and is best treated as an idiomatic expression.[8]   The popular χθες variant to ἐχθές is the Attic form. -- The A *n* + reading of και for οὐδέ is a stylistic one; using και rather than the negative οὐδέ makes clear that the second

7. Cf SS 160.
8. Note Aq's καίγε ἀπὸ τότε λαλήσαντός σου.

πρό phrase is coordinate with the first one. -- The second οὐδέ joins what follows with the coordinate πρό phrases. Within the second οὐδέ clause ἀφ' οὗ is an idiom meaning "since" representing the Hebrew מאז. as also at 5:23 9:24.

Exod's ἤρξω λαλεῖν makes explicit what is implicit in MT's בדרך. An F M C s reading changes ἤρξω to the perfect, probably to show that God is still speaking, but Exod understands the verb as showing the time when God began speaking. The O tradition has the aorist λαλησαι possibly under the influence of the aorist ἤρξω.

θεράπων is the characteristic rendering in Exod of עבד, just as παῖς is characteristic of Gen. Only seldom (eight times) does Exod use παῖς, and never Aq's word, δοῦλος, and when עבד means "slave, hireling," he uses οἰκέτης (5:15 12:44 21:7,26,27 32:13). Elsewhere for the idiom "house of servants" (13:3,14 20:2) Exod has οἶκος δουλείας.

The last clause is independent in Exod, but in MT is a כי clause. Hex "corrects" Exod by inserting a postpositive γάρ. -- The two adjectives "thin voiced and slow of tongue"[9] are renderings of כבד פה and כבד לשׁין.[10]

4:11 The addressee is specified as Moses in Exod (with Tar[P]) rather than the pronoun "him." The n λεγων gloss is the common Hebraic marker for introducing direct speech in LXX.

In MT the two מי clauses have the same verbal root as predicate, but Exod distinguishes by using ἔδωκεν and ἐποίησεν resp. The former is an excellent choice since it is often used to render שׂים in the sense of "put, place," but its primary intent "give" also fits well in the context. Exod understood the inflection ישׂום as an old preterite form, probably correctly. MT joins the two clauses as well as the four nominals in the second clause by או; Exod uses only καί, and renders the four nominals not as a series but as two pairs. -- Exod has δύσκωφον καὶ κωφόν "deaf and dumb" which reverses the order of MT.[11]

9. For the compounds see SS 70.
10. Translated by Aq as βαρὺς στόματι and βαρὺς γλώσση.
11. Apparently The Three corrected the order since they used μογιλαλός to represent the first one (אלם).

The last clause is an οὐκ question, i.e. one expecting an affirmative reply. MT has "Is it not I, Yahweh?" Exod uses κύριος ὁ θεός. The κύριος is of course necessary in the argument, since the τίς questions must be answered by a name, and its omission by B z is simply a careless mistake. Why Exod should have added ὁ θεός is not as obvious, but possibly the designation of deity was thought appropriate in a creation context.

4:12 The command πορεύου for the Hebrew לך is a word of encouragement and should be understood in the sense of "go ahead, come on." Moses can proceed since God will not only help him with his speaking, "will open his mouth," but will even instruct him in those things he is to speak. The collocation ἀνοίξω τὸ στόμα σου concretizes the Hebrew אהיה עם פיך "I will be with your mouth." The emphatic ἐγώ before the first person singular verb is especially appropriate in view of the divine affirmation of the preceding verse.

For συμβιβάσω a popular F variant has the Attic future inflection συμβιβῶ. The verb renders the Hiphil of ירה.[12] -- A B b variant reads the singular o for ἄ.[13]

Exod's rendering μέλλεις λαλῆσαι is most appropriate for the Hebrew תדבר. The n reading λαλειν for the infinitive λαλῆσαι is tautological in view of μέλλεις.

4:13 This verse represents a change of speaker which Exod in contrast to MT shows by Μωυσῆς. A popular F M reading omits the subject, an omission which is probably recensionally inspired.-- For δέομαι κύριε, see the note at v.10. δέομαι interprets the Hebrew בי correctly.[14]

MT simply has "send, pray, through whom you would send" which Vulg neatly translated by *mitte quem missurus es.* Exod translates the

12. Aq translates by φωτίσω, but Sym, by ὑποδείξω; this is also the case at v.15 and at 24:12 (where, however, Exod has νομοθετῆσαι).
13. See THGE VII.G.6 for a discussion of this variant.
14. Aq and Theod take it as the homonymous prepositional phrase, and renders by the thoroughly unintelligible ἐν ἐμοί. This is, however, also the rendering for it in LXX at Jdg 6:13,15 13:8 1Kgdm 1:26 25:24 3Kgdm 3:17,26 as well. More intelligible is ἐπ' ἐμέ κύριε for עלי אדני at 2Kgdm 14:9, probably in the sense of "on me (rest the responsibility), Lord" is intended.

relative clause literally, but amplifies the first part freely though not incorrectly by "appoint another capable one," which by contrast to his own pathetic οὐχ ἱκανός εἰμι of v.10 clearly tells God "anybody but me, pray." Incidentally the *f* pair 53' substitutes μηδαμως κυριε οτι ου δυναμαι for the entire statement of Moses, which is not even a paraphrase, and its source is obscure.

4:14 The Hebrew idiom אף חרה "anger became hot" occurs six times in Exodus and in every case but one a noun in the dative is used as part of the translation in Exod: ὀργῇ here and at 32:10.11, and θυμῷ at 22:24 32:19. In 32:22 the expression is translated by the imperative ὀργίζου. For the verbal idea (finite verb or participle) either ὀργίζω or θυμόω obtain. The dative nouns throughout stress the verbal idea, thus "becoming really angry."

For ἰδού see the note at 3:9. The order οὐκ ἰδού is the question order contrasting with καὶ ἰδού later in the verse. The question is syntactically ambiguous; it is probably to be analyzed as a nominal sentence with the first cut after ἰδού. The question being asked is "Is not there Aaron your brother the Levite?"

For cognate participles rendering Hebrew free infinitives see note at 3:7. -- Exod uses αὐτός to indicate the subject both for λαλήσει and for ἐξελεύσεται thereby calling attention to Aaron as the new character in the narrative. Exod also adds over against MT a σοι to modify λαλήσει; after all, what concerned Moses was not that Aaron was an able speaker, but that he would stand in for him.

Exod uniquely interprets the participle יצא as an imperfect verb, probably done on the analogy of the future verbs in the context. According to MT Aaron is already on the way, whereas in Exod this is still in the future.

The *f n x* variant σου for the dative σοι after συνάντησίν is possible but unusual.[15] -- The interpretation of the Hebrew בלבו as ἐν ἑαυτῷ is not incorrect;[16] what Exod is saying is that Aaron will be *inwardly* glad, which is probably what שמח בלבו really means.

15. Cf Johannessohn, Gebrauch 295f.
16. Cf SS 95.

4:15 The rendering ἐρεῖς for דברת is rare though Pesh also attests to it. Certainly εἰπεῖν regularly renders אמר. In the first ten chapters אמר is translated by εἰπεῖν 100 times but εἰπεῖν equals דבר only six times. On the other hand throughout Exod λαλεῖν is the rendering for דבר 62 times, and only once, at 31:12,[17] does it correspond to אמר in MT. An M C tradition adds τους λογους τουτους to the verb as an epexegetical explanation since ἐρεῖς used absolutely is unusual. Exod's τὰ ῥήματά μου makes explicit what is implicit in את הדברים. Moses is to feed Aaron the divine message; cf also 7:2; in fact Moses must put them into his mouth.

For the clause καὶ ἐγώ as well as for συμβιβάσω see notes on v.12. -- Since the phrase καὶ τὸ στόμα αὐτοῦ is here added to "your mouth" the pronominal modifier is plural: ὑμᾶς (ἃ ποιήσετε). The A f variant ποιησεται for the final verb makes sense but it is rooted in itacism and need not be taken seriously.

4:16 The first clause is explicative of and summarizes the preceding verse. Exod places the two pronouns αὐτός σοι next to each other to emphasize the relation of Moses and Aaron; the speaking is of Aaron, but it is performed for Moses. A popular F M hex variant places σοι after the verb to conform to MT, thereby losing the point of Exod's ordering. A very popular B* F M variant changes the verb to a simplex stem; in spite of its strong support it is clearly secondary. The προσ- compound plus πρός was a stylistic nicety on the translator's part. Another popular F variant, probably a Byzantine text revision, adds τα before πρός. The variant arose under the influence of τὰ πρός later in the verse, and though it makes a nice balance over against the last clause, it is the wrong balance; the final clause is contrasted with the preceding one as the δέ after σύ makes obvious.

Exod simplifies the syntax of the parent text by omitting היה from והיה. V.16b of MT is best analyzed by making the first cut after והיה. The rest of the verse is then the compound subject of היה. This compound subject consists of two clauses which are coordinate and parallel. Each has a nominative pronoun + an imperfect inflection of היה, ל + a pronoun

17. See THGE VII Q.

referring to the subject of the other clause, and a second ל + a nominal. The היה + the second ל means "become" rather than "is." Exod changes the intent of the Hebrew in a subtle fashion. Rather than using a form of γίνομαι to indicate היה ל, Exod uses a form of εἰμι + a predicate nominative. In the first clause for לך "for you" Exod has σου so that the clause must be rendered "and he will be your mouth." The second clause is similarly constructed but does have the dative αὐτῷ for לו. An *n* variant has αυτου for αὐτῷ probably due to the influence of the genitive σου in the preceding clause; here the genitive is, however, inept. Exod also avoids the crassness of "shall become a God" by rendering לאלהים by τὰ πρὸς τὸν θεόν which is also the interpretation of Vulg: *in his quae ad deum pertinent.*

4:17 Exod amplifies "this Rod" of the Hebrew by an explanatory τὴν στρα-φεῖον εἰς ὄφιν, thereby identifying it as the rod of vv.2--4. Its omission by an F M^txt + variant is likely due to MT. -- Exod often avoids the Hebraism by which Hebrew's inability to inflect the relative pronoun is overcome such as in אשר ... בו of 17b. Exod has ἐν ᾧ[18] which should have been sufficient; the recapitulative prepositional phrase ἐν αὐτῇ is a Hebraism.

4:18 The new section in the narrative begins with a transitional δέ construction. For ἀπέστρεψεν the tradition supplies compounds with various prepositional elements: επεστρ., ανεστρ., and even υπεστρ., but none with much support, nor with any real difference in meaning.[19]

For ᾽Ιοθόρ as well as for γαμβρόν and its *b d x* variant see notes at 3:1. -- For καὶ λέγει as a rendering for ויאמר (לו) see note at 2:13. The popular και ειπεν αυτω is probably due to recensional activity based on Hebrew influence.

πορεύομαι is future indicative in form but in the context it ought to have hortatory meaning.[20] Here the verb probably simply signifies strong intent to go: "I am going to go," i.e. Moses informs his father-in-law that he is leaving and his mind is made up.

18. As instrumental; cf SS 120.
19. Cf. THGE VII.Q.
20. Unfortunately examples of a hortatory use of the future indicative cannot be substantiated in the papyri according to Mayser II.1.213f.

The intent of ὄψομαι must be to express the reason for the return, i.e. "that I may see," but again Exod uses a coordinate future indicative. -- ὑγιαίνων, present participle, is used idiomatically for לשלום, i.e. "(go) staying healthy." Hex sources render the phrase literally as εἰς εἰρήνην (with εν ειρηνη probably an internal variant within it).[21]

The last clause, μετά -- fin, has no Hebrew counterpart. It is taken from 2:23 and serves as a bridge to the following verse which in MT follows with harsh abruptness, with Yahweh ordering Moses to do what he has just informed Jethro he is going to do.

4:19 In the tradition a popular M reading amplifies Μαδιάν by placing γη before it, as in 2:15. -- Exod renders האנשים המבקשים simply by οἱ ζητοῦντες; the hex tradition of course prefixes it with οι ανδρες so as to correspond exactly to MT. Hex also reorders σου τὴν ψυχήν to fit that of נפשך.

4:20 By using ἀναλαβών as a translation of the neutral ויקח of MT Exod adds the notion of accompaniment, i.e. taking along; cf the same usage in Gen 24:61 46:6 and 48:1 and compare 50:13. -- Exod disregarded the pronominal suffixes of אשתו and בניו as unnecessary; the wife and sons are of course his. -- The pronominal object of ἀνεβίβασεν is the neuter αὐτά to agree with παιδία as the nearer coordinate antecedent. The *x* reading αυτας takes on the gender of γυναῖκα, which is strange. The bizarre υπο of *n* for ἐπί is simply a careless error.

Exod interpreted החמר as a collective and so used a plural τὰ ὑποζύγια in which surprisingly Vulg's *asinam* did not share. -- Exod apparently chose ἐπέστρεψεν for variation over against ἀποστρέφω in v.18. There is no semantic difference involved, though the text is not fully certain. A widespread F M variant witnesses to an απ- compound; *n* reads ανεστρ., and *f* uses υπεστρ. In such cases the combined witness of A B + is determinative. Furthermore it also fits into Exod's pattern of free variation.

21. The full statement πορεύου εἰς εἰρήνην is attested by F[b] anonymously but is certainly Aq.

Exod interprets the polysemantic Hebrew phrase מטה האלהים as τὴν ῥάβδον τὴν παρὰ τοῦ θεοῦ, "the staff which is from God"; the C text has απο for παρά without change of meaning. Tar also were dissatisfied with the phrase and have "the staff with which signs were done before ייי." Exod's τὴν παρὰ τοῦ θεοῦ does prepare the way for it as an instrument used by Moses with wondrous effect later on with the plagues as well as during the wilderness journey.

4:21 Exod uses a compound genitive absolute construction to translate ב + bound infinitive with pronominal suffix + marked bound infinitive.[22] The σου of the genitive absolute construction is identical with the subject of (ὅρα) ποιήσεις, an unclassical phenomenon. The participles are both present inflections, presumably since going and returning are processes and not simply accomplished actions. But the *d* text has the second participle in the aorist, presumably on the presumption that the going and returning would be completed before the wonders were to be performed before Pharaoh.

The syntax of ὅρα -- Φαραώ is not immediately obvious. The object of ὅρα is all of πάντα -- Φαραώ; the first cut comes immediately after ὅρα. What is intended is "take care that you do all the wonders...," with the object of ποιήσεις preposed, and a recapitulative αὐτά after ποιήσεις to remind the reader of that preposed object. Exod has the plural ταῖς χερσίν instead of the singular of MT, as does Pesh. There is no particular rationale for the plural; in any event the word must be metaphorical for "power."

Exod introduces the next clause with the pronoun ἐγώ to lay stress on the contrast: *you* will perform ... but *I*. The τέρατα will be unconvincing because God will harden Pharaoh's heart. Exod's σκληρύνω is precisely what MT means.[23] Exod is throughout the narratives concerning Pharaoh and the exodus (chh.4--14) true to the recurring theological theme that the Lord hardened (σκληρύνω) Pharaoh's heart. The theme recurs at 7:3 9:12 10:20, 27 11:10 14:4,8,17 and Exod consistently renders the Piel of חזק by

22. For examples for the former see SS Infin. 88--91.
23. Aq translates אחזק by his usual rendering ἐνισχύσω "I will strengthen" which is not overly appropriate in this context. Sym's rendering is somewhat better: θρασύνω "I will make bold, rash," then "audacious."

this verb; note here Vulg's *indurabo*. The *f* text reorders αὐτοῦ before σκληρυνῶ. This places the αὐτοῦ close to ἐγώ, but that makes the wrong contrast; the ἐγώ contrasts God's action with that of Moses, not God vs Pharaoh. More significant is the reordering of αὐτοῦ before τὴν καρδίαν by an A *n z* tradition, an order commonly found in Exod, and it could here easily be defended as Exod. The order adopted has, however, such overwhelming support including our oldest Greek witness, Cod B, that it is probably original. -- A *C* reading specifies αὐτοῦ as φαραω; it is indeed a correct identification, but no reader could possibly be misled by αὐτοῦ.

4:22 Exod continues to stress the contrast between God's action and the activity of Moses by introducing the verb ἐρεῖς by the pronoun σύ, whereas MT simply has ואמרת. -- Over against MT which has both "my son" and "my firstborn" Exod has μου only with the second. Hex of course "corrects" this by adding μου after υἱός as well. -- The messenger formula τάδε λέγει κύριος occurs ten times in Exod (also in 5:1 7:17 8:1,20 9:1,13 10:3 11:4 32:27), sometimes with further identification, but at times without. It represents a formulaic rendering of the Hebrew כה אמר יהוה.

4:23 The *n* tradition consistently substitutes the classical ειπον for εἶπα.[24] -- Only Exod has the τὸν λαόν μου tradition for MT's בני,[25] but this is not an improvement. The identification is correct but only υἱός would tie the υἱός of v.22 to the τὸν υἱόν σου of 23b. Exod has probably used λαόν for variation for the middle member; it is also consistent with later references such as 5:1 7:16 8:1 9:1,13 10:4. -- In the tradition *O* has reordered μοι λατρεύσῃ to fit the order of MT.

The next clause in MT is difficult because the verb is preterite; ותמאן means "and you refused" as Jerome recognized: *et noluisti dimittere eum*.[26] So instead of a statement of fact Exod has εἰ μὲν οὖν μὴ βούλει, i.e. if Pharaoh refuses to comply, God will kill his oldest son. A majority F M text in the tradition is συ δε ουκ εβουλου; this represents a more classical usage

24. For the originality of the Hellenistic form cf TGHE VII.M.9.
25. The Later Revisers also have λαόν.
26. Note also Aq's rendering of the verb as ἀνένευσας or that of Sym ἠπείθησας, both of which translate תמאן correctly.

than Exod with its unusual μή + present indicative. Other attempts to improve the text are: ου for μή (in *b*), and βουλη for βούλει in the A *f* + text.

Exod also uses a plural pronoun αὐτούς to designate τὸν λαόν μου even though the singular verb was employed in λατρεύσῃ. The fact that MT continues with a singular suffix in לשלחו promoted the correction to αυτον in another very popular F M variant. -- Within the conditional sentence οὖν is used as a balancing particle both in the protasis and the apodosis, "if on the one hand ... then actually."

For the syntax of ὅρα see the note in v.21. Here too the first syntactic cut in the apodosis is to be made immediately after ὅρα. -- The change from the future to the present αποκτεινω in the Byzantine tradition may well be recensional since MT has a participle. Hebrew participial predicates are often rendered in Greek by a present tense form of the verb.

4:24 For ἐγένετο δέ see note at 2:11. For the second place designation, καταλύματι, *f* arbitrarily adds αυτου. Throughout the episode, vv. 24--26, the antecedent for any third masculine singular pronoun must be Moses of v.21. -- MT identifies the one who met him as Yahweh,[27] but Exod together with Tar have ἄγγελος κυρίου, probably to mitigate the harshness of the account; it is the messenger of the Lord, not Yahweh in person, who met Moses. An F M *oI* C variant goes even further by omitting κυρίου, so that all reference to the Lord is absent from the account.

In the second clause the main verb occurs in the imperfect since "was seeking" as well as "trying to kill him" is a process rather than a simple event. -- A popular hex variant transposes αὐτὸν ἀποκτεῖναι to conform to the order of MT.

4:25 Sepphora, Moses' wife, took a ψῆφον which means "a pebble,"[28] and with it she circumcised her son. In contrast to v.20 where Moses' sons are

27. Sym and Theod confirm this by their κύριος, but Aq renders it doubtful by his ὁ θεός.
28. Aq corrects to πέτραν "rock." Sym simply added πετρίνην, thus "a rocky pebble," whereas Theod with good rational instinct has σκρότομον a "cutting instrument," presumably meaning a "sharp stone."

mentioned, here the singular is used, and only the eldest son, Gershon, is meant.

Exod apparently interprets MT's תגע as a Qal though the Masoretes vocalized it as Hiphil. But it has no object suffix in Hebrew and Exod's προσέπεσεν "she fell down at" makes good sense.[29] Exod did not translate the suffix of רגליו, and a popular hex tradition has added αυτου, which does not clarify much of anything. One still does not know whether it refers to Moses or the angel or to her son.

The statement made by Sepphora in Exod represents an attempt to make some kind of sense out of the Hebrew but independent of the actual Hebrew lexemes. The Greek may be translated as "The blood of the circumcision of my child is staunched." In v.26 exactly the same words are repeated. Exod took the reference to circumcision from למולת of v.26 and has disregarded all reference to "bridegroom" and made the reference to blood refer to the circumcised son, which makes more sense than the "bloody bridegroom" of MT. In fact, instead of חתן Exod has ἔστη "has stood still, is stauched," and some misreadings have been suggested. Suggestions made include חתם - to stamp, seal, or חסן - be strong, hence firm, but these have no basis in LXX anywhere.[30]

4:26 The verse has been omitted by B + in the tradition, but this is simply an error due to homoiot, and the variant text may be dismissed out of hand. Problematic is the intent of the opening clause. In MT it is clear that the angel withdrew from Moses but Exod has an ambiguous καὶ ἀπῆλθεν ἀπ' αὐτοῦ. The references could indeed be the same as in MT but since Exod and MT represent separate traditions this is by no means assured. Equally possible and probably to be preferred is that the subject is Sepphora; the translation would then be "and she went away from him." This would fit in

29. Cf on the other hand the discussion in Helbing 298f. Sym translates the phrase by ἀψαμένη τῶν ποδῶν αὐτοῦ, i.e. "touching his feet," whereas Theod has used the finite inflection ἥψατο "she touched." In neither case is it clear whether "she" or "it" (i.e. the foreskin) is the subject of the verbal idea since the Greek word ἀκροβυστία is also feminine (as is the Hebrew ערלה!).
30. The Three render MT literally by ὅτι νυμφίος αἱμάτων σύ μοι which is no more luminous than is MT.

56

much better with the account of ch.18 where Jethro arrives at camp bringing Moses' wife and two sons, note especially 18:2 μετὰ τῆς ἄφεσιν αὐτῆς. In the text tradition a popular variant clarifies the text by adding ο αγγελος; in Byzantine times the interpretation that it was the angel that went away predominated. At least this tied vv.25 and 26 more closely to v.24 and corresponds to MT.[31]

In any event the parting took place διότι...; why what Sepphora said should be the reason for the departure is not at all clear, but then neither is אז of MT obvious since this means "at that time, then." What Sepphora said is in Exod an exact repetition of what she said in v.25 which in view of διότι is proper. In MT where Sepphora says something mysterious a second time the text is also different.[32] -- The omission of μου in A + is a scribal error due to homoiot, the preceding word also ending in ου.

4:27 The narrative reverts to Aaron's role (see vv.14--16), who is divinely ordered to join Moses. The δέ construction which introduces the verse shows change of subject. -- The change of καὶ συνάντησεν to εις συναντησιν in the Byzantine text tradition is directly due to its occurrence in the preceding clause; it does not change the meaning of the passage.

This is the first mention of τῷ ὄρει τοῦ θεοῦ; at 3:1 MT did designate Horeb by this term but Exod did not; see note at 3:1. Pesh here adds "Horeb," probably on the basis of the 3:1 tradition, and also adds "your brother" after Moses.

The final clause is pluralized in Exod: "and they kissed each other," over against all other ancient witnesses "and he kissed him." An early preOrigenian correction to κατεφιλησεν αυτον made heavy inroads in the tradition. Exod simply makes explicit that the greeting was mutual.

4:28 A hex addition of τω before Ἀαρών represents the Hebrew preposition אל.[33] -- The words which Moses related to his brother were not his own but

31. Neither Sym nor Theod clarify this either by their καὶ ἀφῆκεν αὐτόν.
32. This is reflected in the other traditions. The Three have νυμφίος αἱμάτων as in v.25 but Aq and Theod continue with εἰς περιτομός, whereas Sym has τῆς περιτομῆς; these are renderings of למולת.
33. For its secondary character in the B + tradition see THGE VII.D.1.

κυρίου, which the *f* group for no apparent reason changes to του θεου.

The Hebrew שלחו אשר is ambiguous; it is more readily rendered by who had sent him," but the larger context makes it unlikely that this was intended; the parallel clause also has such a clause אשר צוהו which cannot possibly mean "who had commanded him" since the אשר must modify האתת. So here the אשר clause must modify דברי (יהוה). Exod understood this and has οὓς ἀπέστειλεν without rendering the suffix, which lack the hex tradition filled by adding αυτου. Exod's text is not as clear as Vulg: *quibus miserat eum*. The *z* tradition eased the lexical difficulty of Exod by changing the verb to ελαλησεν, while the *f* group subordinates the next clause by changing the conjunction καί 2° to ποιησαι. -- Cod B uniquely changed σημεῖα to ρηματα probably because of the verb ἐνετείλατο; "words" are more readily commanded than "signs."

4:29 Sam Pesh and Vulg have the first verb in the plural as well as the second. When a verb has a compound subject in Hebrew the verb preceding is usually singular to agree with the nearer subject; when the verb follows it must be plural. Exod followed the pattern of MT in this respect. -- Exod does not render the word כל to characterize the eldership, but a popular hex reading does so.

4:30 In accordance with the arrangements which the Lord detailed in v..15--16 it is Aaron who serves as mouthpiece for Moses so that the words which Moses had received from God are spoken by Aaron to the γερουσία. The noun ῥήματα is not only modified by πάντα but also by the demonstrative ταῦτα. The omission of ταῦτα by an M *b x* + variant may simply be due to homoiot rather than a revision due to the Hebrew.

The subject of the relative clause is ὁ θεός whereas MT has יהוה. All other ancient witnesses agree with MT. One might expect this to be a textual matter, except that the same thing is true in the following verse, as well as at 5:17 and 21. Not until 6:9 is there an indication that Moses has communicated the name "Lord" to Israel (compare 6:6--8 with 9); prior to this Moses and Aaron used ὁ θεός in speaking of God to the Israelites; compare 3:13,14.

It is also Aaron, not Moses, who performed the signs which were detailed in vv.4--8(or 9). An *n* reading has the verb in the plural, εποιησαν, making Moses and Aaron joint performers, while the *b* text makes μωυσης the subject of ἐποίησεν.

4:31 Exod uniquely has καὶ ἐχάρη whereas MT and all other ancient witnesses attested to וישמעו. The verb χαίρειν is a common rendering for the root שמח as at v.14, which must also have been presupposed here. The people rejoiced because God (cf note at v.30) looked upon the Israelites, and saw their affliction. For ἐπεσκέψατο see note on the root επεσκοπε- at 3:16. -- The phrase αὐτῶν τὴν θλίψιν has been reordered by hex to conform to the suffixed noun of MT.

For the final clause not only is a δέ construction used to indicate change of subject but ὁ λαός is added to make certain that the subject of the preceding clause, ὁ θεός, was not bizarrely taken as continuing subject. The aorist participle of κύπτειν with the finite verb προσκυνέω also occurs at 12:27 34:8 as well as in Gen 43:28; comp also later occurrences in Isa 46:6 and Judith 13:17 for the same collocation. -- An *f* reading added τω κ̄ω̄ at the end of the verse, a gloss also found in Pesh.

Chapter 5

5:1 The phrase μετὰ τοῦτο renders אחר; for the contrast with μετὰ ταῦτα
see note at 3:20. According to 3:18 Moses and the γερουσία of Israel were
to approach Pharaoh for leave to depart; here Moses and Aaron
representing the people without the elders go in to Pharaoh, and in the
name of the Lord ask release for his people in order to make a feast to him
in the desert. For a singular verb before a compound subject in Exod
(though not here in MT), and the one following in the plural, cf note at
4:29. MT uses the verb באו absolutely and only has אל פרעה after the
second verb. Exod quite rationally has πρὸς Φαραώ modifying εἰσῆλθεν
and then an αὐτῷ after εἶπαν. Hex corrects by reordering πρὸς Φαραώ to
modify the first verb, and of course then omitting αὐτῷ. An F *b d n* variant
has the classical ειπον instead of Exod's εἶπαν.[1] -- For the τάδε formula see
note at 4:22. -- The order "Send my people away" occurs in the quoted
divine order to Pharaoh throughout the Exodus story (4:23 7:16 8:1,20
9:1,13 10:3), but only here with the purposive clause with ἑορτάσωσιν
rather than the verb λατρεύω; the notion of making a feast is of course an
act of worship. -- The reordering of μοι ἑορτάσωσιν by the majority A F M
reading is hex to fit the Hebrew text.

5:2 A tradition of uncertain origin but probably hex adds κ̄ς after ἐστιν,
which equals MT. An A text adds θ̄ς the origin of which is independent of
the κ̄ς tradition. The failure to render יהוה may be textual in origin; Exod
often uses ἐστιν to render הוא used as predicate of a nominal clause, and
he could have misread יהיה as such.

Exod has the common phrase τοὺς υἱοὺς ' Ισραήλ for the first ישראל,
thereby contrasting with the τὸν ' Ισραήλ in the last clause. -- The use of
the present tense for ἐξαποστέλλω shows the adamance of Pharaoh's
refusal; the popular future variant, εξαποστελω, is probably a scribal error
rather than a recensional change due to Hebrew influence;
haplography/dittography of *lambda* is a common scribal error for this root.

60

5:3 For the use of the historical present λέγουσιν see note at 2:13. -- Exod as often adds the addressee, αὐτῷ (Pharaoh). In the narrative portions of Exod εἶπεν/λέγει or εἶπαν/λέγουσιν occur 192 times of which 124 name the addressee. In fact, Exod tends to name the speaker as well.

The clause ὁ --- ἡμᾶς is exactly the same as in 3:18, but here it is a literal rendering of MT. The perfect tense προσκέκληται is contextually fitting; the divine summons has created a present imperative for the pilgrimage festival. An F *b s* text changes the prepositonal element in the compound to επι- and ἡμᾶς to the dative with no change in meaning. The tendency to elaborate compounds in Byzantine Greek is well illustrated by *C*'s προσεπικεκληται, again with no real change in lexical content.

For πορευσόμεθα in the future indicative see note at 3:18. The aorist subjunctive variant with a great deal of scattered support is homonymous and secondary. -- The particle οὖν is well-chosen since the πορευσόμεθα clause is the logical consequence of the divine summons of the preceding clause.

As at 3:18 Exod simply has τῷ θεῷ ἡμῶν modifying θύσωμεν; a very popular variant has supplied κ̄ς̄ to conform to MT.

In the final μήποτε phrase Exod has θάνατος ἢ φόνος as subject of συναντήσῃ,[2] i.e. "lest death or the sword should overtake us." In this way Exod avoids the harshness of MT where Yahweh is the subject and רבד or ברח are the means by which Pharaoh is made existentially aware of the divine confrontation.[3] θάνατος is a standardized translation for רבד; רבד "pestilence" occurs 46 times in LXX; once at Hab 3:5 it was misunderstood as dābār, λόγος; 11 times it is omitted from the triad "sword, pestilence and famine" in Jeremiah, and in the remaining 34 cases LXX has θάνατος. In each of these cases the word means "fatal illness, pestilence."[4] -- φόνος "murder, slaughter" is also unexpected for the concrete ברח where μάχαιρα or ρομφαιά would be expected.[5] φόνος did not become popular for ברח, howver; it only occurs elsewhere at Lev 26:7 and Deut 28:22.

---

1. See the discussion in THGE VII.M.9.
2. Cf Helbing 229.
3. Cf SS 124f.

5:4 The Hebrew תפריעו means "cause to let hang loose, be slack"; so here Moses and Aaron are accused of being responsible for the people slackening up their efforts. Exod's διαστρέφω also has a pejorative sense of "distort, render twisted," hence here "to divert."[6]

Exod's τὸν λαόν μου for את העם contrasts with the Lord's τὸν λαόν μου of v.1 and emphasizes the arrogance of the monarch in claiming the Israelites as his people. The omission of μου in a popular F M variant may well be a preOrigenian revision.

A hex plus added a third person genitive pronoun after ἔργων, but whether in the singular or the plural as in Tar is uncertain; the evidence of the O mss is divided.[7]

The final clause is a free but idiomatic rendering of MT's לכו לסבלתיכם "go to your burdens." Exod's choice of the compound verb ἀπέλθετε "go away!" is somewhat more scornful than the neutral לכו of MT. -- For the noun τὰ ἔργα here and in v.5 cf note at 1:11. In the tradition a popular A B F variant has the Hellenistic aorist form απελθατε.[8]

5:5 Exod renders the opening nominal clause of Pharaoh's statement by a verbal one, but the sense is satisfactorily given by the present tense indicating the process of "multiplying, becoming many." -- The particle νῦν is here one of stress rather than of time, i.e. like "now" in English but without major stress.[9]

The last clause completely reinterprets MT; it accuses Moses and Aaron in terms similar to v.4, i.e. of interrupting the work pattern of the people, but Exod has "we shall certainly not let them rest," i.e. as an emphatic future expressed by a subjunctive. Pharaoh states his intention to increase the work load of the Hebrew slaves to such an extent that their numbers may gradually decrease. Note again the use of οὖν as a word showing this clause as logically following the preceding one. -- The addition of αυτων after ἔργων in the tradition is a hex plus to fit the Hebrew.[10]

---

5. Aq and Sym have μάχαιρα, and Theod has ρομφαιά.
6. See Helbing 165. Aq uses the rare word ἀποπετάζετε "diffuse, spread out;" Sym has the straightforward ἀποτρέπετε "turn aside," and Theod διασκεδάζετε "scatter, disperse."
7. See SS 95.
8. See the discussion in THGE VII.M.9.
9. For the omission of τῆς γῆς by a B z text see THGE VII.P.

5:6 The hex tradition made two additions to Exod to "correct" its shorter (than MT) text. After Pharaoh it added εν τη ημερα εκεινη and αυτου after γραμματευσιν. -- To translate נגשים Exod uses ἐργοδιῶκται "taskmasters" as in 3:7 and in vv.10 and 13 but not in v.14.

For the second class of officials, the שטרים, Exod consistently uses γραμματεύς "scribe" but in the sense of overseers who kept the record of works and therefore in charge of the corvee; cf also vv.10,14,15,19. Throughout the Pentateuch and Joshua this is consistently used to render שטרים except for four instances in Deut (1:15 16:18 29:10 31:28), where γραμματοεισαγωγεῖς is used.

5:7 The use of the verb προστίθημι + infinitive is idiomatic for LXX in the sense of "repeat" or "again, anymore"; in origin it is a Hebraism for Hiphil יסף + infinitive. Exod here combines it with οὐκέτι, thus "no longer shall there be," with the ἔτι particle added for emphasis. The future passive verbal inflection is used indefinitely, which in the tradition has been popularly emended to second plural forms of the three voices, thereby conforming more exactly to MT; the second plural is an early (probably preOrigenian) change.

Exod renders תבן by the singular ἄχυρον the first time since it is intended as a generic or collective concept, but as ἄχυρα the second time since it refers concretely to the individual serfs gathering straw.

The term πλινθουργίαν is a hapax legomenon in LXX but its meaning is clear: "brickmaking"; it translates the cognate phrase ללבן הלבנים "to brickmake bricks." -- For καθάπερ --- ἡμέραν see note at 4:10.[11] A popular A M plus after ἡμέραν, και το της σημερον, has come in from v.14.

Exod use of a nominative pronoun is inspired by the parent text and serves to contrast the new subject with the indefinite passive construction of

---

10. Cf SS 95.
11. The phrase in Aq is a literalistic rendering of MT: καθὰ ἐχθὲς τρίτην, whereas Theod revises Exod by τῆς τρίτης for τὴν τρίτην ἡμέραν. Sym has an idiomatic καθάπερ καὶ πρότερον which may have influenced Vulg's *sicut prius*.

the preceding clause. -- Exod changes from a present stem πορεύομαι[12] to an aorist stem for συνάγω, which is voided by *C*'s συναγετωσαν. The contrast is, however, meaningful in Exod, since semantically πορεύομαι is a process, a continuous action, whereas συνάγω "gather, collect," need not be such.[13]

5:8 A very popular A F M variant has a synonym πλινθουργιας for πλινθείας. Exod, however, used that word for the cognate phrase in v.7, here using a simplex to designate the single lexeme הלבנים.

MT has the nominal pattern: pronoun + participle three times within this verse, but Exod uses three different ones: αὐτοὶ ποιοῦσιν, σκολάζου-σιν, and κεκράγασιν. The last-named changes the sense of the parent text with its timeless nominal into a perfect verb, a past idea with continuing effect. The other two patterns: a pronoun + present tense verb, and a simple present tense, are commonly used by Exod to translate a nominal clause with participial predicate.

The relative pronoun ἧς is not accusative but genitive by assimilation to its genitive antecedent. A popular F reading has added ποιησουσιν after ποιοῦσιν. This divides the first part of the verse into two parts: "and the levy ... they shall perform each day" and "you shall place on them; nor shall you remove anything." That it is secondary is clear from the resulting awkwardness of the ἐπιβαλεῖς clause.

Exod renders תמול שלשם not as might be expected from v.7 as a reference to past custom, but to the present arrangement, "according to each day." The Hebrew phrase in contrast to v.7 is an adverbial one, which difference Exod recognized.

Exod apparently overlooked the fact that Pharaoh was addressing the ἐργοδιῶκται and the γραμματεῖς and has ἐπιβαλεῖς and ἀφελεῖς in the singular. A very popular F M variant constitutes an early correction to the plural probably simply made for good sense. An *f* addition of απ αυτων after ἀφελεῖς makes explicit what is already implicit in the verb.

---

12. Of The Three only Sym changes Exod's πορευέσθωσαν to a subordinate participial construction ἀπερχόμενοι.
13. The Three translate קשׁשׁו by καλαμάσθωσαν "let them gleam," a more literal rendering of the Hebrew verb.

The *b* text has a doublet και σκολασται εισι which barely differs lexically from the verb σκολάζουσιν; it is probably based on v.17. -- Hex added αυτοι before κεκράγασιν so as to correspond to MT. Exod introduces direct speech by the marker λέγοντες, which is hardly necessary in view of the verb "cried out."

5:9 The Hebrew text is somewhat more graphic with its prepositional phrase עַל הָאֲנָשִׁים, whereas Exod has no preposition, τῶν ἀνθρώπων τούτων. Hebrew lacks a pronoun, but it is sensible for indicating the people. The verb is singular in congruence with the neuter plural subject τὰ ἔργα. -- Exod has μεριμνάτωσαν twice, positively with ταῦτα (ἔργα), and negatively with ἐν λόγοις κενοῖς, following Sam Tar^O and Pesh which presuppose ישעו in both places rather than MT and Tar^P with יעשו in the first instance. The parent text for Vulg's *expleant* is not fully certain. An A reading has a middle rather than an active form in both cases but with no semantic change.

The last phrase interprets דברי שקר "words of falsehood" as λόγοις κενοῖς, i.e. empty discourse, therefore "vain, useless talk." Pharaoh characterizes all this talk about an exodus for cultic purposes as so much useless talk. An *n* variant substitutes the homonym καινοις for κενοῖς, a mistake, though "new discourse" would not be meaningless.

5:10 Exod now switches to the imperfect in describing the actions of the foremen and overseers - "they were urging them on and saying." The same verb is used here as in v.13, κατέσπευδον, but here MT has ויצאו "they went out" probably read as יאצו (אצים) in v.13). An *n s* reading has κατασπουδαζον which is semantically related but not as fitting in the context as the Exod text, since an accusative of person is unusual with κατασπουδάζω. One might, however, compare Gen 19:15 where the Hiphil of אוץ is translated by ἐπεσπούδαζον (τὸν Λώτ). -- The compound subject occurs here without modifiers; Hex has added του λαου to the first and αυτου to the second in accordance with MT.

Direct quotation is again introduced by the marker λέγοντες; cf v.8. Pharaoh is quoted by means of the messenger formula τάδε λέγει, as saying οὐκέτι δίδωμι ὑμῖν ἄχυρα, which varies slightly from MT with ἔτι as a sensible exegetical plus; after all Pharaoh had provided ἄχυρα hitherto. For the plural ἄχυρα see the note at v.7.

5:11 The verse explicates the previous statement by Pharaoh. Exod uses the double pronoun αὐτοὶ ὑμεῖς (for אתם)[14] with the former in its original reflexive sense, i.e. "you yourselves"; its omission by a *b* text is only formally equivalent to MT.-- Exod has recast the paratactic "go, take" of MT into a good Greek construction: a nominative participle + present imperative. The harshness of Pharaoh's order is made more vivid by the judicious use of pronouns: αὐτοὶ ὑμεῖς ... ἑαυτοῖς. Within the relative clause[15] a variant with scattered support is an itacistic ευρηται for εὕρητε; since the antecedent of the clause is the neuter plural ἄχυρα this is a sensible variant.

The concluding statement is a γάρ clause in imitation of the כי clause of MT. Normally a γάρ clause supplies the rationale for a verbal idea, here the collecting of straw, but this can hardly be the case here. The statement can best be understood then as an elipsis of some kind,[16] probably for something like "So get going"! -- The use of τῆς συντάξεως is probably occasioned by v.8, but it is well-chosen; a literal των εργων for עבדה would not have made a great deal of sense.

5:12 Exod understood ויפץ as a Qal, which is possible from the consonantal text; it has the aorist passive form διεσπάρη. MT's Hiphil can also be used in a middle sense, hence "scatter," i.e. the Israelites scattered (themselves). Exod also failed to render ארץ, which hex corrected by adding γη before Αἰγύπτῳ. The purposive infinitive συναγαγεῖν uses the synonym for συλλέγετε of v.11 for the same Hebrew verb, once again showing Exod's tendency to vary his translation.

5:13 -- For the imperfect κατέσπευδον see note at v.10.[17] Here too an *s* reading substitutes κατεσπουδαζον. The Greek verb requires an object,

14. See SS 72.
15. For ἄν rather than εαν in relative clauses see THGE VII.B.
16. See LS s.v. I.3.
17. Aq translates its subject הנגשים by οἱ εἰσπράκται, for which see Job 39:7.

αὐτούς, which is lacking in MT but supplied in Sam by בעם.

Direct speech is again introduced by the marker λέγοντες. -- Exod's τὰ ἔργα is a good rendering for MT's מעשיכם,[18] though a popular F M hex reading adds the expected υμων. ἔργα is modified by an attributive participial phrase "those which are daily due," an idiomatic translation of the Hebrew idiom דבר יום ביומו. This daily quota is not to be changed but is to continue as καὶ ὅτε τὸ ἄχυρον ἐδίδετο ὑμῖν. MT has a shorter text: בהירת התבן, but all other ancient witnesses agree with Sam which adds נתן לכם.

The conjunction καί is used in the sense of "even, also," thus "as even when." -- ἄχυρον is here again generic and therefore singular; see note at v.7. The verb is in the imperfect middle since the provision of straw had been an ongoing process. An A f variant to the verb shows the gradual loss of -μι stem inflections, ἐδίδετο presupposing a root δίδω.

5:14 Exod makes the distinction between שטרים and נגשים clear by adding τοῦ γένους before "of the Israelites"; i.e. the γραμματεῖς belonged to the race of the Israelites and were appointed by Pharaoh's נגשים, called ἐπιστάτεις "superintendents" rather than the usual εργοδιωκτεις. So these Egyptian officials carried out Pharaoh's wishes and were put in charge over the Israelite overseers. When the serfs did not fill their unreasonable quotas it was the γραμματεῖς who were beaten. -- Φαραώ is articulated by τοῦ, which a d reading changes to an improbable dative.

A popular F M variant has the direct speech marker, λέγοντες, inflected in the genitive; this makes clear that it is not the γραμματεῖς but the ἐπιστάτων who are the speakers.

The question again refers to the levies, τὰς συντάξεις, as in vv.8 and 11. In each case MT has a different lexeme; here it has חק, i.e. the inscribed regulation. The noun is here in the plural, presumably because each overseer had his own assigned quota. For the Byzantine variant της πλινθουργιας see note at v.8.

For καθάπερ --- ἡμέραν see note at 4:10. MT continues with גם תמול גם הירם neatly rendered by Vulg: *nec heri nec hodie*. The point is that neither yesterday nor today did you fill the quotas as formerly. Exod simply has καὶ τὸ τῆς σήμερον omitting all reference to yesterday. Within the καθάπερ clause a popular M 835 variant has added a καὶ; this balances ἐχθές and τρίτην ἡμέραν as a και ... και construction admittedly, but it is rare in this idiom.

5:15 With change of subject Exod again uses δέ. The change of εἰσελθόντες to the simplex in the *x* tradition is not an improvement. The subject expressed is "the overseers of the Israelites," appropriate since they were the ones who were beaten. The *b* group adds "the Israelites," thereby making it a popular complaint to Pharaoh. This complaint is introduced by the direct speech marker and a question phrase ἵνα τί, a synonym of διὰ τί of v.14. Within the question hex corrects the word order of οὕτως ποιεῖς to conform to MT. -- The *f* tradition has created a sensible variant to οἰκέταις in ικεταις "suppliants," but this is simply an itacism.

5:16 For ἄχυρον in the singular see note on v.7. -- In contrast to v.13 δίδοται is in the present tense since it is a present reality about which the complaint is made. -- τὴν πλίνθον rather than the expected πλινθείαν is used to translate the plural לבנים; presumably πλίνθος is here used with ποιεῖν in the sense of "to make brick" rather than "to make bricks."

No subject is named for λέγουσιν but the context makes clear that the ἐπιστάτεις of Pharaoh are meant. -- MT twice refers to עבדיך but Exod uses two different terms, changing from ταῖς οἰκέταις to οἱ παῖδές;[19] for these terms see note at 4:10.

The final clause concludes with a statement having a verb in the future, though a present tense would be expected. The future is probably intended to show Pharaoh what the continuation of these unjust requirements will involve, and οὖν relates the clause logically to the preceding statements: "so you will be doing your people wrong." The statement is difficult in MT and Exod has made good sense of it.[20]

---

18. Cf SS 95.
19. For the second The Three all have οἱ δοῦλοί.
20. It is of some interest to see what The Three have made of it. Aq has καὶ ἁμαρτία λαῷ σου which Theod smooths out to καὶ ἡ ἁμαρτία εἰς τὸν λαόν σου. Both seem to represent the preposition ל before עמך. Sym renders the phrase quite differently by καὶ ἁμαρτίαν ἔχεις presupposing a different vocalization for עמך to mean "with you."

5:17 The subject changes and Exod shows this by adding αὐτοῖς; a pair of *b* witnesses makes doubly sure by inserting φαραω as the named subject. -- The Hebrew uses a repeated participle נרפים with the pronominal subject אתם between the two: "idle are you, idle." Exod varies this by making two clauses with little difference in meaning: a present tense verb "you are unoccupied," and the second a derivative noun "an unoccupied one" + ἐστε. The Byzantine text by repeating σχολασταί makes a triplet, which would be too much even for Pharaoh. The repeated use of the present tense: σχολάζετε ... ἐστε ... λέγετε makes for a lively narrative style. -- Stylistic improvements change the first of the hortatory subjunctives in the final statement to a participle, an *n* variant to πορευθεντες and a *b* one to απελθοντες.

5:18 Exod neatly presents Pharaoh's resulting orders "go and get to work" by the introductory particles νῦν οὖν "now then."[21] The asyndeton verbs of MT are brought together into a single clause by using a participle for the first one. The following clause is made into a γάρ clause by Exod whereas MT simply has a *waw*. What Exod conveys is "return to work because your requests are not going to be met."

For ἄχυρον in the singular see note at v.7. -- A popular variant places ὑμῖν after ἄχυρον instead of after the verb, but for what reason is not clear.

The last clause reproduces the word play of MT's תתנו over against the Niphal ינתן of the preceding clause by using the same root as well. The choice of ἀποδώσετε vs δοθήσεται is well chosen; the levy must be returned.

5:19 The overseers now realize that they were worse off than previously. The verb ἑώρων is rightly in the imperfect contrasting aspectually with the aorist verb of v.20. The *n* text inflects the verb as though it were derived from an -εω root rather than from ὁράω, whereas a *b* tradition inflects with the Hellenistic ending -σαν.

21. That πορευθέντες rather than the majority A F M reading απελθοντες is Exod is fully argued in THGE VII.Q.

The τοῦ γένους gloss before τῶν in the *f* text is borrowed from v.14. -- The *n s* variant λεγοντων for λέγοντες has the Israelites making the following statement, but the Exod text is rather an elliptical reference to the ἐργοδιῶκται of v.13.

The verb ἀπολείψετε with the genitive occurs in the sense of "to come up short, leave off" and thus "to fail in." The well-supported itacistic M reading, απολειψεται, seems to be supported by יגרע of Sam, but this is simply coincidence.[22] Not to be overlooked is a very popular F M gloss απο before the genitive[23] which since it equals MT is clearly hex in origin. Also hex is the *O* reading υμων after πλινθείας. -- For the semantics of τὸ καθῆκον see note at v.13. It is here inflected as neuter singular accusative and used adverbially. Note, however, the variation in its modifier τῷ ἡμέρᾳ over against the καθ' ἡμέραν in v.13.

5:20 The subject is the same as in v.19, but Exod continues with a δέ construction since the logical relationship to v.19 is not simple parataxis, but rather one of building on what v.19 states.

For the Hebrew נצבים Exod uses ἐρχομένοις which fits well into the context but has quite a different nuance. In MT Moses and Aaron were "standing, waiting" as the Tar קימין (also Pesh) shows. But "standing to meet" is ambiguous, and so Exod chose a lexeme indicating movement. -- Exod then uses another participial construction, a genitive absolute, indicating time when something is happening;[24] its antecedent is not the Μωυσῆς καὶ 'Ααρών of ἐρχομένοις, but the overseers of v.19.

5:21 A popular reading has the classical second aorist ειπον.[25] -- The use of the aorist optatives ἴδοι and κρίναι represents the classical means of expressing a future wish: May God see you and judge! A very popular F M compound επ(ε)ιδοι for ἴδοι could be recensional; it is closer to MT which has ירא plus עליכם, i.e. "look" plus "on you." Exod, however, used ὑμᾶς as direct modifier which is a freer rendering. But if the compound were due to

22. Aq translates here by ὑφελεῖτο from ὑφαιρέω "take away, remove by stealth."
23. For the genitive as partitive see SS 164.
24. Cf SS 177-180.
25. For which see the discussion in THGE VII.M.9.

70

Hebrew influence one might also have expected a change of ὁ θεός to κ̄ς̄
for יהוה, though of this there is no trace in the tradition. Why Exod should
have used ὁ θεός here is not clear; possibly it is intended to show that the
Israelite overseers still have not accepted the revealed name κ̄ς̄.

The use of a ὅτι clause after the optatives is somewhat ambiguous.
The clause could be taken as an object clause, i.e. "May God see you and
judge that you have ...." But it could also be taken as a causal clause in
which the ὑμᾶς of the main clause would be taken as direct modifier of the
coordinate ἴδοι καὶ κρίναι, and the ὅτι clause not a judicial conclusion but a
statement of fact occasioning the judgment. This is more likely to be what
Exod intended.

Exod uses ἐβδελύξατε "you made loathsome" for הבאשתם.[26] An
itacistic *oI d x* variant changes "our odor" to "your odor," referring it to
Moses and Aaron, but this cannot be intended since the last word in the
verse is ἡμᾶς.

בעיני is correctly understood as ἐναντίον (twice);[27] -- The text
follows with two unarticulated infinitival constructions but quite varied in
usage. The first of these, δοῦναι, shows the result of Moses and Aaron's action, viz. "thereby giving placing a sword into his hands."[28] The second
infinitive simply modifies ῥομφαίαν; it is a sword "for killing." Note that
Exod has αὐτοῦ, i.e. of Pharaoh, whereas MT has בידם, i.e. the hand (power) of Pharaoh and his servants. There is uncertainty among the ancient
witnesses: Sam and Tar[O] agree with MT, whereas Tar[P] and Pesh have
בידיהון "in their hands"; Vulg simplifies by *ei* presupposing a singular
referent.

5:22 The verse begins with a δέ construction since the subject is now
Μωυσῆς. Aaron is omitted from the narrative not to reappear until the
Lord orders the two of them to go to Pharaoh in 6:13. From the Exod text
there is no way of realizing that κύριον and κύριε represent יהוה and
אדני of MT resp. Cod B has added δέομαι before κύριε, but this is an
import from 4:10,13.

26. Aq together with Sym substitutes the more literal rendering of MT
ἐσαπρίσατε "you made to stink."
27. For the usage cf Sollamo 132f.

For the question phrases διὰ τί vs ἵνα τί see v.15. The former occurs four times in Exod, twice for מדוע (5:14 18:14) and twice for למה (2:13 5:22). The latter occurs six times in Exod, three times for למה (5:4,15 32:11) and three times for למה זה (2:20 5:22 17:3). One can hardly draw any conclusions from these equations; the choice is probably random.

In the tradition a *C s* text has added σου after λαόν, which makes the question even more accusatory. -- Exod joins the two questions by καί. Since the conjunction is supported by Sam Tar[P] Pesh, as well as some Hebrew mss, the καί is probably textually based. Moses' questions demand an accounting from the Lord on two counts, as though he is accusing God of having commissioned him to bring evil rather than good upon the people.

5:23 For ἀφ' οὗ see note at 4:10. The verb εἰσπεπόρευμαι is in the perfect, which rather exaggerates the matter of Moses' activity, but it is clearly so intended. In the tradition some variants represent a present tense, which would emphasize Moses' continual going in to Pharaoh, but this is hardly justified with only one such recorded visit (vv.1ff).[29] A *b z* variant ονοματι σου for σῷ ὀνόματι represents a more common idiom in LXX.

Moses querilously makes a double complaint; Pharaoh has afflicted this people and God has not fulfilled his promise to rescue them. The Hebrew makes the second complaint even more accusatory by means of a cognate free infinitive, i.e. "you haven't rescued your people at all." Hex accordingly added a cognate participle from Aq and Theod, ρυομενος.

---

28. See SS 136.
29. For the simplex A B variant see THGE VII.N.

Chapter 6

6:1 This verse is, as the paragraphing shows, the conclusion of the preceding pericope; the new section begins with v.2.

The adverb ἤδη is here used in the sense of "now" as opposed to "presently, shortly." It therefore delimits ὄψει as the immediate future, i.e. "right now you will see." Since the σημεῖα are what is to be done to Pharaoh Exod uses the plural relative pronoun ἅ.

As at 5:11 a γάρ clause is not quite what one might expect since the clause is not really the reason for Moses' seeing God's wonders; it is rather their result. The elipsis is, however, easily understood.

The text of MT has ביד חזקה twice,[1] which is also presupposed by The Three. Exod, however, (and Pesh,) presupposes the common Deuteronomic ביד חזקה ובזרוע נטריה (for the second phrase cf v.6). Exod's text is stylistically a great improvement over the tautology of MT. The antecedent for αὐτούς (twice) is τὸν λαόν of the preceding verse. An *n* variant has απο instead of ἐκ but the latter is original in view of the verb ἐκβαλῶ which it modifies. -- The *x* text identifies αὐτοῦ as αιγυπτου, which was never in doubt!

6:2 Exod has ὁ θεός as subject which agrees with MT and Pesh[2] over against a *b n* reading κ̄ς̄ with Sam Tar Vulg. The collocation ἐλάλησεν ... εἶπεν followed by direct speech occurs only here in Exod, whereas λαλέω followed by the direct speech marker occurs fairly frequently (16 times).

The independent nominal clause of self-identification, ἐγὼ κύριος, also occurs at vv.6,8,29 12:12 and 35:3, and as ἐγώ εἰμι κύριος at 15:26 20:2 and 5. It should be carefully distinguished from its use after ὅτι which often occurs in Exod, always after the verb γιγνώσκω, i.e. in a recognition formula.

1. See SS 120.
2. Koster's emendation to **mry'** is dubious.

6:3 The aorist passive ὤφθην is regularly used in LXX for the notion of a divine appearance, shown in MT by the Niphal of ראה.[3] -- The construction πρός --- ʾΙακώβ is identical with 2:24 but here as objects of divine revelation. Hex has added the preposition προς before ʾΙσαάκ and ʾΙακώβ to equal MT.

The phrase θεὸς ὢν αὐτῶν "being their God" is odd as an interpretation of באל שדי; θεός does reflect אל, but ὢν αὐτῶν is more difficult. In Genesis אל שדי occurs six times and is always rendered by ὁ θεὸς + the pronoun "my" or "your." A continuation of the Gen pattern here would have demanded ο θεος αυτων, but Exod leaves θεός unarticulated, and inserts ὤν which possibly reflects the ὁ ὤν of 3:14 which obtains as an interpretation of אהיה as a divine appellation. Or does ὤν possibly reflect the first element of שדי? The sentence as a whole makes good sense. God says "I appeared to Abraam and Isaak and Jacob (as) being their God."[4]

The second clause being negative contrasts with the first one. The nominative κύριος, since it defines τὸ ὄνομά μου, is taken by Exod as an indeclinable noun; it is what "I did not disclose to them." So what Exod is saying is that God did reveal himself as being their God but did not disclose his name κύριος to them. A variant in the *b* tradition changed οὐκ to κυριος ων thus making the clause mean "and my name κύριος I disclosed to them (as) being κυριος, an exegetical attempt to contrast θεός with κύριος, i.e. κυριος ων and θεὸς ὢν αὐτῶν. But this is not what Exod meant.

6:4 This verse is a positive counterpart to the last clause of v.3, i.e. "but I did establish...." God's covenant is directed πρὸς αὐτούς; for this use of πρός see note at 2:24.[5] αὐτούς refers to Abraam (Gen 17:1--8), Isaac (Gen 26:2--5,24) and Jacob (Gen 35:11f.,46:2--4). ὥστε with infinitive expresses intended result. The infinitive's subject being the same as that of the main verb is not expressed. The land of promise is τῶν Χαναναίων, used only here for כנען in Exod. In fact כנען occurs only here and at 15:15 in Exodus.

3. Aq has ὡράθην, an aorist passive built on the ὁρα- stem; cf Dan θ' 1:15 and Ezek 21:24.
4. Aq interprets באל שדי as ἐν θεῷ ἱκανῷ.
5. See also Johannessohn, Gebrauch 269.

Verse b of MT interprets "land of Canaan" as "the land of their so-journings in which they sojourned." Exod makes a double point: for "land of their sojournings" he has τὴν γῆν ἣν παρῳκήκασιν,[6] a perfect tense, and for the remainder he has ἐν ᾗ καὶ παρῴκησαν ἐπ᾽ αὐτῆς with an aorist tense. The first verb is antecedent to the aorist, i.e. the land in which "they had so-journed" - the reference is to the patriarchs which the Byzantine text makes quite explicit by inserting αυτοι. The next verb is then contemporary to the patriarchs. At first blush the construction seems Hebraic, but Exod knew what he was doing and makes a neat point. The appositional construction as a whole may then be rendered: "the land (in) which they had been sojourning, in which also they were sojourning on it."

6:5 Though this verse is paratactically joined to the preceding it contrasts with it. God's establishment of the covenant was with the patriarchs, but (now) I have heard; an emphatic ἐγώ calls attention to the subject. The *b* group changed the verb to εωρακα, for which cf 3:9 where that verb is more appropriate; presumably what was meant is "I have observed, i.e. taken note of."

Since the Hebrew relative is uninflected its antecedent could in theory be נאקת or בני, but the recapitulating אתם makes clear that it is בני, i.e. "whom the Egyptians were enslaving." Exod, however, made στεναγμόν the antecedent thereby creating a clause difficult to understand. Presumably it can best be understood as an elipsis: "which (they suffered in that) the Egyptians were enslaving them." The tradition reflects the difficulty of the construction and variants to ὅν include not only ων, but also ω, ου, ους, and α. The verb in the present is sensible since the enslavement is contemporary to the main verb. An *f* variant unnecessarily makes the verb imperfect; it is already a past progressive in the context.

The last clause is paratactic to the first one. (τῆς διαθήκης) ὑμῶν is unique to Exod, all other ancient witnesses having a first singular pronoun. Exod has interpreted בריתי not in terms of a subjective genitive but rather as an objective one, i.e. the covenant involving you. In fact only seldom is the divine covenant referred to by an objective genitive; the only ones I found were Lev 26:42 "covenant of Jacob and the covenant of Isaac and the covenant of Abraham"; Lev 26:45 "their former covenant"; Deut 4:31 "covenant of thy fathers"; Ps 88:40 "covenant of thy servant"; and "covenant of (our) fathers" in Mal 2:10 1Macc 2:20,50 4:10. A revision towards MT has μου; its support is scattered and includes La and all the Egyptian versions except Sa but not Arm and Syh; its source is puzzling.

6:6 βάδιζε or its plural is commonly used by Exod to introduce another imperative (4:19 10:24 12:31 19:24 32:7, 34, and cf 4:18). Undoubtedly the translator misread לכן as an imperative of הלך.

Before the direct speech of the Lord Exod placed its marker λέγων. The word was omitted in a popular F M^txt variant which may represent an old revision based on MT. -- For ἐγὼ κύριος see note on v.2.

The promise of divine deliverance is made in three coordinate clauses. The exodus is characterized as a bringing out from the domination of the Egyptians, a rescue out of bondage, and a redemption by a display of power. The first of these means a removal of the people from Egyptian power. The preposition ἀπό is well-chosen (much better than the x variant ἐκ) since it involves a physical removal away from Egyptian rule. The second clause is a promise to rescue out of their current state of enslavement. The variant n s preposition απο is here idiomatically inferior to the ἐκ of Exod. The noun δουλείας is made more emphatic by the epexegetical plus of τῆς σκληρᾶς in the x family. Note also the majority F M hex addition of αυτων corresponding to MT. The last clause is a pledge to redeem the people ἐν βραχίονι ὑψηλῷ καὶ κρίσει μεγάλη.[7]

The phrase ἐν -- μεγάλη is an unusual variant of a common Deuteronomic phrase "with a strong hand and an outstretched arm," for which see note at v.1. The Hebrew word for "outstretched" is normally rendered by ὑψηλός as here. Somewhat puzzling is Exod's use of the singular κρίσει μεγάλη in the light of the plural in all the other ancient witnesses. Rather than making reference here to the plagues, Exod speaks of a great judgment in the abstract; God is not just sending a number of plagues to redeem his people; redemption means a display of divine power, βραχίονι ὑψηλῷ, one of great judgment.

6:7 The second part of the statement of divine intention concerns the establishment of a covenant relation with the people. It also consists of three clauses: God's adoption of the people as his very own, the promise that he will be their God, and the intended popular response of recognition of the Lord by the people not only as their God, but more particularly as their redeemer God.

The first clause might seem overloaded with first person references with both ἐμαυτῷ as well as ἐμοί. This is also reflected in the text tradition in a variety of ways. The Byzantine text has omitted ἐμοί and reordered the modifiers as υμας εις λαον εμαυτω. The *f* text has put ἐμαυτῷ after λαόν and omitted ἐμοί. A popular A F M reordering of ἐμαυτῷ ὑμᾶς is hex in origin in view of לי אתכם. Also hex is the prefixing of εις before λαόν; cf לעם in the Hebrew. The source for the popular omission of ἐμοί is uncertain; it might stem from the Byzantine tradition. It need not be based on anything more than an attempt to simplify the text. And an F *ol* C reading radically simplifies by omitting both ἐμοί and λαόν: "I will take you to myself."

The text of Exod can, however, be defended in its own right. It should be noted that ἐμαυτῷ modifies the verb, but that ἐμοί must modify λαόν. The clause may then be rendered: "And I will take you to myself as my own people."[8] Exod in other words intentionally emphasizes the first person, thereby effectively placing all the impetus for covenantal action in God's hands; all that the people need do is respond in terms of the last clause.

The response is put in terms of the recognition formula: "And you shall know that I am the Lord." κύριος has two modifiers. The first one, ὁ θεὸς ὑμῶν, is directly in response to the second clause in which God promises "and I will be your God." The second modifier is the recognition of the Lord in the light of v.6, i.e. the God who effects the exodus. In contrast to v.6, Exod uses the compound καταδυναστείας. The compound is semantically distinct from the simplex of v.6 in that it has a pejorative sense which the simplex does not have. So God is the one who brings his people out of the context of oppression. A popular F M reading voids the distinction by changing it to the simplex. Of greater import is a very popular

---

6. Cf SS 70,95.
7. Dative of instrument, cf SS 95 as well as 120.

F M gloss after ἐξαγαγὼν ὑμᾶς, viz. εκ γης αιγυπτου και, coming from the popular phrase "bring you out of the land of Egypt."

6:8 The final promise is the land of inheritance which God had promised to the patriarchs. The two parts of the promise are: I will bring you into the promised land, and I will give it to you ἐν κλήρῳ.[9] The land is identified by means of an εἰς ἥν clause, thus recapitulating the antecedent εἰς τὴν γῆν. Within the clause the Hebrew idiom "I raised my hand" is rendered by ἐξέτεινα τὴν χεῖρά μου "I stretched out my hand"; this is an oath formula as the gloss in Tar[P] בשבועה makes explicit. A popular variant has simplified the construction by substituting εφ for εἰς; cf Vulg: *super quam levavi manum meam.* Both Isaac and Jacob are objects of the preposition ל in MT, which also lacks a conjunction before "Isaac." A very popular hex tradition has added τω before both names.

The second independent clause explicates the complementary infinitive δοῦναι of the relative clause by the future δώσω. The oath was to give it to the patriarchs; this was to be redeemed by giving it to you, their descendants. This is thus not a direct gift but one that is ἐν κλήρῳ; the gift to the patriarchs was *in spe*; it is now *de facto* to be realized in their offspring. This phrase occurs only here in Exod, to reappear as a common idiom in Num, Deut and Josh.

The Lord's speech ends with the statement of self-identification ἐγὼ κύριος with which his speech began in v.2; it also began the divine speech which Moses was told to transmit to the Israelites in v.6, and it is that which Israel is to recognize and accept in response to the covenantal promises in v.7. It is thus formally a framework for the whole of the Lord's speech; cf also the comments at v.2.

6:9 The opening δέ is appropriate for the change of subject to Μωυσῆς. The change to a και pattern in the *b* tradition is not an improvement. The compound εἰσήκουσαν is particularly appropriate here since it signifies "pay close attention to" rather than the simplex notion of "hearing" of the *f* text.

8. Cf Helbing 53.
9. See Helbing 52.

Exod interprets the first cause of their inattention as being ὀλιγοψυχίας "faintheartedness," which is probably not a bad rendering for the hapax legomenon קֹצֶר רוּחַ, literally "shortness of spirit."[10] -- The second cause for the Israelites' failure to attend to Moses was their hard labors. The preposition ἀπό here designates the cause or occasion.[11]

6:10 For the unusual εἶπεν δέ for וַיְדַבֵּר see note at 4:15. The reading may well have a textual origin.

6:11 The asyndeton imperatives represent the Hebrew text. The addressee is indicated by the dative case in Exod. The majority variant text changes this to προς and the accusative, a change due to the occurrence of אֶל in MT and possibly hex in origin.

The ἵνα construction shows that λάλησον is meant in the sense of "order, command," which is acceptable usage for Hellenistic Greek.[12] This is undoubtedly what the paratactic construction in MT also meant.

The textual tradition has changed αὐτοῦ of the prepositional phrase at the end of the verse. An F + variant has (εκ γης) αιγυπτου, whereas an *oI* reading changes it (referring to Pharaoh) to αυτων, thereby making it refer to the land of the Israelites!

6:12 The B *f* text has εναντι instead of ἐναντίον.[13] -- The omission of οι before υιοί in a number of witnesses is clearly an itacistic error.[14]

Exod contrasts past experience as εἰσήκουσάν with an anticipated one εἰσακούσεταί, effectively using the same compound to make the contrast compelling. Interference with this balance in the text tradition, both the *b* ηκουσαν for the first and the *f* επακουσεται for the second, produces a weaker contrast.

For the colorful עֲרַל שְׂפָתַיִם "uncircumcized of lips" Exod has ἄλογος which usually means "thoughtless, mindless" but here must be intended as

10. Aq's κολοβόπητος "being curtailed, shortened," only represents the קֹצֶר; the expected πνεύματος is lacking in our sources.
11. See LS s.v.III.6.
12. Cf LS sub ἵνα B.II.1.
13. For the variant preposition and its unusual use in Exod see THGE VII.L.3.

"being without λόγος" as "lacking verbal fluency."[15] Tar^O has יקיר ממלל both here and in v.30, i.e. "heavy of speech," while Tar^P has חגר ממלל "halting of speech" in both places.

6:13 For εἶπεν see note at 4:15. With change of subject δέ is appropriate. -- Exod in the interest of good style does not repeat the preposition in "to Moses and Aaron" as MT does.

In Exod's version of the second part of the verse God gave them orders for Pharaoh king of Egypt so as to send away the Israelites from the land of Egypt. This gave trouble in the text tradition on two levels. First of all, συνέταξεν is modified by αὐτοῖς and by πρὸς Φαραώ; the Byzantine text simplified this by inserting πορευεσθαι. This was only a partial solution and did not solve the second difficulty, viz. that the MT had a different version. MT states that he gave them orders for the Israelites and for Pharaoh; the hex text accordingly added προς τους υιους ιηλ και before "for Pharaoh." But the Hebrew text does not read "so as to send away" but להוציא "to bring out"; i.e. MT means "he gave them orders over against the Israelites and Pharaoh ... that they (i.e. Moses and Aaron) should bring out the Israelites." But in Exod the subject of the infinitive is Pharaoh. An early very popular (preOrigenian) revision toward MT changed ἐξαποστεῖλαι to εξαγαγειν to conform to MT.

The tendency of the *d* text to abbreviate the Greek text is shown by the omission of βασιλέα Αἰγύπτου and abbreviating "the Israelites out of the land of Egypt" to τον λαον αυτου, the pronoun referring to κύριος.

6:14 Exod begins this new paragraph with καί as Sam Pesh, and so it is probably textual. The first clause is a heading for the section ending with v.27. For a parallel to vv.14--16 cf Gen 46:9--11. The list consists of ἀρχηγοὶ οἴκων πατριῶν αὐτῶν, i.e. "chiefs of their ancestral houses." In the tradition ἀρχηγοί is popularly articulated but the οι is a dittograph from the preceding οὗτοι. Similarly υἱοί is articulated in an M + tradition but this is an itacistic error. For the reverse error cf v.12.

---

14. For the articulation of υἱοί see *ibid* D.2.
15. Aq of course renders the Hebrew with coarse literalism ἀκρόβυστος χείλεσιν, whereas Theod does very little better with his ἀπερίτμητος

The spelling of ʽΡουβήν wherever it occurs engenders at least the following in the tradition: ρουβιν, ρουβημ, ρουβιμ and ρουβειμ. Eth Arab and Syh (equals Pesh) always end the name with an *l* rather than a nasal. The origin of the tradition is unknown to me. -- The sons of Rouben are given in two pairs both in Exod and MT. Only a *d x* variant omits the καί between the first pair.

The second name Φαλλούς has a Graecized ending. The dropping of the final consonant in F[b] and 426 is a revision based on MT.[16] The spelling of the name with a single *lambda* by C *n x* is a case of haplography. A *d* spelling φαλες shows minuscule misreading of -ους as -ες.

The third name, Ἀσρών, represents an old pronunciation of MT's ḥeṣrōn. A popular variant with final *mu* is the result of scribal confusion of *mu* and *nu*. Particularly in final position the nasals are easily confused, so that at times almost all extant witnesses have the wrong nasal, e.g. Μαδιάν as μαδιαμ for מדין throughout LXX.

The last name is χαρμί which in the text tradition often has the usual itacistic misspellings of χαρμει or χαρμη. -- These four are then called ἡ συγγένεια or "family" of Reuben.

6:15 The sons of Simeon are all careful transliterations of the names in MT except for the fifth one. Σάαρ with its αα shows an old /cacc/ type of word rather than the /cucc/ or /cocc/ type which the MT ṣōḥar represents.

The name Συμεών is a good approximation of the Hebrew spelling though why the first vowel should be an *upsalon* is not clear. In Hellenistic or Byzantine Greek it is homonymous with the *iota* row, but in the tradition the vowel never changes to ι, ει or η as one might expect.

The first name ʼΙεμουήλ appears with a different middle vowel in a unique B reading as ιεμιηλ and in 76' as ιεμετλ. The origin of the former is puzzling, whereas the latter illustrates scribal confusion of ου and ε. The *f* pair 53' has misread μ as β; in 12th and 13th century mss these are very similar in some scripts.

The names are all joined by καί in Exod (equals MT), but in a *d x* tradition all but the last καί are omitted; the Catena text omits only the first one.

The second name, Ἰαμίν, shows the usual mistakes of spelling in the tradition particularly in itacisms, and in nasal confusion for the final *nu* as *mu*. Some witnesses, especially *C*, omit the initial letter, which is simply a haplograph after καί.

The third son is Ὤαδ representing אֹהַד of MT, and popularly appears as αωδ through transposition.[17]

Ἰαχίν for יכין has the usual itacistic misspellings as well as final nasal confusion. Aphaeresis of initial *iota* occurred in some spellings through haplography after καί. Quite unusual is αχειρ in 799 which has *rho* for *nu*.

For Σάαρ the tradition has produced occasional errors, with only σαωρ showing unusual change of *omega* for the second *alpha*.

Σαούλ also has hardly any variants; odd is the extra vowel in σαουηλ in 68', spelled thus under the influence of the common -ηλ ending in proper names. -- He is designated by Exod as son of the Phoenician woman. The *b* text by changing ὁ to οι makes her the mother of all six sons. -- The designation τῆς Φοινίσσης as an equivalent for הכנענית is uncommon in LXX. The name Phoenicia and Canaan were synonymous in ancient times with the name Phoenicia in origin merely a translation of כנע "place of purple"; comp also 16:35. The Catena reading has the adjectival form φοινικισσης, and two *O* mss have της χαναναιος, under the influence of The Three.

The term משפחת is translated by αἱ πατριαί "ancestral lineages"; the word משפחת occurs six times within this paragraph, and the translation varies each time: v.14 ἡ συγγένεια; v.15 αἱ πατριαί; v.17 οἶκοι πατριᾶς; v.19 οἶκοι πατριῶν; v.24 αἱ γενέσεις and v.25 γενέσεις without an article. It is thus clear that Exod had no clear understanding of the sociological concept of משפחת; it was some kind of unit consisting of clan fathers, but the Greek of his day had no exact equivalent for it. The *b* reading αρχαι πατριας is an exegetical attempt at defining this concept more precisely as "heads of the lineage." It should be noted, however, that Exod refers the πατριαί not to Simeon but to the Simeonites, a tradition which it shares with Tar[P]:בנוי דשמעון.

6:16 Exod here uses συγγενείας to translate not מִשְׁפָּחֹת but תֹּלְדֹת "generations." MT, however, uses תֹּלְדֹת because geneologies are to be given, a
distinction which Exod missed. The variant *x* text has the singular
συγγενειαν, betraying thereby lack of understanding of the term.

The name Γεδσών for גֵּרְשׁוֹן shows a misreading by the translator
of ר as ד; the original misreading occurred with Exod and is then taken
over throughout in Num, Josh and 1Chr (except at 15:7). An early
correction based on the Hebrew (or on Gen 46:11) in an A F *O C* variant
has changed the *delta* to *rho*. The *d t x* spelling γεδεων betrays an uncial
parent text since *sigma* and *epsilon* are easily confused only in uncial form.
Other variants γεθσων and *getson* show devoicing by assimilation to the
voiceless *sigma*. The spelling γηρσαμ is probably based on Γηρσάμ, son of
Moses, at 2:22.

Καάθ is a transliteration of קְהָת. One might note that *kappa* occurs
for *qoph* over against *chi* for *kaph* in vv.14 --15.

For μεραρί itacistic spellings occur as might be expected; otherwise
only μαραρι in two mss changes the first vowel by attraction to the second.

The final clause is nominal with ἑκατὸν τριάκοντα ἑπτά as the
predicate. A popular Byzantine text has changed the syntactic pattern by
adding ταυτα before τὰ ἔτη, thereby making ταυτα the subject, "the years
of Levi's life" the predicate, and "one hundred thirty-seven" is in apposition
to ταυτα. MT adds a repetitive שָׁנָה at the end of the compound number
which Exod naturally omits, but a popular hex text dutifully added ετη.

6:17 For Γεδσών see note in v.16. The pattern of spelling variations found
in v.16 recur here, with a few new patterns added, e.g. the 318 spelling
γελσων which presupposes confusion of Λ and Δ in an uncial parent.

Variants in the spelling of Λοβενί show the usual itacisms of *iota* as
well as *omega* for *omicron*, all rooted in homophony. Also to be noted is the
dittography of *nu* in the *n s* tradition, and the dropping of a syllable in
λωβει, λαβεν and *lobon*.

The second son is Σεμεΐ. Spelling variants are mainly itacistic, but ms
59 separates the last two vowels by a *nu* and F^b adds a syllable βε before
με, presumably a dittograph based on a μ - β confusion; see note on

Ἰεμουήλ at v.15.

The term οἶκοι πατριᾶς is levelled to correspond to v.19 by the Fᵇ reading οικοι πατρων. The change in number of the genitive noun is not significant; both would mean "ancestral houses," i.e. sublines of descent from the original patriarch.

6:18 For Κααθ see note at v.16. As in v.14 so here Exod divides the names into two pairs over against all the other ancient witnesses. A hex plus has added και before Χεβρών so as to conform to MT.

For Ἀμράμ a popular A B spelling inserts a *beta* between the two spirants μρ. When the first of these is a nasal Greek tends towards inserting a related stop, e.g. μρ, νρ to μβρ, νδρ resp. It is then not surprising that the variants αβραμ leading to αβρααμ should also develop. Confusion of final nasal also leads to such spellings as αμβραν and αβραν. And the misspelling αμιαμ of 76' must be based on an uncial parent since in many Greek hands the uncial *rho* is very narrow and looks almost like *iota*.

Dittography has created the popular M spelling ισσααρ for Ἰσαάρ,[18] whereas uncial confusion of Ε - Σ resulted in the spellings ιεσσααρ in F and ιεσαρ in 59. From ισσααρ one easily arrives at the patriarchal name ισσαχαρ in B 55.

The *d* group misspelled Χεβρών as χευρων; the two are homophonous since both εβ and ευ were pronounced /ev/ in Byzantine Greek.

For Ὀζιήλ, aside from various itacistic spellings, only ο εζιηλ of some *z* witnesses needs explanation. Since *omicron* and *epsilon* are both "round" letters and look alike in the uncial script an *epsilon* has entered as a dittograph. Since the combination οε is nonGreek writing the successor scribe took the *omicron* as an article thereby producing ο εζιηλ.

Exod has the lifespan of Καὰth as 130 years though all other ancient witnesses have 133. The dropping of the "three" may have been due to parablepsis caused by homoiarchon. Note MT's ושלשים שלש. The lacuna has been filled by a very popular hex plus of τρια. It has, however, been placed after rather than before τριάκοντα.

χείλεσιν. Sym tries to interpret the figure by οὐκ καθαρὸς τῷ φθέγματι "impure in utterance."

6:19 For the articulation of υἱοί in the tradition see note on v.14. -- For Μεραρί see note on v.16. -- Μοολί has an "o" vowel tradition instead of the "a" vowel of MT. The doubling of thé vowel is common for a syllable closed by Π. Other spellings of the name involve itacisms for *iota*, doubling of *lambda* in the *n s* tradition as well as haplography producing a single *omicron* spelling. Also to be found are ου for οο probably due to auditory confusion, ομολι and ομοαι due to transposition of μο, and spellings showing aphaeresis of *mu* in *x*, and of *mu omicron* in ολει of 72. Both ομοαι and μοθαι are based on the confusion of Α - Λ in an uncial parent. Furthermore in the uncial forms Ο - Θ are both rounded letters and very similar resulting in μοθαι.

᾿Ομουσί is a transliteration of רמושי. The initial consonant was intended as a conjunction and it is twice represented, both in transliteration and in translation by καί. A few witnesses have corrected it, presumably on the basis of MT, by omitting the first letter. Otherwise misspellings are mainly itacistic.

A summary statement states that these are the ancestral houses of Levi according to their families. For Exod's use of συγγενείας for תלדת see note at v.16. In the tradition a *t* reading of οικου instead of οἶκοι is almost certainly based on a scribal misreading of οι as ου since οικου is barely intelligible. An *s x* variant changes πατρῶν to the singular under the influence of v.17. For the singular συγγενειαν reading see note at v.16.

6:20 For ᾿Αμράμ and its variant spellings see note at v.18. -- The name of Aaron's wife ᾿Ιωχάβεδ gave rise to a number of variant spellings. Devoicing of the final consonant produced both the popular Byzantine ιωχαβεθ as well as ιωχαβετ. Uncial confusion of Δ - Λ created the *C f x* spelling ιωχαβελ. The β - μ similarity in certain cursive hands brought about such oddments as ιωχαμελ and ιωχαμεθ. And by apocopation ιωχαβε and ιοχαβε were produced.

According to MT Jochabad was the דדה of Amram, i.e. his agnate aunt. This, however, contravened the law concerning incest in Lev 18:12, and Exod led the way in changing it to an agnate cousin. This interpretation was followed by Tar[P] Pesh as well as Vulg: *patruelem*.

In the tradition ἑαυτῷ is contracted in a very popular F M variant to αυτω. Since the pronoun must be reflexive αὐτῷ must be meant. The *d* substitution of αυτην for ἑαυτῷ is difficult to justify; the object of ἔλαβεν has been named and a recapitulating pronoun is quite otiose.

The phrase εἰς γυναῖκα is a Hebraism for לאשה. Elsewhere Exod renders this phrase simply by γυναῖκα (vv.23, 25 22:16). In Gen the phrase לאשה in the sense of as "wife" is rendered by εἰς γυναῖκα only at 12:19 20:12 34:4,12, but without the preposition ten times.

In the next clause Exod adds καὶ Μαριὰμ τὴν ἀδελφὴν αὐτῶν (cf 15:20) as does Sam; Pesh has "and Mariam" only. The *ol n* spelling μαριαν is due to *mu - nu* confusion.

The last clause begins with a δέ construction showing change of subject (but not in the parallel clauses in vv.16 and 18). Amram lived 136 years according to Exod and Sam, but in MT 137 years; the F M majority text has corrected the ἕξ to επτα. Variation in the tradition has B *f* with δυο, Ach with "three" and an Arm ms with "five."

6:21 For οι before υἱοί see note on v.14. For 'Ισαάρ see note on v.18. Variant spellings not attested there are εσσααρ and ασσααρ where the initial vowel has been changed, the latter presumably by regressive assimilation. Attenuation of /i/ to /ε/ is not uncommon and produced the former. Aphaeresis of the initial letter created the F + variant σααρ. -- The three sons of Isaar are connected by conjunctions in all the ancient witnesses; the omission of the first καί in *x* yields the pattern: a b + c.

The name Νάφεγ for נפג has undergone a variety of transformations in the tradition, mostly concerning the final consonant. Names with final *gamma* are fairly unusual and it is changed to *sigma* (a common ending for Greek names), or to *tau* (confusion of T - Γ in uncial script), or to *rho*, but principally by devoicing as *kappa* in the majority ναφεκ spelling.[19]

The last name is Ζεχρί for זכרי. Aside from itacistic spellings for *iota*, it also appears as *alpha* in ζεχρα. Ach and Sa transpose the final syllable. Ms 59 adds a syllable -σι to produce ζεχρισι. The scrambled form of 246 ζεγρευγρι has a partial dittograph of εγρ as ευγρ in which the

16. Or possibly based on Gen 46:9?
17. For the originality of "Ωαδ and its misspellings see THGE VII.K.

original *chi* had been voiced by attraction to its voiced environment. Some witnesses add και μισαηλ borrowed from v.22.

6:22 For οι before υἱοί see note on v.14. -- For ' Οζιήλ see note on v.18. An odd gloss in 527 adds after ' Οζιήλ "Maara and Sabara, and Sabara took Elisa daughter of Aminadam, sister of Naason, to himself as wife and she bore to him Taath." It seems in part to reflect a scrambled version of v.23, but some of the names such as Maara, Sabara and Taath are not attested anywhere in LXX.

The first son Μισαήλ is (together with the following καί) omitted by a well-supported A B variant.[20]

The second son is ' Ελισαφάν for אלצפן. The vocalization of MT lacks the glide vowel after אל which is, however, represented in Sam, Pesh and Vulg. The opening vowel through an E - O confusion in a parent uncial produced ολισαφαν in 376. Other variants concern the final syllable, apocopation producing both ελισαφα and ελισαφ; similarity between *rho* and *phi* in the cursive script resulted in ελισαραν, and knowledge of the name Shaphat probably created ελισαφατ.

The third son Σετρί produced a large number of variants. Besides itacisms, consonants are also changed. Voicing of *sigma* produced a number of spellings beginning with ζ. Misreading of *tau* through T - Γ confusion produced σεγρι, σεγρει, ζεγρει and then by further devoicing of the *gamma* ζεχρι. Closing the final syllable yielded σετριν and σερειν. Variants admitting of no palaeographic explanation are σεμισεηλ or σεμησεηλ in 76' and ζεμιναδαβ or ζεμιδαβ in 53'.

6:23 A δέ construction shows change of subject. -- Most witnesses close the final syllable of ' Ελισάβε with a dental stop.[21] -- For ' Αμιναδάβ a *C* variant prefixed an *iota* probably under the influence of the name ' Ιαμίν, and then transposed the last two consonants thereby producing ιαμιναβαδ. Another *C* variant also omitted the last consonant and transposed δα to create ιαμινααδ. An A M + variant read the final *beta* as *mu* in cursive form; the resultant final *mu* was then further corrupted to *nu*, as αμιναδαν.

---

18. For the original spelling of ' Ισαάρ see THGN 115f.
19. For this variant see THGE VII.K.

The Byzantine plus of δε after ἀδελφήν creates a contrast: "daughter of A. but sister of N." -- The change of the first αὐτῷ to the reflexive in *n x* is good Greek; cf v.20. The change to αυτην in *d* is odd, since it unnecessarily recapitulates ' Ελισάβε pronominally.

The majority text has τε after τόν.[22] -- The name Ναδάβ is corrupted in different ways in the tradition. The spelling ναδαμ again reflects confusion in the cursive β - μ. Some witnesses transpose *delta* and *beta* so that ναβαδ (or αβαδ) results. Aphaeresis of *nu* in the name is the result of haplography after τόν. -- Nadab as the first in a list is articulated to represent a preposed את; comp v.20.

' Αβιούδ is throughout LXX the Greek form for אביהוא as though it were אביהוד (1Chr 8:3). The correction to αβιου in 426 is under Hebrew influence. Odd errors are αβλουδ, αβιουμ and αβισουρ, explicable only as based on a badly written parent text.

The καί before ' Ελεαζάρ is not represented in BHS Sam Tar[O], but is in Hebrew mss Tar[P] Pesh and Vulg. Its omission by *d x* is probably mere coincidence. Eleazar and Ithamar are transposed in *d* which is unusual, Ithamar always being listed after Eleazar in LXX.

For ' Ιθαμάρ the presence of καί before it has by haplography created the variant θαμαρ. The spelling ιαθαμαρ has treated the initial *iota* as consonantal, which is common in Hebrew names.

6:24 The three sons of Kore are in the common mode all joined by καί. The first καί is omitted by a few witnesses creating the pattern: a b + c. The first son ' Ασίρ is misspelled itacistically in the majority of witnesses. The weakly supported spelling with double *sigma* follows the Masoretic pointing. -- ' Ελκανά is almost universally supported in its spelling; variation in the first vowel occur in αλκανα and ηλκανα and in the second with ελκωνα.

' Αβιασάφ created trouble for copyists. An old misspelling in A B + misread the final *phi* as *rho* which is possible both in uncial and cursive scripts. Apocopation created αβιασα, whereas the wellknown name Shaphat influenced the spelling αβιασαφατ. The *x* + spelling αβιαθαρ is simply the better known name Abiathar.

---

20. See the discussion in THGE VII.P.
21. For the originality of' Ελισάβε see THGE VII.K.

88

The articulated הַקָּרְחִי of MT appears as a simple קרח in Tar Pesh, and this is what the second Κορέ in Exod seems to represent. -- For αἱ γενέσεις "the generations" see note at v.15.

6:25 The notion "take a wife to himself" occurs only in this chapter (vv.20,23,25). In each case the pronoun precedes, before εἰς γυναῖκα in v.20 the reflexive ἑαυτῷ occurring, but in the other two before γυναῖκα the simple αὐτῷ. In both cases a variant text reads εαυτω, but this is secondary.

The genitive τῶν θυγατέρων is a partitive genitive, i.e. "one of the daughters" is meant.[23] An f reading makes an απο phrase; cf the Hebrew מבנות.

The name Φουτιήλ becomes φουτουηλ by progressive assimilation in the Catena tradition. Unusual is the variant in the z group φουτηνα. That lambda should be misread as alpha is easily understood as from the uncial forms Λ - Α. but a misreading of ιη as ην is puzzling.

The Byzantine text witnesses show two variants in the change of αὗται αἱ to αυται δε: the omission of αἱ and the addition of δε. Since the omission of αἱ was a haplograph after αὗται, the addition of δε must have occurred subsequent to it. The particle is not inappropriate for signaling a new sentence.

The phrase ἀρχαὶ πατριᾶς "ancestral chieftains" is made to conform to MT by pluralizing the genitive in F +; cf note on v.17. -- For γενέσεις see note on v.24.

6:26 The singular οὗτος, as is the more literal variant αυτος, is based on the Hebrew הוא which in turn is singular by attraction to the nearest member of the compound subject אהרן. Change to ουτοι in some witnesses is not surprising.

The relative clause is not only introduced by οἷς which is quite correct but also has the recapitulating pronoun αὐτοῖς hebraistically reproducing the להם of MT. Its omission by a b f + variant is better Greek. The pronoun precedes the subject ὁ θεός in Exod but within the text tradition the majority transposes the order which is a hex correction in agreement with MT. -- The subject within the relative clause is ὁ θεός, although MT has the tetragrammaton. This is not unusual in Exod; in fact of the 182 times that θεός occurs in Exod 43 obtain where MT has יהוה.[24]

In MT הוציא is vocalized as an imperative, i.e. representing direct speech. Exod translates this by a complementary infinitive ἐξαγαγεῖν with the subject understood as Moses and Aaron. An *n* variant εξαγαγετε could be recensional based on MT.

Exod renders the MT מארץ literally by ἐκ γῆς.[25] The popular A variant εξ is probably due to the common expression ἐξ Αἰγύπτου; cf especially v.27.

This is the first use in MT of על צבאתם; it recurs at 12:51 and is often used throughout Numbers. Exod's translation σὺν δυνάμει αὐτῶν was destined to become a standardized idiom for "with their host(s)." Though MT has the word in the plural the collective singular is used consistently. Cf also 7:4 12:17,41 where צבאת also occurs in MT, always rendered by δύναμις.

6:27 The verb διαλέγομαι in the sense of "converse with" takes either πρός with the accusative or the simple dative, and a popular F M variant supports the dative rather than Exod. There is no lexical difference between the two.

The second clause has the verb in the aorist which contrasts with the present tense εἰσιν of the coordinate first clause. MT has an infinitive להוציא subordinating the notion of bringing the Israelites out of Egypt as the purpose of the conversing with Pharaoh. By making the notion coordinate the sense is changed to "These are the ones who ... and they did bring out." Exod changes the potential of MT to an actual exodus event. This was "corrected" by changing καὶ ἐξήγαγον to ωστε εξαγαγειν in an early (preOrigenian) popular F M variant text. Exod has εξ here in view of MT's "from (Egypt)"; a B + variant has εκ γης as Sam, but see note on v.26.

An odd use of αὐτός (for הוא in MT) obtains in the final phrase of the verse; it really means "that is, namely." It calls attention to the identification Ἀαρὼν καὶ Μωυσῆς of v.26, which unusual order is retained here rather than the more common order of MT: "Moses and Aaron"; hex

---

22. For its secondary character see THGE VII.O.
23. See SS 160.
24. For a discussion of θεός vs κύριος see THGE VII.O. sub 3:18.

has naturally transposed them. -- That αὐτός should become ουτος in *s x* is not surprising in the light of v.26.

6:28 For the rendering of ויהי with preposition and infinitive see note at 2:11; here, however, Exod by beginning with a relative pronoun subordinates v.28 to the following verse, i.e. "on the day that ..., the Lord did speak."[26]

The addressee is given in the dative Μωυσῇ, but an F *x* tradition has προς with the accusative with no change in meaning. -- A group of scattered mss changes Αἰγύπτῳ to the genitive, i.e. reading "in the land of Egypt."[27]

6:29 The initial καί beginning the main clause (cf note at v.28) is a Hebraism impelled by MT. -- The Catena text group omits the direct speech marker λέγων;[28] -- For ἐγὼ κύριος see note at v.2. The self-identification formula sets in relief the order to speak to Pharaoh the Lord's words. The address is to Moses since Aaron is simply to be Moses' mouthpiece; cf 7:1 below.

The relative adjective ὅσα as neuter plural is often used as an indeclinable to represent either כל אשר or simply אשר. In the hex tradition a παντα obtains to show the כל of MT.

The omission of ἐγώ by the *f* text does not change the sense since the verb is inflected for first person singular, but the pattern: pronoun + present tense is a common Exod pattern for rendering Hebrew's nominal clause: pronoun + participle.[29] The verb is here most unusual, however. The root דבר is normally rendered in Exod by λαλεῖν whereas λέγειν equally consistently translates the root אמר. Exod may have intended to break the repetition of the root since it would otherwise occur three times in the verse.

6:30 This verse is a shorter version of v.12. For the popular εναντι variant for ἐναντίον see note on v.12. -- MT again has the phrase ערל (אני

---

25. For Exod's exactness in connection with the phrase "from (the land of) Egypt" see the discussion in THGE VII.O., first entry.
26. Cf SS 109.
27. That this is contrary to Exod usage is demonstrated in THGE VII.H.3 sub 12:1.

שפתים) as in v.12 but here Exod translates by ἰσχνόφωνός "having a speech impediment" rather than ἄλογος; see note at v.12.[30]

Exod adds εἰμι after ἐγὼ ἰσχνόφωνός; a number of witnesses omit the word but this does not change the sense of the passage. -- An *n* variant rather elegantly reads πως ουν instead of Exod's καὶ πῶς in the last clause, thereby showing the reasonableness of Moses' petulant question: "then how will Pharaoh pay attention to me?"

---

28. Though cf Mayser II.3, p.63 for non-Biblical occurrences.
29. Cf also SS 82.
30. Sym translates the clause by οὐκ εἰμὶ καθαρὸς φθέγματι as at v.12. The anonymous reading ἀκρόβυστος ἐν χείλεσιν in F^b is clearly Aq.

Chapter 7

7:1 Exod has added against the Hebrew the direct speech marker λέγων. Its omission by a very popular F M text is probably a preOrigenian revision based on the Hebrew. -- ἰδού is Exod's translation for ראה here as well as for הנה elsewhere.[1] -- The word δέδωκα here takes on the meaning "I have set, appointed" a meaning which the root takes on from the Hebrew נתן, and it is often used in the LXX in this sense.[2] The Antiochian Fathers here use the more classical τεθεικα.

The case of Φαραώ is ambiguous and theoretically could be vocative, genitive, dative or accusative. The Byzantine text, as Aq, articulates the name with τω to render MT's לפרעה.

Only Tar avoid the literal rendering of אלהים, TarO using רב to which TarP adds ושליט, i.e. "teacher and ruler." Exod renders literally, reserving for v.2 the explanation of the relationship: God and Prophet, as it applies to Moses and Aaron. -- Hex has transposed the order of σου προφήτης to conform to MT.

7:2 Now it becomes clear that Moses is not really θεόν but is himself a mediator of the divine word, i.e. he is God's prophet to Aaron, will speak to Aaron, who in turn will speak to Pharaoh; i.e. to Pharaoh Aaron is Moses' medium - the actual words belong to Moses. The God-prophet relationship is now clear. The prophet is one who faithfully speaks the message which he has received from God. Rather than a classical μέν ... δέ construction Exod uses a δέ construction for both independent clauses with σύ (Moses) subject of the first clause and Aaron of the second. The *n* pair 75' substitutes ουν for the first δέ thereby indicating that this verse is the logical conclusion to v.1, but in Exod (and in MT) it is rather an explanation of v.1.

---

1. Aq uses ἰδού only for הנה and here he, as does Sym, uses ἴδε.
2. For נתתי Aq naturally also uses δέδωκα whereas Sym uses a contextually more fitting κατέστησα.

Exod also adds a necessary αὐτῷ after λαλήσης even though the Hebrew uses תדבר absolutely. Its early and very popular F omission, though equal to MT, is not an improvement.

In contrast to 6:29 (cf note ad loc) Exod does render כל before אשר by πάντα. -- The Byzantine text added εγω as subject before ἐντέλλομαι probably to balance the σύ of the main clause. -- Hex has transposed the word order of σοι ἐντέλλομαι so as to equal MT.

The last paratactic clause in MT is changed into a probable result clause in Exod, which is not at all inappropriate. No subject of the infinitive is stated since its subject, Φαραώ, comes immediately before the ὥστε clause. The translator is careful to use an infinitive rather than a finite verb, since Pharaoh's dismissal of the people was not really the result of Aaron's speaking Moses' words but rather of the divine signs.

7:3 For the first clause see the note at 4:21. -- The divine promise to multiply his signs (cf also 11:9) is particularly appropriate at the beginning of the narrative of the plagues here called τὰ σημεῖα (μου) καὶ τὰ τέρατα (only elsewhere in 11:9,10). The double designation is appropriate since the plagues were not only signs accompanying the communicated orders to release the people but were in themselves "portents, wonders" displaying the divine power. In MT both nouns have the first singular suffix and the popular hex A tradition has added μου to τέρατα so as to equal MT more exactly. -- For Αἰγύπτῳ and the variant genitive in a number of disparate witnesses see note
at 6:28.

7:4 Though MT again uses נתתי here the Hebraism of v.1, δέδωκα, would not be sensible, whereas ἐπιβαλῶ in a pejorative sense fits nicely, i.e. "I will impose my will upon Egypt and bring out."

For the phrase σὺν δυνάμει αὐτῶν as standard idiom see note at 6:26. Exod interpreted את צבאתי uniquely as similar in structure to על צבאתם 6:26 12:51; all other ancient witnesses with greater plausibility translate את by the accusative case or its counterpart, e.g. Vulg: *exercitum ... meum*. These take את עמי as being in apposition to את צבאתי.

The change of ἐξάξω, future indicative, to εξαγαγω aorist subjunctive in 53' means that ἐπιβαλῶ is also so understood but as expressing simple future.[3] -- The Catena text by placing καὶ before the concluding σὺν ἐκδική-σει μεγάλη[4] understood this σύν phrase as coordinate with σὺν δυνάμει μου, i.e. taking δυνάμει μου in the sense of "my heavenly host," i.e. the angelic army; compare 4Reg 6:15--17.

Exod has the singular ἐκδικήσει μεγάλη instead of MT's plural; the plagues to Exod constitute the great divine vindication of his people at Pharaoh's expense.

7:5 The concluding verse of the divine speech. The recognition formula gives a theological basis for the plagues; all the Egyptians will recognize that it is the Lord who is afflicting Egypt. As in MT syntactically the last clause is paratactic and so coordinates not with ἐκτείνων ... Αἴγυπτον but with καὶ γνώσονται; the plagues have the double result of recognition and the exodus. "All (the Egyptians)" has an equivalent in Sam, but not in MT. Its omission by *b* may be recensional.

For εἰμι see note at 6:2. Its omission in the F O C s text may have been influenced by the repeated ἐγὼ κύριος in ch.6; cf note at 6:8. -- An unarticulated ἐκτείνων is used to indicate occasion, time when, for the Hebrew בנטתי, i.e. "when I stretched out (my) hand." Exod does not translate the suffix of ידי since it is contextually obvious; the Lord does not stretch out someone else's hand. --   For the unambiguous ἐπ' Αἴγυπτον *d* has επ αυτους, by which the referent changes to Αἰγύπτιοι.

The last clause reiterates the promise of an exodus (cf v.4) with the referent in αὐτῶν being Αἰγύπτιοι as well, not as in A, αυτης, which makes it Αἴγυπτον. The *x* text has changed the future indicative verb ἐξάξω into a present participle εξαγων; the syntactic pattern thereby has the syntagm coordinate with ἐκτείνων; there is then a double occasion for the recognition of the Lord on the Egyptians' part.

7:6 A general statement that Moses and Aaron carried out the divine in-struction; this is probably a reference to v.2. The syntactic structure of the

3. Cf the discussion of tenses in Bl-Debr 318.
4. Cf SS 128.

verse is also not very clear. Does the καθάπερ clause go with ἐποίησεν or with ἐποίησαν? The punctuation given to Exod is intentionally ambiguous, though it might seem easier to take it as MT does with the οὕτως clause. But this leaves the ἐποίησεν used absolutely which is highly unusual. I would suggest taking the entire καθάπερ --- fin as modifying ἐποίησεν, as an explanation of what Moses and Aaron did.

The pronominal modifier αὐτοῖς is kept close to the modified verb within the καθάπερ clause, but hex reorders it to conform to MT. -- A variant with only scattered support omits οὕτως ἐποίησαν, which solves the syntactic difficulty of the verse by eliminating the problem.

7:7 For the use of δέ in two successive clauses to show contrast see note on v.2. The two clauses use parallel patterns: subject + ἦν + ἐτῶν + number. This contrasts with the Hebrew pattern for denoting one's age: subject + nominal predicate consisting of בן + number + "years."[5] Hex has changed the order by placing ἐτῶν after the number in both clauses to equal MT.

Only Exod among the old witnesses attests to ὁ ἀδελφὸς αὐτοῦ (comp vv.1,2,9,19), and its omission by a majority F M[txt] may well be an early preOrigenian revision based on the shorter Hebrew text.

The tradition had trouble with the ἦν in the second clause. An A b s tradition placed it at the end of the clause; a B tradition simply omitted it as unnecessary in view of ἦν 1°, and hex inserted it between the number and ἐτῶν.

The temporal clause at the end of the verse shows how carefully Exod interpreted his text. All other ancient witnesses attest to a plural subject in agreement with בדברם of MT. But it was not Moses and Aaron who spoke to Pharaoh according to v.2, but only Aaron, and so Exod has ἐλάλησεν. A very popular A M variant changes this to ελαλησαν; this need not have been recensional, but may have been due to ἐποίησαν at the end of v.6.

7:8 The b text has substituted ελαλησε for εἶπεν; it is unlikely that וידבר in Sam had anything to do with it; the b text is at times quite erratic.

5. Which pattern Aq copies exactly by his υἱός before "80."

7:9 The first sign. Unexpected is the unique opening καί since this is the beginning of direct speech, and its omission by a number of witnesses is probably a stylistic improvement rather than recensional. The pronoun in the construction δότε ἡμῖν is ad sensum, though probably occasioned by לכם in the Hebrew. This represents a common usage in Hebrew by which the prepositional phrase contains the pronoun with the same referent as the verb.[6] A few mss actually have δοτε υμιν, but this is simply an itacism error for ἡμῖν, rather than based on the Hebrew.

Exod's σημεῖον ἢ τέρας indicates a parent text like Sam: אות או מופת rather than MT's מופת. The omission of σημεῖον ἤ by two *O* mss must be due to Hebrew influence, possibly a post-hexaplaric omission of an obelized phrase. -- For τῷ ἀδελφῷ σου over against all other ancient sources, see note at v.7.

Not Moses but Aaron as his prophetic agent is to perform the first sign. The instructions which Moses is to give Aaron show a number of differences between Exod and MT. 1) ῥάβδον is unaccompanied by a genitive pronoun,[7] though hex has added σου to conform to MT; 2) αὐτήν is added as object of ῥῖψον (as also in Tar[P]); MT lacks it since "staff" occurs in the preceding clause; its omission in B 53' formally equals MT; 3) The phrase ἐπὶ τὴν γῆν has no counterpart in the other ancient witnesses, but is consistent with the original account in 4:3 where it occurs both in the order and in its execution. Its omission by a popular F M variant is apparently an early preOrigenian revision towards MT. 4) Not only is the sign to be done "before Pharaoh," but also καὶ ἐναντίον τῶν θεραπόντων αὐτοῦ, for which see also vv.10,20 5:21 8:3,4, 9,11,21,24,29,31 9:8,14,34 10:1,6 11:3 14:5.

The last clause is simple future "and it shall be a serpent."[8] MT and Tar[O] have יהי "let it be"; this is often changed either knowingly or otherwise to ויהי "that it might be" by translators. Whether Exod's parent text had the conjunction or not cannot be determined since he simply tried to make good sense.

6. Which older grammarians often called an ethical dative; cf GK 119s.
7. Cf SS 94.
8. Aq renders this as κῆτος.

7:10 For the singular εἰσῆλθεν cf note at v.6. The δέ construction shows change of subject. A *d* text characteristically abbreviates init --- ᾽Ααρών to ειϲηλθον δε. -- For καὶ τῶν θεραπόντων αὐτοῦ and its omission by F M *O C s* see note at v.9.

In the second clause a *d* text lacks οὕτως for which one might compare v.6. -- *C* variants, καθα and καθως for καθάπερ, occur with no distinction in meaning. Within the καθάπερ clause Exod expresses the addressee for the verb ἐνετείλατο by αὐτοῖς, making explicit what is already implicit in MT. A few scattered witnesses attest to an article before κύριος, but κύριος as the divine name is ordinarily not articulated; it only occurs twice with postpositive γάρ, and otherwise only at 9:27: ὁ κύριος δίκαιος, which see.

As in v.6 τὴν ῥάβδον without a genitive pronoun is in accordance with good Greek style,[9] but hex added αυτου conform to MT.

7:11 According to Exod Pharaoh called together three classes of people: experts, mixers of magical potions and enchanters, all presumably magicians of some sort who did likewise with their magical arts. Precisely what distinctions were originally intended is no longer clear. Thus Tar[O] uses the same root to translate the second and third members, calling them both magicians, but then using a different word in the prepositional phrase "with their charms." Tar[P] and Pesh abandon any attempt at distinctions and use the root חרש for all but the first class.[10]

Exod designates the σοφιστάς as being Αἰγύπτου, which a popular F M text omits, thereby conforming to MT. Two mss identify these experts as being Jannes and Jambres; compare 2Tim 3:8.

A popular F variant has omitted the καί before οἱ ἐπαοιδοί as otiose, but the omission changes the sense. In Exod οἱ ἐπαοιδοί are a third class who also performed, but the shorter text implies that numbers one and two are included in οἱ ἐπαοιδοί as an inclusive cover term. The καί renders גם גם in MT.[11] The spelling ἐπαοιδοί is the Hellenistic form for the Attic ἐπῳ-

9. Cf SS 94.
10. For MT's חרטי (οἱ ἐπαοιδοί in Exod) Aq has κρυφιασταί while Sym leaves Exod unchanged.
11. Cf SS 73. Aq has καίγε αὐτοί but Sym simply has καὶ αὐτοί.

δοί.[12] --   For MT's בלהטיהם Exod has ταῖς φαρμακείαις (αὐτῶν)[13] using the same root as the second class of magicians τοὺς φαρμάκους "the mixers of magical potions."[14]

7:12 The use of ἔρριψαν in the plural is in imitation of the common Hebrew pattern: "they did each his...." The popular A reading of the singular brings the text into grammatical congruity with ἕκαστος. The obverse to this is the B *d* plural αυτων for αὐτοῦ. In spite of the singular ἕκαστος ... αὐτοῦ the overall context is plural as the next clause makes clear.

The article before ' Ααρών is used as a relative pronoun, and stresses the contrast between Aaron's rod and the rods of the others (the magicians of v.11). A majority tradition eliminates the ἡ, and thereby loses the stress intended by Exod though it formally equals MT.

Exod uses ἐκείνων to render the suffix of מטתם, and places it before ῥάβδούς so as to stress the contrast between Aaron and "those." Hex simply changed the order to conform to MT.

7:13 κατίσχυσεν for יחזק occurs only here in Exod though in later translations, particularly 1 and 2Chr and some of the prophets it is regularly used for חזק. With one exception חזק always occurs in connection with the hardening of Pharaoh's heart in Exod, either in the Qal (7:13,22 8:15 9:35) or transitively in the Piel with God as subject (4:21 9:12 10:20,27 11:10 14:4,8,17), and in all cases but 7:13 Exod uses σκληρύνω. This verb obtains as well for הכביד (10:1) and הקשה (7:3 13:15) but also in connection with Pharaoh's heart. Presumably Exod here used κατίσχυσεν to set the scene of the struggle beween the divine signs and the stubborn heart of Pharaoh; in spite of the powerful sign Pharaoh won the first round, a struggle which he would certainly lose in due course to God's signs. -- The *x* text substitutes

12. See LS s.v.
13. An instrumental dative according to SS 124.
14. This was unsatisfactory to both Aq and Sym. Aq has ἐν ἡμεραίοις which he uses to represent the hapax legomenon להטים, possibly in the sense of לחש "whisper," thus "with whispered or quiet incantations". On the other hand Sym has διὰ τῶν ἀποκρύφων presupposing בלליהם of 8:3,14 from the root לוט.

εθρασυνθη "became emboldened, over-confident" which points in the same direction.[15]

The antecedent of αὐτῶν is Μωυσῆς καὶ ᾽Ααρών of v.10, and not the nearer references of vv.11 and 12, as common sense dictates.

Exod alone indicates the addressees αὐτοῖς after ἐλάλησεν in the καθάπερ clause; an F M *O C s* text omits the pronoun, probably an early revision based on the Hebrew.

7:14 The verse begins with a δέ construction indicating change of subject. It also serves to introduce the story of the next sign: the plague of water turned to blood.

βεβάρυνται occurs here as a literalism for כבד. The root is used seven times in Exod for כבד in the Qal or Hiphil always of Pharaoh's heart. The perfect is appropriate since the effect of Pharaoh's heart has been "weighted down" and therefore is "stubborn, immovable." By assimilation of *nu* into the *tau* the tradition has produced a number of variant spellings of the root βαρέω which means the same as βαρύνω.[16]

The marked infinitive with negative particle is used to render מאן "he refused"; i.e. Exod uses the infinitive marker τοῦ plus μή in the sense of "so as not to."[17]

7:15 Exod uses the adverb τὸ πρωί either with or without the accusative neuter article τό as an accusative of time when to indicate the morning. An itacistic variant has the dative article τω which is a more classical usage, but LXX only attests the Hellenistic accusative article.

For ἰδού in narrative see note at 3:9. The *C s* prefixing of ἰδού by a conjunction is also found in a Qumran ms but this is a mere coincidence.

The pattern αὐτός + present indicative verb for a Hebrew participle occurs only here in Exod; since Sam has הוא before the participle it may have had a textual basis.

The third clause is paratactically joined to the second, i.e. the ἰδού modifies both clauses, thus making it impossible to take the second clause

15. Sym translates by ἀντέστη "stand up against, oppose."
16. See Thack 261; for a discussion of the tradition see THGE VII.Q.
17. This of course could not do for Aq who translated by means of an aorist

as parenthetic. Its main verb is inflected in the middle voice followed by the participle συναντῶν, i.e. "you shall set yourself in meeting." An old B *f z* variant has εση instead of στήση probably due to palaeographic conditioning, though it also simplifies the phrase as a paraphrastic "you will be meeting."

For the preposed direct object in the last clause comp 4:17. The future indicative verb parallels στήση of the preceding clause. The *f* text changes it to the imperative λαβε, thus in odd fashion making it parallel to the first clause.

7:16 Now for the first time "the god of the Hebrews" is identified as κύριος (as in 9:1,13 10:3); cf note at 3:18. The real struggle between Israel's God κύριος and Pharaoh is joined by means of the plagues which are about to begin; cf v.17. Moses (the notion that it is Aaron who does all the talking has now been abandoned) is to mediate the divine message. The perfect tense of ἀπέσταλκεν in Exod is well-chosen, and the change to the aorist in *b* neutralizes the effect intended by Exod.

The order to Pharaoh to release God's people that they might worship him, first occurring at 4:23, is thematic throughout the narrative of Moses' meeting with Pharaoh. -- Hex has changed the word order of μοι λατρεύσωσιν to conform to MT. The verb is in the plural as throughout the plague narrative (8:1,20 9:1,13 10:3,7); an old A B *x* reading has the singular making it congruent with λαόν, possibly under the influence of 4:23.

For ἰδού see note at 3:9. -- An *n* reading has the perfect εισακηκοας for εἰσήκουσας; this is an attempt at stylistic improvement since it is clear that Pharaoh continues to pay no attention; ἕως τούτου, however, does impose a limit to the verbal effect, i.e. "up to this point," and the aorist is in order.

7:17 The *b* text has added a transitional και νυν before the messenger formula, probably intended as a stylistic gloss. -- For the self-identification formula ἐγὼ κύριος see note at 6:2. -- For ἰδού see note at 3:9. -- ἐγὼ τύπτω represents a common pattern for rendering a Hebrew pronoun plus

---

indicative ἀνένευσεν "he refused;" cf also note at 4:23.

participle, the present tense being appropriate for a tenseless participle. Here the present tense is one of incipient action "I am about to...."

The subject ἐγώ must refer to the Lord even though in the ensuing narrative the divine striking "with the rod which is in my hand" refers to Moses (cf v.15). The language is hyperbolic; Moses and Aaron are viewed as the Lord's instruments and when they carry out the divine orders it is the Lord who is here pictured as the one doing it. In fact in v.20 ' Ααρών is the one who strikes the water with the rod. The sign is described in the last clause "and it (i.e. the water) shall turn into blood." The verb μεταβαλεῖ is intransitive and is an adequate rendering for the Niphal of הלך.

7:18 As in the preceding verse MT's relative clause modifying a noun is rendered by an article plus a prepositional phrase. The *oI* text omits the οἱ; the prepositional phrase ἐν τῷ ποταμῷ then modifies the verb τελευτή-σουσιν, whereas in Exod it refers to οἱ ἰχθύες. -- The verb in the second clause ἐποζέσει "to stink" becomes slightly less graphic in the *C* text; αποζεσει means "to smell," though not necessarily offensively.

In the last clause MT has נלאו with a marked infinitive modifying it. The usage is not elsewhere attested and the interpretation of Exod, οὐ δυνήσομαι, based on v.21, probably comes close to what MT meant. Vulg has *affligentur* (*bibentes*), presumably drinking river water made the Egyptians sick. -- The preposition ἀπό designates the river as source of the drinking water. A majority F M text has εκ which is equally possible.

7:19 A δέ construction introduces a new command to transmit orders to Aaron. Moses in turn is to speak to Aaron. For τῷ ἀδελφῷ σου and its omission by F M *oI C s* see note at v.7.

Aaron is told "Take τὸν ῥάβδον σου"; the Byzantine text omits the σου as being obvious. Similarly Exod itself does not add σου after χεῖρα, though the majority of witnesses do so in an early preOrigenian adaptation to MT.

The imperative ἔκτεινον is modified by five ἐπί phrases strung along paratactically; the conjunction between the first and second ones is supported only by Exod and Vulg, whereas the one between the second and third is lacking only in MT (i.e. BHS). The first water sources given are τὰ ὕδατα, τοὺς ποταμούς, τὰς διώργας, τὰ ἕλη and πᾶν συνεστηκὸς ὕδωρ, the first being called "of Egypt" and the others all with αὐτῶν apparently referring to ὕδατα. The spelling of the third item is uncertain and a popular M variant has διωρυχας.[18] The word which means "canal," particularly "artificial canals," is a translation of יארים by which the Nile canals are meant.[19] The next item τὰ ἕλη "marshlands" is Exod's choice for אגרים "reedy pools." The last item is the perfect participle of συνίστημι for מקוה; it refers to the collecting of water in man-made cisterns or reservoirs.

The sign is then ἔσται αἷμα, the referent being ὕδωρ; what is meant is that all the water contained in these various sources will be blood.

The verb in the last clause is ἐγένετο; the sign was now effected, though it is not until vv.20--21 that the orders are executed. Exod takes the ἐποίησαν οὕτως as substantiating what has taken place and then recapitulates the details of its taking place. The Byzantine text has a future γενησεται, corresponding to MT, i.e. the clause explicates the preceding clause καὶ ἔσται αἷμα.[20]

The blood is to be "in all the land of Egypt." Variants articulating or omitting γῆ are palaeographically conditioned. A popular F M variant has changed Αἰγύπτου into the dative.[21] -- The statement is then further defined as ἔν τε τοῖς ξύλοις καὶ ἐν τοῖς λίθοις "both in things made of wood and in things made of stone." Tar[O] makes clear what is meant by its ובמני אעא ובמני אבנא, which understanding is shared by Vulg: tam in ligneis vasis quem in saxeis. The b text has substituted τοις ποταμοις και εν τοις ελεσις αυτων, a doublet based on the earlier part of the verse.

7:20 Exod now uses a plural verb with a compound subject; for his frequent use of the singular cf e.g. v.10. Exod simply imitated MT which is also inconsistent in this regard. --   For the O b n καθα variant see note at v.10. The αὐτοῖς within the clause is also supported by Pesh. Its omission by a d reading equals MT, though this is probably mere coincidence.

18. See Thack 150.
19. Sym renders the word by ῥεῖθρα "streams."
20. Theod supports Exod, whereas Aq and Sym have a future tense.
21. For its secondary nature see the discussion in THGE VII.H.3.

For the second independent clause MT does not designate the subject of the singular verbs וירם and וירם, an ambiguity intensified by Sam and Tar^P which also have "his (rod)." Exod clarified the text by adding ' Ααρών after ἐπάρας in agreement with v.19; only Pesh shares Exod's text here. An early revision shown by a B + reading has restored the ambiguity of MT by deleting ' Ααρών.

The dative case modifying ἐπάρας in imitation of MT's במטה is questionable Greek; an accusative is standard and the change to την ραβδον was made by a popular A variant. Exod again uses τὸ ἐν τῷ ποταμῷ (twice) to render a nominal relative clause; cf note at v.18.

The *d* text characteristically shortened the text both by omitting the ἐναντίον phrases, and abbreviating the last clause by making it simply και μετεβλήθη εις αιμα "and it was changed into blood." Three mss doubled the *lambda* in μετέβαλεν, but an imperfect ("the water was changing into blood") must be a copyist's error.

7:21 The first three clauses are the aorist counterpart to the predictions of v.18, and the last clause is the same as καί ult --- Αἰγύπτου of v.19 except that its ἐγένετο is here ἦν. The only other difference between this verse and its model is ἐκ instead of ἀπό. -- For *C*'s απωζεσεν see note at v.18. The spelling εδυναντο in the *t x* text is the classical spelling.[22] -- The *C* text changed Exod by transposing οἱ Αἰγύπτιοι and πιεῖν thereby placing the complementary infinitive next to the finite verb. -- For the variants τη before γῇ and the dative for Αἰγύπτου see notes at v.19.

7:22 With the change in subject Exod uses a δέ construction. -- Though the καί before οἱ ἐπαοιδοί has no basis in MT it makes good sense in the context with the meaning "also." -- The change in *s* from ὡσαύτως to ουτως is no improvement; it probably came in under the influence of ἐποίησαν οὕτως in v.20 where οὕτως is fitting. For ἐπαοιδοί and ταῖς φαρμακείαις see notes at v.11.[23]

For the use of חזק in Exodus see note at v.13. When the root σκληρύνω is used to translate it the active translates the Piel or Hiphil, and

22. For the augment in ἠδύναντο cf Thack 197f.
23. For Aq and Sym see footnotes 10 and 14 above.

104

the passive as here (and at 8:19 9:35), the Qal; the unique B reading, εσκληρυνεν, is a careless mistake.

εἰσήκουσεν correctly interprets שמע here.[24] -- For the unusual εἶπεν for דבר see note at 6:29. -- For the articulation of κύριος in C see note at v.10.

7:23 The new subject is Φαραώ. He "turned and entered his house and paid no attention (ἐπέστησεν τὸν νοῦν αὐτοῦ) even to this"; an *x* + variant has omitted αὐτοῦ as unnecessary. -- The last phrase οὐδὲ ἐπὶ τούτῳ renders גם לזאת; usually Exod disregards גם but here he uses οὐδέ by which he picks up οὐκ and applies it to the final phrase. -- Scattered witnesses have the accusative τουτο but this is merely an itacism.

7:24 The δέ shows a new subject. All the Egyptians dug around the Nile. The purpose of the digging in MT is stated as מים לשתות, "for drinking water." Exod expresses this rather awkwardly by ὥστε πιεῖν ὕδωρ which is really a result clause "so as to drink water." Hex has transposed this so that ὕδωρ comes first to conform formally to MT but the ὥστε makes the construction somewhat peculiar.[25]

In the last clause Exod has the preposition ἀπό governing "the river" rather than "water" for MT's היאר ממימי.[26] εκ for ἀπό in the F C s text does not change the meaning. -- For the augment in εδυναντο in M + see note at v.21.

7:25 This verse seems to indicate a transition period of seven days between the time of the fouling of the waters and the next confrontation. It can be taken either as a conclusion to the story of the first plague or as a statement introducing the onset of the second. The former is presupposed by the

24. Sym renders freely by προσέσχεν "hold to."
25. The Three correct the order with Sym retaining ὥστε and having εἰς ὕδωρ before it which makes much better sense. Aq as might be expected makes it ὕδωρ τοῦ πιεῖν which Theod improves by changing τοῦ to εἰς τό. For the first part of the verse only Aq has significant differences from Exod. The subject in Aq is πᾶσα ἡ Αἴγυπτος, which literally reproduces MT's כל מצרים, followed by κυκλόθεν τοῦ ῥείθρου for היאר סביבת. Aq uses either κυκλόθεν or κύκλος for סביב/סביבת.
26. There has been no attempt to revise this on the basis of MT on the part

paragraphing of the text. -- It might also be noted that the real confrontation is now clear; it is the Lord who is the effector of the plague; not the instrument, Aaron. The struggle is really between the Lord and Pharaoh.

---

of The Three all of whom substitute ἐκ τοῦ ὕδατος for ὕδωρ ἀπό.

Chapter 8

8:1(7:26) The δέ construction shows change of subject. For ἐξαπόστειλον κ.τ λ. see note at 4:23 and 5:1. Hex reorders μου λατρεύσουσιν to conform to MT. In contrast to 4:23 and with 5:1 Exod has a plural verb, since the subject λαόν is viewed as a collective.

8:2(7:27) A threat of frogs. -- In the protasis with εἰ an indicative is normal, but βούλει is negativized by μή to render מאן idiomatically.[1] Since the pattern: μή + subjunctive is a very common one the itacistic spelling βουλη in A F M *fs* + is not surprising; furthermore, βούλει is one of only a few verbs to retain the -ει spelling for the second singular present indicative middle rather than -η.

The complementary infinitive is used absolutely in imitation of the Hebrew לשלח; since ἐξαποστεῖλαι usually has an object expressed, the tradition has variously supplied one, though it is clear from v.1 who is meant.

Though both protasis and apodosis use a pronominal subject plus an inflected present indicative verb, both representing pronoun + participle in Hebrew, their intent is different. In the protasis the tense expresses simple condition of fact, but in the apodosis the verb shows intention "I am going to smite."

For ἰδού see note at 3:9. -- The verb τύπτω is difficult to distinguish from πατάσσω in meaning, and Exod seems to have used them indiscriminately. Here τύπτω uniquely renders נגף; elsewhere in Exod it always renders the Hiphil of נכה. On the other hand נגף also occurs in 12:23(twice),27 21:22, 35 32:35 and except for the special case of 21:35 is always translated by πατάσσω (which is regularly translation for נכה Hiphil).

τὰ ὅρια, except for three occurrences at Deut 3:16,17 where a specific border is described, always occurs in the plural in the Pentateuch, even though גבול is always in the singular. -- Exod follows the articulation pattern of MT with respect to "frogs" meticulously throughout the account, although here most witnesses omit the article.

8:3(7:28) Exod is most expressive having the river's belching forth - ἐξε- ρεύξεται - frogs. An F + scribal error makes this verb εξερευσεται, but having the river redden the frogs can hardly have been intended! -- For the secondary Byzantine articulation of an unarticulated βατράχους cf note at v.2.

The collective nouns in MT, בית, חדר, משכב and מטה are quite properly rendered by plural nouns in Exod. -- The spelling ταμιεῖα is to be preferred to the contracted spelling ταμεια of B + attested in the papyri only from the first century B.C.[2] The term refers to "inside" or even to "secret rooms" and is appropriate with τῶν κοιτώνων for "bedrooms." Frogs were everywhere - not just in the bedrooms, but even on (ἐπί) the beds themselves, and in the ovens. Exod uses different prepositions: εἰς, εἰς, ἐπί, εἰς, ἐν and ἐν to show where the frogs got to, but why he did so is not always clear.[3]

The A and C traditions have added "cisterns" to the list as also being invaded by frogs. Exod has transposed the last two items of MT, i.e. φυρά- μασίν "bread dough" (presumably here for the dough containers) and κλιβάνοις "ovens," Hex of course transposing them. The spelling κριβανοις in Cod M is the Attic form.

8:4(7:29) The preposing of the coordinate prepositional phrases effectively places emphasis on the ones to be affected by the plague of frogs. Only Exod has the same order as in vv.9 and 11 with "your servants" before "your people"; all the other witnesses, except for Pesh with a different text, transpose them here. Exod clearly makes all three references alike.

8:5(1) The δέ construction introduces the next scene in which Moses is told to tell Aaron to carry out the threat by stretching out with (his) hand his staff and effect the plague of frogs. For τῷ ἀδελφῷ σου see note at 7:7.

---

1. The particle μή is the standard negative particle in protases.
2. Cf Bauer s.v. and Thack 63.
3. But cf SS 138.

MT has as modifiers of נטה in the imperative אֶת יָדְךָ בְמַטְּךָ, i.e. "your hand with your staff." Exod with better logic has τῇ χειρὶ (σου has been added by hex to equal MT) τὴν ῥάβδον σου. The Byzantine text omits σου but this is no real improvement -- For the items διώρυγας and ἕλη see 7:19.

In the last clause Aaron is told: "bring up the frogs." The wonder working rod is to be raised and the plague brought on. Cod A thoughtlessly changed ἀνάγαγε to συναγαγε, but collecting the frogs signified the end of the plague (v.14) not its beginning. The x text has changed the clause to επι τους βατραχους αναγαγε, thereby making it an unintelligble text. -- MT has a prepositional phrase at the end "upon the land of Egypt," which Exod does not represent, but it is supplied by hex.

8:6(2) In this verse Aaron is said to stretch out τὴν χεῖρα, not the rod as in v.5, over the waters, to which hex added αυτου to represent the suffix in יָדוֹ. -- In response to v.5 Exod uniquely adds καὶ ἀνήγαγεν τοὺς βατρά-χους "and he brought up the frogs" as the wondrous result of stretching out his hand. The next clause ἀνεβιβάσθη ὁ βάτραχος "and the frogs were brought up" is then in the collective singular as in MT and pairs with the final clause "and covered the land of Egypt," in which the verb is also in the singular. The neat balance of the two clauses (with plural frogs) plus two clauses (with singular frogs) is destroyed by the Byzantine text which has the plural εκαλυψαν.

8:7(3) The first clause is an exact copy of 7:22 for which see notes. -- The omission of τῶν Αἰγυπτίων by an *oI* text could be the result of revision based on MT. -- MT is also the source for the hex addition of εν before the dative phrase. -- Both φαρμακείαις and the variant φαρμακιαις are possible with the former better attested.[4] Change to επαοιδ(ι)αις in an A 970 *x z* variant was influenced by ἐπαοιδοί in the verse.

For the second clause the *f* pair 53' has changed the text to give it a meaning almost opposite to Exod. According to 53' "they were not strong enough to withstand the frogs," whereas Exod has the magicians able to

4. Cf LS s.v.

imitate Aaron's wonder. Was this a pious revision to make the magicians' powers of no effect?

8:8(4) The δέ construction signals change of subject.⁵ -- An F *b* variant adds an otiose αυτοις as the addressee after εἶπεν as do Pesh and Vulg.

Exod alone of the ancient witnesses has περὶ ἐμοῦ modifying εὔξασθε. Pharaoh realizes that his prayers to the Lord would be unthinkable, that he needs a mediator. Exod's version puts Pharaoh into the prayer relationship, not just as the one who orders prayer to be performed, but as the one on whose behalf the prayer is to be made. The omission of the phrase by *O b* must be recensional.

The Byzantine text has an accusative τον κ̄ῡ for πρὸς κύριον; this is unusual though possible, in the sense of "to beseech someone."⁶

Pharaoh understands that the Lord is directly behind the plagues, and so he wants to strike a bargain with him. The Lord is to take away the frogs, "and I will release the people." The present tense of *C*, εξαποστελλω, is the result of a copyist's dittograph of the *lambda*.

Cod B uniquely substitutes αυτους for τὸν λαόν; this must have been created by inattention since this creates an ambiguous text. -- Exod's καί plus subjunctive correctly interprets MT's *waw* plus ויזבחו as showing intent "that they may sacrifice." Exod reflects a syntactic pattern of future tense + καί + subjunctive mode: "I will ... that they may";⁷ this is voided by the popular F M future indicative, θυσουσιν, which puts the two clauses at the same level.

8:9(5) Change of subject is again shown by δέ. Exod renders the polite התפאר in blunt fashion: τάξαι "set, arrange, order." The modification of τάξαι by a πρός phrase is unusual and betrays a zeugma: "arrange (and tell) me when."

The verb in the indirect question is in the subjunctive, which presupposes that the direct question would be πότε εὔξωμαι περὶ σοῦ "When should I pray for you?" rather than the majority A F M indicative:

5. For the secondary character of the και construction in the A B 970 + variant cf THGE VII.E.1.
6. Cf LS sub εὔχομαι.

"When shall I pray for you?" Both are sensible, but the variant arose by homophony in Byzantine times. -- The B *d f s* text adds περι before τοῦ λαοῦ 1°.8

A complementary infinitive after εὔχομαι is a normal syntactic pattern.9 For parallels cf Num 6:2 1Esdr 4:43--45 5:43. Exod has three prepositional phrases modifying the infinitive ἀφανίσαι: for you, and from thy people and out of your houses; MT has only two, lacking the second and with the last one as "from thy houses." Both Sam and Vulg add to MT"s text: "and from thy servants and from thy people." Whether the added "and from thy people" of Exod is textually based text cannot be determined.

The πλήν clause is only loosely connected with the preceding: "-- only in the river shall they be left."10 The normal situation is to be restored; it is the point of the prayer: removal of the frogs from their unusual locations means limiting them to their usual ones.

8:10(5) Change of speaker occurs in rapid succession. The first speaker, Pharaoh, is clear from the δέ construction. His short reply "Tomorrow,' is immediately followed by εἶπεν οὖν. This created some confusion and there were various attempts to clarify it. The simplest was to add μωυσης as subject. A few witnesses changed to ο δε ειπεν; others changed to a plural verb ειπον or ειπαν which made Moses and Aaron the subject. But Exod allows the context to make it obvious that it is Moses who is now speaking, and he uses οὖν to show the intimate relation of this to Pharaoh's reply. The actual reply is elliptical: "As you said" for "It will be as you said."11 That the reply is an ellipsis is clear from the ἵνα clause; what Exod says is "It will be as you said in order that you may know." The itacistic variant ιδης for εἴδης in B *C x* is not to be taken seriously, as is clear from MT's תדע.12

In MT the object clause of "know" is "that there is no one like Yahweh our God," i.e. Yahweh is incomparable, whereas Exod has a monotheistic statement: ὅτι οὐκ ἔστιν ἄλλος πλὴν κυρίου. The attributive "our God" is

---

7. Cf Thack 91.
8. For its secondary character see THGE VII.L.1.
9. Cf LS sub εὔχομαι 2.c.
10. Cf v.11 below.
11. See also SS 95. Jerome prosaically added *faciam* after "according to your word."

omitted since that detracts from the absoluteness of the statement; hex supplied it by ο $\overline{κς}$ ημων. To Exod what is really important is that Pharaoh recognize Israel's monotheistic faith as correct: "there is no one else besides the Lord." A popular A F tradition has changed κυρίου into $\overline{κς}$, taking πλήν as a conjunction rather than as a preposition (governing a genitive).

8:11(7) This verse is paratactically joined to the preceding, and thus continues Moses' statement. In MT **סור** makes the frogs turn away, but Exod has a future passive περιαιρεθήσεται which involves a divine agent; it is after all a "sign" from the Lord; the frogs "shall be removed." In the prepositional phrases which modify the verb Exod has been careful to distinguish between people and places. The frogs are to be removed ἀπό, "from" you, people, servants, but ἐκ, "out of" houses, villages; comp also vv.8 and 9. Popular traditions have failed to observe Exod's careful distinction. The prepositional phrases καὶ ἐκ τῶν ἐπαύλεων is here unique to Exod, who also uses it in v.13. It could be taken as secondary, but it does fit well into its context; its omission by an F *b* tradition is probably due to homoiot, i.e. it is neither original nor a revision inspired by MT.

The πλήν clause with which the verse ends is exactly the same as in v.9, only here it fits the context better than there. The clause balances with the first sentence: the frogs shall be removed ... only in the river shall they be left.

8:12(8) Again δέ shows change of subject. The verb is singular by attraction to the nearer member of a compound subject. A majority reading has the compound ανεβοησεν for ἐβόησεν; there is no real change in meaning. The simplex does occur four times in Exod for the verb **צעק** (also at 14:15 15:25 17:4), but the compound only once (14:10).

Exod is much more specific than is MT as to the subject of Moses' call to the Lord. Exod defines MT's "concerning the matter of" by a concrete περὶ τοῦ ὁρισμοῦ "concerning the limitation of, the setting up of boundaries for"; Exod recalls the specifics of vv.9 and 11 - the frogs are to be kept in bounds, "only in the river will they be left."

---

12. Cf Walters 197ff.

The verb ἐτάξατο is somewhat ambiguous in the final clause. At v.9 the middle imperative occurred with active meaning. If that is here intended Φαραώ would be the subject. Much more likely is the understanding of Φαραώ as in the dative, as understood by the popular F M τω φαραω; the clause would then mean "as was arranged for Pharaoh."

8:13(9) The Lord ended the plague as requested by Moses on Pharaoh's behalf. Change to κύριος as subject is shown by the δέ construction. -- For the variants καθα and καθως see the note at 7:10.

The last clause with the verb ἐτελεύτησαν modified by three ἐκ phrases contains an ellipsis which is based on the Hebrew. What is meant is that they died (and disappeared) from. Instead of οἰκιῶν the Byzantine text has οικων; the distinction between the two is minimal, since both must here mean actual buildings.

8:14(10) The subject of the first clause is indefinite, presumably it is the Egyptians. The verb συνήγαγον "they gathered together" is not as expressive as the Hebrew יצברו "they heaped up," but Tar Pesh Vulg all agree with Exod.13 -- θημωνιὰς θημωνιάς represents a Hebraic usage in which a repeated word occurs with distributive sense; in ordinary Greek this would be represented by a κατά phrase. The words are the second of a double accusative modifying συνήγαγον, i.e. αὐτούς and θημ. θημ.; the meaning is "in piles." As might be expected haplography has produced a single reading of θημωνιάς in the tradition in a number of witnesses.14

In the second clause Exod has the simplex ὤζεσεν but a popular variant has the compound επωζεσεν; this may well be an attempt to intensify the meaning; cf note at 7:18. The *b* text has εξωζεσεν which is probably an internal variant in the επωζεσεν tradition.

---

13. But not Aq who has συνέχωσαν.
14. Theod adopted the reading of Exod in his revision, whereas Aq has κόρους κόρους, i.e. "in homers" for Hebrew חמרם חמרם. Cod M preserves the reading σωροὺς σωρούς "in piles" but wrongly attributes it to Aq. Other sources attribute the reading to Samariticon which could be correct. At least the A tradition of the Sam Targ has כרוא כרוא which means the same thing.

8:15(11) Pharaoh's obduracy. The δέ construction shows change of subject to Pharaoh. Rhetorically the verse is loosely constructed. Φαραώ is the stated subject of ἰδών, but the subject of the main clause is ἡ καρδία αὐτοῦ (referring to Pharaoh), and only in the next clause is the subject of εἰσήκου-σεν again Pharaoh. MT has Pharaoh as subject throughout and the Byzantine text revises towards MT with its εβαρυνεν την καρδιαν αυτου. In spite of the loose construction the verse is easy to comprehend.

The Hebrew הרוחה is well rendered by the ἀνάψυξις of Exod "respite."[15] -- The reference in αὐτῶν is of course Moses and Aaron. The genitive modifying εἰσήκουσεν is classical usage..

8:16(12) The plague of gnats. Change of subject to κύριος is shown by δέ. -- Again Aaron is the one to perform the signs; cf 7:9,19 8:5, even though Moses apparently now does all the speaking to Pharaoh in spite of 7:1,2. -- For ἔκτεινον τῇ χειρὶ τὴν ῥάβδον σου see note at v.5. The Sam reading את ידו is probably parent for τῇ χειρί, since MT lacks it. The C b text has added σου and conforms more exactly to Sam, though it is simply added *ad sensum*.

Aaron is to smite τὸ χῶμα of the ground. The subject of ἔσονται must be χῶμα "dust," probably considered congruent because it consists of particles. -- Whether σκνῖφες or σκνιπες was written by Exod is uncertain; both spellings are attested for the root as early as the third century B.C.[16] Approximately half the Greek witnesses have the σκνιπες spelling but the uncials all follow Exod.[17]

Exod alone has "even on men and on animals and," which is consistent with v.17, and cf also v.18. The translator did not simply look at his parent text phrase by phrase but tried to make a narrative consistent within itself.

An F d variant has changed the case of Αἰγύπτου to the dative.[18] -- After Αἰγύπτου hex has added και εποιησαν (or -σεν as in Pesh) ουτως to

15. Aq is determined to render words with רוח as root by the Greek root πνευ- and so has ἀνάπνευσις "recovery of breath, respite." Sym has ἄνεσις "relaxation," hence "abatement, remission," whereas Samariticon has εὐρυχωρία "roominess, spaciousness"; note that Sam Targ A has נפרוש "enlargement, breathing space."
16. See Mayser I.1, 146.
17. The Samariticon has φθεῖρες "vermin."
18. That this could not be Exod is clear form THGE VII.H.3.

conform to the ‏ויעש כן‏ of MT.

8:17(13) Aaron accordingly (οὖν) carries out the divine orders mediated through Moses. For τῇ χειρὶ τὴν ῥάβδον cf notes at v.5. Neither suffix of ‏ידך‏ or of ‏מטהו‏ is translated, since in the context such repetitions of σου would be otiose; hex, however, added for both nouns. The *d* text has created an unfortunate ambiguity by placing the subject ᾽ Ααρών between the two modifiers, and ᾽ Ααρών could then momentarily be misunderstood to be in the genitive.

In the next clause the *C* text added παν before τὸ χῶμα, i.e. "all the dust," which would be quite a feat for Aaron! *C* has the feminine article for σκνῖφες (σκνιπες) in this verse in both instances, which is simply a mistake since in v.18 *C* correctly has the masculine. For the popular variant spelling σκνιπες see note at v.16. It might be noted that Exod carefully distinguishes between εἰμι and γίνομαι; in v.16 the future existence, ἔσονται, of the σκνιπες is predicated, but in vv.17 and 18 they have become, ἐγένοντο, an itching reality. -- The omission of τε by B + means that the "both" of a "both ... and" pattern is omitted; this is closer to MT which has no conjunction here.

The last clause involves a reinterpretation of MT. According to MT and all the other ancient witnesses all the dust of the land became gnats in all the land of Egypt. But if all the dust had become gnats there would be no dust left (to one living in Egypt quite inconceivable!); far more dramatic and far more believable would be for all the dust of the land to be crawling with insects; so Exod renders this as "and in all the dust of the land there were gnats in all the land of Egypt.

8:18(14) Change of subject to οἱ ἐπαοιδοί is shown by δέ. The clause ἐποίησαν -- αὐτῶν is exactly the same in v.7 and 7:22; see note at 7:22. But ἐποίησαν is here modified by a complementary infinitive and differs from v.7 and 7:11,22 where ἐποίησαν was used absolutely. What is here meant is that the magicians acted likewise, i.e. as Aaron had done, to produce (ἐξαγαγεῖν) gnats but could not (i.e. produce them). The word for gnats is τὸν σκνῖφα (but with a feminine article in a *b* variant; cf note at v.17), i.e.

singular because it is used generically. In the last clause where actual gnats are referred to, the plural is again used. MT does not make this distinction but has the plural in both instances. For the popular spelling with *pe* for *phi* see note at v.16. An *f* + variant gloss identifies the ἐπαοιδοί as των αιγυπτιων, probably on the basis of 7:11.

ἠδύναντο is also spelled with single augment in the tradition.[19] -- For the last clause cf notes on its identical counterpart in v.17. The Byzantine text mistakenly continued with the rest of v.17: "and in all the dust of the land there were gnats."

8:19(15) Exod now uses οὖν, since the conclusion which the magicians reached from the foregoing is given. This conclusion is put in anthropomorphic terms: "this is the finger of God," which Tar^O prosaically but correctly interprets as "the plague is from ייי." The use of "finger" rather than "hand" to indicate action or deed here is unique. Note the frequent use of יד /χείρ in the sense of "power" in OT.

The subject of the nominal clause in MT is הוא; Exod has two words for it, ἐστιν τοῦτο, and accordingly Origen marked one of them, τοῦτο, with an obelus, which shows how purely mechanically he operated, paying little attention to the sense of the passage.

For the remainder of the verse cf notes on its identical counterpart in v.15. For the change in *b* of ἐλάλησεν to ειπεν also see note at v.15.

8:20(16) The plague of dog flies. Change of subject is shown by δέ. Its change to ουν by a *b* reading probably shows an attempt to tie this plague to the preceding one, but this is not legitimate; v.20 clearly begins a new paragraph.

The phrase ὄρθρισον τὸ πρωί is an idiomatic rendering of השכם בבקר "rise early in the morning." For the phrase τὸ πρωί and its dative variant cf note at 7:15. -- Exod's στῆθι "stand" (before Pharaoh) is somewhat blunter than the reflexive Hithpael התיצב of MT; cf also 9:13. Moses is supposed to interrupt Pharaoh as he is going.

19. For which cf Thack 197f.

For ἰδού see notes at 3:9 and 4:14. A popular B reading has καὶ before it against MT.[20] -- The ἰδού clause has αὐτὸς ἐξελεύσεται for MT's participle יוצא; there is a הוא, however, in 4Q364 as well as in Sam Tar[P]; for the pattern see 7:15. Exod correctly interprets the tenseless participle here by the future; Pharaoh will be going out by the water (Tar[P] has also added the reason: למתקוררה "to cool himself off").

For the previous plague no warning to Pharaoh is recorded, but here the messenger formula with the demand for release is given in terms identical to that of v.1; for the messenger formula see note on 4:22; for the message itself see notes on 4:23 5:1. -- As elsewhere (4:23 7:16 8:1 9:1) μοι stands before the verb; hex changed the order to conform to MT. -- A well supported A B M addition after λατρεύσωσιν is ἐν τῇ ἐρήμῳ.[21]

8:21(17) Instead of the simple "If you do not send away" of MT Exod has added a complex verbal figure ἐὰν δὲ μὴ βούλῃ ἐξαποστεῖλαι, as in the parallels in 4:23 8:2 9:2; see also 10:4. The construction differs from the parallels only in the use of ἐάν + subjunctive instead of εἰ + indicative. -- For ἰδού see notes at 3:9 and 4:14.

The Hebrew pattern: pronoun + participle משלח is rendered by the usual pronoun + present tense. Idiomatically Exod uses ἐπαποστέλλω modified by ἐπί in the sense of "I am going to send against"; The variant compound ἐξαποστελ(λ)ω in C n x can also mean "send upon." Other readings (O d t) omit a *lambda* to make a future inflection, but these are all secondary.

The four prepositional objects are: you, your servants, your people, your houses. As in vv.9 and 11 only the last "your" is plural, ὑμῶν, since Pharaoh hardly needed more than one house, although in v.24 οἴκους Φαραώ does occur. -- An early correction towards MT in O C corrects this plural ὑμῶν to σου.

A Byzantine gloss adds καὶ επι πασαν γην αιγυπτου after "your servants"; this is clearly wrong, since it is contradicted in the next verse where Goshen is excluded from the plague.

20. For its secondary character see THGE VII.E.3.
21. For a discussion of this gloss see THGE VII.O.

The plague according to Exod is to be one of κυνόμυιαν, "dog flies." The word stands for the Hebrew ערב which probably means "a swarm" (of some kind of insects).[22]

The word κυνόμυιαν[23] is unarticulated the first time since it is generic; thereafter it is always articulated. --MT has וגם הארמה after "the houses of the Egyptians shall be filled with the insect swarms," in which the וגם shows that the word הארמה stands on the same level as "the houses," so "even the land," or "namely, the land." Exod interprets this differently by καὶ εἰς τὴν γῆν, "even within the land (on which they are)," probably because the plague is to affect only that part of Egypt not occupied by the Israelites.

8:22(18) The verb παραδοξάσω "I will deal gloriously, render glorious" apparently reflects the root פלא rather than MT's הפליתי "I will set apart, treat differently." Exod's text is reflected in Vulg: faciamque mirabilem; cf also 9:4. -- The M + spelling γεσσεμ is due to dittography.

The phrase ἐπ' αὐτῆς within the first ἐφ' ἧς clause is in imitation of MT's אשר ... עליה. A popular M reading of the simplex εστιν for ἔπεστιν is an attempt at simplification. The Byzantine text's omission of the verb is probably within a parent εστιν text, since it is easier to understand the omission of εστιν than of ἔπεστιν.

The second ἐφ' ἧς is an adaptation to the first one; the construction of MT is quite different: לבלתי היות,[24] but Exod's ἐφ' ἧς οὐκ ἔσται brings out what MT intends: "where (on which ...) there will be no (dog flies)." The repetitiousness of ἐφ' ἧς led to a number of variants including εφ η, εν η, and εφ ην, none of which changes the meaning; an x + reading actually changes the gender, εφ ω; this must presuppose λαόν as antecedent.

The purpose of the foregoing is recognition by Pharaoh that it is the Lord, the lord of all the land who is in charge of affairs. -- For the popular itacistic variant ιδης for εἰδῆς see note at v.10. -- For a discussion of ἐγώ

22. Sym adopted Exod, while Aq and Theod, basing their interpretation on a root ערב meaning "to mix," translates resp. by σύμμικτον and μίγμα (cf also Aram and Syriac ערב Pael "to mingle, or mix"). The Samariticon misunderstood ערב as עורב "crow" and reads κόρακα.
23. For the late Hellenistic spelling κυνομυιης adopted by a B + variant see THGE VII.H.1.

εἰμι κύριος see note at 6:2. A majority A M text omits εἰμι with no difference in meaning.

Exod ends the verse with an attributive phrase ὁ κύριος πάσης τῆς γῆς modifying κύριος 1°, i.e. it is not Pharaoh but the Lord who is master of all Egypt. This interprets MT's בקרב הארץ "in the midst of all the land," in that being κύριος in the midst of the land means his complete mastery; when κύριος, Israel's God, is present he is automatically in charge. A variant tradition of uncertain origin makes this even more emphatic by inserting (rather awkwardly one must say) the participle κυριευων before πάσης, i.e. the Lord ruling over all the land.[25] Incidentally Tar[O] shares Exod's understanding of the phrase; it has שליט בגו ארעא "ruler in the midst of the land."

8:23(10) Exod states that the Lord will set a distinction, διαστολήν, between the two peoples. The word in MT is פדת which usually means "redemption," but this is ill-fitting in the context. Tar[O] paraphrases with פורקן לעמי ועל עמך איתי מחא, i.e. "redemption for my people, but on your people there will be the plague," which interpretation certainly shows that "a distinction" is intended. The noun is modified by two ἀνὰ μέσον phrases with the pronouns in both phrases preceding the noun; hex transposes them to conform to MT.

The last clause begins with a δέ construction, thereby showing change of subject from first person to τὸ σημεῖον τοῦτο. The temporal ἐν phrase is preposed in order to emphasize it. The adverbial αὔριον is uninflected but is treated as a feminine noun "the morrow."

A *b* variant has ποιησει κ̄ς instead of ἔσται, i.e. "tomorrow the Lord will execute this sign," as an exegetical comment. -- Exod uniquely among the ancient witnesses adds ἐπὶ τῆς γῆς at the end of the clause, thereby avoiding what would otherwise be a case of ἔσται being used absolutely. A popular M tradition omits it, possibly as a recensional change based on MT.

---

24. Theod rendered it literally by ὥστε μὴ γένηται
25. The Three of course corrected the Exod text. Apparently (based on Syh) Aq had ἐν ἐγκάτῳ τῆς γῆς; Sym, ἐν τῇ γῇ, and Theod, ἐν μέσῳ (τῆς) γῆς.

8:24(20) Change of subject is shown by δέ. Though the speech of the Lord in vv.20--23 gives Pharaoh the alternative: to send away or not to send away the people, the opening statement takes for granted that Pharaoh is unwilling to obey and so the Lord carries out the threat. In the next clause πλῆθος is used adverbially modifying the verb, thus "came in great numbers." בית twice occurs as singular, but Exod has the plural τοὺς οἴκους for both even though the plural is fitting only for the second; cf note at v.21. The *d* group omits the second "into the houses"; i.e. has "into the houses of Pharaoh and of his servants."[26]

The last clause in the verse is introduced by καί; there is no conjunction in MT or Tar, and the form תשחת is an old preterite, correctly translated by ἐξωλεθρεύθη.[27] -- ἀπό here designates the cause, i.e. the land was destroyed because of the dog flies.[28]

8:25(21) The subject change to Pharaoh is signaled by δέ. -- The direct speech marker λέγων correctly represents the ויאמר of MT. This quoted speech begins with the participle ἐλθόντες which is unusual for לכו, though it does occur in a similar context at 3:16 "come (or go), assemble," and compare 2:8 ἐλθοῦσα ... ἐκάλεσεν, where it means "going." Usually it renders the verb בוא. The verb can mean "come" or "go," but the former is far more common throughout the LXX. The popular M variant απελθοντες makes it clear: "go away, leave, depart."

Moses and Aaron are told to "sacrifice to your God in the land." A popular A M variant identifies "your God" by adding κω before it as in Tar[P] Pesh; this is dramatically wrong in view of v.22. The real struggle between the Lord and Pharaoh is Pharaoh's constant refusal to recognize ὅτι ἐγώ εἰμι κύριος.

The last phrase is the real point of Pharaoh's statement. Do your religious rites ἐν τῇ γῇ, not outside Egypt. The phrase is somewhat ambiguous and the tradition has tried to make it more specific in various ways, thus "in my land, "this land" (also Vulg), "that land," "land of Egypt" (as in Tar[P]).

26. For the articulation of γῆν in B *C f x* see the discussion in THGE VII.D.4.
27. Sym translates it somewhat more literally by ἐφθάρη.

8:26(22) A *b* δε construction shows change of subject. The *x* text has ειπαν for εἶπεν Μωυσῆς, making the subject Moses and Aaron. -- The subject of the introductory statement made is γενέσθαι οὕτως "to take place thus," but in MT it is לעשות כן "to do thus"; the predicates are also distinct: οὐ δυνατόν "is impossible" vs לא נכון "is not upright, correct." But to Exod acting in a not upright fashion is not quite the point; rather to Exod for the suggestion of Pharaoh to take place in such a context is simply not possible; note Vulg: *non potest ita fieri* which comes close to the interpretation of Exod.

The reason for this being impossible is clear from the next clause: "because we would be sacrificing the abominations of the Egyptians to the Lord our God." The word תועבת in MT is, intended as a collective.[29]

A B variant with a good deal of scattered support for the future has the future indicative θυσομεν instead of the homophonous aorist subjunctive.[30] A *b* + variant which has ου θυσωμεν was probably influenced by the οὐ δυνατόν with which Moses' reply began; it might then be understood as "for we would (hardly) sacrifice, etc."

Exod twice has τῶν Αἰγυπτίων;[31] for Exod's variation between "Egypt" and "Egyptians" to render מצרים see notes at 1:13,15.

Within the protasis of the conditional clause variations in the tradition have resulted from the influence of the preceding clause. Thus the verb has been placed after Αἰγυπτίων by the *C* mss and a few witnesses have added κω τω θω ημων after the verb.[32] -- For לעיניהם Exod idiomatically has ἐναντίον αὐτῶν.[33]

For the verb λιθοβοληθησόμεθα in the apodosis the *d* text has the homophonous aorist subjunctive, whereas the *x* tradition represents a

---

28. For the variant spelling κυνομυιης in B 82' see THGE VII.H.1.
29. Of The Three Aq alone changes τὰ βδελύγματα (twice) to the singular to conform to MT.
30. That this is secondary is discussed in THGE VII.H.6.
31. Aq Theod have Αἰγύπτου.
32. Since MT simply has הן for ἐάν Aq naturally omitted the γάρ which followed it; Sym changed it to δέ, whereas Theod has καί instead of ἐὰν γάρ.
33. Aq in his usual literalistic fashion has τοῖς ὀφθαλμοῖς αὐτῶν, and Theod, πρὸ ὀφθαλμῶν αὐτῶν.

recensional change based on MT; it has λιθοβο+ λησουσιν ημας.[34]

8:27(23) For ὁδόν ... ἡμῶν see notes at 3:18 and 5:3. The use of the future indicative expresses the certain intention. An A reading with a great deal of support in the tradition has the homophonous aorist subjunctive for both verbs. This would weaken the intention and make the course of action a potential mood. -- The omission of κυρίῳ by B 56* is an error made under the influence of the shorter text at 3:18 5:3. -- For the *b x* reading καθα see note at 7:10.

8:28(24) The compound ἐξαποστελῶ is regularly used for the Piel of שׁלח, whereas αποστελω occurs for the Qal.[35] An A *d t x* text has the present tense which is the product of dittography of the *lambda*.

Exod uses the aorist imperative θύσατε as a command based on the prior Pharaonic action. Pharaoh says: "I will send you away - so worship." The popular Byzantine θυσετε, which is indeed closer to MT's וזבחתם, is probably merely a simplification of the text. -- For the omission of κυρίῳ by Cod B see note at v.27.

Exod has idiomatically avoided potential Hebraisms in his translation of the רק clause; רק has been translated by the adversative ἀλλ', and the cognate free infinitive plus negated finite verb has lost all traces of the cognate construction in Exod's "not far away shall you extend (your) going." Exod has expressed the intent of MT in good Greek fashion.

MT's final instruction: "pray for me" is enhanced in Exod by the logical particle οὖν as well as by πρὸς κύριον at the end. The former ties the clause to its context, whereas prepositional phrase makes Pharaoh recognize once again that the Lord is in control; compare v.22.

8:29(25) Change of subject is here shown by δέ.[36] -- Exod sharpens the narrative by using ὅδε "right now, immediately" for הנה rather than the usual ιδου read by *O C*, which may well be an early correction towards

34. As in The Three. Aq and Theod also have the literal καὶ οὐ introducing the apodosis. The readings of The Three in this verse are all taken from Syh and are retroversions.
35. For the *s* variant αποστελω or the B *f* αποστελλω cf THGE VII.N.
36. Aq and Theod change to a καί construction.

MT.[37] A well supported variant is ὧδε "thus, in such a way," but this is simply a misspelling of ὅδε, the two being homophonous in Byzantine times. The pattern: pronoun + future verb sensibly interprets the Hebrew: pronoun + participle as "I shall be leaving you forthwith and." ἐγώ is lexically otiose and is conditioned by the Hebrew.[38]

Moses accedes to Pharaoh's request to pray for him, though not to κύριον as requested but to τὸν θεόν.[39] A b variant changes the verb to the compound προσευξομαι probably under the influence of its modifier πρὸς τὸν θεόν.

The remainder of the verse is in third person in all other ancient witnesses, and Exod alone continues with the more consistent and from the point of view of the narrative the more direct and personal second person. Various attempts at partial revision towards MT obtain in the tradition, but none is complete.

For the Hebraistic idiom προσθῇς ἔτι see note at 5:7. The infinitive ἐξαπατῆσαι "cheat, deceive" occurs in the majority A M variant in the simplex, which is almost identical in meaning.[40]

The τοῦ μή + purposive infinitive expresses both the content and intent of ἐξαπατῆσαι, viz., not sending away the people. In turn θῦσαι κυρίῳ also expresses purpose, as was fully understood by the Byzantine text which has οπως θυσωσιν κυριω.

8:30(26) Though Moses remains the subject he now leaves Pharaoh's presence and prays to τὸν θεόν instead of to יהוה as all other ancient witnesses attest, probably because he had promised Pharaoh εὔξομαι πρὸς τὸν θεόν in v.29, and so here he uses the identical phrase.

---

37. Aq and Theod also read ἰδού, whereas Sym changes the entire הנה clause into a temporal clause ὡς ἂν ἐξέλθω παρὰ σοῦ "when I go out from you."
38. Since the Hebrew has the long form אנכי Aq has his usual rendering ἐγώ εἰμι, which is unacceptable in normal Greek, but is also found in Theod. For Exod's ἐξελεύσομαι both Aq and Theod have a present indicative verb in first singular to agree with ἐγώ (εἰμι), Aq with ἐξέρχομαι and Theod with ἐκπορεύομαι.
39. Aq corrects to κύριον. Neither Sym nor Theod change Exod's εὔξομαι "I shall pray," but Aq translates by ἱκετεύσω "I will beseech."
40. Aq and Sym translate by παραλογίσασθαι "to defraud."

8:31(27) The δέ construction shows change of subject to κύριος. -- For the καθα variant see note at 7:10. -- The clause is a rendering for a prepositional phrase in MT: "according to the word of Yahweh," probably on the analogy of the καθάπερ clauses in the chapter (vv.13,15,19, 27). For εἶπεν as rendering for דבר see note at 6:29.

περιεῖλεν is modified by three coordinate ἀπό phrases. The καί before the second phrase is supported by all the old witnesses except MT Tar^O. A variant tradition in B + omits the second and third instances of ἀπό.[41]

The last clause is asyndetic in MT but is paratactic in Exod (and Pesh). For καταλείφθη "was there left," the *C* tradition has απελειφθη with a slightly which different nuance: "was there left behind."

8:32(28) That Pharaoh should "weigh down, make heavy his heart as a figure for his obduracy is due to the Hebrew which has כבד in the Hiphil. It is indeed a striking figure; cf also 9:34 10:1, and for the passive 8:15 9:7. -- The final clause in MT is a simple statement of fact: "and he did not send away the people." Exod on the other hand stresses Pharaoh's attitude by οὐκ ἠθέλησεν ἐξαποστεῖλαι "he did not want to send away," which is particularly fitting in the context.

41. For the secondary nature of the shorter text cf THGE VII.L.2.

124

Chapter 9

9:1 The plague on cattle. Change of subject to κύριος is signalled by δέ. --
For εἴσελθε ... κύριος 2° see 8:1. -- For the messenger formula see note at
4:22. -- For "God of the Hebrews" see note at 7:16. -- For the message itself
see notes at 4:23 5:1 and 8:1. The reordering of μοι λατρεύσωσιν in the
majority tradition is hex.

9:2 The verse begins with εἰ μὲν οὖν and has no δέ counterpart, which
might be rendered "yet if then," with the verse closely related to v.1, as the
οὖν shows.[1] The same construction occurs at 4:23. The *b* tradition simplifies
this by ει δε.

For μὴ βούλει cf note at 4:23; for the well supported A variant
spelling βουλη as though it were a subjunctive see note at 8:2.[2]

The verb in the adversative clause, ἐγκρατεῖς, a hapax legomenon in
LXX, means "hold on to, retain control over" with the genitive.[3] When it is
modified by an accusative it means "master, overpower," and the popular
variant αυτους does not fit well; it is probably due to a partial correction
from one of The Three where a different verb obtained.[4] An *x* + variant
spells the verb as though it were aorist subjunctive, but this is simply an itacism. The clause is an adversative one in Exod, though paratactic in MT; a
popular A M variant "corrects" ἀλλ᾽ to και in order to equal MT.

9:3 This verse along with v.4 constitutes the apodosis of v.2. Though the
verse is not without possible syntactic ambiguity, Exod probably intended
the list of animals ἔν ... προβάτοις to be explicative of and thus in
apposition to κτήνεσίν, and θάνατος μέγας σφόδρα similarly to χείρ. This
is also the way in which the Masoretes interpreted the Hebrew text.

1. Cf LS sub μέν B.II.2.
2. Sym translates אתה מאן by ἀπειθεῖς, and with Exod does not render
the pronoun independently.
3. See Helbing 122.
4. E.g., Aq renders מחזיק by ἐπιλαμβάνη "hold fast, grasp," which is a
literal rendering. Sym uses κατέχεις "hold fast, hold back."

For ἰδού see note at 3:9. χείρ is articulated in *oI C*; either is good usage (contrast 4:6 15:9 with 19:13). -- The B *x z* variant ἐπεστιν is an attempt at a stylistic correction.[5] ἔσται is modified by an ἐν phrase which is a Hebraistic rendering of MT's בְ phrase. More idiomatic would have been ἐπί, and the ἐν must be translated "upon, on" throughout. The generic term מִקְנֶךָ is correctly interpreted by the plural τοῖς κτήνεσίν (σου), since it includes the various species that follow. Similarly בַּשָּׂדֶה within the relative clause is taken as collective: ἐν τοῖς πεδίοις.

The nouns apposite to κτήνεσίν are five in number with the first three governed by ἐν and all five joined by καί. In MT Sam Tar and Pesh all five are governed by the preposition בְ, while Vulg has *super* only for the first in accordance with good Latin style. Both Pesh and Vulg join Exod in joining all five nouns by conjunctions; Sam lacks a conjunction before the fourth; Tar[P] joins one and two, and four and five; MT and Tar[O] join only the last pair. Anyone of these patterns can be defended stylistically. Some changes in the tradition affect the prepositions: the *b* text (as Vulg) leaves out all but the first; Cod B *f z* omit the ἐν before ταῖς,[6] and the ἐν before τοῖς ὑποζυγίοις is omitted by *f x z*. Such omissions are stylistic in nature.

The *b x* text transposed ἵπποις and ὑποζυγίοις for no apparent reason. -- Also the gender of καμήλοις is uncertain. Exod made them female camels, whereas an A *f* + variant makes them male - the difference is ταῖς as τοις, the article alone indicating gender. --   The affliction, i.e. χείρ κυρίου, is then dubbed as θάνατος μέγας σφόδρα "a very great pestilence."[7]

9:4 Exod makes the verse continue as speech of the Lord instead of the third person with יהוה as subject of MT and the other ancient witnesses. For παραδοξάσω (also Sam Vulg) see note at 8:2. Obviously MT's "make a distinction" fits better than Exod's παραδοξάσω "I will set up something wonderful (between the cattle, etc.)." This wonderful thing is then explained in the final sentence. Exod also differs from the other ancient witnesses in naming the cattle of the Egyptians before those of the Israelites. And since

5. See the discussion in THGE VII.N.
6. Cf THGE VII.L.2.
7. The Hebrew דְבַר כָבֵד is more literalistically rendered by Aq and Sym as

מצרים is here (as often) understood as Egyptians, rather than Egypt, the term "Israel" is also interpreted as τῶν υἱῶν ᾿Ισραήλ. An early popular correction makes this του ισραηλ so as to conform to MT, and subsequently hex has transposed this term and τῶν Αἰγυπτίων to equal MT. -- An early gloss is found in B z +, viz. εν τω καιρω εκεινω after ἐγώ, but as (εν) τη ημερα εκεινη in b.[8]

The last sentence is asyndetic in Exod, and the majority text with και before οὐ is an early preOrigenian revision based on MT. -- The pattern of the noun phrase τῶν τοῦ ᾿Ισραήλ υἱῶν is excellent Greek but nowhere else in the Pentateuch is the article and the noun υἱός ever separated by a genitive modifier. The phrase has created a great deal of difficulty for the tradition. It became του οικου ιηλ in x; a popular A variant had των κτηνων (των υιων) ιηλ, and the majority tradition has the common idiom των υιων ιηλ. The unusual pattern of Exod does place strong stress on τοῦ ᾿Ισραήλ - it is Israel and not the Egyptians who will escape the plague. -- Changes of the subject ῥητόν to ουδεν or μηδεν in the tradition are instances of simplification.[9]

9:5 The verb ἔδωκεν is rather unexpected as a rendering for שׂים, but it does occur seven times in Exod (also at 4:11,15,21 8:23 17:14 21:13). Throughout the LXX (including Exod) it is the standard rendering for the root נתן. The root נתן can mean either "to give" or "put, place," which is then readily transferred to LXX's δίδωμι. Nonetheless the use of δίδωμι for שׂים is uncommon. Outside Exod it only occurs 17 times according to HR: once each in Num, Kgdms, Chr, Dan; twice each in Josh, Ps, Jer, and seven times in Isa.

The subject is uniquely ὁ θεός over against MT's יהוה. A popular Byzantine variant does make it κς ο θς. -- What God did set was a ὅρος, a temporal limit, an adequate (though unique) rendering of the Hebrew מועד. -- For ἐν τῇ αὔριον cf note at 8:23, the only other instance in LXX.

λοιμὸς βαρύς "a heavy plague."
8. Cf THGE VII.O.
9. Samariticon apparently has ῥῆμα instead of ῥητόν; this is a far more common rendering of דבר than ῥητόν.

9:6 Exod here uses τῇ ἐπαύριον rather than ἐν τῇ αὔριον of v.5, thus distinguishing between מחרת and מחר; in v.6 the time reference is "on the morrow" ἐπαύριον, whereas αὔριον is simply used as "tomorrow." MT is quite correctly rendered by these adverbs.

The verb ἐτελεύτησεν "came to an end, i.e. died" is intransitive, and the *C* text which adds κ͞ς in the second clause is an anachronism; there is no evidence elsewhere as far as I can discover that the verb can be transitive. Classically a neuter plural subject is congruent with a singular verb, and the plural M variant is unnecessary (though not incorrect).

The final clause contrasts with the second as the δέ structure shows. A popular variant for the subject οὐδέν as ουδε εν reminds one of Tar^P Pesh: אף לא חד "not even one." The reading ρητον of the *x* text is taken from v.4.

9:7 Exod has simplified the opening part of the Hebrew: "And Pharaoh sent and behold" to ἰδὼν δὲ φαραὼ ὅτι "but when Pharaoh saw that"; this shows up the relation of the two parts of the verse more clearly. ἰδών is a much more idiomatic structure than the finite verb ειδεν of *n*, which is then paratactic with the ἐβαρύνθη clause in Hebraic fashion.

The ὅτι clause virtually repeats the final clause of v.6. A popular B variant added παντων before τῶν κτηνῶν on the basis of v.4.[10] -- Exod follows the Sam tradition of τῶν υἱῶν ᾽Ισραήλ instead of simply "Israel" as MT and Tar. As in v.6 a popular variant for οὐδέν obtains as ουδε εν. -- For the ἐβαρύνθη clause see note at 8:32.

9:8 Boils on man and beast. Change of subject to κύριος is shown by δέ. -- The direct speech marker is attested in 4QpaleoExod^m, and its origin may well be textual. -- MT makes use of the so-called ethical dative לכם after "Take";[11] Exod preferred the nominative ὑμεῖς. The sense of Exod can be conveyed by "do you take!"[12]

The phrase πλήρεις τὰς χεῖρας "handfuls" represents the bound

10. See the discussion in THGE VII.O.
11. For the ethical dative cf GK 119s.
12. Aq and Sym render לכם literalistically by ὑμῖν.

phrase מלא חפנים in MT.[13] In the text tradition hex has added υμων after χεῖρας to conform to MT.

Moses and Aaron are to take "furnace soot" which Moses (not Aaron) is to sprinkle (aorist of πάσσω) heavenward. The adjective καμιναῖος is formed from κάμινος, and the popular variant καμινιαιος would presumably ultimately derive from the adjective.[14] Hex has added αυτην to the verb πασάτω to show the object suffix of זרקו; Exod also has a fuller text than all other old witnesses in its "and before his servants"; cf 5:21 7:9,10,20.

9:9 The subject of γενηθήτω is the αἰθάλη of v.8: "Let it become a dust cloud." -- In the nominal "all the land of Egypt" γῆ is never articulated when it is modified by a genitive Αἰγύπτου.[15]

In MT the next clause has a היה + ל construction and the clause means "and it (the dust cloud) shall become boils." In Exod the preposition is disregarded and ἕλκη "festering sores" is the subject of ἔσται. The sores are defined as φλυκτίδες ἀναζέουσαι "blisters oozing." The words are reversed by hex so as to agree with the Hebrew.[16] MT has פרח "sprouting" and refers mainly to plants and flowers, but here used figuratively. -- Exod alone modifies φλυκτίδες ἀναζέουσαι by three coordinate εν phrases instead of merely by "in all the land of Egypt;" Exod's "in men and in animals," is based on the next verse. -- The majority M variant omits the last καί, agreeing with MT; this omission is hardly recensional, but rather a revision by which "in all the land of Egypt" no longer coordinates with "both in men and in animals," but modifies the two nouns. -- A B x variant omits the final εν, but is probably merely the result of an auditory lapse. A C d x variant articulates γῆ for which see note on γῆ above. -- The change of Αὐγύπτου to the dative in d s t after πάσῃ γῆ is secondary.[17]

---

13. The Three all attempted to show the bound relationship by a genitive. The Syh source for these readings probably represents the following Greek: Aq, πλήρωσιν θενάρων ὑμῶν (cf Prov 30:4 in Field); Sym, πλήρωσιν χειρῶν ὑμῶν, and Theod, πλήρωμα χειρῶν ὑμῶν.
14. Cf Palmer 255.
15. See the discussion in THGE VII.D.4.
16. Instead of ἀναζέουσαι Aq has πεταζόμεναι "being spread out"; for Aq the blisters were growing larger. Sym translated by ἐξανθοῦσαι "blossoming," i.e. "ripening blisters."

9:10 The instructions given by the Lord are being now carried out. Exod, however, abbreviates the MT account by making the first two clauses into a single one by omitting ריעמד; hex has of course added καὶ εστησεν (after "furnace"). Exod also changes the subject from plural to the singular, which is inconsistent over against the λάβετε of v.8. In fact, a popular A variant has ελαβον, probably an early revision towards MT. -- The C text has changed "the soot of the furnace" to "the furnace soot," simply by changing the case from a genitive to the accusative.

The subject is not named until the next clause where Μωυσῆς is given as subject of ἔπασεν; cf again v.8. An f variant has moved Μωυσῆς to the first clause, thus removing the awkwardness caused by making the first singular verb without a named subject. -- The C tradition also attempted to make the first clause clearer by omitting ἐναντίον Φαραώ, a phrase which fitted in MT where the verb modified was "they stood," rather than "he took."

In the last clause a popular variant changed ἐγένετο into the plural because of the plural subject ἕλκη, but a neuter plural is in order. For ἕλκη ... fin see v.9 where exactly the same collocation obtains.

9:11 For the Hellenistic ἠδύναντο a number of scattered witnesses have the classical εδυναντο.[18] -- For φάρμακοι see note at 7:11. -- For the variant plural εγενοντο see note at v.10.

Exod states that the magicians could not stand before Moses "because of the sores." But the next clause is a γάρ clause, and might seem repetitious, and it may better be understood as an explanation as to why boils should have affected the magicians; they themselves had boils. The construction ἐγένετο ... ἐν is a Hebraism; ἐν (τοῖς φαρμάκοις) would have been better served by επι.

The last phrase reads καὶ ἐν πάσῃ γῇ Αἰγύπτου, exactly as in v.9. MT, however, has no equivalent for γῇ; since 4Q365 does, however, the basis for γῇ is probably textual. For the Byzantine αιγυπτω see v.9.

---

17. See THGE VII.H.3. sub 12:1.
18. Cf Thack 198.

9:12 Change of subject is shown by δέ. -- For the theme of the Lord's hardening the heart of Pharaoh see note at 4:23.

The second clause also occurs at 7:13,22 8:15,19; as at 8:15 the reference in αὐτῶν is to Moses and Aaron, even though only Moses is involved in vv.10 and 12.

In the καθά clause Exod uses the verb συνέταξεν though all other old witnesses support דבר of MT; see comment at 1:17. -- The verb of ordering always includes the addressee throughout Exod, and the popular B variant omitting τῷ Μωυσῇ is not Exod but a later change within the tradition.[19]

9:13 The subject changes from Pharaoh to the Lord which is indicated by δέ. The stretch ὄρθρισον ... Φαραώ is also found in 8:20, for which see the notes ad hoc. The language of τάδε ... fin is an exact replica of v.1b except for the word order of λατρεύσωσίν μοι which follows the order of MT; see references at v.1.

9:14 The initial γάρ construction seems to take for granted that Pharaoh will not obey the divine orders, since it really gives the result of and not the reason for v.13.

The phrase ἐν τῷ νῦν καιρῷ is Exod's rendering of בפעם הזאת. The phrase may well originate with Gen 29:34 30:20; in the former case it renders עתה הפעם, and presents a striking phrase for "at the present time."

The words ἐγὼ ἐξαποστέλλω translate the MT pattern: pronoun + participle, and show intent, but the numerous variants retain the stem, and none needs to be taken seriously nor greatly affects the text lexically.

Somewhat surprising is Exod's use of συναντήματα to translate מגפה "plagues"; the word means "encounters, happenings, incidents"; so in the present context it must mean "plague-encounters."[20]

These plagues the Lord intends to send εἰς τὴν καρδίαν σου; here καρδία like ψυχή simply means "the self," and the phrase then means "to you." The reflexive use of καρδία is not uncommon in the Pentateuch, and does occur e.g. at Deut 8:17 9:4 18:21. Exod also simplifies MT's אל לבך

19. See the discussion in THGE VII.P.
20. Aq followed by Theod translates by θραύσεις which according to Hesych has the same meaning as Sym's πληγάς "plagues."

followed by וּבְעַמֶּךָ וּבַעֲבָדֶיךָ by making the nouns coordinate not to καρδίαν but to σου, i.e. καὶ τῶν θεραπόντων σου καὶ τοῦ λαοῦ σου.

For εἰδῇς and its popular itacistic variant ἴδῃς, see note at 8:10. What Pharaoh must recognize is "that there is no other one like me in all the land." ἄλλος is not represented by MT and a early popular A M text omits it to conform to MT. The ὅτι clause stresses the incomparableness of the Lord, and may be compared to 8:10. An interesting variant of 53' Arab has αλλος θ̅ς̅ instead of ὡς ἐγὼ ἄλλος, threby denying reality to any of the gods of Egypt.

9:15 God might justifiably have destroyed Pharaoh and his people. The verbs are aorist subjunctives and must be translated as potentials and contrary to fact, i.e. as "I might have ... you might have been." What God is actually doing was stated in v.14 as ἐν τῷ νῦν καιρῷ. Then v.16 is to say why God did not do what he might well have done.

The initial participial phrase modifies the subject of πατάξω. τὴν χεῖρα has no μου modifier, it being quite unnecessary, though the majority text does have it, a gloss at least as old as hex, and based on MT.

For ἀποστείλας an *s x* tradition has the more common εξαποστειλας, probably influenced by vv.13 and 14, but there the words are in a context of physical movement: "send away my people," "send plagues to."

The main verb of the first clause, πατάξω "I would have struck," has two accusative modifiers "you and your people" and a dative of means[21] θανάτῳ;[22] cf v.3. A popular B variant divides the clause into two by changing θανάτῳ to θανατωσω, the aorist subjunctive of θανατόω. The resultant text might then be translated: "I would have struck you and have put to death your people," making perfectly good sense, but it is simply the result of a careless copyist's misreading of Exod.

9:16 Exod joins this verse to the preceding by καί whereas MT shows the adversative relationship much more clearly by its וְאוּלָם. One might well have expected Exod to have had ἀλλά. -- The referent in the demonstrative τούτου is kataphoric, i.e. to the ἵνα and ὅπως clauses which follow. The

21. Cf SS 124.
22. Aq has ἐν λοιμῷ for MT's בַּדֶּבֶר.

verb διετηρήθης "have you been spared" is a clear rendering of MT's
העמדתיך "have I let you stand"; though it puts the idea in the passive there
is no doubt that it is the Lord who alone is responsible; he alone is the
effective actor in vv.14--16. An *s* reading διετήρηξα σε reflects some other
translation, probably one of The Three, since it is a more literal translation
of MT.

The reason for sparing Pharaoh from destruction is twofold shown by
a ἵνα and by a ὅπως clause. The two particles here represent two different
purposive particles in Hebrew בעבור and למען resp. The first clause "that
I might display in you my power" differs from MT which has "to show you
my power." The Hebrew again reflects the theme of Pharaoh's forced
recognition of Yahweh; it is Pharaoh who is to see God's power. In Exod
Pharaoh is simply the occasion, the arena, where God displays his power.

In the tradition a *d* + variant has the homophonous future indicative
ενδειξομαι instead of the aorist subjunctive.[23] A popular A M[txt] variant has
δυναμιν instead of ἰσχύν. The word δυναμιν, however, is never used for
the Hebrew כח in the Pentateuch where it remains the normal rendering
for צבא. In fact δυναμιν does not occur as a rendering of כח until Chr (five
times according to HR, and once each for Neh and Eccl). The second
reason is given as "and that my name might be proclaimed in all the land."
The verb διαγγελῇ is a second aorist passive subjunctive. In MT an active
Piel infinitive ספר is used to proclaim my name" but the different syntactic
pattern gives the sense of the parent text.

9:17 This verse sets out the status of things which occasion the predicted
judgment of v.18. The particle οὖν leads from the general statement to the
specifics of the present situation: "Moreover you are still holding on to."
The pattern of pronoun + inflected present tense is regular, but MT's
participle מסתולל emphasizes Pharaoh's arrogance over against the
people. Instead of ἐμποιῇ the Byzantine groups have αντιποιη; with a
genitive modifier this verb means "lay claim to."[24] -- The articulated infin-

23. For the occasional occurrence of the indicative future after ἵνα see Bl-
Debr 369.2.
24. Apparently Aq in origin; Sym reads κατέχεις "you are holding back,"
which may well have inspired Vulg: *retines*.

itive modifies ἐμποιῇ, and simply explicates it; Pharaoh "is holding on to my people so as not to send them away."

9:18 For ἰδού see note at 3:9. Here the pronoun + present tense verb recurs, a present tense of incipient action as is clear from the adverb αὔριον. Instead of ὕω a *b n* text has ποιω; it may well have arisen by auditory confusion: /hi-o/ as /pi-o/, though it does make good sense: "makes hailstones" instead of "rain hailstones." An *f* variant has the synonyum βρεχω - from one of The Three?[25] The phrase ταύτην τὴν ὥραν designates the time during which something happens; cf also 10:4. The more usual designation would probably be a κατά phrase. The *O* text has a dative phrase, signifying time when.

The plague is to consist of a divinely given rain of very much hail. The Hebrew describes the hail(stones) as being כבד.[26] Since the hail was to be extremely destructive either their large size or that they were πολλήν makes good sense. Exod further characterizes the coming storm by a ἥτις clause: "the like of which had not happened in Egypt from the day it was founded until this day." The last phrase is slightly different in MT which has "until now."[27]

9:19 Instructions on how to avoid the coming catastrophe. The opening particles νῦν οὖν are used to present a conclusion: instructions based on what has been said. The command "Hurry to gather up" is a free rendering of MT's rather ambiguous "send (out), bring to safety." The point of שלח is not fully luminous; does it mean "send out instructions," or "send your servants," or is it simply used as an idiom ordering action? Exod has a clearer order with its κατάσκευσον. The second Hebrew imperative העז occurs rarely; it is the Hiphil of עוז "to seek refuge," hence "to bring to safety." For Exod this was expressed by συναγαγεῖν, an interpretation shared by Tar כנ(ו)ש.

25. For the distinction between ὕω and βρέχω see Lee 122-124; cf also Thack 262.
26. Aq and Sym have βαρεῖαν instead of πολλήν (cf also v.3 where they translate similarly).
27. Aq Sym have a different lexeme in ἐθεμελιώθη; this is somewhat more literal for יסדה than ἔκτισται.

Syntactically the subject of the γάρ construction is all of πάντες ... χάλαζα and its predicate is τελευτήσει. Within the subject ὅσα governs both the εὑρεθῇ and the μὴ εἰσέλθῃ clauses, and the πέσῃ δέ structure stands in contrast to it. The structure of the complex subject may be shown as follows: "As for man and cattle, whatever is found and has not entered, but hail has fallen, - shall die." The verbs within the ὅσα clause are singular, congruent to a neuter plural τὰ κτήνη, the nearer of the compound subject. -- The A B + text has τω πεδιω for the plural τοῖς πεδίοις, which equals MT.[28]

For the passive תאסף Niphal "be collected" Exod has an active εἰσέλθῃ in "and has not entered a dwelling" (i.e. "come home"). -- For εἰς οἰκίαν the x text has εν τη οικια, but a locative notion is not overly fitting. -- The δέ clause shows what happens to those who disregard the instructions of the first sentence - hail falls on them - ἐπ' αὐτά, a neuter plural to agree with τὰ κτήνη, the nearer referent. -- A variant subjunctive spelling of the predicate, τελευτηση, is not suitable; it is simply an itacism. A suggested translation for the second sentence might be: "For all people and cattle, i.e. whatever might be found in the fields and not have entered shelter - but hail would have fallen on them - shall die."

9:20 Exod along with MT begins the verse without a conjunction, and a *d* text fittingly has a δε structure. The subject ὁ φοβούμενος means "one who respects." Here the reference is to the individual who accepted the "word of the Lord" as a true warning and responded to it.

The genitive τῶν θεραπόντων is a partitive genitive modifying the subject.[29] -- MT used the verb הניס "caused to flee"; they made their servants and cattle to flee into houses. Exod in line with v.19 has "collected" - συνήγαγεν, an interpretation shared by Tar[O] כנש.[30] Exod also limited the rescue operation to τὰ κτήνη αὐτοῦ; presumably the servants could fend for themselves. The hex tradition of course added τους παιδας αυτου και before τὰ κτήνη to equal MT.

28. But see THGE VII.H.2.
29. See SS 164.
30. Sym translated the word by διέσωσεν "preserved," which was at least

9:21 Though the expression προσέσχεν τῇ διανοίᾳ is unusual (the accusative is standard), it does occur in the papyri in the sense of "pay attention to."[31] MT has לבו and so hex added the expected αυτου.[32] Over against v.20 here the action of those who disregarded the divine warning is portrayed. As in v.20 Exod omits reference to servants entirely, hex adding the lacking τους παιδας αυτου και. Hex also supplies αυτου after κτήνη to conform to MT.[33] -- A popular B variant has the plural τοις πεδιοις for τῷ πεδίῳ.[34]

9:22 A new stage of discourse is introduced by a δέ structure. The Lord now speaks to Moses; even the pretense that Aaron is in any way mediator between Moses and Pharaoh, or the one who performs the signs, is abandoned. Moses is to stretch out his hand heavenward and the hail will come down on all the land. What this really involves is that this hail's destructive power will be "both on men and cattle and on all herbage," which differs somewhat from MT's "on man and on cattle and on all herbage." By adding the particle τε after the first ἐπί and omitting a preposition before "cattle" Exod has made a bipartite distinction between animate life and plant life. A popular hex reading has added the failing επι. In the description of the βοτάνην "herbage" Exod has also gone his own way over against other ancient traditions with its modifier τὴν ἐπὶ τῆς γῆς instead of MT's "of the field in the land of Egypt." Note the subtle distinction in case usage with ἐπί. The hail will come down "on the land" (accusative). But here the herbage is "on the land" (genitive), i.e. no motion is involved. Hex has corrected differences between the two either by "of the field" or as the *O* mss have it την εν τω πεδιω for τήν, and then adding αιγυπτου at the end. There is some uncertainty about the first "correction."[35]

---

the point of "causing to flee."
31. Cf Helbing 294.
32. Cf SS 93.
33. Cf SS 94.
34. See THGE VII.H.2.
35. Syh notes on the margin that for του πεδιου Aq and Sym have τῆς χώρος and Theod, τοῦ ἀγροῦ. But then where did hex take του πεδιου from? It occurs for שדה as a Theod reading at 2Kgdm 10:8 but for Sym at Ps 77:43, whereas ἀγρός frequently translates שדה in both Sym and Theod.

9:23 Change of speaker is shown by δέ. -- Exod has leveled the text to make it agree with v.22, where Moses was ordered to stretch out his hand heavenward, not his staff as in MT. Once again Origen's quantitative way of dealing with his LXX text is seen here; he does not change τὴν χεῖρα to την ραβδον (though one can be quite certain that The Three did), but simply added αυτου since MT had מטהו.

In the second clause the subject also changes, and so an *O n* tradition has made καὶ κύριος into a δέ structure. ἔδωκεν appears as perfect δεδωκεν in the *b* tradition, but this fits oddly into the context. -- What the Lord produced was φωνὰς καὶ χάλαζαν. The φωνάς are the sounds of thunder, as an anonymous marginal reading of βροντάς makes clear.[36]

The third clause refers to the lightning flashes over the land. The Hebrew verb form is highly unusual in the Masoretic tradition, it being vocalized on the pattern *yiqtal*; cf also Ps 73:9. Exod's translation is a graphic one διέτρεχεν "run across"; i.e. "the lightning (literally "the fire") ran about over the land." An *s* variant has εν τη χαλαζη instead of "over the land," i.e. this tradition has the lightning flashing in the hail. This may have originated in a gloss to the text from v.24 as part of the *n* tradition (which adds εν τη χαλαζη after γῆς) shows. -- The concluding clause states that the Lord rained hail on all the land of Egypt. The word πᾶσαν is not represented in MT but results from a leveling with the prediction in v.22.

9:24 The opening clause shows change of subject by δέ, and the verb ἦν is used absolutely "and there was hail," whereas the second clause is nominal with φλογίζον as predicate nominative to the subject τὸ πῦρ. The omission of the article by *d x*, which equals MT, changes the syntax radically; πῦρ φλογίζον is now the second element of a compound subject (with ἡ χάλαζα) in the first clause. The clause in Exod has the lightning flashing in the hail; cf the *s n* variant in v.23. Exod's text though difficult is intelligible, since it deals with lightning (see also Ezek 1:4).[37]

There is a real possibility that τοῦ ἀγροῦ was Sym and τοῦ πεδίου Theod, but there is no actual evidence for this intriguing notion.
36. See Bauer sub φωνή 1.
37. For φλογίζον Aq has συναναλαμβανόμενον, reflecting a literal interpretation of MT's מתלקחת, i.e. "a taking hold of oneself, taking oneself back and forth," hence "flashing." Sym's translation ἐνειλούμενον, from

ἡ δὲ χάλαζα was necessary to show that the subject is no longer τὸ πῦρ. In MT no subject is given since the subject must be ברד.

Exod has the intensifier σφόδρα repeated for greater emphasis; a B C b f text has it but once to agree with MT, but the shorter text is almost certainly due to haplography, and not to Hebrew influence. -- For πολλή as a rendering for כבד see note at v.18. -- For ἥτις ... ἀφ' οὗ see note at v.18.

The phrase ἐν Αἰγύπτῳ levels with the phrase at v.18 over against MT's "in all the land of Egypt," and hex corrects to εν παση γη αιγυπτου to equal MT. Furthermore τοιαύτη stands before οὐ γέγονεν as in v.18, which a popular A M hex variant has transposed to agree with MT.

The prepositional phrase ἐπ' αὐτῆς between γεγένηται and ἔθνος has no counterpart in MT. MT takes מצרים to mean the people and not the land, since it concludes with "from the time that היתה לעם - it had become a people." Exod changes this somewhat; by disregarding the preposition ἔθνος becomes the subject, making the local reference of ἐπ' αὐτῆς necessary, i.e. limiting the reference thereby to Egypt.

9:25 The verb ἐπάταξεν plus ἐν indicating the object of the smiting is the same in meaning as ἐπάταξεν plus an accusative. For a good example of these two usages in adjacent clauses see 1Kgdm 23:2. In MT this is followed by את כל אשר בשדה which a popular hex variant supplies by its παντα οσα εν τω πεδιω.

Just what smiting all the land involved the last two clauses show in detail. The first involves all herbage which was ἐν τῷ πεδίῳ, and the second concerns all the trees which were ἐν τοῖς πεδίοις. When the antecedent is singular (βοτάνην), בשדה is rendered by the singular in Exod, but if it is plural (ξύλα), it is translated by the plural.[38] This nice distinction was not always understood in the tradition and the number is sometimes arbitrarily changed. -- In both clauses the subject ἡ χάλαζα is added though it would have been obvious from the context; an early popular A* M variant omits the last ἡ χάλαζα thereby equalling MT, a revision probably earlier than Origen since it is found in most hex witnesses as well.

ἐνειλέω, means "to be wrapped up in, entangled with" and simply paraphased freely on the basis of the context.
38. For a discussion of πεδίῳ vs πεδίοις see THGE VII.H.2. Aq rendered

9:26 Γέσεμ occurs ten times in LXX; seven times in Gen (45:10 46:34 47:1,4,5, 27 50:8), and only once is there any Greek text which records a *nu* rather than a *mu* as a final consonant; MT always has גשן. In Exod Γέσεμ occurs twice (also at 8:22). There Compl γεσεν is almost certainly a correction based on the Hebrew text; here ms 319 has γεσεν; all other Greek witnesses end with *mu*. This is also true of Jud 1:9 for which no Hebrew text is extant. -- Exod adds the verb ἦσαν in the οὖ clause for good sense even though MT has no verb here. -- The hail did not fall on the land where the Israelites lived. A *b* variant has χάλαζα unarticulated which does equal MT, though it is unlikely that the Hebrew inspired the omission of the article.

9:27 Change of subject is shown by δέ. Presumably the fact that the hail fell only on land where the Israelites did not live convinced Pharaoh that he had better acknowledge his fault. So he sent and summoned Moses and Aaron. The *b* tradition articulates Μωυσῆν, but this is otiose since the name is itself inflected.

Pharaoh states that he has sinned τὸ νῦν. The phrase means "the present time"; what is presumably meant is "I have sinned this time" (in contrast to earlier encounters?). Attempts to improve the phrase include τα νυν as well as *b*'s simple νῦν, but they all mean "now."

Pharaoh admits that the Lord (here articulated since it is the subject of a clause with a predicate adjective) is δίκαιος whereas he and his people are ἀσεβεῖς. He admits that not only that he is in the wrong (which is what MT means), but that he and his people are actually impious. Vulg follows this contrast by using *iustus* vs *impii*. -- In the tradition ἀσεβεῖς becomes the singular ασεβης in a number of scattered mss; this is a possible variant by attraction to the nearer of a compound subject, ὁ λαός μου, which is grammatically singular. It is, however, not a serious variant but merely an itacism.

9:28 The logical consequence of the preceding confession is the demand for intercession, and so Exod uses οὖν. For the addition περὶ ἐμοῦ see note at

8:8. It is omitted by an early (preOrigenian) A O C b revision towards MT. Its repositioning after κύριον by the z text is a matter of taste. A b d tradition used the compound προσευχασθε instead of Exod's simplex, a development typical of Byzantine Greek's love for compounds; there is no difference in meaning between the two.

The second clause in Exod gives the content of the desired prayer: "and may God's thunder and the hail and fire cease to be." This is formally quite different from MT which makes it a statement justifying the request for intercession, i.e. רב מהית "enough of there being," i.e. we have had enough of.... Vulg follows Exod: *ut desinant tonitrua*. Tar[P] translates similarly with וימנע מן למהוי.

An n variant has γενεσθαι for γενηθῆναι. There is no distinction between the two as far as meaning is concerned. The aorist passive was particularly in vogue in the third and second centuries B.C. after which it became less popular in usage.[39] In Exod it appears over against the middle inflection in a ratio of 1 to 4, i.e. 12 vs 48 times. It is articulated here but μένειν in the same verse is not. Articulation of infinitives in Exod seems to be without significance.

The compound subject has three units over against MT's two; to God's thunders and hail there is added "and lightning," for which see vv.23 and 24. The words καὶ πῦρ are omitted by A* but this is due to homoiot. The b tradition carelessly omitted θεοῦ after φωνάς; it would hardly have been intentional.

In return Pharaoh promises that he will send them away; the future alone can be correct for the verb, and the dittography of the *lambda* creating a present form in the f tradition is a scribal mistake.

The last clause shows what Pharaoh's sending them away means. For the idiom οὐκέτι προσθήσεσθε see note at 5:7. The verb appears as a future passive προστεθησεσθε in a popular B M variant. Either form is possible and both are used by Exod on occasion. The middle form with infinitive occurs three times in Exod (also 9:34 14:13), twice in the active (8:29 10:28), and twice in the passive (5:7 23:2).

---

the word by τῇ χώρᾳ, Sym, by τῷ χώρῳ, and Theod, by τῷ ἀγρῷ in retroversions according to Field from Syh.

9:29 Change of subject to Moses is indicated by δέ. The *b* text omitted αὐτῷ (as Vulg), which also makes good sense. -- The ὡς ἄν plus subjunctive indicates time in the future when something is to take place.[40] It is when Moses leaves the city that he will pray and the plague of hail will cease.

Exod uses ἐκπετάσω, future of ἐκπετάννυμι "to spread out," rather than the more common root ἐκτείνω. (פרש not הטה). The *b* text does have εκτενω here. "To spread out the hands towards the Lord" is a graphic description of prayer posture; the A + tradition makes this even stronger by adding the phrase εἰς τον ο̅υ̅ν̅ο̅ν̅. Cod B, on the other hand, abbreviates by omitting the addressee πρὸς κύριον.

The result of Moses' spreading out his hands towards the Lord is introduced by καί (as Sam Vulg), whereas the clause is asyndetic in MT. -- Now the thunder is referred to without θεοῦ, it being unnecessary in view of v.28 where it was so defined.

The parallel clause states that "the hail and the rain will no longer obtain," Exod adding ὁ ὑετός from v.34 thereby making the account complete.

The purpose underlying the display of divine power over the forces of nature is that Pharaoh "may recognize that the land is the Lord's." The object clause is lexically ambiguous because ἡ γῆ, as well as הארץ, may mean "the land" or "the earth"; cf e.g. Ps 23:1. In this chapter γῆ has been used only to indicate the land of Egypt, and that is most likely intended here as well.

9:30 The verse begins with a nominative pendens construction which identifies the subject of πεφόβησθε more closely. -- Moses states that he knows that Pharaoh and his servants have not yet learned to fear the Lord; the reference is to the past and so οὐδέπω is used. In a popular variant text ουδεποτε obtains but this commonly refers either to the present or the future in the sense of "never." In later Greek the two are sometimes confused.

The verb πεφόβησθε is appropriately perfect; the point is that Pharaoh should long since have learned that the Lord is in control. An *O* + variant φοβεισθε is in the present; all witnesses attesting to the present also read ουδεποτε. So the accent shifts from the learning process continuing to the present moment over to the present situation itself.

Exod uses the verb with an accusative of personal modifier, whereas MT has the verb modified by a prepositional phrase מפני יהוה אלהים.[41] It will be noted that Exod has an equivalent only for יהוה, hex adding θεον to conform to MT. A B + text has θεον rather than κύριον, possibly because of the article. κύριον when referring to God is hardly ever articulated in Exod (elsewhere only at 5:2 and 14:31), whereas θεόν lacks the article only once (7:1) where the unarticulated form is exegetically necessary.

9:31 This verse and the next describe which of the cereals were damaged by the hail and why. -- A new subject is indicated by δέ. The damaged cereals were flax and barley. The particle γάρ is causal; the two nominal clauses give the reason for the hail's destruction: the barley was standing παρεστηκυῖα,[42] and the flax was forming seed. Thus the barley had formed stalks; at this stage it begins to form awned ears; this is the time of אביב. The flax was גבעל, a hapax legomenon probably referring to the seed pod of the flax; in any event Exod understood it thus as σπερματίζον shows. The two clauses are contrastive as the δέ of the second makes clear, but a majority reading has changed this to a και clause.

9:32 A new subject is indicated by δέ. Wheat and spelt[43] were not damaged by the hail. The predicate ἐπλήγη is singular by attraction to the nearer unit of the compound subject. Cod B has the plural επληγησαν, which Sam TarP also show. Puzzling is the *b* variant which has επληγην, which simply makes no sense; possibly a plural verb was intended. The inflection is a second aorist passive. In the second aorist active the third plural and the

39. See Mayser II.2.157f.
40. Cf Bauer s.v. IV.c.
41. Cf Helbing 29. Aq renders this literally by ἀπὸ προσώπου κυρίου θεοῦ (from Syh).
42. See Lee 56f.
43. ἡ ὀλύρα is the Greek word for "spelt," but so is ἡ ζέα (and ἡ ζειά). Syh gives us readings for Aq Sym and for Theod. Unfortunately Syriac uses *kwnta* to translate both ὀλύρα and ζέα, and so Syh reads Aq Sym *kwnta* Theod *kwnta* in its note. The text in Syh is of course for ἡ ὀλύρα.

first singular are identical (as e.g. εἶπον). Apparently this was formed on that analogy, though I have found no other instance of such an inflection.

The reason for these two grains not being destroyed by the hail is given by Exod as ὄψιμα γὰρ ἦν. The adjective is in the neuter plural since two grains of different genders are referred to; the singular predicate is congruent with the neuter plural subject. The word ὄψιμος means "late, slow," and the clause may be translated: "for they were late crops." Neither wheat nor spelt were sufficiently developed for the hail to do damage, i.e. they were still in the grassy stage.

9:33 The particle δέ shows a new subject. The difficult ויצא plus את is clarified by Exod with ἐξῆλθεν ... ἐκτός: "Moses departed from Pharaoh outside the city," which reflects the ἐξέλθω τὴν πόλιν of v.29. The verse describes the carrying out of the intentions given to Pharaoh in v.29. -- Instead of ἀπό a popular Byzantine variant has παρα with little change in meaning. For ἐκτός a popular variant has the synonym εξω, whereas the C n text has εκ.

Moses then "spread out hands to the Lord"; of course they were his own hands, which a popular hex variant by adding αυτου to conform to MT makes doubly certain. -- The consequent halt to the hail plague is described on the basis of v.29 rather than MT. Thus αἱ φωναί precedes the predicate over against MT (and hex!). Furthermore the next clause adds an ἔτι, which a C + variant omits to equal MT. The verb in this clause is much milder in meaning than MT. For MT's נתך Niphal "was poured out," Exod used ἔσταξεν, i.e. the rain (articulated with Sam against MT) no longer dropped on the land.

9:34 The word δέ shows change of subject to Pharaoh. The participial clause is temporal. The order of items in the compound subject of the object clause is rain, hail, thunders as in MT, but the b text transposes the first two for no discernible reason. -- For προσέθετο plus infinitive see note at 5:7. Only here, however, is the infinitive articulated (cf 5:7 8:29 9:28 10:28 14:13 23:2).

Fortunately we know from ms 108 that Aq Sym read ἡ ζέα, so we may conclude that Theod retained the Exod text.

The last clause defines what Pharaoh's sinning again consisted of: he hardened his heart as well as that of his servants. MT defines the subject of the verb in larger detail as "he and his servants"; what MT means is that Pharaoh and his servants hardened their hearts, but Exod has καὶ τῶν θεραπόντων αὐτοῦ joining it to αὐτοῦ 1°, which αὐτοῦ precedes τὴν καρδίαν in good Greek style; a popular A M hex text transposes it to equal MT.

9:35 The account of the hailstorm plague ends with the summary statement that the status quo remains as predicted. -- ἐξαπέστειλεν becomes ἀπέστειλεν in an ƒ reading. Another variant in the tradition, mainly marginal, has τον λαον instead of τοὺς υἱοὺς ('Ισραήλ), which makes good sense but the source and/or reason for the variant is puzzling.

In the καθάπερ clause "the Lord spoke to Moses," i.e. Moses is the addressee. But Exod has changed the intent of MT which has "spoke by the hand of Moses"; i.e. Moses is the medium through whom the Lord spoke; compare 35:29 συνέταξεν κύριος ... διὰ Μωυσῆ. Whenever Moses is involved in connection with the Lord speaking Exod makes him the addressee, and Exod was simply leveling to the usual pattern. The hex tradition has εν χειρι instead of τῷ, thereby emending to the MT pattern, and a popular A variant omits the article but this does not change the sense.

Chapter 10

10:1 The locust plague. A δέ structure shows the beginning of a new section. -- Exod has added λέγων to the opening statement as a direct speech marker; the direct speech extends through v.2. The opening instruction "go in to Pharaoh" is amplified in the Byzantine tradition by inserting λαλησον before "to Pharaoh," probably due to the influence of v.3. This is followed by a γάρ clause, which explains the reason underlying the continued contact with Pharaoh. The verb within the clause is ἐβάρυνα, not εσκληρυνα as a popular B text has it; Exod does not use σκληρύνω to translate the Hiphil of כבד.[1]

Hex has not only emended the order of αὐτοῦ τὴν καρδίαν, but also inserted a την καρδιαν before τῶν θεραπόντων, thus fully conforming to MT.

The ἵνα clause gives the purpose for the divine hardening of Pharaoh's heart; this is only the mediate purpose, with the ὅπως clause of v.2 expressing the reason for the occurrence of the plagues. The ἵνα clause differs considerably from its equivalent in MT: "that I myself might put these signs of mine among them." Exod makes "these signs" the subject of the clause, chooses the verb ἐπέλθῃ "may come upon," adds the adverb ἐξῆς as a verbal modifier, and for בקרבו "among them" has the phrase ἐπ' αὐτούς. The Greek text may then be translated: "that these signs may successively come upon them."[2] All reference to God's involvement in the action has been removed. So God has hardened Pharaoh's heart in order that the plagues might take place. Exod has intentionally avoided first person references: אני is disregarded, the first person suffix of the infinitive שתי is changed to a third person, the first person suffix of אתתי is dropped, and stress on the plagues is added by ἐξῆς "in order, one after another." -- The tradition shows some recensional change in a majority hex variant which adds μου after σημεῖα. The *b* change of ἐπ' to εις is somewhat closer to בקרב but this is probably coincidence.

1. See the discussion in THGE VII.Q.
2. Cf SS 95.

10:2 Exod makes the verse a final clause modifying the preceding final clause, i.e. "(the plagues happened) in order that you might relate." This contrasts with MT which coordinates this clause with the preceding, i.e. למען ... ולמען. In MT the second person references are all singular up to the final "you may know" which is plural. Exod simplifies this by making all of them plural. The *ol* text has διηγησθε for the aorist subjunctive διηγήσησθε, but the perfect hardly fits in this context, and is simply a scribal error palaeographically inspired. -- Incidentally the Byzantine text has added αν after ὅπως.[3]

The concrete figure διηγήσησθε εἰς τὰ ὦτα reflects the Hebrew and simply means "to relate to." Two matters are to be related to the next generations: how God had mocked the Egyptians as well as God's signs (or his plagues) which he had perfomed; in fact, ἐμπέπαιχα, "I have mocked" makes the divine arbitrariness even more marked than MT's התעללתי "I acted ruthlessly with." The second object of διηγήσησθε is "my signs which I performed in them"; the καί before it coordinates it with the preceding ὅσα clause.

The last clause states the consequence of the preceding in future terms: "and you shall know that I am the Lord." Here it is no longer Pharaoh who through divine coercion is forced to recognize that it is the Lord who is active in the plagues, but the Israelites who will acknowledge that he is the Lord. A Byzantine reading changes the future indicative into an aorist subjunctive, γνωσησθε, which would make the clause coordinate with the διηγήσησθε clause, i.e. a second clause governed by ὅπως. For the A *b* + addition of ειμι in the formula ἐγὼ κύριος, see the discussion at 6:2.

10:3 The δέ particle shows change of subject. The first verb is singular by atraction to the nearer unit of a compound subject. -- Exod has Moses and Aaron go in ἐναντίον Pharaoh as at 7:10, rather than πρὸς Pharaoh as 5:1 7:15 and MT's אל. The notion of going in before may well represent a zeugma for "go in and stand before"; compare 8:20 9:13. -- Instead of Exod's

3. For this usage see Mayser II.1.254--258 together with his references.

εἶπαν many witnesses support the Byzantine reading of the classical second aorist ειπον.[4]

For the messenger formula see note at 4:22. -- For "God of the Hebrews" see note at 7:16. The use of a negative particle and βούλομαι to render מאן is common in Exod (4:23 8:2 9:2 16:28 22:17); in fact, only twice is מאן not so translated (7:14 by τοῦ μή; 10:4 μὴ θέλῃς). Exod has found a simple but elegant translation for לענת מפני "to humble yourself (Niphal of ענה) before me" in its ἐντραπῆναί με "to revere me, stand in awe of me." -- For the formula ἐξαπόστειλον ... fin see note at 5:1.

10:4 The δέ indicates contrast to the preceding command. For μὴ θέλῃς as rendering for מאן אתה see note at v.3. The variant reading βουλη for θέλῃς comes from v.3. Since אתה is not independently rendered by Exod a B hex tradition has added σου.

For ἰδού as clause modifier see note at 3:9. -- ἐγώ + first person present tense verb is a standard pattern for Hebrew: pronoun + participle. -- The phrase ταύτην τὴν ὥραν has no equivalent in MT but levels with 9:18, for which see note.

Exod amplifies the MT account by adding πολλήν to ἀκρίδα ("a locust swarm") for MT's ארבה and adding πάντα before τὰ ὅριά σου.

10:5 The subject of καλύψει is the ἀκρίδα of v.4. The ἀκρίδα will be so πολλήν that the face of the land will be covered. -- For the indefinite יוכל Exod has second person (as does Tar^P), which is sensible since Pharaoh is being addressed.

The third clause details the destruction which the locusts will enact. They will devour πᾶν τὸ περισσὸν τὸ καταλειφθέν "all the left over surplus." MT has no equivalent for πᾶν but has את יתר הפלטה "the remainder of that which escaped" to equal τὸ περισσόν. The B *f x* + text has an epexegetical gloss, της γης, modifying περισσόν.[5] τὸ καταλειφθέν is then defined as ὅ κατέλιπεν "which (the locusts) left (for you). A well

4. For the priority of the Hellenistic εἶπαν see THGE VII.M.9.
5. For its secondary character as well as its meaning see THGE VII.O. Aq has (τὸ) λεῖπον instead of τὸ καταλειφθέν which means about the same.

supported A variant has the imperfect spelling of the verb, κατελειπεν, but this is inappropriate and is merely an itacistic spelling.

The last clause extends the destruction to all the trees. A popular A variant adds the article to ξύλον under the influence of the three cases of τό within the verse. The last phrase, ἐπὶ τῆς γῆς, has the noun in the genitive, appropriate since the participle which it modifies is not transitive. The *b* text has the accusative and is not as idiomatic as Exod.

10:6 σου αἱ οἰκίαι was reordered by hex so as to equal MT. -- Exod differs from MT which has כל before עבדיך instead of before (ו)בתי 2°, but the tradition is unanimous in supporting Exod, and it may well have had a textual basis.

The prepositional phrase ἐν πάσῃ γῇ Αἰγύπτου has "of all Egypt" as its counterpart in MT. No witnesses in the tradition attempt to "correct" it, though some deviation does obtain, e.g. instead of Αἰγύπτου a B *f x* variant has των αιγυπτιων; but των αιγυπτιων is never used by Exod to modify γῆ.[6] For the relative pronoun ἅ which is here used indefinitely in the sense of "whatever" a popular A M tradition has the singular ο. This conflicts with Exod usage. The relative ὅ occurs 23 times in Exod and always with a clear neuter singular referent. In 18 cases ἅ occurs with a clear plural neuter referent. In seven instances (4:12,15 6:1 10:6 14:31 16:5,5) the neuter relative pronoun obtains with no particular referent named, but only at 16:5 does Exod has ἅ.[7]

Exod appropriately has οὐδέποτε "never" for the simple negative of MT; see note at 9:30. -- The pattern ἀφ᾽ ἧς ἡμέρας ... ἕως is used as in 9:18; compare the usage of ἀφ᾽ οὗ (4:10 5:23 9:24) without a given antecedent but also without a ἕως phrase. -- The ἕως phrase is a literal translation of MT: "until this day," for which the *b n s* text has εως της σημερον ημερας.

The last clause has the pattern: participle + subject + finite verb, which an *n s* variant text has changed to finite verb (εκλινεν) + subject + infinitive (εξελθειν), which is a stylistic change. An early (preOrigenian?) A M *O C* revision omits Μωυσῆς as named subject to conform to MT.[8]

6. See the discussion at THGE VII.Q.
7. See also THGE VII.G.6.
8. Aq also lacks the subject but retains the remainder of the pattern in

10:7 Change of subject is shown by δέ, which a B *f n* variant changes to a και structure.[9] For the historical present λέγουσιν see note at 2:13. -- Exod has interpreted זה in the question not as referring to Moses but as τοῦτο, i.e. this situation. The Hebrew pronoun admits of either interpretation; the Greek does not. Furthermore Exod disregarded the preposition in למוקש, which modifying יהיה means "to become." Exod renders the phrase by σκῶλον "stumbling block." The question has undergone some change in the tradition. By transposing τοῦτο ἡμῖν an *n* variant puts τοῦτο next to σκῶλον and "this stumbling block" becomes subject. A popular A* reading omits τοῦτο, i.e. "will be a stumbling block to us," and an *f s* tradition articulates σκῶλον which also makes the phrase subject.

The last clause in MT הטרם תדע "have you not yet recognized" has given translators some trouble. Exod has ἢ εἰδέναι βούλει "or do you want to experience." This is presumably meant ironically.[10] The servants themselves understand that Egypt is already destroyed, ἀπόλωλεν; only Pharaoh seems not to realize that Egypt is finished. The locust plague was the final coup de grace.

10:8 The opening clause in MT begins with a Hophal form ויושב followed by a compound את structure. The preposition את must here denote the subject, i.e. "And there was returned Moses and Aaron" with the verb in the singular by attraction to the nearer unit. Exod has rendered this by the indefinite plural active modified by a compound accusative phrase: "And they turned back both Moses and Aaron (to Pharaoh)." The majority of winesses have επεστρεψαν "they turned around."

Instead of πρὸς Φαραώ the *b n s* text has εις προσωπον φαραω, an interpretative variant which is a somewhat more courtly way of expressing what happened. Upon their arrival they were addressed by Pharaoh, i.e. Pharaoh εἶπεν, which the *b n y* tradition expresses by the historical present as in v.7. That it is Pharaoh who now speaks could only be made clear by adding the subject specifically in the case of the *d* text which had substituted

---

Exod exactly.
9. See THGE VII.E.1.
10. Sym renders it exactly by ἄρα οὕτω οἶδας, whereas Samariticon has πρὶν

τον λαον for Φαραώ. -- A popular B text has connected the two imperatives "go serve" by και.[11] The two imperatives are present and aorist tense resp. When πορεύεσθε (or βαδίζετε) introduces a second imperative it is always present tense in Exod and the second one aorist.

In the tradition a weakly supported B variant omits κυρίῳ from "the Lord your God." In view of the weak support (four mss) it is unlikely to be Exod text. -- Exod quite rightly translates מי רמי by the plural τίνες δὲ καὶ τίνες "but exactly who (are the ones going)?"

10:9 For the historical present λέγει see note at 2:13. Moses replies naming six groups who are to go on the planned journey: young ones, elders, sons, daughters, sheep and cattle. Only the last one has ἡμῶν attached, though MT has the first plural suffix for all six nouns, hex also adding ημων to the other five. Each of the nouns in MT has the preposition ב prefixed; Exod has σύν and the article τοῖς prefixed only to the first and, since πορευσόμεθα intervenes after the second, to the third as well. MT parallels the first two and the last four by ending both rows with נלך; Exod (as Vulg) does not repeat πορευσόμεθα at the end, but hex supplies it. In the tradition numbers two and four have been articulated as well, particularly by the Byzantine groups. It should be also noted that the lists are joined throughout by καί, whereas MT has the second list of four in two pairs.

The justification for this huge company is made in MT by "because a feast of Yahweh we have (לנו)." Exod does have ἔστιν γὰρ ἑορτὴ κυρίου but instead of לנו it adds τοῦ θεοῦ ἡμῶν, Vulg following Exod, but which B* omits; this is surely a copyist's error, not a recensional correction.

10:10 From the context it is clear that Pharaoh is now the subject, but there are no formal marks to show the change, although two mss and Eth do add φαραω in the tradition. The pious wish: "May the Lord thus be with you" is not really explained until v.11 in πορευέσθωσαν ... καὶ λατρεύσετε. What intervenes is the negative part to which Pharaoh says μὴ οὕτως. I would translate Exod as "As I send you away, should I also send away your possessions? Take note that you prepose evil intents." The word ἀποσκευή

γνῶς "before you might realize."
11. For a discussion of this see THGE VII.E.3.

150

refers not only to material possessions but to people who are part of the tribe as well, i.e. to dependents.[12]

The C text has εσται instead of ἔστω, which is also represented by Sam. -- For ἀποστέλλω in the καθότι clause a popular reading has the future, which formally conforms to MT, but is probably simply the result of scribal haplography. In the ὅτι clause B d t x + have πρόσκειται "lie by," hence "bound up with." It is a possible reading: "evil matters are bound up with you," but it is obviously due to scribal confusion with πρόκειται of Exod.[13]

10:11 The μὴ οὕτως applies to the foregoing. In MT הגברים is vocative as the imperatives לכו and עבדו make plain. Exod has retained an imperative for the second but the first has been rendered by a third person plural imperative with οἱ ἄνδρες as subject: "Let the men go and (do you) serve." Note the same tense pattern as in v.8 for πορεύω plus another verb: πορευέσθωσαν as present, but λατρεύσατε as aorist. The B* x reading λατρευσατωσαν is a simplification of Exod. -- The modifier of λατρεύσατε, τῷ θεῷ, is changed by A b + to (τω) κω, thereby equalling MT. If this is a recensional change it is impossible to identify it more closely.

The γάρ clause that follows makes plausible the limitation to the proposed journey by Pharaoh. The use of αὐτοί as a substitute for the second personal pronoun (MT has אתם) is also reflected in the *ipsi* of Vulg. A B d x text has the imperfect ἐζητεῖτε for the present ζητεῖτε. Either makes sense in the context but the present is the more usual Exod rendering for the participle.[14]

In the last clause the indefinite plural ἐξέβαλον is used: "they cast them (i.e. Moses and Aaron) out of Pharaoh's presence"; MT (against Sam and Pesh) has the singular which is more difficult. In any event the meaning is clear. The change to εξεβαλεν in three s mss presumably derives from one of The Three.

12. See Lee 103ff; Sym translated טף "children, little ones" by ὄχλον "crowd," whereas Aq predictably has a literalistic νήπια.
13. Against Helbing 296.

10:12 Change of subject is shown by δέ. -- Exod simply has ἔκτεινον τὴν χεῖρα since a σου is hardly necessary, though hex supplies one so as to equal MT. -- γῆν Αἰγύπτου is never articulated after its first occurrence at 8:6; on the other hand, when γῆν has no modifier it always has the article; thus ἐπὶ γῆν Αἰγύπτου and ἐπὶ τὴν γῆν always contrast as in this verse. Incidentally γῆς Αἰγύπτου is never articulated in Exod either, nor is γῇ Αἰγύπτῳ (or Αἰγύπτου). In the tradition this distinction is not continued, since a popular tradition articulates the first γῆν.

MT has an odd text with respect to "the locusts." It has בארבה as part of the נטה clause, and then begins the next clause with ויעל: "... concerning locusts, and let them come up." Exod simplifies the whole matter by making the locusts subject of the second clause and removing the reference in the first: "and let locusts come up." The hex text shows again how mechanically Origen often acted; it simply transposes ἀναβήτω ἀκρίς.[15]-- The *d* text characteristically abbreviates with επ αυτην for ἐπὶ τὴν γῆν.

In the following clause the *f* text has articulated βοτάνην, whereas a *b x* variant has added επι before τῆς γῆς. Neither has a basis in the Hebrew. -- The second element of the compound accusative modifier is based on the Sam tradition ואת כל פני הארץ rather than the כל את of MT. MT makes "even all that the hail had left" explicative of the עשב, i.e. it has no compound modifier of the verb at all, whereas Sam and LXX do; compare v.5.

The relative clause refers to καρπόν. Variants have arisen under the misunderstanding that ξύλων was the antecedent (as though locusts would destroy the trees rather than the fruit), leading to ων, a genitive by case attraction in the *C* tradition, as well as to the A *O z* + variant α. The former is, however, homophonous with ὄν in Byzantine Greek. Also inspired through homophony is the itacistic popular A variant imperfect spelling υπελειπετο, which does not fit the context at all.

10:13 The opening clause in Exod describes Moses' action differently from the other ancient witnesses. MT has "And Moses stretched out his staff over

---

14. Sym and Theod have "desire, ask for" according to Syh.
15. Aq along with Theod did a much better job of recreating MT with ἐν

the land of Egypt"; Exod has "And Moses raised the staff heavenward."
Unique is the use of ἐπαιρέω to render the Hiphil of נטה. In fact, the verb
occurs only three times elsewhere in Exod; at 7:20 the verb is also modified
by "staff," at 17:11, by τὰς χεῖρας, and in 14:16 the collocation "raise the
staff" actually contrasts with "stretch out the hand." An O b text with
εξετεινεν δε for καὶ ἐπῆρεν must be an early (preOrigen?) correction
towards the Hebrew. An x + text (as Sam) has χειρα instead of ῥάβδου,
probably due to the influence of v.12, whereas the hex addition of αυτου is
made to conform to MT. The origin of εἰς τὸν οὐρανόν is difficult to explain. The raising of the hand heavenward does occur at vv.21,22 and 9:22,-
23 but this can hardly have created this text. If the phrase is not textually
based it may be intended to contrast with: "stretch the hand over the land of
Egypt" of v.12. This gesture towards heaven is then immediately followed by
καὶ κύριος, thereby dramatically tieing the gesture to the immediately
following divine action.

To an Alexandrian an east wind producing locusts would not make
much sense and so instead of רוח קדים Exod has ἄνεμον νότον "a south
wind";[16] so too ὁ ἄνεμος ὁ νότος occurs later in the verse.[17]

For the usage of the passive ἐγενήθη see note at 4:6. The fact that the
south wind had blown on the land that whole day and night had produced
the result: the locusts were in place; i.e. the aorist ἀνέλαβεν together with
those of v.14 must be understood as past to ἐγενήθη; thus "it was morning
and the south wind had taken up the locusts, etc." For τὸ πρωί see note at
7:15.

10:14 The first clause is coordinate with the last one of v.13, sharing the
same subject. This differs from MT in which the subject changes from the
wind to the locusts. In MT the locusts came up and settled; in Exod the
wind brought them up and they settled. Revision based on MT is evident in
the b n reading, επληθεν η ακρις for ἀνήγαγεν αὐτήν; cf also the related s
reading εξηλθεν η ακρις which looks like a variant to the b n text.

ἀκρίδι καὶ ἀναβήτω (from Syh).
16. See SS 65.
17. This becomes a "burning" wind in Aq and Sam (as well as in Pesh and
Vulg).

The subject of the first clause is the αὐτήν of the second clause, as is clear from the πολλὴ σφόδρα at the end; since this is nominative feminine singular the subject must be ἀκρίς. An *x* tradition has πολλην, i.e. it takes the verb κατέπαυσεν as transitive with ὁ ἄνεμος (as in the two preceding clauses) as subject: "it deposited a great many on all the borders of Egypt." Exod's text must be rendered "and there settled on ... a great many (i.e. locusts)."

The following clause has a rather swollen phrase in MT about the locusts: כן ארבה כמהו "thus locusts like it," which Exod simplifies as τοιαύτη ἀκρίς; compare 9:18,24 11:6. -- The words προτέρα and μετ᾽ are prepositions with pronouns referring to ἀκρίς: thus "before these ... after these." For μετ᾽ αὐτήν a popular μετα ταυτην as well as a B + μετα ταυτα are attested in the tradition.[18] -- Instead of οὐκ ἔσται an *n s* text has ου γεγονεν, an error based on its occurrence in the preceding clause.

10:15 The subject of the first clause remains ἀκρίς. Within the clause MT had "all" before "the land," and hex has added πασας; Arm and 53' mistakenly have "all" before τὴν ὄψιν instead.

The translation of the second clause in Exod needs comment. Instead of MT's "and the land was darkened" Exod has "and the land was destroyed," ἐφθάρη. That the land was wasted is then explicated in the rest of the verse; in the context ἐφθάρη fits much better than MT,[19] though it is useless to suppose a parent תשחת instead of תחשך; Exod was simply trying to make sense.

In the third paratactic clause the subject reverts to ἀκρίς. A popular M variant articulates βοτάνην (because the coordinate καρπόν is articulated?). The relative pronoun ὅς is masculine singular by attraction to καρπόν the nearer antecedent. The clause itself is structured differently from MT. There the pronoun is the object of הותיר (with הברד as subject). Exod makes the pronoun nominative and the verb passive (cf the next clause where the verb is repeated but there appropriately for the Niphal נותר).

18. For these see the discussion in THGE VII.G.10.
19. Cf also its equivalent in Aq and Sym ἐσκοτάσθη (or possibly the active ἐσκότασεν attested by M^mg, which is just as possible).

Because of this Exod is required to render MT's subject הברד by a prepositional phrase ἀπὸ τῆς χαλάζης.

The next clause is asyndeton in Exod (against MT), which as a summary statement on the extent of the locust destruction is appropriate. A popular A M variant changes the ὑπελείφθη of Exod to κατελείφθη with no real lexical change.

Double negatives οὐχ ... οὐδέν simply stress the negative, and the omission of οὐδέν by an *ol C b* tradition weakens the statement. -- The two conjoined ἐν phrases which modify χλωρόν are ἐν τοῖς ξύλοις and ἐν πάσῃ βοτάνῃ, whereas a last one modifies the verb. Exod has πάσῃ before βοτάνῃ over against all other ancient witnesses, but this is consistent with his practice elsewhere (9:22, 25 10:12).

10:16 Change of subject is shown by δέ. The verb κατέσπευσεν is rightly aorist rather than the imperfect κατεσπευδεν of the A B s + tradition.[20] -- The use of the direct speech marker λέγων for ויאמר is almost zeugmatic; it usually occurs after a verb of saying, but καλέσαι here is not.

Pharaoh admits "I have sinned before the Lord your God and against you."[21] -- In MT the verb is followed by two prepositional phrases, ליהוה and לכם. These are carefully distinguished by Exod. Sinning "against Yahweh" is quite different from sinning "against you"; accordingly the first is translated by ἐναντίον κυρίου (compare ἐνώπιόν μου of 32:33), and the second by εἰς ὑμᾶς.[22] This same distinction is found in Tar: קדם/קרם יוי ייי vs לכון, but not in Pesh and Vulg.

10:17 The logical consequence, οὖν, of admission of sin is a desire to escape its consequences, and Pharaoh now asks Moses and Aaron προσδέξασθε "expect," hence "bear with, endure." MT's אך הפעם "only this time" stands over against Exod's ἔτι νῦν which indicates that this was not the first time. The verb is in the plural (over against MT Tar) since both Moses and Aaron are being addressed; cf the plural verb in the coordinate clause (in all witnesses). Both imperatives are in the aorist since a present tense would

20. See note at THGE VII.M.5.
21. For ἡμάρτηκα Sym has ἀσφάλην from σφάλλω "to trip up," and so "I have been tripped up," hardly a confession of sin on Pharaoh's part.

be inappropriate, Pharaoh does recognize that it is to κύριον τὸν θεὸν ὑμῶν that prayer must be directed; gradually he is learning the role that the Lord, Israel's God, plays in the plagues. -- For θάνατον see comments at 5:3.

10:18 Change of subject is shown by δέ, which contrary to MT is expressed as Μωυσῆς (as Pesh Vulg), not as "Moses and Aaron" as vv.16 and 17 would seem to demand; Aaron is obviously only a secondary figure in the narrative. -- Exod does not have Moses then pray to the Lord but rather to τὸν θεόν, though a popular A M variant has κ̄ῡ, probably a preOrigenian revision based on MT.

10:19 The Lord answers the prayer by turning a vehement wind from the sea which took up the locusts and cast them into the Red Sea. The opening verb is somewhat unusual; μεταβάλλω only occurs twice elsewhere in Exod (7:17,20) both times of changing water into blood. Otherwise it occurs in the Pentateuch only throughout Lev 13 in the laws concerning leprosy. It is throughout used to render הָפַךְ, Qal or Niphal. The notion of changing the wind reflects v.13, where a south wind brought the locusts; now the Lord changes it to a wind from the sea. MT simply refers to "a west wind," but Exod renders יָם as ἀπὸ θαλάσσης. This makes sense to an Alexandrian; a wind from the sea is either north or west; such a wind towards the ἐρυθρὰν θάλασσαν would have to be from the west and slightly north. -- The wind is described in MT as חָזָק מְאֹד "very strong," for which Exod uses a single adjective σφοδρόν "violent, vehement"; this occurs only rarely in LXX, in fact, only three other instances, all in the context of ἐν ὕδατι σφοδρῷ, obtain (15:10 2Esd 19:11 Wis 18:5). Very common is the adverb σφοδρα, the standard rendering for מְאֹד, which the *C* text attests. -- An A + text reorders ἄνεμον after ἀπὸ θαλάσσης, a stylistic change to place ἄνεμον next to σφοδρόν.

The phrase τὴν ἐρυθρὰν θάλασσαν is always used by Exod (see also 13:18 15:4 23:31) to represent יָם סוּף, i.e. the order is always ἐρυθρ. θαλ. (except in 15:22), whereas in MT it is throughout in reverse order. In later

---

22. But see Helbing 217, who makes no such distinction.

books the order often follows that of MT. A popular A M tradition does have την θαλασσαν την ερυθραν here as well.

The result of the vehement wind is stated in the last clause which is paratactically tied to the preceding (as in Pesh), while MT is asyndetic. The verb ὑπελείφθη is again used here (as twice in v.15, which see) but this time to represent נשאר. Exod repeats v.15 in ἐν πάσῃ γῃ Αἰγύπτου, whereas MT uses גבול "border(s)" rather than ארץ.

10:20 For the theme of the Lord hardening Pharaoh's heart see note at 4:21.

10:21 The plague of darkness. A new section is indicated by δέ. Moses is told to stretch out the hand heavenward, as signal for a new plague to be imposed. Hex has added σου after τὴν χεῖρα so as to conform to MT.

The use of a third person imperative, γενηθήτω after καί, is a Hebraism for a final clause, i.e. Moses is to stretch out his hand ... :"that there may be (darkness)." This darkness is to come "upon the land (of Egypt)"; an M *ol C* variant has γης instead of γῆν after ἐπί, for which see note at 9:22.

MT has a two word clause at the end of the verse which might be literally rendered as "let there be felt a darkness," or more idiomatically "a darkness which could be felt"; this is exactly how Exod understood it with its ψηλαφητὸν σκότος, a phrase in apposition to and explicative of σκότος 1°.

10:22 Change of subject is shown by δέ. For the first clause see notes on v.21. -- The resulting darkness is defined in MT as אפלה "deep, gloomy darkness." Vulg rather colourfully has *tenebrae horribiles* which is probably close to what MT had in mind. Exod uses two words to describe the darkness, γνόφος θύελλα.[23] The first word is simply a synonym, whereas the second indicates a kind of storm with a great deal of wind such as a hurricane or a wind squall.[24] That a darkness which is defined in such a way should be called *horribiles* is indeed appropriate. Exod's rendering by these two words was then taken over by Deut (4:11 5:22) to translate two

23. Sym translates by ζόφος "gloomy darkness."
24. Hesychius defines the word as a "twisting, a rushing or a squall of wind.

different Hebrew words. -- Note that the ἐπί phrase modifying ἐγένετο uses the accusative rather than the genitive.

10:23 The verse begins with καί though MT is asyndetic. The first two clauses have plural verbs, ראו and קמו, which Exod renders by the singular in congruence with οὐδείς. An *s* variant, probably from The Three, has ειδον for the first one. At the end of the first clause a B *f* variant adds τρεις ημερας which is borrowed from the second where it belongs.[25] -- Exod interprets תחתיו as κοίτης αὐτοῦ; this makes good sense since MT says that no one rose from his תחת - that which is under one, i.e. a sitting or a lying down place.

Again the miraculous contrast between Goshen and the rest of Egypt is brought out. The terrible darkness did not effect the area which the Israelites occupied. Exod has ἐν πᾶσιν οἷς κατεγίνοντο "in all (the regions) which they were inhabiting"; note the use of the imperfect. The πᾶσιν renders explicit what is only implicit in MT.

10:24 According to Exod (and Sam Tar^P Vulg) both Moses and Aaron were summoned to Pharaoh; MT has only Moses. Since the imperatives addressed to him are in the plural (of course Moses and the people are meant), the inclusion of "and Aaron" is easily understandable as a later attempt to lighten the text. For λέγων for ויאמר see the note at v.16 for a similar context.

For the aorist imperative after βαδίζετε see note at v.8. The majority variant λατρευετε is an adaptation by attraction to βαδίζετε. -- MT has את יהוה modifying the imperative, whereas Exod (and a Pesh ms) amplifies κυρίῳ by τῷ θεῷ ὑμῶν as in vv.25, 26; in fact Exod always has "worship the Lord" with the accompanying modifier "your (or their) God."

Pharaoh still sets conditions for Israel's departure. Their sheep and cattle are to remain presumably as surety against the people's return. In MT צאנכם and בקרכם constitute the compound subject of the Hophal יצג, singular by attraction to the nearer unit: "your sheep and your cattle will be detained." Exod has quite a different construction. The pronouns are omit-

25. Cf THGE VII.O.

ted both for προβάτων and for βοῶν,[26]though supplied by hex, and the genitive nouns modify the verb ὑπολείπεσθε, a present plural imperative: "only the sheep and the cattle leave behind." The itacistic variant υπολιπεσθε of B + is merely a misspelled imperfect.[27]

The word ἀποσκευή here refers only to the offspring; at least it contrasts with "sheep and cattle" so that it can hardly be intended as broadly as at v.10.[28]

10:25 An *s* variant has the historical present λεγει instead of εἶπεν, for which see note at 2:13. -- Exod renders **ܕ** here by the sensible ἀλλὰ καί "but also." A *C z* gloss has ου before it, probably a scribal attempt to clarify Pharaoh's role: "but neither will you give..., (v.25) and therefore our cattle will go with us." But the sense of Exod lies in the understanding of δώσεις as "but also you must grant us," i.e. a cultic journey without the accoutrements of sacrifice is meaningless.

The sacrifices are called "holocausts and sacrifices" in Exod, whereas in MT these are reversed, and so too hex reorders them. -- The relative pronoun referring to these sacrifices is ἅ, i.e. neuter plural - neuter because the two items are of disparate gender. An *ol f y* variant has ας by attraction to the gender of the nearer unit θυσίας. The verb within the relative clause, ποιήσομεν, is future indicative, not a potential mood as the popular A variant ποιησωμεν is, i.e. simply "we shall make."

10:26 This verse is tied paratactically to the preceding thereby echoing MT, though one might have expected an οὖν "therefore, so." The second clause is also introduced by καί even though it is asyndetic in MT. The statement "we shall not leave a hoof behind" makes clear that more than a temporary cultic journey is intended. The verb is future middle, but B has the rare future passive inflection.

The γάρ clause explains why all the cattle must accompany the Israel-ites: "because we will be taking from them (the cattle) in order to serve."

26. Cf SS 94.
27. See THGE VII.M.5.
28. But see Lee 104.

The δέ is adversative: "but we do not know." ἡμεῖς reflects MT as did
σύ in v.25, but the pronouns do help to set up a contrast in stress between
the two protagonists. -- The object clause modifying οἴδαμεν contains a
grammatical difficulty in that λατρεύσωμεν is modified by an accusative
and a dative of person. In LXX this verb never has an accusative but always
has a dative modifier to indicate the one who is served, except for a cognate
accusative at Jos 22:27 τοῦ λατρεύειν λατρείαν κυρίῳ. Possibly the τί
should here be taken adverbially: "how we should serve." The verb is in the
aorist subjunctive; the potential mood is much more appropriate than the
popular M homophonous future indicative λατρευσομεν. The *d* reading,
λατρευσαι, is simply a scribal error based on the infinitive in the γάρ
clause.

The final structure is a prepositional one, with ἕως governing the
genitive. The infinitival structure is a good rendering of MT's infinitive. The
accusative ἡμᾶς is the subject of the infinitive, and should not be changed
to the nominative of the *C* text, which would be abnormal Greek.

10:27 Change of subject is indicated by δέ. -- For God's hardening of the
heart of Pharaoh see note at 4:21. -- Instead of ἐβουλήθη a popular variant
has ηβουληθη.[29]

10:28 Exod again uses the historical present for which see note at 2:13. The
addressee (Moses) is not given in Exod, and the לֹ of MT has promoted
the popular A M hex addition of αυτω.

πρόσεχε σεαυτῷ[30] became almost a set translation for הִשָּׁמֶר לְךָ not
only in Exod (see also 23:21 34:12) but particularly in Deut; it had already
been used in Gen 24:6. Here it is used with a complementary infinitive, and
is a negative warning: "watch out for."

The text in MT is peculiarly vocalized; instead of an expected negative
particle אַל the Masoretes vocalized it as the preposition אֶל, which is
baffling. The Tar Pesh Vulg all took it as the negative. Exod has for אַל
חֹסֶף ἔτι προσθεῖναι, literally "yet to add." The verb προστίθημι is regularly

29. For the *eta* augment as early as 300 B.C. in Attic inscriptions see LS sub
βούλομαι.
30. Helbing 291 calls this "der Dativ des Reflexivums beim Imperativ."

used as an equivalent for the Hiphil of יסף in the sense of "to repeat." The Greek is thus a Hebraism; but the construction is quite different. Probably Exod understood אל as the negative particle though the use of the otiose ἔτι makes this unclear. An *f* variant adding μη before προσθεῖναι may well be a revision based on MT.

The infinitive is in turn modified by the complementary infinitive, ἰδεῖν, which designates what is not to be repeated; the words do rather pile up "again to repeat to see," all of which simply means "to see again."

Hex reordered the phrase μου τὸ πρόσωπον with μου at the end so as to equal MT. -- The relative clause which follows is a translation of a preposition with infinitive in MT; it is introduced in MT by a causal כי, but Exod uses δέ. Furthermore Exod uses the aorist passive ὀφθῆς in second person plus μοι: "(in the day that) you appear to me," whereas the Hebrew has the Qal infinitive ראתך "your seeing (my face)." Exod realized that it was Pharaoh's seeing Moses that was dangerous, not the reverse.

10:29 The δέ indicates change of speaker. The historical present is continued here; see note at 2:13. MT has Moses saying כן דברת "so you have spoken," for which Exod simply has εἴρηκας "you have said (it)." *x* has changed this to first person ειρηκα, "I have said (it)." Aside from the fact that this verb is usually used for אמר, whereas λαλέω is the regular rendering for דבר, Exod has also disregarded the כ, and so hex has added ουτως.[31] Exod is abrupt indeed.

The ὀφθήσομαί σοι of the last clause parallels ὀφθῆς μοι of v.28. So too MT with its לא אסף עוד ראות פניך parallels the אל תסף ראות פני of v.28 except for the added עוד, which may be the source for the peculiar ἔτι of v.28. Over against v.28 Exod abbreviates considerably. The verb "to repeat" is omitted in favor of the ετι in οὐκέτι, admittedly a much better rendering. But the σοι εἰς πρόσωπον is also peculiar, and the clause probably means "I will not again appear to you in person," i.e. visually. The hex attempt to fix this up to fit MT by its εις προσωπον σου does not create a particularly intelligible rendering after ὀφθήσομαι.

31. This is what Aq and Theod also have, whereas Sym has ὀρθῶς.

Chapter 11

11:1 The last plague foretold. The beginning of a new section is shown by
δέ. The addressee is shown by πρός plus the accusative, which *C* changes to
a simple dative. There are 37 cases without addressee in Exod where
ויאמר occurs in MT (plus those rendered by λέγων). For the rest if the
addressees are proper nouns (in cluding three cases of יהוה) 55 instances
use πρός with accusative, and only three use the dative. There are 16 cases
of πρός plus accusative other than proper nouns, of which three are τὸν
θεόν, three are τὸν λαόν, two involve all the congregation of the Israelites,
and the other eight are pronouns. On the other hand, there were 27
instances of the dative not involving proper nouns. It is clear that for proper
nouns the πρός construction is preferred to a dative. This may be due to the
fact that this often mirrors the distinction between אל and ל in the Hebrew.

The adverb ἔτι along with the preposed modifier μίαν πληγήν serves
to lay stress on the fact that the plagues are nearing an end. -- The μίαν
πληγήν phrase is transposed by hex to conform to MT.[1] The verb ἐπάξω is
modified by two prepositional phrases "on Pharaoh and on Egypt"; *C* omits
the second preposition thereby making it a single prepositional phrase.

The next clause is asyndetic in BHS Tar[O] and Pesh. In Exod whenever
μετὰ ταῦτα introduces a clause it is always preceded by καί (3:20 5:1 11:1,8
34:32). The phrase μετὰ ταῦτα is an idiomatic rendering for אחרי כן
meaning "afterwards."

The temporal condition with ὅταν + subjunctive verb renders the
Hebrew כ + infinitive. Variant renderings for such a construction are
subjunctive verb introduced by ὡς ἄν (9:29) or by ἡνίκα δ᾽ ἄν.[2] A ὅταν
construction also occurs twice at 28:39 for כ + infinitive, whereas ὡς ἄν at
13:11 translates כי. ἡνίκα δ᾽ ἄν occurs at 33:8,22 34:34 40:30 but each time
for כ (+ infinitive.) The verb in the clause is appropriately in the present
subjunctive (as at 28:39) rather than the aorist εξαποστειλη of *d t z*. It
might be noted that after the other two particles mentioned the present

1. Instead of πληγήν Aq Sym have ἀφήν; cf also 12:17.
2. See SS Inf 95f.

subjunctive is not used by Exod but rather the aorist, and in 33:8 34:34 the imperfect obtains. In the tradition the *f* pair, 53', has the first singular ending (as Pesh). Exod supplies ὑμᾶς as its object over against MT, correctly interpreting what was intended.

The last clause begins with an unusual expression, σὺν παντί for כלה, which Exod must have understood as related to כל. I have not found σὺν παντί elsewhere; it here modifies ἐκβαλεῖ in the sense of "with everything," and contrasts with past attempts on Pharaoh's part to keep back parts of Israel's encampment as hostage for their return. Exod placed the phrase immediately before the verb with the cognate noun in the dative at the end. Hex reordered the noun to equal the Hebrew order of גרש יגרש. Hex also supplied an εντευθεν at the end of the verse under the influence of MT.

11:2 The particle οὖν is used to show that this instruction follows logically on v.1. Its omission by an *f* variant may be due to homoiot. Exod also adds κρυφῇ, i.e. "speak secretly," though MT simply has דבר נא. The translator thereby makes explicit what is implicit in MT.

The second clause constitutes the instruction in λάλησον κρυφῇ. For the Hebrew pattern: plural verb + "each his" see comment at 7:12. -- Exod has the grammatically congruent singular αἰτησάτω. Each one is to ask of (παρά, but in the *C* text changed to απο) his neighbour. Exod does not translate "his" nor "her" in the parallel phrase of MT,[3] which are added by hex. -- The indeclinable πλησίον occurs both for male and female neighbour, case and gender being shown by the articles τοῦ and τῆς resp. -- As to what they are to ask for MT says "vessels silver and vessels golden." Exod omits the repeated "vessels" as does Vulg: *argentea et aurea*; hex adds σκευη before χρυσᾶ to equal MT. Then at the end of the verse Exod (as Sam) has καὶ ἱματισμόν; cf the note at 3:22.

11:3 Change of subject is shown by δέ. Exod has changed the usual order: verb - subject, with κύριος standing first, thereby paralleling the second clause pattern where ὁ ἄνθρωπος Μωυσῆς also precedes the predicate; hex has changed the order to fit MT. The fact is that all of v.3a is based on a

3. Cf SS 94.

parent text equalling 12:36a. Incidentally the *C* text has omitted δέ, possibly through confusion with the immediately following ἔδωκεν.

Exod has simplified MT's bound phrase הֵן הָעָם (את) by τὴν χάριν τῷ λαῷ αὐτοῦ, correctly understanding the bound phrase as an objective genitive relationship but with an epexegetical αὐτοῦ added by which the relation between the Lord and Israel is subtly stressed; its subsequent omission by a *b* + variant conforms to MT.

The clause καὶ ἔχρησαν αὐτοῖς is based on וישאלום; see Sam and 12:36.[4] The itacistic spelling in *d t*, εχρισαν, makes very little sense here.

The predicate of the clause in v.3b in MT is גדול מאד which Exod renders by μέγας ἐγενήθη σφόδρα, i.e. inserts a verb, with the adverb modifying the predicate μέγας ἐγενήθη. -- The remainder of the verse is only explicable on the basis of a different parent text. All other ancient witnesses have "in the land of Egypt (or "the Egyptians") before the servants of Pharaoh and before the people." Exod has "before the Egyptians and before Pharaoh and before all his servants." (It is in fact not certain who "the people" in MT are, Egyptians or Israelites). Hex has added και εν οφθαλμοις του λαου at the end of the verse, and may also have been responsible for omitting πάντων and for changing αὐτοῦ 2° to "Pharaoh" as well.

11:4 The addressee is not given and it is only made clear in Exod that it was Pharaoh from v.8. -- For the messenger formula see note at 4:22. -- The phrase μέσας νύκτας "midnight" obtains in the *d x* tradition with νύκτας as νυκτος, as though μέσας were nominalized.

The usual pattern of pronoun + present tense verb for MT's pronoun + participle is changed to pronoun plus future εισπορευσομαι in a *z* text. The intent of the present is of course future as the time indicator περὶ μέσας νύκτας shows.[5]

---

4. The verb is probably correctly understood by Schl: *mutuum sumo*, i.e. the Israelites asked of the Egyptians what they felt was their due, their fair return.
5. Cf SS 67.

164

11:5 The divine entrance into Egypt means that every first born in the land of Egypt will die. Exod always uses Αἰγύπτῳ after ἐν γῇ, not the genitive of a popular variant.[6]

All three instances of πρωτοτόκου are left unarticulated in Exod though in the case of the first and second popular variants do add the article. It would be odd for the translator to have articulated some and not others.

The articulated participle הישב modifying "Pharaoh" is adequately rendered by a relative pronoun and a present tense verb, ὃς κάθηται. That Pharaoh should sit on his own throne is obvious, and Exod simply has τοῦ θρόνου,[7] but hex has dutifully added αυτου to equal MT.

The word עד can be rendered either by ἕως or by καὶ ἕως, but in the pattern: "from x up to y" Exod only uses καὶ ἕως when a coordinate ἕως phrase obtains, i.e. "up to y καὶ εως z." A popular B addition in the tradition of και before the first ἕως is then secondary.[8] -- The word השפחה "maidservant" is rendered in Exod by τῆς θεραπαίνης, for which a marginal variant in a number of mss substitutes (της) αιχμαλωτιδος "the captive"; presumably this is an exegetical comment; the lowest class of people in society is the slaves working at the mill. -- The final phrase in the verse is "firstborn of all cattle" (as Sam), a sensible reordering of MT's "all firstborn of cattle"; hex transposes παντός to conform to MT.

11:6 A great outcry will obtain in the whole land. -- The ἥτις clause has two parts in coordination, and thus differs from the similar expressions in 9:18,24, but only in the second part: τοιαύτη οὐκέτι προστεθήσεται "such will not again be repeated." For MT's לא יסף Exod not only uses the negative οὐκ and the verb but adds ετι to the negative to reinforce the notion of repetition as at 8:29 10:28.

11:7 Change of subject is indicated by δέ, but a popular B variant changes it to a και structure.[9] -- Presumably the omission of πᾶσιν from the phrase "among all the Israelites" by the *b* text was simply a matter of abbreviation.

6. See the discussion in THGE VII.H.3 sub 12:1.
7. Cf SS 94.
8. Cf the discussion in THGE VII.E.3.

-- That "not a dog should growl with his tongue" apparently puzzled some scribe which then promoted the M + variant βρυξει "bite" for γρύξει. -- That "from man to cattle" should follow created some ambiguity which a popular Byzantine variant tried to remove; by prefixing ουδε it became clear that it does not modify γρύξει, but rather the initial prepositional phrase. -- For the popular itacistic variant ιδης for εἴδης see the note at 8:10. MT anachronistically has the plural, but only Sam agrees with Exod; the plural is incongruous with v.8 where the suffix on "servants" is second masculine singular.

For παραδοξάσει see the note at 8:22. A B *n* + variant reads the present tense παραδοξαζει. Since the context throughout is future the present is probably merely a palaeographically inspired error. -- The wonderful thing that the Lord is to effect is "between the Egyptians and Israel." Exod does not repeat the "between" before the second noun as MT does, but a majority hex tradition adds ανα μεσον before τοῦ ' Ισραήλ for an exact correspondence with MT. Actually Exod otherwise always repeats the ανα μεσον before a second noun! The tradition also witnesses to an A *O C s* variant omitting τῶν before Αἰγυπτίων. Exod usually articulates "Egyptians"; in fact, only four times (3:8 14:30 18:9,10) does the unarticulated form (and that only in the genitive) occur in Exod.

11:8 Instead of "shall come down" a *C f* variant has καταβοησονται "shall call down," an excellent example of palaeographic confusion, ie. -βησονται as -βοησονται. -- The noun phrase is ordered exactly like its Hebrew parent with οὗται at the end. An *s* variant omits πάντες without disturbing the overal sense of the phrase.

Somewhat unusual is the use in the second clause of προσκυνήσουσίν με. It would normally mean "shall worship me" but it can hardly mean that here. It translates the Hebrew הוחתשהו; in fact, that Hebrew verb is only rendered by προσκυνέω in LXX (except for the Aramaic part of Daniel where the verb translates סגד). Obviously here "bowing down" does not mean "doing obeissance," but rather "begging, pleading, imploring," as the context makes fully clear.

---

9. See the discussion in THGE VII.E.1.

That plea is put in the imperative singular, but with a compound subject σὺ καὶ πᾶς ὁ λαός σου, the σου with no equivalent in MT. -- The imperative is modified by a οὖ clause, whereas MT has אשר ברגליך, an idiomatic phrase meaning "who are in your train," i.e. "who are following you."[10] Exod makes of this something different; after the adverbial οὖ he has σὺ ἀφηγῇ, a subjunctive from ἀφηγέομαι "to lead away from," thus "where you might lead away." -- For μετὰ ταῦτα see note at v.1.

The last clause is a δέ structure, the subject changing to Moses. The verb is again ἐξῆλθεν, the third occurrence of the root in the verse, first as imperative, then as future, and here as aorist. -- A d x reading adds προσωπου after ἀπό under the influence of the common LXX phrase "from the face of." --Moses' departure was μετὰ θυμοῦ, a simplification of but just as effective a phrase as MT's בחרי אף.

11:9 Change of subject is shown by δέ. -- The Lord assures Moses that Pharaoh "will not listen to you"; the "you" is plural, though throughout the chapter thus far only Moses and God (Pharaoh only secondarily) are involved. But here ὑμῶν refers to Moses and Aaron. The divine purpose underlying Pharaoh's continued refusal to listen is stated in the ἵνα clause, "that I may multiply my signs and wonders in the land of Egypt." MT has a slightly more neutral statement, with למען governing the infinitive רבות whose subject is מופתי, i.e. "that my wonders may abound in the land of Egypt." For the fuller phrase "signs and wonders" here and in v.10 see note at 7:3. Exod also used a first person verb which makes κύριος the subject, and signs and wonders" the object of the verb. Most variant traditions are obviously secondary. A B f + variant has through dittography added πληθυνων before πληθύνω.[11] Furthermore the majority text has rearranged μου τὰ σημεῖα (which is not in MT at all) with μου at the end. τέρατα becomes εργα in oI, a scribal error due to visual confusion. More significant is the very popular hex addition of μου to represent the suffix of מופתי.

---

10. Cf SS 83.
11. See the dicussion in THGE VII.O. where the entire ἵνα clause is discussed as well.

11:10 Change of subject is twice indicated by a δέ structure, first to Moses and Aaron, and in the second clause to κύριος. For "signs and wonders" see note at v.9. The compound phrase is modified by πάντα preceding it and by ταῦτα after it; the omission of τὰ σημεῖα καί by a popular A* text would equal MT, but it is probably due to homoiot. Similarly the transposition of πάντα to precede τὰ τέρατα in the Byzantine text seems closer to MT but it is doubtful that it was inspired by the Hebrew.

Early revision towards MT does seem to be at work in the very popular omission of ἐν γῇ Αἰγύπτῳ. Exod was intent on a close parallel with the preceding verse where the phrase follows "signs and wonders"; cf comment on v.9. -- The omission of ἐναντίον Φαραώ by *oI* which would make the verse even more closely parallel to v.9 is, however, unwarranted, since this is represented in MT.

For the Lord's hardening of Pharaoh's heart see comment at 4:21. -- MT simply makes the blunt statement "he did not send away (the Israelites)," but Exod expands this to "he was unwilling to send away" by which Pharaoh's wilfulness is stressed. A B + variant changes ἠθέλησεν to εισηκουσεν "listened to, obeyed," making Pharaoh's refusal a matter of disobedience. The infinitive ἐξαποστεῖλαι is modified by ἐκ γῆς Αἰγύπτου; all other ancient witnesses have "from his land," also supported by an A M *b d t* + variant, probably recensional (Byzantine?) so as to conform to MT.

Chapter 12

12:1 Change of subject is shown by δέ. -- The preposition אל is repeated before Aaron in MT, though not in Exod, but supplied by hex according to Syh. The phrase ἐν γῆ Αἰγύπτῳ is strictly Exod usage; the εν γη αιγυπτου of B *O s* is secondary.[1]

12:2 The subject of the nominal clause is ὁ μὴν οὗτος; Pesh makes this clear by adding the verb "shall be" after οὗτος. -- By "this month" is meant the present month, which Tar[P] identifies as *Nisan*.

ἀρχὴ μηνῶν "the beginning of months" is explicated in v.2b. Not fully clear is the syntax of ὑμῖν in the phrase πρῶτός ἐστιν ὑμῖν; does it modify the verb or the adjective? In MT this is obvious; the nominal clause has with ראשׁון as subject and הוא לכם as predicate. An *f s* variant clarifies the syntax by placing ἐστιν after ὑμῖν, i.e. ὑμῖν must modify πρῶτος; actually this may well have been intended by Exod as well. -- Significant is a *C x* variant which has εσται for ἐστιν; i.e. the priority of the Passover month is a prediction rather than a statement of present reality. Both Pesh and Vulg also have a future verb.

*12:*3 Only Exod of the ancient witnesses begins with a singular imperative; though Moses and Aaron are addressed, only one can speak to the Israelite assembly; mss 58' add δη which equals the נא of Sam. -- Over against BHS and Tar[O](txt) Exod has υἱῶν before 'Ισραήλ; this may well be textual in origin. -- The specific "time when" is defined by a dative construction: "on the tenth of this month."

Over against MT Exod does not have a reflexive pronoun modifying the verb λαβέτωσαν; hex, however, has added an otiose εαυτοις to represent the לכם. The explication of the "taking" is set in the singular, i.e. "let them take, each...," a common Hebrew pattern designating distribution; in fact, ἕκαστος, except for 11:2, always (24 times) modifies a plural verb in Exod. Since ἕκαστος πρόβατον is modified by a plural construction, κατ' οἴκους πατριῶν, the Byzantine text "emended" πρόβατον to προβατα, creating a hybrid construction which is neither good Greek nor Hebrew. -- This is then explained by a singular formula πρόβατον κατ᾽ οἰκίαν "a sheep per household." An early B x variant has added ἐκαστος before the expression, a copyist's error due to the preceding phrase ἕκαστος πρόβατον.

12:4 The verse explains what is to be done when a household, οἱ ἐν τῇ οἰκίᾳ, is too small to carry out the general rule of the preceding verse: "a sheep per household." The b f n text omits οἱ, thereby making the prepositional phrase modify ὀλιγοστοί. -- The ὥστε clause interprets MT correctly as pertaining to sufficient numbers of people for a single sheep.[2] Should the number be too small for eating a sheep he shall take with himself[3] the next door neighbour κατὰ ἀριθμὸν ψυχῶν, "according to the number of persons." Precisely what that number should be is not specified but was probably known to the community. According to an old Jewish tradition the minimum number was ten.[4] The phrase for next door neighbour in MT is literally "his neighbour, the one near to his house"; Exod simplifies the construction by τὸν γείτονα τὸν πλησίον αὐτοῦ. -- A popular variant for the compound verb συλλήμψεται is the προσ-compound, but with no substantial change in meaning.

The final clause of the verse centers around the verb συναριθμήσετε with the modifier εἰς πρόβατον.[5] Preposed is the norm to be employed for the counting: ἕκαστος τὸ ἀρκοῦν αὐτῷ. Syntactically the structure is loose, which has led to third singular middle and passive variants. The syntax is best understood by consulting MT which has איש לפי אכלו "each according to his eating." The clause as a whole can be rendered: "As for each one according to what is sufficient for him shall you count up together for a sheep."

---

1. For this pattern see the discussion in THGE VII.H.3.
2. Cf the discussion of the clause in SS 147.
3. See Helbing 310.
4. According to Josephus, Jewish Wars VI.9,3.
5. For the verb and the popular passive variant συναριθμηθησεται see the discussion in THGE VII.M.7.

12:5 The paschal animal, the πρόβατον, must have three characteristics: τέλειον, ἄρσεν and ἐνιαύσιον, i.e. without imperfections, male and a yearling. The Byzantine group has added αμωμον after ἄρσεν, which is tautologous in view of τέλειον. Furthermore, the animal may be taken either from the ἀμνῶν or the ἐρίφων. A B *f* variant has αρνων "lambs" which, however, Exod reserves for גדי, whereas כבש is rendered by ἀμνός throughout.[6]

12:6 Only here in the entire LXX is משמרת rendered by the participle of διατηρέω (perfect passive), but it is appropriate as a complement to ἔσται: "and it shall be observed by you." The word also occurs in ch.16 in connection with the manna story, twice as ἀποθήκην, and twice as διατήρησιν. The word often occurs in Numbers where it is usually rendered by φυλάκη, though διατήρησιν does obtain at 17:10 19:9.

The animal is to be kept until the fourteenth of the month; Exod does not translate "day," since that is obvious from the context, but hex adds ἡμερας to equal MT. On that day the paschal lamb is to be slain. The verb is plural active with the collective noun τὸ πλῆθος as the subject. The rendering is unusual; in fact, only in 2Chr 31:18 is קהל also rendered by πλῆθος, where it is appropriate since the reference is a collective for Levites enrolled with all their offspring εἰς πᾶν τὸ πλῆθος. Exod was faced with the highly unusual collocation קהל עדת; it occurs only once elsewhere in MT, at Numbers 14:5, where the translator simply used συναγωγῆς, i.e. he omitted it as otiose. συναγωγή is used in the only other occurrence of קהל in Exodus, 16:3. Exod by his "all the multitude of the congregation" neatly avoided the apparent tautology of MT.

The slaughter is to take place according to MT "between the two evenings," the meaning of which is disputed. Does it mean between sunset and darkness, or between the sunset beginning and that ending the day? Exod has πρὸς ἑσπέραν (also at 16:12), τὸ δειλινόν at 29:39,41, and ὀψέ at 30:8. Num always has πρὸς ἑσπέραν (except at 9:5 where it is omitted). The only other occurrence of the Hebrew phrase is at Lev 23:5 where Lev renders literally by ἀνὰ μέσον των ἑσπερινῶν which is not particularly luminous. Exod is fully decisive; it is at dusk.

12:7 The preposition ἀπό is here used as partitive,[7] thus "some of the blood." The πλῆθος συναγωγῆς are to take some blood and put it on the two doorposts and on the lintel of the houses.[8] -- The prepositional phrase ἐν τοῖς οἴκοις is somewhat ambiguous; does it modify both σταθμῶν and φλιάν or only the latter? Since a house would usually have one entrance it is quite rational to speak of the two doorposts and the lintel as being in the house, i.e. they are part of the house structure, and it is likely that the ἐν phrase is meant to modify the compound structure rather than only φλιάν. The ambiguity was felt in the tradition as well and a popular variant added και before the ἐν phrase. This does remove the ambiguity but it radically changes the intent of Exod. A *b* variant of this popular reading has επι instead of ἐν thus making it fully parallel with the other two phrases. This reading has nothing to do with the על of MT; it is rather a secondary variant within a variant text.

The relative clause has ἄν plus the subjunctive.[9] The pronominal object of φάγωσιν is αὐτά, plural because the πλῆθος eats the paschal sacrifices "in the houses" with one animal per house; cf v.4. In v.6 the πλῆθος slaughtered αὐτό, but plurality (τοῖς οἴκοις) has now intervened. A popular A variant does have αυτο, which could well be an early prehexaplaric revision towards MT's אתו, though it could just as well be due to the influence of v.6. -- The inclusion of ἐν αὐτοῖς is a Hebraism pure and simple made even more awkward since Exod had ἐν governing the relative clause.

12:8 They are to eat the flesh τῇ νυκτὶ ταύτῃ, i.e. the night of the fourteenth day. MT indicates the time by a prepositional phrase, and the Byzantine text's prefixing of εν conforms to it. A *b f s* reading reorders the pronoun to the beginning; either order is acceptable Greek and the variant order involves no semantic shift. -- That the animal was roasted in the fire and eaten with unleavened cakes and bitter herbs was certainly by Exod's time long established and Exod is faithful to MT even to the extent of using a prepositional phrase ἐπὶ πικρίδων to represent על מררים when one

---

6. Cf THGE VII.Q.
7. Cf SS 160.
8. For "lintel" Aq uses τὸ ὑπέρθυρον, a more descriptive term than the τὴν

might expect a simple conjunction. The meaning is clear: "and unleavened cakes with bitter herbs shall they eat"; comp ἐπ' ἀζύμων καὶ πικρίδων of Num 9:11.

12:9 The preposition in ἀπ' αὐτῶν is partitive, "any of it"; the pronoun refers to κρέα. An M s variant has απ αυτου which formally equals MT (since הבשר is singular), but in Greek it can only be a copyist's error. -- What is forbidden is eating the flesh raw or boiled in water. MT has prefixed a free infinitive בשל to the Pual participle, but Exod simply has ἡψημένον, hex prefixing εφθον to equal MT. The perfect passive participle of ἕψω can also appear as εψημενον as in the C s text.[10]

The positive counterpart follows the adversative particle ἀλλ' ἤ which indicates "but" after a negative (like the German *sondern*). But ἀλλά by itself in C is also used thus and does not change the sense.

What is ordered is that the paschal animal be roasted whole in the fire, "whole" being defined as "head with feet and intestines";[11] for each of these three the hex tradition has added an αυτου to conform to MT. What it does not mean is Vulg's *caput cum pedibus eius et intestinis vorabitis*; Jerome obviously never observed passover.

12:10 Nothing of the meat may be kept beyond the night festival; all that remains to the next morning must be burned. Between these two statements Exod has repeated from v.46 the clause καὶ ὀστοῦν οὐ συντρίψετε ἀπ' αὐτοῦ. Exod probably added it here as the one instruction concerning the preparation, use and disposal of the paschal animal which was part of the passover lore but not included in the body of instructions of vv.3--11. With v.12 the subject changes, and only with vv.43--49 is the ordinance of the feast set out. The only instruction concerning the passover itself occurs in v.46. Exod has brought together all the relevant material in a single block.

The text tradition presents some confusion with respect to the opening clause. The οὐκ ἀπολείψετε has been misread by the C tradition as ου καταλειψετε; it was, of course, palaeographically inspired. Also the result

---

φλιάν of Exod though it means the same.
9. Not the B x + variant εαν for which see the discussion in THGE VII.B.
10. For the variation see LS s.v.

of a copyist's error is the M *b* variant ουχ υπολειψετε. Neither reading affects the sense of the passage.

Only Exod begins the verse asyndetically, all other witnesses beginning with "and." Exod also carefully distinguishes the number of the pronouns. V.9 forbade eating ἀπ᾽ αὐτῶν but here what is forbidden is leaving ἀπ᾽ αὐτοῦ,[12] the antecedent now being πρόβατον

ἕως πρωί occurs twice within the verse as a literal rendering for עד
בקר. In both cases a variant tradition εις το πρωι (at 34:2,25 for לבקר)
occurs - for the first case with popular support.[13]

For the middle clause the verb is συντρίψετε, a second plural verb. Through itacism a third singular middle form, συντριψεται is supported by A B plus scattered support. A further variant then developed as συντριβησεται in the *oI C* tradition, a future passive form based on the second aorist passive stem. Both variants make a sensible text, since they take the neuter singular ὀστοῦν not as accusative but as subject of the verb.

Exod refers in the last clause to τὰ καταλειπόμενα, a present middle participle. A B *b t* variant reads the aorist τα καταλιπομενα, which is an itacism. The present form is lexically preferable though the aorist, being colorless, is also possible. The term is an accusative, modifying the verb κατακαύσετε "you shall burn," for which the A *b* text has the itacistic third singular middle form. This too makes good sense; the accusative participle is then taken as nominative, a plural neuter subject being congruent with a singular verbal predicate.

12:11 Change of subject is shown by δέ. The opening clause is introductory, the οὕτως pointing forward. It (the paschal animal) is to be eaten in a state of preparedness for departure, loins girded, feet sandalled, staff in hand. The three conditions are all joined by καί as in Sam Pesh, whereas MT and Tar do not have the first two joined, i.e. the pattern is 1 2 + 3. Either pattern is sensible, and both are attested throughout Exod.

In accordance with good rhetoric Exod does not repeat the unnecessary ὑμῶν after ὑποδήματα and βακτηρίαι,[14] but to conform to MT

11. Cf SS 93.
12. See SS 164.
13. For a discussion of this variant see the discussion in THGE VII.Q sub

popular hex traditions have added pronouns. It might also be noted that both "staffs" and "hands" are in the singular in MT, only Tar^O among the ancient witnesses supporting MT, and that only for the latter.

Twice the Israelites are told "you shall eat it;" the first time the verb is φάγεσθε, the second, ἔδεσθε. Exod preferred to vary his translation, the words meaning exactly the same. In the second case MT describes the manner of their eating as בחפזון, a word usually interpreted as "with haste." Though it occurs only three times in OT the verbal root is well known and means "to hurry." Exod renders the word by σπουδῆς (cf also Deut 16:3); they were to eat on the run.[15]

The final clause simply states "it is a *pascha* to the Lord." It is apparently a concluding statement to the description of the feast described and ordered in vv.2--11, and now for the first time receives a name. The word πάσχα is simply a transcription of פסח in its Aramaic form פסחא, undoubtedly a well known word in the Jewish households of Alexandria.[16] -- For κυρίῳ a very popular του κυριου obtains, but it is secondary.[17]

12:12 Εωδ uses ἐν γῇ Αἰγύπτῳ, not the variant εν γη αιγυπτου, for which see Note 1 above. -- The focus for this final plague is now centered solely on the Lord; there is no Moses or Aaron to serve as mediator; the verbs are all in the first singular future, διελεύσομαι, πατάξω, ποιήσω, and the statement ends with the self-identification formula ἐγὼ κύριος.

The plague includes effecting judgment on all the gods of the Egyptians. The plagues are now complete and this signalizes the power of Israel's God to impose his will on all the Egyptians' gods, since the eventual outcome of the struggle, the exodus of the Lord's people from the house of bondage has arrived. The struggle is fundamentally not between the Lord and Pharaoh with his people; it is the struggle between the faith of the Is-

---

16:23.
14. Cf SS 94.
15. Sym renders it by (ἐν) ἐπείξει, a synonym of σπουδή. Theod and Aq, however, translate the phrase by ἐν θάμβω "in amazement." This probably reflects the fact that the haste of the root חפז is often a haste occasioned by fright or alarm; cf e.g. Deut 20:3.
16. Simple transcription was not enough for Aq and Sym, however. Aq added his translation ὑπέρβασις, a "passing over" (cf v.27), but Sym idiosyncratically adds ὑπερμάχησις, "defence." It is not clear how Sym came

raelites and the religion of the native populace. -- τοῖς θεοῖς τῶν Αἰγυ-πτίων is popularly revised by omitting both articles. This formally equals MT, and the revision could well be the result of (preOrigenian?) recensional activity. It is not Exod, however, which always articulates both plural nouns when modified by "all."

12:13 Here the point of v.7 becomes clear. Blood was to be placed on the two doorposts and the lintel because this would become (ἔσται ... ἐν) a sign for you on the households (οἰκιῶν rather than οικων "houses"). The πάσχα is now defined as a sacrificial sign; cf v.27. -- The οἰκιῶν is designated as ἐν αἷς ὑμεῖς ἐστε ἐκεῖ, a rather cumbersome way of saying "where you are." The ἐκεῖ is a Hebraism tacked on at the end to represent שׁם.

The signal character becomes evident when the Lord says that he will see the blood and σκεπάσω ὑμᾶς, "I will protect you."[18] The Hebrew verb is פסח, i.e. it is an interpretation of pesaḥ; to Exod the passover constitutes a divine shelter or protection of the participants (cf Tar[O] with its איחוס). This is probably anticipatory of the next clause, viz. "there will be no πληγὴ τοῦ ἐκτριβῆναι in you when I smite...." That no plague of eradication or destruction will affect those households with the smeared blood is due to God's protection.[19] -- For ἐν γῇ Αἰγύπτῳ see Note 1 above.

12:14 The opening clause presented a problem in the tradition. The subject is ἡ ἡμέρα αὕτη, but the position of αὕτη is changed in *b* which has the pronoun at the beginning of the phrase which is equally possible, whereas cod B uniquely has it after ὑμιν; this is simply a thoughtless copyist's error. -- μνημόσυνον is the accusative modifier of ἔσται, representing the prepositional phrase לזכרון in MT; hex has prefixed the preposition εἰς to equal MT.

The memorial is to be festively celebrated - ἑορτάσετε; the verb occurs twice, and in both cases an *O* variant with scattered support has the aorist imperative εορτασατε, a possible but unlikely reading in a context consistently future. In the first instance it is modified by a double accusative αὐτὴν ἑορτήν. The noun is omitted by the Byzantine text either as otiose

___

to this rendering. Vulg adds (in agreement with Aq) the interpretation "id est transitus."

or because of homoiot. In turn ἑορτήν is modified by κυρίῳ which hex has articulated, doubtlessly to represent the preposition in ליהוה of MT.[20] -- All this is to be done εἰς τὰς γενεὰς ὑμῶν "throughout your generations." A B f variant has inserted πασας.[21] -- In fact, this celebration is to be an eternal νόμιμον.[22]

12:15 Unleavened cakes are to be eaten for seven days. For the φαγεσθε of the f text cf comment at v.11. -- MT continues with the rather odd אך בירם הראשון "already (or indeed) on the first day"; Exod simplifies this by ἀπὸ δὲ τῆς ἡμέρας κ.τ λ., i.e. "but from the first day (on)." On day one MT orders תשביתו שאר "you shall put away leaven (from your houses)"; Exod has ἀφανιεῖτε "do away with, hide, remove."[23] -- Exod uses his favorite pattern: article + noun + article + ordinal throughout this verse. A popular A M text has the pattern: article + ordinal + noun, equally valid in Greek and with no semantic difference.

MT continues with a כי clause as though the reason for getting rid of leaven was the threat of excommunication from the community. Exod removes such fear as the basis for obedience by leaving out the כי, making the simple statement: everyone who eats leaven, that person shall be destroyed from Israel. -- The b x text has εαν for ἄν within a relative clause.[24]

MT distinguishes between שאר "leaven" and חמץ "something leavened," but Exod uses ζύμη for both. -- The verse ends with a loose construction "from the first day up to the seventh day"; this is somewhat awkwardly placed at the end in imitation of MT; it modifies the πᾶς ὅς construction, and the ἐξολεθρευθήσεται clause must be parenthetic.

---

17. See the discussion in THGE VII.H.3.
18. Cf Lee 77.
19. Aq has θραῦσμα, "a shattering, breaking up," hence "destruction."
20. The Three all have the τῷ as well.
21. For the probable NT source for this variant cf THGE VII.O.
22. Aq and Sym have their own regular renderings for חקה (or חק). Aq uses ἀκρίβειαν which means "exactness, precision," thus an exact formula to be followed; Sym prefers πρόσταγμα, "ordinance, commandment."
23. Aq oddly has διαλείψετε, i.e. "leave off for a while"; the word really means "to leave a gap," presumably chosen by Aq to show the temporary nature of the ban on leaven in the households. Sym has the literalistic

12:16 According to Exod both the first day and the seventh shall be called holy; Exod varies the predicate by using κλητή plus ἔσται for the seventh day, but κληθήσεται, future passive of καλέω, for the first. For the latter the majority A M text has κεκλησεται, a variant future passive inflection for καλέω. Both forms existed in Classical Greek, but in LXX the latter occurs only at Lev 13:45 and Hos 11:12, in both cases with κληθη- as a substantial variant tradition. In both cases MT has מקרא קדש, a holy assembly. Later the designation κλητὴ ἁγία became a regular translation of the phrase; thus in Lev passim the phrase probably took on the MT meaning of "a holy assembly." The same translation occurs in Num 28:25 though elsewhere Num preferred ἐπίκλητος ἁγία (28:18,26 29:1,7,12).

No service work is to be performed on those days, i.e. they are holy in the same way as the Sabbath is holy. The majority A B M variant ποιήσεται is the itacistic second plural active ποιησετε, but the middle is original.[25]

Exod defines the exemption as ὅσα ποιηθήσεται πάσῃ ψυχῇ "what must be done for any person," broadening it to include all service work necessary for human life, rather than limiting it to the preparation of food as MT does. Tar[P] supports the Exod reading, though I suspect that יתעביד is due rather to the occurrence of the same form (though defectively written) twice within the verse.

12:17 Instead of המצות "unleavened cakes" Exod follows Sam: המציה "commandment," which also makes good sense; the addition of ταύτην is epexegetical.[26] For φυλάξεσθε, a B n variant has the active future with no significant lexical difference, whereas the A b f x text has the aorist middle imperative, φυλαξασθε.

The γάρ clause gives the basis for the required observance. God says that on this day "I will bring out your host from the land of Egypt"; the exodus as a promise is viewed as the basis only for the inaugural festival. All the other ancient witnesses have the verb in past tense, by which the exodus is defined as the basis for the cultic event for all time - an eternal ordi-

---

rendering παύσετε "stop."
24. See the comment in THGE VII.B.
25. That the variant is secondary is clear from the discussion in THGE VII.M.7.
26. See Prijs 38 on this point.

nance. Exod's "your host" must be a reference to the military host, the army, as is clear from MT which has צבאות.

The last clause also shows Exod's individuality in interpreting a text. It has "and you shall make (ποιήσετε) this day an eternal ordinance throughout your generations." MT uses the verb שמרתם, i.e. "you shall observe," though Sam uniquely has a conflation of the two: ושמרתם ועשיתם.

In the text tradition a popular C tradition articulates γενεάς as in v.14. Exod seems quite arbitrary on the matter, and there seems to be no real distinction between the two lexically.

12:18 The verse gives the duration of the feast, appropriately placed in the genitive "beginning ... from evening ... until the 21st day of the month (i.e.) until evening." The time frame of the feast is thus starting from the evening of the 14th day and continuing up to the evening of the 21st of the first month of the lunar calendar.

The tradition produced only minor changes of little significance except for a b n s variant which changed the genitive participle ἐναρχομένου to the dative feminine singular to agree with τῇ ... ἡμέρᾳ, thus changing the genitive of time within which to a dative of time when; this is a possible construction, but in view of the ἀφ' ... ἕως structure clearly not intended by Exod.

12:19 The verse begins with an accusative of extent of time "for seven days"; during this time "no leaven is to be found in your households." An s x variant has οφθησεται "is to be seen" for εὑρεθήσεται, a variant based on Deut 16:4.

The second clause should be compared with its parallel in v.15. Here too the כי of MT is disregarded; in fact, the materials from πᾶς ... ἐκείνη are almost word for word the same as in v.15 (except for ζυμωτόν), and notes on v.15 should be consulted. -- In the 13 instances in which the noun συναγωγή refers specifically to Israel in Exod, only here is Israel not designated as υιων ισραηλ, and it is not surprising that a C s variant should have υιων inserted in συναγωγῆς 'Ισραήλ.

A new element over against v.15 is the addition of ἔν τε τοῖς γιώραις καὶ αὐτόχθοσιν τῆς γῆς, "both among the resident aliens and the natives of the land," the terms representing גר and אזרח resp. in MT. For גר Exod uses the rare word γιώραις, found elsewhere in LXX only at Isa 14:1 and on the margins of four mss as a variant text to προσήλυτοι in Lev 19:34. גר occurs only twice in Gen (15:13 23:4) and is translated by πάροικος. This translation also occurs in Exod in the popular etymology for Γηρσάμ at 2:22 18:3. Otherwise Exod introduces the term προσήλυτος which thereafter became standard for the later books of the Pentateuch.[27]

12:20 V.20 restates negatively and positively the rule on leavened food. In the positive statement בכל מושבתיכם is rendered by the singular ἐν παντὶ κατοικητηρίῳ ὑμῶν; as far as I know this noun occurs only in the singular (at least throughout the LXX), and must here be taken as a collective. A B x + variant has added a contrastive δε after παντί; this though secondary correctly interprets the intent of Exod.[28] The tradition did have some trouble with κατοικητηρίῳ. The *b* tradition has the simplex form, whereas an *s* tradition has οικηματι. Both words basically mean "dwelling place," i.e. the same as the text of Exod, though οἴκημα has a wider semantic range.[29]

12:21 Change of subject is shown by δέ. Moses now passes the instructions which the Lord had given to Moses and Aaron (cf v.1) on to the elders of Israel. For the term γερουσίαν see notes at 3:16. Its articulation by *C b* + is simply stylistic. -- As in v.18 the word υιων is inserted in the text tradition before ʼ Ισραήλ and supported by B *C f*.[30]

Direct speech is introduced without a marker. The coordinate verbs are put into good Greek by making the first one a participle; literally "going away take," i.e. "go and take." λάβετε is modified by the dative ὑμῖν ἑαυτοῖς.[31] The reflexive as a substitute for the second personal pronoun is

27. Cf Bauer s.v. Aq and Sym attest to τῷ προσηλύτῳ here as well (the word גר being singular).
28. See the discussion in THGE VII.E.3.
29. See LS sub οἴκημα and οἰκητήριον.
30. Its secondary nature is clear from the discussion in THGE VII.O.
31. For this unusual usage see the discussion in THGE VII G.10.

characteristic of Hellenistic Greek in general.[32] A popular A M text spells it in its Attic form, αυτοις, and *b* omits as otiose.

What is to be taken is a πρόβατον κατὰ συγγενείας ὑμῶν "a sheep according to your families." That a popular A variant read the plural προβατα is not surprising; it betrays the kind of rationalization which finds the plural reference in λάβετε, ὑμῖν ἑαυτοῖς, συγγενείας overwhelming. Of course Exod's use of the singular is just as logical; no family had to take more than one sheep. A B + variant tackled the seeming inconsistency in a different way by reading the singular συγγενειαν. -- Exod then adds καὶ θύσατε τὸ πάσχα using the imperative in balance with the coordinate λάβετε. The B *f* variant θυσετε, a future indicative, does not improve the style. -- Exod here uses the word πάσχα for the first time to indicate the sacrificial sheep.

12:22 The particle δέ occurs twice as a coordinating conjunction. -- The people are to take a bundle of hyssop and dip (it) in the blood and touch lintel and doorposts with it. Exod does present some difficulties. The blood is twice located παρὰ τὴν θύραν, as rendering of בסף. The word סף can either mean "threshold, doorsill" or "basin, container"; MT is usually understood as intending the latter, but Exod took it in the former sense. Why the blood should have been "by the door" is not clear. -- Furthermore the prepositional phrase modifying βάψαντες is ἀπὸ τοῦ αἵματος. Since one would expect either εἰς or ἐν Exod must have intended the blood as source, i.e. "dipping from the blood" in the sense of soaking up the hyssop bundle with some of the blood.

The words καὶ θίξετε exactly reproduce MT's והגעתם "and you shall touch." Exod seldom uses καί to introduce a finite verb after a participial construction, and the tradition soon ran into trouble when a copyist dropped the *iota* of καί to create a new form καθιξετε, presumably from some such root as καθίγω.[33] This even produced an *f* variant καθιζετε which must have troubled readers considerably since it means "to seat."[34] The verb θιγάνω does take the genitive, thus "and you shall touch the

32. For its use for the second person see Bauer sub ἑαυτοῦ 2.
33. The root is not recognized in LS.
34. For a fuller discussion of this passage see THGE VII.Q. See also

lintel[35] and the two doorposts with the blood (which is by the door)." The Byzantine text has added του οικου after door, under the influence of θύραν τοῦ οἴκου in the next clause.

The last clause presents no problems of interpretation. It represents a common LXX syntactic pattern with ἕκαστος, for which see note at v.3.[36]

12:23 The clauses are all paratactically set forth: "and the Lord shall pass by ... and he will see ... and pass by ... and not permit." There is a fine balance in the verse in that clauses one and three both have the identical subjects and predicates, though MT uses different verbs. Then in clause one the purpose of the "pass by" is πατάξαι, whereas in clause four πατάξαι also occurs as a purposive infinitive modifying εἰσελθεῖν. Clause two is then the condition for clauses three and four.

The translator uses παρελεύσεται to translate both עבר and פסח (thus interpreting πάσχα), but in two different senses, since in the second case the verb is modified by an accusative τὴν θύραν,[37] whereas in the first it is modified by a purposive infinitive πατάξαι. The latter is a destructive passing by; the former is salvific.

In the mythology of the rite it also appears that the Lord is not himself the one who kills, but rather works through an agent, τὸν ὀλεθρεύοντα "the destroyer": "when the Lord passes by the door he will not permit the destroyer to enter your households to destroy."

12:24 A summary injunction to practice this rite ἕως αἰῶνος. The injunction is in the future, φυλάξεσθε, modified by a double accusative τὸ ῥῆμα τοῦτο and νόμιμον. A popular A reading has changed the verb to aorist imperative, φυλάξασθε, whereas an *n* variant has φυλάξετε, i.e. active instead of middle; the latter is obviously correct as the modifiers σεαυτῷ and τοῖς υἱοῖς σου demonstrate. -- An A variant with scattered support has added αιωνιον after νόμιμον as in v.17. The *d* text articulates the noun in the unique ἕως αἰῶνος, probably under the influence of the common phrase εἰς τὸν αἰῶνα in which the noun is always articulated in Exod.

Helbing 125.
35. As in v.7 Aq has τὸ ὑπέρθυρον for τῆς φλιᾶς here and in v.23 according to Syh.

12:25 The particle ἐάν + subjunctive can and here does serve as a temporal condition, so "when you come into the land."[38] -- The relative clause contains ἄν + subjunctive verb δῷ, thereby showing divine intentionality.

The apodosis is in the future indicative φυλάξεσθε. For variant readings see notes on v.24 which also apply here. -- The term τὴν λατρείαν ταύτην in a religious context means service, cult practice;[39] specifically it refers to the passover ritual described in vv.21--22.

12:26 This verse is the protasis for v.27. The initial καὶ ἔσται is a Hebraism. MT often places והיה before a כי conditional clause, which Exod usually omits as being otiose as in v.25, but here he has it. -- For ἐάν + subjunctive see note at v.25. -- The question that children in the future might ask is τίς ἡ λατρεία αὕτη. For the relevance of the note on λατρείαν in v.25 note Vulg: *quae est ista religio.* -- Hex added υμιν at the end of the question so as to equal the לכם of MT.

12:27 The apodosis is introduced as so often in LXX by καί in imitation of Hebrew usage; the *C* text improves the Greek by omitting it. -- The epexegetical αὐτοῖς in "you shall say to them," is supported by Pesh Vulg but not by MT.

In the reply the πάσχα is actually called a θυσία; this predicate is modified by κυρίῳ, with the subject of the nominal construction intervening. κυρίῳ is in turn modified by a relative clause explaining the origin of the festival. The majority A B M text has ὡς instead of ὅς introducing the clause. Contextually this would make excellent sense: "since he..." instead of "who...," but Hebrew has אשר, so that the relative pronoun must be original, and the variant arose through homophony.

For ἐσκέπασεν see the note on σκεπάσω at v.13. The בתים are here taken as οἴκους "houses" rather than οικιας, because they are the units for celebrating the feast.

For the populace's response of bowing and worshipping see note at 4:31; a *b* reading has the plural, προσεκυνησαν, the subject ὁ λαός being a

---

36. See also Helbing 86.
37. Cf Helbing 86.

collective; the participle κύψας, however, was not changed.

12:28 The section concludes by stating that the Israelites went and did as the Lord had commanded. In the tradition καθά appears both as καθώς and καθαπερ; all three mean the same thing. For ἐνετείλατο an *s* reading has συνεταξεν. The two are synonyms and Exod uses both. συντάσσω is the more commonly used by Exod (33 times), whereas ἐντέλλομαι occurs only 14 times. The verb is modified by the compound indirect objects τῷ Μωυσῇ καὶ ᾽Ααρών, of which A and B uniquely omit καὶ ᾽Ααρών, which is odd in view of v.1.

The concluding οὕτως ἐποίησαν is difficult to justify from the point of view of Greek rhetoric; it is completely otiose in the context, and is simply a Hebraism taken over from MT.

12:29 The death of Egypt's firstborn. The opening clause is typically Hebraic; "and it happened at the middle of the night and" simply means "at midnight."[40] For ἐγενήθη *n s* have εγενετο; for their use and meaning in Exod see note at 2:10.

In the second clause the subject κύριος precedes the verb; the unusual order simply follows MT. -- The popular variant αιγυπτου for Αἰγύπτῳ is contrary to Exod usage, though perfectly good Greek.[41] -- Throughout the verse πρωτοτόκου is left unarticulated as perforce in MT, and the occasional articulation in the tradition is simply a stylistic variant. -- Exod in the interest of good style renders בכאו by τοῦ θρόνου, and as expected hex has added αυτου.

The pattern: ἀπό ... ἕως ... καὶ ἕως makes excellent sense but a popular variant has also added και before the first ἕως.[42] -- Unusual is the attributive phrase describing the slave τῆς ἐν τῷ λάκκῳ "the one in the pit" for בית הבור in MT. The term was apparently used for prison already in Gen 40:15.[43]

38. Cf Bauer sub ἐάν 1.d.
39. Cf Schl: *cultus religionis.*
40. Cf SS 179.
41. As is clear from the discussion in THGE VII.H.3. sub 12:1.
42. That this is secondary to Exod is clear from the statement in THGE VII.E.3.

The pattern's last element is the καὶ ἕως phrase, which in MT is simply the conjunction *waw*: "and all the firstborn of cattle." This undoubtedly is the basis for the well supported A M *O C b* variant παν πρωτοτοκον for Exod's ἕως πρωτοτόκου παντός (cattle), an early revision towards MT; note also the "correction" of word order.

12:30 The initial καί construction is changed to ανεστη δε in *n*, thereby showing change of subject. A B *x* variant has αναστας for the verb, which would create an anacoluthon.[44] The subject of the verb is Φαραώ which is then compounded by adding "and all his servants and all the Egyptians";[45] in MT this is preceded by אוה and hex accordingly adds αυτος, thereby placing αυτος ... Αἰγυπτίοι in apposition to Φαραώ.

The second clause has the adjectival phrase κραυγὴ μεγαλή as subject; a *b* reading omits the adjective, probably a scribal error due to homoiot. -- In the phrase ἐν πάσῃ γῇ Αἰγύπτου the last word is always genitive in Exod when γῇ is modified by πάσῃ, and the A B + variant, αιγυπτω, is secondary in Exod.[46]

The final clause gives the reason (γάρ) for the great outcry. The word for "one dead" is masculine since the dead was the firstborn son. The relative clause contains an unnecessary ἐν αὐτῇ, as a recapitulatory phrase reflecting ἐν ῇ, a Hebraic usage. MT, however, does not have a "which ... בו" construction, but rather "which ... שם." Tar[O] and Pesh have the former construction, and this must have been the text which Exod translated.

12:31 Exod (as Pesh) removes any possible ambiguity from the opening statement by naming the subject. The narrative disregards the apparent discrepancy with 10:28f. The reaction is pictured as immediate; it is still νυκτός. -- Both Exod and Pesh add an unnecessary αὐτοῖς after εἶπεν.

Twice in this verse two imperatives occur as compound predicates; in the first case ἀνάστητε and ἐξέλθατε are joined by καὶ against MT; the parent text may have had an extra *waw* by dittography. Both verbs are in the aorist, there being no particular call for stressing continuity of verbal action.

---

43. This promoted the literalism of Aq and Theod ἐν οἴκῳ τοῦ λάκκου. Sym has the more idiomatic ἐν τῷ δεσμωτηρίῳ "in prison."
44. This would be quite contrary to Exod practice as THGE VII.M.1. shows.

A popular M variant supports the classical ἐξέλθετε instead of the Hellenistic form favored by Exod.[47]

The second pair of imperatives are asyndetic in Exod. In MT a conjunction precedes the first one, ולכו, but not the second עבדו. A weakly supported B x reading joins the two imperatives by καί.[48] The Byzantine text has added a καί before βαδίζετε thereby conforming to MT. The imperatives are in the present and aorist resp., showing fine perception on Exod's part; "go" involves process, whereas this need not be so for "serve." A popular A F M variant has λατρευετε for λατρεύσατε but this is due to an unreflective adaptation to βαδίζετε. -- Exod's expansiveness over against MT in this verse is also apparent from the τῷ θεῷ ὑμῶν after κυρίῳ for which Exod is sole witness.

12:32 The pronoun ὑμῶν occurs only after the second noun of the opening pair. The *b* text omits it, whereas hex has also added it after πρόβατα to equal MT. -- The preposed accusatives are the object of the participle ἀναλαβόντες with the present imperative πορεύεσθε following immediately, i.e. "having taken, be gone." This is dramatically rather stronger than MT's "take as you said and go." The כאשר דברתם in MT is largely repetitive of the כדברכם (καθὰ λέγετε) with which v.31 had ended, and Exod does well for the narrative by omitting it. Hex added καθαπερ ειρηκατε after the participle so as to equal MT; this in turn popularly followed πορεύεσθε, probably as a stylistic improvement.

The final clause shows how deflated the arrogant monarch has become: "and bless even me." Pharaoh is now overwhelmed by the power of Moses and Aaron, and seeks their blessing. A well supported B F variant intensifies this cowed attitude on Pharaoh's part by reading the particle of entreaty δη for δέ.

12:33 The main verb of the opening clause is in the imperfect since the action is a process: "they were constraining (τὸν λαόν)"; constraining the people meant urging them on. The infinitive ἐκβαλεῖν is a purposive

---

45. Cf SS 74.
46. Cf THGE VII.H.3. sub 12:1.
47. Cf THGE VII.M.9.

infinitive in the aorist, which is in turn modified by σπουδῇ in the dative to show manner of action, "to throw them out with speed."

The reason for the panic and haste is clear from what they said. γάρ syntactically describes the εἶπαν clause but lexically the cause lay in what they said. The popular variant ειπον is the classical inflection.[49]

What is said is introduced by ὅτι as at 36:5. This use of ὅτι to express the content of the verb is particularly common in Exod after verbs of knowing such as οἶδα 3:19; ἐπίσταμαι 4:14 9:30; γνωστόν 33:16; εἴδης 8:10, 22 9:14; εἰδέναι 10:7; ᾔδει 34:29; γινώσκω in the aorist often, and verbs of seeing such as ὁρᾷ 3:2; ἰδών 8:15 and often; εἶδον 34:35; εἶδεν 3:4; ἴδετε 10:10 and ἑωράκατε 20:22. But it is also used to indicate what is said even occurring after the direct speech marker λέγων at 3:12. Other instances occur after ἐρεῖς 13:14; ἐροῦσιν 4:1. These cases of ὅτι must be carefully distinguished from instances where ὅτι is causal; cf especially 2:22 and 18:15 where ὅτι is part of the quotation. -- The desperate panic of the Egyptians is clear from what they say: "all of us are dying," with the verb in the present.

12:34 Change of subject is shown by δέ. The people were in such a hurry to leave that they took along their dough before it was leavened. Exod does not use an otiose genitive pronoun with "dough," but a very popular hex plus of αυτων obtains to equal MT. An odd *C* variant has αλευρον instead of σταῖς, i.e. "wheat-meal," or "meal" in general. But the context demands a σταῖς with the yeast not yet added or at any event not yet spread through the dough rather than the dry meal.

In MT kneading troughs are used as containers tied up in their garments and carried on the shoulders. Exod refers to τὰ φυράματα αὐτῶν rather than to kneading troughs. A φύραμα is a mass of dough, but Exod uses the plural; are these then stacks of flat pieces of dough? Somewhat similar is the interpretation of Tar[O] which has מרתר אצורתהון, i.e. "the overflowing of their (bread) batches." -- Exod locates these ἐπὶ τῶν ὤμων; MT of course has a pronominal suffix and hex has added αυτων.

---

48. See the note in THGE VII.E.3. sub 10:8.
49. See the discussion in THGE VII.M.9.

12:35 Change of subject is shown by a δέ structure. This verse along with the next reflects the instructions of 3:21--22 11:2. In the καθά clause Exod uses συντάσσω to render דבר which is unusual; see the note at 1:17, and for the αὐτοῖς the note at 9:12.

The "despoiling" of the Egyptians is put in less detailed fashion than in 3:22 11:2: "they asked from the Egyptians...." An *n* reading attempts to improve the text by its middle ητησαντο "they claimed for themselves." What they demanded were "vessels of silver and gold and raiment," exactly the text of 3:22 11:2, which see. A popular A M tradition has transposed the metals as "gold and silver" presumably as the more common collocation. Only Vulg agrees fully with Exod: *vasa argentea et aurea.* MT's שמלת is rendered by the singular collective ἱματισμόν; Vulg also has the singular but interprets as *vestemque plurimam*; cf note at 3:22.

12:36 For the first clause see notes at 11:3. The F *b* tradition has a δε construction in place of καὶ κύριος thereby showing change of subject. In the clause "and the Lord gave favor" the word χάριν is articulated as in 11:3, though in the prediction at 3:21 it is not. Usually χάρις is not articulated; e.g. it never is in Gen nor is it in Exod when modifying εὑρίσκω. -- The identification of the people as αὐτοῦ actually emphasizes the covenantal relation between God and the people, a stress not clear in MT.

The second clause καὶ ἔχρησαν αὐτοῖς also occurs at 11:3; it is not as ambiguous as the difficult MT text; neither text has an external indication as to subject or indirect object, but one presumes that the subject must be "the Egyptians" with αὐτοῖς referring to τῷ λαῷ. An *f* variant has changed ἔχρησαν to the middle εχρησαντο, i.e. "they lent to them." This is a possible mitigation of the despoiling, but it is doubtful that this is what was intended. What Exod means is that the Egyptians gave them whatever they asked. The difficult MT text has the Hiphil of שאל "made to ask," presumably meaning that the Egyptians begged the people to ask whatever they wanted.

The last clause also has no expressed subject, but it can only be the people since "the Egyptians" is the object of the verb ἐσκύλευσαν. The verb is the usual word for stripping the fallen enemy on the battlefields of weapons and clothing; the Israelites stripped, despoiled the Egyptians.

12:37 For the finite ἀπῆραν a B *f n x* variant has an anacoluthic participle απαραντες which is contrary to Exod usage.[50] -- For ʽ Ραμεσσή as one of the storage cities built by Israelite slave labor see note at 1:11. Its spelling with double *sigma* is assured by the Hebrew רעמסס. The spelling with a single *sigma* is well supported in the tradition but is the result of haplography. -- The spelling Σοκχώθα must be original since the final vowel can only derive from the Hebrew סכתה. Admittedly the final *he* is doubly rendered both by an unstressed final *alpha* and by εἰς. The tradition gives a wild variety of spellings which can be understood either as corrections towards MT by which the final vowel is excised or as errors of transcription palaeographically or phonetically inspired. Palaeographically inspired are those spellings which have lost the initial consonant by reason of haplography, or which have changed σ to ο in οοκχωθ, a case of uncial confusion from a parent text. Phonetically based are confusions of ο-ω, change of κχ to χ, χχ, or κγ. Unclear is the source of the doublet *b* reading εις σολχωλ εις εκχωθα.[51]

The use of εἰς with numbers means "about" and correctly interprets the Hebrew כ. The number applies only to πεζῶν, i.e. "those on foot" and here means men of army age, the infantry. These are further defined as men besides τῆς ἀποσκευῆς. As at 10:24 the term applies to human baggage,[52] i.e. people possessed by men, viz. women and children.[53]

12:38 The term ἐπίμικτος "mixture" refers to the mixed lot of peoples who attached themselves as camp followers to armies on the move; cf also Num 11:4. Also accompanying the Israelites were πρόβατα and βόες and a great deal of cattle. The flocks and herds are hardly distinguishable from the

50. Cf the discussion in THGE VII.M.1.
51. Aq has translated the phrase by εἰς σκηνάς.
52. See Lee 105.
53. Aq renders the Hebrew לבד מטף literally by χωρὶς ἀπὸ νηπίων, a phrase which is much better Hebrew than Greek. Sym interprets טף by τοῦ ὄχλου "crowd"; possibly Sym thought of the term as indicating "camp followers" as used in Xenophon; cf v.37.

κτήνη, and the last element in the list may well be a summary statement, i.e. "flocks and herds, even a great deal of cattle."

12:39 That v.38 is syntactically a parenthetical statement is clear from the unexpressed subject of v.39. This can hardly be ἐπίμικτος of v.38 but must be the οἱ υἱοὶ ' Ἰσραήλ of v.37. -- Now they baked the dough (ἐπίμικτος as "sent" in scattered mss is not sensible) into unleavened cakes. This statement is followed by two γάρ clauses, the first explaining the unleavened nature of the cakes; this in turn was due to the fact that "the Egyptians had thrown them out...." In MT and Tar the statement is in the passive. The active statement is more in line with the opening statement of v.33 καὶ κατεβιάζοντο οἱ Αἰγύπτιοι κ.τ.λ.

In the following clause ἠδυνήθησαν with double augment is well attested as Attic by the third century B.C., though the form with single augment is better known from early times.[54] The single augment spelling is found in A *t x y*. The inflection ηδυνασθησαν is a variant of the aorist passive and obtains in A M *x y z* +. The complementary infinitive ἐπιμεῖναι "to stay on, abide" is a hapax legomenon in LXX; the majority reading has the common υπομειναι "to stay behind." The two prefixes are quite similar in Greek cursive writing and the direction of error would almost certainly be towards the better known word. In any event the pressure on the Israelites to leave Egypt had been so great that they could not stay on long enough to prepare bread adequately.

The last clause further explains what their hasty departure had involved: "they had prepared no provisions for themselves for the road." The final phrase εἰς τὴν ὁδόν is an epexegetical plus correctly interpreting the reason for provisions.

12:40 Change of subject is shown by δέ. The cognate structure κατοίκησις ... ἣν κατῴκησαν "the dwelling (time) which they dwelt" has been replaced in a popular A F tradition by παροίκησις ... ην παρωκησαν "the sojourning which they sojourned." Either reading would make sense but usage makes clear which is original. The root שׁב is translated hundreds of times by κατοικέω but only rarely by παροικέω (only once in the Pentateuch (Num

190

20:15), which commonly renders גור. Cf, however, πάροικος for תושב in v.45.

κατοίκησις must mean the time of dwelling since the predicate is ἔτη τετρακοσία τριάκοντα. Exod found some difficulty with a period of 430 years for the Egyptian sojourn and has added καὶ ἐν γῇ Χανάαν, i.e. the 430 years are made to cover both the patriarchal period (215 years) and the Egyptian sojourn, thus two periods of equal length. This tradition at least partially relieves some of the chronological difficulty of only four generations from Jacob to Moses in 6:16--20. Sam shares the expansion though it more logically puts the reference to the land of Canaan ahead of Egypt. Sam also adds ואבחם after ישראל. This tradition also obtains in the text tradition of Exod; a popular tradition has added αυτος και οι πατερας αυτων immediately after the verb, and another popular tradition places it after Χανάαν.

12:41 Exod has a condensed version of MT. For מקץ "at the end of" Exod simply has μετά. And after ἔτη MT has ויהי בעצם הירם הזה "and it happened on that very day" which has no counterpart in Exod, nor is it in any way necessary to the story; hex, however, has added και εγενετο εν τη ημερα ταυτη.

The initial καὶ ἐγένετο is changed in an A + reading to a δε structure. The date given is the date of the departure of "the entire army of the Lord." MT has "army" in the plural הצבאות.[55] Over against MT's "and it happened on that very day" Exod has νυκτός "at night"; Exod uniquely joins the first word of v.42 as a time indicator for the exodus itself; cf note on v.42.

12:42 The verse begins with προφυλακή "a vigil,"[56] whereas MT has ליל שמרים, but see note at v.41. Exod emphasizes the cultic nature of the event - "it is a vigil to the Lord so as to bring them out from the land of

---

54. For the double augment cf Thack 137f and Bl-Debr 66.3.
55. Theod has πάντες οἱ ἄνδρες (according to Syh), whereas Aq and Sym have πᾶσαι αἱ στρατίαι.
56. The separation of ליל from שמרים by Exod was not followed by Aq and Sym, though Theod retained Exod at this point. Aq has νὺξ παρατηρήσεων "night of observations," but νὺξ παρατετηρημένη "a closely

Egypt," though this really only becomes clear in the second part of the verse. In the first part the vigil probably is intended to define the watch of the night referred to at the end of v.41.

This is then restated in cultic terms as applicable to the Israelites for all times. The collocation ἐκείνη ἡ νύξ refers specifically to the actual night of deliverance. That night is now defined as being "this vigil to the Lord." The syntax is made clearer by a Byzantine group variant which adds εστιν after προφυλακή 2°.

The ὥστε clause ending the verse defines the προφυλακή as a continuing, i.e. a cultic, event in the life of all Israelites for all times. The infinitive has no expressed subject but must refer to the προφυλακή, i.e. the passover vigil is to be for all Israelites throughout their generations.

12:43 Change in section is shown by δέ. The direct speech marker λέγων is present in Exod but not in MT. A popular A F M variant omits the word, rprobably a revision towards MT. νόμος as translation for חקה is not unexpected (though it does occur at 13:10 as well), since Exod uses this for תורה and prefers νομιμόν for חקה. The law of the πάσχα is designed to keep its celebration unprofaned by carefully excluding from it everyone who is uncircumcized (vv.43--49). This first of all excludes every ἀλλογενής "one from another tribe or race"; in MT it is "a stranger."

12:44 MT then deals with the עבד איש מקנת כסף, ״someone's slave bought with money"; Exod uniquely among ancient witnesses has two classes of servants here: οἰκέτην τινός, referring to a household servant, i.e. one born in the household, and ἢ ἀργυρώνητον "or one purchased." Note that πᾶν modifying οἰκέτην is not an error for παντα, the majority reading in the tradition; this usage does occur in LXX, though this is the earliest example of its usage. It can best be explained as a neuter substantive in apposition with the masculine noun.[57] The majority of mss substitutes και for the conjunction ἤ, thus coordinating the two classes of slaves: houseborn and purchased.

Such a slave must first be circumcized and may then take part in eating the sacrifice. The accusative compound object is preposed to the verb περιτεμεῖς; this in turn is, however, also followed by a recapitulatory pronoun, αὐτόν, reflecting the Hebrew idiom. -- For "then he shall eat of it" Tar[P] nicely gets the point by its "and he shall be *kosher* for eating of it."

12:45 A second class of those forbidden to partake: πάροικος ἢ μισθωτός, a sojourner or a hireling. A very popular variant changes the conjunction to καὶ, which equals MT. This is hardly recensional, however, since ἤ is comparatively rare over against καί in the LXX in general, and the tendency to level to καὶ must have been strong. -- Though I have translated πάροικος as "sojourner" it probably should be kept distinct from προσήλυτος, the standard rendering for גר. The word תושב is also an inhabitant of a land but not yet of the גר class of "resident alien."

12:46 Regulations concerning the sacrifice itself are three in number. A paschal feast must be held within a single household; the meat may not be taken outside, and no bones may be broken. A very popular A M variant adds a fourth though in second place: και ου καταλειψετε των κρεων εις το πρωι, a gloss taken from Lev 22:30, but compare also v.10 and Num 9:12.

The second statement appears asyndetically but a substantially supported B variant has a και before it.[58] The verb is ἐξοίσετε and an *O* itacistic variant with scattered support has εξοισεται, which is barely sensible with the same subject as that of βρωθήσεται. -- τῶν κρεῶν is a partitive genitive: "any of the meat."[59]

In the third statement the itacistic A M + variant συντριψεται makes excellent sense. The accusative ὀστοῦν as object of συντρίψετε now becomes the subject of the verb. It is, however, the product of an itacistic spelling as MT makes clear.

12:47 The συναγωγή is defined by υἱῶν Ἰσραήλ, as in Vulg and some Hebrew mss, all others having simply "of Israel." Similarly Vulg joins Exod in having a singular predicate; all other witnesses follow MT's יעשו, a plural in view of the collective nature of עדה. -- The verbal modifier αὐτό

---

observed night" is the rendering of Sym, a reading which may well be reflected in Vulg: nox ... est observabilis.
57. But cf Thack 173--175.

refers to the πάσχα; presumably the A + variant τουτο would have the same referent.

12:48 For the Hebrew cognate expression יגור ... גר Exod coins προσέλθη ... προσήλυτος; the latter remains thereafter the normal translation in the LXX for גר.[60] The context is the protasis of a future more vivid condition and concerns the approach of a προσήλυτος to celebrate the Passover. The Hebrew term refers to a resident alien, someone who had certain rights in the community but not full rights of citizenship. Such a גר though not an Israelite was a resident but could by circumcision become a proselyte. Initially, howver, the προσήλυτος was only one who had approached, come to the community, and was residing there for the time being. The infinitive ποιῆσαι is purposive, and renders MT's coordinate finite verb "and he would keep the Passover," i.e. a second condition governed by כי. A very popular variant does read και ποιη, an early change in the direction of MT. The articulation of κυρίῳ in the tradition is hex; Origen often felt that the preposition ל had to be represented by the dative article. A C reading has the optative προσελθοι instead of Exod's προσέλθη; the optative is unusual in a protasis with ἐάν and is simply an itacistic spelling of the subjunctive.

The prepositional phrase πρὸς ὑμᾶς was chosen to modify a προσ-compound verb; change to υμιν by the Byzantine text is lexically insignificant, whereas the *b* reading εν υμιν may be the result of understanding the προσήλυτος as residing among the Israelites, i.e. an exegetical improvement of the text, or more likely it was simply due to the influence of ἐν ὑμῖν in v.49.

The apodosis has the future verb περιτεμεῖς modified by πᾶν ἀρσενικόν and it in turn, by αὐτοῦ. Since αὐτοῦ must have an antecedent προσήλυτος that word must now be taken as collective and should be rendered as plural: "you shall circumcize (among) them every male." Only after circumcision may the resident alien celebrate it, i.e. προσελεύσεται ποιῆσαι αὐτό. The stated conclusion that "no uncircumcized shall eat of it" is by now fairly obvious.

12:49 What this verse says is that exactly the same rule, νόμος εἷς, is to apply to the native and to the προσήλυτος. Exod uses the word ἐγχωρίῳ as a substantive, it being an adjectival formation, rather than the αὐτόχθων of v.48 so as to avoid restating what had already been said in v.48; MT uses the same word.

The προσήλυτος is defined as τῷ προσελθόντι προσηλύτῳ ἐν ὑμῖν, again showing his independence from the Hebrew patterning. MT has the pattern: articulated noun + articulated participle, which is usually the favored pattern for the adjectival phrase in Exod as well. But Exod uses another good Greek pattern: article + participle + noun. Hex "corrects" the Greek so as to conform to MT.

12:50 Israel fully complied with the divine demands. It is almost word for word the same as v.28 which, however, added ἀπελθόντες before the main verb, whereas here Exod has added an otiose πρὸς αὐτούς after "to Moses and Aaron,"[61] which an A F *O z* variant omits, one suspects, not to conform to MT but for stylistic reasons.

The concluding οὕτως ἐποίησεν is also otiose, for which see the notes at v.28.-- Exod does not render the כל which precedes "Israelites," and hex supplied πάντες.

12:51 A final statement that "on that very day the Lord brought the Israelites out of the land of Egypt with their host. For a discussion of σὺν δυνάμει αὐτῶν see the note at 6:26.

---

58. For a discussion of this see THGE VII.E.3.
59. See SS 160.
60. See Muraoka in Cox, VI Congress, 260-261.
61. Which pattern Helbing 206 renders by "einem etwas an einen auftragen," which seems to me difficult to apply here.

Chapter 13

13:1 Change of subject is shown by δέ. -- For εἶπεν as rendering for ידבר see note at 4:15. -- The direct speech marker at the end of the verse introduces the divine speech of v.2.

13:2 A general statement about the tabu nature of all firstborn. Moses is ordered to sanctify such; precisely what this "render holy" involved in practical terms is not said, but compare vv. 11--13 as well as 22:29--30 and 34:19--20. The term πᾶν πρωτότοκον is defined by an appositional construction as "πρωτογενές opening up any womb among the Israelites from man to beast." The term πρωτογενές is rare in LXX occurring elsewhere only at Prov 31:2, where it also has no Hebrew equivalent. To distinguish it from the more common word it might be rendered "the one born first." This in turn is modified by the participle διανοῖγον "one opening up a womb." The divine claim to the firstborn is all-inclusive of humans and animals. -- With ἐμοί ἐστιν the case is closed; just what belonging to the Lord means is not stated. Even the fact that only males are thus involved is not told until vv.12--13.

13:3 A new section is introduced with a δέ structure. The imperative μνημονεύετε is in the present since memory is a process. This is neatly shown by the Tar which use the imperative (ו) הוו plus the participle זכירין "be remembering." -- Exod uses the classical second aorist forms for ἔρχομαι and its compounds consistently, and not the Hellenistic variant form ἐξηλθατε of A B F *s y*.[1] Exod is also remarkably consistent in distinguishing ממצרים from מצרים מאר'ץ.[2] MT has ממצרים here, and the B *n s* reading ἐκ γης (Αἰγύπτου) is secondary.

The phrase (ἐξ) οἴκου δουλείας was created by Exod to represent בית עבדים "house of slaves," and thereafter became a standard translation of the phrase as describing Egypt, not only in Exod (v.14 20:2) but wherever

---

1. For a discussion of these forms see THGE VII.M.9.
2. This is fully documented in THGE VII.O.

196

the Hebrew phrase recurs (except at Jos 24:17 where it is left out, though added by hex). An expected οικου δουλων never occurs throughout LXX.

The γάρ clause gives the reason for remembrance; it is the exodus by God's powerful hand. χειρὶ κραταιᾷ is used to render the bound phrase חזק יד. In fact, throughout the Pentateuch κραταιός is used only (except for Deut 7:21 describing ὁ θεός) to modify χείρ, after which the word is used frequently in other contexts and only occasionally to describe χείρ.

ὑμᾶς κύριος represents the normal pattern after a verb: personal pronoun in the accusative + subject; in fact 5:21 is the only exception in Exod. A popular hex text has transposed these two words to conform to MT.[3]

The final clause forbids the eating of leaven; though it is not expressly stated the time element must be τὴν ἡμέραν ταύτην. The statement is in the passive with ζύμη as subject, but a Byzantine reading levels this to its context (μνημονεύετε ... ἐξήλθετε ... ἐκπορεύεσθε) by its φαγεσθε, "and not shall you eat (leaven)."

13:4 The reason given for the leaven prohibition is that "today you are going out in the month of new (grains)." ἐν τῇ σήμερον is most unusual, occurring elsewhere in the Pentateuch only at Deut 4:4. In fact, the expression at most occurs at only six other places in LXX. Nor is it due to Hebrew pressure since MT simply has היום. For the use of a nominative personal pronoun + inflected present tense verb see note at 6:29.

MT's month of "Abib" occurs here for the first time (see also 23:15 34:18 twice Deut 16:1 twice) and is always translated by τῶν νεῶν; the phrase mean "new grains" as in Vulg: *novarum frugum;* comp also Lev 2:14 νεά.[4]

13:5 After ἡνίκα the particle ἄν rather than the popular εαν is used by Exod throughout.[5] -- The subject of the verb of the protasis is κύριος ὁ θεός σου (as Sam), all other witnesses having the single name. -- γῆν is modified by a list of seven nations in the genitive plural. This does not conform to MT

3. Cf note in THGE VII.F.1.
4. Aq has τῶν νεάρων which means the same thing.
5. Cf THGE VII.B.

which has only the first five but in a different order, with each one in the singular and all articulated. The tradition had great trouble with the list, omitting some, probably because of homoiot, as well as reordering the list in various ways.[6]

Also modifying γῆν is the relative clause "which he swore to your fathers to give you," a favorite of Deut; comp also v.11. For the phrase γῆν ῥέουσαν γάλα καὶ μέλι see note at 3:8. -- For λατρείαν see the note at 12:25.

13:6 According to MT the people are to eat unleavened cakes for seven days, but Exod follows Sam's "six days," an old text also reflected in Deut 16:8. It is of course quite clear that on the seventh day the people are also to eat unleavened cakes as v.7 makes clear, but what Exod means is: six days of eating unleavened cakes + the seventh as a special day, a total of seven days of unleavened cakes.

The seventh day is a feast of the Lord; in MT this is called a חג which is really a pilgrimage festival, but Exod uses the general word ἑορτή, accurately reflecting what is meant here, since no pilgrimage is envisioned. -- A number of scattered witnesses have κυριω for κυρίου, which reflects the ליהוה of MT more literally. This is, however, coincidence rather than reflection, probably palaeographically inspired since the abbreviated forms of κύριος in the genitive and the dative are easily confused.

13:7 MT has a Niphal inflection in each of its three clauses. Exod follows this pattern only for the middle one by its ὀφθήσεται. Exod changes the first one to an active second plural (ἄζυμα ἔδεσθε), the noun being taken as an accusative, and the last one, presumably for variety's sake, is changed to a neutral ἔσται. In the first clause the verb is modified by an articulated accusative of extent of time, τὰς ἑπτὰ ἡμέρας, articulated to refer to the six days plus seventh discussed in v.6. The omission of τάς by B b is due to a failure to understand the allusion to v.6.

The second clause, in contrast to MT, is asyndetic. What is not to appear is ζυμωτόν, something leavened, whereas ζύμη of clause three is

6. For a full discussion of this list here and elsewhere in Exod see THGE VII.D.5.

the leaven itself; one eats ζυμωτόν but not ζύμη.

The last clause is made even more absolute in Exod: "ζύμη is not to exist for you in all your borders. The *d* reading υιοις for ὁρίοις is palaeographically inspired; "among your sons" is not impossible, but it was certainly not intended.

13:8 As part of the ceremonial of the feast day (ἐν τῇ ἡμέρᾳ ἐκείνῃ) the head of the household is to explain to his son (plural in the *b* text) the rationale of the feast. The statement is given as direct speech as the marker λέγων shows. The explanation is unfortunately rather cryptic; I would translate it as "(It is) because of this (namely that) the Lord God did to me when I went out from Egypt." This is apparently also the way Vulg understood it: *hoc est quod fecit mihi dominus quando egressum sum de Aegypto.* Syntactically ἐποίησεν ... fin is explicative of, or in apposition to, τοῦτο.

Exod also attests to "Lord God" for MT's "Yahweh." This has led to a popular Byzantine variant adding μοι after ἐποίησεν and reading μου for μοι; this then reads: "the Lord my God did to me when...." -- For the expansion of ἐξ to εκ γης, i.e. "from the land (of Egypt)," see comment at v.3.

13:9 The subject of ἔσται is not given; presumably it is the observance of the feast of unleavened cakes. The language is symbolic; the observance is to serve as a sign on one's hand and a memorial before one's eyes, i.e. it must always be kept in mind. That this is what was intended is clear from the variant version in v.16 where for "memorial" it reads ἀσάλευτόν "immoveable.

These constant reminders are to serve a purpose shown by the ὅπως clause, "that the Lord's law may be in your mouth", i.e. that God's law may be a regular topic of conversation.

For the final statement cf comment on v.3. As in v.8 the single divine name of MT becomes κυριος ο θεος (σου) in a substantially supported B variant.[7]

13:10 For φυλάξεσθε an A reading with scattered support has the aorist imperative φυλαξασθε, but the future is usual after καί in Exod. The *n* text with the active φυλάξετε does not change the sense. The singular imperative, φυλάξαι in *f*, is probably a derivative of the A reading. -- For νόμος as a rendering of חקה see note at 12:43.[8]

The phrase κατὰ καιροὺς ὡρῶν is unique in the LXX; the MT reading is למועדה "at its set time," and the doublet rendering represents Exod's attempt at describing the time of the recurrent festival in the cultic year. Already at Gen 1:14 εἰς καιρούς occurs for למועדים. One might have expected either κατα καιρον by itself or καθ ωραν as later in Num 9:2, but Exod has "according to the times of the seasons." This is then further defined by the expression ἀφ᾿ ἡμερῶν εἰς ἡμέρας; this means "from year to year," as a comparison with Jdg 11:40 21:19 1Kgdm 1:3 2:19 proves.

13:11 The use of והיה followed by a protasis of a condition is commonly employed in MT, but it is usually omitted in Exod. Only here does the Hebraic καὶ ἔσται ὡς appear. The other instances in Exod are καὶ ἔσται ἐάν at 4:9 12:26 and καὶ ἔσται ἡνίκα at 13:5.

The subject of εἰσαγάγῃ is the double name κύριος ὁ θεός σου as in Sam; other witnesses have only a single name. -- Only here is τὴν γῆν solely modified by τῶν Χαναναίων; elsewhere the genitive is only one of a list. As elsewhere, however, it represents the singular gentilic of MT, הכנעני.

Within the ὃν τρόπον clause only one dative, τοῖς πατράσιν σου, modifies ὤμοσεν, as in v.5. This "corrects" MT which has לך ולאבתיך; after all the divine oaths were to the patriarchs and not to the people themselves; cf 6:8. Hex duly inserted σοι και so as to equal MT.

The last clause is still part of the protasis and subject to ὡς. Two variant traditions, δωσει as third person and δωσω as first, change the verb to a future indicative, making the clause part of the apodosis[9]

13:12 The apodosis for the ὡς clause of v.11. It consists of two parts, an ἀφελεῖς clause and one with ἁγιάσεις. In the first all male firstborn are to be set aside to the Lord; in the second all male firstborn from the herds or among the cattle are to be sanctified to the Lord. The term for firstborn is

7. For a full discussion of the double name see THGE VII.O. sub 3:18.
8. Instead of νόμον Aq has ἀκρίβασμα, and Sym, πρόσταγμα; these are their usual translations.

"one opening the womb" for which see note at v.2. In the second clause as well as in v.13 MT lacks the word for womb רחם, but Exod Tar and Pesh use the full phrase throughout. Exod uniquely adds τὰ ἀρσενικά to the first clause as well as to the second.

The majority of Greek texts has αφοριεις instead of ἀφελεῖς. Both might be considered possible renderings for עבר, but in LXX only ἀφαιρέω is ever used for עבר (seven times for the Hiphil and three times for the Qal), whereas ἀφορίζω never is. The latter does occur in Exod, twice for הגביל (19:12,23) and three times for the Hiphil or Hophal of נוף in ch. 29. On the other hand, ἀφαιρέω is used to represent seven different Hebrew verbs in Exod. The variant probably arose as an attempt at exegetical clarification. The basic meaning of ἀφαιρέω is "to take away, remove," whereas ἀφορίζω is "to separate," and the latter might be considered more appropriate.

The second clause is asyndetic, over against MT, hex prefixing καὶ. The firstborn are here given as ἐκ τῶν βουκολίων ἢ ἐν τοῖς κτήνεσίν σου "from the herds or among your cattle," where MT has שגר בהמה "litter of cattle." βουκόλια is always used to render שגר (Deut 7:13 28:4,18, 51), but one would expect it to be modified by a genitive, here by τῶν κτηνων. An *f* variant does omit ἢ which at least comes somewhat closer to what MT says. When two classes of animals are given in LXX they are usually τὰ πρόβατα and τοὺς βοάς, and this is probably the distinction which Exod had in mind.

Within the ὅσα clause[10] ἂν is of course original rather than the B *b* + ἐάν.[11] -- The change of σοι to σου in *d* really does not change the sense since the σοι is here a dative of possession.

The main verb for the second clause is ἁγιάσεις, but this has no counterpart in MT; MT attaches the b part of the verse to the first part by means of *waw*, thereby making it a second modifier of העברת. An early tradition omitted ἁγιάσεις and may well betray recensional activity.

13:13 The specific cases of the donkey and that of mankind. That all firstborn belong to the Lord is now clear. But the donkey is an impure animal and may not be sacrificed, nor is human sacrifice permitted. This

---

9. For these see the discussion in THGE M.5.
10. For the clause see SS 59.

verse gives the solution. In the case of the firstling of the donkey one may exchange it for a sheep,[12] or failing that one must pay a ransom. For human firstborn a ransom must be paid.

This is somewhat gentler for donkeys than the rule in MT. Instead of "redeem" the verb is "exchange"; in other words the sheep is a ransom price for the donkey. Alternatively a ransom may be paid instead of וערפתו "and you shall break its neck."[13] After all, donkeys were too valuable to permit their wanton destruction.

The second regulation like the first is also asyndetic over against MT. Human firstborn must be redeemed. The relevant class is here defined as ἀνθρώπου τῶν υἱῶν σου, i.e. the rule of the first born applies only to males. MT's syntax is somewhat clearer since the limiting element is a prepositional phrase בבניך. For a parallel version of this rule see 34:20.

13:14 The protasis contains a time indicator μετὰ ταῦτα "afterwards," a phrase translating כי אחרי at 3:20 11:1,8 34:32, but אחר at 5:1, i.e. with an אחר element in it. Only here does it appear for מחר. In the other ten instances of its occurrence in MT of Exodus it is always rendered by αὔριον. Here, however, the word does mean anytime in the future, and μετὰ ταῦτα carries this sense much better than αὔριον would have done.

The potential question "what is this" asks for the rationale behind the regulation. The first direct speech is marked by λέγων, and the second, unmarked in MT, by ὅτι. For the reply ἐν χειρὶ κρατεῖα κ.τ.λ. see note at v.3. -- The phrase ἐκ γῆς Αἰγύπτου is exceptional in that MT simply has ממצרים.[14] -- For the phrase ἐξ οἴκου δουλείας see note at v.3.

13:15 Change of subject is shown by δέ. The verb ἐσκλήρυνεν is used here in a peculiar way; the verb is transitive and usually has "heart" as object. Here it occurs absolutely and must mean "hardened himself," and then by

---

11. See the evidence given at THGE VII.B.
12. Cf Helbing 246.
13. Aq has this literally as τενοντώσεις "you shall cut through the neck," whereas Theod effects the same result with νωτοκοπήσεις "you shall cut through the back," and Sym calls a spade a spade by his ἀποκτενεῖς. The Three also render all instances of תפדה in the verse by λυτρώσῃ.
14. See the discussion of the problem in THGE VII.O.

202

extension "to refuse."[15] Cf also the note at 7:22. Thus with the complementary infinitive ἐξαποστεῖλαι, "refused to send (us) away."[16]

The subject of the apodosis is uniquely unstated in Exod, but sensibly it could not be the same subject as in the protasis. Hex has added κυριος to conform to the other old witnesses, as the context suggests. -- ἐν γῇ Αἰγύπτῳ appears in *n s* as εν γη αιγυπτου which cannot be Exod.[17]

In MT the word בכור occurs four times in the verse; in Exod the plural πρωτοτόκων occurs when the word is modified by a generic plural, ἀνθρώπων or κτηνῶν, but when it is modified by "all," the singular πρωτότοκον is used. An early popular revision uses the singular in accordance with MT throughout; this probably in turn promoted the variant singular ανθρωπου (for אדם) and κτηνους (for בהמה) in the tradition as well.

The διὰ τοῦτο conclusion is twofold: the firstborn of both animals and man belong to God, but the Israelite speaker deals differently with them. As for animals ἐγὼ θύω, but for people λυτρώσομαι. The former phrase is in the usual pattern for rendering the Hebrew pronoun plus participle. -- The verb is modified by τῷ κυρίῳ, the article representing the preposition in the phrase ליהוה. Exod is by no means consistent in this regard. In fact, of the 50 occurrences of the dative κυρίῳ representing the tetragrammaton, only 11 are articulated.

In the second part Exod designates those who are to be redeemed by class membership, i.e. τῶν υἱῶν μου. The διὰ τοῦτο part of the verse parallels the ἀνθρώπων/κτηνῶν distinction of the preceding clause.

13:16 The phrase ἔσται εἰς is probably to be taken in the sense of "become" as is the Hebrew: היה ל. The subject is still the practice or regulation referred to in τοῦτο of v.14. -- The coordinate term is ἀσάλευτόν "immoveable." This is an interpretation of the more concrete term טוטפת of MT as being constant reminders of the divine act of redemption;[18]

15. Schl renders the clause as *cum obduraret se Pharao, et nollet vos dimittere.*
16. Cf also Thack 54.
17. The discussion in THGE VII.H.3. sub 12:1 demonstrates this clearly.
18. Aq has the translation νακτά "closely pressed materials" as a description of the phylacteries of his day; cf also Deut 6:8 where Aq also has νακτά and

whether Exod actually had something more concrete in mind, i.e. something visible, which might serve as a sign and a constant memorial, is unclear.

The γάρ clause with which the section on the feast of unleavened cakes closes is an exact repetition of v.9, for which see the discussion at v.3. -- The object of the verb in MT is "us," but Exod (as Sam Pesh) has σε, for which see v.9. A popular variant makes it με, and a few witnesses have ημας which equals MT. The textual history is not clear on the matter of the pronoun.

13:17 The beginning of a new section is shown by δέ. Note the different ways in which Exod rendered the Hebrew construction of ב + bound infinitive. The first one follows on ויהי which is normally disregarded by Exod when it is followed by an infinitival construction; בשלח is then rendered by a temporal protasis structure ὡς ἐξαπέστειλεν. Later in the verse בראתם occurs as a temporal condition for the repentance of the people, and Exod renders this well by an attributive participle (τῷ λαῷ) ἰδόντι.

The most direct road from Egypt to Canaan was the coastal road, here called the ὁδὸν γῆς Φυλιστιίμ. It might have been the expected route for the Israelites ὅτι ἐγγὺς ἦν "because it was nearby." Yet God did not lead them along the expected road, but insisted on a desert journey.

God's statement itself is a μήποτε governing two clauses, the first with the impersonal verb μεταμέλει, but in the aorist subjunctive with a dative of person in turn modified by an attributive participle ἰδόντι πόλεμον,[19] and the second with ἀποστρέψῃ with the τῷ λαῷ of the first clause as subject. The participle gives the condition which might promote the repentance. What is meant is that God feared that the people might repent when "they saw war" and in consequence would return to Egypt. Future indicative spellings for the aorist subjunctive verbs in the tradition are simply itacisitic; after μήποτε the subjunctive was standard usage.

As for the various spellings of Φυλιστιίμ in the tradition all of them are itacistic. Th ending -ιίμ for the transcription of the plural gentilic ending is conventional. Actually I suspect that -ιειμ might well have been used originally. After all, phonetically a semivocalic glide did and does separate the two /i/ phonemes, and the almost universally appearing -ιειμ ending makes one wonder whether it might not have been original.

13:18 This verse is the positive counterpart to v.17. Exod has ὁδὸν εἰς τὴν ἔρημον for MT's "way of the desert."[20] The phrase εἰς τὴν ἐρυθρὰν θάλασσαν is appositional to the preceding εἰς phrase; i.e. the way leading into the desert is also the way leading to the Red Sea. Hex changes the word order of the noun phrase to conform to MT's יַם סוּף. For the translation see note at 10:19.

The second sentence introduces a different idea entirely as the δέ structure shows. It begins with a dative of time when, πέμπτῃ γενεᾷ, "in the fifth generation," Exod's interpretation of the controversial חֲמֻשִׁים of MT.[21] More commonly the word is thought to mean "armed in battle array," an interpretation followed by the ancient witnesses, thus **mzynyn** Tar[P] Pesh; **mzrzyn** Tar[O]; Vulg: **armati**.[22] This meaning for the Hebrew word is secure elsewhere as at Jos 1:14 and 4:12 where LXX has εὔζωνοι and διεσκευασμένοι resp. But Exod's interpretation is consistent with the tradition of four generations of Israel's stay in Egypt; cf 6:16ff. -- Instead of ἐκ γῆς (Αἰγύπτου) an A *n* reading has ἐξ.[23]

13:19 Moses in accordance with the demands of Joseph in Gen 50:25 took the latter's bones along with him. Instead of μεθ' ἑαυτοῦ an *O b* text has the more usual μετ αυτου, with no change in meaning.

Exod twice uses identical patterns to render MT's pattern: cognate infinitive + finite verb, using a cognate dative noun to render the free infinitive. The first one is in a γάρ clause giving the reason for the transport of the bones; viz. Joseph had made the Israelites swear an oath. Exod (as Sam) names the new subject since without it one might momentarily think that Moses was also the subject of ὥρισκεν. Both B* and Eth omit ' Ιωσήφ; this equals MT, but is probably mere coincidence.

Deut has ἀσάλευτά (plural because of MT).
19. Cf Helbing 112.
20. See SS 69.
21. Theod also felt that the word had something to do with "five," rendering it πεμπταίζοντες "on the fifth day."
22. Cf also Aq:ἐνωπλισμένοι, and Sym: ὁπλῖται.

The direct speech marker λέγων introduces the exact words of Joseph. It is indeed closely similar to Gen 50:25. In Gen the cognate dative is introduced by ἐν τῇ and succeeded by ᾗ; furthermore the subject of ἐπισκέψεται is ὁ θεός rather than κύριος, the latter being unique here among the old witnesses. One might well suspect that Exod knew the Gen text.

The translation of the root פקד by ἐπισκοπέω was also made at 3:16 and 4:31 (see note at 3:16); the translation has become a cliche, and so here has taken on the meaning of פקד; i.e. God not only watches over, but actively comes to his people in redemptive fashion, he visits them.[24] -- Exod uses his common pattern: verb + accusative pronoun + subject instead of MT's: verb + subject + prepositional (את) phrase. A popular A F M hex text "corrects" the order to conform to MT.

The last clause is almost identical to that of Gen 50:25. An A d n itacistic variant has συνανοισεται, thus taking the accusative τὰ ὀστᾶ as nominative. This makes good sense, but it is not Exod. The original μου τὰ ὀστᾶ is only sparsely supported; the popular rendering with μου at the end is probably hex, but could be based on Gen.

13:20 Change of subject is indicated by δέ. Exod alone of the old witnesses identifies the subject as οἱ υἱοὶ ' Ισραήλ, though the context makes this obvious. According to 12:37 the people had proceded from Egypt to Succoth. Now they move from Succoth to a place on the edge (παρά) of the desert called Othom. For moving, ויסעו, from a place, i.e. pulling up stakes, Exod uses ἐξάραντες, aorist participle of ἐξαίρω, which had already been used in Gen 35:5 in a similar way. Presumably it meant "to raise, lift up" the tent or tent stakes preparatory to moving. -- For variant spellings of Succoth cf the notes on 12:37.-- For ויחנו Exod here uses the excellent translation ἐστρατοπέδευσαν "they encamped"; it also occurs at 14:2, but it never again occurs as a translation for the root חנה; instead παρεμβάλλω becomes popular, especially throughout Num; cf Gen 33:18 as well as its first use in Exod at 14:9.

---

23. See discussion in THGE VII.O.
24. For the broad usage of this verb as an equivalent for פקד see J.W.Wevers in the Orlinsky Festschrift, ERETZ-ISRAEL XVI, pp. 235*ff.

Their next encampment was at ' Oθόμ. Since the place was totally unknown to Greek copyists, errors of transcription are numerous. Some are phonetically based, those in which one or both *omicron*s become *omega*. Since the preceding word is ἐν, dittography also produced νοθομ, which in turn by transposition could produce ονθομ, ονθωμ, developing into αναθομ and αναθωμ as well. The spelling ιωθομ is the result of partial dittography based on EN appearing before the name. Still more removed from the original are οθωθ and αθωθ, and one spelling even revised on the basis of the Masoretic pronunciation ηθαμ. The name also occurs at Num 33:6--8 but there the translator went wild.[25]

The final prepositional phrase παρὰ τὴν ἔρημον is a good rendering of MT's בקצה המדבר "on the edge of the desert."[26] Of some interest is an anonymous reading on M[mg]: (εἰς) τὴν ἐρημοτάτην, the superlative of ἔρημος, thus "to a very dry place." Sine קשה means "limit," hence "edge," the translator has understood קשה המדבר as "the limit of the dry place," i.e. the very driest of places.

13:21 Change of subject is shown by δέ. Exod uniquely has ὁ θεός as subject for יהוה of MT. The reverse was true in v.19, and it seems evident that Exod did not always carefully distinguish between יהוה and אלהים; only where it was important to use κύριος rather than ὁ θεός did he carefully reflect his parent text. That variations between Exod and MT in this regard always reflect a different parent text for Exod is most unlikely, particularly in view of the fact that the opposition in such cases is almost always Exod over against all the old witnesses.

The predicate is ἡγεῖτο, an imperfect representing the Hebrew participle, since continuity of action is implied for past time: "God was leading them"[27] for MT's "Yahweh was going before them." This is then explicated by a contrastive μέν ... δέ structure. The first of these is in the genitive, i.e. "during the day," but the second is in the articulated accusative τὴν (δέ) νύκτα which designates the extent of time involved, thus "throughout the night." The raison d'etre for the "pillar of cloud" is given by

25. According to cod M The Three read ' Hθάν; the tradition is probably corrupted from *ηθαμ.
26. Cf SS 69.

a purposive infinitive "to show them the way," but for the pillar of fire, no such explanation is given in Exod, though all the other witnesses do supply it. Hex has dutifully filled (from Sym Theod) the lacuna: του φαινειν αυτοις οδευειν ημερας και νυκτος. It is difficult to imagine Exod's intentionally excising this statement, and his parent text was probably defective as the result of homoiar, skipping from (האיר)ל to (א)ל.

13:22 A concluding summary statement. The verb is ἐξέλιπεν "failed, left." An A F O *n y* variant text has the imperfect εξελειπεν, which is an itacistic spelling error for the aorist. The aorist is a good rendering for ימיש which must be understood as an old preterite tense "did not depart, move" (cf also 33:11, where, however, Exod renders by an imperfect). The continual presence of these two pillars by day and night resp. is said to be ἐναντίον παντὸς τοῦ λαοῦ. Other witnesses have no equivalent for παντός.

---

27. See Helbing 117.

Chapter 14

14:2 Directions for a new encampment. According to 13:20 they were at Othom on the edge of the desert. Now they are to "turn back (from the edge of the wilderness) and encamp in front of the settlement between Magdol and the sea, opposite Beelsepphor," and then "before them you shall encamp by the sea." This is obviously intended to prepare the way for the wondrous crossing of the sea. Somewhat puzzling is τῆς ἐπαύλεως. The word refers to an unwalled settlement or village,, and stands for the Hebrew פי החירת usually taken as a place name. ἔπαυλις often translates חצר (or חוה), and החצרת (or החורת) is often suggested as parent text here, but had this been the case here it would also have had to have been present in v.9. Exod apparently understood פי החירת to be an unwalled settlement; after all he rendered it by ἐπαύλεως twice, here and in v.9.

The name Magdol preserves the contemporary pronunciation of Masoretic *Migdol.* A few witnesses have assimilated the second vowel to the first and have μαγδαλ(ου), and some *C* mss have lost the *gamma* to produce μαδωλου. -- By "the sea" is meant the ἐρυθρὰν θάλασσαν (ים סוף), for which see note at 10:19. The *C* variant which changed (ἀνὰ μέσον) τῆς θαλάσσης to της επαυλεως is simply a senseless mistake based on its occurrence a line earlier.

The place Βεελσεπφών is unfortunately just as unknown as the places designated "the settlement" and "Magdol." It was obviously near the Sea. It was popularly misspelled without a *pi.* Odd misspellings are βεελσεφωρ and a unique βεθλεπφων.

In the final clause the Israelites are told to encamp ἐνώπιον αὐτῶν, the αὐτῶν presumably referring to "the settlement" and Βεελσεπφών.[1] -- In changing from third to second person Exod uses the singular; presumably the translator had "people" as a singular word in mind, but it remains odd.

---

1. Syh yields some evidence on The Three and their rendering of נכחו. Aq rendered it by "straight over against him," whereas Sym had "opposite him" (ἐξ ἐνατίας αὐτοῦ), and Theod left Exod unchanged.

14:3 This verse and the next continue the speech of the Lord. Exod solved the problem of the peculiar Hebrew text which has Pharaoh speaking to the Israelites, which is absurd. The other old translations have taken לבני ישראל as though the preposition were על, i.e. "concerning the Israelites." Exod simply added τῷ λαῷ αὐτοῦ as addressee and then made "the Israelites" nominative, i.e. subject of πλανῶνται. But Exod has also rendered הוא by an otiose οὗτοι; it would seem that he did have MT as parent text. The tradition shows different attempts at fixing up the text. A very popular B reading omitted τῷ λαῷ αὐτοῦ, apparently an early attempt at revising towards MT. Another popular A F M tradition has περι των υιων instead of οἱ υἱοί, approximating the על interpretation referred to above.

The Exod pattern: present tense + pronoun renders MT: participle + pronoun; this pattern is syntactically the predicate for οἱ υἱοί 'Ισραήλ. It could then be rendered as "As for the Israelites they are wandering about in the land."

The final clause is asyndetic in MT but is a γάρ clause in Exod, i.e. giving the reason for the wandering about. An A F z variant omits γάρ which does equal MT but the causal relationship between the desert enclosing them and their wandering about is not immediately obvious and the shorter text may be a simplification. For συγκέκλεικεν an s reading has a blend form συγκεκλεισεν, i.e. a perfect prefix with an aorist inflection.

14:4 Change of subject to ἐγώ is shown by δέ. For ἐσκλήρυνω see note at 4:21. God's hardening of Pharaoh's heart now will involve his pursuit after the Israelites. An f variant has υμων instead of αὐτῶν, as does Pesh, but Pesh also reintroduces the verse with "And the Lord said to Moses," making "your" contextually acceptable.

The real point behind the hardening, behind the entire confrontation between God (through Moses) and Pharaoh from chapter 5 onwards is here bluntly stated: "And I will be glorified by Pharaoh and by all his army, and all the Egyptians shall know that I am the Lord." It is now quite clear that the Exodus account is *ad maiorem gloriam dei*. Pharaoh and his army by their annihilation will be the instruments by which God is glorified, and in turn God will be recognized by all Egyptians as the Lord. But "the Lord" represents here the divine name; not rule or sovereignty is the primary issue, but recognition, identification.

An A F + reading has στρατεια for στρατιᾷ. The itacism does produce a sensible text, since στρατεια means "expedition, campaign" which might well characterize Pharaoh's pursuit of the Israelites.

Only Exod witnesses to παντές (the Egyptians), but its omission in a *b* variant is not necessarily a revision towards MT. -- A popular F M reading omits the verb in ἐγώ εἰμι and technically equals MT's אנ י. But אנ י is sometimes rendered by ἐγώ and at times by ἐγώ εἰμι, and the shorter text is merely a stylistic variant.

The final statement records the Israelites conpliance with the orders to encamp; cf.v.1.

14:5 The subject of the passive ἀνηγγέλη is the ὅτι clause. -- The second clause also has a passive verb "was changed"; its subject, ἡ καρδία, is modified by two genitives Φαραώ and τῶν θεραπόντων αὐτοῦ, and a B + variant unnecessarily repeats η καρδια before the second one as well. The prepositional phrase, ἐπί with accusative, means "as over against the people"- signifying wherein the heart of Pharaoh and his servants had changed.

This is then explained by what εἶπαν.[2] The main verb in the direct speech is in the perfect, for which the B *z* text has the inferior aorist form εποιησεν.[3] The verb is modified by a marked complementary infinitive τοῦ ἐξαποστεῖλαι with τοὺς υἱοὺς ᾽Ισραήλ as object, which is what ישראל of MT intends. -- The final marked infinitive with negative particle modifies the earlier infinitive; it is purposive in character, or more specifically shows the outcome or result of the dismissal of the Israelites.

14:6 Pharaoh suited the deed to the word; the relationship is indicated by οὖν: "so Pharaoh readied his chariots." Exod alone names Pharaoh as subject, thereby removing all possible ambiguity. Its omission by *x* is unlike-

2. For the secondary character of the variant second aorist ειπον see the discussion in THGE VII.M.9.
3. See the note in THGE VII.H.5.

ly to be the result of MT influence. Another text, *oI C y*, has δε instead of οὖν, by which change of subject would be shown. -- The verb used really means "to tie up as a yoke," hence "to span in," i.e. Pharaoh hitched up his chariots.

The second clause has the object preposed, in which Exod's unique "all" represents the same impulse that in v.4 promoted παντές before "the Egyptians." The compound verb chosen for the gathering of the people for departure was συναπήγαγεν; an F *n s y* variant simplified this by συνηγαγεν, whereas the C text, probably the result of careless copying, had συνεπηγαγεν, though its meaning is close to Exod. -- The change of ἑαυτοῦ to αυτου in F *t* in the phrase μεθ᾿ ἑαυτοῦ represents the Attic elided αὑτοῦ, rarely found in the Greek of the LXX.

14:7 A third clause describing Pharaoh's preparations for pursuit of the people. A B *x* variant has a participle λαβων for the finite ἔλαβεν which is quite at odds with the style of Exod.[4] Exod's "and all the cavalry" is rather more sensible than MT's "and all the chariotry." Though רכב means "chariotry" and not "cavalry" there are occasional instances of ἵππος used for רכב in the later books; cf ἵππος ἐπίλεκτος for רכב ברזל at Jos 17:16, 18, as well as 3Kgdm 16:9 and 2Chr 21:9.

Also included were the τριστάτας ἐπὶ πάντων. The noun was chosen to represent שלשם;[5] these are officials of some kind in charge of πάντων, i.e. of chariots and cavalry. In origin the word may well mean an officer of the third rank.[6]

14:8 Here the first two clauses of v.4 are reported in third person with a few differences: Pharaoh is here identified as βασιλέως Αἰγύπτου, and (ὀπίσω) αὐτῶν becomes τῶν υἱῶν ᾿Ισραήλ. In the tradition αιγυπτιων occurs as a popular variant to Αἰγύπτου, but this is almost certainly not original. Αἰγυπτίων occurs frequently in Exod, but is always articulated except in the

---

4. See the discussion of participial variants for finite verbs in THGE VII.M.1.
5. Note Sym's rendering by ἀνὰ τρεῖς. From Syh Aq's reading may be restored as τρισσούς; Theod retained the reading of Exod.
6. Though Schl's translation *tres regni proceres* can hardly be correct. Interesting is a definition in a Lex. of Cyril quoted by Schl as τοὺς παρὰ

set phrase ἐκ χειρὸς Αἰγυπτίων. -- Another popular B variant has added καὶ θεραποντων αυτου after Αἰγύπτου; this is obviously added under the influence of v.5. This in turn led to κατεδιωξαν for the singular in the next clause; the singular is original, however, with Pharaoh as the unstated subject.

The δέ construction of the last clause indicates change of subject to οἱ υἱοὶ ᾿Ισραήλ. The verb is appropriately imperfect as a rendering of the Hebrew participle יצאים. The clause is probably best taken in conjunction with the next clause rather than with v.8. Thus: "The Israelites had been going out defiantly (literally "with a high hand"), and the Egyptians pursued."

14:9 The main verb of the second clause is εὗρον, the classical second aorist form which represents Exod usage rather than the Hellenistic ευροσαν of the B x z text.[7] The perfect participle παρεμβεβληκότος is now used to represent חנים; cf the comment on חנה at 13:20. The word has been simplified in *f x* by omitting the middle element of the compound, i.e. παραβεβληκοτος, but the root παραβάλλω is used in LXX only rarely and never for חנה.

The prepositional phrase is with παρά rather than with επι as in v.2, but with no change in meaning. A *d* reading rather oddly has εις την θαλασσαν which seems to have the Israelites tenting in the sea; of course, "near" or "by" the sea is meant.

The compound subject of the nominal clause differs somewhat from MT; Exod has the first two elements "all the cavalry and the chariotry of Pharaoh," whereas MT has "all the horses of the chariotry of Pharaoh." With this one might also compare MT at v.23: "all the horses of Pharaoh, his chariotry," which Exod renders by "all the cavalry of Pharaoh and the chariotry." Exod throughout renders סוס by ἡ ἵππος, "cavalry," except for the plural סוסים at 9:3 which is of course rendered by "horses." -- The third and fourth items of the subject are "the horsemen and his army," hex also having "his" with "horsemen" to conform to MT. A popular Byzantine group variant has transposed the two nouns for no obvious reason, possibly to separate ἡ ἵππος and οἱ ἱππεῖς as much as possible.

The predicate is ἀπέναντι τῆς ἐπαύλεως which is in turn modified by ἐξ ἐναντίας Βεελσεπφών; for both of these phrases see notes at v.2.[8] -- Variants in spelling of Βεελσεπφών include not only the popular βεελσεφων as in v.2, but by haplography in the opening syllable as βελ., by assimilation of π to φ for βεελσεφφων, by apocopation of the final consonant, βεελσεπφω, and even such oddities as βεελσεφωρ and βελσεεφωμ.

14:10 The first clause is a transition statement related both to the preceding and the following statement. The verb προσῆγεν is here used without an accusative modifier. The verb is usually transitive and presumably it here means "brought (himself) near," i.e. advanced, came near.[9] προσάγω is commonly used for the Hiphil of קרב in the tabernacle accounts later in the book, but even more regularly in the sense of "bring near" a sacrifice in Lev and Num. A popular variant omits the *sigma*, i.e. προηγεν, but this is certainly the result of a copyist's error.

The idiom "looking up with the eyes" occurs only here in Exod but was common in Gen, as a rendering for raising the eyes" in Hebrew. A few witnesses omit τοῖς ὀφθαλμοῖς as tautologous, and a hex plus of αυτων is a revision towards MT.[10] A *b* variant reorders τοῖς ὀφθαλμοῖς after ὁρῶσιν which is no improvement whatsoever. -- There is no equivalent for ὁρῶσιν in MT though Sam has וירא before יהוה. On the other hand Exod has no equivalent for הנה having only καί after ὁρῶσιν; hex as expected does add ἰδού.

A popular tradition has changed the καὶ οἱ of Exod to οι δε, thereby showing the change of subject. Oddly the coordinate clause "and they were very afraid" shows no change in subject, but the last clause is not only a δέ structure but also names οἱ υἱοὶ ' Ισραήλ as subject. From this it would appear that "the Egyptians" is the subject of ἐφοβήθησαν, though the sense demands otherwise. One can only conclude that Exod did not translate

χεῖρα τοῦ βασιλέως τοὺς ἔχοντας λόγχας ἀνὰ τρεῖς κατὰ χεῖρα.
7. Cf THGE VII.M.9.
8. For the first of these Aq and Theod have ἐπὶ Φιϊαρώθ, a literal rendering of MT. Sym translates the first element of the place name, ἐπὶ τοῦ στόματος τῆς ' Ιαρώθ.
9. Aq and Sym sensibly have ἤγγισεν "came near," this in spite of the fact

214

clearly at this point. It should also be said that ἐστρατοπέδευσαν does not accurately represent נסע which means the opposite of "encamp"; viz. "to pull stakes, move." But the Exod account says that the Egyptians were encamped behind them.

The final clause can best be taken as the beginning of v.11, i.e. "the Israelites called out to the Lord; and they said to Moses"; the calling out to the Lord meant in real terms a bitter complaint to Moses.

14:11 That Exod preferred the Hellenistic εἶπαν to the classical ειπον of the Byzantine text is well established.[11] -- The prepositional παρά construction with which the speech of the Israelites begins gives the "necessary and sufficient cause or motive."[12] Exod idiomatically disregards the tautological אין after מבלי in MT simply by παρὰ τὸ μὴ ὑπάρχειν "because there were no (graves)."

The popular omission of γῆ in ἐν γῆ Αἰγύπτῳ is a posthexaplaric revision to produce a text closer to MT. The word is under the obelus in Syh, showing that the word though absent in the Hebrew was present in Origen's text. The verb which the prepositional phrase modifies is ἐξήγαγες, in turn modified by the accusative ἡμᾶς plus purposive infinitive θανατῶσαι; a Byzantine text variant which changes the infinitive to αποκτειναι changes the sense. ἡμᾶς is then no longer the subject of the infinitive but its preposed object: "to kill us"; compare 16:3.

In the final querulous question introduced by the interrogative τί "why," the nominative participle is explicative of the ἐποίησεν ἡμῖν; the majority reading adds an expected ημας which is a hex addition made under MT influence. -- The F s variant εκ γης for ἐξ is not original.[13]

14:12 The demonstrative pronoun in the opening statement is proleptic, anticipatory of the direct speech introduced by its marker λέγοντες. Then τὸ ῥῆμα is defined by πάρες ... Αἰγυπτίοις 1°. Exod puts "the word" in the past by adding ἦν. A b reading puts this in the present which negates the nice distinction which Exod made, viz. this was the matter we had already

---

that MT has הקריב.
10. Cf SS 93.
11. See the documentation in THGE VII.M.9.

raised in Egypt. A z variant places the verb after τὸ ῥῆμα which change is unfortunate since this would make the pronoun attributive. -- A well supported M variation in word order has πρὸς σέ after Αἰγύπτῳ, thereby unnecessarily separating the addressee from the verb of speaking.

The direct speech introduced by λέγοντες ends with the ὅπως clause. That the Israelites had been unhappy with Moses' interference is clear from 5:21; compare also 6:9. -- πάρες is an aorist imperative which is modified by a final clause, ὅπως with an aorist subjunctive. What the Israelites had said was "Leave us alone in order that...."

The γάρ clause gives the rationale for what the Israelites had said. One might be surprised that the Israelites wanted to be left alone to pursue their enslaved existence, but the alternative was worse, viz. "to die in this desert." The comparative κρεῖσσον[14] occurs in an *n* variant in its Attic spelling κρειττον.[15] A popular M Byzantine reading has added ην after γάρ, a stylistic variant probably influenced by ἦν earlier in the verse whereby a specious balance might be achieved. The first infinitive, δουλεύ-ειν, is in present tense, but the second, ἀποθανεῖν, is aorist, since the former is a process, but the second is not. The subject of the first infinitive is stated as ἡμᾶς, and carries over to the second as well. Exod (as Pesh) has added a demonstrative modifying ἐρήμῳ over against MT, thereby heightening the tension of the narrative.

14:13 Moses' words of encouragement to the people are stated positively in Exod; instead of the negative "do not be afraid," Exod has θαρσεῖτε "take courage"; compare 20:20 and Gen 35:17. The second imperative is στῆτε, for which a popular A variant has στηκετε, from στήκω, a verbal root formed from ἕστηκα, the perfect of ἵστημι; it is a present imperative and makes just as good sense as the aorist of ἵστημι of Exod. It translates התיצבו, for which equation see also 8:20 9:13.

The act of redemption, σωτηρίαν, is characterized as τὴν παρὰ τοῦ θεοῦ, used to call special attention to the source of the saving act which is about to be enacted. MT simply has את ישועת יהוה. The Exod text is but sparsely supported by the witnesses but that it is original is clear from

12. LS s.v. C.III.7; cf also Bauer s.v. III.5.
13. See the discussion in THGE VII.O.

the pattern of support in the tradition. Eleven mss have κυριου for τοῦ θεοῦ but over 80 mss have του κυριου; but κυρίου is anarthrous in Exod. What seems to have happened is that an early prehexaplaric revision changed θεοῦ to κυριου on the basis of MT, with a further correction, mainly C, dropping the article. -- σωτηρία is also modified by a relative clause: "which he will perform for you today." In the tradition ὑμῖν has become ημιν in the majority of witnesses. The two forms are homophonous; to know which is original one does not count mss, but one looks at the Hebrew which is לכם.16

The nature of the saving act which God is presently going to perform is rather delicately stated in the rest of the verse, given as a γάρ statement, though it really does not give a reason at all but rather an explanation. "For," says Exod, "as you have seen the Egyptians today, you will not ever again see them any more." Exod's προσθήσεσθε ἔτι represents MT's תסיפו "add, do again" plus עוד "yet, again," somewhat tautologous but intentionally used for emphasis. ἔτι follows immediately on the verb in Exod, but is reordered by hex to follow αὐτούς as in MT. Neither the passive προστεθησεσθε of s nor the active προσθησετε of n is lexically significant.

What I have rendered by "ever ... anymore" is an attempt to render the phrase εἰς τὸν αἰῶνα χρόνον. The usual phrase for עד עולם found in LXX is εἰς τὸν αἰῶνα. The full phrase does not occur until Isaiah where it occurs (seven times) for different Hebrew phrases, but all in the sense of "for a long time." The only other occurrence in LXX is in Bar 3:32. But compare also εἰς τὸν ἀεὶ χρόνον in 3Macc 3:29 as well as its concluding words (7:23) εἰς τοὺς ἀεὶ χρόνους.

14:14 A promise and an admonition. Israel can take courage since "the Lord will fight for you." There is some uncertainty as to the preposition "for." Instead of περί a popular F M reading has υπερ. Both mean "on behalf of, about, for," but the older texts have περί. The itacistic ημων of C f for ὑμῶν is sensible but wrong as the Hebrew לכם shows.

---

14. Cf SS 146.
15. For a discussion of κρεῖσσων vs κρειττων see Thack 121--123.
16. Cf also THGE VII.G.9.

The admonition ὑμεῖς σιγήσετε refers to clamorings and complaints. Israel is to trust the Lord and remain quiet. A popular variant to the verb is the more common future σιγησεσθε.[17]

14:15 Change of section is shown by δέ. The question "why do you call out to me?" interrupts the usual formula: "The Lord said to Moses: speak to the Israelites." Since a new section starts here the question is unexpected as the beginning of divine speech. In any event the Israelites are to move on.[18]

14:16 Moses' instructions. He is to raise his staff, stretch out his hand over the sea and break it up. For the accusative τὴν ῥάβδον (σου) B 129 have the dative, probably under the influence of 7:20; but here MT does not have the במטה of 7:20 but rather את מטך which is normally rendered in Greek by a direct object of a transitive verb; for the same idiom cf 10:13. Each of the three imperatives is in the aorist as might be expected: raise, stretch out, break up.

The point of all these actions is given coordinately in the last clause that "the Israelites may enter the middle of the sea on dry ground." Semantically these symbolic actions are used to change the course of nature; the raising of the staff and the stretching out of the hand both play this kind of role throughout the plague story; both are involved in 7:19 8:5,16,17, as well as the staff in the hand at 7:17; the staff is also used singly at 7:9--12,20, 10:13, while the hand is stretched out at 8:6 9:22,23 10:12 and 14:26; at 17:9 the staff is called ἡ ῥάβδος τοῦ θεοῦ (ἐν τῇ χειρί μου). The Hellenistic εισελθετωσαν of A B F for the classical second aorist form is clearly secondary.[19] It is modified by εἰς μέσον; the C variant εν μεσω seems quite inappropriate after εἰσελθέτωσαν; it demonstrates that the ἐις/ἐν distinction had completely broken down in Byzantine times.

14:17 For God hardening Pharaoh's heart see note at 4:21. A *b* variant changes the initial καί to a δε structure, thereby showing change of subject. An interesting reading is that of *b n s* στερεω for σκληρυνῶ. The form is

17. According to LS the active ending is a later form.
18. For ἀναζευξάτωσαν The Three have *tollent* (for ἀράτωσαν?; from the Syh) "let them raise."

the present tense of στερεόω, showing the common LXX pattern for rendering the Hebrew participle. One suspects its source to be one of The Three, but compare also Jer 5:3 (and 10:4 52:6).

MT does not refer to the heart of Pharaoh, but only to the "heart of Egypt," whereas Exod has Φαραὼ καὶ τῶν Αἰγυπτίων πάντων. The addition of Φαραὼ καί may well be textual since a Qumran ms (4Q 365) also attests to it. πάντων is probably an adaptation to v.4 which this verse and the next reflect.

For ἐνδοξασθήσομαι ... στρατιᾷ αὐτοῦ see the comments on v.4. V.17, however, amplifies the statement of v.4 by "and by the chariots and by his horses." The first "and" (also in Pesh Vulg) represents a coordinate string of four prepositional phrases, whereas the other old witnesses have two pairs. Only Exod and Vulg lack a possessive pronoun with "chariots," hex of course adding αυτου. The last unit, τοῖς ἵπποις αὐτοῦ, both here and in v.18, stands for פרשיו "his horsemen" in MT; in v.9 the Hebrew noun is more literally rendered by οἱ ἱππεῖς.

14:18 The main clause is word for word the same as the fourth clause of v.4 and the first part of 7:5; cf note at 7:5. For ὅτι ἐγώ εἰμι κύριος see note at 6:2. -- For πάντες, represented only in Sam of the other old witnesses see note at 7:5.

The genitive absolute construction is appropriate being set over against the subject "all the Egyptians"; i.e. the ἐγώ εἰμι κύριος which immediately precedes the construction is not directly related, but is a ὅτι clause modifying γνώσονται. Over against v.17 only three phrases modify the participle instead of four, though it might be noted that Sam and Pesh add ובכל חילו after "Pharaoh," obviously taken from v.17. -- ἐν τοῖς ἅρμασιν has no genitive pronoun but hex supplies an αυτου; the ἐν in the phrase governs both τοῖς ἅρμασιν and ἵπποις and a popular hex reading adds εν τοις before ἵπποις as well so as to conform to MT.

14:19 ἐξῆρεν δέ occurs twice, in both cases with change of subject. This verse is the first reference to Israel's guiding angel; cf also 23:20,23 32:34, whereas in 33:2 God's angel has a different function. Here he is "the one who goes before the camp of the Israelites" (not simply "Israel" as the other old witnesses). Both angel and pillar of cloud (cf 40:30--31) went up before the Israelites, and both moved to a position behind them. The end phrases differ, however, as ἐκ τῶν ὄπισθεν "at the rear" and ἐκ τῶν ὀπίσω αὐτῶν "behind them" resp.; in MT these are both מֵאַחֲרֵיהֶם. Both phrases in Exod have the unusual ἐκ τῶν to begin the phrase, presumably to represent the initial preposition מִן as well as the plural form אַחֲרֵי. The phrase ἐκ τῶν ὀπίσω also occurs at 26:22 but for quite a different Hebrew. Beyond that it occurs in the LXX only five times. With ὄπισθεν it occurs only here in the Pentateuch, though seven times elsewhere in LXX.[20] The hex tradition has added αυτων after ὄπισθεν, thereby recognizing the suffix in the Hebrew phrase. The καί in ἐξῆρεν δὲ καί is omitted by C presumably since it seemed otiose.

14:20 The subject of the first clause though unspecified must be the ὁ στύλος τῆς νεφέλης of v.19, which came in between the two camps. Now the action in (at least the second part of) v.19 becomes clear; by moving behind the camp the cloud now separates the two. The Byzantine text included the angel as well by making the verb εἰσῆλθεν plural. At the end of this statement a B *f z* variant introduced a gloss και εστη from v.19.[21]

The next part is quite obscure in MT. What it says is "And there was the cloud and the darkness, and it made light the night." Tar[O] interpreted this as "and there was the cloud, and it was dark to the Egyptians, and to Israel it was light all night." Tar[P] at rather greater length has the same notion.[22]

Exod has a different interpretation: "and there was gloom and darkness, and night intervened." The first clause reflects on the pillar of cloud; for those behind (the cloud had moved to the rear) it meant σκότος καὶ γνόφος. A popular F M variant has transposed the two nouns but this really makes no great difference; it could in no way have been inspired by

---

19. See THGE VII.M.9.
20. According to HR.
21. Cf THGE VII.O.
22. Aq has translated word for word: καὶ ἐγένετο ἡ νεφέλη καὶ τὸ σκότος καὶ ἐφώτισε σὺν τὴν νύκτα. Sym did try to make some sense out of it: καὶ ἦν ἡ νεφέλη σκότος μὲν ἐκεῖθεν φαίνουσα δὲ ἐντεῦθεν "and there was

220

the Hebrew! καὶ διῆλθεν ἡ νύξ serves as the setting for the final clause, and one might then translate as "since the night intervened, they (unspecified, but the Egyptians and Israel are obviously meant) could not mix with one another during the entire night.[23]

14:21 Change of subject is shown by δέ. That the stretching out of the hand by Moses was symbolic of a divine action, as the note at v.16 suggests, is clearly shown here. "Moses stretched forth..., and the Lord reduced the sea...." Exod in good Greek style simply has "hand," but hex adds αυτου to conform to MT.

The verb in the second clause, ὑπήγαγεν, is particularly appropriate since it means to "bring under (the power)." That is more than can be said for the well-supported *f* reading, επηγαγεν, "to bring in, bring forth"; the variant is palaeographically inspired, copyists often confusing the two prepositional prefixes. -- As means for controlling the sea the Lord used a "strong south wind" blowing all night; for the Alexandrian use of νότῳ "south"[24] instead of "east" קדים, see the note at 10:13.

The omission of ἐν by a *C x* text is probably palaeographically inspired with the letters αυ both preceding and following it; the meaning does not change, since it leaves a dative of means (without ἐν).

The result of the blowing of a strong south wind was twofold: the sea became dry and the waters were split. The first of these is stated somewhat ambiguously since the subject of ἐποίησεν is not given; the clause is joined to the preceding by καί so that one might take the subject to be the same for both clauses, viz. κύριος. This clearly is so in MT, but in Exod the subject could also be the wind. Or did Exod intentionally leave it ambiguous, since the wind was, after all, the Lord's instrument? -- For "dry" Exod has ξηράν, whereas MT has a prepositional phrase לחרבה.[25]

For the second result Exod used the simplex ἐσχίσθη, "was divided, separated"; a popular A F M variant has a compound, διεσχίσθη, which

---

the cloud: darkness thence but shining hence"; Sym reflects the interpretation of Tar.
23. Aq renders in crass Hebraic fashion by καὶ οὐκ ἤγγισεν οὗτος πρὸς τοῦτον.
24. For νότος used as adjective see SS 65.
25. Both Aq and Sym translate by an εἰς phrase, Aq also changing the noun

intensifies the verb as "was cleft, rent asunder," a somewhat overblown statement if the division of the waters was the result of a strong wind blowing all night.

14:22 The logical consequence of divided waters: the Israelites entered the middle of the sea on dry ground, carrying out the divine orders of v.16. For the C variant εν μεσω for εἰς μέσον see comment at v.16.

The second clause is nominal with τεῖχος ... τεῖχος as predicate of the subject τὸ ὕδωρ. An *f* variant makes the clause verbal by adding εγενετο before he first τεῖχος, i.e. the waters became a wall. Over against MT Exod repeats τεῖχος also for the left side. The second τεῖχος is omitted by a variant reading, which equals MT but is not necessarily due to its influence, the omission being stylistic. The phrases ἐκ δεξιῶν and ἐξ εὐωνύμων both have plural substantives. When these adjectives are used absolutely in the sense of "right or left side" they are usually plural.[26] In MT both nouns have plural suffixes, and hex has accordingly added αυτων to both.

14:23 Change of subject is shown by δέ. A B *x z* variant has a και structure here even though δέ is particularly appropriate in showing change of subject; the variant is probably due to the monotonous frequency of the paratactic και structures throughout the book. -- The "Egyptians" are then delineated by a compound appositional structure as consisting of "all the cavalry of Pharaoh and the chariots and the riders." For this see the note at v.9. αναβάται is unusual as a rendering for פרש, and except for Isa 36:9 is limited to Exod (also vv.26,28, 15:19) in the context of being cast into the sea. Both "chariots" and "riders" have a pronominal suffix in MT, and so hex has added αυτου after both nouns.

14:24 A δέ structure introduces a new theme. The use of ἐγενήθη with an ἐν phrase indicating time is unique in Exod. It does occur at 12:29 with a genitive of time during which, μεσούσης τῆς νυκτός. The usual form with time indications is the middle ἐγένετο: with ἐν at 2:11 12:51 16:22,27 19:16 40:15, and with μετά at 12:41 18:13 32:30. For usage in Exod of ἐγένετο vs ἐγενήθη see note at 2:10. -- The time indication was the morning watch;

the night, from sundown to sunset, was divided into three watches, this one being the last one; thus some time before dawn. The general pattern "and it happened" + time indication + καὶ + finite verb is a common Hebrew pattern which is here borrowed into Greek. The verb used is ἐπέβλεψεν, used for שָׁקַף in the same sense as in Gen 19:28 where Abraham looked down upon Sodom and Gomorrah, and only occurs here in Exod, as is also true for שָׁקַף Hiphil. Variant readings include κατεβλ. "look down" of *t*, εισεβλ. "look towards" of *b n*, and an incomprehensible επεβαλεν of *oI*, obviously a copyist's error.

The verb is modified by an ἐπί phrase, which a very popular A F M variant has changed to an εἰς one, i.e. the Lord looked "towards," not "upon," a rationalization based on the relative positions of pillar and Egyptian camp. The Lord is shown as looking on the Egyptian camp ἐν στύλῳ πυρὸς καὶ νεφέλης; i.e. a pillar which was fire on the Israelite side and cloud on the Egyptian side. The "looking on" is an active activity; by it he brought the camp of the Egyptians into disarray, συνετάραξεν.

14:25 Exod's καὶ συνέδησεν "and tied together (the wheels)" is based on וַיֶּאְסֹר of Sam rather than on MT's וַיָּסַר; in other words God clogged up the wheels, which makes good sense in view of the next clause "and he made them go with difficulty." The picture envisioned by Exod is one in which the dry ground was no longer so dry, but muddy.[27] - It should be noted that references in the plural all presuppose reading מִצְרַיִם not as singular but as οἱ Αἰγύπτιοι; cf the comment at 1:15.

The A *O n* text has the imperfect ηγεν for the aorist ἤγαγεν. This was probably palaeographically inspired rather than exegetically; the imperfect is semantically possible but unlikely. -- The reaction of the Egyptians was one of fear. -- Exod prefers the Hellenistic εἶπαν to the classical form ειπον.[28]

The hortatory subjunctive φύγωμεν correctly interprets the long form of the imperfect אָנוּסָה. In turn the γάρ clause, also part of what the Egyptians said, gives the reason for the flight proposal. The former slaves

---

to χέρσον; since χέρσος specifically refers to dry land over against water, it is an excellent choice.

26. With an understood μέρη? Cf Bauer sub δεξιός 2b.

have the Lord fighting the Egyptians for them. Implicit in the statement is the Egyptians' recognition of the superiority of Israel's God, a motif that has occurred oftener in the narrative; cf comment on v.4.

14:26 Change of subject is shown by δέ. For the relation between stretching out the hand and moving the waters see note at v.16. Instead of the one verb ישב of MT Exod uses two coordinate verbs in third singular aorist imperatives: ἀποκαταστήσω (τὸ ὕδωρ) and ἐπικαλυψάτω (τοὺς Αἰγυπτίους) "let the water return and cover the Egyptians," thereby rightly interpreting MT as expressing a zeugma, but compare v.28. An F + variant has the passive for the first verb, with good sense "let be restored." The *d* variant αποκαταστησω is first person singular future; the variant would make sense, but it really is simply a scribal mistake. Hex has added the preposition επι before "the Egyptians" to equal על of MT, but this is in disregard of the fact that על modified not a verb "to cover" but rather ישבו. Origen was also responsible for another επι before ἀναβάτας as well, which corresponds to MT.

14:27 With δέ change of subject is shown. At the signal of Moses' raised hand the routing of the enemy takes place; the Egyptians are destroyed in the Lord's great act of deliverance; the sea returned to its normal levels thereby catching the Egyptians.

Exod as usual does not translate the suffix of ידו, and also as usual hex supplies αυτου. -- The verb ἀπεκατέστη has a double augment which an M C d t reading changes to a single. Admittedly the augment of the prepositional element κατ- is unnecessary. More meaningful is the απεκατεσταθη of *b*, i.e. a passive form. The Hebrew לפנות בקר is well rendered by the phrase πρὸς ἡμέραν "towards day," i.e. at daybreak. So too Exod used a good idiom to translate לאיתנו "to its accustomed station" by its ἐπὶ χώρας "to its place."[29]

With the third clause the subject change to οἱ Αἰγύπτιοι is signalled by δέ. They are said to have fled ὑπὸ τὸ ὕδωρ, i.e. "under the water"; in MT they were fleeing לקראתו, i.e. the water was coming in on all sides, so that even though they presumably were trying to return the way they came the waters met them. Exod expresses this by an even more impressive picture; the waters returned so suddenly that their flight was under water. A popular variant has επι instead of υπο, as though the flight attempted was over the waters.

The last clause has the Lord shaking out, or shaking off the Egyptians right into the sea; the picture is vivid, with the Lord shown as though shaking crumbs from a cloth. It represents MT's נער literally.[30] -- Not unexpectedly a popular Byzantine text variant adds εις before μέσον which is not only closer to MT's בתוך but is also much more common in LXX than the absolute use of μέσον, though lexically it means the same.

14:28 The first verb in MT is rendered by a second aorist passive participle modifying the subject ὕδωρ. The object is threefold, τὰ ἄρματα, τοὺς ἀναβάτας and πᾶσαν τὴν δύναμιν Φαραώ, followed by an appositional phrase "those (i.e. all three) which had entered the sea after them (i.e. the Israelites). This differs somewhat from MT which has a twofold object: the chariotry and the horsemen, followed by a prepositional phrase which means "of the entire army of Pharaoh," in turn followed by an appositional phrase (but to the twofold object of the verb). A popular reading of a present participle εισπορευομενος for the perfect middle participle εισπεπορευμένος is fully possible, but the perfect is more fitting since entering the sea preceded the waters covering them

The final clause is asyndetic both in Exod and MT, though a B *O f* variant has added a και.[31] The statement is a powerful dramatic conclusion to the story of the God of the Israelites vs the arrogant Pharaoh and his people: "there was left of them not even one!"

14:29 Change of subject is indicated in both clauses by δέ. The second clause, except for the δέ structure is identical with the second clause of v.22; cf commentary there.

The first clause is also similar in content to the first one in v.22, but differs in form. The verb is ἐπορεύθησαν rather than εἰσῆλθον. This is

27. Sym obviously translates MT's ויסר with his μετέστησε "changed," hence "turn aside."
28. See THGE VII.M.9.

modified by two prepositional phrases διὰ ξηρᾶς "across dry ground" and
ἐν μέσῳ (τῆς θαλάσσης) "in the midst," whereas the phrases in v.22 are εἰς
μέσον and κατὰ τὸ ξῆρον; note also the reverse order.

14:30 Exod used ἐρρύσατο "rescued" to render MT's ויושע. The Hiphil of
ישע occurs only three times in the Pent; it also occurs at 2:17 where Exod
used the same verb and at Deut 20:4 (as διασῶσαι). Oddly enough though
the verb occurs a great deal throughout MT outside the Pentateuch it is
rendered by ῥύομαι only once (Jos 22:22), the verb σώζω being the usual
translation. The direct object τὸν 'Ισραήλ immediately follows the verb
unlike MT where ביום ההוא intervenes. The word order is made to fit
that of MT by hex. A B *f z* variant has articulated Αἰγυπτίων in the phrase
"from the hand of Egyptians."[32]

14:31 The introductory δέ showing change of subject becomes a και
structure in A *f*. The Hebraic "and Israel saw the great hand" is literally
transferred to Exod. The nominal is of course metaphorical. Tar[O]
understood this well as its גבורת ידא רבתא shows. Vulg handled the
difficulty by translating אשר עשה as *quam exercuerat*. Exod fully understood
the problem as shown by his use of ἅ. The change to the plural neuter
inflection is intentional. The verb within the relative clause is ἐποίησεν.
One cannot "do a great hand," but one can refer to having done those things
which the powerful hand of the Lord did. In other words Exod understood
MT in the same way as Tar[O] did. I would translate the problematic phrase
by "the display of great power which the Lord exercised." Incidentally an *f*
reading betrays awareness of Exod's syntactic difficulty by adding και before
the pronoun.

The subject of the next clause changes to ὁ λαός. The majority of
witnesses changes the δέ to a secondary και structure. -- The effect on the
people of their seeing the saving act of divine power was twofold: "they
feared (i.e. in a religious sense) the Lord and trusted in God and Moses his
servant." All the other witnesses have "in the Lord" for "in God." The terms
"the Lord" and "God" ought to represent יהוה and אלהים resp. and usually

---

29. Sym renders it literally by εἰς τὸ ἀρχαῖον αὐτῆς "to its original state."
30. Aq also uses a strong figure by his ἀνέβρασεν "seethe, throw up, shake

do, but the amount of variation in Exod is sufficiently large to distrust suggestions of differences from MT in the parent text in this regard.

---

violently," a term more appropriate to the waters of the sea than to God's actions.
31. Its secondary nature is argued in THGE VII.E.3.
32. That the article is secondary is argued in TGHE VII.D.1.

Chapter 15

15:1 That ישיר must be an old preterite was understood by Exod which has
ἦσεν. שירה is rendered by ᾠδή, which first occurs here, and was later taken
over to designate the liturgical odes in the liturgy of the Christian Church,
the Song of Moses being in most rites the first ode. In the Eastern churches
the ode is still part of the daily liturgy. The ode was sung τῷ θεῷ, which in
the majority tradition was corrected to τω κω to correspond to the ליהוה
of MT, though *C* omitted the addressee entirely.

The *C* text also omitted καὶ εἶπαν λέγοντες. The popular Byzantine
tradition has the second aorist ending ειπον.[1] The direct speech marker,
λέγοντες, suffered a great deal of change in the tradition,[2] with the
majority of witnesses omitting the word entirely as otiose.

The Song itself begins with a hortatory subjunctive in the plural, an
adjustment which Exod makes over against the singular of MT, legitimate
in view of the plural speakers, Moses and the Israelites. -- The pattern: free
infinitive + cognate finite verb in MT is rendered by an adverb + finite
verb, "gloriously has he glorified."[3]

The second line "horse and rider has he thrown into the sea" is an
accurate rendering of MT except for the failure explicitly to render the
suffix of רכבו,[4] which hex has made up for by adding αυτου.

15:2 The first half of the verse in MT is syntactically two coordinated
clauses: "Yah is my strength and (my) protection(?); and he has become my
salvation." The word זמרת in some mss has a suffixed form זמרתי, a
reading supported by Sam, Tar^O and Vulg. Exod has made a single clause
out of the line. It has omitted יה and made the compound phrase βοηθὸς
καὶ σκεπαστής modifier of ἐγένετο, eliminating the conjunction of ויהי.
Hex has added μου after the second noun as well as κυριος, as though the

1. See THGE VII.M.9.
2. Aq's (τω) λεγειν in particular has influenced the tradition.
3. The use of an adverb to render a Hebrew free infinitive is rather
uncommon in LXX; cf Thack 47.
4. See SS 93.

228

Hebrew had זמרתי יה at the time of Origen. Exod interprets זמרת as σκεπαστής "protector"; this seems to support the understanding of זמרת by some modern scholars as "defense, protection." The first line in Exod may be translated as "A help and a protector did he become to me for salvation."

The next two lines are a literal rendering of MT. Exod understood אנוהו correctly as his rendering δοξάσω αὐτόν shows. The Hebrew root does not mean "to adorn" as DBD, but is probably cognate to the Arabic nawwaha; cf the Arabic tanwīh meaning "praise, tribute."

15:3 In the first line the predicate is the participle συντρίβων modified by πολέμους, thus: "The Lord shatters wars (i.e. warfare)," a unique rendering of MT יהוה איש מלחמה. Exod interprets the predicate as one who crashes, and so one who is victorious in warfare; cf Tar^O נצח "victorious." -- In line two Exod renders שמו by ὄνομα αὐτῷ, though one might have expected a genitive pronoun rather than a dative of possession.

15:4 The first line with the coordinate accusative modifiers preposed renders MT in literal and exact fashion. The second half of the verse begins with three accusatives as direct modifiers of a singular transitive verb; the parallelism with the first line is carefully made: preposed accusatives + singular verb with κύριος as subject continued from v.3. The three accusatives constitute an extra one over against MT in ἀναβάτας. For τριστάτας see note at 14:7. It is presumably in apposition to ἀναβάτας, and the phrase might be rendered "choice riders, even officers." The verb is κατεπόντισεν "he sank," i.e. "drowned." MT has a plural Pual verb, with "choice of officers" as subject. Attempts to correct Exod to a plural passive obtain in κατεπον-τισθησαν and in a B variant κατεποθησαν "they were swallowed up" from καταπίνω, but the the three preposed accusatives are retained. Accordingly these texts can only be understood by taking these words as an elaboration of line one, i.e. as objects of ἔρριψεν, which represents a substantial reinterpretation of the text. For ἐρυθρᾷ θαλάσσῃ see note at 10:19. Note also the use of ἐν with a verb of action.[5]

5. Cf SS 136.

15:5 Exod continues to accent the divine action. Whereas MT begins with
תהמת "abysses, floods" as subject,[6] Exod has κύριος as subject with πόντῳ
simply the means which God used. He correctly understood the prefix
verbal inflection of MT as preterite. The word תהמת is difficult to translate.
It occurs in v.8 as well where Exod has τὰ κύματα. In the Creation Story in
Gen 1:3 the singular is rendered by τῆς ἀβύσσου, with τοῦ ὕδατος in the
parallel line. In our verse Exod uses πόντῳ rather than θαλάσσα which he
reserved for ים. The line probably means "with the sea he covered them."
The change of πόντῳ in a variant text to the nominative ποντος is the result of Hebrew influence.

In line two the verb is in the plural, κατέδυσαν "they sank down,"
which is more graphic than the Hebrew ירדו. A *C* reading κατεβησαν is a
synonym, though closer to the colorless verb of MT.

15:6 Both lines have as stated subject ימינך "your right hand," but Exod
with feeling for poetic variation has ἡ δεξιά σου for the first line but an
expanded ἡ δεξιά σου χείρ for the second.[7] -- Exod again uses δεδόξασται
which in v.1 rendered גאה, but here used for נאדרי, an old Niphal free infinitive.[8] I would translate the line in Exod by: "Your right hand, o Lord, has
been rendered glorious in (or by) power," i.e. in the display of power in
overcoming the enemy.

The second line correctly interprets תרעץ as a preterite, i.e. "shattered
(the enemies)." The two lines are neatly parallel both in structure and
meaning.

15:7 Again the prefix tenses of MT (there are three) are to be taken as
preterite; accordingly Exod has συνέτριψας, ἀπέστειλας and κατέφαγεν.
The verse continues to refer specifically to the deliverance at the Red Sea
experienced by the Israelites. Again the stress is on the divine action: "You
did crush ... send out your anger, and it (the anger) devoured." In the first
line a preposed dative modifier to the verb is probably a dative of means,

6. The Three according to Syh had ἄβυσσοι.
7. The Three on the authority of Syh omitted the χείρ as might well be
expected.
8. According to W.J.Moran, in *The Bible and the Ancient Hear East*
(Albright Festschrift, New York, 1961), p.60.

i.e. "by the plenitude of your glory you did crush the opponents." The object needs no σου in spite of MT's קָמֶיךָ, since the opponents are God's own; after all, at the Red Sea God had identified himself with Israel's cause; their opponents are his automatically.

The second line has two cordinated clauses, with the second "and it devoured them like stubble" semantically the result of the first. In MT the two clauses are asyndetic.

15:8. The term אַפֶּיךָ "your nostrils" is a common figure for divine anger; MT means "by the breath (snort) of your nostrils." Exod has avoided the crass figure by the ren dering "by the wind (breath, blast, snort) of your anger,"[9] a not overly appropriate means for parting waters. Exod translates נֶעֶרְמוּ "were heaped up" by διέστη "stood apart, separate," thus showing the picture of 14:29b.[10]

Lines two and three both have the same verb, ἐπάγη, the second aorist passive of πήγνυμι, i.e. "became stiff, congealed"; this is appropriate for קָפְאוּ of line three which also means "to congeal," but hardly for נִצְבוּ "stood up." The picture in Exod is a vivid one: "the waters became stiff like a wall; the waves became stiff in the middle of the sea." For the former MT uses a different figure: "the streams stood up like a hill"; Exod, as in line one, has the picture of walls of water on either side, avoiding such terms as "heaped up" and "hill." Both lines two and three are asyndetic, though a majority variant adds an emphatic καὶ before τὰ κύματα in the last line.

15:9 The statement of intention by the enemy is presented in MT almost staccato like by a series of six verbal units asyndetically strung along, Exod combining the first two by a subordinate participle + finite verb. Exod, on the whole, makes the enemy even more insolent. In line two where MT makes נַפְשִׁי "my appetite" subject of the verb, Exod renders by "I will fill up (i.e. satisfy) my appetite." In the last line for "I will unsheath (my sword)" Exod has ἀνελῶ "I will kill (with my sword)." The old uncial texts have the Hellenistic μαχαιρη for μαχαίρᾳ.[11]

9. Cf SS 124.
10. The Three translate the Hebrew literally by ἐσωρεύθη.
11. See note in THGE VII.H.1. Cf also the discussion in Thack 141.

The final verb in Exod is κυριεύσει with ἡ χείρ μου as subject, "my hand shall dominate." The Hebrew, however, probably means "my hands shall destroy (literally, disinherit) them." But this had already been said by ἀνελῶ, and so Exod took the Hiphil of ירש in the Qal sense as "my hand shall inherit them," therefore "be master, dominate."

15:10 The opening hemistich in MT is highly anthropomorphic: "you did blow with your breath." Exod avoids the notion of God's blowing by a neutral ἀπέστειλας. Tar⁰ went much farther with its אסרת במימרך "you did destroy by your word"; this is the effective word by which the victory was achieved, by which the sea covered them.[12]

The second line has its parallel in verse 5b, though the vocabulary is quite different. Here the simplex verb ἔδυσαν is used to translate the hapax legomenon צלל which from the context must mean "to sink," as all the old witnesses render it. -- Exod has them sink in violent water,[13] water which quickly submerged the enemy ὡσεὶ μόλιβος; lead, being heavy, would quickly sink.

15:11 These hymnodic lines are nominal clauses, with attributive modifiers emphasizing the point of comparison in the question "who is like you." The first instance is modified simply by a prepositional phrase ἐν θεοῖς "among the gods." This in turn influenced the ἐν phrase which follows in the next line, i.e. ἐν ἁγίοις, where MT has a singular word קדש "holiness." This might then be translated "(rendered glorious) among the holy ones," presumably taken as parallel to ἐν θεοῖς.[14]

The second attribute θαυμαστὸς ἐν δόξαις "wonderful in glorious deeds," is Exod's translation of נורא תהלת. The participle is seldom translated by θαυμαστός, though Exod also uses it at 34:10 to describe the works of God; the root ירא is usually rendered by φοβέω (or its derivatives). The prepositional phrase becomes ενδοξως in a *d* + reading,

12. According to the Latin of Procop The Others apparently translated the verb by ἐφύσησας, i.e. a literal translation.
13. Cf SS 138.
14. Sym has a different version. Instead of ἐν θεοῖς he translates באלים by ἐν δυναστείαις "among the powers" interpreting אלים on the basis of a presumed root meaning "to be strong." For בקדש Sym has ἐν ἁγιασμῷ "in a

for which see v.1; it is obviously the product of a copyist's mispronouncing the text. -- The final attribute, ποιῶν τέρατα rightly interprets פלא as a collective, and therefore to be translated by a plural noun.

15:12 The second line appears asyndetically on portraying the effect of the first line. An A M *f s t* variant adds και to introduce the line. Similarly an A M C *s t* reading articulates γῆ as a stylistic improvement, since the unarticulated γῆ is a slavish imitation of MT's ארץ.

15:13 With v.13 the Song no longer rhapsodizes the Red Sea deliverance but speaks in more general terms of God's guidance of his people, and the terror inspired by him among the foreign tribes in the vicinity.

The verb in line one, ὡδήγησας, is modified not only by an expected accusative, but also by a dative of means τῇ δικαιοσύνῃ σου "by your righteousness";[15] this translates חסדך.[16] The word really means steadfast love, loyal graciousness, but Exod uses "righteousness" as a better parallel to the dative τῇ ἰσχύι of line two. Also to be noted in line one is the double translation of זו, both as a demonstrative τοῦτον and as the relative ὅν following it. The result "this people which" simply makes the contrast between God's people and the ἔθνη of the following verse sharper.

In line two MT's verb means "to guide, lead," and serves as a good parallel to נחית of line one, Exod has παρεκάλεσας "you did summon, invite."[17] The verb is not inappropriate to the εἰς phrase modifying it, i.e. "to your holy lodging place." The summons is more than invitation, however; it is an effective one τῇ ἰσχύι σου.

15:14 Vv.14--16a present the reactions of the heathen neighbours. In line one MT has: "Nations heard, they trembled" ירגזון. The ancient witnesses all rightly understood the verb as preterite, but Exod's translation is surprising: καὶ ὡργίσθησαν "and they became angry."[18] The use of ὀργίζω for this verb was already shown at Gen 45:24. Schl suggests that the Exod

sanctuary" as though the Hebrew had במקוש.
15. See SS 127.
16. This is more exactly rendered by Aq as τῷ ἐλέει (σου).
17. Sym renders the verb by διεβάστασας "you did carry over," or "through."
18. Aq translated by ἐκλονήθησαν "driven into confusion," and Sym, by

translation may be in the sense of *metu percelli, perterreri,* in the manner *quavis vehementione animi commotione ac perturbatione*; thus in the same sense as in Ps 4:5. An A *y* variant reads εφοβηθησαν "and were afraid," showing a similar understanding.

In the second line ὠδῖνες is the subject; since the line parallels the ὠργίσθησαν of line one, the Schl interpretation of that verb receives added support. The object of the verb is designated as κατοικοῦντας Φυλιστιίμ, the inhabitants of (the land of) the Philistines. Only here is the land of פלשת called Φυλιστιίμ, for which term see comment at 13:17. The translator mistakenly used the transliteration for פלשתים. A *d* variant has the nominative for κατοικοῦντας, an error probably promoted by v.15. Presumably the line would then treat ὠδῖνες as a pendant nominative, but it still makes very little sense. For a parallel cf line two of v.15.

15:15 In the first line Exod understood נבהלו in the Late Hebrew sense of "hasten, hurry" rather than the intended meaning "be dismayed." Accordingly Exod has ἔσπευσαν, by which the parallelism with the other lines is destroyed.

The second line begins with a pendant nominative (introduced as in Pesh with a conjunction) "and as for the rulers of the Moabites." Here as in the case of Φυλιστιίμ in v.14 the people rather than the country named in MT is used. -- Exod renders אילי "the strong ones" by ἄρχοντες "rulers"; the interpretation is undoubtedly valid.

In the last line the strong figure of the Hebrew is literally rendered into Greek: "all the inhabitants of Canaan were melted away," a figure for extreme fright, i.e. dissolved in fear.

15:16 Exod interprets this verse as an imprecation which is fully possible in view of MT's verbs תפל and ידמו in the first two clauses. Accordingly the first line has an aorist optative ἐπιπέσοι, and the second an aorist passive third person imperative ἀπολιθωθήτωσαν. The compound subject is φόβος καὶ τρόμος; the terms are reversed in a B variant with scattered support.[19] MT has two synonyms אימתה ופחד. The word φόβος has been used to

---

ἐταράχθησαν "became troubled, shaken," both close to ירגז.
19. This is also followed by Theod. Aq apparently (from Syh) had θάμβος

translate either word in LXX; contrast 23:27 with Gen 31:43,53. On the other hand, τρόμος never occurs as a translation of אימה in LXX, and only seldom for פחד.[20]

The second line has as rendering for ידמו כאבן "let them be still as a stone," ἀπολιθωθήτωσαν "let them be petrified," obviously a free translation.[21]

Lines three and four are in climactic parallelism, the ἕως ἄν παρέλθη ὁ λαός σου being repeated, first with a vocative, and then with οὗτος ὃν ἐκτήσω. Variant readings with much scattered support have an optative παρελθοι, which as a potential mood is quite possible. Since παρέλθη and παρελθοι were pronounced exactly alike in Byzantine times it is unlikely that the optative was ever actually intended. The verb is used in both cases in a absolute sense. This raised questions for the Targumists who add an object. Tar[O] has "the Arnon" for the first case, and "the Jordan" for the second. Tar[P] with greater exactness has ית נחלי ארנונא and ית מגזתה דיירדנה resp. Observe the progression towards the promised land!

In the final line MT has עם, not עמך as in the previous line, but Exod has σου in both lines. As in v.12 Exod translated זו doubly by οὗτος ὄν. For the verb in the relative clause ἐκτήσω an A variant has ἐλυτρωσω which came in from v.13.[22]

15:17 The initial verbs are paratactically joined imperfects in MT; Exod subordinates the first by an attributive participle and translates the second as an imperative: "bringing in, plant them."[23] Since the first also had a pronominal suffix in MT hex has supplied an αυτους for the participle as well.

The second line is parallel to the εἰς phrase of the first line. For the phrase מכון לשבתך Exod has an unexpected εἰς ἔτοιμον κατοικητήριόν σου "for your ready dwelling." Exod has taken מכון as cognate of כוננת in

καὶ φόβος.
20. According to HR only three times.
21. For the Hebrew verb Aq has something like σιωπήσονται, whereas Sym had ἀκίνητοι ἔσονται (both from Syh); presumably they had ὡς λίθος as well.
22. According to Field Origen and Theod also read this, which I do not believe. If his source (Montefiore) can be trusted a mistake was made, since this could only apply to v.13.

the latter part of the verse, which he translated by ἡτοίμασαν "(which your hands) made ready," a fully valid rendering of כוננה. Then he rendered מכון by ἕτοιμον, an adjective modifying οἰκητήριον. The point made is that "the mount of inheritance" of line one, and the ἁγίασμα "sanctuary" of line three become a "ready dwelling" for God.[24]

15:18 The Song ends with a statement that "the Lord is ruling for ever and forever," a nominal clause with a present participle of βασιλεύω as predicate, i.e. as a continuous fact. This kind of doxological statement seems more appropriate than the future sense of the Hebrew verb ימלך.[25] -- The temporal compound modifier τὸν αἰῶνα καὶ ἐπ' αἰῶνα καὶ ἔτι is one of the ways in which LXX says "for ever and ever."

15:19 The verse begins with ὅτι as a causal particle, which does not tie in very well with the Song which precedes it. Possibly the verse could be taken as the reason for v.20, i.e. "because Pharaoh's cavalry entered ..., Mariam ... took." The *n* + reading οτε is much simpler; it clearly means "when Pharaoh's cavalry entered ..., then the Lord brought upon them the water of the sea." ἵππος, though unarticulated, must equal ἡ ἵππος, i.e. "cavalry," rather than "horse"; so too MT's סוס must be taken as a collective.

The prepositional phrase with coordinate dative nouns translates coordinate prepositional phrases of MT, Exod idiomatically not repeating the preposition with the second noun. Hex adds αυτου to both nouns so as to equal MT.

In the second clause the verb ἐπήγαγεν is an unusual choice by Exod for rendering the Hiphil of שוב, an equation otherwise found only in the collocation "bring back my hand" (Am 1:8 Zech 13:7 Isa 1:25). Exod does not emphasize the return to a former state, but rather suggests the active

---

23. See Lee 58.
24. Aq also interprets the cognate noun and verb in cognate fashion: ἕδρασμα "seat" and ἕδρασαν "he sat," This, however, does get Aq into some difficulty since he rendered לשבתך by εἰς καθέδραν (σου), resulting in ἕδρασμα εἰς καθέδραν "a seat for a chair," an obvious tautology.
25. For "Lord" The Three all have πιπι (i.e. a transcribed יהוה into Greek) according to Syh, but differ in the predicate. Theod does not change the Exod reading, but Aq and Sym both have a future βασιλεύσει. According to Syh Sym inserts σου between the two words; this seems to me quite

divine intervention by which the waters are brought upon the Egyptian forces. -- An A F reading changes the word order so that the subject κύριος immediately follows the verb as in MT.

The last clause is introduced by a δέ construction, emphasizing the contrast between the safe conduct of the Israelites and the destruction of the Egyptian forces. The statement is the climax of the Lord vs Pharaoh narrative of the first 15 chapters.

15:20 The δέ particle shows change of subject. The verbal form is aorist indicative, though a B *b* variant changes ἔλαβεν to the subordinate participle λαβουσα which produces an ungrammatical construction of a type rarely found in Exod.[26] -- τύμπανον is the regular rendering for the Hebrew תף; in fact only twice is another Greek word used to translate it: ψαλτήριον in Job 21:12 and αὐλός in Isa 30:32, in both cases coordinated with κιθάραν (-ρας) "lyre(s)." The tambourine was commonly used to accompany a cultic song and/or dance. The word is articulated in imitation of MT's את התף; the article is omitted in *x*, thereby improving the sense.

The second clause has the Attic second aorist ἐξῆλθον, for which B *b* *f z* read the Hellenistic εξηλθοσαν.[27] -- The Israelite women following Mariam are said to have been μετὰ τυμπάνων καὶ χορῶν, which nouns represent תפים and מחלת. Though the latter term is often taken as a plural of abstraction "dancing" Exod with good plausibility rendered it by χορῶν "dances."

15:21 The subject change is again shown by δέ. For MT's ותען להם "and she sang to them" Exod has ἐξῆρχεν δὲ αὐτῶν. ἐξάρχω with the genitive means "to begin, take the lead in," and here probably means "she was taking the lead in their singing."[28] Since it is a process the imperfect tense is appropriate. A C *n s* variant has the dative pronoun αυτοις instead of αὐτῶν; the expression might then be rendered by "she was teaching them."[29] Exod also used the direct speech marker, λέγουσα, to introduce

---

improbable; the tradition recorded in Syh must be in error.
26. See the discussion of the variant in THGE VII.M.1.
27. Cf THGE VII.M.9.
28. Schl defines the verb here as *incipiebat vel praecinebat*.
29. Aq and Sym have κατέλεγεν, imperfect of καταλέγω "to recount,

the Song in contrast to the other ancient witnesses; this makes clear that the subject was indeed Mariam.

The Song itself was taken over bodily from v.1, although in MT the verb is now imperative. As in v.1 hex has added αυτου after ἀναβάτην to conform to MT.

15:22 A new section is introduced by a δέ structure. The wilderness journey from the Red Sea now continues. The verb ἐξῆρεν is regularly used in the Pentateuch as a rendering for נסע; it can mean "move" as an intransitive verb, and is regularly so used for Israel's movements from one place to another. It can also be used transitively "remove" as here with an accusative object; note that the MT verb is vocalized as Hiphil. In MT the object is את ישראל; Exod enlarges this to τοὺς υἱοὺς 'Ισραήλ, and Pesh, to "house of Israel." -- The term θαλάσσης ἐρυθρᾶς here uniquely follows the order of MT in Exod; for the usual rendering see note at 10:19.

The second clause also has a transitive verb with object in ἤγαγεν αὐτούς, agreeing with Sam: וירצאהו against the intransitive of all other old witnesses. An F M + reading has the imperfect ηγεν instead of ἤγαγεν; the imperfect is not overly appropriate and was probably due to parablepsis. -- The prepositions εἰς and ἐν are used here in the classical sense, εἰς of movement into, and ἐν as place where. -- The verb in the third clause is with fine feeling in the imperfect; after all, going for three days is progressive action indeed. The aorist of *x* is hardly an improvement.

In the last clause the verb is also imperfect since for three days they were not finding water. The verb εὕρισκον occurs with Attic augment as ηυρισκον in an A B M *y* variant.[30] -- The verse ends with ὥστε πιεῖν which is not found in any other old witnesses. Exod added it in the interest of exactness. After all the Israelites did find water but it was brackish; what they could not find was drinkable water.

15:23 The δέ is probably intended contrastively; there was water but it was not potable. The name Merra, both here and later on with the genitive in-

relate," probably understanding תען as from ענה "to respond, answer," whereas Theod did not change the Exod text.
30. That the Hellenistic form is original to Exod is clear from THGE

flection, has been variously misspelled in the tradition as could be expected since the name is only meaningful in a Semitic language.[31] The name was easily Hellenized since it ended in the feminine -α, and could be inflected as a first declension noun. A B variant with scattered support has the uninflected μερρα but only for the first instance. It is clearly the result of a copyist's error; a final *nu* was often shown in the mss by a small horizontal stroke over the preceding vowel and was easily overlooked.

In the second clause an A F *n* variant has εδυναντο for ἠδύναντο.[32] -- The infinitive πιεῖν has ὕδωρ as its object in common with all other old witnesses, which was omitted by a B + text but this was probably influenced by the absolute use of πιεῖν at the end of v.22.[33]

The name מרה means "bitterness" and MT makes an aetiological explanation. This might well be lost on a Greek reader; Exod solves this neatly by translating the name the last time it appears in the verse as Πικρία, i.e. since the water was bitter the name of the place was called "Bitterness." -- Exod also clarified MT's קרא שמה, literally "one called its name," i.e. its name was called" by the unambiguous ἐπωνομάσθη τὸ ὄνομα τοῦ τόπου ἐκείνου. The verb is changed to the active by B +, επωνομασεν (and in the plural by five scattered mss as well). This unusual exact equivalence also occurs in Arm and Syh, and could well be a preOrigen revision towards MT.

15:24 The verb διεγόγγυζεν describes a process and is therefore in the imperfect. The verb is plural in MT and Tar but not in Sam. When ὁ λαός is subject in Exod it takes a singular predicate. There are four exceptions to this in Exod, and each has a rational explanation. In 16:4 the relevant text has ἐξελεύσεται ὁ λαός, καὶ συλλέξουσιν. Once the singular agreement has been expressed, the people as individuals are to collect the daily manna portion. The same syntactic pattern obtains in the other three: 20:18 32:3 and 33:10. Accordingly the fact that Sam has a singular verb in our verse is irrelevant for Exod. The verb is a rendering for the root לון which occurs

---

VII.M.9.
31. Why the place name Merra should be spelled (on the authority of Syh) as though with an "o" or "u" vowel instead of ε in both Sym and Theod is puzzling.
32. For this see the discussion in THGE VII.M.5.

in MT either as Niphal or Hiphil; except for Jos 9:18 it is limited to Exod and Num and is always rendered by the above verb or its simplex stem. This is the first instance of the murmuring motif, though complaints directed to Moses already occurred at 5:20,21 14:11,12. The verb is modified by ἐπὶ Μωυσῆν as at 16:2 17:3. In our verse most witnesses have ἐπί with the dative (though B as our oldest witness does have the accusative), but in the other instances the accusative is clearly original, and it is probably the text of Exod as well.

The question asked "what shall we drink?" is quite properly put in the indicative. The popular present subjunctive spelling πωμεθα "what should we drink," though possible, is simply an itacism for πιόμεθα.

15:25 Subject change is shown by δέ. Though MT does not name the subject, Sam and a Qumran ms do, and the name was probably in Exod's parent text. The verb ἐβόησεν more accurately reflects the Hebrew root צעק than does the צלי of Tar, though Moses' calling out to Yahweh could certainly be called "prayer."

A textual problem obtains in the second clause with the verb. MT has ויורהו "and he taught him" which the Tar also presuppose: Tar^O has ואלפיה, and Tar^P, ה סב מיניה with the object מלה דאורייתא. Sam, however, has ויראהו "and he showed him" which Exod's καὶ ἔδειξεν αὐτῷ presupposes (also followed by Pesh and Vulg), but cf 1Kgdm 12:23 and Mic 4:2 where the Hiphil of ירה is also rendered by the future of δείκνυμι, but in both cases with τὴν ὁδόν as object, and the rendering does not presuppose a different parent text. The object of the verb here is ξύλον, "a piece of wood" which he (i.e. Moses) threw into the water with wonderful results: the water lost its bitterness. The verb ἐνέβαλεν has αὐτό after it, a necessary addition required by the verb, though in MT וישלך is used absolutely.

Vv.25b and 26 seem to interrupt the context in MT and Exod reproduces its ambiguities faithfully. V.25b begins asyndetically with ἐκεῖ. Though the context makes it clear that the subject of ἔθετο and ἐπείρασεν as well as of εἶπεν of v.26 must be the κύριος of the second clause of 25a it is in no way indicated. Similarly the antecedents of the pronouns αὐτῷ and

240

αὐτόν must be the ὁ λαός of v.24, and not Μωυσῆς who is subject of clauses one and three in 25a. This is fully clear from v.26 where the people are addressed in the singular throughout. The only tie that v.25b has with the narrative of vv.22--25a is the verb ἐπείρασεν by which the Merra incident is interpreted as a case of God tempting the people. Oddly in the tradition the majority of witnesses have the imperfect επειραζεν for the original ἐπείρασεν.[34]

What the Lord set before the people were δικαιώματα καὶ κρίσεις "ordinances and judgments," representing ומשפט חק "statute and ordinance." Exod interprets these as collective, which is fully possible. Unfortunately there is no consistency in Exod as to the translation of these terms. Leaving out of consideration technical and non-legal uses of these terms חק is rendered by δικαιώματα in 15:25,26, by νόμιμον in 12:24 29;28 30:21, and by προστάγματα in 18:16,20. On the other hand, משפט is translated by κρίσεις at 15:25 28:30, by κρίμα in 23:6, but by δικαιώματα in 21:1 24:3. When כמשפט occurs in the sense of "(according to) custom" δικαίωμα is used, 21:9,31. No clear pattern emerges, and one can only conclude that they were not carefully distinguished as legislation terms.

15:26 The cognate noun in the dative in the expression ἀκοῇ ἀκούσῃς stands for the free cognate infinitive of MT and is a common way of rendering such in LXX. As in Hebrew it simply intensifies the verbal notice, thus "if you really listen to." The protasis consists of four conditions with verbs in the second singular and the clauses syndetically joined. The second of these is unusual in that the accusative modifier, τὰ ἀρεστά, is preposed, and the verb (in all the other clauses standing first) is at the end. The verb's position may well have promoted the itacistic spelling ποιησεις as future indicative of the verb. The modifier τὰ ἀρεστά is the common translation for ישר in the Pentateuch, Deut 9:5 ὁστότητα (τῆς καρδίας), 32:4 ὅσιος (κύριος) and Num 23:10 (ψυχαῖς) δικαίων being the only exceptions. ἐναντίον has a popular variant, ενωπιον, which is synonymous.

In the third clause the verb ἐνωτίσῃ is modified by an unusual dative ταῖς ἐντολαῖς, a Hebraism based on MT's למצותיו. The dative has been stylistically improved in a popular Byzantine variant, the accusative τας εντολας which is standard usage. The last clause in the protasis has φυλάξῃς as verb; in the tradition an *oI C* reading has φυλαξη which is second singular future middle, with no change lexically. For τὰ δικαιώματα see note on v.25.

The apodosis has the accusative modifier preposed to the subject - predicate οὐκ ἐπάξω, viz. "every sickness which I brought on the Egyptians." The care with which Exod translates is well illustrated by the modification of ἐπήγαγον and ἐπάξω, both from ἐπάγω. The aorist form is modified by τοῖς Αἰγυπτίοις, but the future form by ἐπὶ σέ.[35] In both cases the lexical relation of the modifier to the verb is "on, upon," but the former represents במצרים and the latter עליך.

The reason for the divine promise is given in the concluding γάρ clause.[36] God as divine healer would hardly have been the one to have brought sickness on the people in the first place.

15:27 The B *f z* tradition has the Hellenistic inflection εξηλθοσαν.[37] -- The place name Αἰλίμ has undergone numerous itacistic spelling variations; the vowel αι of the first syllable allows for ε, and the vowel of the second syllable can appear as ει or η as well. Besides these various spellings there is σελειμ, the product of phonetic assimilation to the preceding ξ; cf also σαλημ where the first vowel has lost the *iota* of αι, whereas λειμ has lost the first syllable. -- Exod has added the verb ἦσαν in the second clause for good sense. The C tradition has the singular ην as though the subject, πηγαί, were neuter; the second element in the coordinate, στελέχη, is neuter, but it is unusual for a verb to be attracted in number to the more distant member of a compound subject. -- For תמרים Exod has the phrase στελέχη φοινίκων, literally "(tree-)trunks of date palms." -- The last clause begins with a δέ construction since the subject is turned back to "they," viz. the Israelites.

---

33. See the discussion in THGE VII.P.
34. For the secondary character of the majority variant see THGE VII.M.5.
35. See Helbing 276.
36. Cf SS 79.
37. See the note in THGE VII.M.9.

Chapter 16

16:1 A new section is introduced by δέ. The verb ἀπῆραν is regularly employed along with the related compound ἐξαίρω to indicate moving camp; cf note on ἐξῆρεν at 15:22. For the various itacistic spellings for Αἰλίμ 1° and 2° see the note on 15:27. One might also note the erroneous εδεμ in ms 318 for Αἰλίμ 1°. Once the *lambda* was misread as a *delta*, /edim/ easily led to the well-known εδεμ (Edom).

In the second clause the Attic ἦλθον appears in the B z tradition in Hellenistic dress as ηλθοσαν.[1] The plural verb is used as in MT, since συναγωγή is a collective concept, though the grammatically correct singular is found in a *b f* reading. A popular F tradition articulates συναγωγή, but this is contrary to Exod usage. When συναγωγή is modified by "all" it is never articulated in Exod except once; in v.3 πᾶσαν τὴν συναγωγήν is modified by ταύτην thereby making articulation normal.

For the name Σίν the usual itacisms ει and η occur in the tradition as well as the common confusion of final *nu* and *mu*, producing both σειμ and σημ. The variant σουρ in ms 15 is based on 15:22. -- The relative clause is introduced by the neuter pronoun ὅ referring to Σίν; an *n* reading has the feminine η, thereby making ἔρημον the antecedent. The wilderness of Sin is said to be between Ailim and (between) Sina; the repeated ἀνὰ μέσον is in imitation of the Hebrew. Σινά is the usual transcription for סִינָי, not σιναι as one might expect; in this verse only two mss have a -ναι ending; cf note at 19:1.

V.1b is a dating formula not for 1a but for v.2 as the δέ structure shows. Thus what Exod means is that in the 15th day ... the whole congregation ... was murmuring. The use of "in the ... day to the ... month" is a literal rendering of the Hebrew. The use of a perfect participle ἐληλυθότων αὐτῶν "of their having left" betrays a fine feeling for the exact nuance of MT's לְצֵאתָם.

1. See THGE VII.M.9.

16:2 The verse begins without a conjunction since the dating formula of v.1b modifies the verb; in this Exod stands alone. The verb διεγόγγυζεν is in the imperfect which in view of the reinterpretation is sensible. The Byzantine group has changed it to the plural thereby conforming to MT. As in v.1 a popular F tradition has articulated συναγωνή, for which see v.1. The *f* text articulates υἱῶν undoubtedly because the word is usually with an article. In fact, υἱῶν is always articulated in Exod except when preceded by "all (the) congregation of" (in any case) where (12 times) it is never articulated.

Two hex additions to the text were made where Exod was shorter than MT. Exod has "against Moses and Aaron," but MT naturally repeats the preposition before the second name, and hex added επι; and after "Aaron" MT has במדבר for which hex has supplied εν τη ερημω.

16:3 Exod throughout uses the Hellenistic εἶπαν rather than the popular Attic form ειπον.[2] -- There is no obvious reason for the Byzantine variant omitting πρὸς αὐτούς, but an *x* variant changing it to προς αυτον does change the sense; presumably Moses is then the sole addressee.

ὄφελον is probably a neuter participle in origin but became a fixed form to express contrary to fact wishes, an excellent rendering for the equally idiomatic Hebrew מי יתן. Here it occurs with an aorist to indicate past time: "Would that we had died." The variant *n* reading in the subjunctive would be unusual Greek though it ought to be sensible. -- Nowhere else in LXX does the unusual but fitting translation of ביד by πληγέντες ὑπό "smitten by" occur; the usual rendering is the literal (ἐν) τῷ χειρί.

The temporal ὅταν clause, translating a Hebrew coordinate pattern: ב + infinitives, has verbs in different tenses, the aorist "when we resided" and the imperfect "and we were eating," distinguishing carefully between simple residency and the process of eating regularly. This fine distinction is voided by the Byzantine reading οτε εκαθημεθα, imperfect of κάθημαι. This text is a bit of pseudo-scholarship: a) change to the intransitive κάθημαι, and b) making the coordinate verbs both imperfect.

2. Cf THGE VII.M.9.

The final ὅτι clause gives the factual reason for the initial "would that we had died," viz. "because you brought us...." The charge is a horrendous one, that Moses and Aaron had brought "the people into the desert in order to kill (ἀποκτεῖναι as a purposive infinitive) this entire assembly by famine." An *f* reading, επηγαγες, attributes the "brought" only to Moses.-- The *C* text changing ὅτι to οτε would make the clause a temporal clause subject to the preceding ὅταν clauses which can hardly have been intended.

16:4 The δέ particle shows subject change. The use of subject pronoun plus inflected present tense renders MT's pronoun + participle; here it signifies incipient verbal action, "I am about to rain."[3] -- The omission of ἄρτους from the phrase "bread from heaven" in a *d* reading leaves the reader to guess from the context whether the ὕω is transitive with an implied object or simply intransitive.

In the next two syndetic clauses a typical construction for Exod obtains; in the first the verb is singular preceding the subject ὁ λαός, and in the second with the same referent the verb is in the plural. This reflects exactly MT's pattern: יצא and לקטו. An *n* variant has a synonym συναξουσιν for συλλέξουσιν; cf vv.5,16.

The phrase τὸ τῆς ἡμέρας εἰς ἡμέραν "the daily requirement" renders דבר יום ביומו literally "the matter of a day in its day," i.e. "a day's portion";[4] cf Vulg: *sufficient per singulos dies.* For a more idiomatic rendering of the Hebrew phrase cf 5:13,19. This translation failed to satisfy Origen's quantitative norms; there was no equivalent for דבר nor was the suffix of the last word rendered. Accordingly hex added ρημα at the beginning and αυτης at the end, producing a barely sensible text.

The final purposive clause, ὅπως πειράσω, refers specifically, as the later narrative indicates, to the Israelites following the instructions concerning τὸ τῆς ἡμέρας εἰς ἡμέραν; cf especially vv.19 and 23.

16:5 The verse in Exod is ambiguous because of the translator's literalism. By rendering the parataxis of MT by καί throughout it is unclear how the second and third clauses are intended to relate to the first clause seman-

3. For the use of the archaic ὕω see Lee 122--124.
4. Cf SS 95.

tically. The first clause simply designates the occasion: "It will happen on the sixth day." A *C* text, as well as Pesh, has clarified the intent by omitting the second conjunction, i.e. "on the sixth day they shall prepare ... and there will be double...." This is also Vulg's interpretation: *die autem sexto parent.* But it is also possible that clause two is to be understood as basic to the intent of clause three, i.e. "as they shall prepare ... there will be double." Since on days one through five the people also get ready whatever they bring in, the latter interpretation is probably what Exod intended, but it remains uncertain. Possibly the A *x* + reading of the aorist subjunctive ετοιμασωσιν intended to support the suggested intent for the Exod text: "when they would be preparing ... then there will be double," but it is more likely rooted in copyist error.

Both relative clauses contain ἄν plus a subjunctive mood verb to indicate the potential nature of the verbal action.[5] An *n* variant has transposed the verbs "bring in" and "gather" but this, though possible, is clearly a mistake.

In the final clause τὸ καθ' ἡμέραν εἰς ἡμέραν means "daily" and is Exod's rendering for the distributive ‏יוֹם יוֹם‎; as such it is unique for LXX. The phrase occurs in MT also at Gen 39:10 and Ps 61:9 (translated by ἡμέραν ἐξ ἡμέρας), Ps 68:20 (by ἡμέραν καθ' ἡμέραν) and in Prov 8:30,34 (by καθ' ἡμέραν). Similar phrases are ‏ליום ביום‎ in 2Chr 24:11 (translated as Gen above) and at 30:21 ‏יום ביום‎ (as Ps 68), and at Neh 8:18, by the literal ἡμέρας ἐν ἡμέρᾳ. The Exod passage does make good sense: "that by a day for a day," and illustrates how Exod tried not only to make sense but also to keep as nearly as possible to the Hebrew original.[6]

16:6 Change of subject is shown by δέ; the variant B *O n z* και structure is secondary.[7] -- The verb εἶπεν is singular with a compound subject in imitation of the Hebrew. The addressees are called πᾶσαν συναγωγήν of the Israelites in agreement with vv.1 and 9 where, however, the word "congregation" also obtains in MT.

5. For the secondary character of εαν within a relative clause cf THGD 99--102.
6. Aq followed by Theod apparently had ἡμέραν ἡμέραν, whereas Sym had ἐν πάσῃ ἡμέρᾳ according to Syh.
7. See THGE VII.E.1.

What Moses and Aaron said is in direct contradiction to the false charges brought by the murmuring Israelites in v.3; it is the Lord, not we, who brought you here, and by evening (cf v.13) the Israelites will acknowledge this. The *b* text identifies κύριος as ο θεος υμων, a common designation known to every copyist. The *oII* + reading ημας for ὑμᾶς makes perfectly good sense but is a copyist's error; the two words are homophonous.

16:7 In the *O* tradition the contrast beween πρωί and the ἑσπέρας of v.6 is stressed by changing the original καί to a δε structure. -- With the appearance of the heavenly manna (vv.14--15) the Israelites will see the δόξαν κυρίου; i.e. their God will reveal himself by means of the wonderful food. -- The subject of the infinitive in the phrase ἐν τῷ εἰσακοῦσαι τὸν γογγυσμὸν ὑμῶν is not expressed (as it must be in MT), since it is contextually obvious. That the very popular A M gloss κυριον as subject of the infinitive was borrowed from v.8 and is secondary is obvious from the fact that αυτον was added by hex under the asterisk.

Exod characterized the Israelites' murmuring as ἐπὶ τῷ θεῷ; Exod may have used τῷ θεῷ here rather than κυριω for MT's יהוה in order to make the contrast between God and ἡμεῖς particularly clear. The rest of the verse emphasizes this contrast: "But we, what are we that you are murmuring against us?" -- The *b* text has τινες for τι, i.e. "who (are we)," but it is not identification that is asked for, but substance, i.e. we are but men. -- For the A *n* simplex γογγυζετε, see comment at 15:24.

16:8 This verse seems to be an expansive doublet of the preceding verses, but if so, it is in the parent text since Exod simply translates. Vulg has solved the repetitiveness by rendering MT's בתת construction by *dabit*; the statement becomes a simple prediction of what is going to happen. Exod retains the subordinate syntax of the clause by its ἐν τῷ διδόναι and thereby creates an ambiguity; to what precisely is the structure subordinate? it might seem possible that it be the διά clause, i.e. "when the Lord gives ... it is because the Lord has listened..." Or it could be the ἡμεῖς δέ question, i.e.

"when the Lord gives ... because the Lord listened ... then what are we?" The latter is grammatically more feasible.

The d text had a singular collective αρτον for the more usual ἄρτους. That MT has the singular is irrelevant, since לֶחֶם only occurs as singular. -- The verse makes explicit what was only implicit in vv.6 and 7; at evening he will give you κρέα φαγεῖν, and in morning ἄρτους εἰς πλησμονήν. And over against v.7 Moses says that it is because of (διά, not ἐν τῷ) the Lord's listening to your murmurings, murmurings καθ' ἡμῶν. Note the usual pattern of pronoun + present tense for MT's pronoun + participle. The d text's imperfect is no improvement on Exod. The n gloss καθ ημεραν is palaeographically conditioned by the καθ' ἡμῶν which follows immediately.

The clause "but we, what are we?" is an exact repetition from v.7. The reason for the repetition is to give a basis for the important γάρ clause which is the point of the verse, viz. "because your murmuring is not against us but against God." Exod quite intentionally uses "God" as he did with the ἐπὶ τῷ θεῷ in v.7, for which cf note at v.7.

16:9 Change of speaker is indicated by the δέ structure. Aaron is again used as Moses' spokesman; Moses tells Aaron what to say to the people; cf 4:15--16. -- As in v.2 the entire assembly of the Israelites is involved. -- The b text has εκκλησια for συναγωγῇ; its readers would understand this as "church"; was the creator of this variant possible identifying the Israelites as God's OT church?

The imperative προσέλθετε becomes the Hellenistic προσελθατε in the A B F + text.[8]-- As in vv.7 and 8 Exod has "(before) God" for MT's tetragrammaton. -- The reason for the summons is given in the γάρ clause: he has listened to your murmuring. Hex has rearranged the pronoun in ὑμῶν τὸν γογγυσμόν to agree with the Hebrew.

16:10 As usual Exod disregarded initial וַיְהִי as otiose, but begins with ἡνίκα δὲ ἐλάλει for כְּדַבֵּר; note δέ showing subject change to Aaron. The imperfect verb is correctly used, since it was while Aaron was speaking that they (the people) turned themselves around (aorist passive). ἐπεστράφησαν is introduced by an otiose καί in imitation of the Hebrew.[9] Exod states that "the people turned themselves about towards (εἰς) the desert, i.e. in the direction of their forward travel towards Mt. Sinai.

The cloud was the Lord's pillar to lead the people, but here "the glory of the Lord appeared in a cloud"; what is not clear in Exod is whether this was the cloud which led the people or just "a cloud," since the word is left indefinite. In MT the clause is introduced by וְהִנֵּה, but Exod does not translate הִנֵּה, and ἰδου is accordingly added by hex. The appearance of the Lord's glory refers to his actual presence in a revelatory sense; presumably this meant a display of fire; cf 19:18.

16:12 V.11 ended with the direct speech marker λέγων, showing that v.12 is the Lord's direct speech to Moses. The use of the perfect, εἰσακήκοα, is exactly right since he has heard and so things are about to happen in response to the divine audition. -- A popular F M tradition omits the articulation for υἱῶν; see note at v.2.

Moses is then told to speak to the people with a specific message, which is also introduced by the direct speech marker. Prediction is made largely in terms already given in v.8, i.e. meat at dusk and bread to satiety at daybreak. The time designation πρὸς ἑσπέραν renders the Hebrew phrase "between the two evenings" for which see note at 12:6. New in the context of the double promise of food is the recognition formula. This recognition of the Lord as "your God" is theologically central to the narrative. The verb "to know" is used in the Hebraic sense of יָדַע, not so much of intellectual perception as of a person-to-person knowledge. The object clause of γνώσεσθε is a nominal clause. The *f* text adds ειμι to ἐγώ. Exod sometimes uses ἐγώ εἰμι and at times only ἐγώ. There seems to be no particular reason for the choice; Exod is quite impartial; 12 times the εἰμι is present, and 12 times it is not.

16:13 Although MT subordinates the time indications as prepositional phrases Exod makes both independent clauses; the arrival of quails is preceded

---

8. Cf the discussion in THGE VII.M.9 for Exod usage.
9. Aq translates by ἔνευσαν "they inclined towards," whereas Theod apparently used the verb ἀποστρέφω, probably in the passive as

by ἐγένετο δὲ ἑσπέρα, whereas the arrival of manna is introduced by τὸ πρωὶ δὲ ἐγένετο. Both use δέ constructions showing fine balance. A popular A F variant upsets this by changing the first one into a καὶ structure, while a popular B F variant also destroyed it by omitting the second δέ. The hex tradition attempts to bring the Greek closer to MT by adding ἐν before ἑσπέρα which would of course make the noun dative. No such change is made with the adverb πρωί.

The advent of quails is detailed in two clauses; presumably the people caught them and ate them, but this is not stated. The parallel account in Num 11:31--34 places the provision of quails quite separate from the giving of manna. -- ὀρτυγομήτρα is articulated by b as in MT, which is, however, irrelevant since the article η probably is a dittograph of the final letter of ἀνέβη.

The morning event is told in more complex fashion. It begins with a genitive absolute construction which must be taken with the following verse. Exod has condensed MT's somewhat verbose "the dew was laying around the camp, and the dew went up (i.e. evaporated)" into "(when) the dew had ceased (i.e. dried up) around the camp," and then proceded directly to the "and behold" clause of v.14.

16:14 This shorter text naturally demanded fixing up by hex, and what happened illustrates the mechanical way in which Origen operated. At the beginning of the verse hex added καὶ ανεβη η θεσις της δροσου which is really a doublet; after all, the absolute construction at the end of v.13 had said exactly that, viz that the dew had gone.[10]

The verse in Exod begins then with "and behold on the face of the desert λεπτὸν ὡσεὶ κόριον λευκὸν ὡσεὶ πάγος on the ground," i.e. the strange new substance was "fine like coriander seed, white like hoar frost." This is based on understanding the Hebrew text in the light of v.31 where MT refers to manna as being "like coriander seed white." MT here has דק מחספס דק ככפר, i.e. λεπτόν renders דק and ὡσεὶ πάγος equals ככפר, but the rest is different. Precisely what the second word means is not clear.

ἀπεστράφησαν, (cf 32:15), whereas Sym used some form of κλίνω (as 10:6); these latter are based on Syh.
10. The text added by hex was apparently taken over from Sym, whereas Aq

Tar^O has מקלף "flaky" (also in Pesh), and Tar^P has מפספס "shredded."[11] In short the Hebrew is obscure and Exod avoided guessing by using his knowledge of the description later in the account. Similarly λευκόν represents no effort to render MT here which repeats דק. MT's comparison "fine as hoar frost" is not overly apt. Quite different is the *d* variant which has wool" for "coriander," an auditory error of εριον for κόριον.

16:15 Exod twice uses δέ to show subject change, after ἰδόντες and after εἶπεν. The participle ἰδόντες is given an object αὐτό simply for good sense; its omission by the majority of witnesses may well be a prehexaplaric revision towards the Hebrew. -- For εἶπαν the popular F M reading has ειπον.[12] The Hebrew idiom איש אל אחיו "one to another" is rendered here by ἕτερος τῷ ἑτέρῳ; this is highly unusual, occurring only once elsewhere (at Num 14:4). Usually את is rendered literally in the phrase; e.g. at Gen 42:21 43:33 ἕκαστος πρὸς τὸν ἀδελφὸν αὐτοῦ. -- The question posed τί ἐστιν τοῦτο gives no hint of the Hebrew word play involved. MT could just as well be rendered by: "it is *man*." Exod simply translated the word *man* as being the Aramaic interrogative pronoun, thereby making good sense in the narrative.

In the γάρ clause Exod naturally put the object clause modifying ᾔδεισαν into the past as τί ἦν. The Byzantine text changed the verb to εστιν, a pedantry which does not change the meaning in any way.

Moses' reply identifies the *man* as the food "which the Lord gave you to eat." Exod strictly follows the Hebrew order: verb + subject + dative pronoun; the more common order would have been: verb + pronoun + subject; an M *b x z* variant does precisely that, i.e. εδωκεν υμιν κυριος. -- The subject of Moses' reply, הוא, is rendered by οὗτος, since in such contexts Exod makes no distinction between הוא and זה; cf (הדבר) זה of v.16 which is also rendered by the pronoun of nearer definition τοῦτο.

16:16 τοῦτο is proleptic in its reference, viz. the orders given about gathering manna. They are to gather from it (the manna), each לפי אכלו

---

had καὶ ἀνέβαινε τὸ κοίμημα τῆς δροσοῦ, and Theod had καὶ ἀνέβη κοίμημα δροσοῦ according to Syh.

11. Aq followed by Theod has λελεπισμένον ("flaked") according to Syh),

"according to his eating," i.e. as much as he needs. Exod understood it differently in ἕκαστος εἰς τοὺς καθήκοντας "each for the appropriate ones," i.e. each for his own family. The tradition is peculiar since Exod did know what the phrase meant; at 12:4 exactly the same phrase is rendered by ἕκαστος τὸ ἀρκοῦν αὐτῷ. Hex tried rather unsuccessfully to get closer to MT by adding παρ αυτω, for which see παρ᾽ ἑαυτῷ in v.18.[13]

The manna to be used was a γόμορ per head, i.e. about two liters per person. That κατὰ κεφαλήν means "per person" is clear from the κατὰ ἀριθμὸν ψυχῶν ὑμῶν which follows immediately. In the tradition the Byzantine text has prefixed the phrase with και, but this is merely a partial dittography.

The last qualifier reads ἕκαστος σὺν τοῖς συσκηνίοις ὑμῶν "each of you with your tentmates." MT has איש לאשר באהלו "each for those who are in his tent." Thus according to MT one person does the collecting for a household, whereas in Exod the collecting apparently is done in concert. Hex added τοις serving as a relative pronoun after ἕκαστος so as to conform to MT. -- For σύν a very popular A F variant has εν which does represent MT more closely and may be an early revision towards the Hebrew. -- Textually uncertain is the word συσκηνίοις; at least half the Greek witnesses support the A variant συσκηνοις. The two mean the same, but συσκηνίοις is less common, is supported by B, the oldest extant witness, and is thus probably to be preferred.

16:17 δέ shows change of subject, but the majority A F M text has changed it to a και structure. That the γόμορ of v.16 signified the measure in which the manna was to be collected and not the amount of manna gathered is clear from what the people collected - it all depended on individual appetites, ὁ τὸ πολὺ καὶ ὁ τὸ ἔλαττον, "the one much and the other less"; i.e. the gomor could be heaping full or half empty.[14] For ἔλαττον the *b* text has the non-Attic ελασσον. The latter is used in Gen, though the Attic spelling is used for the verb (8:3,5 18:28), whereas in Exod, Lev and Num only the

and Sym rendered by ἀνασυρόμενον "exposed."
12. See the discussion in THGE VII.M.9.
13. Aq as usual translated word for word: ἀνὴρ εἰς στόμα βρώσεως αὐτοῦ, while Theod tried to make sense by his ἀνὴρ εἰς τὴν βρῶσιν αὐτοῦ (these both from Syh). Sym rendered by ἕκαστος εἰς λόγον τῆς βρώσεως αὐτοῦ.

Attic spelling obtained. Oddly enough for all other words with Attic -ττ-
only the non-Attic -σσ- occurs in the Pentateuch.

16:18 For the verb in the opening clause a B *f n* variant has substituted a
participle which does subordinate the action to the succeeding finite verb.[15]
-- The second clause is introduced asyndetically in contrast to MT, but hex
prefixes καί. The measurement by the gomor showed οὐκ ἐπλεόνασεν the
one with much and the one with less οὐκ ἠλαττόνησεν,[16] a chiastic arrangement; the translator may well have omitted an introductory καί simply
to bring out this arrangement more clearly. The first verb may have been
chosen to serve as antonym for the second, i.e. "to have abundant" vs "to
have less (than enough)."[17]

The final clause uses the same idiom "each for the appropriate ones"
as in v.16 for which see its note, except that παρ' ἑαυτῷ is added, for which
a popular A variant has παρ αυτω which in v.16 was added by hex. Presumably the phrase "with himself" makes it clear that τοὺς καθήκοντας were
συσκήνιοι; cf v.16.

16:19 Change of subject is shown by δέ. -- The third singular imperative
καταλιπέτω is aorist, and not present as the well-supported A F M variant
καταλειπετω would have it. The two forms are homophones and only the
context can really decide. The present, however, shows a process, and is not
overly sensible; the variant text is simply an itacistic spelling of the aorist.

Also presenting a problem is the order of the two prepositional
phrases modifying καταλιπέτω. A very popular B tradition follows MT in
having "until morning" in second place. But if that order were original what
would have propelled the other order? Whereas if εἰς τὸ πρωί came before
απ' αὐτοῦ hex would naturally have reordered the text to fit the Hebrew
and that is what must have happened.

---

14. Cf SS 74. Sym shows the contrast by a μέν ... δέ construction, probably
as ὃ μὲν πολὺ ὃ δὲ ὀλίγον (from Syh).
15. But this is not Exod according to THGE VII.M.1. Sym adds an αὐτό as a
pronominal object after the verb as an ad sensum reference to the manna.
16. Cf remarks in SS 147.
17. The Hebrew העדיף is rendered by Sym according to Syh as εὗρον

16:20 The subject of εἰσήκουσαν is not stated; it is the αὐτούς of v.19, the υἱοὶ Ἰσραήλ of v.17. The simplex *f* variant to the verb is not an improvement. -- The opening statement is then explicated by the adversative clause that follows it. In contrast to the preceding verse εἰς τὸ πρωί comes at the end; Exod has probably varied the order to avoid monotony. The ἀπ' αὐτοῦ is best understood as a partitive construction; i.e. "but some people kept some of it until morning." For the A F M + variant κατελειπον, see comment on καταλειπετω in v.19.

The result was that the food became inedible, it became wormy and stank.[18] An *n* + variant εξωζεσεν for ἐξέζεσαν is actually a synonym of the second verb ἐπώζεσεν "stank, smelled."

In the last clause Exod uses the expressive ἐπικράνθη "became embittered" to render the root קצף "became angry." Two *f* witnesses changed it to εθυμωθη, probably derived from one of The Three. For the order: subject + prepositional phrase after the verb, cf comment on υμιν κυριος at v.15. A popular B reading reorders them to equal MT. Whether this was hex or not is not certain. -- The phrase ἐπ' αὐτοῖς "against them" is changed to δι αυτους by the *C* text, i.e. "on their account."

16:21 The daily pattern for gathering manna. This was done πρωὶ πρωί, the rendering for the distributive בבקר בבקר "morning by morning"; cf also comment on יום יום at v.5. The phrase also occurs in the Pentateuch at 30:7 36:3 and at Lev 6:12, but only here without τό. The repetition of a word to show distribution is a Hebraism. The omission of the second πρωί in a number of witnesses is due to haplography. The verb is then modified by the phrase ἕκαστος τὸ καθῆκον αὐτῷ; איש לפי אכלו had also occurred in vv.16 and 18, but was translated in quite a different fashion. The point had already been made in vv.19,20 that it was bootless to collect more than one day's ration, and and so "his appropriate portion" made good sense.[19]

περισσόν (?) "found more," whereas the respective subjects in Sym are ὁ τὸ πλέον and ὁ τὸ ὀλίγον. Sym thus has "and not did they find superfluous the one with more, and the one with little did not have too little."

18. Instead of ἐξέζεσεν (σκώληκας), Sym used the synonym ἀνέβρασεν "seethed."

19. According to Syh Aq rendered the phrase literalistically by κατὰ στόμα

254

The final statement, a temporal condition, represents two paratactic clauses in Hebrew. The δέ not only shows change of subject but is also contrastive. The verb in the ἡνίκα clause is appropriately imperfect "when the sun was getting hot, (it melted)"; the aorist read by a d f variant is quite inferior, as is the change by s of the active to the middle (imperfect), διεθερμαινετο.

16:22 The verse begins with ἐγένετο δέ, the δέ probably being contrastive. -- The time indication τῇ ἡμέρᾳ τῇ ἕκτῃ can modify either ἐγένετο as MT presupposes, or the following verb συνέλεξαν. An n variant prefixes the verb with a και, which then modifies ἐγένετο, but Exod probably intended otherwise.

What they (the people) gathered is idiomatically called τὰ δέοντα διπλᾶ, i.e. "double what was required." δέοντα, plural of δέον, is the participle of the impersonal δεῖ.[20] MT, however, has לחם משנה "bread double."[21] A C variant treated δέον as indeclinable and reads τα δεον. This "double quantity" is then defined by content as "two gomors for one (individual)," i.e. a double ration.

Change of subject in the next clause is shown by δέ. Its verb appears in B f z in the Hellenistic inflection εισηλθοσαν.[22]-- There is nothing in the narrative that would impel the collection of a double ration on the sixth day, and the chieftains of the assembly inform Moses only after the fact.

16:23 Change of subject is shown by δέ. The subject is not given in other ancient witnesses except for a few Hebrew mss, Tar[P] and Pesh. B has κυριος as subject - the work of an inattentive scribe since it is so obviously wrong. And the same scribe added ου before τουτο! -- There is no counterpart to τὸ ῥῆμα in MT but it is good Greek sense; cf also vv. 16 and 32 for similar constructions though without an ἐστιν, which a C variant omits.

βρώσεως αὐτοῦ, whereas Sym repeated his rendering of v.16, while Theod paraphased by εἰς τοὺς ἐσθίοντας αὐτό.
20. See LS sub δέον.
21. Sym rendered by ἄρτον διπλοῦν, whereas Aq literalistically had "bread second," possible ἄρτον δισσόν, according to Syh; in any event Aq wanted to represent the root for "two" in some way.

The term σάββατα first occurs here and was coined by Exod to represent שבת. The ending has been interpreted as based on the Aramaic šabbota, or the emphatic form šabbatta, as the community word for Sabbath among the Jews in Alexandria. The explanation shatters, however, on Exod's own usage, since both at 20:8 and 35:3 Exod speaks of the day τῶν σαββάτων; to Exod, creator of the term for the LXX, it is the plural of σάββατον; the singular does not occur in the Pentateuch, but first occurs in Isa 66:23 and becomes quite common in later books such as 4Kgdm, 1 and 2Chr, Neh, in Ps titles, but also in 1 and 2Macc.

It is then defined as an ἀνάπαυσις ἁγία to the Lord, a definition which was normative for Judaism and its observance a distinctive badge of its culture. In order to observe the Sabbath rest food preparation was to take place in advance. This was ordered by a series of imperatives: πέσσετε ... ἕψετε ... καταλίπετε.[23] -- The statements are abrupt without time designations except at the end of the verse, but the implication is clear "do it before the Sabbath arrives."

The provisions for the Sabbath must be kept overnight from the preceding day as an exception to the prohibition of v.19. By τὸ πλεονάζον "that left over" is meant that which was not eaten on the sixth day of the two gomors of v.22. For the popular F M itacistic spelling καταλειπετε, see comment at v.19. The imperative is modified by εἰς ἀποθήκην "in store, storage," representing MT's למשמרת. The time indication added, both here and in v.24, is ἕως πρωί, rather than the B f + variant εις το πρωι which came in under the influence of vv.19--20.[24]

16:24 In both vv.23 and 24 MT has a different verb for "leave" than in vv.19--20, but Exod throughout uses the same verb καταλείπω, and always in the aorist. This repetitiveness with its solemn sonority extends even to not using αυτο for אתו but retaining the partitive phrase ἀπ' αὐτοῦ of vv.19 and 20. For the A F M + variant imperfect spelling κατελειπον see comment at v.19. The B f z text has the Hellenistic inflection κατελιπο-

22. See the discussion in THGE VII.M.9.
23. For the variant texts with εαν for ἄν 1° and 2° within relative clauses see THGD 99--102.
24. Cf discussion in THGE VII.Q.

σαν.[25] Note that an M^mg s^mg + variant does have αυτο instead of ἀπ' αὐτοῦ; its source is probably one of The Three.

The καθάπερ clause also shows deviation from a literal rendering of MT in that Exod adds a dative pronoun αὐτοῖς to modify συνέταξεν. Curiously both in this as well as in the use of ἀπ' αὐτοῦ for אחד Pesh follows Exod. The oI text omits αὐτοῖς which could be due to Hebrew influence though it is more likely a coincidence. Variations in the conjunction are shown by B's καθως and the καθα of O; these are synonyms of καθάπερ and do not change the sense.

The divine hand in affairs is clear from the fact that exceptionally manna whether baked or boiled kept over to the Sabbath day neither stank nor had worms come into it. -- For the concluding ἐν αὐτῷ B and d t read the plural εν αυτοις. But manna is not referred to pronominally except by the singular.

16:25 Change of subject is shown by δέ. -- φάγετε is used absolutely which is rather unexpected. A few z witnesses added αρτον epexegetically, and hex added αυτο to equal MT. The command pertains to the πλεονάζον, the left over manna as baked or boiled from yesterday. That this is lawful is argued in the γάρ clause: "For today is a Sabbath to the Lord; it will not be found on the field." Exod separates Sabbath from "to the Lord" by the word "today" following the order of MT. The majority of witnesses place σήμερον at the end, i.e. immediately after κυρίῳ. In fact MT has היום in both places, and hex has added it there. So it is not clear whether the transposed text referred to above is really that or that it has filled only positions one and three, i.e. omits σήμερον 2°.

The last clause represents a passive equivalent in Greek "it shall be found" for MT's active "you shall find it." A majority A F M variant text has, however, an active second person plural ευρησετε.

16:26 The verse echoes the Sabbath commandment: ἐξ ἡμέρας + imperative + τῇ δὲ ἡμέρᾳ ... σάββατα οὐκ ... ἐν αὐτῇ; comp 20:9, 10. The command is future indicative συλλέξετε, though an n + variant has the aorist imperative συλλεξατε. Exod does not render MT's pronominal suffix, but hex added αυτο. As at 20:10 the simple dative instead of εν + dative suffices to render בּרים. The δέ shows change of subject to σάββατα.

The final statement is absolute: "not shall (it) be in it." The subject is understood as manna, and "in it" refers to the sabbath. A B *f z* reading has οτι preceding the clause, an attempt to relate this to the preceding. Actually the gloss produces a false interpretation.[26]

16:27 The syntactical pattern of the opening structure is identical in MT to that of v.22, and Exod treats it in the same way except that an ἐν is added before the dative phrase. The parallel even extends to the initial ἐγένετο δέ structure. And a *b f x* text makes the parallel complete by omitting ἐν. For the main verb ἐξῆλθον the B *f z* tradition has the Hellenistic ἐξηλθο-σαν.[27] In MT the subject of יצאו is only given as מִן העם, a partitive construction here serving as a nominal. This was understood by Exod which has τινες ἐκ τοῦ λαοῦ, a fully adequate reading.[28]

Naturally "they found nothing." A *b* variant has the Hellenistic inflection ευροσαν. The augmented ηυρον of cod M is but rarely found in LXX.

16:28 Change of subject is shown by δέ. MT's מאנתם is translated by οὐ βούλεσθε. The negative plus βούλομαι is used similarly at 4:23 8:2 9:2 and 10:3, whereas at 7:14 the negative particle μή occurs alone to render the root מאן. At 10:4 μὴ θέλῃς is used, and at 22:16(17) מאן ימאן is rendered by ἀνανεύων ἀνανεύσῃ; this instance is, however, in a legal context: "if he really refuses ..., then." In general it is clear that a negative plus a verb meaning "desire, wish" is Exod's usual way of dealing with מאן.

God's instructions are called τὰς ἐντολάς μου καὶ τὸν νόμον μου, the usual equivalents for מצותי and תורתי.

16:29 ἴδετε is probably to be understood as "take notice," "pay attention." In MT the כי following the imperative can best be taken as asseverative, but Exod produces a γάρ clause, explaining why one should take notice:

25. See THGE VII.M.9.
26. Cf THGE VII.O.
27. For this usage see THGE VII.M.9.

"Because the Lord gave you this day as Sabbath," with a double accusative modifying ἔδωκεν. The phrase "this day" is unique to Exod, and it makes excellent sense in the context, contrasting perfectly with "on the sixth day" of the next clause. A popular F text omits the article before σάββατα; usage on the articulation of σάββατα is inconsistent in Exod, both the unarticulated and articulated forms occurring.

In the "therefore" clause Exod again has an aorist verb with the pronominal subject αὐτός referring to the Lord.[29] In the vocalization of MT the root is made a participle, i.e. "he is giving you on the sixth day." Either interpretation can fit the context. Exod can justify the past tense as a reflection on the disobedience shown in v.27, and the narrative of vv.22--26.

The instructions for the observance of the Sabbath rest is given in two clauses: a) remain, each (of you) in your houses, and b) let no one go from his place on the seventh day. The first of these begins with the imperative καθήσεσθε, to which the *b n* text prefixed και, a partial dittograph; note that the text of *x* has read the word as και θησεσθε! -- The phrase "in your houses" is Exod's interpretation of MT's תחתיו "(each) his place"; the translation is fully reasonable. -- A popular Byzantine tradition substitutes for the prepositional phrase παρ εαυτω, whereas it occurs as a doublet in the F *z* text. The variant traditions are explicative of the text.

In the second clause a majority tradition has added υμων after μηδείς as an epexegetical gloss. Two major at tempts to correct the text obtain in the tradition. Since MT has איש following the verb יצא the hex text changed the word order, leaving a μη before the verb but placing μηδεις after it. Another very popular A F M tradition has added εκαστος after the verb; this also conforms to MT though it is not hex; it also seems recensional in character.

16:30 The verb ἐσαββάτισεν is a denominative verb from σάββατα. The verse concludes the Sabbath motif. Exod has a singular verb by grammatical attraction to the singular subject ὁ λαός as does Sam. MT, Tar and Pesh have the plural which is also possible, since "people" is a collective.

---

28. Cf SS 157f.
29. SS 82 makes the point that the pronoun "stört den Zusammenhang."

16:31 The subject of the first clause is οἱ υἱοὶ 'Ισραήλ which agrees with a few Hebrew mss, Tar^P and Pesh, the other witnesses having "house of Israel." A B *t z* variant has an otiose αυτο after the verb ἐπωνόμασαν, otiose since the accusative modifier τὸ ὄνομα is given immediately after the subject. It was called μάν, a transliteration of the Hebrew מן. In the tradition this also becomes μαννα, the later form found in Num and Deut, from which the word came into English as "manna."[30] Exod abides by the transliterated Hebrew word throughout.

This manna is then described in the next two clauses, both introduced by δέ structures showing change of subject. The first describes what it looked like; it was white like coriander seed. The clause opens with ἦν δέ; since MT has והוא this is changed by Origen's hex to αυτο δε ην. Baffling is the *d* reading μαγον δε; I can make no sense out of it, except to relate it to the stem μεγα, and cf the Latin stem *magn*, possibly in the sense of "size"? -- It was ὡς σπέρμα (κορίου), which the *f* scribe misheard as ωσπερ![31] -- The second clause describes its taste: "its taste (was) like a cake with honey."[32]

16:32 Change of subject is shown by δέ. The opening clause up through κύριος 1° is identical with the opening of v.16, for which see comment there. The phrase τὸ γόμορ τοῦ μάν occurs both here and in v.33 but only in the latter does MT have מן as equivalent for τοῦ μάν; here MT has ממנו, but Exod identifies the pronoun in the light of v.33: "fill a gomor τοῦ μάν,"[33] and this "for storage for your offspring."

The ἵνα clause gives the reason for preserving the measure of manna, viz that they (the offspring) may see the bread. An A *b* + reading has ειδωσιν instead of ἴδωσιν; but the text demands "see" not "know," and the variant is simply an itacism for ἴδωσιν.

In MT Moses is presented as quoting Yahweh directly, whereas Exod makes this indirect discourse; all first person references are removed.

---

30. Cf also מנא and מנה of Tar^O and Tar^P resp.
31. For κορίου the Samariticon had ὀρύζης "rice."
32. Aq translates the clause as ἡ δὲ γεῦσις αὐτοῦ ὡς ἄμυλος ἐν μέλιτι. The term ἄμυλος literally means "unground," then by extension "a cake made of meal ground by hand," thus a specially fine cake. Sym compares its taste ὡς μελικήριον "like a honeycomb."

Exod's ἐφάγετε ὑμεῖς removes the Lord's role in the giving of the manna entirely over against all other ancient witnesses. In the ὡς clause the first person reference is changed into third person by ἐξήγαγεν ὑμᾶς κύριος, i.e. the clause is part of the indirect discourse.

16:33 Moses (changed to κυριος by *d t*) now addresses Aaron ordering him to take a golden vessel and to put into it a gomor full of manna. The word which Exod renders by στάμνον[34] is צנצנת, a hapax legomenon; from the context it must be a container of sorts and all the ancient witnesses so understood it. That it is χρυσοῦν seems to be a free invention of Exod, possibly in view of the gold of so many of the tabernacle utensils, and cf also the use of gold for the ark itself 38:1--8. At Hebr 9:4 reference to the στάμνος χρυσῆ ἔχουσα τὸ μάννα is made but that is based on Exod. The gender of στάμνον created some difficulty; the pronoun referring to it is αὐτόν but a *b n x* variant has the neuter αυτο, and some scattered witnesses even have αυτην.

What is to be put into it is πλῆρες τὸ γόμορ τοῦ μάν. The word πλῆρες is neuter agreeing with γόμορ. A B *s t* variant has πληρης since it often appears later as an indeclinable. For μάν as μαννα see comment on v.31.

The last clause is also an imperatival one in MT but is second person future in Exod. Admittedly this is a substitute for an imperative, but it is unusual for the change to be inaugurated by the Greek rather than the Hebrew. Aaron is told to place it before God. The "it" is neuter αὐτό and must refer either to γόμορ or to μάν; cf also MT. Presumably it is "manna" which is intended to be placed "before God"; all the other witnesses have "before Yahweh/Lord." To place something before God is clarified by v.34 where this becomes "before the testimony," which see. The placement is εἰς διατήρησιν for your offspring. The word in MT is למשמרת which in vv.23 and 32 was rendered by ἀποθήκην "storage," a rendering avoided here and in v.34 because the cognate verb was being used and the expression would be misunderstood.

---

33. The genitive is partitive; see SS 161.
34. Here taken as masculine; cf Bauer s.v.

16:34 The first part of this verse, the ὃν τρόπον clause, belongs to the preceding verse. Only the second part of the verse is the response to the orders given Aaron in v.33. The response, however, only refers to the καὶ ἀποθήσεις clause of v.33. This seemed unsatisfactory to *d* which filled in the missing "so Aaron took the vessel and put into it from the manna a gomor full." Exod used the aorist middle ἀπέθετο "put aside" for וינחהו of MT; a popular B variant has the active απεθηκεν which really requires an accusative modifier; hex supplied an αυτο to equal MT. Aaron put (it) aside before the testimony, i.e. before the ark in which τὰ μαρτύρια were placed; cf 25:15,20 40:18 as a result of which the ark was often called "the ark (τοῦ) μαρτυρίου 25:9,21 et al. The statement here made is proleptic; the ark of the testimony was not yet built, but from the point of view of the reader this is irrelevant. The B 29 reading θεου for μαρτυρίου is an error influenced by the θεοῦ of v.33.

16:35 Change of subject is shown by δέ. For *man* as μαννα see comment on v.31. The Israelites ate manna ἔτη τεσσαράκοντα, which hex transposed to equal MT. In MT עד occurs twice as a preposition with a bound infinitive, i.e. עד באם "until their coming." Exod rendered both cases of עד as conjunctions with aorist verbs, as ἕως ἦλθον and ἕως παρεγένοντο resp. The two parts of the verse are parallel. For the first verb a *b* text has εισηλθον, i.e. "entered" for "came." The "inhabited land" is of course Canaan, and the variant has the manna continuing up to the entrance into Canaan. In the second half ἔφαγον is changed by a B *f* text to the Hellenistic εφαγοσαν.[35]

The final prepositional phrase is a surprising tradition. It reads εἰς μέρος τῆς Φοινίκης for MT's אל קצה ארץ כנען. Elsewhere ארץ כנען is rendered by τὴν γῆν τῶν Χαναναίων 6:4; cf also 3:17 13:5,11, and in 12:40 the phrase ἐν γῇ Χανάαν occurs. So Exod had no difficulty with "land of Canaan" as such, but here he gives it the old name Phoenicia; cf also Jos 5:1 for its use.[36]

35. See the discussion in THGE VII.M.9.
36. Sym renders the phrase by εἰς τὰ ἄκρα τῆς (γῆς) Χανάαν "to the borders of the land of Canaan," a literal rendering of the Hebrew text.

262

16:36 The learned statement is added that "the gomor was the tenth part of three measures," whereas MT has the omer as the tenth part of the ephah.[37] The τρίμετρος seemingly was a measure of capacity for oil,[38]though that hardly seems relevant here. Tar[P] states that the Omera is one tenth דחלת סאין, i.e. of three Seahs; this in turn was supposed to equal one ephah, so if "the three measures" of Exod are three seahs, the equation of an ephah is assured.

37. Aq has τοῦ οἰφί instead of "three measures."
38. According to LS.

Chapter 17

17:1 Vv.1--7 narrate the account of the water provided from the rock. The Israelite congregation moved on from the desert of Sin and in due course arrived at Rephidin where there was no water. The initial verb is ἀπῆρεν in the singular in grammatical agreement with the subject συναγωγή, whereas MT is plural. An *O b* variant has the plural which may represent an early correction towards the Hebrew, but cf 16:1. Since συναγωγή is a collective noun either number is possible. For the articulation of συναγωγή in a popular F tradition see note at 16:1.

The move was made κατὰ παρεμβολὰς αὐτῶν "according to their encampments." The phrase is a peculiar one; in fact it is unique in LXX, and only here is it used to render למסעיהם "by stages, stations." What is probably meant is "according to the places where they bivouacked," i.e. according to the way-stations where they encamped. The journey was made by divine orders, διὰ ῥήματος κυρίου, and eventually they encamped at Rephidin. -- A B + variant has the Hellenistic inflection, παρενεβαλοσαν.[1] -- The place name is given as Rephidin for the Hebrew רפדים. Some mss, mainly belonging to *O* do spell the name with a final *mu*, but this is probably a hex correction. Other spellings are itacistic and are not unusual.

The point of the narrative comes in the final clause "but there was no water for the people to drink." Change of subject is indicated by δέ. Over against MT Exod has τῷ λαῷ before the infinitive πιεῖν, which hex transposed to accord with MT.

17:2 Exod uses the imperfect middle of λοιδορέω to translate the verb ריב; cf also 21:18, in quite a different context. The Hebrew verb is a juridical term, whereas the Greek simply means "to rail at." The imperfect is appropriate since the railing was a process. The particular complaint is introduced by the direct speech marker which Exod substitutes for the Hebrew paratactic "and he said." A majority A F M text has και ελεγον which may well be an early revision towards MT. Since only Moses is addressed Exod uses the singular imperative δός even though BHS and Tar^O witness to the plural. As in MT the indirect pronominal object precedes the direct object.

Moses' reply illustrates Exod's tendency to vary patterns of translation. In MT the preposition modifying the verb ריב occurs twice as עם. Exod had used πρὸς Μωυσῆν the first time, but in his reply to the raillery changes to the simple dative μοι. Note that here, Moses uses the present tense to parallel the imperfect of ἐλοιδορεῖτο. This raillery against Moses is placed in the proper theological perspective in the coordinate question (the conjunction is lacking in BHS Tar^O and Vulg) "and why are you tempting the Lord"? πειράζετε means "put to the test, try, make trial of." Moses accuses Israel of attempting to put the Lord on trial by their railing against himself.

17:3 Change of subject is shown by δέ. The verse is a doublet account of vv.1b and 2, but here the raillery becomes a murmuring; compare 16:2,3. ἐγόγγυζεν is the simplex form, for which a *y* reading διεγογγυζεν is a free variant; cf note at 15:24. Since murmuring is a process it was placed in the imperfect rather than the aorist. A B *b* text has added an otiose εκει after the verb under the influence of its earlier occurrence in the verse.[2] -- The murmuring is made ἐπὶ Μωυσῆν "against Moses," which the B F *x* text changed to προς μωυσην; this is simply a careless mistake and ought not to be taken seriously.[3]

As in v.2 Exod uses the direct speech marker instead of MT's paratactic "and said." The long form of the question phrase ἵνα τί τοῦτο is best interpreted as a simple Hebraism, a literal rendering of למה זה. The reading τι τουτο οτι of the *b* pair 19' is an attempt to put the phrase into better Greek. -- For a similar "murmuring" cf 16:3 and the comments on it. The deliverance from Egypt is given an evil twist as intended not for good but ἀποκτεῖναι ... τῷ δίψει. The infinitive is purposive. Murmuring is exemplified by interpreting a salvific act as a destructive one.

Exod along with all other old translators except Tar^O have levelled the peculiar change in MT of plural to singular first person suffixes; i.e. MT

1. See the discussion on usage in THGE VII.M.9.
2. Cf THGE VII.O.

has "bring us up ... kill me ... my sons ... my cattle" which is not sensible. Exod does omit as otiose a ημων after κτήνη, but this is supplied by hex. -- There is a great deal of uncertainty in the tradition as to whether the dative of means[4] should be τῷ δίψει or τη διψει. The uncertainty is aggravated by the fact that in the dative singular the neuter and the feminine nouns, both meaning "thirst," are homonyms, and only the article can distinguish which lexeme is intended. τη διψει has substantial support in the tradition though τῷ δίψει is almost certainly the form which Exod used.

17:4 Change of subject is shown through δέ. The verb ἐβόησεν occurs four times in Exod and always for the Hebrew צעק. The *O* text has the compound ανεβοησεν as a free variant; it is also freely used throughout LXX for צעק, though only once, at 14:10, in Exod.

Apparently the incident was turning ugly; at least Moses desperately asks God for advice, complaining ἔτι μικρόν and they will stone me. The Greek is a word for word rendering of MT, "they are almost at the point of stoning me." The verb used is a compound καταλιθοβολήσουσίν, which is unusual since Exod otherwise always used the simplex form to render the root סקל (8:26 19:13 21:28,29,32). The compound is rare, occurring elsewhere only in Num 14:10. Both there as well as here the tradition yields a reading of the simplex.

17:5 The *b* text sensibly changed the initial καί to a δε structure. The verb προπορεύου is present imperative and translates עבר לפני. The verb was already used by Gen to render עבר at 32:16 where the following לפני is translated by ἔμπροσθέν (μου). The more usual rendering for עבר is the παρα- compound (cf 30:13,14 39:3). The *C* variant with the simplex is the result of copyist confusion, a reduction of the syllables προπορ to πορ. After the προ compound the use of the genitive is expected. The popular A F M omission of τούτου in τοῦ λαοῦ τούτου may well be a prehexaplaric revision towards the Hebrew.

The ἀπό phrase in the second instruction is used as a partitive construction.[5] The δέ structure seems to serve no special purpose beyond

---

3. As against Helbing 185.
4. Cf SS 124.

parataxis.

In the third imperatival construction the accusative along with a descriptive relative clause is preposed with chiastic effect. The reference to ῥάβδον ties this narrative in with the plague narratives. -- The hex text has added σου to ῥάβδον to equal MT.[6] -- The concluding instruction (καὶ) πορεύσῃ in imitation of MT is in a finite (future) inflection, though an *n* variant has for stylistic reasons changed it to a present imperative πορευου.

17:6 Exod shows some dissatisfaction with a literal rendering of MT in which God is pictured as standing before Moses on the rock, and interprets the Hebrew first as a reference to God's earlier presence, i.e. ὅδε ἐγὼ ἕστηκα "here I did stand," but also as an instruction for Moses to come on to the rock at Horeb.[7] What Exod seems to have had in mind is to identify the rock where Moses is to go. The difficult construction has given rise to numerous attempts to fix up the text. The homophonic ωδε became a popular variant for ὅδε, though adverbializing the word did not simplify the reading. Only the F^b reading ιδου is a correction towards MT. Little was done in the tradition about the verb ἕστηκα though the participle עמד in MT clearly implies incipient action, but only Arm and Bo interpret the verb as a future.

The phrase πρὸ τοῦ σέ (ἐλθεῖν) "before you (come)" substitutes for the prepositional phrase לפניך in MT.[8] This has created much confusion in the tradition; the most popular variant is to substitute εκει for ἐλθεῖν. This may well be an early preOrigenian attempt to correct the text. The B *b f* tradition has added εκει in the text before πρό, whereas a *C n s* variant has added εκει after ἐλθεῖν. I would translate the text of Exod as: "Here I did stand before your coming on to the rock at Horeb." Note that the accent is on God's former station; it locates precisely where Moses is to come.

The divine instruction to Moses is clear; he is to strike strike the rock, and water for the people will result. A B *f* text adds an epexegetical μου

---

5. See SS 155.
6. Cf SS 94 and 120.
7. Cf the discussion in THGE VII.Q.
8. Aq naturally rendered this literally as εἰς πρόσωπόν σου (from Syh), whereas Sym and Theod have ἔμπροσθέν σου. Of course they would not have retained ἐλθεῖν which has no counterpart in MT; it has שם at this

after λαός. The variant text is an early one; in fact it is quoted in Isa 48:21, but the μου is not overly appropriate in God's reaction to the faithless murmuring of the people.

The concluding statement, with δέ showing change of subject, states that Moses carried out God's instructions publicly ἐναντίον τῶν υἱῶν ᾽Ισ-ραήλ. This is more public than in MT where Moses did so before the elders of Israel. -- The hex text also changes the word order of Μωυσῆς οὕτως to conform to MT's כן משה.

17:7 Moses gave the double name "Temptation" and "Raillery" to the place, reflecting the double question posed in v.2: "why do you rail against me and why do you tempt the Lord?" A C tradition has the verb as an indefinite plural, επωνομασαν, making the statement a popular aetiology. Exod also adds a demonstrative "of *that* place" over against MT, giving greater precision to its location; it is clear that these are not new names for Raphidin but for the rock at Horeb.

Exod correctly interprets the Hebrew names Massah and Meribah, thereby preserving the sense of the etymologies given in the text. The text presents the material in chiastic fashion, i.e. in an a-b-b-a pattern; the etymology of the second name Raillery is given first, and the first name Temptation follows. For the meaning of the verbs (and therefore of the names) see comments at v.2. The infinitive πειράζειν lacks a subject, and hex has added αυτους so as to correspond to the subject given in נסתם. Hex also articulated κύριον so as to represent the את before יהוה. The Byzantine text has also changed the direct speech marker λέγοντας to the indeclinable nominative form λεγοντες, admittedly the more common form in LXX generally.

The particular form of the πειρασμός on the part of Israel was questioning the reality of the divine presence, i.e. Is Yahweh בקרבנו אם לא? Exod quite correctly translated the question, simply rendering בקרבנו by ἐν ἡμῖν "among us."[9]

---

juncture.
9. According to Syh Aq had ἐν ἐγκάτω ἡμῶν, whereas Theod had ἐν μέσῳ ἡμῶν, both attempts at rendering קרב in some more literal way than as a

17:8 The battle with Amalek is introduced by a δέ structure. Exod adds a fine exegetical note by using the imperfect ἐπολέμει rather than the simple past of MT; after all the narrative of vv.9--13 only makes sense as taking place during the battle. An *oI C* variant has the more literal aorist form επολεμησεν. Cod A's unique επορευθη is the product of an inattentive scribe; by it ' Ἰσραήλ is taken as subject: "Amalek came and Israel went!" -- A popular F reading has added the accusative article τον before "Israel" ensuring the interpretation of the verb (quite correctly) as "to make war on."[10] -- Hex added πρός as a rendering for עם.[11] -- For variation in the tradition on the spelling of ' Ραφιδίν see comment at v.1.

17:9 Change of subject is shown by δέ. Moses tells Jesous (for MT's Joshua) "Choose for yourself able men." MT has "for us," which Exod rejected in favor of the idiomatic reflexive pronoun. This in turn made attractive the popular middle επιλεξαι for Exod's active ἐπίλεξον. Exod's characterization of the men to be chosen as δυνάτους does not equal MT though the interpretation is hardly contrary to the intention of MT's simple אנשים. Its omission may well reflect a revision of the text towards MT.

παράταξαι is Exod's rendering for הלחם "fight." Its modification by αὔριον is assured in Exod. In MT מחר could modify either the clause before it or the one after it, though the Masoretes by placing the preceding word under the **ethnaḥ** intended it to modify the following clause. That same uncertainty obtains in Sam and Tar[O], but not in Tar[P] and Pesh which both agree with Exod, whereas Vulg's *ego stabo* takes it with the following. MT continues with אנכי נצב, i.e. with pronoun + participle, which Exod usually renders by pronoun + present tense, but Exod (with Tar[P]) here adds καὶ ἰδού before ἐγὼ ἔστηκα (in form a perfect of ἵστημι, i.e. I have stood, and so am standing). The tense of ἔστηκα is coterminous with παράταξαι ... αὔριον, and one should render the Exod clause by "when behold I am (i.e. will be) standing on the top of the hill, i.e. Joshua is to engage the Amalekites while Moses is standing on the hilltop.

---

mere long form of the preposition ב.
10. Cf LS s.v. II.
11. Taken from Sym.

17:10 This verse explicates the preceding one. All the tenses are now in the aorist. What Jesous "did" is expressed paratactically: "and he set up in battle array with Amalek." In v.9 παράταξαι was preceded by a subordinate participle ἐξελθών; this was the source for the popular B gloss of ἐξελθων before παρετάξατο. Exod simply followed MT which had אֵצֵ in v.9 but not in v.10.[12]

In the last clause the verb is again aorist, as in v.9 coterminous with Jesous' entering the fray against Amalek. The three members of the subject are joined in both cases by καί as in Sam Tar[P] Pesh and Vulg, whereas MT and Tar[O] have "Moses, Aaron and Hur."

17:11 The introductory formula καὶ ἐγένετο ὅταν before a past tense verb must have the aorist, and never the well supported A B F imperfect variant ἐγινετο.[13] The unusual imperfect may well have arisen through a partial dittograph in an uncial parent. An original ΕΓΕΝΕΤΟ could easily by doubling the left leg of *nu* become ΕΓΕΙΝΕΤΟ, the itacistic spelling of ἐγινετο which both B and F actually have. Since this is pronounced *egineto* the imperfect would automatically follow. In any event only the aorist can be original.

Exod has interpreted the entire verse as narrative past, whereas MT has the entire verse in the potential mood; note the imperfects יָרִים and יָנִיחַ and the contextually neutral יִגְבַּר (twice). Exod with fine feeling uses the aorist in the ὅταν clauses but in the apodoses the imperfect κατίσχυεν (not the aorist κατισχυσεν of the *x* + text). These would contrast as follows: "when Moses held up (his) hands Israel was prevailing; but when he let down (his) hands, Amalek was prevailing." In neither temporal clause does Exod have the "his" of MT, and in both cases hex has supplied an αυτου. The genitive pronoun is quite otiose in Greek; Moses would hardly be raising and/or lowering someone else's hands.

17:12 Change of subject to χεῖρες is shown by δέ. When Moses' hands became heavy they took a stone which they placed under him. The antecedent of "they" must be the Aaron and Hor of v.10. An A B *x y* reading

12. Cf also the discussion in THGE VII.O.
13. For a full discussion of this formula in Exod see THGE VII.M.5.

has επ αυτον for ὑπ' αὐτόν, but this must be a mistake; υπ and επ are often confused by copyists. On the other hand the change of ἐπ' in the next clause to επανω in an *oI C b* variant is fully sensible even though unnecessary.

With the mention of Aaron and Hor as new subjects δέ is appropriate. A popular B variant changing the δέ to a και structure was probably created to avoid a δὲ καί collocation.[14]

στηρίζω occurs only here as a rendering for תמך, but it is a good translation; Aaron and Hor "propped up" Moses' hands, one on either side, or as Exod picturesquely renders the Hebrew, "here one and there one." The verb is in the imperfect, signaling that this was a continuing support. A *b* variant, υπεστηριζον, intensifies the notion of "support" for the arms of Moses.

In the last clause the subject ידיו is fully spelled out as αἱ χεῖρες Μωυσῆ; see the opening clause. The narrative flow from the preceding clause is upheld by the use of the same root for the participle complementing ἐγένοντο as that of ἐστήριζον, though in MT the roots are different. Here MT has אמונה "steady, firm."[15] The perfect passive participle in Exod does make good sense: "the hands of Moses were held fast." -- The term δυσμῶν ἡλίου is a good idiomatic rendering of MT's בא השמש, with δυσμη always occurring in the plural in LXX.

17:13 Exod's ἐτρέψατο "put to flight, routed" is a good contextual rendering of MT's יחלש which means "weaken" and so "defeat"; Exod makes a stronger, dramatic finish to the story: Jesous routed Amalek and all his people; the word "all" is a plus in Exod and fits in well with his version. Exod also heightens the tension of the statement by his rendering of the phrase לפי חרב "at the edge (literally mouth) of the sword." For this Exod created a much stronger idiom ἐν φόνῳ μαχαίρας "by the slaughter of the sword," a phrase adopted by Num 21:24 and by Deut 13:15 20:13. The phrase לפי חרב occurs 31 times, and is occasionally rendered by omitting פי, i.e. "with the sword," but otherwise פי is always rendered literally by ἐν στόματι. In the Pentateuch ἐν στόματι μαχαίρας occurs once at Gen

14. Cf THGE VII.E.1.
15. Aq in typical literalism rendered this by πίστις.

34:26. Other instances of ἐν στόματι are found principally in Jos and Jdg, but also in 1 and 4Kgdm and Jer.

17:14 Change of section is shown by δέ. The majority of witnesses supports a καὶ structure but this was due to the influence of the prevalent paratactic pattern. Moses is told to do two things: "write this down" and "put in the ears," and the object is in both cases the same: the statement ἀλοιφῇ ... οὐρανόν. The first command is less ambiguous in Exod than in MT; by means of τοῦτο εἰς μνημόσυνον Exod makes clear that he interpreted the Hebrew text זאת זכרון as a double accusative, which may well be what MT means. Inscribing the message in a book would ensure a permanent reminder of God's intention for Amalek. The Byzantine text has ἐν βίβλω. There is no distinction in meaning though the Exod form, βιβλίω, is morphologically its diminuitive. The B z variant εἰς βιβλιον accents the fact that Moses was to write down into a book; the variant shows how εἰς and ἐν coalesced in Byzantine Greek.

The Hebrew of the second command is unique; שים באזני occurs only here. Verbs modified by באזני include דבר, קרא, שמע and אמר as the more frequently used, and rare combinations include הגיר, גלה, ענה, בכה, נתן, צוה, שוע, and הקשיב. Thus one speaks, calls out, hears, says, weeps, commands, calls out, relates, but one also puts or gives in the hearing of. Furthermore, Exod has δὸς εἰς τὰ ὦτα; presumably what Exod means is "recite in the hearing of (Jesous)." Exod frequently used δίδωμι (seven times) to render שים; it also occurs seven times in Isa, whereas in other parts of LXX it is only rarely used: twice each in Jos, Ps and Jer and once each in Num, 1Kgdm, 2Chr and Ezek. δίδωμι is the regular equivalent for נתן which can mean "give" or "place," and by extension "put, place" is also intended by δίδωμι; this is in turn extended to שים which means "put, place" but not "give." So the use of δός here is a Hebraism.

The message to be written and recited is introduced by ὅτι which here introduces direct speech. The cognate free infinitive מחה is translated by a dative noun cognate to the verb, and it serves a purpose similar to the

Hebrew infinitive. I would render it by "I will completely wipe out (the memory)."

Of interest is the clever way in which Exod translates the compound preposition מתחת "from under." By inserting a feminine article between ἐκ and ὑπό the phrase "from under heaven" of MT becomes "from the (earth) under the heaven." The τῆς automatically calls τῆς γῆς to mind.

17:15 The instinct that Moses built an altar κυρίῳ was undoubtedly sound but there is no ליהוה in MT. And the articulation of κυρίῳ by *d n* + can only be secondary. An A F M *O C x* variant omits the word, and may well be a preOrigen revision towards MT.

This verse along with the next one gave trouble to the Alexandrians. A name for Moses' altar "The Lord is my banner" seemed to make little sense. But if one read נסי as נוסי it means "my refuge," and so Exod has "the Lord is μου καταφυγή." Hex has of course transposed the phrase as καταφυγη μου.

17:16 MT presumably intended v.16 to clarify the reader's understanding of the name given the altar in v.15, and accordingly begins the verse with ויאמר כי. What follows as יד על כס יה is totally obscure. Many scholars emend כס to נס, thereby making the statement an aetiology, though the resultant explanation is not particularly luminous either. None of the ancient witnesses supports the emendation, all but Exod understanding כס as כסא "throne," though this is no great improvement as Tar by their homiletical expansions demonstrate. Exod read the text of MT combining כס יה as one word, i.e. כסיה "hidden." Exod also did not understand the statement as an explanation of the name in v.15; by omitting ויאמר and taking כי as a causal particle, the line becomes the reason for Moses' giving the name. -- To Origen the text of Exod failed in two respects; he added και ειπεν at the beginning to make up for the absent ויאמר; he also found no equivalent for יה and so added κυριου after κρυφαίᾳ.

MT then goes on with מלחמה ליהוה "Yahweh has a war." Exod interprets freely by a verbal construction πολεμεῖ κύριος. What Exod seems to say is that Moses named the altar which he had built to the Lord "The Lord is my refuge" because from now on the Lord would by his hidden power perpetually fight against Israel's enemy Amalek. The notion of perpetuity is shown by the modifier ἀπὸ γενεῶν εἰς γενεάς "from generations to generations." Note that Exod renders the nouns of MT's מדר דר as collectives, i.e. in the plural. For דר דר cf also 3:15.

Chapter 18

18:1 The beginning of a new section is shown by a δέ structure. Jothor is Exod's name for יתרו.[1] Spellings in the tradition mainly concern interchanges of *omega* for *omicron* since to copyists the two vowel signs represented the same sound. Jothor is called both priest of Madian and Moses' father-in-law, for which see 3:1; for γαμβρός see note at 3:1;[2] cf also the account at 2:16--21.

The clause modifying πάντα has κύριος as subject, as do Tar, whereas MT has אלהים.[3] Exod also has no reference to Moses as MT has, i.e. only "Israel his own people" is mentioned as modifying ἐποίησεν. Hex adds τω μωυση και before "Israel," thereby equalling MT. A *b* variant omitted Ἰσραήλ leaving only "his own people." The use of the reflexive pronoun emphasizes the close relation of the Lord and Israel.

The last clause of the verse presents a difficulty in interpretation. It is given as a γάρ clause which is not overly fitting as the reason for the foregoing. In order to clarify this the Byzantine group has ως εξηγαγεν instead of ἐξήγαγεν γάρ, i.e. "how the Lord brought Israel out from Egypt"; this now explicates the preceding "all that the Lord did." Actually the logical continuation of v.1a is v.5 "and came Jothor ... to Moses ...," with vv. 1b--4 as a parenthetical statement explaining inter alia why the sons and wife of Moses were not in the Israelite camp. If the γάρ clause is understood as an unusually preposed clause the sense is much clearer. In fact MT can also be understood in this way; the כי clause can easily be taken as part of v.2; thus "because Yahweh brought out ..., Jethro had taken Zipporah ... and his (i.e.Moses') two sons..."; in the dangerous days of the plagues, the exodus and the crossing of the sea Moses was well rid of family.

18:2 The δέ shows change of subject. The *d* text not only changed it to a και structure but also shortened the text: "and he took Sepphora ...." For the

---

1. The spelling is corrected to conform to that of MT by Aq but not by Sym who retains Ἰοθόρ.
2. Sym apparently used πενθερός, whereas Theod did not change Exod.

spelling of Jothor see note at v.1. -- Sepphora is inflected as a first declension noun in the accusative. Some witnesses take it as an uninflected noun; others insert a *mu* either before or instead of the *pi*. Sepphora's return to her father's house (along with the two children; see v.3) is dated as taking place μετὰ τὴν ἄφεσιν αὐτῆς "after her release." ἄφεσις is the technical term for divorce, but that can hardly be meant here. The Hebrew term used is שלוחיה, a term used for a father's gift to a daughter at the time of her marriage, a going away present, but here it must mean "her being sent away," i.e. dismissal for her own safety.[4] The word in Exod is clearly a reflection of 4:26; cf the discussion there where it is said that "she left him." An *n* variant has αφιξιν, usually meaning "arrival," but here "departure" as at Act 20:29.

18:3 The first phrase "and his two sons" belongs to the preceding verse. Exod betrays his patriarchal attitude by changing the gender of the possessive pronoun, MT having "her two sons." Exod was influenced by the naming of the sons and the explanation for the names which only make sense as coming from Moses. The masculine is then continued in λέγων which correctly attributes the aetiology to Moses.

In MT the phrase שם האחד occurs for both sons, the first in v.3 and the next in v.4. The first is rendered by ὄνομα τῷ ἑνὶ αὐτῶν[5] and the second by τὸ ὄνομα τοῦ δευτέρου; the latter is of course quite correct in the context. There is no basis in MT for the αὐτῶν; an early A F majority reading omitted it, possibly as a preOrigenian revision towards MT. Exod also interprets כי אמר simply by the direct speech marker λέγων. In the parallel passage at 2:22 λέγων also occurs but it is followed by ὅτι which is, however, part of the direct speech. The aetiology here uses πάροικος, for which see the note at 2:22. The statement differs in other aspects from 2:22 only in the use of the imperfect ἤμην instead of the present εἰμί. Either tense can be defended as a rendering for הייתי. An *ol C x* variant actually has εμι.

---

3. According to BHS a Genizah fragment also has יהוה.
4. Aq and Theod have the literalistic (μετὰ) ἐξαποστολάς; the word means "sending away" reflecting in this way not only the Hebrew root but even the plural of the Hebrew noun. What was meant by the plural is unclear except as a copy of the Hebrew as closely as possible.

18:4 A *b n* variant has a δε structure for καί, which would make sense as contrasting with the name of the first one. The omission of τό by the *oI C* text is due to the unarticulated ὄνομα of v.3. Similarly the γάρ clause has been influenced by v.3 in the introductory λεγων of B *f z*, which has no basis in MT.[6] The explanation for the name is only sensible in Hebrew, and the best that Exod could do was simply to translate what MT said as a statement of faith. The statement is in two parts: a nominal one "the God of my father is my help," and a verbal one: "he rescued me from the hand of Pharaoh." The aetiology rightly has "God," not "Lord"; cf 3:13--16. Nor does he use the plural "fathers," but rather "my father," which is probably to be taken literally as referring to Amram, Moses' father.

The second statement speaks of God's rescue of Moses from the power (literally "hand") of Pharaoh. MT has "from the sword of Pharaoh," which is figuratively meant. The phrase מיר פרעה does occur in vv.9 and 10. Exod's rendering rightly understood the figurative use, and rendered it by another figure. -- ἐξείλατό is inflected with first aorist ending on a second aorist stem, a typical Hellenistic Greek phenomenon. A popular M text has the older classical εξειλετο.

18:5 With v.5 the narrative of v.1a continues. Having heard all the reports of divine activity on Israel's behalf Jothor now, together with Moses' wife and sons, comes to visit Moses in the wilderness. The verb is simply ἦλθεν which The Three all support. It is the regular translation of the verb בוא in Exod. A B *f z* variant has εξηλθεν.[7] The verb is preceded by καί but Vulg changes to an *ergo* construction.[8]

Coordinated with Jothor are "sons and wife," both with a third masculine singular suffix in MT. From the context (vv.2--3) it is clear that τὴν γυναῖκα Μωυσῆ ... καὶ τοὺς δύο υἱούς are intended. By not adding a genitive pronoun αυτου in either case it is clear that they belong to Moses,

---

5. See SS 68.
6. For a discussion of the variant see THGE VII.O.
7. For its meaning and secondary character see discussion in THGE VII.N.
8. Possibly based on Sym who changes the construction to ἦλθεν οὖν. Sym clearly felt the need for showing the resumption of the narrative taking place.

whereas by adding αυτου (which hex has done to equal MT) the wrong intepretation that they were sons and wife of Jothor might be promoted.

The relative clause is a good translation of MT. οὗ is an idiomatic rendering of the Hebrew construction אשר plus שם, and the pattern in MT: pronoun + participle is rendered by an aorist verb παρενέβαλεν, the past tense being demanded by the context. The subject is presumably Moses who has just been mentioned. A popular M variant has the plural; this variant makes the people subject of the verb (the ᾿Ισραήλ of v.1), but it could create a great deal of unwitting confusion since the closest plural referent would be the compound ᾿Ιοθόρ ... καὶ οἱ υἱοὶ καὶ ἡ γυνή earlier in the verse. -- The locative phrase is "at the mountain of God" for which a majority variant has εις το ορος του θεου. The εις construction may be due to the earlier εἰς τὴν ἔρημον

18:6 Exod uses a passive construction ἀνηγγέλη plus a plural direct speech marker λέγοντες to introduce the actual message; Pesh also has a passive verb but no marker; all others follow MT's ויאמר. In using the passive the verb could no longer be the usual ειπ- root, and he used an idiomatic ἀνηγγέλη. The Α + απηγγελη does not change the meaning. An *O* variant has a plural active ανηγγειλαν which is another way of saying the same thing.

Instead of MT Tar and Vulg's אני Exod followed the text of Sam Pesh and a Qumran ms reading הנה. The subject of the statement is Jothor which is followed by the appositional phrase ὁ γαμβρός σου. Exod always has Jothor before appositional modifiers (vv.1,2,5,12 and 3:1 4:18), but hex has transposed the text to equal MT. For γαμβρός a *d* + variant has πενθερος, for which see note at 3:1.

Exod has no genitive pronoun σου after γυνή over against MT but does have it after υἱοί. A popular hex text has supplied σου after γυνή, but left υἱοί σου in adherence to Origen's principles of text criticism, though MT has בניה. Only Pesh and Vulg follow Exod in reading "your (i.e. Moses') sons." This change is consistent with Exod's change of gender in a similar context at v.3; cf comment there. This downgrading of Sepphora's role must have been intentional in view of Exod's unique rendering of עמה

"with her" by μετ' αὐτοῦ; Moses' sons came not with her but with Jothor their grandfather.

18:7 Change of subject is shown by δέ. Moses responded by going out to meet his father-in-law. Nothing more is said about wife and children who are from this point on completely disregarded, since the point of the narrative is, after all, the role of Jothor's meeting with Moses. And in the niceties of greeting one another it was the younger man who "bowed down to him (the "to him,"referring to Jothor, is an epexegetical plus in Exod and Pesh) ...." Exod has simplified MT's "and they asked each of his fellow as to peace (i.e. health) by ἠσπάσαντο ἀλλήλους. To Origen there was no equivalent for לשלום, and so hex added εις ειρηνην, an addition which hardly clarified the Greek.

   The last clause is also a free rendering of MT which has "and they entered the tent." Since Moses was the host Exod (as Sam) changes the construction to a transitive verb plus object. Presumably the complete disregard of wife and sons was disturbing and the majority tradition has αυτους for αὐτόν.

18:8 Exod does not translate the suffix of חתנו since it is otiose in Greek, but hex supplies an αυτου. The *d* + text again has the more specific word πενθερω for "father-in-law," for which see comment at 3:1.

   A second matter that Moses told Jothor about concerned "all the trouble which had happened to them on the way." This is joined paratactically to the preceding ὅσα clause as in some Hebrew mss, Pesh and Vulg, which is not unexpected. The *b* text has the present tense participle γινομενον "had been happening" for γενόμενον, but stress on the process of happening was hardly intended.

   The third matter included was the important statement "and that the Lord had rescued them from the hand of Pharaoh and from the hand of the Egyptians." Exod limits the realm of divine rescue by the two prepositional phrases to the dealings with Pharaoh and Egypt, whereas MT does not, and by implication also included divine intervention after the Red Sea deliverance. The limitation is, however, part of the larger context; cf vv.9

and 10 where these phrases are also present in Exod. An *O* reading simplified the text by changing ὅτι to ὡς: "and how the Lord rescued," tying this more clearly to the initial διηγήσατο. And as in v.4 a popular M variant attests to the classical second aorist ending, i.e. ἐξειλετο, rather than the Hellenistic ἐξείλατο.

18:9 Change of subject is shown by δέ. The initial verb in MT is a peculiar formation; cf also Job 3:6; in both cases the root חדה is involved, and the formation probably developed from yiḥde(h) to *yiḥd to yiḥad without removing the daghesh lene. That Exod understood the verb as from √ חדה "to rejoice" is clear from his ἐξέστη "he was amazed, astounded." Exod also correctly took טובה as a collective and translated by the plural τοῖς ἀγαθοῖς (as Pesh Vulg). -- ἐποίησεν is followed by αὐτοῖς κύριος, Exod's normal order of pronoun + subject after the verb, but MT has "Yahweh to Israel." Origen changed the word order to conform to MT, which order is attested by the majority of witnesses.

The verse then repeats with slight differences the ὅτι clause of v.8, the differences being the omission of the named subject and the reordering of the prepositional phrases and the omission of τῶν. As might be expected each of these differences is erased in the tradition: a popular A reading added κυριος; an A M *C f* variant articulated Αἰγυπτίων, and an *f* text reordered the phrases. And as in vv.4 and 8 the classical inflection for ἐξείλατο is found in a popular M variant text. It should also be noted that the source for καὶ ἐκ χειρὸς Φαραώ is v.10.

18:10 Exod's use of εὐλογητός is limited to this one case but it was already the form used by Gen in praise of God (9:26 14:20 24:27,31) for the Hebrew ברוך. In MT Yahweh is modified by doublet אשר clauses: 1) "who has redeemed you from the hand of Egypt and from the hand of Pharaoh," and 2) "who has redeemed the people from under the hand of Egypt." Of the ancient witnesses only Exod sensibly reduces this to one clause though not as a ος but as a ὅτι clause in terms similar to vv.8 and 9, but taking τὸν λαὸν αὐτοῦ from the second clause instead of υμας; cf the העם את of the second clause. A popular Byzantine text variant has corrected the ὅτι to ος towards MT. Also a correction towards MT is the weakly supported variant υμας by three *O* witnesses, while B *x* + have αυτους. For the popular M variant εξειλετο see comments at vv.1,8,9. It should be noted that Αἰγυπτίων is unarticulated in Exod as it was in v.9 but in contrast to vv.7 and 8. A popular variant has added an article, probably due to v.8.

That Exod omitted the doublet version was not left unnoticed. Hex added ος εξειλατο τον λαον υποκατωθεν χειρος αιγυπτιων, a word for word rendering exactly reproducing MT.

18:11 Exod uses ἔγνων "I know" rather than οἶδα, since γιγνώσκω means to know by observation whereas οἶδα means to know by reflection.[9] Jothor's recognition with its νῦν ἔγνων implies that prior to this he did not personally know that the Lord was superior to all the gods,[10] but now Moses' testimony has confirmed it.

The reason for this is given in the rather difficult second part of the verse. MT is especially obtuse here. MT introduces it by כי בדבר אשר "because by reason of the fact that"(?); Exod simplifies the construction by ἕνεκεν τούτου ὅτι "on this account, (viz.) that" (possibly without the כי?).[11] But then MT continues the relative clause with זדו עליהם "they were arrogant (insolent) against them," a phrase which has led to various attempts at midrashic paraphrase by the Tar.[12] Vulg rendered literally by *superbe egerint contra illos*. The verb זדו occurs only twice in the book, both cases being rendered by ἐπιτίθημι. At 21:14 it is modified by להרגו and refers to a wilful attack on a neighbour which Exod renders by ἐπιθῆται τῷ πλησίον ἀποκτεῖναι αὐτόν. Here ἐπέθεντο αὐτοῖς probably should be interpreted as "they set upon them."[13] Neither in MT nor in Exod are the antecedents given. In MT it is clear that "they " refers to the Egyptians and "them" to the Israelites, which was probably also intended by Exod. A popular Byzantine variant changes the verb to the singular επεθετο; "them"

9. Cf LS sub γιγνώσκω I.1.
10. Cf SS 146.
11. Aq has of course rendered all of this literally by ὅτι ἐν τῷ ῥήματι ᾧ, an incomprehensible construction which I shall not attempt to translate.
12. Both Aq and Sym translate the verb literally, ὑπερηφανεύσαυτο; for the prepositional phrase Sym has the idiomatic κατ' αὐτῶν, Aq and Theod, the more literal ἐπ' αὐτούς.
13. Cf LS sub ἐπιτίθημι B.III.2.

would then refer to the Egyptians and the subject would be "the Lord." The verb in Exod was intended in a military sense; "to set upon" meant "to prevail over," and the reference was taken to be to the Red Sea episode; cf also Tar^P with its טמע ית ארתכיהרן בימא דסוף.

18:12 In MT the sacrifices which Jethro took are designated as עולה וזבחים; Exod puts both into the plural, taking עולה as a collective which is plausible. When Exod says that "Jothor took holocausts and sacrifices to God" it is simply reproducing MT's hendiadys for "took and offered." -- For the variant πενθερος see note at 3:1.

The second clause begins with a δέ structure showing change of subject. The verb is put into the singular as in MT by attraction to the nearer member of the compound subject. This is changed to the plural, however, in a *C s* reading, precisely because it is a compound subject. A popular A F M variant adds και before Aaron, creating a και ... και pattern. -- It might be noted that Sam's text not only has no כל in the phrase "all the elders," but substitutes מזקני, i.e. "some of the elders of".

Presumably the sacrifices brought, though in part called עולה, were some kind of communion sacrifice since the common meal was part of the ritual. Exod emphasizes the commonality of the meal by the use of the compound συμφαγεῖν which a popular A F variant voids by the neutral simplex φαγειν. -- The word for food is the symbolic ἄρτον/לחם "bread" which the *C* text unimaginatively made into the plural αρτους "loaves." The ceremonial, or sacrificial, nature of the common meal is emphasized by the local phrase ἐναντίον τοῦ θεοῦ.

18:13 Exod translates the ויהי by καὶ ἐγένετο without a conjunction to introduce the coordinate verb which is, however, rendered by a finite verb. The pattern ויהי + *waw* + finite verb is usually rendered in Exod by omitting ויהי. Besides this verse there are eight more instances in which the pattern is translated with καὶ ἐγένετο (2:11 12:41,51 16:22,27 19:16 32:30 40:17); in each case the ויהי is followed by a time indication, with the verb following without a και, and this verse follows exactly this same pattern. The time indication is μετὰ τὴν ἐπαύριον, with which the parallel at 32:30 should be compared. The μετά is a Hebraism. The main verb of the opening sentence is συνεκάθισεν plus a purposive infinitive κρίνειν, i.e. "Moses sat to dispense justice";[14] a minor b variant substitutes the simplex but with no semantic change.

The second clause with change of speaker shown by δέ has παρειστήκει as its verb, a pluperfect inflection (of παρίστημι) emphasizing that all the people "had been standing by, near at hand." Only Exod attests to "all," a bit of poetic exaggeration. The time indication for all day long is ἀπὸ πρωίθεν ἕως ἑσπέρας. ἀπὸ πρωίθεν is a tautological phrase since the adverbial alone means "from morning" as well; the O C n variant απο πρωι came in from v.14. The other element of the scale, ἑσπέρας, means "evening" for which cod B uniquely substitutes δειλης "afternoon," also an intrusion from v.14.

18:14 Within the narrative of Jothor's giving advice on administration to Moses Exod adopts the lively style of the historical present: ἰδών ... λέγει ... (15) καὶ λέγει. -- Exod uniquely uses the name "Jothor" rather than "the father-in-law of Moses," though later in v.17 (see also v.15) he follows MT in using the descriptive title rather than the name. -- Within the relative clause, which is in turn a grammatical element within the participial clause modifying πάντα, the verb is inflected in the imperfect, showing Moses' habitual action. The B f text has the present tense ποιει, probably simply a copyist error for Exod's ἐποίει; the unimaginative aorist εποιησεν also occurs in z +, but this is not overly appropriate here.

What Jothor says is "What is this that you are doing for the people?" Hex added το ρημα before τοῦτο since MT has הדבר הזה.[15] Within the relative clause Exod has σὺ ποιεῖς, his more usual way of rendering the pattern: pronoun + participle.

In the second question the question marker διὰ τί is best interpreted as covering two clauses, both the σὺ κάθησαι which represents the same kind of pattern as σὺ ποιεῖς, and the λαὸς παρέστηκεν, wherein Exod has

14. Cf Helbing 96.
15. Aq is the source for the hex reading, whereas Sym and Theod preferring ὁ λόγος had to rewrite the first part of the question as well: τίς ὁ λόγος οὗτος ὄν.

understood the Hebrew נצב as a finite verb rather than as a participle. The Byzantine text has παρειστηκει under the influence of v.13.

The time designation is similar to that of v.13, but Exod prefers to vary the diet. For בקר he has πρωί though a popular B F M variant changes it to πρωιθεν to agree with v.13.[16] Similarly ערב is rendered by δείλης and an F + reading has εσπερας, again under the influence of v.13.

18:15 For the use of the historical present λέγει cf v.14 and especially 2:13. The addressee is τῷ γαμβρῷ for which as usual the more specific τω πενθερω receives scattered support in the tradition; cf note at 3:1. Hex has added αυτου so as to represent MT more precisely.

It might be possible to interpret ὅτι as introducing an object clause after a verb of saying. Then the direct speech would begin with the verb. This is not what the context demands, however; since Moses' reply is a direct answer to the διὰ τί question of v.14 one expects an answer with "because"; the ὅτι is then part of the reply: "Because the people come to me." παραγίνεται is rightly in the present; Moses' reply reflects an ongoing situation.

The reason for the people's coming to Moses is given in MT as לדרש אלהים "to make enquiry of God." The idiom is commonly used of seeking an oracle from God; here Exod probably interprets more accurately than some of the other old witnesses; it has ἐκζητῆσαι κρίσιν παρὰ τοῦ θεοῦ "to seek judgment from God," i.e. a legal decision. Moses acts as God's representative in the settling of disputes. Other witnesses refer rather to instruction: Tar to אולפן; Vulg has *sententiam,* or simply a "word" in Pesh.

18:16 Exod has two clauses in the ὅταν condition, and two clauses with first person verbs in the apodosis. All the other old witnesses make the second clause part of the apodosis. Exod's interpretation may well have been textually based since a Qumran ms does read ובא. Exod also relates this verse to the preceding by incorporating a γάρ after ὅταν, i.e. this verse gives the reason why the people come to him to seek judgment from God. Exod also defines what kind of דבר constitutes the occasion for approaching Moses; it is an ἀντιλογία, a "dispute, controversy."

In MT the subject of בא is דבר, whereas in all the others the verb is plural with the people as subject. The sentence is neatly balanced in Exod with two plural verbs in the protasis, and two first singular present verbs in the apodosis: διακρίνω ... καὶ συμβιβάζω, thus a present general condition. -- MT has ושפטתי for the first verb in turn modified by "between a man and (between) his neighbour." Exod abbreviates this considerably by a simple διακρίνω ἕκαστον "I decide for each (person)," correctly interpreting the intent of MT. In the coordinate clause Exod uses συμβιβάζω with double accusative modifiers,[17] over against MT which lacks the personal referent αὐτούς; it is, however, normal Greek usage for this verb; the clause explains how Moses rendered decisions; he taught the appellants "God's ordinances and his law." These ordinances are inter alia those found in chh.21--23. In MT the second element is also plural, תורתיו, and roughly equivalent to the חקי האלהים, but in Exod the singular is used as an overall cover term.

18:17 Change of subject is shown by δέ. Scattered witnesses change γαμβρός to the more exact term πενθερος for which see comment at 3:1.

18:18 The first clause is part of v.17 in MT. Exod renders MT's "not good is the thing which you are doing" freely, by using an adverb ὀρθῶς and omitting the relative pronoun, though the general statement has the same semantic content: "not rightly are you doing this thing." Origen could hardly let this stand; since there is an equivalent for לא טוב οὐ ὀρθῶς remains, but the rest is rearranged to fit the Hebrew order and the lacking relative pronoun is added in its place, resulting in ου ορθως το ρημα τουτο ο συ ποιεις. The fact that the result is not fully grammatical did not trouble him.

MT's v.18 is also not literally rendered into Greek. MT begins with a cognate free infinitival construction "you will actually wither away"; Exod translates this by φθορᾷ καταφθαρήσῃ ἀνυπομονήτῳ "you will be completely destroyed by an unbearable (task)." The Byzantine group has ανυπονοητω, a copyist error palaeographically inspired; "unsuspected" does

---

16. Cf also THGE VII.Q.
17. Cf Helbing 39.

not make much sense. An A F *oI C* variant which omits the last word may well be a revision towards the Hebrew. -- The A z text adds an unnecessary σου to λαός, whereas a few scattered mss including B* omit οὗτος.

MT continues the second part of the verse with a causal clause "because the matter is too heavy for you." Exod makes this a simple statement of fact without a causal particle, nor is the comparative taken over into Greek, and a demonstrative pronoun τοῦτο is added. And the final clause in turn explicates this statement. Exod adds σύ to explicate μόνος for rendering לבדך, "by yourself alone," though in v.14 he uses μόνος without a pronoun to translate the phrase. The omission of σύ by B* + is probably stylistically inspired. The pronoun is unnecessary but must be original, since no one in the tradition would have added an otiose pronoun at this juncture.

18:19 Exod uses οὖν as an inferential particle which following νῦν carries the narrative forward: "now then," "so now." -- For שמע בקולי Exod simply has ἄκουσόν μου which is unusual; Exod normally translated the קול by τῆς φωνῆς (3:18 4:1,8,9 5:2 15:26 18:24 19:5 23:22) or the accusative (32:17, 18), and only twice disregards it (also 23:21). The translation without φωνή is idiomatic Greek and adequately represents the Hebrew.

The third clause reads as a promise in Exod; Jothor says that his counsel will result in God being with Moses,. i.e. he is giving good advice. But MT's יהי is a wish: "may God be with you," which two scattered witnesses also suggest by their εστω, though the agreement with MT is pure coincidence.

The elaborate advice, extending through v.23, which Jothor gives Moses, begins with γίνου σὺ τῷ λαῷ τὰ πρὸς τὸν θεόν "be for the people the things that pertain to God," which is Exod's attempt to render MT's "be for the people מול האלהים," i.e. "in front of God." Vulg approximates Exod with: *in his quae ad deum pertinent*. What all three mean is that Moses is to continue to act as legal arbitrator, on the one hand bringing their cases before God, and on the other instructing the people in the ordinances and law(s) of God in turn. Other witnesses also found the phrase difficult. Tar

286

have תבע אולפן "seek instruction (from ירי)," and Pesh has "a teacher from God."

This role of being τὰ πρὸς τὸν θεόν involves first of all bringing up their cases to God, and secondly, an interpretative role of communicating the demands; this second matter is dealt with in v.20. Vulg makes the relationship much clearer by *ut referas quae dicuntur ad eum* (20) *ostendasque*.... Exod differs only slightly from MT; it does not render the otiose אתה after the verb,[18] and it adds an αὐτῶν after λόγους for clarification, i.e. not Moses' own λόγους, but the people's.

18:20 MT begins with הזהרתה which only occurs here in the Pentateuch; in fact it was a word favored by Ezekiel and only rarely found elsewhere. It generally means "to warn," though in a few cases it is clearly related to the Arabic *zahara* "to shine, be light," and so in the causative "to give light, make to shine"; it is not clear how these are related. Here it must mean "to make clear," hence "to instruct."[19] But Exod renders this by διαμαρτυρῇ "you shall attest to," a root normally reserved for translating העיד, and never elsewhere in LXX used to render הזהיר. Vulg correctly understood the Hebrew as *ostendas*.[20] To Exod Moses' role was to attest to God's ordinances and his law and explain (or interpret) the paths in which they are to walk and the works which they are to do. For the second verb הורעת Exod chooses an unusual word as well, σημανεῖς, again an equation found only here in LXX. Exod then adopts the phrase used in v.16 as object of συμβιβάζω, viz. "the ordinances of God and his law," though MT has "the ordinances and the laws"; cf comments there. Moses' role with respect to the communication of God's demands on his people is one of attestation and of explication. The latter involves a double object τὰς ὁδούς and τὰ ἔργα, both modified by relative clauses. MT has singular nouns in both cases הדרך and המעשה but presumably both can be understood as collectives.

18. The omission may be textual, since a Qumran ms apparently also lacks it.
19. Cf Helbing 226.
20. Aq translates by διαστέλου "delineate, define"; this is also used in LXX of Ezek 3:17,18,21.

18:21 Exod understands the rather odd חתה (presumably plus לך as Sam) "look, gaze," hence "look out for," as σεαυτῷ σκέψαι "look out carefully for yourself," which then has accusative modifiers. The *b* reading επισκεψαι does not clarify the text, and involves no real change in meaning.

Those who are to be searched for must have four qualities; they must be "able men, pious, righteous men, hating arrogance." The first of these translates אנשי חיל "men of ability"; this translation had already been used in Gen 47:5 in the context of able cattlemen among the relatives of Joseph. The second characteristic, θεοσεβεῖς,[21] is a rendering for יראי אלהים, and is a good translation.[22] The third qualification, ἄνδρας δικαίους,[23] is for אנשי אמת "trustworthy men," and though an unusual rendering, does well by the Hebrew text. One who is δίκαιος is one who is observant of custom or rule;[24] such a one does his duty, and so is righteous. The last characteristic is "hating ὑπερηφανίαν, Exod's substitution for MT's בצע "unjust gain, bribe."[25] Exod may well have thought of ὑπερηφανία as the basic characteristic of those who gather בצע.

The last clause advises Moses to establish (appoint) αὐτοὺς ἐπ' αὐτῶν. MT has no equivalent for αὐτούς, though the sense demands it; a Qumran text does , however, support it as well. -- The pronoun in ἐπ' αὐτῶν is changed to the dative in *f*, and to an accusative in the *z* text; all three are possible but a genitive has overwhelming support. -- These were to be appointed to one of four ranks: chieftains of thousands, of hundreds, of fifties, or of tens. In Exod as in Tar[P] Pesh and Vulg these are all connected by καί, whereas MT and Tar[O] have the pattern: 1 2 3 + 4. Sam as well as some Hebrew mss including one at Qumran represent the pattern: 1 + 2 3 + 4. A popular A tradition has added a fifth rank as και γραμματοεισαγωγεις "and governors," which is borrowed from Deut 1:15.

---

21. Cf SS 70.
22. This did not satisfy later Jewish revisers who insisted on the literalistic φοβουμένους τὸν θεόν.
23. Cf SS 65.
24. Cf LS s.v. A.
25. Not surprisingly the Jewish revisers changed this to πλεονεξίαν "excess gains, greediness."

18:22 The ranks named in v.21 will be the contact judges for the people on every occasion, with Moses himself only serving as referral judge for difficult cases.

Exod contrasts the cases by τὸ ῥῆμα τὸ ὑπέρογκον and τὰ βραχέα τῶν κριμάτων over against MT which has simply "the large case" and "the small case," each case beginning with a δέ construction contrasting change of object, as though it were a μέν ... δέ pattern. Exod by using ὑπέρογκον for the first class hints at a kind of case too large for ordinary judges.[26] Exod designates the second class by a plural term, and so contrasts the occasional overly difficult case with the common easy cases. The first verb ἀνοίσουσιν is unidiomatically modified by ἐπὶ σέ in the sense of "to you"; the normal usage would be εἰς σέ.[27]

The lower rank judges κουφιοῦσιν ἀπὸ σοῦ, a construction in which the Hebraic comparative מן is literally reproduced "they will make it easier for you."[28] The Attic future is replaced in A C b by the Hellenistic κουφίσουσιν, an inflection which became common in A.D. times. This help is also designated as συναντιλήμψονταί σοι; i.e. they will take over a lot of your burdens.[29]

18:23 Exod found difficulty with the second clause, וצוך אלהים, understanding it as introducing the apodosis as the omission of the conjunction ensures, though a popular M tradition does prefix a και probably in order to equal MT. But MT apparently includes this clause as part of the protasis. Pesh and Vulg also omit the article taking the clause as part of the apodosis.

The ἐάν clause is introduced by εαν δε in the *f* tradition, probably because δε occurs so often after ἐάν in the Pentateuch. The phrase τὸ ῥῆμα τοῦτο refers to the practice detailed by Jothor in vv.21 and 22.

The next clause introduces quite a different verbal concept. MT has וצוך (אלהים); Vulg takes the clause as part of the apodosis, but

26. The late Jewish revisers with their μέγα kept closer to the neutral גדל of MT.
27. See LS sub ἀναφέρω II.5.
28. See Helbing 165.
29. Sym and Theod translate MT's נשא "they will lift up, carry" somewhat more literally by their συμβαστάσουσιν "they will carry (the load) together

translates by *implebis imperium dei*, thereby at least reflecting the verbal idea of "command, order." Exod abandoned the Hebrew and merely contextualized by "God will strengthen you," choosing a verb which would explain the next clause as well; i.e. the ability to stand is the direct influence of God's strengthening you. παραστῆναι is also an unusual choice in that what must be intended is "to stand" as opposed to "to succomb, be worn out," but this is only on the fringe of the semantic field of παρίστημι.

The advice is especially beneficial for the people as the last clause states. The subject is "all this people," which is not improved by the *b* variant omitting οὗτος; the pronoun in particular indicates the people involved in the cases. Exod placed the verb ἥξει in the position between the subject and the modifiers while in MT the verb comes between the two prepositional phrases. Cod B uniquely placed the verb at the end; hex has reordered the words as well as the order of ἑαυτοῦ τόπον to conform to MT. Exod's use of the reflexive pronoun is intended to suggest an "each to his own place" notion, though without actually using ἕκαστος. -- The phrase μετ᾽ εἰρήνης is a literal rendering of בשלום and should be understood in the Hebraic sense of "with a feeling of fullness, satisfaction," a kind of "at peace with the world."[30]

18:24 Change of subject is shown by δέ. For the literal rendering ἤκουσεν ... τῆς φωνῆς see comment at v.19. For ἤκουσεν the Byzantine text groups use compounds, *n* having εισηκουσεν "listened to," and *d t* having υπηκουσεν "heard, obeyed"; both are attempts to define ἤκουσεν more precisely. The one heard is simply referred to as τοῦ γαμβροῦ, for which the *d* + text has the more specific πενθερου; cf 3:1; hex has added αυτου to represent the suffix in MT.[31]

18:25 Moses now carries out the advice given in v.21; "he chose (ἐπέλεξεν) able men from all Israel."[32] A *d* text changes the verb to εξελεξεν, which is a synonym. For "able men" see note at v.21.

---

with (you)."
30. See SS 128.
31. Cf ss 93.
32. See SS 65 and 155f.

The verb in the second clause is ἐποίησεν, whereas in the instructions of v.21 it was καταστήσεις. The O text witnesses to this same tradition, κατέστησεν, and was probably influenced by it, rather than being a hex revision.[33] MT has ויתן. The verb נתן seldom engenders the verb ποιέω in LXX; ποιέω usually (many hundreds of times) represents עשה, and according to HR occurs as equivalent for נתן only twice in Gen and Lev, and once in Exod, Deut, Jos, Isa and Ezek. Here ἐποίησεν does make sense.

The remainder of the verse has been taken over from v.21 rather than being an independent translation of MT, as is particularly evident from αὐτοὺς ἐξ αὐτῶν which in v.21 had as equivalent עליהם, but here the Hebrew has את ראשים על העם. For variants in the tradition see comments at v.21. Only the pattern of conjunctions joining the four ranks differs slightly in v.25. Both Sam and Tar[O] put them into two pairs. MT alone has the pattern: 1 2 3 + 4. Exod and the other old witnesses join all ranks with conjunctions.

18:26 Moses' setting up ranks of judges corresponds to the advice given in v.22. Exod uses only the imperfect throughout the verse, since the accent falls on the process of judging. In the tradition all three imperfects are inflected in the B f (z) text with the Hellenistic sigmatic -οσαν ending usually reserved for the Hellenistic aorist.[34]

As in v.22 two types of cases are distinguished, and each clause describing these begins with a δέ structure; cf comment on v.22. The first of these is given as in v.22 τὸ ῥῆμα τὸ ὑπέρογκον, which a B f n z text changed to παν ρημα υπερογκον under the influence of the pattern in the next clause, πᾶν ῥῆμα ἐλαφρόν.[35] MT, however, does not have the הגדל of v.22 but has הקשה.[36] This type of case they would bring ἐπί Moses; the Hebrew אל is more commonly rendered by εις which is what the A b x text has, for which see note on ἐπὶ σέ at v.22. For the second type of case MT has the

---

33. Though Sym also has κατέστησεν.
34. These are discussed in THGE VII.M.
35. Cf discussion in THGE VII.5.6.
36. This induced Aq Sym to translate by σκληρόν "hard," and Theod, by δυσχερές "difficult."

same designation as in v.22, where the case is called הקשן, but Exod renders this idiomatically by ἐλαφρόν "easy."

18:27 Change of subject is shown by δέ. Moses' sending his father-in-law back home concludes the story. For the object Exod uses τὸν ἑαυτοῦ γαμβρόν with the reflexive pronoun preposed, possibly under the influence of the same construction in v.23, τὸν ἑαυτοῦ τόπον. The order has been changed by hex to conform to MT.

In the last clause MT has an untranslatable לו after וילך, sometimes called a dative of reference.[37] Exod wisely did not try to translate it but idiomatically used ἀπῆλθεν for the simple "went" of MT.

37. GK 119s calls it a *"dativus commodi...* as an apparently pleonastic *dativus ethicus."* Latin titles do not to my mind clarify the matter one whit.

292

Chapter 19

19:1 A new section beginning is signalized by δέ. The Hebrew prepositional phrase indicating time is translated by a genitive of time in which in Exod. The calendric system is that of לצאת "according to the going out" rendered in Exod by a genitive τῆς ἐξόδου.[1] The lengthy dating formula ends with τῇ ἡμέρᾳ ταύτῃ which must refer to τοῦ μηνός; i.e. "on the day of the month" can only refer to the first day; what Exod is saying is that it was the third month to the day, exactly two months, after the exodus of the Israelites from the land of Egypt. On this day they arrived, ἦλθον,[2] at the desert of Sina. A B ƒ z variant text has the Hellenistic inflection, ηλθοσαν.[3] By "the desert of Sina" is meant the immediate area surrounding the mount. The phrase occurs here and in v.2 as well as in Num 10:12 with a masculine article (τοῦ) before the name. In Num 1:1,19 it has the feminine article, and elsewhere it follows MT in leaving Σινά unarticulated. Presumably in Num 1 the dative article τῇ is understood as a relative pronoun following τῇ ἐρήμῳ. A popular A F variant text omits the article here, which may well be an early, prehexaplaric revision towards MT. Σινά is Exod's consistent spelling for סיני; later translators follow Exod in this spelling. The *n* text regularly changes to σιναι thereby reproducing MT more accurately.

19:2 For ἐξῆραν see note at 13:20. For ῾Ραφιδίν and its spelling(s) see note at 17:1. -- For ἦλθον and the Hellenistic inflection of B 82 see comment at v.1. -- The omission of τοῦ before Σινά by *n* + may be recensional; cf note at v.1. For Σινά also see comment at v.1.

The verb παρενέβαλεν in the final clause is in the singular since the subject is named as "Israel." An M variant with scattered support for the plural takes ᾿Ισραήλ as a collective. The fact that the verb is modified by ἐκεῖ makes it uncertain whether Exod omitted the preceding clause due to an error palaeographically stimulated or he intentionally shortened the text;

1. See SS 206.
2. Cf SS 109.
3. See the discussion in TGHE VII.M.9.

the statement that "they encamped in the desert" is tautologous since MT then says "and Israel encamped there." Hex in any event has added καὶ παρενεβαλον εν τη ερημω. What is, however, a new factor is κατέναντι τοῦ ὄρους. The stage is now set for the divine encounter.

19:3 That Μωυσῆς precedes the predicate is as usual due to the word order of the Hebrew. Exod is consistently careful in this regard. MT, followed by Sam, Pesh and Vulg, states that Moses went up "to God." Tar^O makes this somewhat less bold by לקדם יוי "to before *ywy*," whereas Tar^P expands by "to seek instruction from before יוי," an interpretive expansion which avoids Moses going directly to God. Exod in view of the next clause, which states that "God called him from the mountain," clarifies what MT means by the rendering εἰς τὸ ὄρος τοῦ θεοῦ. If he had already gone up to God, God could hardly summon him. Exod makes the narrative internally consistent.

Exod (as Pesh) makes the subject of the next clause ὁ θεός rather than יהוה, probably to fit the designation "mountain of God" in the preceding clause. A few mss do have κυριος and a few others have κυριος ο θεος, but the scattered nature of the support makes it rather doubtful that this was recensional. -- The summons from God comes "from the mountain"; a B *b* reading has "from heaven," possibly an intentional change.

The divine summons consisted of a message introduced by the direct speech marker λέγων. The order to mediate the message of vv.4--6 is given in parallel clauses as though this were a stich of poetry. -- The phrase τῷ Ἰακώβ is parallel to τοῖς Ἰσραήλ. The verbs are also parallel, ἐρεῖς vs ἀναγγελεῖς, the latter always being used to render the causative stem of נגד.

19:4 Instead of the second person plural pronoun of MT (with inflected finite verb) Exod uses αὐτοί.[4] This is short for ὑμεῖς αὐτοί but the usage is attested,[5] and should be translated emphatically: "you yourselves (have seen)." Both ἑωράκατε and the verb in the subordinate clause πεποίηκα are in the perfect, thus "You have seen what I have done"; the latter verb ap-

4. See SS 72.
5. Cf LS sub αὐτός I,10,b.

294

pears as an aorist in the *f n* text which also makes good sense as a simple past.

The second clause in MT states "and I took you up upon eagles' wings." Of the ancient versions Vulg translates the figure literally, others (Tar⁰ Pesh) follow Exod in inserting ὡσεί "as though on eagles' wings"; the ὡσεί does not misinterpret MT; it simply makes explicit what is implicit.⁶

The last clause refers to God's bringing the people to Sina, i.e. where God is, and so πρὸς ἐμαυτόν. The translator with fine feeling for the context translates the Hiphil אָבִא with an aorist middle προσηγαγόμην, particularly appropriate in view of the modifier πρὸς ἐμαυτόν, rather than the more literal active found in *ol f*, προσηγαγον. Israel has taken note not only of the salvific acts, ὅσα πεποίηκα, but also of God's bringing them as on eagles' wings, i.e. soaring with ease, provident and protective to himself at Sina, where the covenant between God and his people is formally enacted.

19:5 The covenantal promise is conditional doubly stated: "listening to my voice" and "guarding my covenant." The condition is introduced by καὶ νῦν, with νῦν as an adverb of time being used to show the "now" of the argument, almost in the sense of "and now it must be said that."⁷ -- The verbal idea of ἀκούσητε is intensified by a preposed cognate dative ἀκοῇ rendering the Hebrew free infinitive, "if you really hear my voice (i.e. obey me)." -- Exod in good Greek fashion preposed the possessive to the noun, (τῆς) ἐμῆς φωνῆς, which hex transposed as φωνης μου to conform to MT.

The second element "guard my covenant" is not really different from the first; to guard or keep God's covenant means really to hear his voice. These covenantal conditions are outlined in the so-called Ten Words of 20:1--17. The *b f x* variant middle φυλαξησθε for the active is lexically a free variant.

The covenantal status of Israel is defined in the apodosis: you will be to me λαὸς περιούσιος. This is accompanied with an ἀπό phrase. The term περιούσιος, an adjective from περιουσία, "surplus, abundance,"⁸ has the

6. Of The Three Sym adds ὡς, whereas Aq and Theod render MT literally.
7. Cf Bauer sub νῦν 2.
8. See Bl-Debr 113,1.

notion of "above and beyond" in it,[9] and this with ἀπό probably has a comparative sense to it, "above and beyond all peoples."[10] The Hebrew term is סגלה "an acquired property, a personal possession," which Tar translate as חביבין "beloved ones." Elsewhere in the Pentateuch it occurs only three times (in Deut) and is always rendered by περιούσιος, i.e. based on Exod.

A final γάρ clause gives the basis for the Lord's taking on Israel as a personal possession; the entire earth belongs to him (cf Ps 23:1), so that he has every right to choose whatever and whomever he wills.

19:6 Change of subject to ὑμεῖς is shown by δέ. The covenantal promise to Israel is that it will be to God a royal priesthood and a holy nation. The phrase βασίλειον ἱεράτευμα[11] is an unusual pattern in Exod, i.e. an unarticulated noun phrase comsisting of adjective + noun, the reverse of the second phrase which is noun + adjective, thus a chiastic construction. It is a rendering of MT's ממלכת כהנים; this phrase was variously understood in antiquity. In Exod ממלכת is interpreted as descriptive of the body of priests, whereas Tar translate as though the words are in apposition "kings (+ and Tar^P) priests," whereas Pesh has "kingdom and priests," and Vulg takes כהנים as descriptive of ממלכת with its *in regnum sacerdotale*.[12] Exod's "royal priesthood" represents an ideal in which the priesthood is of kingly stock, and in which all Israel constitutes such an ideal. The other term, ἔθνος ἅγιον, also emphasizes that Israel is a λαὸς περιούσιος, a nation set aside, a sacral people especially devoted to God.

A concluding statement serves as part of the inclusio; cf v.3b. In MT "words" is followed by a relative pronoun. Exod, followed by Pesh, does not translate the relative pronoun, which is fully possible in Greek. The appropriate relative would be ἅ, and it might plausibly be argued that it fell out by haplography after ῥήματα. There is, however, not a scintilla of evidence to support such a hypothesis.

9. Bauer defines the word as "chosen, especial."
10. But see SS 147. Sym translates it by ἐξαίρετος "special."
11. But see SS 66f.
12. Aq rendered MT literally by βασιλεία ἱερέων, and Sym Theod have "kingdom. priests."

19:7 Change of subject is shown by δέ. Exod here uses the finite verb ἦλθεν in parataxis with ἐκάλεσεν; this pattern also obtained at 17:8: ἦλθεν ... καὶ ἐπολέμει. Usually Exod subordinates this verb (i.e. when stress does not fall on the actual coming, but the verb is used to introduce another verb), as is seen in 2:8 ἐλθοῦσα ... ἐκάλεσεν; 2:15 ἐλθών ... ἐκάθισεν; 3:16 ἐλθών ... συνάγαγε; 8:25 ἐλθόντες θύσατε, and 35:9 ἐλθὼν ἐργαζέσθω.

For MT's וישם לפניהם Exod has καὶ παρέθηκεν αὐτοῖς, avoiding a literalistic rendering of the prepositional phrase, but using the dative after παρατίθημι, i.e. "to lay before them." -- The reference in "all these words" is specifically to vv.4--6a.

The verse ends with a relative clause modifying λόγους. In MT the subject is יהוה, only Exod being at odds with its ὁ θεός. Scattered mss including *O* may show Hebrew influence either in having κυριος before it or instead of it. -- Exod's αὐτῷ correctly identifies MT's verbal suffix; a popular A F M reading has the plural, making the reference apply to the people rather than to Moses.

19:8 A subject change is twice shown by δέ. The response of the people was given ὁμοθυμαδόν "with one accord"; this was not quite enthusiastic enough for TarP who added בלבא שלמא. -- The Hellenistic ending of εἶπαν is changed to the classical ειπον in *b d f* +.[13]

The popular response differs from MT. As in the preceding verse the subject within the ὅσα clause is ὁ θεός, whereas MT has יהוה. At the end of the verse Exod also has τὸν θεόν for the tetragrammaton. Obviously these three instances form a pattern in which covenant making is put in terms of God and people; why that should be the case is not clear since in parallel passages, 24:3,7, the reference is throughout given as κύριος. Furthermore, the verb in the relative clause is εἶπεν (followed by Pesh), whereas the usual rendering of דבר is ἐλάλησεν; the parent text may have been אמר here. And Exod also has ποιήσομεν καὶ ἀκουσόμεθα though MT only has נעשה. In the three accounts of acceptance of covenant demands on the part of Israel only at 24:7 does MT include ונשמע, but Exod has the full formula in all three cases. The translator clearly wanted to make the response consistent for the book. There is a great deal of support in the mss for the change of both verbs to the aorist subjunctive, but that support changes between the two, showing that the change is simply a misspelling. The two forms are homophonous and it is the future of intention, not the hortatory subjunctive, that is original throughout.

In MT the final verb וישב Hiphil "brought back, returned" is translated by ἀνήνεγκεν. Nowhere else in LXX is this equation made; in fact השיב is most commonly translated by στρέφω and its compounds. Here, however, there is a setting in which ἀναφέρω makes good sense. The people are κατέναντι τοῦ ὄρους (v.1). God is up on the mountain and Moses had to go up the mountain (v.3), and so now he carried the words of the people up to God. Both variants adding παντας before "the words" and τουτους after it come from the fuller expansion in v.7.

19:9 Change of subject is twice stressed by δέ structures. In the Lord's statement to Moses ἐγὼ παραγίνομαι represents Exod's normal rendering of the Hebrew: pronoun + participle. The present tense is here meant to convey a verbal idea of the point of realization, and the phrase means "I am about to come." Exod interprets the tautologous עב הענן of MT by the simpler "pillar of cloud" of 13:21 by which the divine presence was concretized. The ἐν στύλῳ νεφέλης fulfils two necessary conditions: it hides God's presence so that no one can see him, and it permits the people to hear him when he speaks to Moses.

The purpose of the divine appearance is given by a ἵνα clause in two parts: that the people may actually hear the Lord speak, and that they (the people) may believe in Moses in the future. Since ὁ λαός is specified as subject of the first verb, ἀκούσῃ, the verb is singular; then in the next clause - and this is a recurring pattern of usage in Exod - the verb is put in the plural since λαός is after all a collective concept. The verb is modified by the genitive λαλοῦντός μου. Since ἀκούω governs the genitive the phrase need not be taken as a genitive absolute,[14] though MT's בדברי is best understood as indicating time when, i.e. "when I speak."

The second clause is also governed by ἵνα as the subjunctive πιστεύσωσιν shows. The phrase εἰς τὸν αἰῶνα as a translation for לעלם

---

13. See the discussion in THGE VII.M.9.
14. See Helbing 151.

already occurred at Gen 3:22 6:3, and Exod also uses it at 21:6 32:13. It occurs at 40:13 for עולם, and in an unusual context at 14:13 for which see comment there.

The last clause in the verse is ill-fitting in the narrative. The statement is repetitious of v.8, here fitting neither as a conclusion to v.9, nor as an introduction to v.10. The problem is, however, with the parent text; Exod has translated MT literally.

19:10 Change of speaker and section is shown by δέ. Yahweh's instructions in MT begin with "Go to the people," but Exod has καταβὰς διαμάρτυραι τῷ λαῷ; this is exactly the same as in v.21 where MT has רד העד "go down, testify." For a similar case of levelling cf comment on καὶ ἀκουσόμεθα in v.8.

Moses is then instructed ἅγνισον αὐτούς today and tomorrow. The verb occurs only here in Exod and is unusual as a translation for קדש Piel; in fact, this equation only occurs elsewhere at 2Chr 29:17. It does occur at times for the Hithpael, but that equation is clustered in 1 and 2Chr.[15] Exod interprets the state of holinesss as one of purification, cleansing; this is enhanced by the last instruction: καὶ πλυνάτωσαν τὰ ἱμάτια. Presumably ἅγνισον applied to the people just as πλυνάτωσαν applied to the clothing. Cod A changed the third person imperative to πλυνουσιν (future ?), but this does not fit the context overly well. Exod considered MT's plural pronominal suffix on the noun otiose; it has been added as αυτων by hex.

19:11 The divine instructions continue through v.13. The order to be ready for the third day follows naturally on those of v.10, since on day one and two they are to be cleansed and to wash their garments. -- The γάρ clause gives the reason for getting ready for the third day; this is the day in which "the lord will come down on the mountain Sina before all the people." The presupposition is that the Lord is in the heavens (in spite of v.3) and will descend upon the mountain; cf also v.20. Exod has τὸ ὄρος τὸ Σινά for MT's הר סיני; not only is the phrase without an article, but the Masoretic

---

15. The later Jewish Revisers agree on the rendering ἁγιάσεις; it appears as αγιασον in some mss, but this is simply an adaptation to the LXX imperatival form.

vocalization makes it a bound phrase which would presuppose a genitive relation in Greek.[16] The omission of the second τό in the phrase by an A d f variant would permit such an interpretation. For the spelling Σινά see comment at v.1.   -- MT has the two prepositional phrases modifying καταβήσεται transposed, and hex transposed them to equal MT.

19:12 MT's הגבלת "set boundaries" is rendered by Exod's ἀφοριεῖς which literally means "set up limits"; only here, and at v.23 is it ever used for this verb. The word is used to render a variety of Hebrew words, but mainly in the sense of "to set aside, separate"; this is particularly true when it is modified by an accusative of person as here.[17]

In so doing Moses is to issue a warning introduced by the direct speech marker λέγων. The direct speech extends from προσέχετε through αὐτοῦ, after which the warnings (and instructions) continue through v.13. The warning προσέχετε ἐαυτοῖς "be on your guard against" is a set translation for the Niphal imperative of שמר[18] with לך (or לכם), for which see comment at 10:28.[19] The tradition had trouble with the reflexive pronoun; an F b variant has υμιν εαυτοις, whereas the d t text makes it υμιν αυτοις, and the n group, υμεις εαυτοις.

The people are warned both against "going up to the mountain" and "touching any of it";[20] both verbals are infinitives rendering the Hebrew bound infinitives עלות and נגע resp. Oddly the first infinitive is marked, τοῦ ἀναβῆναι, but the second, θιγεῖν, is not. Scattered witnesses add an otiose μη before ἀναβῆναι, otiose because the imperative phrase is already negative. The second infinitive is modified by τι αὐτοῦ "any of it," which stands for בקצהו "its side"; the Greek actually improves the narrative since the next clause refers to "anyone touching the mountain."

The last clause is no longer part of direct speech, but is an explanatory warning. In MT the word for "touching" is the same root as the infinitive

16. According to a Syh note this is what The Three had.
17. This may well have promoted dissatisfaciton on the part of the later Jewish Revisers who translated by ὁριοθετήσεις "you shall set up boundaries."
18. Aq uses the verb φυλάσσω regularly to render the root שמר and according to Syh does so here as well.
19. Cf also Helbing 291.
20. Cf Helbing 125.

נגע, but Exod uses a synonym, ἁψάμενος. It illustrates Exod's love for variation; when a word is used twice in close proximity Exod will often use another lexeme just for variety's sake. Note also θανάτῳ τελευτήσει, where MT has a free infinitive. Instead of a cognate construction, Exod again uses two different roots simply for variety.

19:13 The misreading in *d* οψεται for ἅψεται makes little sense; it is a thoughtlessly made error. The γάρ clause is hardly causal, but confirmatory;[21] what is meant is "in fact he will be stoned...," i.e. he shall be put to death (v.12) but at a distance. Apparently touching the body of someone who had been in contact with deity was itself dangerous; such a one was to be stoned with stones or shot down with a missile. -- For the cognate free noun (יירה) ירה Exod has βολίδι.[22]

The next clause begins with a double ἐάν τε construction; the repeated τε conjunction shows alternation "both ... and"; literally, "both if (it be) cattle and if (it be) man," i.e. "whether it be cattle or man." The two nouns are reversed in an *f n s* variant, probably created by a subconscious urge to place man first.

The second part of the verse is a temporal condition in which the protasis represents a considerable expansion of MT which simply has במשך היבל "when the horn stretches out (its sound)." Exod has "when the thunder and the trumpets and the cloud depart from the mountain." Obviously Exod is at odds with MT, and the reason lies in the seeming inconsistencies with vv.16ff. There the trumpet sound signals the onset of the theophany and when the trumpet sound grew very loud God spoke. Thereafter Moses warns the people not to draw near to God. But in our verse at the sound of the trumpet "they" shall ascend the mountain. So Exod "fixes up" the account by making the verse refer to the conclusion of the theophany. When all the accoutrements of the theophany have disappeared the mountain is no longer surcharged with deity; it is now safe and "they may go

21. See LS sub γάρ I.3.6.
22. Aq translates this by ῥοιζήσει "hurtling, shooting," and Sym, by βέλεσιν "arrows, darts." Theod, however, revises Exod by using a cognate participle τοξευόμενος.

up on the mountain."[23]

Within the tradition a popular variant adds δε after ὅταν to signal contrast over against the preceding. The gloss correctly interprets the passage. An *x* variant has added παυσονται after σάλπιγγες; after all "thunders and trumpets" do not leave - only the cloud can leave - so these are made to stop. -- Within the apodosis the subject is ἐκεῖνοι;[24] its antecedent is the τὸν λαόν of the preceding verse.

19:14 Subject change is signalized by δέ. Moses now carries out the instructions of v.10. The first clause received a great deal of revision in the tradition though the construction could hardly have troubled anyone; Exod simply says: "and Moses went down from the mountain to the people." Most of the changes are fully possibly but hardly improve the original statement; this is particularly true of an *oII f z* text which added και ειπεν αυτοις, an ill-fitting phrase taken over from v.25.

The middle clause "and he sanctified them" has substituted for the repetitious העם את a stylistically superior αὐτούς. Exod does. however, keep close to MT by the use of ἡγίασεν for יקדש rather than ἁγνίζω as at v.10, for which see comment. Also in conformity with the orders given in v.10 the people "washed clothes"; Exod does not say "their clothes" as MT does since that is obvious, but hex supplied an αυτων.

19:15 Exod carefully differentiates here from v.11; the being prepared in v.11 was for the third day, i.e. get ready for day after tomorrow, but here it is to last for three days. This continuous state of readiness is also stressed by the use of the present imperative γίνεσθε, a fine point voided by the Byzantine variant γενεσθε. The reference to "three days" is in the accusative, thus denoting extent of time.

---

23. The Exod version was of course unsatisfactory to the revisers. Sym translated the condition by ὅταν ἀφελκύσθη ὁ ἀλαλαγμὸς αὐτοὶ ἀναβαινέτωσαν εἰς τὸ ὄρος "when the loud noise has been diverted let them come up to the mountain." Theod rendered the protasis by ἐν τῇ ἀπελεύσει τοῦ ἰωβήλ "at the departure of the *Iobel* (transliteration of the Hebrew יבל). Aq uses ἐν ἑλκυσμῷ (a literalism for משך) τοῦ παραφέροντος they shall go up on the mountain. For his rendering of היבל see also Lev 25:10 Num 36:4.
24. Cf SS 72.

19:16 For the translation of וַיְהִי + timer + conjunction + coordinate verb see the comment at 18:13. The time indication is, however, somewhat complex. The dative of time when is straightforward, but this is followed by a genitive absolute construction γενηθέντος πρὸς ὄρθρον with the prepositional phrase as subject of the participle, Exod's rendering of a preposition + bound infinitive construction בִּהְיֹת הַבֹּקֶר. The next verb is ἐγίνοντο without a και before it, though the B *f z* + text does add one.[25] The imperfect is much more appropriate here than the popular F aorist εγενοντο; the thunder and the lightning and the dark cloud were continuously on Mount Sina. Jerome was really caught up in the drama of this clause; he translates: *et ecce coeperunt audiri tonitrua ac micare fulgura et nubes densissima operire montem*! Exod's interpretation of the cloud as γνοφώδης "dark, gloomy," for MT's כָּבֵד is plausible, though Vulg's *densissima* is more accurate. Exod also identifies הָהָר as ὄρους Σινά, undoubtedly correctly though not in MT; for Σινά see note at v.1.

The next clause is asyndetic in Exod, with hex adding και to correspond to MT. The Hebrew's noun clause "and the sound of the trumpet חָזָק מְאֹד" becomes a verbal clause in Exod; it has ἤχει μέγα "echoed greatly."

The final clause states the reaction of the people to all the phenomena; they were terrified, i.e. all the people who were in the tent. The prepositional phrase is introduced by an article ὁ used as a relative pronoun modifying λαός. The Byzantine group made this explicit by substituting ος ην "who were." More problematic is its omission by A *b s x* since this changes the modification to the verb ἐπτοήθη.

19:17 Moses then brought the people out to meet God from the camp. The phrase εἰς συνάντησιν became a set phrase, already found in Gen, to render לִקְרַאת. What created the majority A M text articulating the noun is not clear. The phrase is used to render לִקְרַאת 57 times in LXX according to HR, and another 16 times where no Hebrew parent text is extant, and συνάντησιν is never articulated. The εἰς in the phrase is purposive.

25. For the absence of και in this pattern see the discussion in THGE VII.E.3.

The verb in the second phrase, παρέστησεν, "stood by, near" translates the Hithpael of יצב "to take a stand, station oneself" with τὸν λαόν as subject. The equation also occurs at 34:5 which see. The encounter was to take place ὑπὸ τὸ ὄρος "below the mountain"; what is meant is "at the base of the mountain"; note also בשפולי טורא in Tar^O and Vulg: *ad radices montis*. A B n s z variant identifies the mountain by the gloss το σινα taken from v.18. Another variant in the f x text has επι instead of ὑπό, which can hardly be taken seriously since it contradicts the narrative; it may have come in under the influence of v.13.

19:18 Change of subject is shown by δέ. The verb ἐκαπνίζετο is appropriately imperfect since stress is laid on the process of smoking. The subject of the verb is τὸ ὄρος τὸ Σινά,[26] for which see comment at v.11. For Σινά see comment at v.1. The verb is modified by the neuter ὅλον used adverbially.

The statement is accompanied by a διά clause giving the reason for the smoking mountain. The infinitive is immediately followed by its subject τὸν θεόν and it in turn by two prepositional phrases. MT has a complex equivalent: a prepositional bound phrase plus a relative clause with the subject between the two prepositional phrases.[27] The word order is changed by hex to conform to MT. A marginal M s reading corrects τὸν θεόν to κυριον, undoubtedly taken from The Three.

In the next clause a majority A F M text has a δε for the opening καί structure, a plausible reading with a change of subject that could be original, though the oldest witness, cod B, supports καί. The verb is imperfect since the ascent of the smoke was a process. The particle of comparison used here by Exod is ὡς which he prefers to the very popular M variant ωσει; The word ὡς occurs 18 times in Exod, and ὡσεί, 11 times. -- A popular variant has ατμος instead of "smoke." The source of the variant is puzzling since καπνός is so obviously right for a furnace.

26. Cf SS 67.
27. Theod revised Exod somewhat substituting κύριον for τὸν θεόν, as well as changing the perfect infinitive to the aorist. Aq made a new and literal translation: ἀπὸ προσώπου οὗ κατέβη ἐπ᾽ αὐτῷ κύριος, exactly retaining the patterns of MT.

The last clause represents a considerable departure from MT's "all the mountain shook exceedingly," using the same verb, ויחרד, as in v.16, where, however, כל העם, not כל ההר, was the subject. There Exod used ἐπτοήθη, but here ἐξέστη. This verb could not take "the mountain" as subject, though ὁ λαός makes good sense. Actually העם is attested in some Hebrew mss and Exod may have had that as parent text. In any event it is clear that at some stage v.16 helped to produce Exod's "and all the people were greatly astonished."

19:19 Change of subject is shown by δέ. Exod uses a verbal figure, i.e. ἐγίνοντο + participle (προβαίνουσαι) + an adjective in comparative degree to render the Hebrew ויהי הולך וחזק. The participle הולך when coordinated with another participle or verbal adjective is often idiomatic for expressing continuation of the verbal idea, which Exod's προβαίνουσαι does explicate, and the clause may be translated "and the trumpet blasts were growing louder and louder." Particularly appropriate is the use of the imperfect ἐγίνοντο in this context, though a popular variant does have the neutral aorist εγενοντο, not surprising since it occurs so frequently in LXX.

Exod introduces an interesting tense distinction in the following clauses. MT had used the imperfect inflections: for Moses ידבר, and for God יעננו, but Exod has an imperfect for the first one, ἐλάλει, and an aorist, ἀπεκρίνατο, for the second; Pesh made the same distinction. Thus Moses' speech is presented as a process, "was speaking," but God "answered him." This distinction is destroyed by an F n t reading which has for the aorist the imperfect απεκρινετο. MT by its prefix tense forms probably intended to show the nature of the communication process: Moses would speak and God would answer him. To Exod God's answering is not specifically a process, i.e. Moses engaged in dialogue; God responded. This is delicately underscored in the text by the use of a contrastive δέ in ὁ δὲ θεός. Furthermore the response is characterized by the dative of means φωνῇ "with a voice,"[28] a literal rendering of MT's בקול. It can hardly mean "thunder" here since references to thunder in vv.13 and 16 were in the plural. Here is probably simply means "audibly."

19:20 Change of subject is shown by δέ. Here the promise of v.11 that the Lord will come down upon Mount Sina is fulfilled. As in v.11 הר סיני is rendered by τὸ ὄρος τὸ Σινά, for which see comment. The second τό is omitted by an A F *O C* text which makes it possible to view Σινά as in the genitive. For Σινά see note at v.1. The exact part of the mountain is specified by ἐπὶ τὴν κορυφὴν τοῦ ὄρους, the preposition ἐπί, as in the next clause, probably being used because the first phrase used it in "upon Mount Sina," although MT has אל.

19:21 Twice in this verse Exod has "God" in place of the tetragrammaton; this had occurred earlier in the chapter as well (vv.3,7,8,18; cf also vv.22--24). There seems to be no particular reason for the change except that one senses a reluctance to mention κύριος in the interchange between God and Moses and so to use the neutral ὁ θεός instead; compare also 20:19,20 where this is true of both MT and Exod. The difference between MT and Exod in the chapter is striking; MT has יהוה 18 times and אלהים three times, whereas Exod has κύριος nine times and ὁ θεός 13 times (one case of κύριος in v.24 has no counterpart in MT). Since the other ancient versions all support MT there must be some tendency here to prefer a reference to deity rather than to the personal name in the description of this theophany by Exod.

   Exod has added the direct speech marker λέγων to introduce God's orders to Moses though it is lacking in MT. Its omission in a *d x* + text may be evidence for revision towards MT.

   The orders are followed by a double negative purpose clause, μήποτε governing both ἐγγίσωσιν and πέσωσιν as the subjunctive inflections show, though the second clause expresses the logical result of the first clause: should the people come near to God to take a good look (κατανοῆσαι) many will die. -- Exod interprets the vivid figure of יהרסו "break through" by the more plebeian ἐγγίσωσιν "come near," an equation found only here in LXX; see note at v.24. -- In the second clause Exod continues the plural of the first clause (its subject is τῷ λαῷ), which is possible since its expressed subject πλῆθος is of course collective. The

306

majority A F M text has the singular πεση; this may be an early grammatical correction to agree with the singular subject πλῆθος, rather than a revision based on MT's נפל.

19:22 The reference here is to the priests who come near (i.e. perform their sacrificial duties) to God.[29] -- Exod again substitutes τῷ θεῷ for יהוה, for which see comment at v.21. The majority reading in the tradition has the double title κυριω τω θεω.[30]

This verse also ends with a μήποτε clause: "lest the Lord ἀπαλλάξῃ from them." What Exod is saying is that priests who are officially taking part in the priestly cultic rights, οἱ ἐγγίζοντες τῷ θεῷ, must be in a ritual state of purity; otherwise the Lord will not accept their cultic exercises. This represents a considerable toning down of the Hebrew tradition, which says that Yahweh יפרץ בהם "will break out (i.e. in violence) on them." In fact, Tar[O] interprets this as יקטיל בהון; compare also Vulg: *percutiat*.[31] At v.24 in the same context Exod uses ἀπολέσῃ, which see.

19:23 For τὸν θεόν see note at v.21. The *b* text changed the καί to a δε structure showing change of subject. Exod translates לעלת אל by προσαναβῆναι πρός; αναβηναι of the *f* text would have done equally well but the extra prepositional element agrees with the preposition in the modifying phrase. The preposition is changed by a popular F text to εις, but πρός is of course original in view of προσαναβῆναι. --For the noun phrase τὸ ὄρος τὸ Σινά see comment at v.11, and for Σινά see v.1.

The γάρ clause gives the reason for the people's inability to ascend the mountain: God had forbidden it. The perfect middle is sensibly chosen

28. Cf SS 124.
29. A marginal note on ms 344 states that Aq read (καὶ οἱ) πρεσβύτεροι instead of ἱερεῖς; obviously there is something wrong with this statement. The nearest reference to "elders" is in v.7 but the note does not fit there either. Possibly the note is misplaced from 18:12 and that Aq's parent text there had וזקני, i.e. without the כל of MT; compare Sam which has מזקני.
30. See the analysis in THGE VII.O. sub 3:18.
31. The Three could not accept Exod's interpretation either. Aq translates the verb יפרץ literally by διακόψῃ, whereas Sym comes nearer to Tar[O] with his διαφθείρῃ "destroy," while Theod according to Syh has "finish off, consume." All of them agree with MT that what is threatened is some sort

to render העדתה; God had done it and it remains effective. A *d* + text has διαμαρτυρησαι, presumably as an aorist middle imperative, but actually a copyist's error in which the reduplicative prefix was accidentally omitted. -- For ἀφόρισαι rendering הגבל see comment at v.12. God himself had made the mountain off limits as well as making it sacral so that anyone even touching it would die; cf comments on vv.12 and 13.

19:24 The initial δέ structure shows change of subject, and the popular καὶ εἰπεν is secondary.[32] For βάδιζε used to introduce another imperative see note at 6:6. The word is idiomatic in the same sense as "come" in "come, try it"; for this βάδιζε is used as equivalent for לך "go," i.e. "go, try it." In such cases the verbs usually follow asyndetically, but an F *d t* reading has καὶ before κατάβηθι, probably a partial dittograph.

Only Moses and Aaron are to ascend the mountain. In contrast - note the contrastive use of δέ - the priests and the people are not to force their way up to God. The verb βιαζέσθωσαν "use force" occurs only here for the verb הרס "break through (i.e. the set boundaries)," but is much more adequate than the tame ἐγγίσωσιν used for the verb in v.21. The *f* reading βαδιζεσθωσαν is barely sensible, and is simply a copyist's mistake. The *s* reading προσαναβηναι for ἀναβῆναι is obviously taken over from v.23. Exod here simply illustrates his preference for variation.

The verse ends in MT with the same פן clause as in v.22 except that יהוה is not here repeated. Exod does take over κύριος from v.22 but translates יפרץ by ἀπολέσῃ "destroy," modified by ἀπ' αὐτῶν as in v.22, but here as a partitive construction "some of them."[33]

19:25 Change of subject is shown by δέ. Moses (nothing is said about Aaron) went down to the people καὶ εἶπεν αὐτοῖς. This odd ending to the account renders MT literally, and shows that at an earlier stage some instructions or the like must have followed. In the present context the account of God's speaking the Ten Words follows.

---

of violent end to the unsanctified priests.
32. Cf THGE VII.E.1.
33. For Aq and Sym see the note at v.22. Theod according to Syh has a different rendering, probably κόψῃ.

Chapter 20

20:1 There is considerable doubt as to whether the introduction to the Ten Words has "God" or "the Lord" as subject of "spoke." Exod has κύριος in which it is supported by the Tar Vulg, whereas MT Sam Pesh support אלהים. Some scattered *O n* texts have the double name κυριος ο θεος which is probably due to the influence of v.2.

20:2 Since the Ten Words also occur in Deut 5:6--21 in a slightly different form, that form at times has influenced the Exod tradition. Instead of ὅστις ἐξήγαγόν a popular A F variant has ο εξαγαγων taken over from Deut 5:6. For ἐγώ εἰμι as a translation for אנכי or אני see comment at 6:2; there is no difference between the two forms of the pronoun as far as the Exod translator is concerned. Thus אנכי occurs both in 4:10 and 11; in v.10 it becomes ἐγώ but in v.11 it is ἐγώ εἰμι; on the other hand, אני is rendered by ἐγώ in 6:8 but by ἐγώ εἰμι in 6:12. -- The verb is inflected within the relative clause to agree with ἐγώ rather than with κύριος; an *s* variant does have the third person. -- For ἐξ οἴκου δουλείας as translation for בית עבדים see discussion at 13:3.

20:3 Exod interprets the phrase על פני as πλὴν ἐμοῦ "besides me," in which it is followed by Tar Pesh, whereas Vulg: *coram me* follows the πρὸ προσώπου μου of Deut 5:7.

20:4 The commandment forbidding any Israelite to make for himself images is referred to in MT as פסל and כל תמונה, i.e. "graven image" and "any likeness" resp. The former is translated by εἴδωλον "idol" in Exod, a term chosen by Exod to emphasize the irreality or phantom-like character of the פסל. The equation only occurs elsewhere in LXX at Isa 30:22, but cf the plural at 2Chr 33:22 34:7. The term is first used in Gen to characterize Rachel's teraphim.[1] The latter becomes παντὸς ὁμοίωμα "of anything a

---

1. The later Jewish revisers have the literal γλυπτόν, for which see Deut 5:8.

likeness." This makes a good antecedent for the ὅσα clause, which presumably refers to παντός not to ὁμοίωμα; an *ol* variant, παν ομοιωμα, equals MT where תמונה is the grammatical antecedent of אשר.

There is little variation in the tradition except for the last ὅσα phrase where Exod's "in the waters" is changed into the singular in an F *z* reading. After all, the form of the Decalogue was very well known and would admit of little change by a copyist.

20:5 The two prohibitions differ in that the first is put in the indicative with οὐ, whereas the second has the double negative οὐδὲ μή with the subjunctive. It is to be doubted that any difference in intensity was intended by the translator. An *n* text has the second one in the first pattern, and the *d x* text triples its negative as ουδ ου μη; neither variant affects the meaning of Exod. Cf also note at 23:24.

The γάρ/כי clause, which becomes a ὅτι clause in Deut 5:9, makes אל קנא the predicate according to the Masoretic accentuation, with "Yahweh your God" in apposition to אנכי the subject. Exod (as Deut) has a different interpretation. The reason for the prohibition of images and likenesses is that "I am the Lord your God"; then in turn θεὸς ζηλωτής modified by the ἀποδιδούς clause is in apposition to "Lord" in the same way that "your God" is apposite. It is the fact that God is "the Lord" that makes the making of images taboo. The only legitimate form of worshipping the Lord, Israel's God, is an imageless cult. Since only the Lord is to be Israel's God (v.3), then only his cult is to obtain among Israel.

This κύριος who is Israel's God is jealous, i.e. ζηλωτής, here used in a pejorative sense of "jealous, envious"; God is jealous of his cult which contrasts with the cult of all other gods. Furthermore this jealous God repays those who hate him with respect to the sins of the fathers. The participle ἀποδιδούς represents פקד in the LXX only in the context of sins of fathers on children, Num 14:18 Deut 5:9, both probably based on Exod, interpreting the notion of divine visitation in the commercial sense of "paying back."

עון "iniquity" is translated in Exod (as well as by the Num and Deut passages) by ἁμαρτίας "sins," which is at best a free rendering of the

Hebrew. Furthermore in MT the participle פֹקֵד is modified by two עַל phrases, "upon the children" and "upon the third and fourth generation," the second one being in apposition to the first. Deut 5:9 interprets these literally: ἐπὶ τέκνα ἐπὶ τρίτην καὶ τετάρτην γενεάν, but Exod differs; the second phrase becomes ἕως τρίτης καὶ τετάρτης γενεᾶς "up to the third and fourth generation," not in apposition to ἐπὶ τέκνα but describing the extent of the repayment upon the sons. The Num passage follows Exod though omitting γενεᾶς (as having no equivalent in MT!); the Deut reading does occur as a majority A F reading in the Exod tradition.

The final phrase is probably an indirect object modifying ἀποδιδούς, though it could also be taken as a dative of reference modifying πατέρων. Since in the parallel in v.6 the dative obviously modifies the participle ποιῶν, Exod probably intended it to modify ἀποδιδούς in v.5.

20:6 This verse gives the contrast to v. 5; God pays back sins, but he also does mercy, ἔλεος, which is Exod's interpretation of the difficult Hebrew word חֶסֶד. Vulg: *misericordiam* follows Exod, whereas Tar have טוּבָא which Pesh also follows.

In contrast to God's paying back sins up to the third and fourth generation, he does mercy to thousands; what is meant is thousands of generations, which Tar Pesh actually add. That this is how Exod also interprets it is clear from v.5 where γενεᾶς was added; here it is unnecessary since it has already been specified. -- The indirect object to whom mercy is done is doubly identified as "those loving me and those guarding my statutes"; the former shows the direct contrast to v.5's τοῖς μισοῦσίν με, and the second one defines what "loving me" involves; it means faithful obedience.

Unusual is the rendering τὰ προστάγματά μου for MT's מִצְוֹתָי. The word מִצְוָה occurs four times (also 15:26 16:28 24:12, but cf note at 12:17), and except for this verse is always rendered by ἐντολή. This then becomes a standard equivalent (eight times in Lev, five in Num, and 38 in Deut according to HR). Possibly Exod wanted to emphasize the notion of order by the choice of this term. Deut took over Exod's rendering of this verse entirely.

20:7 The phrase λήμψη τὸ ὄνομα refers to speech, i.e. take up the name on one's lips. What is forbidden is doing this ἐπ' ματαίῳ "idly, in vain," Exod's rendering for לשוא.[2]

The γάρ clause gives the reason why the Israelites should avoid using the name of the Lord idly; the Lord will not pronounce such a one pure, or clear. καθαρίζω is here used in a juridical sense as at Lev 13:6 καθαριεῖ αὐτὸν ὁ ἱερεύς of the cured leper.

20:8 Instead of μνήσθητι Deut 5:12 has φύλαξαι, representing a different Hebrew text. The *b* text has the plural, which is a copyist's error; the singular is addressed throughout the decalogue, presumably referring to the τὸν λαόν of 19:25, though the individual Israelite could also be intended as addressee. -- For the use of the plural "sabbaths" to render שבת see the comment at 16:23.

ἁγιάζειν is Exod's translation of לקדש; since Exod does not represent the marker hex has supplied του.[3] The infinitive is probably intended as complementary with the αὐτήν recapitulating "the day of the sabbath," and so the line should be rendered: remember to sanctify the day of the sabbath.

20:9 Exod renders MT literally by a singular future indicative, ἐργᾷ, which *d* changes to the present imperative ἐργαζου. -- Greek can also distinguish between "all work" and "any work" by means of number. Here Exod correctly interprets מלאכה by the plural, whereas the same word is (again correctly) rendered by the singular ἔργον in v.10. The text in Deut is exactly the same as that of Exod.

20:10 The particle δέ is used to contrast "seventh day" with the "six days" of v.9. Clearly σάββατα, though plural in form, is understood as a singular.[4] That Exod realized it as singular is clear from ἐν αὐτῇ in the second clause. The Sabbath is designated as κυρίῳ τῷ θεῷ σου; the dative is in imitation of the Hebrew and the genitive of *n s* is a stylistic improvement also found

2. Aq translates by εἰς εἰκῇ "at random, in vain," an attempt at literalness; Greek would normally simply have εἰκῇ.
3. Also attested for Aq and Sym.

312

in Vulg. The phrase ἐν αὐτῇ, though not represented in MT, does have early attestation in the Nash Papyrus, and is thus probably textual in origin; both Pesh and Vulg supply it as the context demands. A pair of *f* mss "correct" the phrase to εν αυτοις in recognition of σαββατα as plural.

The subject of ποιήσεις is of course second person singular, and this subject is then explicated by a long apposite text "you and your son and your daughter, etc." The list is given in three pairs "your son and daughter, your servant and female servant, your ox and ass" to which is then added "and all your cattle and the sojourner who is residing among you."[5] Up through the word "sojourner" Deut has exactly the same text. The third pair is unique to Exod though it equals MT of Deut. -- An *f z* reading has changed "son" to the plural, but not "daughter," so it must be a scribal lapse. Furthermore the *C* text has a και before the second pair, which some Hebrew mss Tar Pesh also support. -- The last phrase, ὁ παροικῶν ἐν σοί, is in apposition to προσήλυτος, a free though not incorrect version of MT's בשעריך. Deut 5:14 renders this more literally by ὁ ἐντὸς τῶν πυλῶν σου.

20:11 The γάρ clause gives the basis for the Sabbath injunction; it is rooted in the creation ordinance, particularly as found in Gen 2:2--3. Here the ὁ θεός of the Gen creation account is identified as κύριος, i.e. Israel's God. The Byzantine text has the variant double designation κυριος ο θεος, whereas *x* + has substituted ο θεος. -- That the Lord made τὸν οὐρανὸν καὶ τὴν γῆν is based on Gen 1:1, and for τὴν θάλασσαν, cf Gen 1:9,10 θαλάσσας, and for πάντα τὰ ἐν αὐτοῖς cf Gen 1:11--21. The word αὐτοῖς refers to the combination "heaven and earth and sea." Pesh was apparently swayed by the pronoun of בם to make הים plural, i.e. "the seas and all that is in them." A popular A F M variant in the tradition adds τε before οὐρανόν. It serves as a conjunction to introduce the first of a pair of accusatives in the sense of "both ... and." The particle is some times (21 times) used in Exod and could be original, but the oldest witness, cod B, does not have it. It is probably secondary, since Exod usually does not use it.

The second clause "and he rested the seventh day" is except for the omission of ἐν before τῇ ἡμέρᾳ an exact copy from Gen 2:2. The divine

---

4. The Three actually read σάββατον.
5. Cf SS 58.

model in the creation story is then six days of work and a seventh day of rest.

In the conclusion (διὰ τοῦτο) MT has "the day of the Sabbath" instead of Exod's "the seventh day" (also in Pesh). Exod's text is, however, (except for the divine name) identical with that of Gen 2:3, and shows Exod's acquaintance with Greek Gen.

εὐλόγησεν appears in a popular A F M reading in the augmented form ηυλογησεν; the aorist form only occurs once elsewhere in Exod (39:23) where the same variant also appears but with different support. Since Gen was probably translated only shortly before Exod its usage should be consulted;[6] the unaugmented form was almost certainly the form used by Gen, and should also be adopted for Exod.

20:12 The Word with respect to parental regard is put in positive terms in contrast to the other commandments. In Exod only πατέρα is accompanied by σου, but not μητέρα, since that is obvious from the context. MT as well as Deut 5:16 do support the pronoun, and the majority (hex ?) tradition has duly added σου. Deut also adds "as the Lord your God commanded you" after σου in conformity to its parent text as shown in MT.

The command is followed by two ἵνα clauses, only the second of which is also attested in MT; the first is, however, found in the Nash Papyrus as well as in Deut 5:16 both in Greek and Hebrew, and could be based on a Hebrew original.

The second ἵνα clause renders יארכון ימיך "your days may be long" by a compound adjective μακροχρόνιος plus a second singular aorist γένῃ "a long time you may be," an idiomatic rendering also followed by Deut.[7] The C text substituted εση for the verb, a future indicative, after ἵνα, which is highly unusual. Exod uniquely speaks of the good land, which notion occurs a number of times in Deut (3:25 4:22 8:7,10 31:20,21), although not in 5:16. The source may well be Deut 8:10 which has the same phrase in a similar context.

6. See the discussion in THGG 187f.
7. Cf SS 95.

20:13--15 The order of the prohibitions in Exod is: adultery - steal - murder, whereas that of Deut is: adultery - murder - steal. The order of MT in both Exodus and Deuteronomy is: murder - adultery - steal. Why the order should vary is not clear. In the Exod tradition the order is also unsettled. The *C n x* text has the order of Deut. The majority text which follows the order of MT is undoubtedly a reordering by the hex recension. One ms puts adultery at the end, and another transposes adultery and steal.

20:16 Exod uses a verb cognate to the object μαρτυρίας ψευδῆ, presumably for emphasis. The verb ψευδομαρτυρήσεις means "testify falsely" but represents the Hebrew חענה. Vulg renders the collocation correctly by *loqueris ... falsem testimonium.*

20:17 Exod is identical to that of the text of Deut 5:21. The Greek texts are on the whole much closer to the Hebrew of Deuteronomy than to that of Exodus. The last-named has the two prohibitions against coveting a neighbour's wife and house[8] transposed, which hex reorders to fit MT. Nor does MT of Exodus have any correspondence to "nor his field." On the other hand over against the Hebrew of both versions Exod has οὔτε παντὸς κτήνεως αὐτοῦ after "his ass," and does not have an equivalent for the כל which the אשר clause modifies.

A pair of *f* mss has the subscription: "(The) ten words the Lord said on Mount Sina to Moses which these are."

20:18 The popular reaction to the theophany. In both the first and the last clauses πᾶς ὁ λαός is given as the subject, but in the first the verbal predicate is singular whereas in the latter the predicate and attribute modifier are plural. MT has a plural participle for the first and the other three verbs paratactically arranged with the first one וירא (preceding the subject) in the singular and the next two plural. The plural participle ראים is translated by the imperfect ἑώρα (the plural εωρων in a variant is a correction toward MT), which is appropriate since a process is involved. The verb must here be taken in the sense of "to perceive, experience," since

8. According to Syh Aq has "house," οἰκίας, in the genitive, and for neighbour he has ἑταίρου, whereas Sym and Theod follow Origen's LXX.

the objects of the verb are auditory and visual ones. Sam in a fit of rationalistic prudery carefully distinguished these by "heard the thunderings and the trumpet sound and were seeing the lightning." Exod singly rendered הקולת את by the singular τὴν φωνήν; cf 19:13,16 where the plural occurs. This is particularly odd since this means that the phrase now occurs coordinately in the same form, once for the thunder and once for the sound (of the trumpet).

The two verbal clauses of the verse are separated by a nominal construction in which the predicate is a participle. This follows MT closely where the nominal predicate is the verbal adjective עשן. An A B *f z* variant has simplified by adding an article before the participle, το καπνιζον; this makes the construction an attributive phrase also modifying ἑώρα.[9] A *d t y* variant has changed the participle to the passive voice, with no change in meaning. Nor does the *C* gloss, ην, change the passage semantically.

The final clause is introduced by a δέ structure showing the resumption of λαός as subject. The first verb וירא is vocalized in MT as representing the verb ראה, and Tar Pesh follow this interpretation. Exod understood the verb as derived from ירא "to be afraid" and translated it by an attributive plural participle φοβηθέντες in which it is followed by Vulg: *perterriti*. The main verb in Exod is ἔστησαν. But MT has וינע "and they trembled" between the two which Exod omits having compressed the two verbs וירא and וינע into the one participle φοβηθέντες. Origen filled in the "omission" by και σαλευθεις,[10] but this is in the singular and so he changed the context into the singular as well: φοβηθεις ... σαλευθεις ...εστη.

20:19 A *b d n* variant has the classical ειπον for the Hellenistic εἶπαν.[11] Rather than have God speak directly to them the people ask Moses to be their intermediary. The opening request: "do you speak to us" is amplified in MT by ונשמעה; hex naturally added και ακουσομεθα. By the shorter text Exod has gained a much better contrast "you shall speak to us but do not let God speak..." -- God's direct address to the people was too danger-

9. See the discussion in THGE VII.D.4.
10. As in Aq.
11. For Exod usage see THGE VII.M.9.

ous and might kill: μήποτε ἀποθάνωμεν. The popular variant ινα μη for μήποτε probably came in from v.20.

20:20 For Exod's occasional use of the historical present see note at 2:13. Its use may well have urged the use of αὐτοῖς rather than a literal rendering of אל העם. In MT the subject משה follows immediately on the verb, and hex has therefore changed the word order, so as to conform.

Exod's translation of the Hebrew "do not fear" by the positive injunction θαρσεῖτε "take courage" shows his relative freedom from literalism. -- The γάρ clause gives the basis for the encouragement; God came to Israel in such awe inspiring phenomena, thunder, lightning flashes, a smoking mountain, "for the sake of testing you."[12] This in turn is so that "his fear may be in you," which in turn is "in order that you may not sin." The first clause is a ἕνεκεν clause with a marked infinitive, the second a ὅπως ἄν plus subjunctive, and the last a ἵνα μή plus subjunctive. This set of successive interlocking clauses differs considerably from MT. There the first clause is a לבעבור clause and the second is a coordinate בעבור clause; in other words there are two reasons for God's coming. The third is introduced by לבלתי which in a most unusual fashion here governs an imperfect,[13] but probably not to be distinguished in meaning from the normal pattern of לבלתי plus bound infinitive, i.e. a negative purpose. Exod also has God coming πρὸς ὑμᾶς, a phrase not present in MT.

Thus according to Exod God's presence and his speaking from the mountain to the people is done to put them to the test. That this testing should make the people fearful (φοβηθέντες, v.18) is a good thing. This fear of God is the fear inspired by the theophany, and this in turn will hopefully result in the people not sinning.

20:21 Change of speaker is shown by δέ. The verb εἱστήκει is an imperfect of ἑστήκω, formed from the perfect of ἵστημι,[14] i.e. the people were standing. A popular variant adds πας before ὁ λαός under the influence of

12. See Bauer sub πειράζω 2.b.
13. Cf GK 152x.
14. See LS sub ἵστημι II.1.

v.18. The statement that the people were standing at a distance had already been made in v.18 but here it is in contrast to Moses' action; note the use of δέ to stress the contrast. -- Moses entered the γνόφον[15] where God was. In MT the contrast is "at a distance" vs "drew near to." Exod used εἰσῆλθεν "entered," which subtly alters the contrast. Over against the people's frightened staying at a distance from God's presence Exod has Moses entering the dark cloud where God was.

20:22 Change of theme and section is shown by δέ. V.22 should be compared to 19:3--4 where a similar context occurs. In both cases Moses was instructed: "thus shall you say to the house of Jacob and relate to the Israelites" followed by a pronoun plus ἑωράκατε. In fact the messenger formula is uniquely taken over by Exod from the earlier passage; cf comment at 19:3 for its analysis.

What is to be said follows up to the end of the chapter. It begins with ὑμεῖς which contrasts with 19:4 where αὐτοί is employed. The verb ἑωράκατε has the same semantic coloration as ἑώρα of v.18, which see. What is perceived is "that from heaven have I spoken to you"; this seems to contradict the fact that God had been speaking from the smoking mountain. Presumably what is meant is God's speaking through thunder and lightning flashes, both heavenly symbols of divine communication. -- The *C* text substitutes the aorist ἐλαλησα for Exod's λελάληκα. The latter was intentionally chosen by Exod to call attention to the fact that what God said is still effective.

20:23 This effective speaking is then outlined in the specific commandments of God found in vv.23--26. The first commandment forbids the making of idols of silver and gold. It is divided into two parallel clauses; the two differ as to the placement of the object: in the first it is final, and in the second it comes first. The reflexive modifiers following the verb also differ; in the first it is ἑαυτοῖς alone, and in the second it has ὑμῖν before it; both, however, mean the same, "for yourselves." These reflexives do give trouble

15. Aq and Theod were satisfied with Exod's rendering of ערפל by γνόφος, but Sym used ὀμίχλην, a lighter form of darkness such as "fog, vapor," which may have led to Jerome's *caliginem* for Vulg.

in the later tradition. A B *d t* text adds υμιν before ἑαυτοῖς in the first, whereas a popular A M variant "corrects" ἑαυτοῖς to αυτοις in the second.[16] For the first one MT has אתי "with me" which has given rise to various interpretations. The Tar have "before me," whereas Pesh has a doublet supporting both Exod and MT. Vulg solves the problem by leaving it out entirely.

The first clause forbids the making of "gods of silver," and the second, "gods of gold." Whenever only the two metals are referred to in Exod (and MT) silver comes first (see also 3:22 11:2 12:35), but when a list of three metals obtain (including bronze) the order is gold - silver - bronze (25:3 31:4 35:5,32). Incidentally Pesh reverses the order here.

20:24 Instructions concerning an earthen altar. With v.24 MT switches to the singular for the second person, whereas Exod continues with the plural for the first part of the verse, but changing to the singular in the last two clauses, and then as in MT continuing in the singular in vv.25 and 26. -- For ἐκ γῆς[17] MT has אדמה.[18] -- For ποιήσετε an M *n x* + text has the aorist imperative ποιησατε, but Exod renders the Hebrew second person imperfects in the commandments consistently by future indicatives. -- Similarly for θύσετε in the next clause a popular F M variant has θυσατε. A *d* variant has θησετε "you shall place; though this makes sense it is merely an itacism for θύσετε. The *b* text has the imperative θυσιασατε, a synonym for θυσατε.

To be sacrificed are τὰ ὁλοκαυτώματα καὶ τὰ σωτήρια ὑμῶν; in MT both nouns have a second person (singular; cf comment above) suffix; hex has added υμων, a plural adaptation to the context. Particularly important is Exod's choice of τὰ σωτήρια as a rendering for the *shelem* offerings. The meaning of שלמים is disputed, some rendering the term by "peace offerings," i.e. related to שלם, or as "thank offerings" from the nature of the sacrifice, particularly as described in Lev 7:11--15, and others as "final

16. For this rare usage see the discussion in THGE VII.G.10.
17. According to SS 63 ἐκ is used here instead of a simple genitive of materials.
18. Syh gives readings for The Three here, but what the Greek of Sym and Theod was is not clear; the Syriac uses the same root as MT. Aq probably read χθονός; compare Gen 2:7.

offerings" as related to the root שׁלם "to be complete." For this term Exod uses τὰ σωτήρια (cf also 29:28) or the singular σωτηρίου modifying θυσίαν (24:5 32:6). This equation became standard throughout the Pentateuch; these two Exod patterns are retained throughout, with but two exceptions: at Lev 7:8 (18 in MT) it is omitted and at Num 6:14 where the prepositional phrase לשׁלמים obtains it becomes εἰς σωτήριον. The term σωτήριον when applied to this type of sacrifice is difficult to translate into English.[19] Since such sacrifices are intended to promote well-being I suppose "peace offerings" is as good a paraphrase as any. In any event it is technical term and must be distinguished from all other types of sacrifice.

Both types of sacrifices are meat sacrifices, as τὰ πρόβατα καὶ τοὺς μόσχους ὑμῶν shows. A B x variant coordinates this phrase by prefixing και; it is then no longer in apposition to the preceding coordinate phrase, which is what Exod intended; after all sacrifice types and animal types belong to different semantic orders. As in the previous phrase, both nouns have pronominal suffixes in MT, and hex accordingly adds υμων (cf comment above) to πρόβατα.

According to the Masoretic accentuation the verse breaks before "in every place"; i.e. what MT has is "in every place where ..., I will come to you and bless you." Exod interprets differently as the καί before ἥξω demon strates. The phrase ἐν παντὶ τόπῳ modifies θύσετε, and its relative clause modifier consists of three clauses: (whenever) ἐπονομάσω ... καὶ ἥξω ... καὶ εὐλογήσω σε.[20]

The first clause governed by the relative οὗ contains the recapitulative adverb ἐκεῖ over against MT; this barbarism was, however, hardly a free invention as Sam's שׁמה shows, i.e. Exod's parent text must have been Sam here. Its verb ἐπονομάσω is cognate to its object τὸ ὄνομά μου; as a rendering for the Hiphil of זכר it is unique in LXX, but this clever choice is not inappropriate; to cause someone to remember a name is more simply effected by naming or mentioning the name.

---

19. Schl translates τὰ σωτήρια ὑμῶν here by *sacrificia vestra pro salute*, i.e. your sacrifices for health, well-being, whereas the singular genitive modifying θυσίαν he renders by *sacrificium pro salute*.
20. That ἄν within relative clauses was Exod and not the popular εαν is demonstrated in TGHE VII.B.

20:25 The δέ is contrastive; this verse speaks of altars made of stone, not of earth. The verb in the protasis of this future more vivid condition is a present subjunctive, the making an altar being viewed as a process; the popular variant ποιησης is not surprising; the aorist occurs far more frequently in LXX than the present.

The apodosis contains an unusual usage. The verb οἰκοδομέω is normally modified by a direct object modifier; it also occurs absolutely. Here, however, the direct modifier refers to the materials used; the object is αὐτούς which can only refer here to λίθων; It is of course possible to have an accusative of materials as at Deut 27:6 λίθους ... οἰκοδομήσεις τὸ θυσιαστήριον, but here there is no θυσιαστήριον though it must be understood since the protasis refers to τὸ θυσιαστήριον ἐκ λίθων. The one other instance I have been able to find where only the accusative of materials is present as modifier of οἰκοδομέω is 3Kgdm 18:32.[21] In any event they may not be τμητούς "cut, hewn."

The reason for the prohibition is given in a γάρ clause.[22] The word for instrument in MT is חרבך which in isolation is usually glossed as "your sword." Exod renders this by ἐγχειρίδιον "a handtool"; hex adds an unnecessary σου because of the Hebrew suffix.[23] The verb in MT is הנפת "you made to move back and forth," which Exod translated somewhat freely but not inappropriately by ἐπιβέβληκας, "you have brought upon." [24] -- The pronoun in the phrase ἐπ' αὐτό has because of homophony become αυτω in the C x tradition, and is in the genitive in *oI z* mss, while in a B *f* reading it is αυτους, making it refer not to "altar" but to "stones."[25]

---

21. Bauer, sub οἰκοδομέω 1.b.γ. does refer to a reference in the vision of Hermes as οἱ λίθοι οἱ ἤδη ᾠκοδομημένοι, where λίθοι refers to stones used in building as well.
22. Sym also uses γάρ, where Aq and Theod use ὅτι.
23. Aq has μάχαιράν σου; Sym also has this but with the article τήν, and Theod has τὴν ῥομφαίαν σου. Of the four renderings Exod is much the closest to what חרב means in this particular context (swords are not very effective for cutting stone!).
24. Theod did not revise this. Aq has ἐξῆρας "raise up"; compare Isa 13:2 where Aq has ἐξάρατε χεῖρα for הניפו יד. Sym is probably closest to the Hebrew with his ἐκίνησας "you moved." All Three are agreed on a literal rendering of the last clause as an active verb and have καὶ ἐβεβήλωσας αὐτό.
25. Cf the discussion in THGE VII.G.6.

20:26 Presumably the prohibition against going up by stairs to God's altar is applicable to celebrants, i.e. priests; at least in the time of Exod this could only apply to such. An *n* variant to the verb has αναβηβασει (presumably for αναβιβαση), but this verb is the causative of ἀναβαίνω and inappropriate here.

The reason for this prohibition given is that "you may not reveal your shame upon it." MT has this as an אשר clause which here expresses purpose; compare Gen 11:7 for a similar case where Gen translates by ἵνα μή.[26] Exod introduces the clause by ὅπως ἄν. The ἄν is not necessary and a popular A F M variant text omits it.

Exod interprets the Niphal תגלה as an active verb with τὴν ἀσχημοσύνην σου as object. The verb ἀποκαλύψης becomes ανακαλυψης in the *oI C* tradition; these two are synonyms. Furthermore the *d x* text omits σου after ἀσχημοσύνην as otiose, a stylistic variant.

26. For אשר in final clauses cf GK 165x.

Chapter 21

21:1 A superscription for chh.21--23. The laws are called δικαιώματα "ordinances, judgments," a good rendering for מִשְׁפָּטִים though throughout the Pentateuch it is relatively infrequently used, κρίμα and κρίσις being far more commonly employed. The C text adds μου, i.e. ordinances of God who is pictured as speaker and Moses is the addressee, as appears from the word παραθήσεις "you (i.e. Moses) shall place before them." The verb follows the relative pronoun ἅ and the combination was misread to produce απαριθμησεις "you shall enumerate, count off" in the C tradition, not overly sensible in connection with δικαιώματα.

21:2 Vv.2--11 deal with laws about slaves. The form of the laws throughout is the future more vivid conditional sentence.

The protasis sets up the general condition for vv.2--6: "if you buy a Hebrew slave," with v.2 giving the general rule about length of service, and the following verses, subdivisions with certain specifics. The general rule is "six years he shall serve you"; the word σοι has no equivalent in MT and Tar[O] but is supported by all the other ancient witnesses.

The last clause contrasts with the first clause of the apodosis, which is shown by δέ in particular. Exod's τῷ ἔτει τῷ ἑβδόμῳ is supported only by Tar[P], all other witnesses omitting τῷ ἔτει. A popular B variant has τω εβδομη ετει.[1] -- In the seventh year the slave shall go out ἐλεύθερος δωρεάν, i.e. "free without (further) obligation"; the debt is now paid. An A F *d t x* reading has εξαποστελεις αυτον ελευθερον (δωρεαν), an intrusion from the parallel law in Deut 15:12.

21:3 Either such a person becomes a slave as a bachelor or as married; each situation is separately dealt with. Exod introduces both apodoses by καί and the second protasis by a contrastive δέ. The *oI C* text also has a δέ for the

1. For usage with respect to the adjective phrase in Exod see discussion in THGE VII.J.

first protasis. By contrast MT has only one conjunction: before the second apodosis.

For the first condition attention is specifically called to the subject, the Hebrew slave, by αὐτός; cf also v.4 where, however, the αὐτός has a basis in MT. By μόνος the translator means "alone" in the sense of "unwed."

The second condition is a free rendering of MT. The protasis in MT says "if he is a בעל אשה (i.e. a married man)," while Exod has "if a wife come in together with him." In MT it is taken for granted that if the man is married the wife also enters slavery with him - that is clear from the apodosis; but Exod expressly states the fact.

The apodosis states that the wife who came in with him shall also go out with him.[2] This is constructed in balanced fashion with the subject preceding the verb as in the protasis and in the first sentence, in contrast to MT, but hex has transposed the order as well as added an αυτου after ἡ γυνή so as to conform to MT. The verb in the protasis used a compound with συν, which then influenced the *oI C* tradition in the apodosis, which has συνεξελευσεται for ἐξελεύσεται.

21:4 The conditional sentence has a two part protasis and a two part apodosis. Since it contrasts with the second conditional in v.3 Exod begins with a δέ structure. The two conditions are a) the master gave the slave a wife, and b) she bore children. The master is the slave's as the masculine pronominal suffix shows; Exod does not specify this so hex has added αυτου after κύριος. The second condition is theoretically ambiguous since αὐτῷ could refer either to the husband or to the master, but one presumes that the former was intended; its omission by A does not really help matters. Cod A also represents a popular tradition by which και is substituted for ἥ, though ἥ is clearly intended.

The apodoses differentiate between wife and children over against the slave; the former belong to the master; the slave shall go free by himself. Over against MT Exod does not state specifically that the παιδία were her children. -- Though the compound subject precedes the verb the verb in imitation of the Hebrew is in the singular, ἔσται;[3] the *f* text has the plural

2. Cf Helbing 308.
3. See SS 196.

εστωσαν. Exod states specifically that the owner is τῷ κυρίῳ αὐτοῦ which Sam also supports; on the other hand MT has לאדניה; a preOrigen popular A F M correction has αυτης for αὐτοῦ. Presumably Exod's parent text was the Sam reading. -- As in v.3 μόνος precedes the verb, and hex has placed it after it to equal MT.

21:5 Again δέ is used to show contrast to the preceding verse. V.5 is the protasis for v.6, and must be read in conjunction with it. MT has a cognate free infinitive preceding the verb יאמר: "(if the slave) should actually say." Exod interprets this cleverly avoiding a cognate construction by using the attributive participle ἀπεκριθείς, thus "in response should say."

Exod uses the perfect ἠγάπηκα and the present ἀποτρέχω to translate אהבתי and אצא resp. with a real sensitivity to the statement of the slave; the slave has loved and still loves wife and children, and so he has no intention of abandoning them as the law would allow; this he expresses with the present tense. -- Exod only has a μου modifying κύριόν though MT also has first singular suffixes for "wife" and "children," the relationship to them being fully clear. Hex has of course added μου to both.

21:6 The Masoretes have an incongruous text with the plural form אדני both times vocalized as a plural noun, although the verbs throughout are in the singular. TarO has levelled the text by using the plural for the first two verbs as well, whereas Exod Pesh and Vulg consistently have the singular. That the singular was intended is clear from the final clause (ἐδουλεύσει) αὐτῷ which is singular.

His master is to bring him to τὸ κριτήριον τοῦ θεοῦ "the tribunal of God." MT simply has האלהים; obviously Exod is an attempt to interpret the ambiguous "to God," particularly since in the next clause he is to lead him τότε "thereupon" (also not in MT), to the door upon (at) the doorpost; one would suppose the θύραν and the σταθμόν to be connected with the κριτήριον in some way, and Exod understood "God" to be an abbreviation for God's place of judgment. The Tar (and Pesh) interpreted the word האלהים as meaning "judges." To Exod it is a place.[4]

4. It should be noted that Aq and Sym rendered MT literally by τοὺς θεούς.

The second clause also differs somewhat from MT. Exod by adding τότε specifies the exact place where the ceremony is to take place after the more general κριτήριον has been reached. He is brought πρὸς τὴν θύραν ἐπὶ τὸν σταθμόν, "to the door" and then even more specifically "at the doorpost," whereas MT simply has "at the door or at the doorpost."[5] A B O z tradition has επι in both places, which levelling process destroys the specific nature of Exod's intent.[6]

The third clause describes the ear-piercing ceremony by which the slave is to be rescued from his lonely freedom. The hex recension is responsible for two readings which bring the Greek into closer conformity to MT: it changed the word order of αὐτοῦ/ὁ κύριος, and has added an αυτου (also referring to the slave) to οὖς.[7]

The final clause states the satisfactory result. Theoretically confusion should be possible: the subject is not defined (it has changed from master to slave), and the antecedent of αὐτῷ must be inferred from the context to be the master, but it is doubtful whether any reader had or has ever felt any real ambiguity.

21:7 Vv.7--11 detail the ordinance about a daughter sold into slavery and her rights. The δέ structure introduces a new section.

The protasis in contrast to MT has the subject τίς preceding the verb ἀποδῶται; hex transposes to equal MT. In fact throughout the entire section, vv.2--11, the verb always has another element preceding it, whether it be subject, modifier, an indirect object or attributive participle, and this positioning over against MT simply conforms to the style of the section. The *d* text has an imperative verb αποδοτω which must be a thoughtless error. Another case of hex interference concerns (τὴν) ἑαυτοῦ θυγατέρα which is changed because of MT to θυγατερα αυτου.[8]

5. See also Prijs 9.
6. Cf the discussion in THGE VII.L.3.
7. See SS 93.
8. Note Aq's style in his translation of the protasis. He begins with καὶ ὅταν πωλήσῃ ἀνήρ which takes each word of MT literally: כִּי = ὅταν; יִמְכֹּר = πωλήσῃ, and אִישׁ = ἀνήρ. Then "his daughter" occurs as in hex, and he adds an εἰς before οἰκέτιν because MT has the preposition לְ before אָמָה.

326

The Hebrew daughter is not to go away as female slaves go; she has a special status.[9] Exod has αἱ δοῦλαι "females slaves" instead of MT's העבדים; i.e. MT distinguishes between the אמה "maid servant" and the עבדים "male slaves." Exod makes quite another distinction between οἰκέτιν "a household servant" and the general class of δοῦλαι; comp also the contrast in Vulg: *in famulam* vs *ancillae*.

21:8 A popular A variant has added δέ in the protasis which is sensible. Exod renders the protasis by "if she should not be pleasing to her master to whom she was betrothed,"[10] MT has רעה for "should not be pleasing"; Exod softens the expression by using a negative plus an antonymous verbal idea (note Pesh's strong word "be hateful").[11] -- The dative modifier translates MT's בעיני; hex adds εν οφθαλμοις[12] before τῷ κυρίῳ. In the tradition the *n* text has an optative inflection ευαρεστειη, and a *z* variant has the present subjunctive ευαρεστη. Neither changes the semantic sense greatly and both are obvious copyist errors. And the verb in the relative clause in MT is יעדה "designated her" for Exod's "was betrothed to him."[13]

The apodosis has two parts: a positive and a negative. Positively ἀπο-λυτρώσει αὐτήν, "he shall cause her to be redeemed," i.e. he shall let her go free, without further obligation. Negatively he has no authority (οὐ κύριός ἐστιν) to sell her to a foreign people. Since this contrasts with ἀπολυτρώσει Exod uses δέ.

9. Aq's translation changes Exod's ἀπελεύσεται to ἐξελεύσεται which is slightly different in intent, i.e. "go out (of the house)" rather than "go away from." The remainder, however is most Hebraic: ὡς ἔξοδος τῶν δούλων. Theod has the same verb as Aq, keeps the ὥσπερ of Exod and "corrects" the remainder to ἐκπορεύονται οἱ δοῦλοι. Sym, of course, goes his own way with a free paraphrase: οὐ προελεύσεται προέλευσιν δουλικήν "she shall not go forth in a slavelike release."
10. See Helbing 245 for this translation of καθωμολογήσατο.
11. The Three render רעה in various ways: Aq by κακίσθη; Sym by μὴ ἀρέσκῃ, and Theod by (εἰ) πονηρά ἐστιν, only Sym adopting the kind of pattern which Exod used.
12. Which The Three also have.
13. None of The Three adopts Exod's rendition of the relative clause. All Three have taken the Kethib לא rather than the Qere לו for their text, i.e. have a negative particle for αὐτῷ. These have in turn influenced the Exod tradition as well. Theod's ἣν οὐ καθωμολογήσατο αὐτήν has become a popular A F variant as well, with C varying that text by making αὐτήν αυτη. Aq has a literal ὃς οὐ καθωμολογήσατο αὐτήν, and Sym much more

The final ὅτι clause gives the reason for the law: "he has broken faith with her." The verb ἀθετέω usually has an accusative modifier impelling the Byzantine text to change the Hebraic ἐν αὐτῇ (for בה)[14] to αυτην.

21:9 A δέ structure shows contrast to v.8. The protasis specifies the case of the daughter sold (cf vv.7--8) being intended as wife for the buyer's son, i.e. "if τῷ υἱῷ he should betroth her"; hex has added an αυτου to equal MT. The C text has mistakenly changed the verb to the active καθομολογηση, which is quite inappropriate. The variant arose by apocopation of the -ται ending.

The law is fully clear; in such a case he must deal with her κατὰ τὸ δικαίωμα τῶν θυγατέρων. These laws are called δικαιώματα, see v.1, and the ordinance concerning daughters has just been enunciated in vv.7--8, and these are also operative for one betrothed to a son.[15]

21:10 The δέ structure introduces another ordinance. The protasis sets the condition, the taking on of a second wife; it simply states: "if another one he should take to him"; the context makes clear that it is another wife. A *b f z* variant has the reflexive pronoun instead of αὐτῷ, but this does not accord with the style of Exod.[16]

The apodosis outlines the rights of the original wife; these are τὰ δέοντα and τὸν ἱματισμόν and τὴν ὁμιλίαν αὐτῆς. In MT each of the three has a pronominal suffix, and so hex has added αυτης to the first two as well. The first two items concern food and clothing. The term δέοντα means the "necessary things," the participle of δεῖ. Here it renders שאר "flesh, meat" rather than לחם "food" as at 16:22. The third item, ὁμιλίαν, refers to conjugal rights to sexual intercourse. These rights may not be withheld. Within the tradition the third right appears in the *s* text as ομολογιαν "agreement," which would not make a great deal of sense to a reader; it is an obvious copyist's error.

21:11 The δέ structure shows the negative contrast to the apodosis of v.10. Should the man not fulfill these three obligations to the first wife, then she

---

elegantly ἡ μὴ καθωμολογημένη.
14. For this Hebraism see Helbing 92.
15. Sym gives the betrothed an even higher status in society; instead of

shall go out free without money, i.e. owing nothing. Instead of τὰ τρία the *s* text has παντα, i.e. "all these," but this still refers to the three conditions outlined. -- It should be understood that the first wife is still the same "daughter" referred to in v.7.

21:12 Vv.12--17 deal with capital offenses. V.12 continues the conditional form of vv.2--11, though MT changes the pattern; in fact, except for v.14 this section avoids conditional sentences, preferring apodictic statements: "the one who ... shall ...." With a new section the initial δέ structure is appropriate; its omission by a popular M text does equal MT, though this need not be recensional.

MT begins with מכה איש which Exod renders by ἐὰν δὲ πατάξη τίς τινα; Exod had to add τίς since there is no antecedent, whereas MT's participle itself constitutes the subject. Similarly for ומת Exod continues with a finite verb: (πατάξη ...) καὶ ἀποθάνη.

The apodosis represents MT's מות יומת, a formula also occurring in vv.15,16,17. In all four cases the free infinitive is translated by the dative noun θανάτῳ, whereas the finite verb is translated here and in v.15 by the cognate θανατούσθω, but in the other two cases by the synonym τελευτάτω. The *n s* reading θανατωθησεται more closely approximates the passive character of יומת. The omission of the cognate noun by *C* is probably due to homoiarcton. -- A gloss in the *f* tradition, ινα μη ως φονευς απολειται, does not fit here and must really belong to v.13.

21:13 Vv.13 and 14 particularize the general ordinance of v.12. Each begins with a δέ structure. V.13 deals with accidental or inadvertent manslaughter; v.14, with intentional killing.

Unintentional manslaughter is doubly described, as ὁ οὐχ ἐκών "the one who (acts) unwittingly," and as "God delivered (him) into his hands." The former is a free rendering of MT's אשר לא צדה. The verb צדה means "to lie in wait," and Exod fairly represents the intent of the Hebrew.[17]

For the latter description παρέδωκεν is used absolutely which is rare indeed. It is not surprising that an A Byzantine variant should have added

"daughters" he has εὐγενίδων "well or nobly born."
16. See the discussion in THGE VII.G.10.

αυτου which in any event had to be understood. The verb is a translation of אנה Piel "cause to meet" (the Piel occurs only here).[18] -- Exod translated לידו as though it were plural; actually a Qumran ms has לידיו and this reading may well have been the parent for εἰς τὰς χεῖρας αὐτοῦ.

Rhetorically the verse is loosely structured. The description of unintentional manslaughter is set up as a pendant nominative before the main clause, viz. δώσω σοι τόπον with a relative clause modifying τόπον; the only element tying the opening description to it is ὁ φονεύσας of the relative clause which is the same referent as the opening ὁ δέ and αὐτοῦ. One can thus render the pattern employed by "As for the one who ... his hands ... I will give to you a place whither the killer may flee." ὁ φονεύσας has no correspondent in MT but is made necessary by the way in which Exod translated his parent text. Exod did imitate the Hebrew in the relative clause, however, where the use of ἐκεῖ is quite Hebraic, and its omission by an A + text is a stylistic improvement.

21:14 This verse not only gives the ordinance for wilful manslaughter; it inadvertently also shows what the τόπον to which the involuntary killer could flee was: it was θυσιαστηρίου μου. The verse is put in the form of a conditional sentence; compare remarks at v.12. A δέ structure emphasizes the contrast between vv. 14 and 13.

The protasis has two parts, the second of which has no equivalent in MT, though καὶ καταφύγῃ is implied by the apodosis in which the flight is presupposed. A *z* variant has a gloss to this verb, επι το θυσιαστηριον; this makes even more explicit what is implicit.

The first (and major) condition is "if someone should attack the neighbour to kill him by deceit (i.e. some kind of strategem)." The verb is ἐπιθῆται for which in a military context see comment at 18:11. Exod is blunter than MT; he calls a spade a spade; what MT really means is an attack! -- The subject τις precedes the verb and hex has transposed them to fit the Hebrew. -- The neighbour is naturally "his neighbour" in MT and hex added αυτου for a more exact representation. The purposive infinitive is unmarked, but the *f* text marks it with του. Actually the unmarked infinitive is much more common in Exod than the marked ones. Only 15 instances of the infinitive marked with τοῦ occur, and only eight with τῷ (after a preposition); for the latter cf comments at 3:12.

The apodosis renders MT literally except for the unmarked purposive infinitive at the end; the verb θανατῶσαι is transitive whereas למות is not. What Exod states renders the implicit of MT explicit: "to put (him) to death."

21:15 MT begins the next three verses with *waw* plus participle. Since each is a new theme Exod has no conjunction but instead uses a relative pronoun plus a verb or an articulated participle, each verse having a different construction. V.15 begins with ὅς plus a present indicative; v.16, with the articulated participle, and v.17 with ὅς plus ἄν and an aorist subjunctive.

V.15 renders literally "his father" and "his mother" but joins them with ἤ which is what the "and" of all the other witnesses really means. It is likely that in native Greek the "his" in either or both cases would not be used. A *d* variant does omit the first one and the A *b n* text omits the second; either one (or both) make for better Greek.

21:16(17) Exod alone of the old witnesses has transposed vv.16 and 17 of MT, ostensibly to bring the two capital crimes against parents together. The *C* text reverses them and represents hex. The crime here is κακολογῶν "abusing," literally "bad-mouthing"; compare Vulg: *maledixerit*. MT has a stronger term מקלל "the one cursing." As in v.15 the tradition (*d x +*) improves the Greek style by omitting the first αὐτοῦ or the second (as the *b* text) or both as in the NT and Philo. For ἤ as conjunction see note at v.15.

Why Exod should change the capital formula is not clear, but it is probably merely for variation's sake. The verb used is τελευτάτω "let him end (life)."[19]

21:17(16) Exod considerably expanded the text of MT on the basis of Deut 24:7. Exod's parent text must have had the words מבני ישראל והתעמר בו after איש which would account for τινα τῶν υἱῶν ᾿Ισραήλ, καὶ καταδυναστεύσας αὐτόν "one of the Israelites, and treating him like a

---

17. Aq was naturally unsatisfied with Exod and translated the phrase by ὅς οὐ μεθώδευσεν "who has not acted guilefully."

slave (he sells)."-- Exod also adds an otiose τίς (a Hebraism for אִישׁ) which a popular text tastefully omits. Exod does not translate the pronominal suffix of מכרו and hex adds αυτον accordingly. -- It is of course obvious that the αὐτόν before ἀποδῶται must be understood after the verb as well.

The next condition imitates MT by rendering the *waw* by καί although in vv.15 and 16 Exod interpreted the intent correctly by using the correlative ἤ.

The clause καὶ εὑρεθῆ ἐν αὐτῷ must be understood as an alternative to καταδυναστεύσας αὐτὸν ἀποδῶται and not as a second condition. The capital formula is the same as that of v.16, though a popular A F variant changes it to the same verb as that found in vv.12 and 15.

21:18 Vv.18--27 deal with bodily injuries involving only people. The section's beginning is shown by δέ. The verse portrays the general conditions basic to the specific ordinance to follow in the next verse.

The subject is set as being δύo ἄνδρες supported only by Pesh, all others lacking δύo; the greater exactness does seem somewhat tautologous. For λοιδορῶνται as translation for יריבן see note at 17:2.[20]

The second condition is πατάξη τις τὸν πλησίον, a good rendering of the Hebrew which, however, has a pronominal suffix on the noun, for which hex adds an αυτου. A B z text (as Sam) has the verb in the plural. The word אִישׁ is correctly rendered by τις.[21] Somewhat surprising is its omission in a B O z text, by which a somewhat unusual idiom is created "and he (or "they" in B and z) smites the neighbour" with no antecedent being given. The blow is described as given by a stone or fist;[22] the attacker used some blunt instrument or simply his own fists.

In the last condition the δέ shows contrast; the one struck becomes bed-ridden. The word for bed is κοίτην, and is commonly used for משכב in LXX. A b + variant has κλινην which is cognate to the verb κατακλιθῆ but this is never used for משכב in the Pentateuch; in fact, it occurs only twice elsewhere in LXX; its Hebrew equivalent is usually מטה.

---

18. Aq rendered it by ἀφῆκεν "he sent away."
19. This as well as the secondary change in word order in the B z text is fully discussed in THGE VII.F.4.

332

21:19 A further condition continues the list in v.18 but is separately recorded with ἐάν. Exod uses an attributive participle plus a finite verb to translate coordinate verbs of MT but adds uniquely the subject ὁ ἄνθρωπος, presumably not only because πλησίον which is the referent is at some distance but also because a new ἐάν clause obtains. The point of the condition is that the stricken man is sufficiently recovered to get up and walk about outside albeit with a staff - in modern parlance "with a cane, or crutches." MT has "his staff" and an αυτου has been duly added by hex.

The apodosis states that the first party is legally innocent, "except that he shall reimburse for his loss of employment as well as the medical costs. Exod uses ἀποτείσει as a more exact term than the general נתן of MT; the *n* reading δωσει betrays some kind of Hebrew influence, probably from one of The Three. The two modifiers of the verb are τῆς ἀργίας and τὰ ἰατρεῖα. The change in case is certainly intentional. The accusative shows direct costs which must be repaid, but the genitive is used to indicate reimbursement for the time lost from work; the interpretation probably reflects usage of the time of the translator. A *d* variant which changes the former to τας αργιας makes it a direct cost, i.e. a salary. The Hebrew equivalent is somewhat ambiguous; the infinitival noun שבת if derived from ישב means his "sitting (still)," whereas if from שבת it means his "resting." In either event ἀργίας makes excellent sense. -- The last item is a paraphrase for MT's ורפא ירפא "and he shall be fully healed"; in other words MT has a verbal clause which relates to the שבתו; the loss of employment is to be fully met, including the entire period of full recovery. The Tar interpret the phrase as Exod: "the cost of complete recovery of health," and Vulg has *impensas in medicos*.

21:20 Vv.20--21 as well as vv.26--27 are ordinances concerning injuries to a slave. V.20 has δέ to show a new ordinance being introduced. The subject, τις, precedes the verb in contrast to MT, and hex "corrects" the order. The usual position of τις is as first element for verbal as well as for nominal clauses; in fact in only seven cases out of 30 in Exod does τις follow the predicate. The protasis describes the condition of someone who beats his male or female servant with a stick and he/she dies under his hands, i.e. in the course of the beating. Both the nouns for servants are modified by an αὐτοῦ following MT. The pattern varies in the tradition in that the first αὐτοῦ appears as the reflexive in the F M *s y* variant text, and the second one is omitted by the *b* tradition. Both are quite possible texts, but they are not Exod.

The apodosis in MT consists of the pattern: cognate free infinitive + finite verb. If the verb of the apodosis is in third person it is usually rendered throughout the ordinances in the third person imperative, in this verse by ἐκδικηθήτω. A majority A F M variant has the future indicative εκδικηθησεται which entered the text from v.21. The cognate infinitive is translated by δίκη, and the clause then can be translated by "let him be punished with a judgement."

21:21 Since v.21 contrasts with the preceding verse a δέ is used. Over against "die under his hands" the beaten servant lives on for a day or two. In MT the verb comes at the end of the protasis and hex also puts it there. The judgment of the apodosis is οὐκ ἐκδικηθήσεται. The reason for no judgment is such a case is given as: "he/she is his money," i.e. the slave was his property.

21:22 A new ordinance is introduced by a δέ structure; it concerns injury to the fetus of a pregnant woman. As in v.18 the subject of the protasis is specified as δύο ἄνδρες; cf comment on v.18. The protasis involves an abortion of a fetus μὴ ἐξεικονισμένον "not fully formed"; the stress is on this last proviso. This final proviso is quite different in MT which has ולא יהיה אסון "and there be no mishap"; this is literally followed by Tar[P] and Pesh, while Tar[O] interprets אסון as מותא, "no death ensues," i.e. the mother survives. This is also the interpretation of Vulg: *et ipsa* (i.e. the mother) *vixerit*. But Exod has understood אסון in a more literal way, as meaning health, i.e. "and it (i.e. the ילד) was not healthy," i.e. a viable fetus. If the aborted fetus was not such it was not fully formed.

The apodosis gives the judgment: he shall be fined a fine. This consists of two parts: "as the woman's husband ἐπιβάλη (might impose)" and "he shall give (i.e. pay) μετὰ ἀξιώματος." MT has for "impose" ישית

עָלָיו; hex added αυτω to equal the prepositional phrase. -- An A F z variant has εαν for ἄν.[23]

Exod does not indicate the second part by an initial conjunction as MT does, though the majority text witnesses to a και. Exod has tried to combine the two parts so that he pays according to the demands of the woman's husband but this is in turn circumscribed by ἀξιώματος, i.e. a judicial assessment. This is somewhat clearer in MT which stipulates בפללים "by arbiters."

21:23--25 The δέ structure shows v.23 contrasting with the last clause of the protasis of v.22. For ἐξεικονισμένον see note on v.22. The verb of the protasis is ᾖ, i.e. the subjunctive of εἰμί after ἐάν, and certainly not the imperfect ην as the B f text has it, which can only be rooted in a careless copyist's error.

The apodosis involves the lex talionis; a payment of a fine is not sufficient as in v.22; the abortion of a fully formed child is if it results in its death murder, or if it has other harmful side-effects is to be punished like for like. The statement of the lex talionis here finds its most expanded form; compare Lev 24:20 with three elements but with explanation, and Deut 19:21 with five over against Exod with eight elements. The first five concern life, eyes, teeth, hand, feet and these also comprise the Deut list. In Lev the eyes and teeth also constitute the second and third elements, but the first, σύντριμμα "fracture" for שבר is unique. Exod amplifies by three further cases of tit for tat, viz. κατάκαυμα, τραῦμα and μώλωτα, "inflammation, wound and bruise." Each adequately represents its Hebrew couterpart.

21:26 Change of ordinance is indicated by δέ. This verse and v.27 revert to the theme of bodily injury to a servant, but the judgment contrasts with the lex talionis of vv.23--25. The protasis begins in the same fashion as v.20 with τις preceding πατάξη for which cf comment at v.20. In both, however, MT uses עבדו and אמתו to designate the servants, but Exod makes a distinction. In v.20 he used the general terms παῖδα and παιδίσκην, but here he uses οἰκέτου and θεραπαίνης resp. for servants male and female in the household, i.e. servants who wait on the master in a domestic context.

The second element in the protasis is that the striking is so severe that blindness results. The verb ἐκτυφλώσῃ is usually transitive, though here used absolutely "and he cause blindness." MT has ושחתה "and he destroy it (i.e. the eye)." Hex has added αυτην to represent the Hebrew suffix. Oddly within the tradition of hex itself the αυτην was changed to αυτου; this constitutes a late rationalization of hex: not as "blind the eye" but "blind the individual."

The judgment is "he shall send them away free for their eye." This must have been what MT meant, though it says "he shall send him ... his eye"; of course what was meant was "him/her ... his/her eye," and Exod solves the matter by using plural pronouns. Only Vulg shares Exod's solution by *dimittet eos liberos pro oculo quem eruit*. Within the tradition evidence of further attempts at levelling occur; the *C d f* text changes τοῦ ὀφθαλμοῦ to the plural, which is quite wrong for the ordinance.

21:27 Though this verse parallels the preceding (i.e. "tooth" instead of "eye") it is a new ordinance as shown by δέ. In the protasis αὐτοῦ obtains only after θεραπαίνης, though a popular hex reading has added αυτου after οἰκέτου as well to equal MT. For οἰκέτου and θεραπαίνης see note at v.26. The protasis does not repeat "should someone strike" since this is understood from its parallel in v.26, and it is a single clause with the verb ἐκκόψῃ "he shall knock out" for יפיל.

The judgment is identical to that of v.26 except for the necessary change of ὀφθαλμοῦ to ὀδόντος; cf comments at v.26.

21:28 Vv.28--36 deal, except for the interruption of vv.33--34, with the goring ox. Within the complex each separate ordinance is indicated by (ἐάν) δέ. V.28 gives the general ordinance and the following verses specify particular conditions within the general theme.

The general protasis: if an ox should gore a man or woman, and he/she die" can be taken as an overall condition governing vv.28--32. Here three rules are to apply. The ox is to be stoned with stones. MT has a cognate free infinitive before the Niphal יסקל, which is translated as in 19:13 by the dative noun λίθοις (but without ἐν; compare also Lev 24:16

336

for גם ר). Furthermore its flesh shall not be eaten, presumably because of the blood-guilt attached to the carcass of the ox; compare Num 35:33. Contrastively - note the use of δέ - the owner shares no guilt; he is נקי, i.e. ἀθῷος ἔσται. The future verb is used since the condition is future more vivid. The *d* variant εστω substitutes an imperative, but that is out of character throughout the entire section.

21:29 The protasis specifies the specific exceptions to the general rule of v.28 for which the owner would not be innocent. The overall condition is "if he should have been a gorer previously."[24] A popular variant has ην instead of ᾖ which represents an attempt at putting the conditional in past time; cf also the comment at v.20. For the phrase πρὸ ἐχθὲς καὶ πρὸ τῆς τρίτης see note at 4:10. The addition by the Byzantine text of ημερας is taken from v.36; compare also 4:10. The popular elided form of ἐχθές as χθες is the Attic form; ἐχθές was the form used in Ptolemaic Egypt; at least the elided form is not attested in its papyri.[25]

Furthermore this information was attested to its master, i.e. he was informed. Exod used a deponent plural verb "they attested" to render the passive singular הועד. In spite of the warning, however, the owner did not put him away, ἀφανίσῃ, probably in the sense of put away under guard; the word can also mean "destroy, kill," but that is hardly intended here, since MT has ישמרנו. The owner should have kept the animal safely out of reach. The *d* text has the unusual variant αποφανιση which should derive from an unattested *αποφανιζω, an -ιζω formation analogous to αποφανη, the aorist subjunctive of αποφαινη. It would then mean "and he would not have made him evident, public knowledge." Readers would connect it with the owner's failure to make clear to the public that the bull was dangerous. -- The translator may have been engaging in some word play, i.e. ἀφανίσῃ vs ἀνέλῃ; in view of the δέ used to show contrast this is quite possible.

The judgment is that the owner is now also guilty and will be put to death, προσαποθανεῖται. The substitution by the *f* text to συναποθανειται does not change the meaning.

---

20. See also Helbing 22. The Sym translation, διαμάχωνται, is a more exact rendering of the Hebrew יריבן.

21:30 In contrast to the capital sentence in v.29 an escape route is possible. Two oddities of translation technique should be mentioned here; the word λύτρα occurs twice in Exod for two different terms in MT, admittedly synonymous: כפר and פריון. If these are to be at all differentiated they might be rendered by "atonement price" and ransom price" resp. A second oddity is the opposite phenomenon. MT twice has the structure ישרן עליו but Exod varies the translation, the first by a literal ἐπιβληθῇ αὐτῷ and the second by ἐπιβάλωσιν αὐτῷ. The latter uses the indefinite plural subject as in "they say, man sagt, on dit," and may substitute for a passive construction.

For ἐπιβληθῇ two z variants obtain: επιβαρηθη and επιβαρυνθη, both meaning "be weighted down," not an overly likely text. The two are variants of a single original error.[26] Of greater significance is the hex plus of κατα παντα before ὅσα, for בכל in MT which Exod had disregarded.[27]

21:31 This ordinance concerns the goring of a son or a daughter. The MT does not formally mark the protasis by the usual כי; instead it uses an או או ... construction, i.e. "either ... or." Exod regularizes this by using ἐάν instead of "either" and omitting the second "he gores." The repetition of κερατίσῃ would be otiose, but whether it should stand after υἱόν or after θυγατέρα could be problematic; in fact, a B b z variant transposes the verb to the latter position.[28]

The judgment is "according to this ordinance," i.e. the ordinance outlined in vv.19--30, "shall they do to him." One presumes that the referent in αὐτῷ is the owner, but this is not at all certain since it could just as well be the ox. A d reading has αυτον for αὐτῷ; this must be thoughtless error, since it is not sensible. -- As for the last clause of v.30 the singular passive verbal idea (יעשה in the Niphal) is translated by the active plural (cf note on v.30).

21:32 The lex talionis does not apply in the case of slaves who are treated in terms of property loss. The format of the protasis is the same as in v.31

21. The Three witness to the Hebraic ἀνήρ according to Syh.
22. Cf SS 120.
23. For ἄν in relative clauses see THGE VII.B.

except that the subject ὁ ταῦρος occurs after the verb; in fact the pattern follows MT, this time וכי introducing the protasis and יגח obtaining only after the first modifier. The modifiers are the broader terms παῖς and παιδίσκη of v.20 rather than the οἰκέτης and θεραπαίνη of vv.25 and 27. The choice is quite deliberate; domestic servants would not normally be found in the vicinity of oxen, whereas ordinary servants such as those working on the land would.

The sentence is a monetary fine; thirty silver drachma were to be paid to their owner. Exod uses the plural pronoun, since either male or female slave is covered by αὐτῶν, whereas MT uses the masculine singular suffix when the gender of the referent is ambiguous. The coin is called a didrachma, i.e. a two drachma piece. The *chi* was sometimes voiced by attraction to the *mu*, producing the variant spelling δίδραγμα.[29]

21:33 This verse constitutes the protasis for v.34. The ordinance concerns injury to an animal fallen into a pit which was left uncovered. For τις preceding the verb see comment at v.20; the word order is changed by hex to conform to MT. λατομήσῃ in the correlative clause has the subject repeated for it in MT as well, and hex has dutifully added τις. -- The λάκκον was probably a storage pit.

21:34 The judgment holds the owner of the pit fully responsible. This involves two conclusions: money (presumably its price) he shall give to their owner, but the dead animal will belong to the pit's owner. The *O* text has combined the first two clauses of the verse by omitting ἀργύριον δώσει, undoubtedly an error due to homoiot, though sensible. Since a particular animal is not mentioned but rather any animal - Sam actually added the gloss בהמה כל או - Exod shows the relationship accurately by using a plural genitive pronoun. Whether the *b* + reading αυτου was due to Hebrew influence or not can not be determined.

Over against this cost - note the contrastive δέ - the dead animal belongs to the owner of the pit. The animal is called τὸ τετελευτηκός "the one killed," an accurate designation for an accident victim; the neuter has been used here since any animal, μόσχος ἢ ὄνος, was involved, making the gender uncertain. A popular A F M text has another perfect participle, τεθνηκος "the dead one," which is somewhat closer to MT's המת, but whether it was due to Hebrew influence is doubtful. Certainly due to MT influence is the hex transposition of αὐτῷ ἔσται.

21:35 Vv.35 and 36 are two ordinances dealing with a goring ox killing another ox. In the protasis the genitive precedes the noun it modifies in τινὸς ταῦρος; this is reversed to conform to MT by hex. Hex has also added a genitive pronoun after πλησίον in view of MT's רעהו.[30]

The judgment calls for full sharing of the accidental loss. The proceeds of the sale of the live ox as well as the dead ox are to be shared. The apodosis reflects the MT text exactly except for the third occurrence of τὸν ταῦρον which MT does not have, it being otiose.

21:36 This ordinance concerns an ox known to be a gorer previously which the owner did not safeguard. Exod continues the conditional form, i.e. ἐὰν δέ, rather than following MT's correlative conjunction. Exod states the protasis largely in the terms used in the parallel protasis concerning a goring ox in v.29. MT has: "it was known that the ox was a gorer previously and his owner has not shut him up." To Exod this protasis was not fully clear nor was it complete. First of all, the verb נודע has no expressed subject; this was clarified by using ὁ ταῦρος as subject; it then reads "the ox was known that it was ..." That simply involved transposing כי שור. But more importantly it was legally not complete. Was the owner aware of the ox's propensity for goring? V.29 gave a much more satisfactory coverage and Exod took that over with three minor changes which the new context made plausible. Instead of ᾖ he used ἐστιν because it was part of the ὅτι clause and not governed by ἐάν; he also added ἡμέρας after τρίτης for which see v.29, and instead of the present subjunctive of διαμαρτύρομαι he used the perfect subjunctive. For the text as translation as well as for the popular variant χθες see the discussion at v.29. -- Hex added ο κυριος αυτου after αὐτόν to conform to MT.

The judgment is one of full restitution in contrast to that of v.35 where the loss was shared between the two owners. Exod renders שלם ישלם

simply by ἀποτείσει, i.e. disregarding the free infinitive. This is not an error on Exod's part but intentionally done. In ch.22 the verb ἀποτείσει occurs a number of times, sometimes for ישׁלם by itself and sometimes (vv.6,14) for the cognate construction; in other words Exod saw no distinction between the two constructions. The guilty owner had to repay according to the lex talionis, ox for ox. Since he had paid in full by having restored an ox he could keep the carcass. The z text has the neuter το τετελευτηκος for ὁ τετελευτημώς, probably from v.34 (understanding σῶμα or πτῶμα?). -- The C text has a doublet here, adding "his owner shall repay silver for the ox," thereby giving the owner an alternative, either replacing the ox or paying in cash.

---

24. Cf SS 76.
25. According to Mayser I.1.125.
26. Cf the discussion in THGE VII.Q. sub 7:14.
27. For the popular but unoriginal B variant εαν for ἄν see THGE VII.B.
28. For a defence of the originality of its position in Exod see THGE VII.F.4.
29. Sym used the later term στατῆρος, "stater."
30. Cf SS 94.

Chapter 22

22:1(21:37) All protases introduced by ἐάν in this chapter add δέ except v.27 which adds οὖν. Vv.1--4 are ordinances dealing with thieves. The first protasis has two conditions: "steal an ox or sheep," and "dispose of it either by butchering it or selling." MT repeats "it" after selling and hex has added αυτο. The reverse phenomenon is also attested by a B *n* + variant which omits αὐτό (after "butcher") as well, clearly a stylistic change by which the Greek is rhetorically improved. The distinction insisted on is the disposal; it is no longer in his possession in contrast to v.4. The pronoun is naturally neuter since the alternatives are of different genders.

In the judgment Exod correctly understood that בקר and צאן were collectives resp. for שור and שה and simply translates them by the plural.

22:2(1) Vv.2 and 3a interrupt the matter of stolen animals to deal with the burglar thief. In the protasis of the first ordinance the word διορύγματι, for "breach," refers as does מחתרת of MT to the break or hole made by the thief in order to get into the house.

The judgment is that there is to him no φόνος, a legal term used for homicide or murder, and the clause could be rendered idiomatically: "he is not guilty of murder (or homicide)." The Hebrew term is דמים, plural of דם, used to indicate "blood shed in violence." Vulg rendered it by *reus sanguinis*, whereas Tar^P makes it fully clear by his "guilty of shedding innocent blood."

22:3(2) The verse has two ordinances. The first still deals with the burglar thief. In v.2 the burglar is killed in the act but in the dark of night. Here the condition, i.e. being caught in the act, takes place after sunrise.

The judgment is now the opposite: he is now liable (i.e. to the charge of murder).[1] The "he" refers to the owner who may not kill a thief in daylight. The verb is ἀνταποθανεῖται, with the unusual αντ- element invoking

---

1. Cf SS 183.

the lex talionis, i.e. life for a life. The A F *z* variant αποθανειται misses the nuance of Exod's longer compound.

The second ordinance reverts to the condition of v.1, and its αὐτῷ refers to the burglar thief caught in the act, not to the owner. This means that vv.2 and 3a must be taken parenthetically. The protasis presents the condition: "but if he should have nothing." The judgment is that he must make restitution by his own enslavement. Exod's term for the thing(s) stolen is τοῦ κλέμματος; the hex tradition has added αυτου since MT has a suffix in גנבתו.[2]

22:4(3) MT begins the condition with a cognate free infinitive plus finite verb: "if there was actually found (alive)." Exod amplifies this by adding καταλημφθῇ to which *b* adds ο ανθρωπος as identified subject; by this addition the sensible change of subject for the coordinate εὑρεθῇ is made explicit. Exod's indifference throughout this chapter to the cognate construction is shown by his failure to render the free infinitive. The condition of this verse contrasts with that of v.1 where the stolen animal was either butchered or sold; here the thief has been caught with the undamaged goods still in his possession. These goods are identified as ἀπό τε ὄνου ἕως πρόβατα and their condition as ζῶντα. The conjunctive particle τε joins the ἀπό ... ἕως construction to τὸ κλέμμα from which it is clear that the stolen goods consists of "from ass to sheep." The majority text omits τε. The hex text has added μοσχου και before ὄνου to represent MT which has "from ox to ass to sheep."

The judgement is that "he shall repay them double."[3] αὐτά has no equivalent in MT, and an early A + variant has omitted it, possibly as a pre-hexaplaric revision toward the Hebrew. A *d x* text has αυτω which refers to the owner, possibly under the influence of αὐτῷ in v.2.

22:5(4) Over against MT Exod has two ordinances concerning grazing in a neighbour's field or vineyard, and follows the longer tradition of Sam. The general condition is that of a man grazing his own field or vineyard. But then he sends (i.e. has carelessly allowed to stray) his cattle into another

2. Cf SS 94.
3. See the discussion in Prijs 5f.

field (i.e. that of his neighbour). The judgment for this carelessness is that he shall repay from his own field according to its yield. Presumably "its" refers to the field of the neighbour. The assessment can easily be made from what remains uncropped.

The second ordinance deals with a more severe case. The straying cattle have effectively cropped the entire field of the neighbour. MT has the equivalent of the second judgment attached to the first condition, the attendant condition and judgment resp. not obtaining in MT.

C has καλλιστα instead of the first βέλτιστα; semantically there is little difference. Within this same expression the B *O z* text has και instead of "or" which may well be a prehexaplaric revision towards the Hebrew.[4]

22:6(5) Fire accidentally spreading to a neighbour's property. Exod subordinates the first verbal idea as an attributive participle. "If a fire spreading should catch on thorns": thorns were used as hedges about a field, being effective in keeping larger animals out. -- ἅλωνα ἢ στάχυς ἢ πεδίον" are Exod's interpretation of MT's גריש "heaped up (grain)" or הקמה "the standing" or השדה "the field." The Greek terms literally mean "threshing floor or stock or field." Exod refers to grain in three forms: that which is threshed, the grain still on the stock but cut and ready for threshing, and the grain still uncut in the field. The first two occur in popular variants in the plural, but these are pedantic changes since the terms are clearly collective in Exod.

The judgment involves cognate constructions both for predicate and subject. The former involves a cognate free infinitive plus finite verb of the root שלם, which Exod always renders simply by the verb ἀποτείσει; cf note at 21:36. Hex has added αποτιννυων, from the root ἀποτίννυμι, undoubtedly related to ἀποτίνω. -- MT's subject has a cognate modifier "the one making to burn the burning." Exod makes no attempt to imitate the cognate construction, but translates by ὁ τὸ πῦρ ἐκκαύσας. Hex emends the order so as to make τὸ πῦρ follow the participle in imitation of the Hebrew.

22:7(6) Vv.7--13 constitute a group of ordinances dealing with deposits. The general conditions in v.7 cover the specific ones of vv.7--8. The term σκεῦος refers to moveable goods or property. For the word order τις δῷ see comment on 21:20; hex transposes to agree with MT. Hex has also added αυτου after πλησίον to correspond to MT's רעהו.[5] Money or goods entrusted to a friend or neighbour for safekeeping particularly before a journey was a common practice, and it was expected that it would be returned in good condition upon return or demand.

A second general condition is followed by the first specific condition without δέ following ἐάν. One would expect that the noun גנב "thief" would be translated by κλέπτης as in v.2, but Exod uses the aorist active participle κλέψας (also in the next verse); in fact κλέπτης is the usual rendering for the noun throughout LXX, whereas κλέψας occurs elsewhere only once in Prov, i.e. three times in all. -- In the judgment a b variant has the neuter plural form for διπλοῦν under the influence of v.4.

22:8(7) The δέ shows contrast to the specific condition of v.7. The condition is that the thief is not to be found. In such a case the neighbour from whose house the deposit had been stolen must go out before God and swear an oath that indeed he had not acted evilly over against the deposit of the neighbour. Exod has expanded somewhat to make clear the intent of the rather cryptic Hebrew, taking the similar judgment of v.11 into account. Exod interpreted אם לא שלח ידו as being an oath formula as indeed the אם could be understood. This is then emphasized by ἦ μήν, the classical expression of affirmation in an oath. Exod took the phrase "sent out his hand" not necessarily in the sense of "sent out the hand to take," but in a more general sense as αὐτὸς πεπονηρεῦσθαι ἐφ᾽, using αὐτός to show that the subject is the same as that of the main verb ὀμεῖται, plus a verb in the general sense of acting evilly or wrongly.

ἐνώπιον τοῦ θεοῦ probably means before the sanctuary court, namely, in the presence of God in whose name the oath of innocence would be taken. The tradition has attempted to clarify the text. Thus *ol C* transpose μὴ αὐτός thereby bringing the negative next to the infinitive which it makes negative. An *n* + variant has made a finite verb, πεπονηρευται, out of the infinitive, probably because of the nominative pronoun preceding it. The Byzantine text has simplified the double compound παρακαταθήκης by omitting the -κατα- element, but παραθηκης also means "deposit." And finally as might be expected hex has added αυτου after πλησίον to agree with MT.

22:9(8) A general statement concerning what must be done in the case of any charge of crime which concerns property. This is called ῥητὸν ἀδίκημα, "a specific charge." Such a charge may be "concerning ox and ass and sheep and clothing and any accusation of loss whatever it might be." The list is based on MT, and only the last item shows a different understanding of what is meant. The matter of "any loss" is modified in MT by a relative clause which may be rendered by "of which one says 'This is it'"; presumably what is meant is that an article which was lost is identified by the accuser as being found in the possession of the accused. Exod makes this τῆς ἐγκαλουμένης "the accused," i.e. any accused loss, ὅ τι οὖν ἂν ᾖ, "whatever it might be." In the tradition the ὅ clause in particular underwent a number of changes: an A *b* variant changes οὖν to ου which can only be characterized as the result of a careless copyist at work; ἂν popularly became εαν,[6] and a *z* variant reads ομη instead of ᾖ probably under the influence of v.8, and then wrongly drew the preposed prepositional phrase modifying ἐλεύσεται within the ὅ phrase.

In the judgment the phrase ὁ ἁλοὺς διὰ τοῦ θεοῦ is according to the Masoretic text "the one whom the gods declared guilty," i.e. the verb is plural, a fact which is recognized by Tar Pesh Vulg as well. Accordingly Tar Pesh interpret אלהים throughout this verse as "judges."[7]

22:10(9) This verse sets up the condition for which vv. 11--13 give the regulations, viz. domestic animals given for safekeeping to a neighbour. Within this general condition hex has made some changes to make it fit the Hebrew: the words τις δῷ are transposed, as are πρόβατον and μόσχον, and an αυτου was added after πλησίον.

The remaining specifications are the particular conditions for which v.11 is the regulation. The three particulars are: should it be hurt, or die, or

---

4. Cf the discussion in THGE VII.E.4.
5. Cf SS 94.
6. See the discussion in THGE VII.B.

taken captive unbeknown to anyone. The first two are transposed by the majority hex tradition to equal MT. The b tradition also has τελευτήσῃ in first place but changes the second to κλαπῇ "stolen." This is clearly wrong as can be seen from v.12.

The last clause is joined to the third particular "taken captive" by καί and applies only to it. Exod has chosen γνῷ to render ראה since to him for anyone to be "seeing" meant "recognizing, knowing." A b s variant has corrected this to ἴδῃ (or εἰδῇ) which does equal MT.[8] -- A b + variant has μηθεις for μηδείς. Exod only uses μηδείς and never μηθεις, though the latter is well attested in B.C. Egypt alongside μηδείς.

22:11(10) For MT's "an oath of Yahweh there shall be" Exod has ὅρκος ἔσται τοῦ θεοῦ.[9] Only Exod among the ancient witnesses changes "Yahweh" to τοῦ θεοῦ thereby making it consistent with the larger context of vv.8 and 9 where ἐνώπιον τοῦ θεοῦ occurs. In fact Exod avoids using κύριος as applied to God in contexts where κύριος occurs in the sense of a human master or lord; God is retained to keep the distinction clear. The phrase modifies ὅρκος and it means (an oath) taken in the name of God. Hex rearranged the expression so that ἔσται comes after θεοῦ so as to agree with MT's word order. This oath is to be "between both," i.e. the oath taken by the neighbour is in the presence of the owner. The actual oath from ἦ μήν to πλησίον is identical to that of v.8 and the comments there may be consulted,[10] with two exceptions: instead of αὐτός the accusative αὐτόν is used as subject of the infinitive, grammatically necessary since here the subject is not the same as that of the main verb; also instead of ἐφ' ὅλης this verse has καθ' ὅλης. A b x z variant does have αυτος wrongly borrowed from v.8; a C variant has αυτο, but there is no neuter antecedent

---

7. The Three, however, interpret the phrase literally according to Syh, i.e. all have (οἱ) θεοί, and all use the same verb, κατακρινοῦσιν (?), except for Sym who has ἄν plus the subjunctive.
8. Even closer to MT is the reading of The Three which also preserves the participial form ὁ ὁρῶν according to Syh.
9. The Three corrected τοῦ θεοῦ to agree with MT which is what Syh's *pypy* intends.
10. Not unexpectedly the oath formula is rendered in The Three in a more literal fashion. Aq rendered אם לא שלח ידו literally by εἰ μή ἐξαπέστειλεν τὴν χεῖρα αὐτοῦ, whereas Theod rendered the verb by ἐξέτεινεν; these are attested by Syh. Sym translated the verb by an

in the context which could make any sense at all. -- A majority text has ολου instead of ὅλης; this is quite wrong in the context and came in under the influence of the common idiom καθ᾽ ὅλου "on the whole, generally" which is hardly what is meant here.

In the next clause the word οὕτως has no equivalent in MT but it is an epexegetical adverb fitting the context. And the oath is not only to be acceptable to the owner, but being in no way at fault the neighbour need not pay the owner for the loss sustained. This is put rather unusually as οὐ μὴ ἀποτείσῃ which the B + text emends to ουκ αποτεισει; the future is in line with the usual judgment, but it is weakly supported.[11] The subject though unstated must be the neighbour, and the gloss in mss 76' ο $\overline{κς}$ αυτου is simply wrong, whereas the gloss in some O mss τω κυρω at least reflects a correct understanding.

22:12(11) The particular condition in this verse deals with the animal being entrusted for safekeeping being stolen. In such a case the neighbour must repay the owner. Hex has made two additions to conform to MT. A dative κλοπη is added before κλοπῇ, as well as αυτου after κυρίω. -- The ordinance of this verse and of the following is subject to the general condition given in v.10.

22:13(12) A further particular condition, viz. "if it become prey to wild beasts." MT as in v.12 has a cognate free infinitive to intensify the verb, but Exod again found it unnecessary to take note of it. The regulation for such a case is "he shall bring him to the prey," i.e. he shall show him what has happened by bringing the owner to the carcass. The Hebrew text could be so interpreted, but the Masoretes vocalized עד not as "up to" but as "a witness," thereby intending the suffix of יבאהו to refer to the killed animal and not to the owner. The phrase עד הטרפה is then divided, עד referring to the suffix and הטרפה modifying the following verb ישלם. Other ancient witnesses are by no means in agreement. The Tar can be understood to support the Masoretes; they do understand עד to mean "witness" though

---

infinitive μετεσχηκέναι αὐτόν "he had shared in." i.e. had misappropriated (that which belonged to the owner).
11. Cf the discussion in THGE VII.M.6.

they have the plural.[12] Pesh also understood it in this way but has "for a witness of the torn." Vulg does not support the Masoretes either, having *deferat ad eum quod occisum est.* -- Hex added μαρτυρα after αὐτόν in support of MT, but left ἐπὶ τὴν θήραν unchanged.

That Exod did not take הטרפה with ישלם is made fully clear by the καί which sepaiates "he shall not repay" and θήραν; Vulg interprets in the same way.

22:14(13) Vv.14 and 15 deal with an animal which was borrowed from a neighbour. Over against the usual pattern the subject τις follows the verb as in MT; for the more usual order see comment at 21:20. -- What someone might borrow from (his) neighbour is not said, but the list of possibles given in v.10 is meant. -- As usual hex adds an αυτου to the noun to equal MT.

Over against v.10 only two further conditions are give.:, καὶ συντριβῇ ἢ ἀποθανῇ. The ἢ αἰχμάλωτον γένηται of v.10 was added in the tradition in second place by the Byzantine text, and at the end by the popular B F text.

The particular condition given is: "but the owner not be with him." A contrastive δέ is used with no equivalent in MT, where the nominal clause appears asyndetically. -- Hex adds αυτου after "owner" to conform to MT. The regulation in Exod is simply ἀποτείσει, but hex has added the cognate participle αποτιννυων to represent the cognate free infinitive before the verb.

22:15(14) The verse gives two specific regulations. First in contrast to the preceding one "if the owner should be with him (i.e. with the animal) he shall not repay." This is the direct opposite of the preceding regulation. As in v.14 MT has a suffix which hex translates as αυτου after κύριος.

The second regulation contrasts with both cases given. These two cases dealt with a borrowed animal which was hurt or died; another possibility is that such an animal had been hired (i.e. the owner accompanied the animal). In such a case the regulation is different; "he shall have it for its hire," i.e. the owner has the risk, and receives only the

12. For a full discussion of Targumic evidence see R. Le Déaut, VT XXII(1972), 164-175.

hire and no further indemnity. The construction in Exod is odd, however, since the μισθωτής refers to the person who borrowed the animal, the αὐτῷ, to the owner, and the αὐτοῦ, to the animal.

22:16(15) This verse together with v.17 deals with the case of the seduced unbetrothed virgin. The general conditions applying to both verses are: "should someone seduce an unbetrothed virgin and lie (i.e. have sexual relations) with her." The rule is that he must by paying the marriage dowry make her his wife. MT reinforces the verb by a preposed cognate free infinitive which Exod represents by a cognate dative noun. The verb is modified by two pronouns, αὐτήν and αὐτῷ. The second pronoun has the same referent as the subject, and a very popular M variant has εαυτω. One might be tempted to regard this as original, but[13] αὐτῷ cannot be misunderstood, and it is hardly conceivable that copyists would change an original εαυτω to αυτω, whereas the reverse is a natural phenomenon.

22:17(16) But a virgin is not a free agent; she is regarded as the property of the father, and so a new possibility emerges: "Suppose her father should adamently refuse and be unwilling to give her to him as wife." Exod's text is longer than MT's; it has added "and be unwilling" and "as wife," the latter addition being made to correspond to v.16. The former addition must be epexegetical, interpreting the adament refusal as an unwillingness to give the daughter to the seducer. Since ἀνανεύσῃ is used absolutely the epexegetical addition becomes intelligible.

The judgment is that the seducer still loses the amount of the dowry which he was to pay according to v.16. In MT this is ambiguous; it is not clear who gets the dowry, father or daughter. Exod not only makes this clear by the dative τῷ πατρί but also renders the verb by ἀποτείσει, i.e. as though MT had ישלם, thereby making clear that seduction of a virgin daughter represents an economic loss to the father. A defiled daughter is hardly a marketable product and she may well remain a permanent burden on him, and so he must be repaid. The standard of repayment is "according to whatever the dowry of virgins is"; the phrase raises certain questions

13. Cf the note in THGE VII.G.10.

350

which the text does not answer: was Is there a standard rate? Does the rate vary at all according to the family's social status?

22:18(17) The δικαιώματα or מִשְׁפָּטִים laws in which the future more vivid condition in third person was the norm end with v.17. From v.18 on, except for v.19, through 23:19, the laws are in second person (some plural and some singular) and are mainly apodictic in character. Only a few instances state a condition but these are all in second person.

V.18 says "you must not preserve (or keep alive) sorcerers." Exod uses the plural φαρμάκους as at 7:11, but there it has the article τούς. MT has the singular feminine "sorceress."[14] The word in Greek can be differentiated as to gender only by the article. For the meaning of φαρμάκους see comment at 7:11. The verb περιποιήσετε[15] also occurs at 1:16 but in the middle with no difference in meaning. An A F popular variant has περιβιωσετε "keep alive," a lexeme somewhat more explicit than the rather delicately put Exod text.

22:19(18) Bestiality is a capital offence. Such a person is described as πᾶν κοιμώμενον μετὰ κτήνους "anyone lying (i.e. having sexual relations) with an animal." The word κοιμώμενον is a masculine accusative participle; what is problematic is the vulgarism of the neuter πᾶν modifying it. The phenomenon does occur in LXX with some frequency.[16] A popular variant in the tradition "corrects" it to the more usual παντα.

The common capital judgment מוֹת יוּמָת is used in MT but Exod renders it by θανάτῳ ἀποκτενεῖτε αὐτούς, i.e. the free infinitive is rendered by the dative θανάτῳ, but the verb is reinterpreted as an active verb with plural pronominal object. Only a C variant makes this αποθανει-ται thereby approximating MT more closely. The αὐτούς means that both parties are to be killed. The Byzantine text has the singular, i.e. the κοιμώμενον alone, whereas a popular A F M text omits the pronoun; this could be a revision based on the Hebrew text, but it must then be posthexaplaric since the word was placed under the obelus by Origen.

14. Cf Prijs, 12, who cites Sanhedrin 67a.
15. Aq renders MT literally by ζώσης.
16. Cf Thack 173--175.

22:20(19) MT begins with "one who sacrifices לאלהים shall be condemned to destruction," and tacks on to the end "except to Yahweh alone." The word order is odd, but it is followed by all the ancient witnesses. The Hebrew is potentially ambiguous since אלהים can mean either "God" or "gods," and only the "except" phrase makes it clear that it refers to gods. Exod makes this fully clear by the plural θεοῖς as does the Vulg: *diis*. Tar Pesh have "idols," and Sam glosses אלהים by אחרים; an A *b f x* variant also adds an explanatory ἑτέροις. But such interpretations make the final phrase even more unusual. One can best understand the phrase as a kind of zeugma for "but you shall sacrifice to Yahweh alone." The verse gives the penalty for breaking the commandment against idol worship, 20:3--5. יחרם is well rendered by ἐξολεθρευθήσεται "shall be rooted out, destroyed."[17] A B *f n* variant has the simplex with no change in meaning. The B *f* text also has θανατω before it which came in under the influence of v.19.[18]

An *ol C n* reading omits the article before θυσιάζων, which happens to equal MT, but this is quite irrelevant. The article ὁ stands between *sigma* and *theta*; the three graphemes are similar in form, and the omission is merely a case of haplography.

22:21(20) For a variant to this verse see 23:9. For προσήλυτον see comment at 12:48. The accusative noun is preposed to the verb as in the next verse for emphasis. The prohibition is put in second plural over against the singular of MT and Vulg; the parent text was probably also plural. The verb κακόω is a general term for "injure, maltreat," and was used to translate particularly the roots ענה and רעע. For הונה it occurs only here in LXX. Lev and Deut used θλίβω, which in Exod is used for לחץ as θλίψητε later in this verse. The verbs κακώσετε and θλίψητε do constitute a semantic pair. The two clauses are connected by οὐδέ which in a popular variant appears as ουτε.[19] An *x +* variant, however, omits αὐτόν in the second clause; then the two verbs have the single object προσήλυτον, and the conjunction οὐδέ joins not two clauses but two verbs.

17. The later revisers render this somewhat more literally as ἀναθεματισθήσεται "shall be put under the ban."
18. For its secondary character see the discussion in THGE VII.O.

The γάρ clause gives the basis for the law as "you were resident aliens in the land of Egypt." Hex has transposed ἦτε and προσήλυτον to agree with MT. -- Instead of Αἰγύπτῳ an *s y z* variant text has the genitive αιγυπτου.[20]

22:22(21) The widow and the orphan are the regular symbols in Scripture, often along with the resident alien, for the helpless. Usually, however, they are in reverse order; in the Pentateuch the two often appear coordinately in Deut but ὀρφανός always comes first; in fact I found only three further exceptions, one each in Ps, Zach and 2Macc. -- κακώσετε here and in v.23 renders the verb עָנָה.[21]

22:23(22) The verse consists of three clauses, the first two giving the conditions, the first in second plural, the second in third plural, and the judgment in first singular with God speaking. Each verb is intensified, the first and third by a cognate noun in the dative, the second by a participle of a synonym to the verb. All three render the Hebrew pattern: cognate free infinitive + finite verb.

There are, however, differences in number between Exod and MT for the second and third person references; Exod has them all in the plural: κακώσετε, αὐτούς, (κεκράξαντες) καταβοήσωσιν, and αὐτῶν, whereas MT has all of them in the singular as does Tar[O]. Sam follows MT except for the first one , תענה, and Tar[P] has the first two in the plural but the last two in the singular. Pesh Vulg follow the pattern of Exod.

The second clause has צָעַק יִצְעַק for which Exod uses different roots. The participle κεκράξαντες is an aorist participle from κράζω; as might be expected a variant *b n y* text has the more usual κραξαντες. The inflection seems to be based on the perfect κεκραγα used as a present stem; note also the future κεκράξομαι. ἐκέκραξα is much more frequent in LXX than is ἔκραξα.[22] Semantically the participle is not far removed from the finite verb καταβοήσωσιν.

---

19. See Bauer sub οὔτε.
20. See THGE VII.H.4. sub 12:1.
21. Aq translates MT's תענון by κακουχήσετε which is semantically barely distinguishable from κακώσετε.
22. Cf Helbing, Gramm. 90--91.

The apodosis has the stem form, ἀκοῇ, for the dative noun, but a compound for the main verb. The semantic pattern is similar to that of the second clause in that the finite verb gives the particular semantic color in the context whereas the rendering of MT's free infinitive is a more neutral word reinforcing the core meaning of the verbal idea, i.e. "call" and "hear" resp. The *b d* simplex for the compound results in a less vivid communication. For צעקתו Exod uses the more neutral phrase τῆς φωνῆς αὐτῶν. The popular F M variant noun βοης is probably an early prehexaplaric revision towards the Hebrew.

22:24(23) An explication of what is involved in the last clause of v.23. The first two clauses are in first person singular with God as subject; the rest of the verse, in third plural, shows the result of the divine action. The idiom חרה אפי with אף "nostril" is regularly used as a figure for "anger." Exod renders this by "I will grow angry with wrath," i.e. very angry. Explicative glosses are inserted to identify the objects of the verb: in *C* as προς υμας and in a *y* variant as εις υμας. In the second clause the term μαχαίρᾳ is used as a figure for "in battle."

The result of this divine action uses the verb ἔσονται only in the first clause, but also intended to govern the second; in both clauses a predicate nominative obtains to explicate the ἔσονται. An *O x* reading τεκνα for παιδία substitutes a synonym.

22:25(24) Vv.25--30 are in second person singular; even where it is plural in MT in v.25b Exod renders it by the singular.

The condition in this verse concerns moneylending. In MT the indirect object is designated "my people, the poor with you," with both phrases preceded by את. This is followed by more or less all ancient witnesses except for Exod; so e.g. Vulg has *populo meo pauperi qui habitat tecum* and Pesh has "among my people to the poor who is with you." Exod simplifies the peculiar Hebrew double phrase by τῷ ἀδελφῷ τῷ πενιχρῷ παρὰ σοί "the poor brother near you." Since את עמי is not overly sensible Exod takes it as someone who belongs to my people, thus "a brother." Attempts to "correct" or clarify the text do occur in the tradition; the most obvious is the change of ἀδελφῷ to λαω in a popular F variant. Marked as a hex addition is the addition of σου, which is actually found in all the major hex witnesses, though only μου would equal MT exactly. And an M C *ol z* reading adds τω before the prepositional phrase making explicit what is already implicit in Exod.

The double role in this situation is that you shall not αὐτὸν κατεπεί-γων, and pressing hard is hardly characteristic of being a brother. The term τόκος is a much more neutral word; it refers to "product," here of capital and so the "interest" that money brings up.

22:26(25) In MT the pattern of cognate free infinitive + finite verb in the protasis is rendered in Exod by an accusative cognate noun plus verb. The verb ἐνεχυράσῃς then has a double accusative which I would translate "as pledge you should take in pledge a neighbour's garment. As usual Exod does not render the suffix of רֵעֲךָ, but hex supplies a σου.[23] The verb ἐνεχυράζω in later Greek also occurs as ἐνεχυριάζω, and this root is reflected both for noun and for verb, particularly by some *f* witnesses which attest to ενεχυρασμα ενεχυριασης (the verbal stem also occurs with the later stem in C *z* texts.

The rule in such a case was that the garment had to be returned by sundown. Exod and Vulg do not render the pronominal suffix of תשיבנו, again because it is superfluous; hex of course added αυτο to make up for the omission.

22:27(26) The reason for the humanitarian rule given in v.26 as γάρ shows is "this is his sole wrap-around," i.e. a robe; περιβόλαιον is used to render כסות "covering." A popular variant has αυτω for αὐτοῦ. That this is his sole robe is stressed in the following nominal clause: this is the garment of his shame, for MT's "garment for his skin," i.e. it is the garment next to his skin, the only one he has. Hex added αυτου after ἱμάτιον because of the Hebrew. MT has skin, עֹר, which Exod in view of the verb עוּר "to lay bare, render naked" has interpreted as his ἀσχημοσύνης, i.e. his private parts, his nakedness. An *f* variant ευσχημοσυνης has certainly changed the sense of the passage.

The question ἐν τίνι κοιμηθήσεται reflects the reality that the poor man, i.e. one who had to give up his περιβόλαιον to a creditor in pledge, used this garment at night as a blanket; without it he could hardly lay himself down to sleep.

There follows the divine reaction. God says "if then he should call out to me I will listen to him, for I am merciful." The οὖν designates this as a logical conclusion to the foregoing. -- Exod does not introduce the apodosis with a καὶ, but hex does, because MT has a conjunction (which Hebrew must have, though not Greek). MT uses שמעתי absolutely, but Exod prudently added αὐτοῦ "to him" in the genitive, since this verb in good Greek governs the genitive.

22:28(27) Exod's text concerns θεούς and ἄρχοντας, whereas MT has אלהים and נשיא. The former can either refer to "God" or "gods," but since נשיא is singular, the first clause must mean "you shall not revile God." Exod understood אלהים as plural in intent and for consistency's sake took נשיא as a collective. Exod's use of the plural may be a reflection on the Egyptian environment in which the translator lived. Incidentally Tar rendered the word by "judges," and Pesh by the singular "judge."[24]

The verb in the first clause κακολογήσεις renders קלל Piel, for which see note at 21:16.[25] -- For the next verb תאר "curse" Exod has κακῶς ἐρεῖς "speak evilly." Rulers and officials should not be evilly spoken about. Actually Exod's statement is more limiting than MT; not only must one not curse rulers, one may not speak evilly about them at all. The majority of witnesses in the tradition transpose κακῶς ἐρεῖς for no apparent good reason.

22:29(28) MT forbids the delay of your מלאה "fulness" and your דמע "tear, drop." These are usually taken to refer to the fulness of the harvest and to the flowing (juice) of the presses (i.e. wine and/or olive presses), resp., thus

---

23. Cf SS 95.
24. Sym did not change Exod's use of θεούς. For ἄρχοντας Sym and Theod have the singular; Aq normally uses the verb ἐπαιρέω for the root נשא and according to Syh used a passive participle such as ἐπηρμένον.
25. Theod accepted Exod as adequate but Sym paraphrases with οὐκ ἀτιμάσεις "you shall not dishonor." Aq naturally translates literally by οὐ

the grain harvest and the liquid harvest.[26] Since the next part of the verse speaks of the firstborn, Exod interprets the first part as applying to ἀπαρχάς "firstfruits" of ἅλωνος "the threshing floor" and ληνοῦ "the press." It probably interprets the rather cryptic Hebrew correctly as referring to the bringing of the firstfruits of the crops without delay. Exod only has a genitive pronoun σου after ληνοῦ whereas MT has a second masculine singular suffix on both nouns. A few scattered witnesses also have σου after ἅλωνος, but the gloss does not seem to be hex. Actually the C text omits the σου after ληνοῦ as being otiose. Neither noun is articulated in Exod but a popular Byzantine text adds της before the second but not the first; the reason for the discrepancy is not clear.

The term "firstborn" is defined in legal terms in 13:2, for which see comment there. A fuller statement on the firstborn occurs at 34:19--20 which see. What giving the firstborn of your sons to me means in practical terms is not stated.

22:30(29) Domestic animals are to be treated similarly. Exod says "so shall you do to your ox and your sheep and your ass." The inclusion of "and your ass" is unique to Exod, and was included in view of 34:19--20 where the firstborn of the three, ox, sheep and ass, are mentioned as being ἐμοί. These are all in the accusative as direct modifiers of ποιήσεις which is surprising in the light of MT where the nouns are governed by the preposition ל.[27]

The first week the firstborn are to remain with the mother; hex added αυτου to conform to MT's אמו. Only on the eighth day ἀποδώσεις μοι αὐτό. Precisely what this involved is not stated; presumably it was to be sacrificed. The phrase τῇ ἡμέρᾳ τῇ ὀγδόῃ occurs in the pattern: article - adjective - noun in the B *b z* text.[28]

22:31(30) This verse is in second person plural, and consists of two statements. "And holy men shall you be to me" has no obvious connection with its context either with v.30 which is still in the singular and deals with

καταράσῃ according to Syh.
26. Cf also the discussion in Prijs, 13.
27. Cf Helbing 4.

rules about the firstborn, nor with the rest of the verse which prohibits the eating of flesh torn (i.e. killed) by wild beasts. Or does eating such flesh render one unholy in the sense of "unclean"? The two statements are both introduced by καί but this is simply in imitation of the Hebrew. The word for flesh is κρέας in the singular; for meat prepared for food the plural κρεα is often used and an *O n* + variant has the plural. Over against MT the prepositional phrase בשדה "in the field" is not found in Exod nor in Tar Pesh Vulg; the phrase is indeed awkward. Hex has supplied εν τω αγρω after κρέας.

The final statement is imperatival: "to dogs throw it." The nominal τῷ κυνί is to be taken as a collective. An A F *b t z* reading changes the imperative to the future απορριψετε which more exactly represents the intent of MT. But the imperative as the more difficult reading is to be understood as original text.

---

28. For a discussion of the attributive adjective pattern in Exod see THGE VII.J, sub 21:2.

Chapter 23

23:1 Vv.1--3 deal with prohibitions against false witness. -- The first verb in v.1, παραδέξη, means "allow, permit" which is somewhat broader in its scope than תשׁא "take up," hence "speak, spread." Exod forbids not just the passing on of idle gossip, but also the receiving of or listening to it. For ματαίαν as translation of שׁוא see comment at 20:7.

The verb in the second clause is συγκαταθήση, "agree with,"[1] a good rendering of the Hebrew תשׁת ידך עם; it has, however, given some trouble in the tradition. An F x + reading has συγκαθηση, from συγκαθέζομαι, "sit down together," and the *oI C* text has συγκαθισεις from συγκαθίζω, "to sit together." These variant texts, though making good sense, are simply errors based on misreading the text.

The compact to be made is "with τοῦ ἀδίκου to become an ἄδικος witness." Exod makes a word play using ἄδικος first as an articulated noun to indicate the class of unjust people and then as an adjective modifying μάρτυς,[2] thus "an unjust witness," whereas MT differentiates completely between רשׁע "a wicked man" and a witness חמס "promoting violence." The rendering of רשׁע by ἄδικος (or by cognates) is highly unusual in LXX, though note the participle of ἀδικέω used thus at 2:13. A popular variant has the noun without the article, thus "with an unjust man"; MT also has the noun unarticulated but one cannot press the distinction between רשׁע and הרשׁע as in Greek.

23:2 The first prohibition reads "you shall not be with the majority for evil." The phrase "with the majority" occurs twice in the verse in both cases translating MT's אחרי רבים "after a multitude." A *b n* reading does substitute πολλων "multitude" for πλειόνων. In the second prepositional phrase, ἐπὶ κακίᾳ, ἐπί designates goal or purpose.[3] The context of the verse

---

1. Cf Helbing 310.
2. See SS 65.
3. See Bauer sub ἐπί II.b.ε.

demands an understanding of κακίᾳ as referring to "evil" in the area of justice, presumably in a case in court.

The second prohibition presents a text at odds with the Masoretic understanding, which in the initial clause לא תענה על רב vocalizes the last word as רִב "a judicial suit." Exod has οὐ προστεθήσῃ μετὰ πλήθους, i.e. reading רב as rōb. The Hebrew תענה in a legal context means "to give testimony," thus "you shall not give testimony in a suit." The Greek verb is an aorist passive of προστίθημι, thus "be added to, be joined with." (cf especially Syriac, as well as Aramaic ענ׳ר), to be understood in the light of συγκαταθήσῃ of v.1. A d s reading made the verb active as προσθῆσῃ which is not impossible, but was created by syncopation of the -τε- syllable and was hardly intentional.

Exod then continues with "to turn aside with the majority so as to turn aside justice." The earlier reading of רב has created a repetitiveness yielding both μετὰ πλήθους and μετὰ πλειόνων. Note also that ἐκκλῖναι occurs twice, both for לנטת and להטת, i.e. a Qal vs a Hiphil marked infinitive; Exod does distinguish them, however; the Qal is used absolutely "to turn aside," but the Hiphil is rendered transitively by adding κρίσιν, i.e. "to turn aside justice."

23:3 Exod translates תהדר "be partial to" somewhat freely by ἐλεήσεις "show mercy" but TarO also has תרחים, and Vulg has misereberis. And בריבו is rendered absolutely by ἐν κρίσει, i.e. without an αὐτοῦ.[4] MT and Exod demand impartial justice even for the poor.

23:4 Together with v.5 help is enjoined for an enemy's animal in distress. Both verses constitute conditional sentences beginning with ἐὰν δέ.

The condition presents an incongruity of number in that the dative modifier to the verb is τῷ βοΐ ... ἢ τῷ ὑποζυγίῳ αὐτοῦ which phrase is modified in turn by πλανωμένοις, as though both ox and ass were wandering instead of only one as in MT. TarP and Pesh also have the plural, however, and it depends largely on one's point of view: does one use the

_____

4. Sym has understood this differently: οὐ τιμήσεις ἐν δίκῃ αὐτοῦ "not shall you assess with respect to his penalty," i.e. Sym takes this line to mean that one should be lenient to the poor when he is in legal difficulty.

singular or the plural for "wandering" when it modifies an antecedent "or" construction?

The apodosis in MT uses the emphatic pattern of cognate free infinitive + finite verb. Exod uses a participle plus finite verb but the two roots are synonyms and not cognates: "turning (it) back you shall return (it) to him." Exod in contrast to MT does not mention the object of the finite verb, which hex does, though it is uncertain whether it was αυτα or αυτο, the tradition having both variants.

23:5 The condition or protasis is fully clear: if you should see the ass of your enemy fallen under his load. MT has "of the one hating you" instead of "your enemy" as a variation from v.4 but Exod retains the same expression. The participle πεπτωκός represents the active participle רֹבֵץ "crouching" of MT; Exod's interpretation is realistic; the animal has fallen and cannot get up by himself.

The apodosis in MT is difficult: literally glossed it says "you shall refrain from abandoning him; abandoning you shall abandon with it (or him)." The first part is quite straightforward, and Exod translates it freely but sensibly "not shall you pass him by."[5] The remainder is quite baffling since it uses the verb עזב in the pattern: cognate free infinitive + finite verb; furthermore this is modified by the prepositional phrase עמו which seems entirely inappropriate. The ancient translations in large part abandon the text and ad lib from the context. Thus Vulg has "(do not pass by) *sed sublevabis eum eo.*" Tar[O] expands by "you shall abandon what is in your heart concerning him," but then gives up adding "and help release him."[6] Exod simply abandons MT and makes sense with "but you shall raise him (the ass) together with it (the load)."

23:6 Exod's use of διαστρέψεις "pervert, distort" to render נטה Hiphil is unique in LXX though it does meet the intent of the Hebrew. In v.2 ἐκκλῖναι had been used for the Qal of נטה but ἐκκλῖναι κρίσιν for the

5. Cf Helbing 86.
6. Dillmann suggests that MT's עָזֹב תַּעֲזֹב must mean "let loose" or "loosen," i.e. "you must loosen the straps, or the load with him (i.e. together with the owner)." This is indeed ingenious but is unlikely to be correct since the verb clearly means "abandon" in מֵעֲזֹב לֹו which immediately precedes.

Hiphil. Here that rendering would be impossible since the object of the verb is expressly given as משפט - κρίμα. Similarly בריבו is here translated in full with an αὐτοῦ but in v.3 simply by ἐν κρίσει. But here in view of the κρίμα already stated an αὐτοῦ becomes necessary to distinguish abstract justice from this particular case. -- Hex added σου after πένητος in view of MT's אבינך.

23:7 In the first clause Exod has added παντός against MT but this is merely epexegetical. Instead of ῥήματος the f text has κριματος; this is contextually conditioned; cf κρίμα and κρίσει in v.6. The verb is a first aorist middle subjunctive which[7] is intransitive in the sense of "keep away from," a good equivalent of MT's תרחק. -- The phrase "an innocent and a righteous one" has a conjunction before it in MT and hex has supplied a καί to equal it.

The final clause is a כי clause in MT giving the theological basis for justice in the courts; it lies in the divine intent: I will not acquit the wicked. Exod has quite a different message: a) Instead of a כי clause Exod simply coordinates the clause by means of καί, i.e. places it on a level with the first two clauses; b) instead of a first person verb (with God as speaker) Exod continues with the second singular, and c) Exod adds epexegetically ἕνεκεν δώρων "for the sake of gifts," i.e. bribes. A popular F tradition omits the phrase which may represent a prehexaplaric revision towards MT. The Exod version: "and not shall you acquit the impious for bribes" fits well into the spirit of v.7, even though it departs radically from MT, and the reference to "bribes" fits the following verse as well.[8]

23:8 The prohibition against taking bribes has as its rationale a bit of proverbial wisdom expressed in the γάρ clause: "(for) bribes blind the eyes of those who see;" only MT Vulg among the ancient witnesses omit "eyes of." The parallel passage, Deut 16:19, has עיני in MT as well, and presumably Exod's parent text also had the word; in fact, a Qumran ms also attests to it. -- The words τῶν βλεπόντων render פקדים (also in 4:11)

7. In spite of LS sub ἀφίστημι B.
8. Cf Prijs 13f. for examples of words being taken both with preceding and succeeeding clauses.

which really means "those who see clearly"; its antonym is עורים "those who are blind" (cf 4:11). The parallel passage, Deut 16:19, has חכמים - σοφῶν. In fact, this seems to have crept into the tradition here as well; Tar⁰ has חכמין (followed by Pesh).⁹ Bribes also "pervert ῥήματα δίκαια"; the nominal phrase translates MT's bound phrase, דברי צדיקים "the case (i.e. the judicial case) of the righteous." Presumably Exod intended by the neuter plural adjectival phrase to express the notion of "justice," i.e. "righteous cases."¹⁰

23:9 The verse is entirely in second person plural. The first clause is paralleled in 22:21 where it is longer, and this longer text has invaded the tradition so that the majority of witnesses read ου κακωσετε ουδε μη θλιψητε (or θλιψετε) instead of οὐ θλίψετε. For the clause in general see comments at 22:21.

The next clause is a γάρ clause giving the reason for not afflicting the resident alien. The expression οἴδατε τὴν ψυχήν is a literal rendering of MT, and means "know how (he) felt," i.e. you can empathize with the resident alien. This clause is in turn followed by another γάρ clause giving the experiential basis for knowing how a resident alien feels: "you yourselves were resident aliens in the land of Egypt." The addition of αὐτοί at the beginning is epexegetical; its omission by the *x* mss does equal MT but this is probably mere coincidence. For the clause in general see comments at 22:21.

23:10 Vv.10--12 deal with the rest enjoined for seventh years and seventh days. These verses revert to second singular again.

V.10 renders MT literally except for omitting the opening conjunction; Pesh and Vulg follow Exod. Since an entirely new subject is introduced Exod shows good sense in omitting it.

In the second clause the verb used to translate אספת is συνάξεις "bring together, gather," a translation hallowed by Gen usage. A popular F M variant substituted εισαξεις "bring in," which makes good sense but is

9. Furthermore Aq has σοφῶν and if the well supported ms tradition is correct in attributing the reading of Aq here (rather than Deut 16:19) it must mean that his text had החכמים as well.

never used in LXX to render the root אסף; it is rather the regular translation for the Hiphil of בוא.

23:11 Change of subject is twice indicated in the verse by δέ. The technical term for the year of release is שמטה which occurs elsewhere only in Deut 15 and is always translated by ἄφεσις. The corresponding verb used here is translated by ἄφεσιν ποιήσεις; cf also Deut 15:3. This is then defined as καὶ ἀνήσεις αὐτήν "and you shall let it go (free)," the antecedent being γῆν of v.1.

Within the tradition ἑβδόμῳ is defined as "year" by adding ετει either before it (in the *n s* texts) or popularly after it. -- An itacistic spelling of ἀνήσεις appears in the *d x* text as ανοισεις, possibly in the sense of "offer up," i.e. the land is to be offered up for a year to God, thus abandoned to natural growth, rather than to human cultivation.

The positive result of the ἄφεσις is shown by the change of subject to third person. The natural growth will be food for the poor of your people and the wild beasts. The object of ἔδονται is ὑπολειπόμενα which refers in turn to the γενήματα of v.1. MT has יתרם, the suffix referring to אביני, i.e. the bound relationship is that of a subjective genitive.[11] This suffix sponsored hex's addition of αυτων, whereas *C* added αυτης, presumably referring to γῆν of v.1.

The B *n x* text also changed τὰ θηρία τὰ ἄγρια to τα αγρια θηρια.[12] The phrase represents the Hebrew חית השדה "beasts of the field."[13] Some Hebrew influence may be reflected in the *z* variant του αγρου for τὰ ἄγρια.

A return to second person orders similar treatment for "your vineyards and your olive groves." MT Tar lack "and" but Sam Vulg sensibly have it. In any event it must be understood.

23:12 A shortened form of the Sabbath commandment (20:9--11) set in the context of the year of release. The second clause begins with a contrastive

---

10. But see Prijs 65f.
11. Cf SS 95.
12. For Exod's usual way of presenting the adjectival phrase see THGE VII.J.
13. Aq rendered the phrase literalistically by ζῷα τῆς χώρας, even reflecting the root of חיה by "living beings."

δέ. Instead of ἀναπαύσῃ a B + variant has the noun αναπαυσις "a rest."[14] The verb in MT is תשבת "you shall keep the Sabbath," i.e. you must rest.

The purpose for the injunction is doubly expressed by coordinate ἵνα clauses. In the first of these the verb of the preceding clause is repeated with respect to domestic animals, whereas in MT a synonym ינוח "may rest" occurs. Exod thus identifies the two as meaning the same: to keep the Sabbath is to rest, i.e. to desist from labors. For the second ἵνα clause the b text omits ἵνα, thereby coincidentally equalling MT. This clause refers to people and a different verb is used, ἀναψύξῃ, "may refresh himself." The "son of the handmaid" is the slave born in the house; see 21:4, and for "resident alien" see the discussion at 12:48.

23:13 The general reference to πάντα ὅσα εἴρηκα can in this context only refer to the laws which precede, particularly those in second person; cf the opening remarks at 22:18. It should also be noted that this verse is in second person plural, a change continued through v.15a in rather arbitrary fashion.

Exod (as Vulg) does not follow MT's initial waw; by not beginning with και the lack of an obvious connection with the preceding verses is brought out. The opening statement is simply a general exhortation. A popular A F M variant has substituted λελαληκα for εἴρηκα, which in turn was further changed by the C text to the aorist ελαλησα. Exod does not normally use λαλέω as an equivalent for the root אמר, but rather for דבר.[15] -- The injunction is put in the imperative which also calls attention to the general nature of the statement. A popular A variant has the future indicative, φυλαξεσθε, which equals MT's תשמרו. It need not, however, reflect revision towards the Hebrew, since the Hebrew indicative has been recurring regularly throughout the preceding verses.

The remainder of the verse forbids the use of the name of other gods by means of two parallel clauses. The first prohibition forbids calling such to mind, ἀναμνησθήσεσθε; instead of the passive, the C text has the middle, αναμνησεσθε, but with no real lexical difference. The Hebrew has תזכירו, i.e. Hiphil in form, which Jerome interpreted in the causative "cause to remember," hence "utter," hence iurabitis. This is closer to the

14. For its secondary nature see the comment in THGE VII.Q.
15. For a discussion of the evidence see the discussion in THGE VII.Q.

second clause "nor should it (i.e. the name) be heard from your mouth."
Oddly enough MT Sam suddenly change to the singular reference in the last
word פיך, all other witnesses agreeing with the plural ὑμῶν of Exod, i.e.
keeping the verse consistent in its second person references. An *n* tradition
shared by 960, a Berlin papyrus fragment, has σου supporting MT.

23:14 Vv.14--17 deal with the three great annual festivals. In v.14 "per year"
comes at the end of the verse in MT, and so hex has moved τοῦ ἐνιαυτοῦ to
the end. Thoug'· MT has the imperfect the imperative is retained here (and
continued in v.15a), possibly under the influence of v.13's φυλάξεσθε. In
fact the majority of witnesses read εορτασετε, i.e. a future indicative
(though MT has the singular).

23:15 The first feast: that of unleavened bread. MT simply has תשמר for the
verb but Exod not only has the plural imperative φυλάξεσθε but adds
ποιεῖν. The collocation is found only here in Exod but is frequent in Deut.
It is, however, probably original here although a popular A F variant text
omits it; the omission mmay well be an early, prehexaplaric revision
towards MT. As in v.13 the imperative φυλάξεσθε appears in a popular A F
M variant as φυλαξεσθε.

　　The specific instruction has the verb in the plural; this is then
followed by the subordinate clause "as I commanded you," but with "you"
now in the singular (the Hebrew has the singular throughout the verse),
with the singular used consistently from here on to the end of the chapter.
The plural up to this point was undoubtedly due to the pressure of v.13
above where it began because of the change in the Hebrew, but the Hebrew
changed back to the singular immediately after v.13 again. -- For τῶν νεῶν
as translation for האביב see comment at 13:4.

　　The γάρ clause, as in 12:17 gives the reason for the observance of the
feast as the exodus from Egypt experience, but not as in 12:17 as divine
action but rather with a neutral ἐξῆλθες. The Byzantine text has the verb in
the plural.

　　The last statement is a general one: God expects his people to appear
in his sanctuary with sacrifices. The word κενός "empty" here means "with-

out the materials for the feast" since the passage says ἐνώπιόν μου, which means "in my presence," i.e. in my sanctuary. MT has the verb in the Niphal third plural, יראו, "and not shall they (indefinite) appear" (or is פני the subject: "my face shall not be seen"?). It is often conjectured that it was originally vocalized as Qal, i.e. "and not shall they see (my face...)." Exod clearly understood it in the Niphal sense since he used the passive ὀφθήσῃ. By changing the person to second singular he avoided the difficulty of the Hebrew, and fitted it well into the context.

23:16 The second feast: that of the reaping of the firstfruits. In MT it is simply called the feast of the reaping with "the firstfruits of your works" in apposition with "the reaping," but in Exod θερισμοῦ is modified by the "firstfruits of your works" in the genitive. Accordingly θερισμοῦ is left unarticulated. A majority variant reading has added the article to equal MT. In v.15 the situation was different; ἀζύμων is indeed articulated but it occurs absolutely, without further modification. The two verses are further differentiated in Exod by making v.16 a separate clause through the addition of ποιήσεις over against MT.

The last element in the description of this feast was τῶν ἔργων σου, which in turn is modified by a relative clause. For ἄν the popular εαν occurs in the tradition.[16] Over against MT Exod defines τῷ ἀγρῷ by the pronoun σου; this brings it stylistically in line with the rest of the verse which contains four cases of σου, but see below.

The third feast: that of completion at the end of the year. This is syntactically joined by καί to the second feast with both modifying ποιήσεις; over against the first one it is presented not as a conjoined clause but as a nominal phrase within the verse containing two coordinate modifiers with a single clause. The word συντελείας like θερισμοῦ is left unarticulated. In MT the feast is called "the gathering."[17] -- The time designation ἐπ' ἐξόδου (of the year) involves ἐπί with a genitive "at the time of." A popular A variant has the dative εξοδω which as a designation of time when became more popular in later forms of Greek.[18]

16. See the discussion in THGE VII.B.
17. This promoted Aq's rendering τῆς συλλογῆς, whereas Sym used a form particularly appropriate to the harvest συγκομιδῆς.

The time is further described as taking place "ἐν τῇ συναγωγῇ of your works which are out of your field." Exod uses the noun συναγωγῇ to render a bound infinitive plus suffix אָסְפְּךָ, a good idiomatic rendering. This in turn meant that he had to use a genitive construction to translate אֵת מַעֲשֶׂיךָ. The remainder of the construction is also freely reproduced. MT simply has מִן הַשָּׂדֶה. Exod has introduced τῶν used as a relative referring to ἔργων, and has added σου after ἀγροῦ in line with the style of the verse. The tradition has an unusual variant in that the principal hex witnesses omit the σου, thereby conforming to MT. This must mean that Origen's parent text already lacked the pronoun.

23:17 This verse is repeated exactly in 34:23 except for σου which there becomes Ἰσραήλ. The initial time designation also occurs at v.14. Problematic in the verse is the designation of the deity. Exod's κυρίου τοῦ θεοῦ σου is indeed a frequent collocation, but for the unusual Hebrew הָאָדֹן יהוה "the Lord Yahweh" Exod's rendering is unique. The difficulty lies in the fact that אָדֹן (or אֲדֹנָי) and יהוה are both rendered by κύριος. In the parallel passage in 34:23 MT also has this designation but adds אֱלֹהֵי יִשְׂרָאֵל, and Exod could solve the difficulty by using only one κυρίου, thus κυρίου τοῦ θεοῦ Ἰσραήλ. The collocation "Lord Yahweh" also occurs five times in Isa but always with צְבָאוֹת added. Twice LXX does not render the word "Lord" (10:16 19:4), and in the other cases (1:24 3:1 10:33) LXX has ὁ δεσπότης κύριος σαβαώθ. Obviously Exod wanted to avoid the collocation κύριος κύριος.

23:18 Exod has taken over from 34:24 the entire ὅταν γάρ clause as the temporal condition for two sacrifice regulations, the only variation being the omission of the article in τὰ ἔθνη here, which is, however, added by the A b s z text. -- A parallel version of the two regulations follows in 34:25 as well. Apparently Exod wanted to harmonize at least partially the two accounts. In MT the regulations follow an order to celebrate feasts (v.16) dealing with crops, and precede an order to bring in firstfruits of the land. For Exod the sacrifice regulations are only relevant in the context of the land of promise, not of the wilderness, and this was made explicit by borrowing the ὅταν clause from the parallel account. -- An F *n x* text omits the clause to equal MT, clearly a revision towards the Hebrew, presumably through the text of one of the later revisers.

The first regulation forbids the offering of a sacrifice in the presence of leaven. The phrase ἐπὶ ζύμῃ immediately follows the verb θύσεις. Usually ἐπί after θύω means place where, i.e. you shall not sacrifice in the presence of or near anything leavened. A few mss actually have θησεις, which is of course simply an itacistic spelling, but promoted by the common collocation "place upon." Other variants include the *C s* text's θυμιασεις, a verb which occurs only here for הזבח in Exod. It is usually reserved in the Pentateuch for translating קטר. Similarly inappropriate is the variant θυμιαματος in B *C f x* for θυσιάσματος, since it too is usually reserved for rendering קטרת.[19] "Blood" would be somewhat bizarre as an incense offering! More unusual is the *z* reading αγιασματος: "blood of my sanctuary" would probably have to be understood as "blood shed on the altar in my sanctuary."

The second regulation forbids leaving "the fat of my feast until morning." In the parallel 34:25 that feast was "of the Passover," but this can hardly be inferred from this verse. κοιμηθῇ means "be left lying" and translates ילין "spend the night." That the verb was thus understood is clear from the *z* reading μεινη "remain."

23:19 This verse is repeated word for word by MT at 34:26; in Exod the collocation τὰς ἀπαρχὰς τῶν πρωτογενημάτων is condensed to τὰ πρωτογενήματα in 34:26; otherwise Exod is exactly the same in the two places.

The first clause refers to the first products of the firstfruits of the land; the two terms used are synonyms as are ראשית and בכורי in MT and they serve to intensify, something like "the very first firstfruits." -- The term "house of the Lord" would mean any sanctuary, not necessarily a Jerusalem temple, but any house of the Lord.

The second statement recurs both in Greek and Hebrew in precisely the same form in 34:26 and Deut 14:20(21). The prohibition "you shall not boil a lamb in its mother's milk" occurs in 34:26 in the same context as here but in Deut it stands between the law concerning anything that dies of itself and the laws on tithing. In all three cases instead of kid, גדי, the Greek has ἄρνα. But גדי is the offspring of goats and one might have expected ἔριφον. In fact ἀρήν occurs for גדי only in this context.[20] -- The statement concludes the laws begun at 20:23.

23:20 Vv.20--33 constitute an admonitory exhortation, a mixture of warnings and of promises for the future, particularly for the promised land. The verbal construction: ἐγώ + present tense commonly translates MT: pronoun + participle. The *d t y* text has the future, a variant formed by haplography of *lambda*. -- Exod has an accusative object of the verb in τὸν ἄγγελόν μου, whereas MT simply has מלאך. Whether this is Exod interpretation or textually based is not clear since Sam has מלאכי. All other ancient witnesses except Vulg follow MT. -- The verb is also modified by a prepositional phrase πρὸ προσώπου σου for לפניך.[21]

The promise is modified by a ἵνα clause in turn modified by a ὅπως clause. This differs from MT which connects the two by a coordinating conjunction thereby making of the two clauses a double purpose for the promise. In Exod God sends his messenger "in order to guard you in the way," and this guarding in the way takes place "so that he may bring you into the land." -- Exod has τὴν γῆν instead of המקום with only Pesh following Exod. "The place" is of course the land, and the common collocation "bring you into the land" undoubtedly influenced the translator. It is in turn modified by the relative clause "which I prepared for you." The *n* text changed ἡτοίμασά to the perfect ητοιμακα. An odd error in the tradition is the *O* variant ωμοσα, possibly palaeographically inspired and influenced by such a phrase as "swore to the fathers to give to you," e.g. at 13:5.[22]

23:21 The opening warning, πρόσεχε σεαυτῷ, does not fully render MT which adds מפניו, i.e. pay attention to him. -- The second injunction, "and

---

18. See LS sub ἐπί B.II.
19. See the discussion in THGE VII.Q.
20. This is what Sym used. Sym also avoided the idea of "boiling" entirely and used a less colorful word σκευάσεις "you shall not prepare a kid..."
21. Sym has quite a different construction using a participle + accusative pronoun, προάγοντά σε, modifying "angel." This is almost certainly the

listen to him," is also a free though adequate rendering of the Hebrew "hear his voice." The imperative is in the present since obedience is a process; so the aorist stem of the *d f* texts is no improvement.

The last instruction is also joined to the preceding clause by a καί over against MT. A popular A F M variant text omitting the καί is probably a revision towards MT. -- The warning "do not disobey him" for אל תמר בו seems based on the verb מרה rather than on the verb מרר which the Masoretic vocalization presupposes.[23] It must be said that Exod makes far better sense in the context.

The negative γάρ clause gives the reason for the threefold injunction. "For not ὑποστείληταί from you"; the verb means "shrink back"; presumably what is meant is that he will not refrain from judging you. MT has "for he will not forgive your (plural) transgression." Since only God can forgive sins Exod avoids a statement that the angel does so. As God's messenger he can, however, be involved in man's lot and will not turn aside, will not be overawed by you (comp Deut 1:17).

The second γάρ clause gives the reason why the angel will not draw back; he is not just any messenger, he is the angel of the Lord. Since he is God's angel he does his bidding, and so you must obey him. An *n y z* reading has εν for ἐπ', which is close to MT's בקרבו "within him." But Exod throughout avoids any interpretation that might identify the angel with Yahweh; his name is not within him; he is not himself the Lord - the name is rather upon him, - nor can he forgive sins; rather he can and must carry out God's orders as his messenger.

23:22 At an early stage in the tradition, i.e. before the time of Origen, the text of 19:5--6 was added at the beginning of this verse; its secondary nature is clear inter alia from the plural references.[24]

MT's text presupposes the essential identity of the angel and Yahweh since in the first clause of the condition it is קלו which is to be heard but you are to guard everything which אדבר "I shall say." Exod in accordance

---

source for Vulg: *qui praecedat te.*
22. See also THGD 86.
23. Only Sym follows the Masoretic tradition with his μὴ παραπίκραινε "be not embittered," all others including Aq's μὴ προσερίσῃς "do not rebel" presuppose מרה.

with his interpretation of v.21 voids this by his τῆς φωνῆς μου; this is not the voice of the angel but God's voice; incidentally Sam also has קולי. The condition begins with ἐάν (without a δε) although MT has כי אם. The dative noun ἀκοῇ renders the cognate free infinitive of MT; its omission by the A F M *oI C b* text is an error due to homoiarchon. The verb is plural in the B *f* text due to the plural of the long gloss from 19:5--6; see above. The verb in the second clause of the condition is popularly misspelled itacistically as ποιησεις. If this were really intended it would have the effect of making this clause the first clause of the apodosis, which is hardly sensible; the clause is parallel to the first clause. -- The relative clause which modifies πάντα contains ἄν plus the subjunctive. The σοι at the end is an epexegetical addition by Exod.[25]

The apodosis consists of parallel clauses, in both cases the verb being modified by cognate dative nominals: "I will be at enmity with your enemies[26] and I will oppose those who are opposing you."[27] The σοι at the end becomes σου in *d n x*; this is closer to MT which reads צרריך.

23:23 MT begins the verse with כי which is ambiguous. It can be taken as introducing the condition, and the apodosis would be either the last clause of the verse or v.24. On the other hand it could be taken as a causal particle as Exod Pesh understood it. Since the verse really begins a new theme the former must have been intended. As a γάρ construction Exod makes v.23 the basis for the promise of v.22. It has three clauses, the first two with ὁ ἄγγελός μου as subject and the last with God himself as speaker. Unusual in the first clause is the rendering of לפניך by ἡγούμενός σου "leading, preceding you." The same rendering occurs elsewhere in LXX only at v.27. The reference to "my angel" ties this verse to v.20 which parallels this verse; particularly one should note the ὅπως clause in v.20, which parallels the second clause. That "he shall bring you in to the Amorite, etc." means "to the land of the Amorite ..." is clear from v.20 with its εἰς τὴν γῆν.

---

24. For a discussion of this long gloss and in particular for an explanation of the false asterisks in the tradition see THGE VII.O.
25. For εαν instead of ἄν see THGE VII.B.
26. See Helbing 213 and 314 for the use of the dative.
27. Aq understood the cognate expression as deriving from the root צרר meaning "to tie up, bind" and translated as ἐνδήσω τοὺς ἐνδεσμοῦντάς σε.

For the list of seven nations including "the Girgashite" against MT but with Sam as well as for the articulation of the list see the discussion at 3:8.[28]

Exod's rendering of the singular suffix of the verb in the last clause of MT as αὐτούς correctly reflects the intent of MT. The singular is induced by the singular number for the individual seven nations; only Sam follows MT, all other witnesses having the plural which alone makes sense.

23:24 The first two clauses constitute a closed pair unlike MT where the third clause begins with ולא (rather than לא). This is further emphasized by the fact that the third clause has οὐ with the indicative over against the second one with οὐδὲ μή and the subjunctive. The C text obviates the full force of this stylistic point by also having ουδε plus the indicative for the second clause. The two clauses are closely parallel; the first verb is a general word for "do obeisssance, worship," whereas the second, λατρεύσῃς, emphasizes religious service, especially cultic worship; cf 20:5. The prohibition against idol worship contrasts with the service enjoined in v.25.

The third prohibition specifically contrasts with the rest of the verse as ἀλλά suggests. For a commentary on the third prohibition see Lev 18:3 where, however, ἐπιτηδεύματα occurs rather than ἔργα. Exod does not use a cognate expression as MT does with its "do according to their doings," which would have required a word like ποίησις (cf 28:8 36:12) or ποίημα (never used in the Pentateuch). But this is not surprising since ποιέω is the regular equivalent for עשה, whereas of the 38 cases of מעשה in Exodus Exod translates 31 by ἔργον.

The contrasting orders are in two parallel clauses which in MT both contain the emphatic pattern: cognate free infinitive + finite verb. Exod renders the infinitive of the first clause by a dative noun and in the second by a participle. In the first clause Exod did not translate the suffix of תהרסם; καθελεῖς is, however, transitive and some object must be understood; the two possible modifiers would be ἔργα and αὐτῶν, and obviously it is the latter which is intended. Hex has supplied αυτους to represent MT. The object in the second clause is τὰς στήλας (αὐτῶν). The word στήλη had already been chosen by Gen to represent מצבה. Whenever this word occurs in Gen or Exod (except at 24:4 where λίθους occurs) it is rendered by στήλη. Here it designates a cultic pillar of some sort used in the cult of Canaanite gods and so must be rendered by "pillars."

23:25 MT has the first clause in the second plural, but the rest of the verse in the singular, in which it is followed by Sam and Tar^O. Tar^P has as usual everything in the plural, and so does Pesh. Exod uses the singular throughout except for the final ἀφ' ὑμῶν, for which see below. The service enjoined (λατρεύσεις; cf comment on v.24) is to the Lord your God, as opposed to τοῖς θεοῖς αὐτῶν of v.24.

The remainder of the verse is no longer injunction but promise. MT has the verb of the next clause in third person "he will bless," and that of the last clause in first person "I shall turn aside." Exod (and Vulg) has the first person for both. The objects of the divine blessing are somewhat sparse in MT: "your bread and your water," which Exod has made more palatable by inserting καὶ τὸν οἶνόν σου; I can, however, find no parallel in LXX for ἄρτος, οἶνος and ὕδωρ anywhere.

The last clause is the divine promise "and I will turn away sickness from you (plural)." The C text has "all sickness from you (singular)," but this is not significant; the addition of πασαν is epexegetical and the change to the singular pronoun is due to the pressure of the singular context. The plural is rather odd since it is one of only two second plurals in the entire section vv.20--33, so it must have been intentional. Possibly it represents a bit of rationalization concerning μαλακίον; sickness is after all an individual affair - one man is sick and his neighbour is not - and so the plural phrase really means "from anyone of you."

23:26 The terms ἄγονος and στεῖρα are synonyms;[29] the former renders משכלה, a Piel participle meaning "one who aborts." Instead of ἐπὶ τῆς γῆς a z variant has εν τη γη which happens to equal MT more exactly. -- The second clause in the verse means that God will not bring the life of the people prematurely to an end; they will live out their days. An M s marginal variant has ετων instead of ἡμερῶν, but this makes no difference to the intent of the verse.

---

28. For the word order see THGE VII.F.4.
29. Aq was dissatisfied with the former and translated משכלה by ἄτεκνος

23:27 Exod introduces the initial clause with καί even though all other old witnesses are asyndetic; it is of course another promise and the conjunction is not inappropriate. Not fully apt is Exod's translation of אימתי "my terror" as τὸν φόβον, for which see comment at 15:16, and compare Gen 15:12.[30] It should be noted that Exod did not translate the suffix; had he added μου (as hex did) the text would have been something foreign to what was meant; the fear of God means reverance, awe for God, whereas אימתי means being "fright, terror," and τὸν φόβον means "fear" in general. In other words the omission of μου must have been intentional. -- For ἡγού-μενόν σου as translation for לפניך see v.23.

In the second clause Exod uses the verb ἐκστήσω "I will confound" but in a bad sense, probably in the sense of "stun, terrify." The peoples of Canaan will be utterly confounded and afraid when the Israelites enter their land. -- Exod uses a Hebraic construction for the relative clause modifying ἔθνη by including the otiose prepositional phrase εἰς αὐτούς after εἰς οὕς, i.e. "to whom you will come in to them." The *C f* text has the surprising variant εκπορευη for εἰσπορεύῃ, i.e. "you will go out," completely opposite to the intent of תבא.

In the last clause Exod uses δώσω with a double accusative[31] in imitation of MT, thereby ensuring the meaning of δώσω not as "give" but as "set, make," and the line may be translated as "And I will make all your enemies fugitives," an idiomatic rendering which renders well the intent of the Hebrew "And I will set all your enemies (with) the nape of the neck to you." Exod has abandoned the Hebrew figure as meaningless for Greek, and chosen φυγάδας to interpret אליך ערף.

23:28 The hornet as an instrument used by God for driving out the peoples of Canaan also occurs at Deut 7:20 Jos 24:12. Apparently this is intended to show how God will make Israel's enemies fugitives (v.27); by sending a horde of hornets before them the inhabitants of Canaan will be driven out. The verb ἐκβαλεῖ is in third person with σφηκίας as subject. An A *b n z* reading has εκβαλω (followed by Pesh), under the influence of the context

"childless."
30. Aq uses a different concept: τὴν κατάπληξίν μου.

which has first person before and after the clause. Cod.B, followed by 76',
simplified the text by changing the verb to second person.

The list of inhabitants is unusual both by having only four nations in
the list and by the fact that they are in the plural.[32] MT has only three in the
list, omitting the Amorite, whereas Sam has the full list of seven and Pesh
has only two (the Canaanites and the Hittites). The Byzantine texts have
more than four: *n* adds three to make the list complete, whereas *d t* only
add "and the Jebusites."

23:29 It is clear that the hornets are but God's instrument; it is really God
who will drive them out, though gradually.[33] The Exod text is shorter than
MT, not rendering מפניך; hex accordingly added απο προσωπου σου after
αὐτούς. The phrase is unnecessary in the context of vv.28,30 and 31.

The reason for the gradual expulsion of the Canaanite peoples is
given in two clauses governed by a single ἵνα μή. The void left by the
exodus of the entire populace could not be filled immediately by the
invading Israelites and wild animals would take over. Exod uses an analytic
tense of adjective plus γένηται to render רבה, rather than a verb such as
πληθύνω. Exod also uses γῆ to translate both ארץ and שדה, whereas one
might have expected τοῦ πεδίου for the latter.

23:30 Exod renders מעט מעט "little by little" by combining the Hebrew
idiom of repeating a word to show distribution with the Greek idiom using
κατά, resulting in κατὰ μικρὸν μικρόν. A B *O C d* variant omitting μικρόν
2° is better Greek but is probably a haplograph rather than conscious
revision. The clause is the positive counterpart to v.31.

The ἕως clause contains coordinate verbs, though the action of the
second is dependent on the first. The first verb is an aorist passive αὐξηθῆς,
which correctly interprets the metonymy of the Hebrew תפרה "you should
be fruitful." The second one can only be meaningful if the population first
increases. What is meant by the ἕως clause is "until you should increase and
so be able to possess (in full) the land."

---

31. Cf Helbing 53.
32. For a discussion of the list and of the others in Exod see the discussion
in THGE VII.D.5.

23:31 In the first clause God promises to set up the borders of the promised land. Exod, as well as Tar^P Vulg, uses the plural "borders" as an ad sensum translation over against the singular of MT. The borders refer to those outside Palestine itself. On the southwest they are to extend from the Red Sea to the sea of the Philistines and on the northeast from the desert to the great river Euphrates. Just what is meant by the "desert" is unclear. Hex has changed the order of ἐρυθρᾶς θαλάσσης to conform to MT's ים סוף.[34] The two pairs are both in the pattern: ἀπό ... ἕως. In MT the ἕως stands for ועד in the first pair but for עד in the second; Exod uses only ἕως regardless of the variation in the Hebrew.[35] The term "the great river Euphrates" is an expansion of MT which merely has "the river," whereas Tar^O has only "Euphrates" and Tar^P has "the great river." The expansion correctly interprets MT.

The second clause of the verse is coordinate with the first clause, whereas in MT it is causal. The causal connection is not overly obvious in MT, and successive coordinate clauses are much clearer. Within the second clause a second instance of the second plural within the section vv.20--33 occurs (see comment on v.25), but this one is due to the parent text (ידכם in MT). Similarly Exod reinterprets the bound structure ישבי הארץ by a participle ἐγκαθημένους, modified by a prepositional phrase ἐν τῇ γῇ.[36] A *d t z* variant makes ὑμῶν into σου, thereby making it consistent with the context.

The last clause has the verb in first person, whereas MT has it in second. Accordingly the clause is no longer the logical result of the second one as in MT: "I will deliver ... and (so) you will drive out," but simply coordinate.

23:32 The verb used for entering into a covenant is συγκαταθήσῃ, the future middle of συγκατατίθημι, which was also used in v.1 in a similar sense[37] but without διαθήκην and for a different Hebrew. The verb is rare

---

33. See SS 112.
34. For the word order of τῆς ἐρυθρᾶς θαλάσσης as well as of τοῦ ποταμοῦ τοῦ μεγάλου see the discussion in THGE VII.J.
35. See the discussion in THGE VII.E.3.
36. Cf Helbing 269.

in LXX only occurring once elsewhere; see discussion at v.1. For the Hebrew idiom "cut a covenant" see Dictionaries and O.T. Theologies. From the literal "lay something down together" the verb in the middle means "to agree on," and so with διαθήκην to enter into a covenant relationship.[38]

23:33 This verse continues the pattern of καί plus future verb; materially it gives the reason why the expulsion of all the Canaanite people from the land was necessary as the ἵνα μή clause makes clear. They are forbidden to dwell in the land lest .... The Byzantine reading, συγκαταθησονται, for ἐγκαθήσονται is not sensible but is an error by assimilation to the συγκαταθήσῃ of v.32. Could a reader possibly have understood such a text as "not shall they make common cause"?

The Hiphil verb of the פן clause is translated by an analytic tense, a complementary infinitive plus the verb "to make": ἁμαρτεῖν ... ποιήσωσιν, which pattern also obtains in Vulg: *peccare ... faciant*; this is the only instance in Exod where ποιέω is used to express the causative stem. The *f* text has the present infinitive αμαρτανειν instead of the aorist; this is no improvement and it is doubtful that it was created intentionally.

The second part of the verse in MT is somewhat difficult consisting of two כי clauses: "for you will serve their gods, for it will become for you a snare." All but Vulg of the ancient witnesses have a plural verb in the second clause: "they will become." The "it" of MT is indeed difficult since there is no masculine gender antecedent in the near context to which it can refer; presumably it is intended as a general reference to your serving their gods. Vulg solves the difficulty by taking the first כי as a conditional particle: *si servieris diis eorum,* as a condition for the preceding clause; it then takes the second כי as a causal particle: *quod tibi certe erit in scandalum.* Exod has made of the two clauses a future more vivid conditional sentence and made the whole sentence a γάρ construction. Exod obviously found the Hebrew difficult and reinterpreted the two כי clauses as an "if ... then" construction and made the conditional sentence the explanation for ἁμαρτεῖν σε ποιήσωσιν of the preceding clause. Exod then adds οὗτοι as subject of the apodosis to make clear who the subject of ἔσονται is; the pronoun is necessary since it defines which of the two plural

378

possibilities, θεοῖς or αὐτῶν, is the subject; it is the nearer one, not θεοῖς but αὐτῶν (the Canaanite peoples) who will be the occasion for stumbling. This now makes good sense; these peoples must not live in your land..., for if you serve ... they will be ...." The change of οὗτοι to αυτοι by the M x text makes it uncertain which of the two is intended; the likely understanding would then be "the gods."

---

37. See Helbing 310.
38. See Helbing 242.

Chapter 24

24:1 The unusual placement of the addressee before εἶπεν is in imitation of MT and serves to place stress on Moses' role. The subject, though one presumes it to be the Lord, is unstated and in the instructions the Lord is twice referred to as "the Lord" rather than in first person. This anomaly led to the *C s* variant "(go up) πρὸς με" instead of πρὸς κύριον (though the variant inconsistently retains τῷ κυρίῳ at the end of the verse). A B *z* reading articulates κύριον but this is hardly Exod; see discussion at 9:30.

Only Pesh follows Exod in connecting all of those who are to go up by καί; all the others lack the "and" between Aaron and Nadab, i.e. present them in two pairs. -- Variations in spelling of the name Nadab can usually be explained palaeographically: confusion of letters which look alike for ναδαμ, and possibly ναδακ, transposition of letters for ναβαδ, ναβατ, influence of letters within the word for δαδαβ, ναβαβ, αναβαδ, αναδαδ and haplography for αδαβ. Similarly explanations of variants for ' Αβιούδ are: devoicing for αβιουθ, and including transposition αβιδουθ, influence of near consonant αβιουβ, dittograph of similar letter αλβιουδ, syncopation αβυδ and aphaeresis for ουδ.

In the second clause Exod has third person instead of the second person of MT. τῷ κυρίῳ also has no equivalent in MT. In MT the second person plural is coordinate with the initial ἀνάβηθι and it is meant to be imperatival. Exod's change to προσκυνήσουσιν is probably made in view of v.2 from which it is obvious that Moses is not involved in the distant worship, so the command to worship involves only the 73 other members of the group going up the mountain. The addition of τῷ κυρίῳ is epexegetical; it is of course the Lord who is to be worshipped.

24:2 Exod uses only the Attic future for -ίζω verbs, so ἐγγιεῖ and ἐγγιοῦσιν occur in this verse. In the tradition only ms 55 uses the sigmatic futures εγγιση and εγγισουσιν. Throughout the entire account of ch.24 all references to יהוה have been changed in Exod to "God" except where he is presented as speaking in vv.3,4,7,12, 16 or as making the covenant with Israel (v.8), and the reference to the glory of the Lord in v.17. Here Moses goes to God; in v.3 he relates to the people all the words and ordinances of God; the young people of Israel are to sacrifice to God (v.5), and it was the glory of God which descended on the mountain (v.15). This is in line with the use of God already in the Hebrew account in vv.10 and 11, for which see notes there. Wherever in the theophany human action is described: Moses ascending, or relating God's words, or people sacrificing, leaders seeing where God stood (v.10) or appearing in the τόπῳ of God, a reference to "the Lord" as the personal name is avoided.

Both the second and the third clauses begin with δέ structures showing both change of subject and contrast, from Moses to αὐτοί, and then to ὁ λαός. The stress is first on μόνος - only Moses, and not the 73 elders who went up with him part way, was to come near to God. And in the last clause the people did not go up along with them; i.e. the people were left at the base of the mountain. Exod clarifies the text of MT by changing "with him" (i.e. "with Moses") to "with them." MT might well be misunderstood as meaning that the people did not accompany Moses on the second stage, i.e. after leaving the leaders behind.

24:3 Change of speakers is shown by δέ, first to Moses and then later also to all the people. With vv.3--8 the narrative of chapter 23 is continued and these verses interrupt the story of the theophany in vv.1--2 and 9ff.

Chh. 21--23:19 constituted "the ordinances," whereas 23:20--33 were "words" which the Lord addressed to Moses; now Moses relates all these to the people. Hex added παντα before τὰ δικαιώματα, since MT has "all" before both noun phrases. For God in place of יהוה see comment at v.2.

Since εἰσῆλθεν has no locative modifier an *f y* text reads the simplex ηλθεν, but רבא is normally rendered by εἰσέρχομαι.

The acceptance of obligations inherent in "the words of God and the ordinances" is made by "all the people," φωνῇ μιᾷ, a dative of means "by one voice," plus the direct speech marker (instead of the Hebrew "and he said") introducing the actual reply of the people. Exod has a fuller response than MT by adding καὶ ἀκουσόμεθα, as in v.7; for a discussion of the fuller form

see 19:8. The coordinate verbs constitute the popular pledge "... we will do
and obey." A number of mss particularly of the Byzantine group, has
misspelled these as though they were hortatory subjunctives: ποιησωμεν
και ακουσωμεθα. This could hardly have been intended, since a pledge is
obviously called for in a covenantal ceremony; these are simply misspellings
of the future indicative.

24:4 The first clause is intended as conclusion for v.3. This is seen from the
use of καί to coordinate the clause to v.3, whereas the next clause not only
begins with a δέ structure to show a new section, but against MT again
specifies Μωυσῆς as subject.

Exod by a subordinating participle ὀρθρίσας makes a single clause
out of the second part of the verse. Exod always rendered the Hiphil of שׁכם
plus בבקר by the verb ὀρθρίζω plus τὸ πρωί. This was already used in Gen
19:27 20:8 though Gen usually used ἀνίστημι plus τὸ πρωί. The phrase
בבקר, however, is always rendered by an adverbial accusative, and the *oII f
n* variant reading τω πρωι, although possible, is actually a misspelling, since
το and τω were homophonous.

The main verb ᾠκοδόμησεν has two coordinate accusative modifiers,
θυσιαστήριον and λίθους; this is to be taken as a hendiadys for "build an
altar and (set up) stones," as was fully understood by *C n s* which added
εστησεν to the second accusative. The main verb is also modified by the
prepositional phrase ὑπὸ τὸ ὄρος "at the base of the mountain," i.e. where
the people were encamped. Its position between the two accusatives makes
it apply to the building of the altar. The coordinate object λίθους is almost
certainly not based on MT's מצבה which is normally translated by στήλη in
LXX, but on Sam's אבנים, which may well be due to the influence of Jos
4:20 where twelve stones were set up as a memorial at Gilgal; there too the
twelve stones were memorial stones "for the twelve tribes of Israel."

24:5 The altar has a different purpose as vv.5--6 show. The second and third
clauses with their plural verbs show the purpose (or result) of the first one,
i.e. Moses sent out the young men to make sacrifices. Why the νεανίσκους
should serve as priests is not at all clear. Tar^O interprets these as the first-

born, which may be an old interpretation of the text. They are not designated as Levites, but simply as τῶν υἱῶν ' Ἰσραήλ.

The second clause in MT has a cognate modifier to the verb: ויעלו עלת, but Exod does not reproduce that pattern. The ὁλοκαυτώματα, as their name implies, were completely consumed by fire. This was not true of the θυσίαν σωτηρίου for which see the discussion at 20:24. -- The last clause in MT also has a verb plus cognate noun, and Exod also adopts that pattern. The modifier in MT is זבחים שלמים, the two words being in apposition. Since ἔθυσαν has a double accusative modifying it (θυσίαν σωτηρίου and μοσχάρια), Exod used the singular (cf also 32:6), and one might well render the line as "and they sacrifice as a peace offering to God bull calves.

24:6 The δέ structure at the beginning not only shows change of subject, but also indicates contrast to the priestly actions of the young men in v.5. Moses poured half the blood into bowls, saving it for the rite described in v.8. The majority of witnesses have κρατηρα instead of the plural κρατῆρας. The plural alone is sensible if one take seriously the fact that the blood of the ὁλοκαυτώματα and the μοσχάρια was involved; furthermore MT has the plural as well.[1]

The second part of the verse also begins with a δέ structure contrasting between the two τὸ ἥμισυ τοῦ αἵματος. The second portion of the blood he poured out over against the altar. The two verbs used in the verse, "poured into" and "pour forth," translate different verbs in MT, the former וישם "he put, placed," and the second זרק "he tossed, threw." For the rite of tossing the blood of the sacrifice against the altar see 29:16 where the verb προσχέω is also used. The C text has προσεχυσεν. The verb προσχύω is usually thought of as a late form of προσχώννυμμι "heap up (mud)" which is not sensible here; the root must here be a variant of προσχέω; compare πρόσχυσις at Hebr 11:28. The prepositional phrase used the preposition πρός through attraction to the verb; a d f variant reading επι is much more usual for על.

1. Aq renders the Hebrew of the first clause by the puzzling ἔθηκεν ἐν προθύμασιν; what προθύμασιν is to mean here is not at all clear; the word usually means "preparatory sacrifices."

24:7 As in v.6 יקח is rendered by (καὶ) λαβών; cf also v.8. Here "Moses" as subject is not repeated, the subject simply continuing from the preceding clause so that the conjunction used is καί, not δέ. The verse as such interrupts the account of what Moses did with all the blood, but it is necessary as the stage for v.8 with its reference to τὸ αἷμα τῆς διαθήκης.

The reference to "the book of the covenant" refers specifically to the document beginning with καὶ ταῦτα τὰ δικαιώματα, i.e. chh.21--23, though possibly the commands and ordinances of 20:23--26 ought to be included. The verse can best be understood as a parallel version of v.3. Now Moses reads the book, presumably what he had written, viz. all the words of the Lord (v.4). The phrase εἰς τὰ ὦτα τοῦ λαοῦ is a Hebraism, metonymic for "in the hearing of the people."

The popular response is the same as in v.3 except that instead of "all the words which," Exod here has the shorter πάντα ὅσα; for the response see the comments at v.3. The coordinate verbs are reversed in the F + text, as in Sam and Pesh, presumably on the understanding that hearing must come before the doing. But נשמע - ἀκουσόμεθα means "hear" in the sense of obedient response, an understanding which Vulg clearly shows: *faciemus et erimus obedientes.* For the variant spelling of the verbs as hortatory subjunctives see remarks at v.3.

24:8 Change of subject is shown by δέ. Exod follows the pattern of vv.6 and 7 in subordinating λαβών to an attributive position with τὸ αἷμα as its modifier, which modifier is then understood but not repeated (by a pronoun) with the main verb κατεσκέδασεν "scattered,"[2] a verb normally modified by an accusative and genitive. It might be added that Sam does add a suffix to the verb ויזרקהו, a reading which renders explicit what was implicit.

Moses concludes the section with an ἰδού pronouncement. Though ἰδού is in origin the aorist middle imperative of εἴδω, when accented with an acute rather than a circumflex it is a demonstrative particle calling special attention to what is said; in LXX it is generally the rendering for

2. Cf Helbing 184. This is its only occurrence in the LXX.

הנה. It occurs here without a finite verb,[3] and so its clause must be analyzed as a nominal clause without a subject (its parallel in verbal clauses would be the imperatival clause). Tar[O] reflects this understanding as well by its הא דין דם "behold this is the blood."

The accent in τὸ αἷμα τῆς διαθήκης falls on the genitive noun; this particularizes the blood as symbolic. By touching the people the blood through its sacrificial devotion to God symbolizes the covenantal bond between God and people. This covenant is one which has κύριος as subject and people as object; it is one which the Lord covenanted (for MT "cut" as at 23:32, for which see note) with you. The final phrase, "concerning all these words" identifies this covenant as related to the laws and ordinances of the preceding chapters.

24:9 This verse brings us back to the orders to Moses given in v.1. Though the verb ἀνέβη has a compound subject, it is singular by attraction to the first member, Μωυσῆς, as in MT. As in v.1 all the members of the subject are joined together by καί (as does Pesh), whereas all other old witnesses make two pairs: Moses and Aaron, Nadab and Abihu." For various spellings of the name Ναδάβ in the tradition see comments at v.1. Oddly ' Αβιούδ (for אביהו) has no variant spellings in the tradition here. -- It will be noted that זקני is here rendered by τῆς γερουσίας rather than the τῶν πρεσβυτέρων of v.1;[4] cf also v.14; the majority of witnesses do read των πρεσβυτερων here.[5]

24:10 What MT actually says, "And they saw the God of Israel," seems to be contradicted by 33:20: "for man cannot see my face and live." So Exod interprets MT to mean καὶ εἶδον τὸν τόπον οὗ εἱστήκει ἐκεῖ ὁ θεὸς τοῦ ' Ισραήλ.[6] The choice of "place where God stood" by Exod was contextually influenced by the following reference to τὰ ὑπὸ τοὺς πόδας αὐτοῦ (i.e. of God); the stress on "those things under his feet" calls attention to the place

3. See Bauer sub ἰδού 2.
4. Cf SS 165.
5. It is argued in THGE VII.Q that the reading is due to the influence of vv.1 and 14 and is therefore secondary.
6. Cf Transl. 5.4.

where he stood.[7] -- The *b* text has the sigmatic ending ειδοσαν for ειδον, but this inflection is alien to Exod.[8] The *C* variant εστηκει has dropped the pluperfect augment of the classical form; this inflection is occasionally attested in the LXX tradition as a variant form. Furthermore the popular B text omitting ἐκεῖ is an attempt to improve the Greek style by removing an obvious Hebraism.[9]

Consonant with the place where God stood a nominal construction makes a double comparison for "the things under his feet." First they are said to be like the work πλίνθου σαπφείρου. The word πλίνθου is a literal rendering of MT's לבנת "brick," which is always rendered in Exod (and LXX throughout) by a word formed from the root πλινθ- (also πλινθεία, πλινθουργία). A לבנה is usually a sundried brick, and by extension any kind of building tile. Since here it is some type of expanse visualized as a floor it is probably to be taken as "of a (sapphire) pavement." It is not surprising that a substantial number of scattered witnesses have changed the word to λιθου "stone."

For the second element the translator has added στερεώματος over against MT so as to define τοῦ οὐρανοῦ a bit more closely; it is not the heavens where God is enthroned, but rather "heaven" in the sense of "the sky."[10] What is meant is clear blue skies, since there is added τῇ καθαρειότητι, a dative of respect, i.e. with respect to purity. The popular variant καθαροτητι means the same thing; it derives from καθαρός, whereas the Exod word comes from καθάρειος, and both mean "cleanness, purity."

24:11 The opening clause in MT seems to mean: "and he (i.e. God) did not send forth his hand (i.e. in a destructive fashion) towards the chieftains of the Israelites." The word translated as "chieftains" occurs only here in the O.T. but both Tar and Exod agree on its meaning as "chieftains, important people, leaders." Exod understood the line fully but avoids making God the subject of any fatal activity by a paraphrase: "and of the chosen men of

7. Aq naturally renders the clause literally as καὶ εἶδον τὸν θεὸν ' Ἰσραήλ, whereas Sym inserts ὁράματι after the verb, i.e. "in a vision," thus denying the reality of actually seeing God.
8. This is clear from THGE VII.M.9.
9. Cf the discussion in THGE VII.P.
10. Theod renders MT by ὥσπερ οὐρανόν according to Syh, whereas Sym

386

Israel not even one was lacking" - a rather delicate way of saying that no one suffered any ill effects (i.e. die not die?) from seeing the place where the God of Israel had stood.[11]

The next clause in MT is similar to the first clause in v.10 and presents the same difficulty of interpretation; cf comment on v.10. It reads "and they beheld God," but using ויחזו rather than the ויראו of v.10. Here Exod again uses the idea of God's place as in v.10, but then interpreted ויחזו as though it were the Niphal of ויראו (the Niphal of חזה is not attested anywhere) rendering the clause καὶ ὤφθησαν ἐν τῷ τόπῳ τοῦ θεοῦ, inferring that beholding God must involve appearing in the place where he was.

With real insight Exod renders the last two verbs ויאכלו וישתו as imperfects: "and they were eating and drinking."

24:12 The Lord gives Moses two commands: ἀνάβηθι ... καὶ ἴσθι, with the latter as imperative of εἰμί intended in the sense of "remain there."

This is followed by the Lord's promise to give them τὰ πυξία τὰ λίθινα; this is then defined as "the law and the commandments."[12] MT, though not Sam, has a conjunction before "the law" as though God were to give the tablets (i.e. with The Ten Words) as well as the law and the commandments. This is difficult indeed since the coordinate phrase is modified by "which I wrote," and only The Ten Words were written by God; cf Deut 5:22. Presumably Exod took the phrase "the law and the commandments" as apposition to "the stony tablets," understanding the co-ordinate phrase as descriptive of The Ten Words. Hex has of course inserted και to equal MT. -- Also unusual is the purposive infinitive, νομοθετῆσαι, modifying ἔγραψα as a translation for להורתם "to teach them." But The Ten Words are not really for instruction in Exod's view but rather give a moral framework for law.[13]

translates עצם by χρῶμα "color (of heaven)."
11. Cf R. Hanhart, Suppl.V.T. 40, p.70 who renders "keiner fiel aus," "keiner kam um"; cf also the remarks in Lee 82.
12. The term τὰ πυξία was considered inadequate by The Three, probably since the noun usually refers to tablets made of boxwood, and they used the more neutral τὰς πλάκας.
13. Aq rendered the infinitive quite differently: φωτίσαι "to illuminate, enlighten," which is close to MT, whereas Sym has ὑποδεῖξαι "to indicate,"

24:13 Exod uses a singular attributive participle with a compound subject "Moses and Jesous" by attraction to the nearer subject, but then has the main verb in the plural. -- Jesous is fittingly characterized as ὁ παρεστηκὼς αὐτοῦ "the one attending him," translating משרתו.[14] The participle also occurs at 33:11 where it is rendered by ὁ θεράπων. Wherever the verb occurs (only in the tabernacle accounts) Exod translates by λειτουργέω.[15]

The main verb is ἀνέβησαν with Moses and Jesous understood as subject, but MT followed by all the other old witnesses has ויעל משה; thus only Moses ascended the mountain of God. But this is inconsistent within the narrative since in the next verse Moses says to the elders: "remain ... until we (i.e. the two of us) return." Exod makes the narrative fully consistent by his ἀνέβησαν. -- A popular A M tradition has επι instead of εἰς in the phrase εἰς τὸ ὄρος, making it "(they went up) on the mountain."

24:14 Exod uniquely also changes אמר (i.e. Moses said) to εἶπαν putting this verb in the plural as in the case of ἀνέβησαν of v.13. The tradition does show revision towards MT in a popular A F M text having the singular ειπεν.

The elders are commanded: ἡσυχάζετε αὐτοῦ for the Hebrew שבו לנו בזה "remain here for us." Exod simply disregarded the otiose לנו; after all, what reason would the elders have for waiting quietly except "for us," particularly in view of the "until" clause which follows. The verb ἡσυχάζετε is unique as a rendering for שבו, though it is contextually not inappropriate.[16]

The "until" clause has an expected subjunctive verb, ἀναστρέψωμεν, though the C variant indicative is not impossible. The f reading, επιστρεψωμεν, is a synonym which also fits into the context. A popular F text inserts ἄν immediately after ἕως, which often occurs in a ἕως clause with a subjunctive; here it precedes the verb and is probably a dittograph of the first two letters of the verb.

hence "teach."
14. See Helbing 315.
15. The Three also use this root and translate the phrase by ὁ λειτουργὸς αὐτοῦ.
16. Aq's καθίσατε is much more usual, and note Sym's περιμείνατε "stay

The ἰδού clause is a nominal one with μεθ᾽ ὑμῶν as the predicate. The clause sets the stage for the conditional sentence which follows. Exod's "if a case for judgement happens to someone" is a free though correct rendering of the Hebrew idiom מִי בַעַל דְּבָרִים. The apodosis is given in the third plural imperative "let them go to them" (i.e. to Aaron and Hur). MT with greater consistency has the verb in the singular. A *d n* variant has προπορευεσθωσαν, which makes sense "let them go forward," but is only a copyist error.

24:15 Again Exod adds καὶ ᾽Ιησοῦς to "Moses," thereby rendering the account consistent with vv.13 and 14. The verb by attraction to the nearer member of the coordinate subject is singular. A preOrigenian popular A F M revision has omitted the reference to Jesous so as to conform to MT.

24:16 That the glory of God "came down" upon Mount Sina is a free paraphrase of the Hebrew verb יִשְׁכֹּן "settle down, dwell"; nowhere else in the LXX is κατέβη used to render this verb.[17] Exod probably used it because of the affinity of the divine glory and the cloud, since the next clause states that the cloud covered it (i.e. the mountain); see particularly the note at 16:10. God's glory is the self-revelatory dimension of deity; divine theophanies (see particularly 19:16--20) occurred in the natural phenomena of cloud, smoke and lightning; for the thick cloud on the mountain see 19:16. Since the cloud covered the mountain it was fully consistent to think of the divine glory as descending; cf also 33:9 34:5.

For "God" instead of יהוה see comment at v.2, but here the change is particularly striking since the phrase δόξα κυρίου occurs at v.17 and 16:7,10 40:28 and seven times further in the Pentateuch but δόξα τοῦ θεοῦ only here. Outside the Pentateuch the term "glory of God" is also infrequent; besides Ezek where "the glory of the God of Israel" (who is of course Yahweh) occurs it obtains five times: twice in Bar where, however, the genitive is an objective one, and once each at Ps 18:1 Prov 25:2 Isa 58:8. On the other hand, δόξα κυρίου occurs 29 times.

---

around."
17. Aq of course could hardly abide such freedom of interpretation and translated the verb by ἐσκήνωσεν "settled down, tented," and Sym by

In the second clause αὐτό must refer to τὸ ὄρος, and the *C y* variant, αυτον, is hardly sensible. The only masculine singular referent in the context is τοῦ θεοῦ, which would be bizarre. Nor can it refer to Μωυσῆς since that name is coordinated with Jesous and a pronominal reference would have to have been αυτους.

As an analogue to the Sabbath commandment in 20:9--10 but in reverse, six days pass by without activity and only on the seventh day does the Lord summon Moses. Exod introduces κύριος into the text over against MT which the latter did not need since יהוה had occurred in the phrase כלוד יהוה earlier, but Exod apparently preferred κύριος when speaking was involved, (cf comment at v.2) and so specifies ἐκάλεσεν κύριος.

24:17 Change of subject is shown by means of a δέ structure. The verse interrupts the account of the meeting of Moses with the Lord by a statement as to what the glory of the Lord looked like to the Israelites. The statement is a nominal clause with ὡσεί introducing the predicate. If the divine glory was in the cloud or appeared in cloudy form (see v.16) it was luminous indeed, since it is likened to a πῦρ φλέγον on the crest of the mountain, i.e. "a flaming fire." An *n s* variant has the mediopassive participle φλεγομενον, thus "an enflamed fire" which is no improvement. The theophany is said to be ἐναντίον τῶν υἱῶν ' Ισραήλ who were, however, encamped at the base of the mountain.

24:18 It is clear that for vv.16 and 18 only Moses is involved in the divine summons; Jesous is now abandoned and Moses alone enters the midst of the cloud, only he ascends the mountain and remains there for forty days and nights. One might note that Exod carefully distinguishes here between the prepositions εἰς and ἐν, the former being used with verbs of motion such as εἰσῆλθεν and ἀνέβη, both of which lexically involving movement, the first movement into and the second movement upward, whereas ἐν with locative sense occurs with ἦν ἐκεῖ. The word ἐκεῖ has no counterpart in MT which along with the other old witnesses has "Moses" in its place. At 34:28 the parallel statement also has ἦν ἐκεῖ Μωυσῆς in a similar context; there MT has שם rather than משה, and Exod has levelled the two passages. The *O* tradition has "Moses" in the place of ἐκεῖ; this means that if Origen"s own statement of his methodology[18] correctly reflects his pattern of work on the Hexapla his parent text must already have been revised towards the Hebrew, i.e. this is a prehexaplaric revision.

18. Comm on Matthew XV.14.

Chapter 25

Chh.25--31 present an account of the Lord's direction to Moses as to the making of the tabernacle and all that pertained thereto, whereas chh. 35--40 recount the carrying out of the divine orders. The former I shall call the A account, whereas the latter will be named B. Since B describes the execution of the pattern found in A it will often use the same language simply changing the imperative or the future indicative to an aorist inflection. The two accounts may well have influenced one another and the symbol "par" will designate the parallel passage in the other account. Should the numbering in MT differ from that of Exod A, the MT designation will precede; e.g. 25:9--13 (10--14; par 38:1--4) means 25:9--13 equals 25:10--14 in MT, and the parallel in Exod B is 38:1--4. The numbering of MT in the B account is not given.

25:2--3(par 35:4--5) Exod has εἶπον which is not normally used to render דבר; Pesh follows Exod and it seems likely that the parent text had אמר. Over against MT Exod uses the imperative λάβετε instead of a third person verb as an *f* variant λαβετωσαν does.

The term תרומה "offering, contribution" is variously rendered in Exod, by ἀπαρχή, ἀφαίρεμα or εἰσφορά, the last-named used only for the census tax of a half didrachma in ch.30. The word ἀπαρχή is simply used as a synonym of ἀφαίρεμα in this account;[1] elsewhere the word more commonly means "firstfruits" (as at 23:19). In the par passage B uses ἀφαίρεμα first but then in introducing the list of offerings τὰς ἀπαρχάς.

Instead of rendering כל איש literally Exod uses πάντων; this then involved introducing the relative clause modifying it with οἷς, plural because of πάντων and dative because of δόξῃ.[2]

---

1. Aq uses ἀφαίρεμα here as being the more exact equivalent rather than ἀπαρχή.
2. Instead of οἷς δόξῃ Aq apparently has ὁ ἑκουσιαζόμενος (according to Syh), whereas Sym has αὐθαιρέτου "voluntary, of free will," which is much closer to ידבנו of MT than Exod.

The last clause of v.2 is introduced by καί even though תקחו occurs in MT without a conjunction. The majority A F M reading omits the καί and is probably a correction towards MT. The word before תקחו is לבו which Exod renders by τῇ καρδίᾳ, i.e. without a genitive pronoun,[3] the final *waw* having been read with the next word as a conjunction, showing that καί is indeed original.

V.3 introduces the list of contributions, which continues through v.7, by means of a superscription designating these as 'ἡ ἀπαρχή which you shall take from them." The "you" in both vv.2 and 3 is in the plural, after which (beginning with v.7) the singular is used. This is done presumably since the Israelites are to be addressed by Moses; this is somewhat incongruous since it is Moses who is to "take from them" with "them" referring to the Israelites. But once the list is ended the addressee is clearly Moses.

25:3b--6(3b--7; par 35:5b--8) The list of contributions to be taken from the Israelites are the same in MT of A and B both having 16 items; the only difference in the two texts concern the absence of a *waw* before items numbered 12,13 and 15 in the A text. The texts of Exod A and B are identical except for item 6 which in B is glossed with διανενησμένον for which see below. Both lists omit items 11,12 and 13; these are the supplies for the lampstand and the incense altar and are probably omitted because they are not construction materials.

Over against MT Exod lacks a conjunction before nos. 2 3 4 5 and 6; a και is supplied in the tradition in each case for which hex is usually the source. It should be added that Sam lacks a conjunction before nos. 2 and 4 as well, and Vulg. before nos. 4 and 8. The list orders materials as metals, cloth goods, skins, wood and stone.

25:4 The Hebrew תכלת which means "violet (stuff)" is rendered only by ὑά- κινθος "blue" or by its adjectival form ὑακίνθινος. In a list it is always followed by πορφύρα "purple" the rendering for ארגמן. The third in the list is the תולעת שני (sometimes the free noun in the phrase is articulated). The phrase occurs 26 times in Exodus, is limited to the tabernacle accounts, and refers to the worm producing a scarlet color, the *coccus ilicis*, and so by extension to stuff dyed scarlet, scarlet cloth. Exod here interprets as κόκκινον διπλοῦν "doubly scarlet," taking the free noun as related to שׁנׁי "second," though at the same time aware that it also means "scarlet."[4] In the parallel passage, 35:6, the word διανενησμένον has been added. Actually διπλοῦν occurs only in these two instances for שׁנׁי. Usually the phrase is rendered by κοκκίνου διανενησμένου (or the simplex form) "spun, spun out" (36:9,10,12,15,32,37 37:3,5,16 and in A 28:8, 29), or the noun alone τὸ κόκκινον (35:35 37:21 39:13). In A the usual rendering is κοκκίνου κεκλωσμένου "twisted by spinning" (26:1,31,36 27:16 28:15), but this never occurs in B. In B this participle is reserved as a modifier for βύσσος, whereas in A it occurs both with κόκκινον and βύσσος.

The fourth in the list is שׁשׁ "linen." The word occurs 33 times in A and B; in 21 of these cases it occurs modified by מׁשׁזׁר of which 19 are rendered by κεκλωσμένης "twisted linen," once, 36:37, it is omitted, and in one case, 26:31, νενησμένης "spun (linen)" is used; there it was used because κεκλωσμένου had just occurred before it to modify κοκκίνου. It is likely that the parent text here as well as in the par text had שׁשׁ מׁשׁזׁר.

The last item, τρίχας αἰγείας "goats' hair" is a correct rendering for עׁזׁים used metonymically for "goats' (hair)."

25:5 The list contains three items, two of skins and one of wood. The first of these skins is of אׁילׁים "rams" and is מׁאׁדׁמׁים "colored red"; this appears as ἠρυθροδανωμένα "dyed red."[5]

The second "skins" is called of תׁחׁשׁים, the meaning of which is completely unknown. Exod rendered it by ὑακίνθινα "blue colored." Tar Pesh have סׁסׁגׁוׁנׁא "red, vermillion," whereas Vulg has *ianthinas*.[6] The Hebrew word occurs 16 times in MT (six times in Exodus, 9 times in Num 4, and once at Ezek 16:10) and is always rendered by ὑακίνθινος (or its noun cognate in Ezek); the Num translation is, however, probably based on Exod. It is usually conjectured that תׁחׁשׁ refers to some kind of animal from which

---

3. Cf SS 93.
4. Aq rather bizarrely renders the bound word by σκύληκος "worm" which is what the isolate word may mean but in the context it is rather meaningless. The Three all take שׁנׁי as related to the root שׁנׁה, Aq rendering it by διάφορον and the other two by διβαφές.
5. The later revisers translated this by the participle πεπυρρωμένα

the skins are derived, but there is no evidence at all for this. The ancients all took it to refer to a color, and they may well have been right.

The last item in the verse is עֲצֵי שִׁטִּים "acacia wood." The word שִׁטִּים often occurs in Exodus either after עֲצֵי or עַמּוּדֵי and is always translated by ἄσηπτος "decay or rot resistant," a not unapt description of the hard wood of the acacia tree. The singular שִׁטָּה occurs once in Isa 41:19 where, however, LXX substitutes πύξον.

The hex text has added the three items which Exod had omitted, viz. (και) ελαιον την φαυσιν θυμιαματα εις το ελαιον της χρισεως και εις την συνθεσιν του θυμιαματος.

25:6 The last two in the list involve stones. The first is the שֹׁהַם, a semi-precious stone of uncertain identity. It is almost certainly related to the Akkadian sāmtu which means a red stone, usually carnelian. An awareness of its red color may appear from its translation in Gen 2:12 by ἄνθραξ. In Exod it is variously translated: by σαρδίου here and par; by σμαράγδου at 28:9=36:13, and 35:27, and by βηρύλλιον at 28:20=36:20. The word σαρδίου does mean carnelian, but the other two words are both green stones. Vulg has *onychinos*,[7] whereas Tar^O Pesh call it "beryl." Apparently there was no clear idea among the ancients as to the names and identification of semi-precious stones.

The second class of stones is called מִלֻּאִים. This is a jeweler's term derived from the root "to be full," hence "to fill," and so it refers to "filling, setting." Exod translates it by εἰς τὴν γλυφήν "for engraving."[8] Exod is quite clear that these stones are in a cutting, i.e. in a setting.

The stones, i.e. of both kinds, are designed לָאֵפֹד and לַחֹשֶׁן, i.e. for the ephod and for the oracle. But to the translator the oracle was really part of the ephod; and the picture of the high priest's robe to a Jew of the third century B.C. would hardly have limited these beautiful stones to the shoulder pieces worn by Aaron and his successors; this kind of adornment extended to the entire high priestly robe, and Exod substitutes for the ex-

---

"reddened.
6. Probably from the later revisers who have ἰάνθινα.
7. So too the later revisers translate the word here by ὄνυχος; the onyx was a stone with dark background but with white spots or veins in it.
8. The Later Revisers rendered it etymologically by πληρώσεως which, as

pected λόγιον the word ποδήρη, the robe extending downward to the feet. That this was a deliberate change made probably for the above reason is clear from the fact that only here and in the par 25:8 does ποδήρη occur in the place of חשן; otherwise λόγιον is always used (except at 28:4 where περιστήθιον occurs) even at 35:27 where the stones are brought on to the ephod and εἰς τὸ λόγιον!⁹

25:7(8) This verse begins the second person singular instructions (to Moses), whereas in MT third plural forms of the verb occur and continue intermittently for three verses after which it too changes to second singular; Sam change over after two verses.

The second clause in MT reads ושכנתי בתוכם. But Exod changes the notion of God's dwelling into a matter of self-revelation by its καὶ ὀφθήσομαι ἐν ὑμῖν. The ἀγίασμα was to be the place where the Lord would show himself to Israel; this accords with 40:28, where the δόξη κυρίου appears and fills the tent.¹⁰ Note that ἐν ὑμῖν is supported by Sam's בתוככם, which is, however, probably the result of dittography.

25:8(9) In MT this verse is syntactically somewhat awkward, beginning as it does with a ככל אשר construction. This could be construed as dependent on the רכן תעשו at the end, though the singular אותך in the אשר clause makes this rather implausible. Exod is probably correct in making the construction dependent on the first verb of v.7; i.e. the second clause in the preceding verse in MT is taken by Exod as parenthetical. Exod makes this understanding clear by repeating καὶ ἐποιήσεις μοι of v.7 at the beginning of v.8 as well.

Within the relative clause the expected pattern: personal pronoun + present indicative verb is found for rendering MT's pronoun + participle. The word order σοι δεικνύω is transposed by the very popular hex text to conform to MT. And over against MT Exod adds ἐν τῷ ὄρει, but this was almost certainly based on a parent בהר which Sam has; note the final statement in 24:18 as well as 25:40.

---

far as I know, is not otherwise used in the sense of the setting of a stone, but see 35:27.
9. Of course the Later Revisers had εἰς τὸ λόγιον, and not τὸν ποδήρη.

משכן is translated in Exod by σκηνή, a word also used to render אהל. Since both occur frequently throughout A and B this might create difficulties, but since to Exod these were two words for the same structure this created no confusion; when e.g. משכן and אהל מועד stood in apposition (40:2) he simply coalesced the two into τὴν σκηνὴν τοῦ μαρτυρίου. Only once does it create a real difficulty, for which see the notes at 26:7.

The final statement "so you shall do" is paratactically joined to the preceding in MT, and a popular hex variant has added και to equal MT.

25:9--21(par 38:1--8) The pattern for the ark.

25:9(10) Moses is to make a κιβωτὸν μαρτυρίου "an ark of testimony," though MT only has "ark." Elsewhere the ark is described as τοῦ μαρτυρίου (v.21 26:33,34 30:26 35:11 40:3,19) but never without the article. In fact in Hebrew as the free form in a bound phrase מועד always has an article; here as the first mention of an ארון the entire phrase is unarticulated. κιβωτός had been used earlier both in Gen as well as Exod but only for תבה. This ark is different; it is the symbol of the Lord's presence, a holy cultic chest to contain τὰ μαρτύρια (v.15), and so the translator added μαρτυρίου to make this clear.[11]

For ἀσήπτων see note at v.5.[12] The dimensions of the ark were to be two and a half cubits in length and a cubit and a half in width and height. A cubit πῆχυς was cir 45 cm. (18 in.) long, so that the ark's measurement in modern terms would be cir 112 x 67 x 67 cm. (45 x 27 x 27 in.). The terms "length, width, height" all had suffixes attached in the Hebrew, and so in each case hex has added αυτης.

25:10(11) The ark is to be gilded with pure gold both on the outside and the inside. The verb "to gild, overlay" occurs twice, once in a compound form καταχρυσώσεις and once in the simplex. There seems to be no semantic difference between the two. The compound is the more popular in Exod (13 times), the simplex occurring only four times. They occur only as rendering

---

10. The Later Revisers used the more literal rendering of the verb, σκηνώσω.
11. Aq used quite a different word γλωσσόκομον "case, chest."

for the root צפה. The terms "outside" and "inside" are in reverse order to that of MT, and so the very popular hex text has transposed them.

The last clause instructs Moses to make a זר of gold round about. A זר is a kind of rim or molding and Moses is to make it עליו. Exod simply says αὐτῇ "for it" and renders זר by κυμάτια στρεπτά, a small twisted cyma, a term also used in connection with the table in v.24. This wavelike twisted molding was to be all around it. At what height this molding was to appear is not stated but presumably it was at the top. The word זר also occurs in connection with the pattern for the incense altar in ch.30 where it is translated στρεπτὴν στεφάνην in v.3, "a twisted rim." This is certainly at the top.[13] Unfortunately none of the five occurrences of זר in B is translated by Exod. The molding was χρῦσα, i.e. "golden," which word follows στρεπτά in Exod, but in a popular variant precedes it for no particularly good reason as far as I can see.

25:11(12) Moses must cast (future of ἐλαύνω) for the chest four golden rings. The d n spelling as an aorist subjunctive ελασης is an itacistic error. These four rings are to be placed on four פעמתיו literally "its feet" which being at the four corners is interpreted by all the ancient versions as "corners" except Exod which has κλίτη "sides."[14] But then two rings are to be put on the one צלעו "its side (rib)" and two on the other צלעו. Exod also has "side" τὸ κλίτος for צלעו which creates a seemingly impossible task unless the phrase τὰ τέσσαρα κλίτη be interpreted as at the extreme edges of the four sides, i.e. at the corners; only in this way could a reader visualize two rings on each of the two sides, presumably the long (or rib) sides, and still have the four rings on the four sides. In each case of "side(s)" hex has added αυτης to represent the suffixes of MT.[15]

25:12(13) The verse begins with a δέ structure which is highly unusual in the tabernacle accounts, occurring only 16 times (12 in A, and four in B); a oI C variant changes it to a και phrase, but then καὶ ποιήσεις occurs with monotonous regularity throughout the A account. ἀναφορεῖς is a

12. For ἐκ ξύλων ἀσήπτων see SS 64.
13. Sym actually has στεφάνην as translation for זר, in which both Pesh and Vulg follow him.

398

particularly appropriate term for the poles since they were used to carry the ark (v.13). For (ἐκ) ξύλων ἀσήπτων see note at v.5. A B *b n s* reading has an accusative of materials but this is inconsistent with Exod elsewhere.[16] The poles as the ark were to be gilded with gold.

The pronoun αὐτά refers to ξύλων; it is the wood which is to be gilded with gold. A *d t x* variant, αυτους, takes the reference to be to ἀναφορεῖς.

25:13(14) The purpose of the rings and the poles are now explained. Exod has added τούς after δακτυλίους simply for good sense. -- Instead of the purposive infinitive αἴρειν, the *d* text has αιρουσιν; a third plural present indicative is possible but hardly expected, nor would it be clear what the subject was intended to be.

25:14(15) Once the poles have been inserted they remain permanently fixed. MT makes two clauses out of the statement, but the second one, "they shall not turn aside from it," is economically rendered in Exod by a single predicate adjective ἀκίνητοι. Hex rather unimaginatively added εξ αυτης to represent "from it" of MT. Emphasis is placed on their position in the rings by preposing the prepositional phrase "in the rings of the ark." A majority A F M gloss adds (τῆς) διαθήκης, a description common in the historical books and already present in 31:7 and 39:15. This verse and the following have no par in B.

25:15(16) Exod correctly interprets the Hebrew נתת by ἐμβαλεῖς. The ark is to be the repository for τὰ μαρτύρια ἃ δῶ σοι. The noun means "testimonies" (to the divine will) and refers specifically to The Ten Words given from Sina in ch.20, which were written ἐπὶ τῶν πλακῶν τῆς διαθήκης, τοὺς δέκα λόγους (34:28). In MT אתן in the relative clause is clearly future, but Exod leaves this indefinite by putting it in the aorist subjunctive.

25:16(17) The term ἱλαστήριον "propitiatory" is used only for כפרת in the Pentateuch. Since this is its first occurrence Exod defines it as an ἐπίθεμα "lid, cover." It lay as a lid on top of the ark as a kind of plate made of pure gold, its dimensions being coincident with the length and width of the ark.

Oddly a *b n s* variant places ἐπίθεμα in front of the word it defines. The nominal χρυσόυ καθαροῦ is a genitive of material,[17] made even more explicit by *n s x* which add ἐκ before it.

The uncontracted form πήχεων is the classical form, but the contracted form of the Byzantine text, πηχων, is well attested by the third century B.C. and is regular in NT.[18] As expected both μῆκος and πλάτος have had αυτου added in hex to conform to MT.

25:17(18) Exod has taken χρυσᾶ τορευτά to modify ἐποιήσεις, i.e. the two cherubs are to be made of golden chased work, whereas MT makes two clauses out of this: you shall make two cherubs out of gold; of beaten (work) you shall make them. The Byzantine group does add ποιησεις αυτα after τορευτά by which χρυσᾶ τορευτά is made to modify the second ποιησεις.

The Hebrew מקשה has to do with metal work of some kind, but exactly what it means is not certain. All the versions agree that the word refers to metalwork, though they seem uncertain as to the precise nature of it. Exod with its τορευτά thought of it in terms of carving, or chasing. A number of scattered witnesses read τορνευτα, but τορευτά is original.[19]

For the rest of the verse MT has "from the two sides (i.e. ends) of the propitiatory." Exod has added καὶ ἐπιθήσεις αὐτά at the beginning to make better sense out of it. And in imitation of the Hebrew which refers to the two קצות of the propitiatory Exod also has τῶν κλιτῶν "sides" which can only be understood as the "ends".[20]

25:18(19) MT begins with an imperative ועשה. Exod, however, followed Sam which has יעשו which Exod interpreted as Niphal. The Byzantine text has this as singular to agree with χερούβ, but Exod uses the pattern: plural verb + compound subject: "one ... the other"; cf the common pattern: plural verb + ἕκαστος. The clause is introduced asyndetically presumably in imitation of יעשו, but an M C x z variant has added δε. Both cases of

---

14. Theod has μέρη "parts" and Sym, πλεῦρας "sides," literally "ribs."
15. Cf SS 94.
16. See the discussion in THGE VII.H.3.
17. Cf SS 63.
18. See Mayser I.2.25 and Bl-Debr 48.2.

χερούβ have been popularly changed in the tradition to χερουβ(ε)ιμ under the influence of the χερουβίμ in the context; the variant proves the copyists to be devoid of any knowledge of Hebrew. The subject is actually compound: χερούβ εἷς ... καὶ χερούβ εἷς. -- For "the second" the *O* text has του ετερου "the other." Exod appends τοῦ ἱλαστηρίου to the preceding, and begins a new clause with καὶ ποιήσεις. By so doing Exod has changed the intent of MT and created a tautological statement, reiterating the making of the two cherubs at the two ends. But MT has מן הכפרת תעשה. By inserting a καί Exod made the prepositional phrase part of the preceding clause, whereas in MT it is part of the next one. MT makes the point that the cherubs are attached to, i.e. are of one piece with, the propitiatory. Note that the par text, 38:7, follows Exod A rather than MT of A or B.

25:19(20) Exod begins asyndetically with ἔσονται, possibly having read והיו as יהיו; it then continues the predicate with present participles modifying ἔσονται in imitation of MT. The first of these participles is ἐκτείνοντες." The subject is οἱ χερουβίμ into which a popular F M variant inserted δυο, from the two preceding verses. A second participial construction follows asyndetically on the first, συσκιάζοντες "overshadowing."[21]

The last two clauses describe the position of the cherubs' faces.[22] The first of these, a nominal clause, has a prepositional phrase as predicate, εἰς τὰ ἄλληλα "towards each other," a good rendering for the Hebrew "each to his fellow." The cherubs thus were facing each other. The second clause has a preposed prepositional phrase (modifying a second ἔσονται), εἰς τὸ ἱλαστήριον. Not only did the cherubs face each other, but their faces were directed towards the propitiatory, i.e. downward.

25:20(21) This verse and the following have no par in B. V.20 itself is a kind of recapitulation, with the first clause drawing the necessary conclusion from ἐπίθεμα of v.16: you shall put the propitiatory on top of the ark. --

19. Aq rendered it by ἐλατούς "beaten work," and Sym and Theod apparently (according to Syh) had τορνευτά "turned" as on a lathe.
20. Sym with fine feeling has ἄκρων.

The second clause repeats v.15 exactly except for transposing the verb and the phrase εἰς τὴν κιβωτόν; cf notes on v.15.

25:21(22) Exod quite intentionally interprets the verb נועדתי "I will meet by appointment" by γνωσθήσομαί "I shall be known, reveal myself." BHS et al suggest that Exod misread the verb as נודעתי, but this is not the case. At 29:42 30:36 the same verb occurs in the context of the אהל מועד, the tent of meeting, regularly rendered by τὴν σκηνὴν τοῦ μαρτυρίου, tent of testimony. MT obviously makes a word play on מועד and the Niphal of יעד. But in both cases Exod translates by γνωσθήσομαι (also at 30:6). It is hardly reasonable to expect Exod to have misread the word in each case. To Exod when Gods meets man, he reveals himself; the impetus for this interpretation may well have been the λαλήσω σοι of the next clause, with the ἐκεῖθεν also finding its parallel in ἄνωθεν τοῦ ἱλαστηρίου κ.τ.λ.[23]

The account of the plans for building the ark with the propitiatory and the cherubs finds its focus in this concluding verse; it is not accidental that the first thing ordered built in A should be the ark because this was the dais from which the Lord would speak, where he would reveal himself, a dais located above the propitiatory and between the two cherubs.

The κατά clause modifying λαλήσω is introduced by an intensive καί, the originality of which is not fully certain. Many Hebrew mss do support it, but MT simply has את. Furthermore καί before κατά is often dubious since it can be taken as a partial dittography; a popular M variant also omits καί. It is, however, the lectio difficilior; it does make sense, and the variant may be an early prehexaplaric revision. The κατά clause then gives the dimensions of the Lord's speaking: Moses will be mediator between the Lord and the Israelites. cf 20:19 24:2--3. A *d* variant has simplified the construction by inserting λαλησεις before πρός, making καὶ κατά ... an independent clause.[24]

25:22--29(23--30; par 38:9--12) The Table of the Bread of the Presence and its vessels. Over against MT of both A and B the table is made of pure gold;

21. These translations did not satisfy Aq who rendered the first participle פרשי by ἐκπετάζοντες "spreading out" and the second סככים, by σκεπάζοντες "covering, sheltering," both literal renderings of the Hebrew.

MT more reasonably had it made like the ark of acacia wood plated with pure gold. The par in 38:9 follows the A account. Exod presumably had an exaggerated view of the splendor of the table. It is possible that the tradition of the table being made of gold is dependent on the account of the Table in Solomon's Temple which according to 1Kgs 7:48 was of זָהָב rather than "plated with gold."[25]

25:22(23) An F *n x* variant adds εκ before χρυσίου καθαροῦ probably from its par 38:9. An early prehexaplaric revision has ἐξ ξύλων ἀσήπτων.[26]

The dimensions of the table are two cubits in length, and one in width (90 x 45 cm.; 36 x 18 in.), whereas the height was the same as the ark, one and a half cubits (cir 67 cm.; 27 in.). Each of the three dimensions has αυτης added by hex to show the suffixes of MT.[27] For the contracted form πηχων see note at v.16.

25:23(24--25a) The first clause in MT is omitted and hex has preposed και καταχρυσωσεις αυτην χρυσιω καθαρω. This creates a most peculiar text since according to the preceding verse the table was already made of pure gold.

For στρεπτὰ κυμάτια see the note on זֵר at v.10. A majority A M tradition has the singular στρεπτον κυματιον χρυσουν, with the O text also changing the order putting στρεπτον at the end. The singular is probably due to its occurrence in v.24.

In addition Moses is to make for the table a border of a span or a palm (one sixth of a cubit, i.e. 7.5 cm. or 3.in.) around it. Presumably this border was intended for bracing the legs; at least it would be senseless at the top with its molding.

---

22. See the discussion in SS 196.
23. The late revisers rendered the verb by συντάξομαι, for which see Exod at 29:43.
24. For the secondary character of the *s y* variant εαν see THGE VII.6.
25. The amount of gold used for the temple is incredibly exaggerated by Eupolemus quoted in Eus, Prep. Evang. 34.16. Compare also Aristeas, 57 where the construction was χρυσίου δοκίμου; in fact, he adds οὐ περί τι περιεπτυγμένου τοῦ χρυσοῦ.
26. Theod also attests this, but Sym has a more exact rendering of the

25:24(25b) The border itself also had a στρεπτὸν κυμάτιον. Here the molding is in the singular. In contrast to the molding referred to in v.23 this one is not golden in Exod over against MT, probably because the border was not designated as made of, or plated with, gold. Hex made it conform to the Hebrew by adding χρυσουν. The molding is made τῇ στεφάνῃ to which hex added αυτης since MT has a suffix referring to שלהן.

25:25(26) Exod did not represent the לו after ποιήσεις, so hex supplied an αυτη. As in the case of the ark, v.11, four golden rings are to be made (but ποιήσεις, not ἐλάσεις as v.11).

The placement of these rings in Exod differs from that of MT. In the Hebrew these are to be put "upon the four corners which are at its four legs." Exod took the phrase לעמת המסגרת to this verse, but reinterpreted it as ὑπὸ τὴν στεφάνην; Vulg also has *subter coronam* but it is joined to the next clause as in MT. Furthermore this modifies the verb ἐπιθήσεις, and not the verb of v.26 as in MT: תהיין. The "corners ... legs" is then translated as μέρη τῶν ποδῶν αὐτῆς, and the positioning thus becomes "at the four parts of its feet under the border," making perfectly good sense. It also makes likely the suggestion in the note at v.23 as to the placement of the border as being part way down from the top and attached to the legs. The rings according to Exod were attached just below the border.

Since Exod had not rendered אשר לארבע, hex has α εστιν των τεσσαρων instead of just τῶν (ποδῶν). -- An *f* variant has added στρεπτην before στεφάνην, for which see 30:3,4.

25:26(27) Since the opening phrase had been taken as part of the preceding clause it made sense to introduce ἔσονται with καί thereby changing the intent of MT. The rings are to serve εἰς θήκας "for sheaths" for the poles, a good interpretation of לבתים; in a similar context at 30:4 Exod used ψα-λίδες; cf note at 30:4. The purpose of this construction was "so as to carry the table with them (i.e. the poles)." The addition of ἐν αὐτοῖς over against MT is simply a clarifying gloss, linking the ὥστε clause more directly to the "poles in the sheaths." The omission of the phrase by A F *b s* could be an old revision towards MT.

25:27(28) The poles are constructed exactly like those for the altar except that these are plated with "pure" gold. Why Exod should have added καθαρῷ here but not at v.12 and that over against MT is not clear. The word is omitted by *x* La and Arab possibly due to mediate influence of MT.

The final clause correctly interprets a Hebrew clause which represents a partial transform from an active verbal statement to a statement with a passive verb component. Exod made ἡ τράπεζα the subject of a passive verb; others, Sam, Tar and Pesh, interpreted the singular passive as an indefinite plural active verb.

25:28(29) The vessels for the table are four in number. 1) קערתיו "its dishes, platters." Exod translates by τὰ τρυβλία αὐτῆς, and except for one instance in 3Kgdm 7:36(50) this is always and only used to render this word. A τρύβλιον is a cup or bowl.[28] 2) כפתיו "its bowls," as τὰς θυίσκας. This occurs 25 times in this sense and except at 3Kgdm 7:36(50) the word is always translated by θυίσκη which is really a censer. But the Exod equation is followed by other translators as well. Hex has added αυτης since MT has a suffix, here as well as for the next two vessels. 3) קשותיו "its jugs, jars," rendered as τὰ σπονδεῖα "cups."[29] The Hebrew word occurs only four times but is always rendered by σπονδεῖα. The Byzantine group has added a doublet και τας φιαλας. 4) מנקיתיו "its pouring bowls" as τοὺς κυάθους "ladles." Like no.3 this word occurs only four times and is always rendered by this word. In fact, these four Greek terms have been used almost exclusively as equivalents for the four Hebrew terms.

The last named vessel, "the ladles," is obviously to be used for pouring as the relative clause makes clear "with which you shall pour (with them)." The ἐν αὐτοῖς is a Hebraism, and the Greek would be better off without it. Remarkably no witness omits it.

The last clause begins with a genitive of material χρυσίου καθαροῦ. A popular variant has changed this into an εκ prepositional phrase, which simply makes explicit what is already implicit.

Hebrew, ἐξ ξύλων ἀκανθίνων. According to LS sub ἄκανθα 2 the noun = ἀκακία; and the adjective means "of shittah-wood" (sub ἀκάνθινος II.)
27. See SS 94.

25:29(30) The verse has no par in Exod B. Moses is ordered to put the ἄρ-τους ἐνωπίους on the table, a term which was coined by Exod to render לחם פנים "bread of presence," and intended to convey what the Hebrew meant, i.e. "the loaves which are in front." Only here is the term rendered in this way. The phrase occurs but twice elsewhere in the book: at 35:13 it is not translated, and at 39:18 τοὺς ἄρτους τοὺς προκειμένους occurs. Otherwise the term occurs only three times, each time being translated differently: 1Kgdm 21:7 ἄρτοι τοῦ προσώπου; 3Kgdm 7:34 οἱ ἄρτους τῆς προσφορᾶς, and 2Chr 4:19 ἄρτοι προθέσεως.[30] A gloss on the margin of cod B has ευθειους; if this was intended to clarify ἐνωπίους it missed the mark; "straightforward loaves" is no improvement.

These loaves are to be ἐναντίον μου διὰ παντός; μου refers here to God. An *f* variant has ενωπιον instead of εναντίον probably under the influence of the preceding word.

25:30--40(31--40; par 38:13--17) The lampstand and its appurtenances. As in the case of the table the parallel in Exod B is much abbreviated, and its relations to the A account will be discussed under B.

25:30(31) The verse consists of three clauses. The first one is a general order to Moses to make a lampstand out of pure gold. This is followed by a nearer definition of the construction materials as being τορευτήν, for which as well as for the variant reading τορνευτην and Aq's ἐλάτην see the note at v.17.

The last clause states that all the components ὁ καυλὸς αὐτῆς, οἱ καλαμίσκοι, οἱ κρατῆρες, οἱ σφαιρωτῆρες and τὰ κρίνα are all to be part of it, i.e. all molded from one piece. Only the first one has a genitive pronoun, whereas in MT all five nouns have a pronominal suffix; hex has added αυτης to the other four nouns as well.

The first component in MT is ירכה, literally "its thigh," and so it refers to the center shaft of the stand. Exod translates this well by ὁ καυλὸς

---

28. This was insufficiently exact for Aq who translated the noun as τοὺς πίνακας "plates."
29. Sym and Theod preferred the noun (τὰς) φιάλας "bowls, saucers."

αὐτῆς "its stem."[31] -- The next component is קנה, or possibly better with Sam, קניה, "its branches." Exod's translation is οἱ καλαμίσκοι, which is only used in the context of the branches of a lampstand in LXX, and only to render קנה; the word is a diminuitive of κάλαμος "reed"; Vulg also has *calamos*. -- The third element in MT is גביעיה "its cups" which Exod renders by οἱ κρατῆρες "bowls."[32] -- The next component is כפתריה "its knobs, bulbs" literally rendered in Exod by οἱ σφαιρωτῆρες, which except for an odd usage in Gen 14:23 occurs only in this chapter and always for כפתר. As applied to flowers it refers to the calyx, whereas the last component פרחיה, translated by τὰ κρίνα "lilies," refers to the corolla. The Tar have "apples and lilies" respectively, presumably then as the rounded bud vs the open flower.[33]

25:31(32) First the positioning of the branches is described. The δέ structure probably was used to indicate change to specific parts of the lampstand. There are six branches going out sideways: three ... from its one side, and three ... from its second side. The translator renders מצדיה from its sides" by an adverbial phrase ἐκ πλαγίων. This was not always understood; thus the Byzantine group articulated πλαγίων, whereas an *s* reading added της λυχνιας under the influence of its later occurrences in the verse; hex has, of course, added αυτης. But Exod has carefully distinguished between ἐκ πλαγίων and the renderings of מצדה 1° and 2° which characterize the three branches; these are rendered by ἐκ τοῦ κλίτους (αὐτῆς), with αὐτῆς not repeated for the second side. The κλίτη are opposite each other so that the lampstand branches were formed much like a modern candelebrum.

The adjectival phrase "the side the one" occurs in the *f n z* text as του ενος κλιτους which is equally legitimate in Greek. An A *ol C b* variant omits the second τῆς λυχνίας as unnecessary, whereas the second τοῦ κλίτους has an αυτης after it in hex to conform to MT.

---

30. Aq of course designated the ἄρτούς as προσώπου "of the face," whereas Sym used προθέσεως "of the placing before, presentation."
31. The later revisers (possibly only Aq is responsible?) have μηρός "thigh" which is a literalism which would make little sense to a Greek reader.
32. This was insufficiently exact for Aq who renders it by σκύφοι "goblets, cups"; cf also Vulg: *scyphos*.

25:32(33) The decoration of the branches. MT repeats "three cups made like almonds on one branch, calyx and flower"; Exod has it but once, but beginning with καί (as in the repeat). The word for "made like almonds" is put into Greek by a phrase ἐκτετυπωμένοι καρυίσκους "modelled in relief with (almond) nuts."[34] -- For the readings of Aq and Sym for פרח/κρίνον see note 33 above. The phrase τῷ ἑνὶ καλαμίσκῳ has been "corrected" in word order to (τω) καλαμισκω τω ενι by hex to correspond to MT. Further intervention by hex made up for the failure to repeat the first clause, by repeating the clause exactly. -- The second clause is also a nominal one with οὕτως as predicate and the remainder of the verse as subject.

25:33(34) On the lampstand itself, i.e. on its shaft (cf note on καυλός in v.30) there are to be four cups precisely like the three on the branches, for which see v.32. The four cups are complete ones, i.e. with buds as well as flowers (lilies). Exod agrees fully with the intent of MT by the σφαιρωτῆρες and the κρίνα components of the κρατῆρες (cf note on these terms in v.30). An early tradition misunderstood this, and under the influence of a similar context in v.32 inserted either εν τω ενι καλαμισκω (in the B *O f z* text) or εν τω καλαμισκω τω ενι (in the A M Byzantine text), thereby creating a confused picture. According to these traditions there are four cups on the shaft, but their buds and flowers are on the individual branches which does not make a great deal of sense.

In Exod an αὐτῆς occurs only after κρίνα, whereas MT has a suffix on both כפתרי and פרחי; hex has accordingly also added αυτης after σφαιρω-τῆρες.

23:34(35) MT in order to specify the placement of a bud under each of the three pairs of branches twice repeats the statement "and a bud under two branches from it (the lampstand)"; then it concludes by saying "for the six branches which go out from the lampstand." Exod added οὕτως before "for the six" as a clarification, a word which had also been present in v.33.

---

33. Sym has ἄνθη "bloom, blossom" instead of κρίνα, whereas Aq has βλαστοί a literalism for פרח the root of which means "to sprout, bud."
34. Aq (also followed by Theod) in imitation of MT made a denominative

Having the opening statement three times was, however, a bit too much for Exod, and he attempted to combine the two repetitions into one by changing "two" into "four" but leaving σφαιρωτήρ in the singular. In spite of this lapse there still must be three buds involved since he does conclude with "thus for the six branches."

There were various attempts to remove the ambiguity in the tradition. Particularly astute is that of the A *O d n* text which (actually probably through parablepsis) omitted "and a bud under the four branches from it," thereby making good sense out of the verse. A popular F M tradition simply changed τέσσαρες into δυο, thereby leaving one repetition but doing nothing about the last one. Hex added a third statement (with δυο), but did not change the "four" to "two" in the second case, which simply increases the confusion.

25:36 The buds referred to in v.34 and the branches under which they were were all made of one piece with the lampstand. The *f* text not only transposed σφαιρωτῆρες and καλαμίσκοι but also had a και at the beginning of the verse. Hex added an αυτων to both words so as to equal MT, whereas the M Byzantine text added και τα κρινα from vv.30 and 33 after σφαιρωτῆρες.

The verse ends with an overall statement that the whole was carved work of a single piece of pure gold. For τορευτή see note at v.17. By the term ὅλη is meant the lampstand as a whole with all its components. The nominal clause is best taken with ὅλη as subject, and τορευτή as predicate, which in turn is doubly modified by ἐξ ἑνός and by χρυσίου καθαροῦ.

25:37 According to MT the second clause refers to the practice, presumably by the priests (cf 30:8), of putting up its lamps (every morning). This was interpreted by Tar⁰ Pesh as "lighting"; העלה literally means "made to go up," and was understood in the sense of make the flame go up, but the text refers it to the lamps which are to be put in place. Only MT, however, has the verb in third person, all other ancient witnesses have second person, i.e. continuing the address to Moses. Exod with ἐπιθήσεις follows Sam, i.e. Moses is directed to place the lamps. This need not be considered inconsistent with the practice shown in 30:8 and elsewhere since the direction refers only to the initial making and placing of the lamps. Exod did not render the suffix since it is otiose after having already appeared in the first clause, though the popular hex variant has added αυτης.

MT continued the third person singular for the third clause as well, whereas all others have the simpler plural, i.e. with the lamps as subject. Of these only Exod Sam Tar[O] have the paratactic "and they shall shine," whereas others have "that they may shine," i.e. showing the purpose of the lamps. This interpretation is of course quite correct and the change from second singular to third plural in Exod should be understood in this way.

The prepositional phrase ἐκ τοῦ ἑνὸς προσώπου modifies φανοῦσιν and is Exod's attempt to render על עבר פניה "on the area before it." These lamps were small hollow dishes, either open or closed, with a nozzle on one side in which the wick would lie. What is meant is that the wick-nozzles all faced in the same direction so that the light would shine in one direction only, presumably towards the interior. Hex added an αυτης to show the suffix of פניה.[35]

25:38 MT has two items or vessels given which are to be used in connection with the lamps, מלקחיה and מחתתיה. The former noun refers to "wick-snuffers" and the latter is the usual word for censers," i.e. holders of the fire from which the wicks would be lit. Exod interpreted the first by τὸν ἐπαρυστῆρα αὐτῆς, i.e. its oil vessel, a container holding the oil supply from which the lamps would be filled. The interpetation is probably based on the root לקח "to take," then "to hold."[36]

The second vessel is interpreted by Exod as ὑποθέματα in the sense of "coasters" on which to set the lamps as he was cleaning and filling them. To the Alexandrian translator lamps required both oil juglets for supplies and "underlays" or "coasters" on which to set the warm/ hot lamps while attending to them.[37]

---

verb based on the root of ἀμύγδαλον "almond" and created ἐξημυγδα-λισμένοι to equal משקדים. Sym rendered the word by ἐντετορνευμένοι ἀμύγδαλα "turned out with almonds."

35. Cf SS 93.

36. A similar understanding seems to underly the reading of Aq and Sym on the evidence of Syh. The Syriac word is mzmkˀ and means "oil dish" used

Exod made this verse a verbal clause (instead of v.39 as MT) by adding ποιήσεις at the end. A popular A F M reordering of the text which would end this verse with καθαροῦ and place ποιήσεις plus the first four words of v.39 at the end of v.39 is undoubtedly the product of hex done to approximate MT; hex also added αυτην after the verb, thereby fully equalling MT.

25:39 In MT the amount of gold used, a talent of pure gold, was the total for the lampstand "together with all these vessels." Exod omitted יעשה אתה and apparently made all these vessels" as consisting of a talent of pure gold, rather than including the lampstand as well. The result would be a nominal sentence with σκευή as subject and τάλαντον as predicate, except that the verb of v.38 is understood as carrying over to v.39 as well. Exod thus does interpret MT correctly.

25:40 This verse has no parallel in B whatsoever. MT begins with a highly unusual construction וראה ועשה; in fact the imperative ראה preceded by the conjunction and followed by *waw* and another imperative is found only here in OT; for the plural cf 1Sam 23:23 and Jer 5:1. Even asyndetically ראה followed by *waw* and another imperative is extremely rare. Exod disregarded both conjunctions, rendered the first literally by ὅρα and the second by a second singular future ποιήσεις. For the pattern see also 4:21,23. ὅρα should be understood as a sentence modifier in the same sense as ἰδού. Neither Exod nor MT has a direct object although an F *b s* variant, probably based on Hebr 8:5, has added παντα.

The verb is modified by a prepositional phrase κατὰ τὸν τύπον. Both Pesh and Vulg follow Exod in not translating the plural pronominal suffix of MT, which is indeed otiose. The relative clause in MT is rendered by an articulated perfect passive participle (the predicate in the Hebrew clause is also a passive participle), and so the subject "you" had to be put into the dative. The NT quotation at Hebr 8:5 has the participle in the aorist, δειχθέντα, which was taken over by the *O f s* text. Only Pesh changes the text radically by rendering the relative clause by "which I am showing you in the mountain," thereby recalling the fact that God is the presumed speaker throughout.

libations, but here for the oil for the lamps. Theod understood the word correctly and rendered it by λαβίδης (αὐτῆς) "tongs," hence "snuffers."
37. The later revisers translated חֹתֹּה in the more usual sense πυρεῖα "censers."

Chapter 26

26:1--30 The pattern for making the tabernacle has no parallel in Exod B except for the summary statement in 37:1--2 (though see also 36:8a) and the free listing of things made by Beseleel given in 38:18--20.

26:1 (par 36:8a 37:1) Moses is instructed to make the tent of ten curtains of spun linen, and blue and purple stuff and spun scarlet stuff. For these terms see notes at 25:4. A *C z* text has simplified the double accusative construction by making τὴν σκηνήν into the dative. The curtains יריעת of the משכן are called αὐλαῖαι, whereas those of the אהל "tent" are δέρρεις. The two are quite distinct in Exod; cf comment at v.7.[1]

In the second clause the making of the tabernacle curtains is particularized as "with cherubs in the workmanship of a weaver." The Hebrew חשב "designer" is rendered by ὑφάντου in Exod A only here; at 28:6,15 the term ποικιλτοῦ is used to render חשב. The adjectival form does occur in B at 36:3,8; The transliterated χερουβίμ is probably to be taken as an accusative, i.e. in the same pattern as the first clause: accusative + ποιήσεις + accusative. A popular variant has changed ἐργασίᾳ to the accusative, presumably taking χερουβιμ εργασιαν as a phrase meaning "cherub workmanship," an error caused by copyists unaware that χερουβίμ was a Hebrew plural noun. -- The *d y* text has αυτα instead of αὐτάς, i.e. referring to χερουβίμ instead of αὐλαίας; only the latter can be correct.

26:2 (par 37:2) The length of a single curtain was 28 cubits (1260 cm; 504 in.) and its width was four cubits (180 cm; 72 in.) The μῆκος and the εὖρος are predicate nominatives of ἔσται. The compound number ὀκτὼ καὶ εἴκοσι popularly occurs in the tradition as εικοσι οκτω which is the usual order for Tar Pesh. For the contracted form πηχων see note on 25:16. The Byzantine text articulated εὖρος but left μῆκος unarticulated; this can hardly be Exod. -- Exod by its rendering of מדה אחת as μέτρον τὸ αὐτό

---

1. Aq translates יריעת here by δέρρεις.

catches the exact intent of MT; the same measure is to govern all ten curtains.

26:3 Exod begins with a δέ structure; Sam also begins with a conjunction. A C b text omits δέ but this is hardly due to Hebrew influence. MT repeats exactly the instructions for the two instances of five curtains, thereby making two large sets of curtains for the two sides of the tabernacle. Exod has an ἐξ ἀλλήλων after ἔσονται for the first clause which has no counterpart in MT but is intended to make completely clear that the five curtains are to be mutually joined together the one to the other, i.e. the first to the second, the second to the third, etc. The ἐξ ἀλλήλων is not repeated in the repetition, since it is now clear that the two sets are to be made in the same way. Cod A has uniquely omitted the phrase probably under the influence of the second clause (and coincidentally agreeing with MT), whereas a number of mss in the tradition has repeated the phrase in the second clause as well.

The word חֹבְרֹת is translated by συνεχόμεναι "joined together." A popular variant has the simplex form; aside from the fact that it would be unlikely that the participle would be changed in the two clauses, the simplex must be unoriginal since the root is always rendered in Exod by a συν-compound.[2] In the second clause the C text in particular goes its own way. It has the article before πέντε (a dittograph after καί); it omits the word συνεχόμεναι, and it substitutes for ἐκ τῆς ἑτέρας the single εκατερας. For the last phrase a B x z variant has the simple dative τη ετερα, which is an attempt at simplification, possibly under the influence of v.6.[3] The overall dimensions of each set of curtains amount to 28 x 20 cubits (1260 x 900 cm; 504 x 360 in.)

26:4 Loops made of blue yarn are to be made αὐταῖς, i.e. for the curtains, these to be woven at the border on the one side, ἐκ τοῦ ἑνὸς μέρους, which is a long side (of 28 cubits) intended εἰς τὴν συμβολήν, i.e. for the joining. These loops woven into the border will then have rings, or links, κρίκους, to link the two sets of curtains together, for which see v.6. It should be noted

2. See the discussion in THGE VII.N.
3. See the discussion in THGE VII.L.2.

that now that the five curtains had been joined (presumably sewn) together the resultant set of curtains is simply called "the one curtain."

The same kind of loops is ordered for the other set (curtain) here called the outer, ἐξωτέρος, curtain. In both sets it is the far edge of the far curtain within the set, i.e. the outside edge which is intended πρὸς τῇ συμβολῇ τῇ δευτέρᾳ, "for the second joining."

26:5 There are to be fifty loops for a set of curtains. The verse is introduced by a δέ structure. Cod B + omit the δέ but this is not original.[4] For the second set of curtains the placement of the loops is described as בקצה "on the border," which Exod renders by ἐκ τοῦ μέρους; the Byzantine group inserts ενος before the noun based on v.4. This "side" is further characterized as being κατὰ τὴν συμβολὴν τῆς δευτέρας "at the joining of the second (set of curtains). An x + variant makes the adjective phrase accusative, thereby conforming to MT, but the more unusual genitive is Exod.

The second part of the verse in MT is a nominal clause with the participial predicate preceding the subject הללאת "corresponding are the loops," and then has an explicative modifier, אשה אל אחתה. Exod also uses a nominal construction but has tried to describe exactly how these two sets of curtains are to be placed over against each other. The predicate is ἀντιπρόσωποι "facing," but for the subject Exod uses a positional description ἀντιπίπτουσαι, present feminine plural participle referring to the ἀγκύλας, and this in turn is modified by ἀλλήλαις; in other words Exod shows in detail how the loops in the two sets of curtains are to be placed; they must correspond, i.e. be facing, and they must fall upon (or over) each other, i.e. the loop of the one over the loop of the other set, and all of this further characterized as εἰς ἑκάστην "for each of the fifty corresponding pairs of loops." This is far more specific than MT, but also gives a clearer picture.[5] A popular A F M text has εκαστη for εἰς ἑκάστην, presumably a dative but with no significant change in meaning.

---

4. See note at THGE VII.E.2.
5. Sym and Theod have a text more closely tied to MT and have (from Syh) συναντῶσαι "meeting" and presumably reading αἱ ἀγκύλαι as well; at least

26:6 Moses is told to make fifty golden links. The *n* text has δακτυλιους "rings" instead of κρίκους, but this cannot be correct since one must be able to open and close these holders which are to be used to join together the two sets of curtains. What is envisaged is putting these links resp. through the fifty pairs of loops on the borders of the sets of curtains, one link per pair. Hex has transposed κρίκους πεντήκοντα to fit the Hebrew order. A variant spelling for κρίκους - κρίκοις is found in the *d* text in which the stem is spelled κρισκ-. It may well represent some local pronunciation.

The second clause details the instructions for joining the two sets of curtains. The adverbial modifier ἑτέραν τῇ ἑτέρᾳ describes how the joining up is to be done, viz. the one to the other. The *C* text changed the dative nominal to a genitive - for no good reason as far as I can see.

The point of all this tying up and joining together is given in the last clause "and so the tent shall be one."[6] From the original ten curtains ordered made in v.1 a single piece now constitutes the σκηνή.

26:7--13 A discussion of the making of the אֹהֶל over the מִשְׁכָּן. Both words are usually rendered by σκηνή but the אֹהֶל is a set of curtains (skins) put over the מִשְׁכָּן curtains; i.e. they are distinct in MT. The term אֹהֶל is often used to indicate the tabernacle, particularly as ἡ σκηνὴ τοῦ μαρτυρίου, so that only occasionally when אֹהֶל and מִשְׁכָּן occur in the same context would confusion ensue. Only four times would such confusion occur where MT has the two words used with the above distinction in the same context: 26:7, its par in 36:14, 35:11 and 39:33. The second of these has no counterpart in Exod. The third has τὰ παραρρύματα for which see comment at 35:10(11), and 39:14(33) has τὰς στολάς, i.e. a different text altogether. Only the first passage needed special attention for which see note on 26:7.

It should also be noted that the יְרִיעֹת which were translated by αὐλαῖαι in vv.1--6, are in this section rendered by δέρρεις.

26:7 Moses is told to make a σκέπην over the tabernacle. Here the אֹהֶל is not translated by σκηνήν since that would be a tent over a tent, but by σκέπην "covering." In the tradition a substantially supported A F variant

hex has added αι αγκυλαι to correspond formally to the הַלֻּלְאֹת of MT.
6. Aq has καὶ ἔσται ἡ σκηνὴ ἕν, having changed Exod's μία to the

has the itacistic spelling σκεπειυ, thereby making a purposive infinitive "to cover over (the tent)"; it makes good sense even though it is rooted in an early misspelling. This אהל is to be made of יריעת עזים "curtain of goat's hair." This is interpreted by Exod as δέρρεις τριχίνας "goats-hair skins," such as still used by bedouin throughout the Near East today. Once having established that the "curtains" are of this kind, the יריעת of the אהל are then throughout the section simply called δέρρεις. These δέρρεις are of course quite different from the αὐλαῖαι of vv.1--6 even though MT uses the same word.[7] Vulg distinguishes these as *saga* over against the *cortinae* of vv.1--6.

This outer cover or "tent" obviously has to be larger than the tabernacle it covers; instead of ten skins (v.10) Moses is to take eleven skins for the σκέπην.

26:8 The length of the skins is to be 30 cubits (135 cm; 54 in.), i.e. two cubits longer than the αὐλαῖαι underneath, thereby ensuring full coverage. The *d* text has δερρης for δέρρεως in the first clause as though it were the genitive of δέρρη;[8] it is probably a dialect variation for δέρρεως. In the same clause B plus scattered support omits ἔσται, which coincidentally equals MT, but Hebrew influence is not likely. For the contracted form πηχων see note at 25:16.

The second clause is nominal with the genitive of measure as predicate in preposed position (as in Sam). This is a simplification of MT which separates רהב from "the one curtain" by "four cubits." It might be noted that MT of B (36:15) has the simplified order as well. Hex has changed the word order to conform to MT.

The last clause is an exact duplicate of v.2, for which see note there.

26:9 The eleven skins are to be joined up (sewn or stitched) to form two large curtains as in the case of the αὐλαῖαι in v.3 but of five and six resp. In both cases these are described as ἐπὶ τὸ αὐτό "together" - literally "on the same," translating לבד "by itself, alone." -- For the second part, καί 2° ...

---

indeclinable ἔν.
7. Sym, though aware that these יריעת are not the same as the αὐλαῖαι, does not want to go as far as Exod and simply renders by καλυπτῆρες

αὐτό 2° the verb συνάψεις carries over. The *C* text changes the verb to συναξεις "bring together," but this variant is palaeographically inspired.

The larger set of skins is to be placed forward, with the extra (the sixth) skin folded over at the front edge. The verb ἐπιδιπλώσεις has an *x* variant reading επιδιπλασσεις, probably a dialect form with the same meaning.

26:10 The making of loops for the two sets of skins is patterned like that for the curtains in vv.4 and 5; though the language differs somewhat, the general intent is the same. Nothing is said of the composition of the loops (in v.4 of blue yarn), but they are to be placed on the edge which is towards the middle where the two sets are to be joined. This edge is described as τῆς ἀνὰ μέσον κατὰ τὴν συμβολήν for the one set, and for the edge of the second set as τῆς συναπτούσης "the one joining up," but the same is intended - it is the side where the two sets are to be joined not by stitching or sewing but by loops and links so that they can be readily taken apart and put together again.

Hex transposes ἀγκύλας πεντήκοντα to equal MT but the unusual order (cf the next clause as well as v.5) is also found in Sam and thus probably reflects the order of its parent text. Also following Sam is Exod's repetition of ποιήσεις for the second clause, where Sam has תעשה but MT does not. B *oI* omit the article before συμβολήν, but this noun is always articulated in Exod.[9]

26:11 As in the case of the curtains fifty links are to be made but of bronze not of gold. For the variant spelling κρισκους as well as the n s variant text δακτυλιους see the notes at v.6.

The next two clauses describe the assemblage of the sets of skins: "you shall bring together the links by the loops and join up the skins." The links are brought together, συνάξεις, and the skins joined up, συνάψεις. The majority text has the latter in both clauses, and that also occurs at v.6, but MT carefully distinguished by הברת and הבאת, and so does Exod.[10] The

"coverings."
8. See LS sub δειρή.
9. Cf the note in THGE VII.D.6.

second of these clauses has as object of the verb τὰς δέρρεις which makes good sense indeed. The skins are to be joined (and it shall be one), whereas MT has אֹהֶל אֶת "the tent," i.e. the tent is to be joined up. Of course the end product is the same, but Exod follows the pattern of v.6 in the understanding that joined-up skins make the tent.

The final clause has no expressed antecedent, and the neuter ἕν is used absolutely. This is even clearer from the Byzantine variant to the clause, και εσονται εις εν.

26:12 What to do with the excess of skins over the dimensions of the curtains underneath. The eleven skins of four cubits width per skin make a set of skin coverings of 44 cubits; the eleventh skin has been folded over and the resultant two cubits hang over the front. It appears then that the width is stretched over from front to back, whereas the length (see v.13) is stretched from side to side.

First the general statement is made that Moses is to put down the excess in the skins of the tent. MT then goes on to say "the half curtain which is superfluous you shall hang over the back of the tabernacle." But this seems to contradict the statement that the eleventh (or extra) skin was folded up and put over the front of the tent according to v.9. Exod solves this neatly by making two statements, one about "the half of the skin," and the other about "over the back of the tent." The first statement deals with the folded over eleventh skin (two cubits); Exod says: "the half skin which has been left over you shall let hang down"; of course this according to v.9 must be κατὰ πρόσωπον τῆς σκηνῆς. This leaves 40 cubits to be accounted for. The tabernacle is probably 30 cubits long and its height was 10. Exod makes the second statement account for this: "the excess of the skins of the tent you shall let hang down behind the tent"; accordingly the skins will exactly reach down to the ground as tent coverings quite properly should. The perfect middle participle, ὑπολελειμμένον, appears in a popular variant as present but this does not change the meaning.

A few scattered witnesses leave out "the excess of the skins of the tent you shall let hang down," which also equals MT. It is, however, an omission caused by homoiot on the repeated verb, and thus simply a copyist's error. --

A popular A F M variant changes the ὑποκαλύψεις of the last clause to ἐπικαλυψεις "cover over," probably simply the result of a careless copyist mistakenly reading the initial υπο as επι, a common error in mss.

26:13 The αὐλαῖαι were 28 cubits in length (v.2), whereas the δέρρεις were 30 cubits long, thus the latter were two cubits longer than the curtains; this makes for a πῆχυν ἐκ τούτου and a πῆχυν ἐκ τούτου defined as "out of that which is extra of the skins (MT lacks "of the skins"); furthermore this is measured as "from the length of the skins of the tent"; thus accounting for the 30 cubits in length. The tabernacle itself was ten cubits wide; with the height of ten cubits on both sides the 30 cubit long skins "will be covering over the sides of the tent hither and yon so as to cover (it)." The "it" is in MT and hex added αυτην so as to equal MT.

It appears from vv.12 and 13 that the skins reached to the ground on three sides with the front having a two cubit overhang of a doubly folded skin, leaving an opening of eight cubits in height.

The tradition shows a great deal of activity. Origen apparently had a text which had omitted ἐκ τοῦ μῆκος τῶν δέρρεων due to homoiot, and according to Syh he added εν μηκει before the first (and his only) τῶν δέρρεων so as to conform to MT. An M x variant omits the ἐκ before τοῦ μήκους, whereas a popular variant transposes the two. Hex added καί before ἔσται, probably from Theod, even though MT does not have a conjunction before יהיה. Possibly Origen's Hebrew text read והיה. A popular text has the homophonous genitive plural for συγκαλύπτον, probably through attraction to δέρρεων. And finally since καλύπτη appears without a modifier the *n s* text has transposed ἔνθεν καὶ ἔνθεν to the end of the verse, thereby making this adverbial phrase modify καλύπτη.

26:14 The verb has both an accusative object and an accusative of materials. A covering is to be made of rams' skins dyed red and a covering of blue skins, and these are to be above and over the tent, i.e. as an outer covering. The first covering is a κατακάλυμμα, and the second, an ἐπικάλυμμα, but both mean the same and are used merely for variation. For "skins dyed red"

10. For further discussion of συνάξεις in preference to συναψεις see discussion in THGE VII.Q.

and "blue skins" see notes at 25:5. Nothing further as to size and construction of these skins for the outside covering is given.

The dative τῇ σκηνῇ appears in an *f x z* variant in the genitive, but the dative is original for rendering לאהל. The Byzantine text has κριων added after the second δέρματα as well as the first, but this was under the influence of the first phrase and hardly original.

26:15--25 The pillars for the tabernacle. The Hebrew word קרשים means "planks" in Ezek 27:6 where it constitutes the deck of the ship of Tyre.[11] The term contrasts with עמרים for the tabernacle court, but both are translated by στῦλοι in Exod. Precisely what the קרשים for the tabernacle were is uncertain; the modern rendering "frames" is a pure guess from the context. To Exod they were pillars distinct from the pillars of the court (in ch.27) in that the tabernacle pillars each had two ἀγκωνίσκους and two βάσεις placed εἰς ἀμφότερα τὰ μέρη αὐτοῦ, whereas the court pillars had κεφαλίδες, κρίκοι, ψαλίδες and βάσεις, but only one βάσις per pillar.

26:15 Moses is told to make pillars for the tabernacle of incorruptible wood. For the use of ἀσήπτων for שטים see note at 25:5. The word στύλους is unarticulated in contrast to MT, and the preposed τους in *O x* is hex in origin. The Hebrew not only uses הקרשים but also characterizes them adverbially by the participle עמרים which Exod does not render, and so hex added εστωσας to conform to MT. Exod's choice of στῦλοι as rendering for קרשים may well have been influenced by עמרים (which could equally be vocalized as the normal word for "pillars").[12] Vulg has *tabulas stantes*. Exod realized that these קרשים were uprights and used for hanging cloth or leather coverings on, just as the עמרים of the court were used for the ἱστία (27:9), and saw no good reason for not using the same noun. It should be noted that στῦλοι, ordinarily rendered by "pillars," - and I shall follow that convention throughout, - can also mean "planks."[13] -- These στῦλοι were τῇ

11. For a discussion of the term see THGE VI.A.3.
12. The Three have τὰς σανίδας "planks" rather than στύλους.
13. Hippocrates (fifth century B.C.) in Περὶ ἄρθρων 47 discusses the correct treatment of curvature of the spine, and there recommends taking οἷον στῦλον δρύϊνον τετράγωνον, on to which the patient is to be strapped and pressure gradually supplied. But soft cloths should be put ἐπὶ τὸν στῦλον.

σκηνῇ; a popular variant has the genitive inflection, but the preposition in MT's למשכן is regularly shown by the dative in Exod, not the genitive.

26:16 The dimensions of a single pillar were ten cubits by one and a half cubits (450 x 67.5 cm; 180 x 27 in.) The "ten" cubits was of course the length, and the one a half, the breadth (τὸ πλάτος), but Exod uniquely has the verb ποιήσεις, as do adjacent verses, in place of the designation "the length." Hex preposed μηκος to the verb as a result, and a popular A F M variant omitted the verb as an early concession to the Hebrew text. Also over against MT Exod designated τὸν στῦλον as τὸν ἕνα, which Sam also supports, i.e. Exod's parent text probably had the Sam reading.

Exod phrased the breadth measurement differently from MT as well. MT has "cubit and half a cubit" whereas Exod has "one cubit and a half." Hex placed ἑνος under the obelus and then added "cubit" after ἡμίσους to represent the Hebrew text. The *b* text has παχη "thickness" instead of πλάτος.

26:17 In MT each קֶרֶשׁ is to have two ידות, probably tenons," intended משלבת "for fitting (insertion) one into the other."[14] Exod visualizes these "hands" as "small hooks," ἀγκωνίσκους, a word occurring only here in LXX; it is a diminutive of ἀγκών "elbow," and so anything which is bent or curved.[15] These are to be placed ἀντιπίπτοντας one to the other. What is meant is that the two small hooks are to be placed on opposites sides of the pillar, i.e. placed in contrary direction on the pillar but exactly corresponding to one another. Syntactically the construction of the first aspect of the verse is a further object of ποιήσεις of v.16.

The verse concludes with orders to do οὕτως for all the pillars of the tabernacle. A *C* variant, ξυλοις for στύλοις, is the result of auditory

---

Later in his lengthy discussion the board is called a σάνις "plank," or more often simply τὸ ξύλον. The book may be found in the Loeb Classics, Hippocrates Vol.III; with an English translation by E.T.Withington, (1944).
14. For ידות as an architectural term see the discussion in THGE VI.A.4.
15. As might be expected The Three did not concur in Exod's rendering of ידות. Aq with no regard for the architectural context rendered the word by χεῖρας "hands," with Theod following his lead. Sym used κατοχεῖς "tenons" correctly interpreting the Hebrew.

confusion; the result is not sensible, and it is difficult to see what readers of a C ms would have understood by it.

26:18 Moses is told to make pillars for the tabernacle, twenty in number for the north side; MT has "for the south side." Exod has reversed the two with "south" occurring in v.20 for MT's "for the north side." The end result is, however, the same since the two sides mirror each other.[16] In MT "pillars (for the tabernacle)" occurs with an article, and the F *f z* variant with τους preposed could be hex. On the other hand many of these same witnesses also read της σκηνης instead of the dative of Exod, and the two variants may simply be a single stylistic variant.

26:19 Forty silver bases are to be made for the twenty pillars. Exod preposes the accusative modifier to ποιήσεις, in imitation of MT. But Exod carefully avoids rendering MT's תחת "under" with respect to the twenty pillars. Throughout the entire account, vv.19--25, where MT repeatedly states that the bases were under the קרשים, Exod always uses a simple dative: "for the twenty pillars ... for the one pillar, etc." The reason for this is his understanding of the two bases for each pillar. In MT these are described as לשתי ידתיו "for its two tenons." Presumably the two tenons were at the bottom end of the קרש and they fitted resp. into the two bases. But Exod understood ידתיו here not as its tenons, but as (εἰς ἀμφότερα) τὰ μέρη αὐτοῦ. The word יד can indeed mean "side," and here Exod renders it by μέρη, i.e. "sides," though both sides of a pillar can only mean "its ends." The pillars for the tabernacle are thus construed with an identical base on each end, and therefore can be turned end for end in assembly. It is thus clear why Exod could not translate תחת literally - "two bases for both its ends" does make good sense.

The statement "two bases for the one pillar for both its ends" is then repeated in imitation of the Hebrew, presumably like the Hebrew in a distributive sense.[17]

16. Once again Syh cites The Three as reading τὰς σανίδας instead of στύλους.
17. Cf GK 123c.

Both patterns for the adjectival phrase: "the" + adjective + noun as well as "the" + noun + "the" + adjective, occur in this verse. The *n* text changed τοῖς εἴκοσι to τ. στυλοις τ. εικοσι, thereby making the patterns consistent within v.19.

26:20 The verse presupposes the continued use of ποιήσεις of v.19, here with two accusatives "And the second side that towards the south (you shall make) twenty pillars." For τὸ πρὸς νότου for לפאת צפון see note at v.18.

MT begins with ולצלע המשכן "and to the side of the tabernacle" for which Exod simply has καὶ τὸ κλίτος. Hex has of course added της σκηνης. The hex witnesses also have κατα δε instead of καί, which one would not expect as hex activity, although the reading does approximate MT more closely. Presumably the parent ms which Origen used already had this reading; Origen on his own testimony did not change the text, but simply filled in lacunae in the Greek from The Three.

26:21 Except for a shortened version of the opening clause: "and their forty silver bases," this verse is a repetition of v.19. Instead of "you shall make for the twenty pillars," v.21 has αὐτῶν. See the comments at v.19. An A F M popular reading has αυτοις for αὐτῶν, whereas a *b* reading omitted the word altogether. An *O* variant by reading αργυραι for ἀργυρᾶς has changed the syntax of the verse entirely. In it the text is a new sentence, whereas the accusative formulation of Exod, as v.20, is dependent on the ποιήσεις of v.19.

Over against MT Exod has εἰς ἀμφότερα τὰ μέρη αὐτοῦ twice, whereas MT omits the phrase entirely. Exod has levelled the account by repeating the formulation on the basis of v.19.

26:22 The tabernacle is oriented towards the east, for which see vv. 36 and 37; thus the rear is towards the west. Exod is somewhat fulsome in designating the side; MT simply has "westward," whereas Exod has "which is towards the west."

26:23 Moses is told to make two pillars for the n.w. and s.w. corners. An *oI C* variant adds δυο before γωνιῶν, which is correct but unnecessary; there are only two corners at the rear.

26:24 MT is difficult to interpret and there is no complete certainty as to what the instructions mean. That there is a problem with corner pillars is clear from the measurements given since six pillars would when placed next to one another make for nine cubits. Presumably the western row would be set inside the ends of the north and south rows of pillars. Since the overall dimensions were ten cubits for the width, for which see the note on v.13, this must mean that the pillars were not round but oblong. The breadth of the pillars was one and a half cubits according to v.16, but this could hardly be the width as well since this would make the tabernacle twelve cubits wide. The pillars then must be pictured as one and a half cubits broad and a half cubit in width.

But how then do corner pillars fit? It is clear that v.24 must describe this. Exod states: "And they shall be even from the bottom up, and at the same time they shall be even from the top ends to one juncture." Precisely what this means is unclear. The words "even from the bottom up" represents MT's תאמים מלמטה.[18] It would seem that these corner pillars in Exod served as buttresses on the inside corners and fitted evenly into the corners both at the top ends and at the bottom ends. On the other hand, it is possible to understand ἐξ ἴσου and ἴσοι to mean that these pillars were of a special kind with the top and bottom ends equal as to breadth and width.

Cod B plus two mss have εσται for ἔσονται 1° which is clearly wrong; in fact it is not clear what a reader would make of the singular verb, there being no singular noun in the vicinity which would make sense as a subject. Cod B x with scattered support have also omitted the καί before κατά which error is due to homoiarcton. Also palaeographically inspired is ἴσοι appearing in a *z* variant as σοι, hardly a sensible variant in the present context. And κεφαλῶν "tops, top ends" is the rendering for ראש, but in the majority tradition easily became κεφαλιδων "capitals"; this cannot be correct since Exod A recognizes no capitals whatsoever for the פרשים pillars.

18. The Three according to Syh render this literally by "twinning from below." Field retroverts as διδυμεύοντες κάτωθεν.

For the second part of the verse Exod has: "So shall you do for both (i.e. corners); let them (i.e. the pillars) be for the two corners." This differs from MT for the first clause which there reads: "so shall it be for both of them (i.e. the pillars)," which is fully clear. In Exod the word for "both" is feminine and must refer to corners. Attempts to remove the possible ambiguity of Exod in the tradition have mainly centered on changing the second clause rather than the first; (All ambiguity would have been removed by changing ἀμφοτέραις to αμφοτεροις as in ms 799.) either by adding ισαι before ἔστωσαν or after it. The *b x* text more sensibly made it ισοι. But none of these is original to Exod which was much closer to MT than the majority of witnesses in having no reference to ισαι or ισοι whatsoever.

26:25 A summary statement about the pillars at the rear: there are to be a total of eight pillars (six plus the two corner pillars). ἔσονται of the first clause carries over to the second clause with ἀργυραῖ as predicate. A popular A F M variant omits the article before βάσεις, a case of haplography after καί (αἱ). MT has אָדְנֵי repeated after "sixteen," and so hex has added βασεις.

As in v.21 MT repeats "two bases for the one קֶרֶשׁ"; there Exod also added εἰς ἀμφότερα τὰ μέρη αὐτοῦ in both cases even though it was absent in MT (but see v.19). Here Exod adds it but once and that only at the end. Cod B with small scattered support has transferred it after the first statement, whereas a *z* variant has it in both places.[19]

26:26--27 Moses is told to make bars of incorruptible wood, for which see note at 25:5. There are to be five such bars for the set of pillars on each of the three sides mentioned in vv.18ff. In spite of MT's use of the plural קַרְשֵׁי for the pillars on each of the sides Exod uses the singular as a collective; in fact, for the first mention he even inserts ἑνί in τῷ στύλῳ. The reason for so doing is clear; Exod realized that the bars were to serve as a unifying force for the entire side so that the individual στύλοι became a single unit. An *f* text does change the phrase to τοις στυλοις here as well as in both cases in v.27, thereby formally equalling MT.

In v.26 an M Byzantine text has added μοχλους after πέντε as an explanatory gloss. The adjective phrases follow the pattern: article + adjective + noun. The first of these is changed into the pattern more common to Exod by the *n* text as τω στυλω τω ενι. Hex changes the order of τοῦ ἑνὸς μέρους τῆς σκηνῆς to του μερους τ. σκηνης του ενος to agree with MT.

In v.27 where five bars are ordered made both for the second and the rear side the tradition records a number of variants. From v.26 a *C s* variant has inserted ενι before στύλῳ for the second side, whereas the Byzantine text has added τω ενι. A B *b x y* reading has inserted ενι before κλίτει, a variant which may be related to the previous (Byzantine) variant but with one less τῷ.

In the last clause the phrase τῷ ὀπισθίῳ is left unarticulated by most Greek witnesses but this is grammatically wrong since adjective modifiers must agree with the modified in articulation. Its position immediately after στύλῳ is, however, at odds with MT, and hex makes it conform by transposing it before πρὸς θάλασσαν.

26:28 Only the middle bar is designated as to its purpose. It is described as ἀνὰ μέσον τῶν στύλων, i.e. in the middle of the pillars, or better said halfway up, thus at the height of five cubits. For this middle bar Exod says διϊκνείσθω "let it reach through (from one side to the other side)," i.e. from one corner (or end) to the other corner. Apparently the middle bar would be twenty cubits long for the side, and ten cubits for the rear. Nothing is said about the other four bars; presumably they would be only half as long and would be fitted, two above the middle and two below. Nor is it specified whether these are fitted on the outside or on the inside, though one would imagine them to be on the outside.

26:29 The first and last clauses order Moses to goldplate pillars and bars, the only difference between the two clauses being the placement of the objects, "pillars" being preposed to the verb.

The middle clause introduces δακτυλίους which are to be made of gold. These gold rings according to MT belong to the קרשים, and hex has added an αυτων to conform to it. These are to serve as בתים "houses," i.e. "holders" for the bars; that is fully clear from Tar⁰ which has אתרא לעבריא, and from Tarᴾ's אתרין לנגריה. Exod makes the relation of rings to bars clear by its εἰς οὓς εἰσάξεις τοὺς μοχλούς. Though it is not stated each pillar must have had at least three rings, one for the middle bar, and two for two of the other four bars; cf comment at v.28. The gold-plated bars held in place by the golden rings are then to serve to hold the entire sides together.

26:30 A concluding statement ordering the erection of the tabernacle according to the form shown on the mountain. MT has כמשפטו "according to its prescription," hence "plan," a rare use of משפט in this sense, but cf 1Kgs 6:38 for which LXX has διάταξιν (3Kgdm 6:1d) with reference to the temple. εἶδος occurs only here in LXX for משפט; usually it renders מראה or תאר. But the term is not inappropriate in that it refers to the dimensions, construction and pattern outlined in the immediately preceding vv.1--29.

The reference ἐν τῷ ὄρει ties these instructions directly to the conclusion of ch.24 (v.18).

26:31(par 37:3) Moses is told to make a καταπέτασμα which alone translates פרכת throughout the LXX, with the possible exception of 40:19(21), for which see note at 40:19. The word does occur at 39:34 but this verse has no counterpart in Exod. פרכת is specifically the inner curtain whereas מסך is the outer curtain in front of the tabernacle. Exod does not make this sharp distinction since מסך is also sometimes translated by καταπέτασμα (cf v.37). The word basically means something that is stretched over (cf καταπετάννυμι), hence, a curtain. For the goods from which the curtain was to be made see notes at 25:4. In the tradition the terms κεκλωσμένου and νενησμένης have been confused, especially by the *fx* texts.

ἔργον ὑφαντόν "woven work" occurs in Exod A only here for מעשה חשב, though scattered witnesses do read υφαντου for ὑφαντόν as in v.1; cf note at v.1. In both cases the work involves cherub figures woven into the curtains. -- Exod has the verb in second person rather than in third as MT;

since ποιήσεις is used throughout the A account regularly, Exod's use is consistent and proves nothing at all about the parent text. For the syntax of χερουβίμ see note at v.1.

26:32(par 37:4) The καταπέτασμα is to be placed (i.e. hung) on four pillars (made) of incorruptible wood gilded with gold. For ἀσήπτων see note at 25:5. These four pillars are not of the same type as those of vv.15--29 with their two bases one on each end, but are the more common type with capital on the top and base on the bottom, the same type as those of 27:10--17. In Exod both are called στῦλοι but they are distinctive in MT, the latter type being עמדים, the term used here.

The distinction is also emphasized by Exod's use of κεφαλίδες "capitals" instead of MT's ווים "hooks." That this is an intentional substitution is clear from the fact that it is also found at v.37 and 27:17. The same substitution is found in the B account here which is clearly based on the A account. Other occurrences of ווים in A are rendered by κρίκοι "links" (for this word see note at v.6), whereas in B, when translated, occurs elsewhere as ἀγκύλαι "hooks." It is clear from the use of κρίκοι at 27:10,11 for ווים that the A translator knew perfectly well what ווים were, but intentionally used κεφαλίδες so as to contrast with the other στῦλοι of the tent. It should be noted that throughout κεφαλίδες contrasts with βάσεις, whereas οἱ κρίκοι contrasts with αἱ ψαλίδες for which see note at 27:10.

The number of στῦλοι, four, contrasts with the solid phalanx of six on the west side for which see the discussion at v.24.

26:33 Rather than putting the veil under קרסים "hooks, clasps," Exod visualized the veil as being placed ἐπὶ τοὺς στύλους. This noun is used both for עמדים as in v.32 and for קרשים as in vv.15--29, and so the suggestion is often made that Exod read קרשים which is a possible auditory error, though this is not necessarily correct. Certainly "under the pillars" would be bizarrre, whereas "under the clasps" identifies the position of the veil. But one can not infer this from Exod who made it "upon the pillars" which also makes sense. In Exod's reconstruction the veil was hung over the pillars (עמדים pillars as v.32, not the קרשים pillars of the tabernacle sides). The preposition appears in *n* as υπο which does equal MT but this is likely to be a copyist's mistake rather than recensional.

The second clause orders Moses to bring the ark of the testimony (for which see note at 16:34) there inside the veil. For ἐσώτερον the *z* text has the synonym ενδοτερον. The ark was the only piece of furniture inside the veil.

The veil was meant to hang in front of the adyton. The verb διοριεῖ is an Attic future which two mss change to the Hellenistic διορισεις. A variant in B* *x z* has the second person διοριεις which would have to be understood as a transitive verb with τὸ καταπέτασμα as object.

26:34 Exod continues the thought of the preceding clause by defining the purpose of the veil through its "you shall cover up by means of the veil the ark ..." The ark is thus to be hidden from view even of those performing in the holy place, a logical conclusion to the instructions of v.33. But this quite disregards what MT says "you shall set the propitiatory upon the ark ...." Tar[P] had פרכת instead of MT's כפרת but if this is what Exod's parent text had it would have been a very odd text.[20] Exod makes fine sense, and obviously meant what it said, since it also change the verb of MT by its rendering as κατακαλύψεις.

26:35 Outside the veil, i.e. in the holy place, Moses is to place the table and the lampstand. The lampstand is to stand ἀπέναντι τῆς τραπέζης, directly over against the table, with the lampstand on the south side of the tabernacle and the table on the north. The directions, τὸ πρὸς νότον and τὸ πρὸς βορρᾶν, are adverbial accusatives in each case following a prepositional phrase: ἐπί with the genitive. This has created some confusion in the tradition. Variant texts have made the phrases adjectival either by changing μέρους to μερος so as to agree with the τό phrases following, or by putting τό in the genitive so as to agree with μέρους.

26:36(par 37:5) Still another curtain is to be made, an ἐπίσπαστρον "a draw curtain" of various kinds of yarn for which see the notes at 25:4. MT calls

19. That it belongs only at the end is argued in THGE VII.F.4.
20. Sym according to Syh had καὶ θήσεις ἱλαστήριον ἐπὶ τὴν κιβωτόν, a

this curtain a מָסָך "covering," located לפתח הָאֹהֶל, which Exod omits. Here הָאֹהֶל must be intended as a synonym for הַמִּשְׁכָּן. Its omission could hardly have created confusion, however, since the front of the מִשְׁכָּן is the only opening left in the structure. Hex has duly added τη θυρα της σκηνης to make up for the omission. ἐπίσπαστρον is a highly unusual term; in fact it is a hapax legomenon for LXX here.[21] The participles κεκλωσμένου/-μένης (as in v.31) have been changed by some witnesses to the stem νενησ-. But MT does not have the same word in both contexts. For the unusual rendering of מָשְׁזֻר see note at 25:4.

This kind of work is called the work of a רֹקֵם in MT, an embroiderer, and in almost every context connected with work in colored stuff. Accordingly except for the par text which has ὑφαντόν it is always rendered in some way by the root ποικιλ-, either ποικιλτῆς or the adjective ποικιλτός or with greater precision at 27:16 by τῇ ποικιλίᾳ τοῦ ῥαφιδευτοῦ.

26:37 Five עַמֻּדִים pillars are to be made לַמָּסָך "for the screen" in MT; Exod renders the prepositional phrase by τῷ καταπετάσματι; clearly this noun is not reserved for translating פָּרֹכֶת; cf note at v.31. In the tradition an F n s x variant has τω κατακαλυμματι "covering"; possible Hebrew influence is not to be excluded.[22]

As in v.32 these pillars are made of שִׁטִּים wood which detail is not noted in Exod; hex has added ασηπτους.[23] -- As in the case of the four pillars in v.32 these two are to be gilded with gold. In contrast to the silver bases of the pillars before the adyton those for the five at the east entrance are to be cast in bronze; presumably the metals nearer the most holy place are the scarcer and nobler ones. For κεφαλίδες as substitute for וָוֵי cf note at v.32.

---

literal rendering of MT.

21. Aq followed by Sym translates by παρατάνυσμα (also in par in B for Aq), "curtain, something which stretches out."

22. According to Procopius Aq had τῷ ἐπισπάστρῳ which is almost certainly incorrect; Theod as the source seems much more likely; cf note on v.36.

23. This was taken from Theod, since according to Syh Aq transliterated as σετίμ and Sym had ἀκινθίνους for which see note at 25:22.

Chapter 27

27:1 The construction plans for the altar are detailed in vv.1--8. With Sam Exod refers to an "altar" instead of MT's אֵת הַמִּזְבֵּחַ. Since the building of an altar of incense is detailed in 30:1--10 it seemed inappropriate to call this altar "the altar." Hex has added το to conform to MT, but Exod had intentionally left θυσιαστήριον unarticulated. The altar was to be made ἐξ ξύλων ἀσήπτων, for which see note at 25:5.

On the horizontal the altar was a square measuring 5 x 5 cubits (225 x 225 cm; 90 x 90 in.). MT refers to these as אֹרֶךְ and רֹחַב, i.e. without article or suffix, whereas Exod articulates both - possibly in contrast with the unarticulated θυσιαστήριον? A well substantiated A F M variant omits the τό in both cases, possibly the result of revision towards MT. Over against the horizontals the vertical reference has a suffix in MT which is recognized in Exod's αὐτοῦ. The height of the altar is given as three cubits (135 cm; 54 in.). For the contracted form πηχων see note at 25:16.

27:2 The altar is to be made with horns on each of the four corners. For altar horns see Bible Dictionaries. Furthermore the horns shall be ἐξ αὐτοῦ. i.e. part of the altar, not as separate attachments, though since the altar was made of wood it is difficult to reconstruct exactly how these horns were to be made. All references to horns and to corners in MT have pronominal suffixes, which Exod does not translate; hex has added an αυτου for each one.

In the last clause Moses is told to cover αὐτά with bronze. Only here is צָפָה (Piel) translated in LXX by καλύπτειν, though it is clear that it is used in the sense of plating. Also unique is αὐτά among the ancient witnesses. All others order the altar to be plated with bronze but in Exod the reference can only be to τὰ κέρατα. It is the more puzzling since everything else, utensils, grating, rings and poles, are made of or plated with bronze. It would be possible to understand αὐτά to refer to both κέρατα and

432

θυσιαστήριον but this is not the plain meaning of the text. An *s* reading does have αυτο as a correction based on the Hebrew.

27:3 In Exod Moses is told to make "a border for the altar," a command which has no basis in Hebrew which has "its pots for clearing it of burnt fat." The text of Exod is fully sensible; a border would be just as appropriate for the altar as for the table (25:23--25).

Four things for altar use are to be made. These are a) καλυπτῆρα "cover, sheath," which has no Hebrew equivalent; it has hardly anything to do with the יעיר of MT. One might compare the Num 4:13 tradition where דשנו את המזבח obtains. The LXX tradition there is highly instructive: "and τὸν καλυπτῆρα he shall place on the altar, (and they shall cover it with a garment entirely purple)." b) φιάλας "shallow bowls, pans" is the usual translation for מזרק "bowl," literally "instrument for tossing (liquids)." c) κρεάγρας "forks (for meat)" almost always occurs for מזלג as here. d) πυρεῖον "censer" the usual translation for מחתה; in fact, it never translates any other word in LXX, but here Exod has the singular for MT's plural. -- Vulg has only three vessels: *forcipes, fuscinulas* and *ignium receptula,* of which the last two are equivalents for c) and d), but *forcipes* which may well be useful instruments at the altar has no equivalent in MT or in Exod.

The last clause simplifies MT which has לכל rather than καὶ πάντα. A popular A F M variant does omit the καί thereby somewhat approaching MT; actually if one understood the preposition as designating the object of תעשה the popular variant would equal MT exactly.

27:4 A bronze hearth with lattice work is to be part of the altar. Presumably what is intended by the dative ἔργῳ δικτυωτῷ is to show with what the hearth was to be made, a compound of lattice work.[1] In MT the construction is different; מכבר is defined (by apposition) as "a network of bronze," but Exod's interpretation makes "bronze" modify ἐσχάραν directly.[2]

1. See Lee 112.
2. The Later Revisers use κοσκίνωμα "grating" which is a more exact equivalent for מכבר of MT.

In the second clause Moses is told to "make for the hearth four bronze rings on the four sides (i.e. corners)." MT has על הרשת instead of τῇ ἐσχάρῃ, but Exod having taken the "network" to be the composition of the hearth, naturally has "for the hearth."[3] MT has a third masculine singular suffix for "sides" which Exod did not render as being unnecessary; hex has added αυτου to equal it.

27:5 These rings are to be placed under the hearth of the altar below. But this only makes sense if one knows the position of the hearth, and the last clause states that the hearth will (extend) up to the half-way point of the altar. Thus the rings are to be put precisely below that point. The hearth is thus a grating constituting the upper half of the altar on which the sacrifices would be made. This is quite a different construction from that of MT where the network (אותה) is to be placed under the כרכב of the altar below, which network is then to extend half-way down the altar. The כרכב apparently was a ledge encircling the altar, and the picture one gets of this altar is of a lattice work grating which undergirds this ledge. Obviously Exod has another kind of altar construction in mind, and the choice of ἐσχάρα as a rendering for מכבר in v.5 proves, since a hearth must be at the top; furthermore Exod also omits all reference to a ledge here, as well as avoiding הרשת entirely, referring only to the ἐσχάρα.

27:6 Poles are to be made for the altar of ξύλων ἀσήπτων for which see note at 25:5. MT repeats "poles" after altar, and hex has added αναφορεις to repair the omission on Exod's part. B x z do not have φορεῖς[4] before τῷ θυσιαστηρίῳ.[5]

27:7 The impersonal Hophal of MT[6] is correctly interpreted by all the other ancient witnesses as active, in Exod also as second person, εἰσάξεις. As in

3. Sym and Theod have "corrected" Exod by their (ἐπὶ τὸ) δίκτυον.
4. For φορεῖς The Three have *portatores* according to Syh. Precisely what the original Greek was is uncertain. Field suggests ἀρτῆρας which is a good possibility. One might think of ἐξαιρέτους as at 36:36(39:28), but its Syriac translation is quite different.
5. For the secondary (hexaplaric?) character of B + see the discussion in THGE VII.F.4.
6. Cf GK 121a.

v.6 a popular variant has αναφορεις for the simplex φορεῖς (in both cases), and hex has added an αυτου to φορεῖς 1°to conform to MT. -- The second clause has as its predicate a third plural present imperative ἔστωσαν instead of a simple future, probably intending the second clause as result, i.e. "you shall insert the poles ... so that the poles will be ...." -- MT has "two" before "sides" but Exod simply has τὰ πλευρά; that the poles are on two sides and not on four is obvious. Nonetheless most witnesses follow A F M in adding δυο, clearly a revision based on the Hebrew.

The C s tradition changed the ἐν τῷ αἴρειν construction, either by prefixing it with ωστε or by changing ἐν τῷ to ωστε. "So as to carry it" is not really an improvement over Exod's "when carrying it," but was probably made because αἴρειν had no expressed subject.

27:8 The construction of the altar itself is doubly characterized: κοῖλον σανιδωτόν, "hollow, made of planks." This must refer to the altar base, since the hearth compound of a brass network was the upper part of the altar. Vulg makes much of "hollow" but nothing of the second element; in fact Jerome expands considerably by his *non solidam sed inane et cavum intrinsecus.*" Presumably it was quite contrary to his notion of an altar to be made of planks but "not solid but empty and hollow inside."

The concluding statement enjoins strict execution of the pattern given. In MT's "as he showed you in the mountain so shall they do," "he" must refer to God and "they" must be impersonal. Exod uses a passive participle instead of "he showed," τὸ παραδειχθέν, and retains the second person singular ποιήσεις of the context instead of יעשׂו. The d text uses a different stem for the participle, παραδηλωθεν "what was made clear," a synonym for παραδειχθέν.[7]

27:9--15(par 37:7--13) The orientation of the court in Exod A is unique over against MT, Exod B and its MT (38:9--15). The long sides (100 cubits) are the west (πρὸς λίβα) and the east (πρὸς ἀπηλιώτην) sides, whereas the short sides (50 cubits) are the north (κατὰ θάλασσαν) and the south (πρὸς νότον) sides, with the gate on the south side. It will be noted that the

7. For the popular addition of αυτο at the end of the verse cf the note in THGE VII.G.3.

seaward side is north, i.e. the orientation is determined by Alexandria.[8]
That Exod intentionally changed the orientation over against MT is clear
from the orientation of the tabernacle in 26:18--22 where Exod uses πρὸς
βορρᾶν and πρὸς νότον for "northward" and "southward," and πρὸς
θάλασσαν for "westward" in agreement with MT. Thus the tabernacle is
oriented from the Palestinian point of view with the front facing east,
whereas the court in which it was to be placed is oriented from the
diaspora, i.e. Alexandrian, point of view. In both cases MT has the same
direction, i.e. in 26:18--20 the directions are resp. נגבה תימנה and צפון
(though transposed in Exod), and ימה, whereas in ch.27 the long sides are
נגב תימנה and צפון, and the short ones, קדמה מזרחה and ים.

It is possible that the Alexandrian translators were subtly saying
something about the relation of Jerusalem to the diaspora in placing a
Jerusalem oriented σκηνή within an Alexandrian oriented αὐλή, but this
should not be pressed.

27:9 The phrase חצר המשכן is introduced by את, but Exod with fine
feeling does not articulate αὐλήν, nor does an expected genitive follow but
rather a dative τῇ σκηνῇ;[9] some witnesses join *x* in reading the genitive but
though closer to MT it probably arose internal to the Greek tradition. For
πρὸς λίβα instead of נגב תימנה see the discussion at vv.9--15. The
preposition has been changed to κατα by the Byzantine text, and as might
be expected an early popular F variant has "corrected" the direction to
νοτου. Oddly the Byzantine group has thoughtlessly changed it to βορραυ
(which it also has at v.11!).

קלעים "hangings" is consistently rendered by ἱστία except at 37:14
where αἱ αὐλαῖαι obtains. These hangings were made of βύσσου
κεκλωσμένης, for which term see the discussion at 25:4. The length for the
one side is given as ἑκατὸν πήχεων (45 m.; 50 yds). For the contracted
spelling πηχων see note at 25:16. Hex has placed μῆκος after πήχεων to

8. For a full and convincing study of these terms in an Egyptian setting see
P.M.Bogaert, L'Orientation du parvis du sanctuaire dans le version grecque
de l'Exode (Ex. 27, 9--13 LXX), L'Antiquité classique 50(1981), 79--85. Cf
also the discussion in THGE VI.A.8.
9. Cf SS 68.

reproduce the MT order. Similarly hex has changed the pattern τῷ ἑνὶ κλίτει to τω κλιτει τω ενι to conform to MT.

27:10 Four items are mentioned all of them articulated: the first two, their pillars and their bases of bronze, and the second pair, their links and ψαλίδες of silver. The term ψαλίδες probably designates a band or molding of some kind, possibly between capital and column.[10] In any event it was a decorative band of some kind. It is the rendering for חשקיהם, usually translated as "(their) fillets," though this is by no means certain.[11]

In MT "pillars" has a singular suffix for which the antecedent must be חצר; logically it ought to be "side" but פאת is feminine. Exod uniquely has a plural pronoun αὐτῶν which refers to ἱστία. This is the tradition for both MT and Exod in B and is a possible way of looking at it. The *x* text has αυτης referring to αὐλή and so equals MT, though Hebrew influence is not proven by it.

For the variant spelling κρισκοι see comment at 26:6. The *n* text consistently avoids the use of κρίκοι, always substituting δακτυλιοι wherever it occurs (26:6,11 27:10,11 37:6 38:19). The word κρίκοι at 26:6,11 translated קרסים "hooks" but here and in v.11 MT has ווי העמדים "clasps of the pillars." In the B account ווים is rendered by ἀγκύλαι (37:15,17 39:6). Neither here nor in v.11 does Exod translate the free element of the bound phrase, here using αὐτῶν and in v.11 omitting it (though having τῶν στύλων after the coordinate ψαλίδες.) Vulg seemed unsure of these terms in the context of pillars and has both here and in v.11 *capita (eorum) cum caelaturis suis.*

A majority A F M tradition adds αυτων after ψαλίδες, thereby conforming to MT; this could be but is not necessarily hex in origin.[12]

27:11 The hangings for the parallel side are οὕτως. For πρὸς ἀπηλιώτην instead of צפון see the discussion in vv.9--15 above. The majority A F reading προς βορραν is probably a prehexaplaric revision made to conform to the Hebrew. -- MT has an odd doublet with באר before "hangings" and

10. See LS sub ψαλίς III.
11. Aq translated by προσκολλήματα which is based on the root חשק "to adhere, be attached," and is a mistranslation.

אָרֶך after מִדָּה. Sam has בָּאַמָּה for אָרֶך, whereas Exod omits בָּאָרֶך and has πήχεων μῆκος in second place, and so makes good sense; cf also v.9 where ἑκατόν separates μῆκος from πήχεων. For the spelling πηχων see note at 25:16.

For αὐτῶν after στῦλοι see comment at v.10. The *oI C b* text designates the στῦλοι as being made of χαλκοι under the infuence of the next segment. An odd *x* variant has ten pillars and ten bases instead of twenty resp.; it is probably due to the influence of vv.12 and 13 but it does result in a peculiar structure with only ten pillars on the long sides as well as on the short ones.

Both κρίκοι and ψαλίδες (τῶν στύλων) are mentioned as in v.10, but instead of ἀργυραῖ Exod's text is amplified by καὶ αἱ βάσεις περιηργυρωμέναι ἀργύρῳ "and the bases silvered with silver." There is no basis for this statement in MT, nor is there any reference elsewhere to the bases being silverplated, though ch. 26 does have the bases of the tabernacle pillars (vv.21,25, 29) made of silver, with the bases of the pillars on the east side, however, cast in bronze (v.37). And here only the east side has the bases of its pillars made of bronze but plated with silver; was this an intentional tie-in with the tabernacle where for three sides the bases were silver but the east side bronze?

A majority A F M text has added αυτων after κρίκοι, undoubtedly under the influence of v.10. For the second mention of αἱ βάσεις the Byzantine text has added πασαι either before or after αἱ. The same texts have with slight variations repeated the entire verse but substituting νοτου for ἀπηλιώτην, thereby creating a doublet tradition. Also to be noted is the majority reading αργυριω for ἀργύρῳ, which must here be synonymous with ἀργύρῳ, though it usually refers to silver money.

27:12 The breadth of the courtyard is introduced with a contrastive δέ structure. The side is יָם which is rendered in Exod by κατὰ θάλασσαν "over against, opposite (the) sea." Exod uses κατά here rather than πρός which he used for the other three sides as well as for the directions in ch.26 (vv.18,20,22,27,35). This change (in Exod B πρός is used for all four directions) was probably calculated to draw attention to the fact that θάλασσαν was not taken in the usual Palestinian sense of "west" but rather as "north"; cf discussion at vv.9--15 above. The broad sides were only half the length of the long side; i.e. the hangings were fifty cubits (22.5 m.; 25 yds) with ten pillars and bases. For the broad sides no reference is made to κρίκοι and ψαλίδες, though presumably their pillars did not differ in construction from those of the long sides.

Oddly στῦλοι is unarticulated, though *oI C* do add the article, whereas βάσεις has the article, though a popular A variant does omit it. It might be thought that the αἱ was a dittograph after καί and that the A text was original Greek, but this same phenomenon occurs in vv.13,14 and 15. Since the construction στῦλοι ... αἱ βάσεις is the more difficult reading it would seem that it is original in all four verses.

27:13 The side designated as πρὸς νότον "to the south" is with the exception of the initial τὸ δέ becoming καί described in exactly the same terms as the side κατὰ θάλασσαν in v.12 in spite of a shorter MT. For πρὸς νότον instead of קדמה מזרחה see the discussion on vv.9--15 above. For the broad sides of vv. 12 and 13 in contrast to the long sides in Exod the word לפאת is not translated.[13]

27:14--15 These verses together with v.16 describe the front or south side.[14] It should be noted that MT as well as the Tar and Pesh refers to the hangings for the second side as being fifteen in number not fifteen cubits. Exod along with Sam and Vulg has "cubits" in both places. The sides are designated לכתף and לכתף השנ ית resp.; these are the "shoulders" or wings of the entrance, i.e. τῇ πύλῃ τῆς αὐλῆς of v.16.[15]

Since the front end is fifty cubits broad and the two sides (τῷ κλίτει τῷ ἑνί and τὸ κλίτος τὸ δεύτερον) are fifteen cubits each in length, this will leave twenty cubits for the entrance itself, for which see v.16. MT does

12. For a fuller discussion of this variant see THGE VII.G.2.
13. This deficiency is rectified in v.13 (according to Syh) by Aq and Theod who add τῷ κλίτει (replacing the τό), and by Sym who has κατὰ πρόσωπον.
14. For the originality of πέντε καὶ δέκα in v.14 rather than δεκα πεντε or δεκα και πεντε see the discussion in THGE VII.I., and for the originality of the word order τῶν ἱστίων τὸ ὕψος in both verses see the note in THGE VII.F.4.
15. The first of these is rendered by The Three as τῇ ὠμίᾳ τῇ μίᾳ and the

not designate these as "lengths," and Exod describes these as τὸ ὕψος. The term probably comes from the weaving trade and designates the position on the loom, the indefinite length being the upright weave. That ὕψος means length of the hangings is clear from fifteen plus twenty plus fifteen constituting the breadth (hardly height) of the south end of the court. Each of the sides are to have three pillars and bases. -- For the spelling πηχων see note at 25:16.

27:16(par 37:16--17) The actual πυλή was twenty cubits wide and it was to have a κάλυμμα "twenty cubits in height." For τὸ ὕψος see comment on vv. 14--15. The word κάλυμμα renders מָסָךְ of MT.[16] -- For the spelling πηχων see note at 25:16.

For the list of fabrics see the notes at 25:4. The *z* text changes Exod's κεκλωσμένης to νενησμενης, thereby approximating MT. These fabrics are called "the work of an embroiderer" in MT which Exod varies by τῇ ποικιλίᾳ of the ῥαφιδευτοῦ, a hapax legomenon in LXX, although the adjective does occur at 37:21. For the translation of רֹקֵם in general see the note at 26:36.

Since the sides (wings) had a total of six pillars (and bases) four remain for the entrance itself to make up the total of ten for the side. With ten pillars each for the broad sides and twenty each for the long sides, sixty pillars would seem to be the total number. This is, however, uncertain since it seems possible that the end pillars would constitute corner pillars and thus be counted twice. That would make the total number of pillars 56. It is uncertain how MT or Exod counted and either number is possible.

The *b f* text has changed αὐτῶν in both cases to αυτου making the antecedent κάλυμμα. The plural pronouns in Exod are based on the parent Hebrew text.

27:17(par 37:15) Exod has interpreted מְחֻשָּׁקִים of MT not as "filleted," for which see note at v.10, but rather as κατηργυρωμένοι "silverplated"; this tradition is also followed in Exod B. Thus all the pillars of the court are to be fully silvered with silver, not just filleted, (For ἀργυρίῳ see note at v.11.)

---

second by Sym and Theod by τῇ ὡμίᾳ τῇ δευτέρᾳ (according to Syh).
16. Aq and Sym translate by παρατάνυσμα "something that is stretched out"

The *C* text has prefixed the participle by και, but this is a case of dittography before κατ-.

MT has "their clasps of silver and their bases of bronze," but Exod followed by Pesh and Vulg has "capitals" instead of "clasps," thereby emphasizing an essential difference between the pillars of the court and those of the tabernacle which had a base at either end but no capitals; cf note at 26:19. This interpretation differs from Exod B where both αἱ ἀγκύλαι are ἀργυραῖ and their capitals are silverplated with silver, a tradition based on the Hebrew of B (=38:17). Exod, followed by Pesh, balances these two phrases by prefixing καί before αἱ κεφαλίδες, i.e. making a "both ... and" construction.

27:18 The dimensions of the courtyard are necessarily determined by the hangings since only they give shape to the court. The length and breadth are given in imitation of an unusual Hebrew construction as ἑκατὸν ἐφ᾽ ἑκατόν and πεντήκοντα ἐπὶ πεντήκοντα resp. What is probably meant is 100 (cubits) over against 100 (i.e. on the parallel side), and so too 50 over against 50. MT actually has מאה באמה for the first phrase which Exod has read as מאה באמה. In any event it is clear that the long sides were 100 cubits and the broad sides 50. Sam has simplified the Hebrew text by twice reading באמה, i.e. "100 cubits ... 50 cubits." For another way of understanding the phrase see comment at 37:7.

The statement καὶ ὕψος πέντε πήχεων shows that the measurement concerns the hangings, which is then confirmed by ἐκ βύσσου κεκλωσμένης. ὕψος is here used literally and not as in vv.14--16; i.e. the hangings when in place were five cubits in height (thus designating the width of the cloth).

The final phrase "and their bases of bronze," simply reproducing MT, probably came into this verse from v.17 where it really belongs. This is obvious since αὐτῶν can only refer to στῦλοι in v.17, whereas this verse deals with "hangings."

Popular variants supported especially by the Byzantine group have articulated εὖρος and ὕψος on the analogy of τὸ δὲ μῆκος. -- For the spelling πηχων see note at 25:16. -- For κεκλωσμένης the *x* text has δεδιπλωμενης. This odd reading seems influenced by 25:4 where (κόκκι-νον) διπλοῦν is coordinate with βύσσον κεκλωσμένην, but here it is not fitting. Why the linen should have been doubled is not obvious.

27:19 Exod concludes the section on the courtyard by "all the equipment and all the utensils and the pegs of the court are of bronze." Precisely what these matters are over against the court is not stated. It is possible to take the nominal τῆς αὐλῆς as applying only to οἱ πάσσαλοι and that κατασκευή and ἐργαλεῖα be taken absolutely, but this is not clear nor would the context make that likely. MT has quite a different understanding in that the references in the verse except for the phrase "and all the pegs of the court" are to the משכן. MT begins with "for all the vessels of the tabernacle in all its service." Exod has "and" both for "for" and "in," and has taken "its service" as plural: τὰ ἐργαλεῖα. Hex has revised this text by adding της σκηνης after κατασκευή and αυτης after ἐργαλεῖα both being based on MT. Not clear is what is meant by עבדתו, though it is clear that τὰ ἐργαλεῖα does not express its intent.[17]

The second half of the verse is shorter in Exod; the initial וכל יתדתיו referring to the tabernacle is omitted, which is consonant with Exod's making the verse refer only to the courtyard. Hex has added και παντες οι πασσαλοι αυτης, and has also added a παντες before οι πάσσαλοι, both equalling MT.

The *f* text has added at the end of the verse the statement: "and you shall make blue and purple and scarlet garments to minister in them in the sanctuaries," a text also found in Sam. It is completely obscure how this Sam text found its way into the *f* tradition.

27:20 Together with v.21 this verse orders oil to be prepared and to be used for a perpetually burning light for the holy place. Moses is, however, not ordered to provide oil but rather told to command the Israelites to provide it, an unusual pattern also occurring in 31:13. The word is imperatival, σύνταξον, even though MT has a second singular imperfect (at 31:13 MT also has an imperative). The change to an imperative is signalized by an

---

from παρατείνω (cf also 37:5 and 40:5).
17. Aq and Theod translate it by δουλείᾳ αὐτῆς, whereas Sym has λατρείαν

initial σύ, though a substantial number of witnesses omit it. Of those that omit the pronoun the C text also changes σύνταξον to συναξον "bring together," obviously an unintentional error since the text keeps the dative τοῖς υἱοῖς.

The subject of the second clause is "the Israelites," and the verb is modified by σοι, a dative of advantage, omitted by the C x z text. MT speaks of the oil as "from olives, pure, beaten" which Exod renders literally except for "pure" which has a double rendering: ἄτρυγον and καθαρόν. -- The B f x text has added the complementary infinitive καυσαι after φῶς; this entered the text from Lev 24:2 where the context is similar. Instead of καυσαι Exod has a purposive clause. -- Codex B has the Attic καηται but it is its sole witness.[18] In fact the κα- stem occurs in LXX only when the next letter is *eta* and I strongly suspect an itacism, i.e. the stem should always be taken in LXX as και-.

27:21 The verse begins with a detailed preposed locative modifier: "in the tent of testimony outside the veil which is before the covenant." σκηνῇ τοῦ μαρτυρίου as a term for the tabernacle occurs here for the first time, after which it occurs 34 times in Exod (and once without an article). MT, however, has אהל מועד "tent of meeting," i.e. the place where God and man meet. Exod takes מועד as though related to עדות "testimony" for which see the note at 25:15. The tent is thus thought of as the place where העדות, the tablets of The Ten Words, here translated τῆς διαθήκης, were placed. As the tent of the divine "testimony" the tabernacle symbolized the centrality of the עדות/τὰ μαρτύρια, or διαθήκη, in the cultic life of Israel.

The constantly lit lamp was to be in the holy place, outside the veil which was before the adytum. διαθήκη is a rare translation for עדת, commonly rendered as μαρτύριον. That it does refer to the tablets of The Ten Words is clear from 31:7 39:15 where the ark is called κιβωτὸν τοῦ μαρτυρίου (the only other certain instances where עדות is rendered by μαρτύριον). The f text actually has της κιβωτου before "the covenant" here as well. To Exod the Ten Words constitute the heart of the covenant between the Lord and Israel; cf 20:2.

αὐτῆς.
18. Cf Crönert 106 for καίω as Hellenistic form.

The verb in the clause is καύσει "shall burn"; MT simply has יערך "shall tend, arrange," and Exod takes "tending a lamp" to mean "keeping the lamp burning," especially in view of v.20b; compare also 30:7. The verb has αὐτό as object, referring to φῶς. A popular A F M variant has αυτου, referring to λύχνος, which is equally intelligible.[19]

Both νόμιμον αἰώνιον and εἰς τὰς γενεὰς ὑμῶν occur at 12:14, and cf also v.17. The genitive pronoun is, however, surprising. MT has the simpler third plural suffix as referring to Aaron and his sons. Sam and Pesh both attest to the more difficult second person and Exod's parent text must have had it; Exod would hardly have changed it on his own.

19. For ἔναντι rather than the εναντιον of the popular B variant see the discussion in THGE VII.L.2. sub 6:2.

444

Chapter 28

28:1 The chapter is devoted to a description of all the priestly garments to be made, and begins with a command to Moses: προσαγάγου πρὸς σεαυτόν "bring to yourself." The modifying prepositional phrase is otiose after a middle imperative. A popular variant text has the neutral εαυτον instead of σεαυτόν, which is synonymous. -- Hex adds μετ αυτου after "his sons" to render the omitted אתו of MT.

The verb is modified by a purpose infinitive ἱερατεύειν.[1] MT has a subject suffix which Exod did not translate but hex, as well as The Three, added αυτον.[2] -- C s used the accented form εμοι instead of μοι.[3]

The names of Aaron and his four sons are all connected by καί in Exod Pesh, but the other witnesses made two pair out of the four sons and also lack a conjunction between Aaron and the sons. The names of the sons created little difficulty in the tradition except for Ναδάβ where ναδαμ, ναβαδ, ναδαδ and δαβαβ are attested. For the tradition see the notes on 6:23.

28:2 Over against the plural of MT Exod followed by Vulg orders the making of a στολὴν ἁγίαν for Aaron. The term is a collective, however, as v.4 shows where the στολαί are individually listed. To Exod the whole set of priestly garments constitutes a single set called στολὴν ἁγίαν.

Although Aaron and his sons are all mentioned in v.1 the detailed priestly garments are intended for the high priest alone; only vv.36--39 describe garments for the sons. The garments are described as εἰς τιμὴν καὶ δόξαν, a collocation repeated with respect to the garments for the sons in v.36. The collocation occurs elsewhere in LXX but in transposed order only four times, Ps 8:5 95:7 Job 40:5 2Chr 32:33. When applied to the priestly garments it refers to their splendor and beauty.

1. Theod preposed an εἰς; it was articulated by Aq, and changed by Sym to the aorist ἱερατεῦσαι.
2. Cf SS 84.

28:3 As in v.1 and 27:20 the verse begins with the pattern καὶ σύ + an aorist imperative. Moses is to speak to (in the sense of to order) all the wise τῇ διανοίᾳ "in understanding," a normal rendering for לב. Exod, followed by Tar Pesh Vulg, has simplified the reading of MT Sam מלאכתיו by which the antecedent of אשר must be לב by making the referent plural, i.e. the חכמי.

The verb ἐνέπλησα is modified by a genitive πνεύματος which an M O n reading has in the accusative, a late change not attested for classical times. It is in turn modified by αἰσθήσεως, thus "(with a spirit of) perception."[4] The choice of αἰσθήσεως to render חכמה is unique in LXX which commonly uses it to render דעת. Its use here shows the lengths to which Exod sometimes goes to avoid the repetitious. An *f* variant has συνεσεως, possibly as an attempt to clarify.

The καὶ ποιήσουσιν clause serves in effect as the result clause of the preceding, i.e. Moses speaks and the practical issue is that they will make the garment. This garment is called τὴν ἁγίαν in imitation of v.2. In MT they are to make Aaron's garments לקדשו "so as to consecrate him"; but the making of garments does not consecrate a priest - anointing does, and Exod "improves" MT by his εἰς τὸ ἅγιον "for the sanctuary" where the holy apparel was to be worn. MT then concludes with the infinitive construction found in v.1, לכהנו לי, which Exod must now tie to ἅγιον; he effects this by using a relative clause "in which he will serve as priest for me."[5] The Three naturally had an accusative αὐτόν as subject of the infinitive to render the subject suffix of לכהנו; Origen could hardly use this with a finite verb so his solution was to add αυτος after the verb.

28:4 A list of six στολαί which are to be made. a) τὸ περιστήθιον which occurs only here in LXX and designates something around the breast. The Hebrew is חשן normally rendered by λόγιον;[6] cf note at v.15 but also the discussion on ποδήρη at 25:7. Exod's unique reading serves to inform the reader where the λόγιον was to be worn.

---

3. As did Sym.
4. The Three have the expected σοφίας.
5. Aq Theod and Sym render the Hebrew by an infinitive; in fact, they use exactly the same translations as in v.1 for which see comment there.
6. Aq naturally corrects here to λόγιον.

446

b) τὴν ἐπωμίδα, the usual rendering for אפוד; cf vv.6--14 for its pattern.[7]

c) τὸν ποδήρη "a foot length robe" for מעיל as at 29:5. Cf the note at 25:6.

d) χιτῶνα κοσυμβωτόν "a tasseled cloak" for תשבץ כתנת. The word כתנת is well known and its Greek rendering χιτῶνα is probably derived from the Semitic word. It is modified by תשבץ which occurs only here but compare the related משבצות in v.11 and the participle of the root at v.20 and the Piel at v.39; it apparently means "chequered (in weave)." Exod's κοσυμβωτόν occurs only here.[8]

e) κίδαριν "turban" for מצנפת as at v.35 and 36:36, but the word is more commonly rendered in Exod by μίτρα, another word for some kind of headdress. Since κίδαρις also occurs for מגבעת (v.36 29:9) one suspects that Exod used either term without much distinction. It should be noted that at 36:36 the two words occur as separate items, but each is described as being ἐκ βύσσου.

f) ζώνην "girdle" for אבנט, which is always rendered by ζώνη in the Pentateuch. The b n text has ζωστηρα, a synonym of ζώνη.

In the concluding clause MT identifies Aaron as אחיך, which only hex recognized by τω αδελφω σου. The concluding phrase in MT is לכהנו לי, exactly the same as in vv.1 and 3, but Exod in each case has a somewhat different translation; here the infinitive is introduced by εἰς τό. Since the subject suffix of MT is not given in Exod hex has added αυτον after ἱερατεύειν.

28:5 The third plural subject αὐτοί continues the reference to "the wise in understanding" of v.3. They are to take over the gold and the fabrics necessary for their work; for these see the notes at 25:4. There is some uncertainty as to the order of the list of colored materials within the tradition; the C mss have κόκκινον before ὑάκινθον, whereas the oI text transposes "blue" and "purple." The list does not deviate from MT except for τὸ

7. Aq rendered it by ἐπένδυμα "upper garment."
8. The Three render by σφιγκτόν or the compound σύσφιγκτον "closely tied up together."

κόκκινον where MT has יִ הַשְׁנִ תּוֹלַעַת אֵת.[9] Hex has added κεκλωσμενον to represent the untranslated הַשְׁנִ י, but its source is not clear since The Three all had a different translation.

28:6(par 36:9,10b) Vv.6--14 describe in detail the construction of the ephod. Exod has considerably simplified the text of v.6 by limiting the materials for the ephod to ἐκ βύσσου κεκλωσμένης, omitting all reference to gold and the colored fabrics of MT. Hex has added χρυσιου και υακινθου και πορφυρας και κοκκινου νενησμενου και before βύσσου thereby equalling MT.

This is called ἔργον ὑφαντὸν ποικιλτοῦ "the woven work[10] of a pattern weaver."[11] -- As a translation for חֹשֵׁב "designer," ποικιλτοῦ occurs only here and in v.15. It is more commonly used to translate רֹקֵם, for which see note at 26:36.

28:7(par 36:11) The ephod must have two shoulder (straps) holding each other together, attached to the two sides. Exod has interpreted חֹבְרֹת by συνέχουσαι ἑτέρα τὴν ἑτέραν; the ἔσονται αὐτῷ which precedes it has been moved after the participle by a B + variant, which approximates the order of MT, but MT has no equivalent for ἑτέρα τὴν ἑτέραν which modifies the participle. An *f* tradition, possibly related to the B + variant, moved only the αὐτῷ after συνέχουσαι. This in turn may be related to a popular A F M reading adding an αυτω after the participle as a clarifying gloss.

Exod has tried to make sense out of the final וְחֻבָּר of MT by its rendering ἐξηρτημέναι from ἐξαρτάω "to attach" and then taking ἐπὶ τοῖς δυσὶν μέρεσιν as modifying it, i.e. connected at the two sides (or edges). Hex added αυτου to represent the suffix in MT's קְצוֹתָי ו. One might also note the very popular A B F M variant participle εξηρτισμεναι. The verb ἐξαρτίζω means "prepare, complete, finish," and is hardly appropriate here.

9. Aq translated this by σὺν σκώληκος τὸ διάφορον; Sym added τὸ δίβαφον and Theod, τὸ διάφορον. For these see the note at 25:4.
10. Cf SS 66.
11. Schl translates this somewhat more exactly by *variegator, qui versicolore ornatu vestes elaborat.*

448

Actually both verbs occur only here in the LXX but only the former can render חבר.

28:8(par 36:12) Exod interprets the bound phrase of MT חשב אפדתו as "the texture of the shoulder straps."[12] The Hebrew noun חשב refers to something well contrived, and Exod's ὕφασμα "texture or web" (also at 36:29) is not inappropriate to the context. What Exod is saying is that the web of the straps is to be of the same fabrication, κατὰ τὴν ποίησιν ἐξ αὐτοῦ (i.e. the same as the body of the ephod itself), viz. of gold and blue, etc.

The singular pronouns αὐτῷ and αὐτοῦ refer to the ἔργον of v.6, and ὅ, to ὕφασμα. MT also has a singular suffix in מעשהו referring to אפד of v.6; Exod does not translate this but hex has added αυτων which makes the fabrication refer to the ἐπωμίδων which is not overly sensible. -- For the materials used see notes at 25:4. The z text has glossed χρυσίου as "pure" gold, and the n s text has used κεκλωσμενου instead of διανενησμένου as a modifier for κοκκίνου; for this phenomenon also see the notes at 25:4.

28:9(par 36:13) Two stones of שהם are to be taken and on them the names of the sons of Israel are to be engraved. The שהם has been variously identified also in the Greek tradition. In Exod A the gem is mentioned three times and is differently rendered each time; cf the note at 25:6.[13]

A b n variant leaves λίθους unarticulated, whereas the majority A B F M text variant repeats λίθους, but this is almost certainly a dittograph with no support in MT. Another popular A M reading has επ for ἐν; this does come closer to על of MT, but it is unlikely to be original since the full phrase would be επ αυτοις. In Exod ἐπί occurs 317 times of which ten occur with indeclinables whose case cannot be determined. Of the remaining 307 the accusative occurs 177 times; the genitive, 111 times, but the dative only 19 times. It is thus almost certain that ἐν is here original text, and επ is either a correction or simply a scribal mistake.

12. Aq keeps the first noun of Exod but renders the second by τοῦ ἐπενδύματος αὐτοῦ, consistent with 28:4.
13. The Three rendered it by ὄνυχος though the Aq tradition is uncertain and may have had σαρδόνυχος.

The term τῶν υἱῶν 'Ἰσραήλ here means "sons of Israel" rather than "the Israelites." The reference is to the 12 sons as the next verse makes clear.

28:10 Exod has simplified the Hebrew by its ἓξ ὀνόματα and τὰ ἓξ ὀνόματα for שׁשׁה משׁמתם and שׁמות הששׁה resp.[14] The only hex change which Origen made was to add αυτων after the first ὀνόματα to represent the Hebrew suffix. The twelve names were to be ordered "according to their generations," i.e. from the eldest to the youngest, the six oldest on the one stone and the remaining six on the second one.

28:11(par 36:13) Again Exod has shortened and simplified the text of MT, this time by omitting all reference to the setting of the stones, and concentrating rather on the actual engraving to be done. The engraving to be done is doubly characterized as an ἔργον λιθουργικῆς τέχνης "work of a stonecutter's craft" and as a γλύμμα σφραγῖδος "engraving of a seal." In MT the former is called the work of a חרשׁ אבן and hex has transposed λιθουργικῆς τέχνης to approximate MT. The term λιθουργικῆς obviously refers to a worker in precious stones, not to a stone mason. The engraving of the names of the tribal fathers was to be done in the fashion of a seal engraving involving fine and careful workmanship.

Hex has added at the end of the verse περικεκυκλωμενους συνε-σφραγισμενους χρυσιω ποιησεις αυτους, i.e. "enclosed, sealed about with gold you shall make them" to make up for the absent second part of the verse in Exod.[15]

28:12(par 36:14) The two stones are to be placed on the shoulders of the ephod. Presumably the ὤμων of the ephod are the same as the δύο ἐπωμίδες of v.7, though the choice of the more literal rendering for כתפה here seems intentional since the stress is now on the placement of the memorial stones rather than on the construction of the ephod. It is

14. Cf SS 165.
15. Presumably this was taken from Theod, since Sym has συνεσφιγμένους "bound up" for the second participle, whereas Aq has for the two μετεστραμμένους ἐσφιγμένους "turned about, bound up," representing MT's מסבת משׁבצות in literalistic fashion.

important that these stones be fully visible, i.e. on the shoulders (i.e. the straps).

Exod continues to stress the memorial stones; these εἰσίν to the sons of Israel; there is no linking verb in MT, but there is a הנה in Sam, so its origin is probably textual. But Exod repeats "sons of Israel" in the next clause as well so as to identify the ὀνόματα, though MT simply has שמות. Exod also adds the phrase περὶ αὐτῶν after μνημόσυνον at the end of the verse - all these are added to emphasize the importance of the twelve names as central to the symbolism of the ephod. These names are to be carried by Aaron as he stands ἔναντι κυρίου in his priestly role as a memorial both to God as well as to the priesthood of the tribes of Israel.

The n + reading of αυτων for τῶν υἱῶν 'Ἰσραήλ may show recensional activity, since it equals MT exactly.

28:13(par 36:23a) The term משבצת presented difficulties of interpretation for Exod since it has something to do with settings for stones which he had omitted in v.11. The word apparently refers to chequered work here made with gold thread. Exod A throughout (vv.13,14,25) has substituted ἀσκιδί-σκας "bosses, small shields" which are meant for ornamental purposes on the ephod. In B the term ἀσπιδίσκας is twice taken over from the par A text (36:23,26), whereas at 36:13 it has an independent translation περισεσιαλωμένους; cf note at 36:13.[16] -- Over against MT Exod has these made of "pure" gold, where MT simply has "gold."

28:14 Further ornamentation of the ephod, particularly with respect to the ἀσπιδίσκας. Moses is told to make two κροσσωτά out of pure gold. The term means something that is fringed or tasselled. The Hebrew has שרשרת "chains," which occurs only four times in Exodus but is always rendered by κροσσωτά (or κροσσούς); cf v.22 and 36:22).[17] Since these are the work of a πλοκῆς, "a braiding," one might think of these κροσσωτά as braided fringes. In composition they were καταμεμιγμένα ἐν ἄνθεσιν "intermixed with flowers" for which there is no counterpart; in its place MT has מגבלת

16. Aq has rendered the word here by σφιγκτῆρας "bands."
17. Aq translated the word by ἀλύσεις, Theod, by χαλαστά, both words meaning "chains" often used as ornaments.

(מעשה אבת) . This noun is usually translated as "cords" which is sensible contextually but could be wrong. Tar have מתחמן from חתם, probably understanding it as "bordered," as related to גבול "border." Pesh interprets it as "twinned, doubled" from the root תאם. The Hebrew word is a hapax legomenon, and there is no certainty as to its meaning.[18]

MT speaks of the chains as being מעשה עבת "corded work." But Exod rendered the second word as an abstract noun πλοκή "a braiding."[19]

The second clause deals with the placement of the κροσσωτά, which in the following section will be seen to be of use for the λόγιον as well. These "braided fringes" are to be placed on the ἀσπιδίσκας; for ἀσπιδίσκας see the note at v.13.[20] Possibly on the basis of v.25b in MT, Exod added κατὰ τὰς παρωμίδας αὐτῶν ἐκ τῶν ἐμπροσθίων "on the shoulder bands on the front sides," which makes definite precisely where these braided fringes are to be placed.

28:15(par 36:15) The most important part of the ephod was the λόγιον, the construction, attachment and use of which is described in vv.15--26. For other notes on חשן see v.4 and 25:6. The חשן is usually translated by λόγιον "oracle" since it contained τὴν δήλωσιν and τὴν ἀλήθειαν used by the priest to obtain a decision from God, hence an "oracle." In fact, the λόγιον is called an oracle τῶν κρίσεων "of judgments, legal decisions," showing the priestly use of the λόγιον; it was a square piece of cloth with a pouch to contain the means for making legal decisions; cf also the note at v.23. A popular M variant has λογειον, an itacistic spelling which really means "a speaking-place," and can hardly have been intended. Its construction was the work of a pattern weaver, for which see the note at v.6, and it is to be made according to the manner of the ephod. ῥυθμόν is an unusual but apt translation for מעשה; it is wrongly taken as a neuter by the *f* text.

The oracle is to be made of the same fabrics as was the ephod in v.8 except that κοκκίνου is modified by κεκλωσμένου though a number of scattered mss support the M variant νενησμενου.

18. According to Syh Theod translated it by συμπεπλεγμένα (ποιήσεις αὐτά), which does seem to support the common understanding of the word.
19. Sym translated this by βροχωτόν "twisted, corded."
20. Aq again has σφιγκτῆρας, whereas Sym used σύσφιγκτα "laced, tied tightly."

452

28:16(par 36:16) The oracle is to be square and doubled, thereby making a pouch. In size it was to be a span squared (22.5 x 22.5 cm; 9 x 9 in.). The words for length and width have suffixes in MT, which only hex supplied as αυτου.

28:17(par 36:17) MT speaks of making a setting ("a filling in") for the stones, while Exod in view of the fabric constituents of the oracle with fine sense has "a texture interwoven"; this ὕφασμα is described by two words in apposition, κατάλιθον "setting for stones,"[21] and τετράστιχον "four rowed," thus a "four rowed composition for holding stones."[22] In MT this is followed by אבן and then to introduce the first three stones by טור. Sam omits אבן, whereas Tar by their ראבן tie it to "four rows (of stone)." Furthermore they interpret טור as "the first row," (but not neglecting "row one" at the end). Exod interprets אבן טור as στίχοι λίθων ἔσται "a row of stones shall be," thereby making good sense out of a rather odd Hebrew text. The hex text has transposed στίχος λίθων so as to conform to the word order of MT.

28:17b--20a(par 36:17b--20a) Four rows of stones are given. In MT all four are presented in the pattern: a b + c, whereas in Exod the first row is completely asyndetic, i.e. a b c, and the others are all joined, i.e. a + b + c. Exod B has all four in the pattern: a + b + c.

The four rows are a) σάρδιον "carnelian," τοπάζιον "topaz" and σμάραγδος "emerald"; b) ἄνθραξ "carbuncle," σάπφειρος "sapphire" and ἴασπις "jasper"; c) λιγύριον "ligure, jacinth," ἀχάτης "agate" and ἀμέθυστος "amethyst," and d) χρυσόλιθος "chrysolite," βηρύλλιον "beryl," and ὀνύχιον "onyx." Admittedly the English equivalents are only approximations. Only two variant spellings received solid support in the tradition: λιγύριον became λιγυρις in the C text, and a C b z + variant misspelled "amethyst" as αμεθυσος. This list of twelve stones was taken over by the translator of Ezek 28:13 in the lamentation for the Tyrian king in complete disregard for

21. Schl has *gemma obsita*.
22. The late revisers translate the first part of the verse literally: καὶ πληρώσεις ἐν αὐτῷ πληρώματα λίθων τεσσάρων ταγμάτων.

his Hebrew text, the only difference between the Greek list of Ezek and of Exod being the insertion of gold and silver in the middle of the Ezek list.

As to the relation between MT and Exod much uncertainty must remain since in many cases the modern equivalent to the Hebrew stone is enigmatic.

a) אדם is a red stone, and both carnelian and ruby have been suggested. The Sardian stone is a good possibility. -- τοπάζιον stands for פטדה a yellow stone of some kind. -- The third stone is ברקת and occurs only here and in par; it is probably a green stone, and KB suggests a dark green beryl. That it was green is supported by Exod's σμάραγδος.[23]

b) נפך is uncertain. Tar[O] translates by "smaragd," thus a green stone, but Exod's ἄνθραξ would suggest a reddish hue. -- ספיר is probably lapus lazuli, in any event a blue stone, which Exod transliterates by σάπφειρος. -- יהלם has no certain identification. Exod called it ἴασπις which is no whit clearer.

c) All three names on the third row, לשם, שבו and אחמלה are obscure, though Exod's λιγύριον, ἀχάτης and ἀμέθυστος are all identified.

d) Chrysolite renders another unknown Hebrew word, תרשיש. -- For שהם see the discussion at 25:6. -- The last stone is ישפה, for which compare Akk. šadi ašpee i.e. "jasper mountain," a designation of a mountain near Lake Van. In Akkadian times it was a highly precious stone, even called a royal stone. From it, probably through Phoenician, the Greek ἴασπις is derived. Here, however, it is translated by ὀνύχιον "onyx." Vulg substantiates the list of Exod entirely except for transposing the last two: *onychinus et beryllus*.

In general, it must be said that one knows very little about these gems, and that throughout the Greek is more readily understandable than is the Hebrew, but that clear distinctions among the stones can not be made.

28:20b(par 36:20b) MT describes these gems as "with a plaited mounting shall they be with gold in their settings." Exod apparently had a text close to the B account where משבצות is preceded by מוסבת "surrounded by." Exod has two participles each modified by (ἐν) χρυσίῳ: "covered about with gold"

23. Sym etymologizes with κεραύνιος but what a "thunderbolt stone" could be is not clear to me.

and "bound up together in gold." In par מוסבת is translated by περι-κεκυκλωμένα "surrounded by," a literal rendering of the Hebrew. Sam has the extra participle here as well and it seems likely that it represents Exod's parent text. The Byzantine text has altered it to περικεκλωσμενα, which is probably the result of the frequent appearance of the participial stem κε-κλωσμεν-, e.g. v.15 above. The majority A F M text has joined the two phrases with και, thereby coordinating the doublets; in Exod the phrases can be understood as in apposition. These participles modify ἔστωσαν, thus making periphrastic verbal constructions. The verb is also modified by the prepositional phrase "according to their row" which has no basis in MT's במלואתם. Exod's text is probably meant to make συνδεδεμένα ... ἔστωσαν intelligent; they (i.e. the stones) must be tied up together not as twelve stones but according to their row, i.e. in sets of three. The C text has added ονοματα after ἔστωσαν so as to make this clear.

28:21(par 36:21) As in the case of the memorial stones of the ephod in vv. 9--12, the stones symbolize the names of the twelve tribes. Both clauses in the verse are put in the third person imperative which interrupts the sequence of ποιήσεις constructions. Somewhat ambiguous is the syntax of the first clause. Does δώδεκα modify ὀνομάτων or ἔστωσαν? Since the clause ends with a κατά phrase which is somewhat repetitive it would seem preferable to take the ἐκ phrase as adjectival and δώδεκα and the κατά phrase as both modifying the verb. -- The tradition has been influenced by κατὰ τὰς γενέσεις αὐτῶν of v.10 in connection with the κατά phrase here, an A b text prefixing, an f text substituting, and the z text adding it to the phrase.

The second clause begins with γλυφαὶ σφραγίδων as predicate nominative after ἔστωσαν, i.e. "let them be engraved like seals each one according to name." The majority text has the genitive for ἕκαστος, probably by attraction to σφραγίδων which immediately precedes it; this would mean: "let the engravings like seals be for each ...," but the Hebraistic ἕκαστος (κατὰ τὸ ὄνομα) is original. A b n s reading has simplified the construction by its γλυφαις, a dative of means "with engravings." An f n x reading has τὸ ὄνομα in the plural probably because γλυφαί is plural, but the singular agrees with ἕκαστος. MT has a suffix and hex has added αυτου to represent it. With the final phrase it becomes clear that the twelve names are the tribal names, not the names of the sons of Israel/Jacob. It might be noted that the B text not only changed δώδεκα to δεκα δυο[24] but also omitted the article, but the article is demanded by the context; in fact, nouns governed by εἰς are usually articulated in Exod.[25]

28:22(par 36:22) Moses is told to make κροσσοὺς συμπεπλεγμένους "plaited fringes" which must be a reference to τὰ κροσσωτὰ τὰ πεπλεγμένα of v.14. The Hebrew has שרשת גבלת as compared with שרשרת and מגבלת of v.14. (Sam has שרשרות גבלות which makes the relationship even more obvious.) Cf the comments at v.14.[26] Exod further defines these as an ἔργον ἁλυσιδωτόν. The change is intentional; since Exod does not intend to include all the intricate details of how precisely the oracle bag was to be attached and fitted on to the ephod, he simply notes that these braided fringes are really a chain-like construction, and the inference that these are to serve usefully for securing the λόγιον though not actually stated can and should be made. For the popular M λογειον see note at v.15. The omission of ἐκ by the popular A F M text is probably secondary since throughout this chapter "made of gold" always has ἐκ before χρυσίου.

[28:23--28] The Hebrew text of vv.23--28 are only summarily dealt with by Exod in vv.24--25, whereas v.23 is a rendering of v.29. When Origen prepared the hex he found no counterpart for vv.23--28 and in accordance with his principles added a translation from one of The Three, viz. Theod. This represents a literal rendering of the Hebrew text[27]. It must be emphasized that this section is not Exod.

When Origen came to vv.24--25 he considered these verses as having no counterpart in the Hebrew and accordingly placed them under the

24. For this see Thack 187f.
25. For a discussion of this see THGE VII.D.
26. Aq and Sym translate שרשת here by ἁλύσεις "chains," and Theod apparently by χαλαστά as at v.14; in other words The Three made no distinction between the שרשרת of v.14 and שרשת here, probably rightly.
27. For readings of Aq and Sym see Apparatus II of the Göttingen edition.

456

obelus.

28:23(29) In v.21 stress had been placed on the twelve stones having the names of the twelve tribal heads on them. Here the reason for it is made clear. Aaron must carry these whenever he performs his priestly duties in the sanctuary. The verse has an obvious analogue to vv.9--12; after all, the λόγιον is part of the ephod; both have twelve stones, both serve as memorials for which see comments at v.12.

Over against v.15 the oracle is called τῆς κρίσεως, i.e. singular rather than plural. There the plural was used since the λόγιον was introduced and its general use for obtaining divine decisions, or judgments, served to define it carefully. Thereafter the singular serves (see also v.26) to indicate judgment in general -- For the variant λογειον see v.15.-- The λόγιον is worn ἐπὶ τοῦ στήθους, i.e. over the ephod on the breast. MT has a suffix and hex added αυτου to indicate it.[28]

The condition for Aaron's taking "the names ... on the breast" is introduced by a dative present participle εἰσιόντι, not the nominative of the popular Byzantine text, εισιων, because the condition modifies the clause rather than ' Ααρών, and means "whenever he enters..."; it is a dative of relation.[29]

Over against v.12 the appearance in the sanctuary is called "before God" rather than "before the Lord," though in both cases MT has לפני יהוה. In v.26 he reverts to "before the Lord." Apparently the distinction was not important to the translator. More significant is the failure to render תמיד at the end of the verse. This could be confusing in the immediate context. If one added δια παντος, as hex did, it might not be understood; a reader could be misled to apply it to εἰσιόντι which would be confusing indeed. Of course, it was to be understood adverbially as modifying the entire verse, but this was difficult to make clear, and omitting it may have seemed the simpler course. -- Hex also added αυτω after εἰσιόντι to represent the Hebrew suffix.[30]

---

28. Aq renders לבו literally by καρδίας αὐτοῦ.
29. Aq rendered בבאו literally by ἐν τῷ εἰσέρχεσθαι αὐτόν.
30. For εναντιον for Exod's ἔναντι see THGE VII.L.3.

28:24--25(24--28) Actually the statement is only vaguely related to vv.24--28 in MT which give a detailed statement on how the λόγιον was to be attached to and positioned on the ephod. Exod only insists on three matters all dealing with placement: a) θήσεις "the κροσσούς on the oracle pouch." These are the ones which v.22 had ordered made, and must be the same as the κροσσωτά of the ephod. b) ἐπιθήσεις "the τὰ ἀλυσιδωτά on both sides of the λόγιον," and c) ἐπιθήσεις the "two little shields on both shoulder bands of the ephod on the front side." From v.22 it is clear that the ἀλυσιδωτά are, if not identical with, at least part of (extensions of) the κρόσσους. The picture which one obtains, though somewhat vague, is one in which the small shields on the front shoulder bands holding up the ephod have attached to them plaited fringes which extend downwards on the side of the ephod but are tied somehow to the sides of the oracle pouch loosely holding it in place on the chest of the priest. Exod here shows no more interest in the details of how to tie on the λόγιον than he did in the fabric settings of the two inscribed memorial stones of the ephod; cf comment on v.11. Similarly he omitted unessential details from the statement on the construction materials of the ephod; cf note on v.6.

At first glance it seems odd that Exod should insert v.23 between vv.22 and 24--25; after all, vv.22,24--25 all deal with the κρόσσους and their relations to the oracle pouch, whereas v.23 deals with the names of the tribes on the pouch. But stylistically vv.24--25 belong with v.26 which is also an ἐπιθήσεις clause. Stylistically Exod has varied the three clauses of vv.24--25 according to three different patterns: a) verb + prepositional phrase + verbal object; b) object + prepositional phrase + verb, and c) object + verb + prepositional phrase. With the first clause of v.26 he reverts to the first pattern.

28:26(30) The verse consists of three statements of which the first is peculiarly difficult to interpret. MT orders the placement of τὴν δήλωσιν and τὴν ἀλήθειαν on (or "in") the λόγιον of judgment. These terms are used by Exod to render הָאוּרִים and הַתֻּמִּים. Whatever may be visualized by the Urim and the Thummim, it is clear that they were used to obtain oracles, or divine decisions, i.e. the κρίσεις of the Israelites could be decided through the priestly carrying of these "before the Lord," i.e. into the sanctuary. This is also apparent from the third statement that Aaron was to carry "the κρίσεις (cases in dispute?) of the Israelites on (his) breast before the Lord continually." But what did the Alexandrian mean by these two terms? Apparently they were thought to be priestly means of settling cases, i.e. a δήλωσις would be "a means of making clear" a judgment, whereas an ἀλήθεια would be "a means of arriving at a true decision"; how this could be done is not stated, and it probably was no clearer to Exod that it is to us.[31]

The second clause has a singular verb ἔσται. This differs from MT which has the verb in the plural, i.e. δήλωσις καὶ ἀλήθεια are to be on Aaron's breast, rather than the λόγιον containing them. MT also lacks an equivalent for εἰς τὸ ἅγιον which is really quite unnecessary since the following ἔναντι κυρίου means the same thing. The term translated "breast" is לב as in v.23.[32] Hex has added an αυτου to conform to MT.

The last clause puts all of this in the proper context; Aaron is to carry the Israelites' κρίσεις continually on (his) breast before the Lord. Aaron is to be the priestly mediator between the Israelite and the Lord on the interpretation of the law, in legal cases of dispute which need divine light and guidance. Here at the end of the description of the λόγιον משפט is again as at the beginning (v.15) rendered by the plural, whereas in the intervening section the λόγιον is described by τῆς κρίσεως. -- For the spelling λογειον see note at v.15.[33]-- In the last clause Exod used the simplex verb οἴσει for נשא, rather than the compound εισοισει of the O text, or the z variant θησει, neither of which would adequately render MT.

28:27(31; par 36:30) A blue ποδήρη, or robe extending to the feet, is to be made as ὑποδύτην, i.e. something worn underneath the ephod and the oracle pouch. In MT this is called "the robe of the ephod," which Exod describes somewhat more specifically, though not incorrectly. In Exod B the same phrase is rendered by "the undergarment under the ephod" which was

31. The later revisers translated the terms as τοὺς φωτισμούς and τὰς τελειότητας, i.e. "lights and perfections."
32. Aq naturally substitutes καρδίου for στήθους.
33. For εναντιον instead of ἔναντι see THGE VII.L.3.

probably influenced by Exod A.[34]

28:28(32; par 36:31) MT has literally for the first clause: "and there shall be the mouth of its head in its middle," i.e. there is to be an opening for the head within it. Exod calls the פי a περιστόμιον "collar," which is modified by ἐξ αὐτοῦ. This is amplified by hex as της αρχης αυτου.[35] Exod simply has μέσον as an adverb of place modifying ἔσται for בתוכו.[36] Hex added αυτου to conform to the suffix in the Hebrew.

MT continues with a verbal clause which Exod renders by a participial phrase "having a hem around the collar."[37] Hex not only adds an αυτου but also places κύκλῳ at the end making it equal MT:s לפיו סביב more exactly.

A second יהיה clause in MT is obscure since it says literally: "like the mouth of תחרא there shall be to it." Tar interpret the word as "coat of armor"; Vulg has the neutral *vestium,* which RSV follows, whereas ZürB follows Tar. Exod has taken its cue from the ἵνα clause at the end, and has τὴν συμβολὴν συνυφασμένην ἐξ αὐτοῦ "with the binding interwoven with it," i.e. the hem has been interwoven with the garment itself so that it will not easily rip. The z text has συμπλοκην "interweaving" for συμβολήν which is somewhat tautologous.[38]

28:29(33; par 36:32--33) This verse and the following describe the various ornamentations on the border or skirt of the ὑποδύτου. MT twice refers to שוליו "its borders, edges" but Exod persists in realizing the suffix by τοῦ ὑποδύτου, throughout insisting on the subordinate relation of the מעיל to the ephod.[39]

MT has as object of the verb "you shall make" רמני "pomegranates"; these are of course fake pomegranates, and Exod makes this clear by its ὡς

34. Aq renders the phrase more literally by ἔνδυμα τοῦ ἐπενδύματος "garment of the upper garment."
35. As in Sym; Aq had τῆς κεφάλης αὐτοῦ.
36. This is rendered literally by The Three by ἐν μέσω αὐτοῦ.
37. The unusual ἔχον occurs only here in Exod; see SS 182.
38. Aq has προσπλοκήν "tightly braided," whereas Sym has σειρωτόν "bound."
39. Instead of λῶμα "skirt, border" Aq has ἀπόληγμα which means the same thing; Sym has (τὰ) πρὸς ποδῶν, for which see Isa 6:1.

ἐξανθούσης ῥόας ῥοΐσκους "knobs as of a flowering pomegranate"; these are to be made of blue and purple and scarlet yarn[40] as well as βύσσου κεκλωσμένης, attested only by Sam elsewhere. These colorful knobs or tassels are to be put on the skirt τοῦ ὑποδύτου κύκλῳ which an *n s* variant reorders to read "around the underrobe."

Further objects of the verb are ῥοΐσκους χρυσοῦς and κώδωνας. Exod differs from MT in having two kinds of "knobs," the one made of variegated thread and the other, also golden, which takes "the same shape"; and between these are bells round about. MT says nothing about "golden knobs of the same shape"; further it has the bells "of gold," about which Exod A in contrast to B has nothing. Hex has at least transferred χρυσοῦς after κώδωνας so that in its reading it is the bells not the knobs that are golden.

28:30(34; par 36:34a) Exod continues with the three objects: "beside a golden knob, a bell and an ἄνθινον which refers back to the knobs described as ὡσεὶ ἐξανθίσης ῥόας, i.e. to knobs made of variegated yarn. What is apparently meant is that round about on the skirt of the underrobe these three types appear in succession throughout: golden knob, bell, flower-like knob. The Hebrew has only the two: "golden bell and pomegranate," but it also indicates that they are to appear alternately by repeating the phrase.[41] An F Byzantine text has και added before κώδωνον; probably a "both ... and" construction was intended by the variant text, but it is quite unnecessary.

28:31(35; par 36:34b) The purpose of the bells is here given. When Aaron is performing his cultic duties, ἐν τῷ λειτουργεῖν, the noise of him shall be heard, i.e. the bells will tinkle. Ἀαρών must be in the dative because the participial modifiers εἰσιόντι and ἐξιόντι are dative. Hex has placed an επι before "Aaron" to show the על of MT. The dative participles render the pattern: preposition ‫ב‬ + bound infinitive, which is a relatively rare rendering in Exod,[42] but the more usual rendering: ἐν + infinitive had already been used to render ‫לשרת‬. Both participles have αυτω added by hex to

40. Instead of διανενησμένου Aq has διάφορον, and Sym, δίβαφον, for which see 25:4; according to Syh Theod had still another rendering, ἀλλοιουμένου, for which compare 35:23,35.
41. Instead of ἄνθινον the Later Revisers have ῥόαν for the Hebrew ‫רמון‬.
42. See SS Inf 91 where the references are given.

represent the suffixes of MT. The *C* tradition has the senseless variant λογιον for ἄγιον, palaeographically inspired by the similarity of the letters A and Λ in the uncial script.[43]

The verse ends with ἵνα μὴ ἀποθάνῃ, which simply translates what MT says, but why Aaron should die if the sound of him (by means of the bells) as he enters and leaves the sanctuary is not heard is puzzling. Presumably some ancient taboo is involved.

28:32(36; par 36:38--39) Vv.32--34 deal with the construction, placing and purpose of a thin plate of pure gold inscribed with the words "holiness of the Lord." The inscription is to be made in the relief work of a seal according to Exod. MT made no distinction between the engraving of stones in v.9 and of the gold plate here using the verb פתח for both, whereas Exod used γλύψεις "engrave" in v.9 and ἐκτυπώσεις "work in relief" here, but the two processes are quite different, and the translator carefully distinguishes them. Note also the use of γλύμμα σφραγῖδες at v.11, γλυφαὶ σφραγίδων in v.21, but ἐκτύπωμα σφραγίδος here. The *b x* text has the simplex for ἐκτυπώσεις but this does not alter the meaning. More significant is a popular *O* variant which changes κυρίου to the dative which more accurately reflects MT's ליהוה; this could thus represent an early, prehexaplaric revision towards the Hebrew.

28:33(37; par 36:40) Its placement. It is to be put on (presumably "attached to") a blue spun (cord?). The word for "spun cord" is simply κεκλωσμένης, the word regularly used with κόκκινον; cf note at 25:4, but here it translates פתיל "thread" as that "made by spinning or twisting." The cord with the plate was to be ἐπὶ τῆς μίτρας. The par presents a much clearer picture; the פתיל is rendered by λῶμα; this blue edging is put on the plate ὥστε ἐπικεῖσθαι ἐπὶ τὴν μίτραν ἄνωθεν "so as to be placed on the headband above." Oddly in *C* ἐπιθήσεις ... ἐπί is altered to υποθησεις ... υπο which would have the plate and its cord underneath the headband.

The final detail orders the plate to be κατὰ πρόσωπον τῆς μίτρας, i.e.

43. For the B + variant εναντιον for ἔναντι see THGE VII.L.3.

462

on the front side of the turban.[44]

28:34(38) The reason for its placement on Aaron's forehead (i.e. the front side of the turban, v.33). Aaron "will carry off the sins of the holy things which the Israelites might dedicate." What this appears to mean is that any faults connected with the presentation of offerings will be taken up and away, i.e. removed through the high priest bearing the inscription "Holiness to the Lord" on his forehead. The high priest, himself ritually pure, will be able through his holiness to present offerings to the Lord on behalf of the people who may themselves not be ritually pure. Thus offerings, τῶν ἁγίων, are defined as παντὸς δόματος τῶν ἁγίων αὐτῶν, "any gift among their holy things."

The inscribed plate is to remain on Aaron's forehead continually; MT has "his forehead" but Exod uses the proper noun throughout the verse by which no mistake can be made - it must be the high priest alone who can in this way represent the people before the Lord. In fact, this role is actually defined as δεκτὸν αὐτοῖς "to make them acceptable." Theoretically either ἁγίων "holy things," i.e. the sacrificial gifts, or υἱοὶ ᾽Ισραήλ could be the referent of αὐτοῖς, but the context suggests that it is the former which is meant.

28:35--36(39-40; par 36:35--37) V.35 begins with a statement that οἱ κόσυμβοι of the cloaks are to be of linen,[45] whereas MT has the verb שבצת "you shall weave in chequered design." Exod not only took the word as a noun, but also understood it differently; cf the discussion at v.4.[46] The *s* text adds κεκλωσμενης after βύσσου under the influence of the oft-recurring phrase.

Also to be made of linen is the turban but of the girdle it is only said that it is ἔργον ποικίλτου. For ποικίλτου as a translation of רקם cf note at 26:36.

44. Aq and Theod do not use μίτρας in this verse (for מצנפת) but κιδάρεως, though the words seem to be synonymous; in this chapter Aq uses μίτρας for מגבעות and κιδάρεως for מצנפת; cf v.36.
45. Cf SS 63.
46. Aq translates the clause by καὶ συσφίγξεις τὸν χιτῶνα τοῦ βύσσου "and you shall bind up closely the cloak with linen." According to Syh Theod

28:36(40) This verse introduces the provision of garments for the sons of Aaron, which in A in contrast to Exod B is quite distinct from the preceding verse. Three pieces of clothing are to be provided: cloaks, girdles and turbans. In MT each is separately ordered, i.e. with "you shall make for ..." but Exod abbreviates by omitting this for the second one; hex prefixes ζώνας by ποιήσεις αυτοις to equal MT.

The third item, κιδάρεις, translates מגבעות, a word which occurs only four times, 28:40 29:9 39:28 and Lev 8:13. At 39:28 it contrasts with מצנפת and Exod (36:36) has κιδάρεις for it and used τὴν μίτραν for פאר המגבעת. The other three cases all have κιδάρεις.[47] -- For the expression "for honor and glory" see note at v.2.

28:37(41; par 40:11--13) The verse renders MT literally except for the word order αὐτῶν τὰς χεῖρας which hex changes by placing the pronoun at the end so as to equal MT, and the rendering of the final clause as a ἵνα clause rather than by και. The interpretation as a purpose clause is quite correct, however, as the change of subject from second masculine singular to third plural in the Hebrew shows.

The literalism of the translation extends to the rendering of the Hebrew idiom מלאת את ידם by ἐμπλήσεις αὐτῶν τὰς χεῖρας; in ch.29 (vv.9,29,33, 35) the verb τελειόω is used for this expression, i.e. "to validate their hands" rather than "fill up their hands" in the sense of "ordain to of fice." In any event the Greek is a Hebraism.[48] -- B + have the present rather than the aorist subjunctive after ἵνα. Both make sense but the majority reading is original.[49]

28:38(42) Exod continues to use the future ποιήσεις even though MT has changed to the imperative for the final item of priestly dress, the linen drawers. The purpose of the drawers is to cover ἀσχημοσυνὴν χρωτὸς αὐτῶν; for the demand for priestly avoidance of exposure of their privy parts see note at 20:26. The Hebrew has the nouns in reverse order: בשר

rendered בתנה in the plural over against Aq.
47. Aq and Sym have μίτρας instead of κιδάρεις, whereas Theod had ὑψώματα, an etymological rendering based on the word גבע "hill, height."
48. According to Syh Theod also had τελειώσεις here, whereas Aq and Sym attest to πληρώσεις (vid).

ערוה; hex has placed ἀσχημοσυνήν at the end, and αὐτῶν under the obelus to show that it had no Hebrew equivalent.

In the second clause the extent of minimum coverage is defined as from ὀσφύος up to the thighs. The noun rendered by ὀσφύος is always dual in Hebrew but is commonly singular in LXX; in fact only ten cases of the plural are attested in HR, and that usually in the sense of "upon the loins" or "girding the loins." Both nouns, ὀσφύος and μηρῶν are unarticulated; the Byzantine text articulates the latter, though not the former.

28:39(43) Exod correctly interprets "they shall be upon Aaron" of MT as ἕξει Ἀαρὼν αὐτά "Aaron shall wear them (i.e. the drawers)." For ὅταν + subjunctive as a translation for ב + infinitive + pronominal suffix see note at 11:1. They are to be worn "whenever they enter the tent of testimony," for which term see note at 27:21, "or whenever they approach to minister πρὸς τὸ θυσιαστήριον τοῦ ἁγίου, i.e. the altar which was described in 27:1--8. MT differs in that the infinitive which follows "altar" is marked, and for τοῦ ἁγίου MT has בקדש, i.e. it modifies לשרת and not המזבח. Ms 376 which probably represents hex here has προς το θυσιαστηριον του λειτουργειν εν τω αγιω which reproduces MT exactly.-- ὅταν 1° is original rather than ως αν (or εως αν) of the B O s text.[50] -- For ἤ an M s text has και, but the *oI* C text has the doublet η και, and a B z reading omits the conjunction altogether. -- And the *d* text has a προ- rather than a προσ- compound for προσπορεύωνται, i.e. "go before" rather than "approach"; this is an error of haplography since *omicron* and *sigma* are very similar in the uncial script.

The following clause together with the ἵνα clause makes the necessity for priests wearing drawers religiously significant. "They shall not bring on themselves sin lest they die."[51] Exposure of one's privy parts by definition brings sin on oneself, a sin which would result in death. Exod not only uses the middle voice, ἐπάξεται, but adds πρὸς ἑαυτούς for emphasis. Instead of πρός most texts have εφ or επ which is probably due to the influence of the compound ἐπάξεται which it modifies.[52]

---

49. This is argued in THGE VII.M.5.
50. As is clear from THGE VII.Q.
51. Cf Helbing 276.
52. For πρός as original text see THGE VII.L.3.

The concluding statement is not a subject-predicate clause, but simply states "an eternal statute for him and his seed after him," as though it were a subscription. The Byzantine group has also changed the case of αὐτόν to the genitive, i.e. "with him" instead of "after him," probably due to the influence of v.37.

466

Chapter 29

29:1--37 The text of vv.1--37 is often similar to that of Lev 8, and mutual influence in these texts is a possibility to bear in mind at all times. As far as Exod is concerned it is earlier than the LXX of Lev but for the text history influence has gone in both directions.

29:1--2 MT's opening words are in the singular אשר הדבר זה ו, but Exod, since it introduces a set of instructions in connection with the consecration of priests uses the plural omitting the noun entirely: ταῦτά ἐστιν ἅ. MT follows with two marked infinitives, the second subordinate to the first. Exod also has two infinitives but introduces the second by ὥστε thereby ensuring the relationship between the two. Both are accompanied by αὐτούς but the first pronoun is the object of the purposive infinitive whereas the second serves as subject of the infinitive ἱερατεύειν. Note also that ἁγιάσαι is aorist since the consecration is a once for all ceremony, whereas ἱερατεύειν is present, the serving as priest being a continual service. The ὥστε construction shows result flowing from the ἁγιάσαι.[1] The B z text under the influence of the frequent use of the second singular future in the context has αγιασεις, but only a purposive infinitive ἁγιάσαι is correct.

The preparations are to begin by taking one bull calf from the herd and two unblemished rams, and unleavened bread (loaves) and cakes. For the first two items Exod puts the numbers at the end of the nominal, whereas MT has them in the middle. Hex changes the word order accordingly to fit MT.[2]

V.2 lists the cereal objects of λήμψῃ. The first of these, ἄρτους ἀζύμους, has a doublet in MT, מצת וחלת מצות לחם; "breads" and "loaves" represent the same thing. Origen added καὶ κολλυρας πεφυραμενους to

1. Since MT has a marked infinitive Aq and Theod render it by εἰς τὸ ἁγιάσαι, whereas Sym apparently had ὥστε ἁγιάσαι.
2. For the latter see also the discussion in THGE VII.F.2.

represent the missing phrase. These are then described as πεφυραμένους[3] ἐν ἐλαίῳ "mixed, kneaded in oil."[4]

The next item is "unleavened cakes anointed with oil." These are to be made from fine wheat flour. The word for "these" is αὐτά and might refer specifically to the cakes, λάγανα, but the pronoun is neuter by attraction to the gender of the nearer referent and applies to ἄρτους as well.

29:3 That αὐτά refers not just to λάγανα but to ἄρτους as well is clear from the instructions to put them in a single basket and bring them in the basket along with the bull calf and the two rams. ἐπί is used once with the accusative and once with the dative, since in the first case the phrase modifies a transitive "put into," whereas in the second case the dative is used since the phrase is locative. The first case undergoes partial change to the genitive in A *d z*, i.e. as επι κανου εν, with ἐν left unchanged.

29:4 The verbal objects, "Aaron and his sons," are preposed for emphasis' sake. For the doors of "the tent of meeting" see note at 27:21. The Hebrew פתח occurs only in the singular in Exodus, but when applied to the tent of meeting Exod A always uses the plural. At 33:10 such "doors" are contrasted with the "door" of an Israelite's tent.[5] By contrast Exod B has the singular at 37:5 39:8 and 40:5, but the plural at 38:26 40:6,10,26.

An *n* + variant has added δυο before υἱούς, an obvious attempt to exclude Nadab and Abihu who were killed for offering unholy fire before the Lord (Lev 10:1--2 Num 26:61). -- The C text has θυσιας instead of θύρας, the result of reading a cursive text; the mistake was made easier since the context does deal with sacrifices.

The second clause orders Moses to wash them with water.[6] This is to be distinguished from the washing demanded at 30:19--21 where the priests were to wash hands and feet in the water of the laver before entering the

---

3. Aq has for the participle ἀναμεμιγμένους "mixed up," whereas Theod has ἀναπεποιημένους "made up"; Sym has the Theod reading but in the feminine modifying his translation of חלת (probably κολλύρας).
4. See SS 123 and Helbing 146.
5. See note in THGE VII.H.2.
6. Cf SS 118.

sanctuary. Here the priests are washed - presumably their entire body - by Moses as first step in the ceremony of ordination to the priesthood.

29:5 Exod uses a subordinating participle to render the first clause rather than the parataxis of MT; the emphasis is rightly placed on the robing of Aaron only, not including his sons; in fact, Exod by added τὸν ἀδελφόν σου, against MT, seems to stress this. The elements of the dress are listed as καὶ τὸν χιτῶνα τὸν ποδήρη καὶ τὴν ἐπωμίδα καὶ τὸ λόγιον. MT does not have a conjunction at the beginning, but has ראת מעיל האפד instead of τὸν ποδήρη thereby making it clear that there are four garments. Exod can be understood as though τὸν χιτῶνα is explicated by τὸν ποδήρη in apposition, thereby making only three pieces.[7]

The last clause in MT is ואפדת לו בחשב האפד "and you shall "ephod" him (i.e. tie on the ephod) with the finely wrought band of the ephod." Exod makes the verb apply to the nearest noun, חשן, and renders "and you shall tie up for him the oracle pouch to the ephod"; see also the note at 28:24--25, for which this statement may be taken as a summary order. For the spelling λογειον see note at 28:15.

29:6 The placement of the headgear: the headband on his head and τὸ πέταλον τὸ ἁγίασμα on the headband. MT calls this נזר הקדש "a holy diadem." This probably refers to the פתיל תכלת "the blue cord" (see note on 28:33) to which the thin plate with the inscription was attached. So the interpretation "the thin plate Holiness," an allusion to the inscription Ἁγίασμα κυρίου (see 28:32), is not out of order.[8] O z read αγιον, which changes the meaning to "the holy plate," thereby losing the reference to the inscription; the reading arose through misunderstanding ἁγίασμα as an adjective. Tar[P] also has a different interpretation with בית קודשא "the sanctuary."

7. The Three "correct" Exod. Instead of τὸν ποδήρη Aq has τὸ ἔνδυμα τοῦ ἐπενδύματος; Sym, τὸ ἐπένδυμα τοῦ ἐπενδύματος, and Theod, τὸν ἐπενδύτην τῆς ἐπωμίδος; cf note at 28:27.
8. Aq and Sym translate נזר by ἀφόρισμα "something set apart" a rendering based on the root meaning "to separate, set apart."

29:7 The verse is a literal rendering of the Hebrew only adding an αὐτό after ἐπιχεεῖς, referring to the ἐλαίου of the first clause. The anointing pertains only to Aaron as high priest, not to his sons.

29:8 The sons of Aaron are to be brought forward and clothed with cloaks. The word "cloaks" is left unarticulated as expected but a popular M reading has the article; this is, however, simply a dittograph from αὐτούς (τους), and need not be taken as an intended reference to 28;36.

29:9 Exod limits the first three clauses to Aaron's sons, i.e. αὐτούς and αὐτοῖς 1° and 2° refer only to the sons. MT, however, has at the end of the first clause the phrase אהרן ובניו, thus making all the pronouns refer to both Aaron and his sons, admittedly sensible since as yet Aaron was lacking both girdle and turban. Hex has added ααρων και τους υιους αυτου to represent the missing words.[9] --For κιδάρεις as a translation of מגבעת see note at 28:36.

The orders to Moses are interrupted by the statement "and they shall have a priesthood to me for ever," i.e. ordination to the priesthood is for life not just for a term of office. The statement is not an exact rendering of the Hebrew which has no basis for "to me," and לחקת עולם becomes εἰς τὸν αἰῶνα. The failure to render חקת does not alter the intent, and ἐμοί is Exod's way of ensuring the purity of the priesthood, not priesthood in general but one which the Lord defines as ἐμοί.

The return to a second future summarizes in command form what all the preceding section has been about, as modern versions recognize, e.g. ZürB has "dann"; RSV has "thus." מלאת יד, a Hebrew idiom meaning "to ordain to office" for which see note at 28:37, is here rendered by τελειώσεις τὰς χεῖρας "validate the hands." The verb is also associated with the mysteries in the sense of being initiated, to become an initiate in the mystery religions, a τέλειος.[10] Vulg translates by *initiaveris manus eorum*; note also that Tar[P] has חשלם קרבן ידוי. Those to be ordained to office are here defined as Aaron and his sons, not just the sons.

---

9. Aq apparently had διαζώναις rather than ζώναις. It actually appears in the sources in the dictionary form διαζώνη.
10. Cf Bauer sub τελειόω 3, and sub τέλειος 2b.

29:10 Moses is to bring the bull by the doors of the tent of meeting. For פר Exod now uses μόσχον rather than the diminutive μοσχάριον as in vv.1 and 3. For the plural θύρας see note at v.4, and for "tent of meeting" see comment at 27:21.

There Aaron and his sons are to lay their hands on the head of the bull, for which see Lev 1:4. Exod, however, adds ἔναντι κυρίου παρὰ τὰς θύρας τῆς σκηνῆς τοῦ μαρτυρίου, for which it is the only witness. This is taken from the following verse, and it is not unlikely that the dittograph was already in its parent text. The O text does not have it, which shows that Origen's text which he used to create his fifth column did not have it.

29:11 Since most of the verse also appeared at the end of v.10, which see, the *ol C b* variant omitting τοῦ μαρτυρίου so as to change the phraseology slightly is not surprising.

29:12 Exod reproduces מדם exactly by a partitive ἀπὸ (τοῦ αἵματος).[11] -- The last clause in MT has "and all the blood you shall pour out towards the base of the altar." To Exod this was not sufficiently exact, and so he characterizes the blood as τὸ δὲ λοιπὸν πᾶν αἷμα; note both the contrastive δέ as well as the addition of λοιπόν - only all the blood that remained could be poured out! An A + reading omits πᾶν and simplifies the text, which Vulg's *reliquum autem sanguinem* also supports. -- According to MT Sam the blood was to be poured אל "towards" the base of the altar; this is also followed by Tar^O, though not by Tar^P Pesh which have על "upon," or "besides"; cf Exod's παρά plus accusative and Vulg: *iuxta.*

29:13 The details of the sacrifice at the altar. Four specific parts are to be sacrificed on the altar. a) all the fat which is on the intestines. MT has "all the fat which covers the intestines," but translating the participle by τὸ ἐπί is adequate. b) the lobe of the liver, for MT's the lobe on the liver. In v.22, however, the bound phrase יתרת הכבד does occur. Elsewhere the liver's lobe is referred to only in Lev, usually as יתרת על הכבד (3:4,10,15 4:9 7:4) but as a bound phrase at 8:16,25 9:19. But the translation there is not consistent either internally or with the Hebrew. The genitival construction occurs only twice (3:15 8:25), all others using a τὸν ἐπί construction.[12] c) the two kidneys, and d) the fat which is on them.

The last clause directs Moses to place (them) on the altar. MT has as verb הקטרת which means "burn up in smoke, burn as incense." Exod's different interpretation is supported by Tar[P] as well. Tar[O] followed by Pesh has חסיק ל which is ambiguous, but Tar[P] has תסדר על גבי. Vulg, on the other hand, has *offeres incensum,* an interpretation shared by the C text with its θυμιασεις for ἐπιθήσεις. Exod's use of ἐπιτίθημι for הקטיר was widely adopted by the Lev translator (12 times), and represents an old understanding of the verb as a technical term for the presentation of an offering on an altar. Only at Num 16:40 is the phrase "upon the altar" not used, though ἔναντι τοῦ κυρίου does occur.

29:14 In contrast - note the contrastive δέ - the rest of the bull is to be burned outside the camp, viz. the flesh, skin and dung. The term for flesh is plural since it is dressed; the singular occurs only twice in the Pentateuch, Gen 9:4 Exod 22:31. The F C variant κερατα "horns" would be possible for a bull, but it is simply a scribal mistake for κρεατα, a rare plural for κρέας occurring here as an *oI* variant. -- τὸ δέρμα and τὴν κόπρον occur without genitive pronouns, and hex added αυτου to both to conform to MT. -- That these should be burned πυρί is obvious, and the *oI C* text omits the word as otiose. On the other hand, hex has prefixed the word with εν in view of the באש of MT.

The word חטאת can mean either "sin" or "sin offering." In the former sense it occurs at 10:17 32:30,32,34 and 34:9 and presented no difficulty; it could simply be rendered by ἁμαρτία. But three times the word occurs in the sense of sin offering and for such Greek had no particular word. At v.36 it occurs in the phrase פר חטאת which Exod renders word for word as τὸ μοσχάριον τῆς ἁμαρτίας; this clearly meant "the bull calf dealing with sin," thus sacrificed on behalf of sin. In 30:10 which deals with the annual rite of atonement reference is made to "blood of the sin offering of atonement." There Exod rendered חטאת by the phrase τοῦ καθαρισμοῦ τῶν ἁμαρτίων

11. See SS 161.
12. Aq and Theod are dissatisfied with τὸν λοβόν and use περιττόν

472

which is really a description rather than an explanation. Here Exod was faced with a nominal phrase, חטאת הוא, which allowed for no dodging. This he rendered astutely by using the genitive: ἁμαρτίας γάρ ἐστιν. The γάρ is Exod's attempt to link this statement as the reason for the regulations concerning the sacrifice of the bull, and the genitive is his way of distinguishing the sacrifice from ἁμαρτία: "for it is that which concerns sin." An *O x* variant voids this distinction by reading the nominative, thereby creating a real difficulty: it calls the regulations "sin."[13]

29:15 Vv.15--18 deal with the sacrifice of one of the two rams mentioned in vv.1 and 3 as a holocaust sacrifice. Exod introduced this in the opening clause by τὸν κριὸν λήμψῃ τὸν ἕνα with the verb separating the elements of the nominal phrase. Hex changes the word order to conform to MT. -- For the rite of priests placing their hands on the head of an animal see Lev 1:4; see also v.10 above.

29:16 Exod takes the three clauses of MT and reduces them to two by mean of a subordinating participle for the second clause. The first clause simply orders Moses to kill "it." Exod uses a pronoun since τοῦ κριοῦ immediately precedes the clause. The majority reading, τον κριον, constitutes an early preOrigenian revision based on the Hebrew.

The subordinate participle λαβών has τὸ αἷμα as object, to which hex adds αυτου to conform to MT. The main clause orders the pouring out of it around the altar, which Vulg follows with *circa altare*. MT has זרקת על "toss against" here and in v.20 (as well as 24:6). Exod pictures the blood being poured out of φίαλας (cf 27:3), shallow bowls used for this purpose. In the Greek there is no hint of throwing the blood against the altar but rather of a pouring πρὸς τὸ θυσιαστήριον κύκλῳ, i.e. about the base, cf v.12. Other compounds for προσχεεῖς occur, notably προχεεις in *b f* +, and εκχεεις in z, but the text of Exod is original.

29:17 In Exod Moses is to cut in pieces the ram κατὰ μέλη "according to limbs." What is meant is "by its natural constituents," heads, legs, etc. MT

"unusual, superfluous part" instead.
13. Sym rendered the word by περὶ ἁπαρτίας, the favorite rendering in Lev

has a cognate term, "into its pieces," hex adding αυτου to represent the pronominal suffix.[14]

The second clause orders washing with water the intestines and the feet. Both terms have suffixes in MT and hex of course adds αυτου. Exod's ὕδατι is an explanatory plus over against MT, which is quite unnecessary, and its omission by F z + probably has nothing to do with Hebrew but rather with good sense.

The last clause orders their placement on the cut up pieces σὺν τῇ κεφαλῇ. MT has instead "and on its head." Possibly Exod read ראשו את. Again the two nouns have suffixes in the Hebrew for which hex adds αυτου. The clause orders the gathering up of all the pieces preparatory to the next clause which opens v.18.

29:18 Exod has taken all but the last three words of the verse in MT as a single clause; thus ὁλοκαύτωμα κυρίῳ is an adverbial accusative modifying ἀνοίσεις, showing how the κριός was to be offered, viz. as a holocaust to the Lord. Then ריח ניחוח which in MT is part of verse b is translated by an εἰς phrase modifying ἀνοίσεις. ὀσμὴν εὐωδίας first occurs in Gen 8:21 as object of ὠσφράνθη, of the Lord God smelling a pleasing smell, and it became the standard translation of the Hebrew phrase. ὁλοκαύτωμα κυρίῳ represents a nominal phrase in MT with הוא inserted; hex changes the pattern by adding εστι after ὁλοκαύτωμα, whereas the C text has added it after κυρίῳ. The Byzantine text makes ὁλοκαύτωμα plural (referring to διχοτομήματα?), whereas a popular A F variant has articulated κυρίῳ, possibly under Hebrew influence in order to represent the preposition in ליהוה. Exod has also against MT put ὅλον after τὸν κριόν; hex has changed the order to equal MT.[15]

The final clause is a kind of subscription to vv.15--18 similar to that at the end of v.14; cf also v.25. θυσίασμα is a general term for sacrifice, here translating אשה "a fire offering." This term also occurs in vv.25 and 41 where it is translated by κάρπωμα, which equation is adopted throughout by Lev.[16] A fourth occurrence is at 30:20 where it becomes τὰ ὁλοκαυτώματα. -- This

---

where it is original text.

14. Cf SS 93,95.

15. Cf also the note in THGE VII.F.2.

θυσίασμα is κυρίῳ "(belongs) to the Lord." The *n s* text has it in the genitive.

29:19 This introduces a third sacrifice (vv.19--34), that of the second ram, the ram τῆς τελειώσεως (vv.26f.) for the priests. V.19 varies only slightly from its counterpart, that of the first ram, in v.15; the word order of the first clause has the verb before the object here, and the number of the verb in the second is singular, ἐπιθήσει. Both of these changes are due to MT.

29:20 Exod's text differs considerably from that of MT. Both order the slaughter of the ram, though Exod simply has αὐτόν; cf note at v.16. In MT the full treatment is ordered for the sons: blood is to be smeared on the lobes of their right ear as well as on the thumbs of their right hand and the big toe of their right foot, but for Aaron this is ordered only for the lobe of the ear. Exod orders the full treatment for Aaron as well in the same terms as for the sons. On the other hand, MT adds "and you shall toss the blood (i.e. the remaining blood) against the altar round about" for which see v.16. Hex has added at the end of the verse και προσχεεις το αιμα επι το θυσιαστηριον κυκλω so as to equal the missing clause. For Exod's omission see the discussion under v.21.

For the first part of the verse Origen was somewhat lost. He placed the entire section about the sons under the obelus, i.e. as not being in the Hebrew. Then he tried to fix up the extra text dealing with Aaron by additions. So after ' Ἀαρών he added του δεξιου και επι τον λοβον του ωτος των υιων αυτου; then after χειρός and ποδός he added αυτων; what he should have done is to have placed του 3° ... δεξιου 2° under the obelus, and nothing more.

Exod used the same word (τὸ) ἄκρον to render thumb(s) and big toe(s), which then becomes the standard rendering for בֹּהֶן which can also mean either thumb or big toe; this shows real skill on Exod's part in finding a single word in Greek which could be understood in both ways.[17]

The *z* tradition has the word "right" modify "lobe" rather than Aaron's ear; the *d* text has transposed the references to "hand" and "foot" as well as

---

16. See THGL 73--74.
17. Aq, however, used τὸν ἀντιδάκτυλον for "thumb"; unfortunately what

adding αυτου in both cases, and ms 75 abbreviated by his των υιων αυτου ομοιως the repeated materials dealing with the sons.

29:21 As in v.21 Exod uses an unnecessary ἀπό instead of a simple partitive genitive in imitation of the Hebrew הדם מן and מאשר. This probably promoted his use of the same preposition in the intervening phrase τοῦ ἀπὸ τοῦ θυσιαστηρίου for the Hebrew "which was על the altar." The odd phrase led to various attempts to improve the text: an *n t* reading has επι which only by coincidence equals MT, an *f* reading has επανω, whereas the A F *b d z* text omitted ἀπὸ τοῦ.

The second clause orders Moses to sprinkle (with the blood) Aaron, his robe, his sons and their robes. The point of this sprinkling is clarified in the next clause, namely that all the aforementioned ἁγιασθήσεται. MT has קדש "shall be holy," but Tar Pesh support Exod. Sam omits the entire verse.

The last clause in v.20 of MT had been omitted by Exod, but here it has a statement similar to that of v.16 to make up for it: "and the blood of the ram you shall pour about the altar." It is now clear why Exod waited until the end of v.21 to make this statement; in v.20 some of the blood still had to be used for sprinkling before the remainder could be poured forth.

29:22 The list of materials to be taken from the sacrificial ram differs somewhat in Exod from MT. The first is simply החלב in MT but Exod adds an αὐτοῦ; MT continues with "and the fatty tail and the fat which covers the intestines," but Exod omits "and the fatty tail"; the result reads "its fat, even the fat which ...." Hex has added καὶ τὴν κέρκον "and the tail" to make up for the omission.[18]

For the rest of the list see note on v.13, except that Exod here added "the right shoulder"[19] instead of "the right thighs" of MT (שוק).[20] The word also occurs at v.27 where Exod also uses βραχίονα, and the equation was also adopted throughout by Lev; Vulg has *armum* following Exod in both verses.

---

he used for "big toe" is unknown.
18. This was taken from Aq, while Sym and Theod had the diminutive (καὶ) τὸ κέρκιον.
19. Cf SS 66.
20. The later revisers rendered the word more accurately by κνήμην.

The verse ends with a γάρ clause which is parenthetical since the next verse continues with more things to be taken (λῆμψη). Exod has "for this is a τελείωσις," a word which must be understood in the light of τελειώσεις in v.9, for which see note. MT has איל מלאים "a ram of ordination," which Vulg renders by *aries consecrationis.* The word τελείωσις usually means "completion, fulfilment," and can be used of the attainment of a state,[21] and is here used of initiation into the priestly office.

29:23 Exod abbreviates MT's ככר לחם אחת וחלת לחם as ἄρτον ἕνα; this is the same pattern as that followed in v.2 where Exod also considered the two phrases to be the same thing and so used a single generic term. Hex added καὶ κολλύραν ἄρτου after ἕνα as well as μιαν after ἐλαίου to modify κολλυραν, thereby equally MT precisely. -- The phrase ἐξ ἐλαίου as applied to bread probably means "smeared" or "anointed with oil."

These (a bread and a λάγονον) are to be taken "from the κανοῦ of unleavened stuff τῶν προτεθειμένων ἔναντι κυρίου." For the basket into which unleavened bread and cakes had been placed see v.3. That these had been set out "before the Lord" presumably refers to these materials brought to the doors of the tent of testimony (v.4). Exod's use of the perfect participle is an exegetical amplification over against MT which simply has אשר לפני יהוה.

29:24 Moses is to put τὰ πάντα, i.e. all the above, "upon the hands of Aaron and upon the hands of his sons." This is the first stage of the תנופה after which they are to be taken away and sacrificed. The so-called "wave offering" presumably refers to this back and forth action.

Exod, however, interprets the second clause "and you shall wave them (as) a wave offering before Yahweh" as an act of ἀφόρισμα, i.e. "and you shall set them aside as a separation before the Lord." By this action Aaron and his sons are set aside as consecrated to God's service, taken out of the realm of the secular into that of the sacred. Vulg translates by *et sanctificabis eos elevans coram domino.*

21. See LS s.v. II.

A popular variant changed αὐτούς as referring to the ordinands to αυτα; thus it is not the priests but all the things offered which become the ἀφόρισμα.

29:25 For the חנופה to be complete the materials presented for sacrifice must be taken back from the hands of the ordinands, and then Moses is to offer them up on the altar. MT adds על העלה "upon, i.e. besides, the holocaust," a reference to v.18's אשה. Exod changes this to a genitive modifier of θυσιαστήριον, i.e. "the altar of the holocaust" or as more commonly known, the altar of burnt offering, thereby distinguishing this altar, for which see 27:1--8, from the θυσιαστήριον θυμιάματος described in 30:1--10. This is to become εἰς ὀσμὴν εὐωδίας, for which see comment at v.18.

The subscription dubs this a κάρπωμα κυρίῳ. κάρπωμα occurs here for the first time as the name for a sacrifice. In ordinary Greek it means "fruit," and then comes to mean the offering up of something one has. Its use in the Pentateuch is, however, much broader. Here it is a translation for אשה, something which is burned on that altar. The word is taken over to mean any kind of sacrifice; in fact it also occurs for עלה not only in Exod but also in Lev and Num, as well as in Jos.[22]

29:26 Moses is to take the breast from the ram of initiation. For τελειώσεως see note at v.22.[23] The phrase ὅ ἐστιν ' Ααρών refers to "the ram," not to τελειώσεως, and ' Ααρών must be taken either as in the dative or the genitive, i.e. the ram pertains to Aaron.

For the second paratactic clause see note at v.24. The last clause states that this ἀφόρισμα will belong to Moses ἐν μερίδι, as his share in the sacrifice, since he is here serving as the priest; cf Lev 8:29, and for the general principle 7:23.

29:27 The syntax of this verse is somewhat loose; the verse has two coordinate relative clauses, the first of which should refer to τὸ στηθύνιον (ἀφόρισμα), and the second to τὸν βραχίονα (του ἀφαιρέματος). But the

22. Suidas actually defines it as θυσία, προσφορά.
23. According to Syh Aq rendered המלאים by τῆς πληρώσεως "completion," whereas Sym simply changed Exod to the plural τῶν τελειώσεων.

relative pronouns are both masculine, ὅς, i.e. referring to βραχίονα (by attraction?), whereas sensibly it is the ἀφόρισμα which ἀφώρισται and the ἀφαιρέματος which ἀφήρηται, or probably the breast as an ἀφόρισμα and the shoulder as an ἀφαίρεμα which are involved; for "shoulder" cf note at v.22. Furthermore the translator has differentiated in the translation of the two bound phrases of MT חזה התנופה and the שוק התרומה, the first one being rendered by a double accusative "(you shall consecrate) the breast as a separation," and the second by an accusative plus genitive modifier "the shoulder of removal." ἀφαιρέματος literally refers to "that which is lifted up from"; of ἀφαίρεμα it is said that הורם "it has been elevated, raised up." The noun is regularly used to render תרומה and though it is usually distinguished from ἀφόρισμα as rendering for תנופה "the wave offering," there is occasional confusion in the B account; cf 35:22 and 39:7 where MT has תנופה but Exod has ἀφαίρεμα. For its definition cf v.28 below. -- For τελειώσεως cf note at v.22.

29:28 The subject of the verb in the opening clause is not stated, though specifically it must be the βραχίονα of v.27 since it is later defined as an ἀφαίρεμα; on the other hand, both breast and thigh become the priestly portion.

This is to be a perpetual allotment because it is an ἀφαίρεμα. In vv.27--28 this refers to that which is taken up out of the θυμάτων τῶν σωτηρίων of the Israelites, called an ἀφαίρεμα κυρίῳ, and therefore it is ἐν μερίδι (v.26) for Aaron and his sons. In Exod B the term ἀφαίρεμα κυρίῳ also occurs, but not of the priestly portion but rather of all the gifts of metal and fabrics which were brought by the Israelites as voluntary gifts for the making of the tabernacle (ch.35 passim 36:3 39:2,7,12); they are even defined (35:5) as "first fruits to the Lord."

The terms ἀφαίρεμα and ἀφόρισμα are often confused. E.g., B O + have αφορισμα for the first, but A B + alone support ἀφαίρεμα for the second, all others having αφορισμα, and for the third all witnesses support ἀφαίρεμα.[24]

24. For the priority of ἀφαίρεμα throughout see the discussion in THGE VII.Q.

θυμάτων is a generic word for sacrifice, or more specifically for that which is sacrificed. The *C* text as the result of a copyist's error has θυμιαματων "incense offerings" which is not overly sensible in the context. These θυμάτων are called τῶν σωτηρίων, i.e. "peace offerings," for which see the discussion at 20:24.

The suffix of שלמיהם occasioned hex's αυτων. A B *f* variant has των υιων ισραηλ here as a gloss under the influence of its double occurrence earlier in the verse.[25]

The final ἀφαίρεμα κυρίῳ is in apposition to ἀφαίρεμα 2° and renders תרומתם ליהוה. Hex has made two "corrections": it has added αυτων to represent the suffix, and it has prefixed the article to κυρίῳ to show the preposition.

29:29 The priestly robe is designated "the robe of the sanctuary which is for Aaron,"[26] so-called since the high priest only wc.e it in the sanctuary; this will remain the high priestly robe throughout the succession, i.e. "to his sons after him."

The verse concludes with two coordinate purposive infinitive phrases. The first phrase represents the Hebrew למשחה בהם "for anointment by them." The term משחה is vocalized by the Masoretes to indicate a passive infinitival noun, and is so interpreted by Tar[P] למתרבי, followed also by Vulg: *ungantur in ea*. The "in them" refers to בגדי, i.e. ἡ στολή in Exod. Exod takes the word as an active concept χρισθῆναι αὐτοὺς ἐν αὐτοῖς, a grammatical infelicity since ἐν αὐτοῖς should be εν αυτη, i.e. the reference in αὐτοῖς is really ad sensum as though ἡ στολή were a collective or τα ιμα-τια.

The second infinitival phrase is τελειῶσαι τὰς χεῖρας αὐτῶν; for the meaning of the phrase see the discussion at v.9. MT, however, has בם after the infinitive for which hex supplies εν αυτοις; for this syntactic incongruity see the preceding paragraph.[27]

25. See also THGE VII.O.
26. See SS 64.
27. As might have been expected from footnote 23 above Aq has for the infinitive πληρῶσαι and Sym, τελεωθῆναι (according to Syh).

29:30 The one who succeeds to the office of high priest after the death of his father is to wear them (for the plural see the note in v.29) for the seven days of the installation ceremony; cf v.35. The successor is called the priest ὁ ἀντ᾽ αὐτοῦ τῶν υἱῶν αὐτοῦ. The rather convoluted phrase represents MT's תחתיו מבניו. Vulg paraphrased in order to clarify what was meant by *illa qui pontifex pro eo fuerit constitutus de filiis eius,* a correct but involved elucidation. The majority hex text has inserted εκ before τῶν to conform to MT's מבניו.

The successor is also called "the one who shall enter the tent of testimony to perform cultic rites ἐν τοῖς ἁγίοις." For "tent of testimony" see note at 27:21. בקדש is usually translated by ἐν τῷ ἁγίῳ, but Exod here used the plural to designate the two holy places in the sanctuary, the holy place and the most holy place. It is the high priest who is being ordained, and not ordinary priests, and so a distinction is made between the high priest who alone can enter both holy places and the ordinary priest who can only serve in the holy place. An *O b* variant has the singular and probably represents an early correction towards the Hebrew, one which is not necessarily an improvement.

29:31--33 For κριὸν τῆς τελειώσεως see comment at v.22. -- Exod simply refers to τὰ κρέα in v.31 whereas MT has בשר; hex accordingly added αυτου.[28] The verb in v.32 is singular in MT by attraction to the nearer noun of the subject אהרן ובניו, but Exod uses the plural; either number is possible in Greek. For the plural κρέα see note at v.14. For the plural τὰς θύρας see comment at v.4, and for "tent of testimony, at 27:21.

In v.33 αὐτά, οἷς, αὐτοῖς and ἀπ᾽ αὐτων refer to the κρέα and ἄρτους, whereas the subject of ἔδονται and ἡγιάσθησαν as well as the referent in (χεῖρας) αὐτῶν and αὐτούς is Aaron and his sons. The otiose ἐν αὐτοῖς which recapitulates ἐν οἷς is a Hebraism which Exod often avoids. It modifies ἡγιάσθησαν, a verb he uses here as well as in v.36 to render the root כפר. The verb occurs only in chh.29 and 30 and Exod uses three different verbs to translate it. At v.37 he used καθαριεῖς as well as τοῦ καθαρισμοῦ for הכפרים. At 30:10 the verb occurs twice, once rendered by ἐξιλάσεται and once by καθαριεῖ, and at 30:15,16 the infinitive ἐξιλάσασθαι obtains. At 32:30 this verb is used of Moses on behalf of the sinful people. The choice of ἁγιάζω here and at v.36 is in the context of the infinitive לקדש; ἁγιάσαι αὐτούς occurs here, and ὥστε ἁγιάσαι αὐτό (the altar), in v.36. Exod was also faced here with the difficulty of reconciling the idea of eating dedicated foods within the initiation ceremony with the clause אשר כפר בהם. The idea of atonement was normally tied to holocausts, not to sacrifices of which parts could be eaten by priests. Since the clause is followed by successive marked infinitives the choice of ἡγιάσθησαν was a neutral one.

The infinitives which follow the relative clause are asyndetically presented, although a popular A F variant tradition does insert a καί. The impulse to join them with a καί is, however, based on a failure to understand the relation between the two infinitive phrases, the second being simply explicative of the first. The first phrase "to validate their hands" for which see comment at v.9 really means ἁγιάσαι αὐτούς. Priests are to eat dedicated foods ... so as to be ordained to priestly office, i.e. to be sanctified, set aside from the profane for sacred service.

These are dedicated foods (ἅγια), and therefore no layman, ἀλλογενής, may eat of them. Exod has added an ἀπ' αὐτῶν simply for clarification. The καί introducing this statement is omitted by a b f n variant text, and the b text has pedantically added πας before ἀλλογενής.

29:34 What is left of the dedicated food on the next day must be burned by fire. In MT the meat is modified by המלאים, but meat "of validation" does not make much sense in Greek and Exod defines it as τῆς θυσίας τῆς τελειώσεως; for the latter noun see comment at v.22. What is left is defined by the partitive ἀπό construction,[29] i.e. it designates the subject, and ἕως πρωί modifies the verb. Within the apodosis a C s variant has transposed τὰ λοιπά after πυρί for no identifiable reason.

The prohibition of eating a sacrifice on the second day was a common one; cf 12:10. The reason given was that "it is holiness"; for ἁγίασμα see note at v.6. An O variant introduces a καί before the prohibition (as in Pesh).

29:35 The use of οὕτως here is proleptic not reflective, and refers to the actions described in vv.35--37. Its omission by the *C* tradition loses this proleptic note since what remains removes the one word connecting the overall command to act in a certain way with what follows. -- One might have expected a present tense instead of ἐνετειλάμην, since what is to follow has not yet been commanded, but the phrase "what I/he commanded" is an oft-recurring one, and one should hardly press for strict consistency. Exod's aorist is of course based on צריתי of MT.

For "you shall validate their hands" see comment at v.9. The popular A F M reordering of αὐτῶν to follow τὰς χεῖρας is probably hex to make the order conform to MT.

29:36 The first clause orders effecting (i.e. performing the sacrifice of) "the bull calf of sin in the day of purification." Exod understands the sacrifice of the bull calf as taking place only once, presumably on the first day of the week-long ceremony. The phrase τῆς ἁμαρτίας represents חטאת in the sense of sin offering; see comment at v.14.[30] For "in the day of purification" MT has ליום על הכפרים "per day for atonement"; Exod has taken ליום not in the sense of "each day" but rather as "at the day" with the prepositional phrase modifying "day" rather than the verb תעשה. For καθαρισμοῦ as a translation of כפרים see the discussion at vv.31--33 above.[31]

The second clause in MT has חטאת "you shall make a sin offering" as its main verb. Greek had no verb with that meaning so the translator used καθαριεῖς "you shall purify, cleanse., which does communicate what the concept of חטא was to bring about.[32] -- Exod does not translate the preposition in the phrase על המזבח but makes τὸ θυσιαστήριον the direct object of the verb. Moses is to "cleanse the altar," rather than "to make a sin offering on the altar" as MT has it. The clause is modified by the temporal phrase ἐν + marked infinitive + accusative subject pronoun, a

28. Cf SS 93.
29. See SS 157.
30. The Later Revisers have rendered the word by περὶ ἁμαρτίας.
31. The Three have as might be expected used ἐξιλασμοῦ "atonement" rather than καθαρισμοῦ.
32. The Later Revisers created a new denominative verb based on the Lev

pattern reflecting the Hebrew: preposition + bound infinitive + pronominal subject suffix. For the infinitive ἀγιάζειν see the comment at vv.31--33.

The last clause orders the anointing of the altar by which it will be set aside for sacred use. The referent in αὐτό is throughout to θυσιαστήριον.

29:37 Here Exod closely reflects the second clause of v.36. Two actions are there reflected: purification of the altar and its sanctification. Though MT changes from חטאת to כפר (in each case adding "upon the altar"), Exod adopts exactly the same phrase used in v.36: καθαριεῖς τὸ θυσιαστήριον.[33] The verb has been prefixed through partial dittography by και in *x* +, whereas an *O* variant changes the Attic future to the Hellenistic καθαρισεις. The addition of επι before "the altar" by some scattered witnesses could be due to Hebrew influence.[34] -- The second clause, καὶ ἁγιάζεις αὐτό, finds its analogue in v.36 in the infinitival construction with ἁγιάζειν.

The third clause is a literal rendering of MT, and the phrase ἅγιον τοῦ ἁγίου is an elative "very holy, most holy." This kind of holiness is magnetic so that anyone touching the holy altar in turn is made holy. MT simply has the Qal יקדש, which Exod translates by a passive, as do Tar[O] Pesh Vulg. The Qal can indeed be so understood.

29:38 Exod begins with the plural ταῦτα ... ἅ for MT's singular זה אשר because what is to be offered is not one, but two lambs. The relative adjective οσα obtains in the majority text instead of the pronoun ἅ; it is frequently used in LXX; in fact it occurs 41 times in Exod as over against 22 cases of ἅ; it is somewhat more specifically allinclusive than the simple relative, i.e. "everything which, all that," and only it occurs after πάντα in Exod.

Exod is expansive over against MT, amplifying the text in three cases: ἀμώμους describing the lambs; the phrase ἐπὶ τὸ θυσιαστήριον between ἡμέραν and ἐνδελεχῶς, and the final phrase κάρπωμα ἐνδελεχισμοῦ. For ἀμώμους its position was uncertain in the tradition; an *O* reading places it

translator's neologism for the חטאת offering τὸ περὶ ἁμαρτίας "that on behalf of sin," viz. περιαμαρτιεῖς.
33. See Helbing 215.

after δύο, whereas the Byzantine text has it before ἐνιαυσίους, which is incidentally easily misread (as in *O C*) as ενιαυσαιους. Both are adjectives, and both mean "a year old." -- The second expansion was "corrected" through the majority text omitting the phrase, probably a prehexaplaric revision towards MT. -- The final phrase probably depended on a parent text עלת תמיד which Sam also attests. For κάρπωμα see note at v.25.

The sacrifices described in vv.38ff. concern the daily sacrifices to be offered on the altar of burnt offering; cf 27:1--8, and more particularly Num 28:3--8. τὴν ἡμέραν means "each and every day" as is clear from the adverb ἐνδελεχῶς "constantly." In fact it is a κάρπωμα ἐνδελεχισμοῦ, "a perpetual sacrifice."

29:39 The terms τὸ πρωί and τὸ δειλινόν are adverbial accusatives indicating time when. The latter term here translates בין הערבים for which see discussion at 12:6.

29:40 The cereal offering and the libation which was to accompany each sacrifice (τῷ ἀμνῷ τῷ ἐνί) are in the accusative and presuppose ποιήσεις from the preceding verse.

The cereal offering was a mixture consisting of a δέκατον of fine flour and a quarter ἵν of oil. The term "tenth" probably refers to an ephah, and is a measure of quantity roughly equal to the γόμορ for which see comment at 16:16 and Bible Dictionaries. The word σεμιδάλεως/סלת means finely ground wheat flour. This was to be "mixed with oil," for which see comment at v.2. This oil is described as "beaten," i.e. it was the very best oil, of a quality which was also to be used for the lamp which burned continually, 27:20 and Lev 24:2. The only other reference to "beaten oil" occurs in 3Kgdm 5:11 as part of a large barter payment made by Solomon to Hiram. The amount of oil used for the cereal offering was a quarter of a hin, a transliteration of the Hebrew הין, a liquid measure of about four liters; cf Bible Dictionaries. τῷ τετάρτῳ refers to ἐλαίῳ; a *z* variant in the genitive is an error influenced by the τοῦ ἵν which immediately follows, and the Byzantine text has the accusative under the influence of τὸ τέταρτον in the coordinate phrase.

The libation is identified as being a quarter hin of wine. which is coordinate with δέκατον, whereas σπονδήν is an adverbial accusative, i.e. "as a libation a quarter hin of wine."

29:41 Instructions about the second lamb. For δειλινόν cf v.40. In the second clause the distinction between θυσίαν, referring to the cereal offering of v.40, and the σπονδήν as the libation is continued. These are both κατά phrases in accordance with MT. MT also has לו after the second תעשׂה which is odd since its anaphoric referent is then עלה in v.42. Sam has לו which is easier since this would refer to כבשׂ. Exod lacks a pronoun, but hex has added αυτω, referring to ἀμνόν. -- Also problematic over against MT is αὐτοῦ which also refers to ἀμνόν, but MT has a feminine suffix, making "its" refer to θυσίαν, i.e. the morning sacrifice and its libation. Sam has a masculine suffix and its reading is probably parent text for Exod. An M s variant reads αυτης, probably a correction twoards MT.[35]

These daily sacrifices are characterized as ὀσμὴν εὐωδίας and as a κάρπωμα κυρίῳ; for the latter see comment at v.25, and for the former, at v.18. In MT the former phrase is a prepositional phrase though not in Sam, and Sam represents Exod's parent text. A widely followed hex reading prefixed εις.[36]

29:42 Exod again uses the term θυσίαν but now for the holocaust עלה rather than for the cereal offering, מנחה of v.41.[37] Since it is modified by τοῦ ἐνδελεχισμοῦ it also characterizes the daily sacrifices; in fact, syntactically the verse as a whole, as are ὀσμήν and κάρπωμα of v.41, is in apposition to τὸν ἀμνόν of v.41.

This θυσίαν is modified by the two prepositional phrases: "throughout your generations" designating time, and "at the doors of the tent of meeting," for which see comment at 27:21, for location. Both γενεάς and θύρας are articulated in Exod but a B oII variant omits both cases of τάς.[38]

---

34. The Later Revisers have as might well be expected translated the verb by ἐξιλάσῃ "atone."
35. Based on Theod, though Aq and Sym agree with Exod.
36. See also the discussion in THGE VII.L.1.
37. Aq and Theod translate more exactly as "holocaust" (ὁλοκαύτωμα or ὁλοκαύτωσιν) according to Syh, whereas Sym had ἀναφοράν, a translation

For "doors" in the plural see comment at v.4.

It is these doors before the Lord that are identified by a relative clause אשר אועד לכם שמה, i.e. God is appointing this place as the spot where he and his people will meet. Exod, however, has avoided the notion of an appointment entirely, and in view of the concluding clause ὥστε λαλῆσαί σοι "so as to speak to you" has interpreted the relative clause in the sense of self-revelation, i.e. ἐν οἷς γνωσθήσομαί σοι ἐκεῖθεν. One should note the use of οἷς which does not refer to θύρας which is feminine, but rather is an indefinite reference to all the foregoing matters, presumably then to the ταῦτα of v.38 which introduced this section. Then the choice of verb is also of note. The idea that God makes himself known is a favored one in Exod (2:25 25:21 30:6, 36), and it is intentionally used as the comment at 25:21 shows; it is certainly not based on a text with אודע instead of אועד.

In the tradition εκει is a popular substitute for ἐκεῖθεν, but the equation with שמה makes ἐκεῖθεν clearly original. At the end of the verse MT did have שם which Exod omitted as otiose, but hex supplied an εκει. A d variant has changed the ὥστε construction to οτε λαλησω σοι "when I shall speak to you," possibly created to avoid any semblance of tautology between γνωσθήσομαί and ὥστε λαλῆσαί.

29:43 Apparently the text of the first verb in MT is not fully certain. Instead of נעדתי "will meet, come together with" Sam has נדרשתי "I will be consulted for an oracle." Exod interprets by τάξομαι "I will order,"[39] i.e. I will give further directions, and its parent text is not certain. Note also Tar: "I will order my word," and Vulg *praecipiam*. What is meant is that where God makes himself known so as to speak is where he will be in charge, will give instructions to the Israelites; by ἐκεῖ is meant at the doors of the tent of testimony (v.42).

The second clause is also in first person with the Lord still speaking; this is an attempt to solve the difficulty of a third person verb (נקדש in MT) which has no obvious subject. Jerome interprets by *sanctificabitur altare* which has led various commentators to suggest that the altar will be sanctified pointing to the שמה of the first clause. Or is the sacrifice intended? In any event Exod makes it fully parallel to the first clause: I will give orders / I will be sanctified. Obviously these are theological concepts. -- The term δόξα has a broad semantic field. It can mean brightness, shining, splendor as well as reputation, honor, renown.[40] Here the problem of its meaning is made more difficult by μου; is the pronoun to be taken as a subjective genitive or an objective? If the former it could be a designation of God's appearance, a revelatory reflection, hence "splendor" in the Hebrew sense of כבוד as holiness, deity revealed. But if it be taken as an objective genitive it could mean "praise" in the sense of "giving glory to the Lord." But the phrase ἐν δόξῃ μου modifies ἁγιασθήσομαι. I would suggest that what is meant is "I will be seen as holy (i.e. recognized as God) by my splendor (i.e. through my appearance)." That the clause was difficult for later readers is clear from a popular doublet which was inserted between the two clauses: και αγιασθησομαι εν τοις υιοις ισραηλ, an epexegetical gloss on the verse as a whole.

29:44 The divine presence at the sanctuary doors affects all that which is cultically involved. God's holiness will make holy, i.e. set aside to sacred service, both tent of testimony and altar as well as Aaron and his sons. That rendering holy means a setting aside for sacred duty is clear from its definition with regard to the designees: ἱερατεύειν μοι which is to be understood as a purposive infinitive; note Jerome's *ut sacerdotio fungantur mihi.*

29:45 Exod avoids the notion that the Lord might dwell among the Israelites; possibly such a notion was a somewhat overly corporeal figure and so instead of שכנתי he has ἐπικληθήσομαι. The Lord's presence at the doors of the sanctuary means that he can be called upon, invoked, by the Israelites; he can be prayed to in the sanctuary; in fact it becomes an οἶκος προσευχῆς, Isa 56:7.

This promise is then stated in covenantal terms: "I will be their God," a simplification of MT which literally says "I will become God for them." The genitive pronoun is changed to αυτοις in scattered witnesses which does conform to MT, but this is probably coincidence.

29:46 For the recognition formula see the discussion at 6:7. The participial phrase ὁ ἐξαγαγὼν αὐτοὺς ἐκ γῆς ᾿Αιγύπτου occurs only here in Exod, though the notion is common throughout the book but only in the more literal relative clause with ὅς or ὅστις, as at 20:2; the participial pattern has, however, been taken over by its parallel account in Deut 5:6.

Exod concludes by giving a double purpose to the Lord's redemptive action. He brings them out of the land of Egypt "to be invoked by them and to be their God." For the first of these Exod is consistent with the previous verse in changing the idea of indwelling, לשכני, to that of being called upon, ἐπικληθῆναι, for which see comment. Exod then continues with the parallel notion at v.45, viz. καὶ θεὸς εἶναι αὐτῶν, i.e. the Lord redeemed Israel from Egypt "to be their God." The text is thus fully consistent with v.45, but it has entirely abandoned MT which has the affirmation formula אני יהוה אלהיהם. Admittedly ולהיות instead of אני יהוה would be a literal equivalent to Exod but the translation is exegetically not textually based.

The text tradition shows a great deal of activity in these infinitival clauses. A Byzantine gloss, θεος after αὐτοῖς, creates a reading "to be invoked by them as God." For the second phrase a *z* variant has ειναι αυτων κ͞ς ο θ͞ς; an *O* reading has ειναι κ͞ς ο θ͞ς αυτων; a *d t* variant has ων θ͞ς αυτων, which *n s* has changed by transposing the first two words. And finally a popular A F M variant has reordered Exod as ειναι αυτων θ͞ς. With such a variety to unscramble it seemed wise to adopt as Exod the reading of the oldest witness, cod B.

which Vulg: *oblatione* also reflects.
38. See the discussion of this in THGE VII.D.6.
39. See Bauer sub τάσσω 2.
40. See Bauer s.v.

Chapter 30

30:1 Vv.1--10 describe the construction and use of a second altar, one for incense. Moses is commanded to build an incense altar; MT has an altar to burn incense, and hex has added θυμιατηριον after "altar" so as to equal MT.[1] The C text omits θυμιάματος so that Moses is simply told to build an altar. It is to be made of rot-resistent wood (cf 25:5). In MT this is a separate clause: "of acacia wood you shall make it," but Exod divides the construction differently, leaving the ἐξ phrase to v.1, and the remainder as καὶ ποιήσεις αὐτό to introduce v.2. This is not due to a different parent text but rather to supply a verb for v.2.

30:2 The dimensions are to be a cubit in length and breadth (45 sq cm; 18 x 18 in.), and two cubits in height. Thus the vertical dimensions are double the horizontal. For all three dimensions hex has added αυτου so as to equal MT. For the horns which are to be ἐξ αὐτοῦ see note at 27:2.

30:3 In contrast to the altar of burnt offering (27:1--8) which was bronze plated throughout the incense altar was to be entirely gold plated, and that with pure gold, i.e. its hearth, its sides and its horns. The altar is actually referred to as αὐτά signifying its various parts. For "hearth" compare the comment at 27:4. Here it refers to the top covering, its ܓܓ "roof" in distinction from its τοίχους "walls, sides." The exact details of the construction of the ἐσχάραν are not given as they are for 27:4, and the hearth is apparently thought of in terms quite different from that of the holocaust altar in 27:5; since it contrasts with "walls" the hearth seems to be thought of as a kind of grating lying on top of the altar. on which only incense (cf vv.34--38) is to be burnt. A popular A variant substitutes εσχαριδα "brazier" for ἐσχάραν, but altars do not usually have braziers.[2]

　　Also to be made was a golden twisted rim around the altar for which see comment at 25:10.

1. Aq has θυμιάσεως for θυμιάματος according to Syh.
2. The Three translate by δῶμα "roof, housetop," a literal rendering for ܓܓ.

30:4 Also to be made for it are two rings of pure gold[3] below its twisted rim; the word "pure" is found only in Exod. B + has omitted αὐτῷ but ל plus a pronoun modifying עשׂה is normally rendered fully by Exod.[4] The Byzantine text has a gloss after it: εν ταις δυσιν πλευραις, a dittograph from the next clause.

The second clause is somewhat ambiguous, both in MT and in Exod. The verb ποιήσεις is modified by two prepositional phrases which seem to say the same thing. Preposed is εἰς τὸ δύο κλίτη and following the verb is ἐν τοῖς δυσὶν πλευροῖς. That Exod, however, distinguished the two is clear from the fact that he changed the preposition. The verb plus εἰς here must mean "you shall make them on to (the two sides)," and the ἐν phrase must be purely locative "at the two flanks"; what this means is "on the two opposite sides, at the ends (i.e. the corners)." This also shows that the first clause does not mean two rings in total, i.e. the second clause defines the first clause as applicable εἰς τὸ δύο κλίτη, making them four rings in all. Note that Tar Pesh interpret similarly though reversing the phrases: "on its two corners ... on its two sides." Hex has added αυτου both to κλίτη and πλευροῖς to correspond to MT. The Byzantine text has ταις δυσιν πλευραις instead of τοῖς δυσὶν πλευροῖς, but πλευρά and πλευρόν mean the same.

In the last clause Moses is told that their rings will constitute ψαλίδες for the σκυτάλαις; MT has "shall become housings for the poles." ψαλίδες was identified at 27:10 as architectural bands on pillars, but here it is a translation for בתים "housings," describing the rings into which the "poles, staves" are inserted for carrying the altar, and open bands are what the word must mean.[5] -- For the ὥστε clause showing the purpose of the poles cf 25:13 27:7.

---

3. Cf SS 63.
4. As is argued in THGE VII.G.5.
5. Sym calls them εἴσοδοι "entrances" and Theod has εἰς θῆκες for which see comment at 25:26. To translate לבדים The Three use the more common term τοῖς ἀναφορεῦσιν instead of ταῖς σκυτάλαις; cf comment at 25:12.

30:5 As for the ark (25:12), the poles are to be made of rot-resistent wood overlaid with gold. A popular A variant changes αὐτάς (referring to poles) to αυτα which refers to ξύλων, probably because ξύλων is nearer than σκυτάλας, but the reference was not so intended by Exod.

30:6 Exod follows Sam's shorter text. The verse orders placement of the incense altar over against the inner curtain (see note at 26:31) which is over (i.e. shields) the ark of the testimonies, after which MT has לפני הכפרת אשר על העדת. The parent text of Exod had omitted the words due to homoiot. As expected hex added κατα προσωπον του ιλαστηριου εστιν επι των μαρτυριων to make up for the lacuna. -- Unique in Exod is the description of the ark as τῶν μαρτυρίων, which is always singular elsewhere, for which see the discussion at 25:9. The plural can, however, be justified since the ark contained τὰ μαρτύρια, for which see note at 25:15.

For the relative clause see the comment at 29:42 where exactly the same text obtains in Exod, though in MT לכם occurs instead of לך. As at 29:42 εκει is a popular variant for ἐκεῖθεν but the Hebrew makes clear that the latter is original.

30:7 Not Moses but Aaron is to burn incense on the altar; this incense is described as σύνθετον λεπτόν "a finely ground compound," whereas MT simply has סמים "a perfume paste." Elsewhere in Exod A when סמים is translated it becomes (v.34) ἡδύσματα "aromatics" or ἡδυσμοῦ "of a sweet smell," or in 31:11 τῆς συνθέσεως. In B only the last-named word occurs (35:28 38:25 39:16 40:25).[6] All the other ancients are agreed that the word means sweet smelling spices or perfumes; cf Vulg: *suave fragrans*.

For τὸ πρωὶ πρωί see note at 16:21; the adverbial phrase modifies the second θυμιάσει as is clear from the further specifications of the ὅταν clause, rendering MT's pattern: ב + infinitive + subject suffix. The infinitive היטיבו is idiomatically reproduced by ἐπισκευάζῃ, a present subjunctive, "(whenever) he makes ready, dresses (the lamps)."

Exod places the emphasis on the place of the altar rather than on the incense which MT does. To Exod the section is about the altar, and so

6. In Aq and Sym it is translated by ἡδυσμάτων and in Theod by the synonymous ἀρωμάτων.

Aaron is throughout to burn incense ἐπ᾽ αὐτοῦ rather than to burn "it."

30:8 That the ἐπ᾽ αὐτοῦ interpretation of v.7 is intentional is clear from v.8 where again יקטירנה is translated by θυμιάσει ἐπ᾽ αὐτοῦ. Exod is followed by Tar Pesh in interpreting MT's בהעלת as ὅταν ἐξάπτη "whenever he lights, burns." The majority of witnesses have the simplex which means the same, but cod B has the compound. This verse is the counterpart to v.7; over against τὸ πρωὶ πρωί here it is ὀψέ, Exod's translation for בין הערבים. The phrase occurs only five times in Exodus; twice (12:6 16:12) it is translated by (τὸ) πρὸς ἑσπέραν, and twice, (29:39,41) by τὸ δειλινόν; cf the discussion at 12:6. A popular hex reading has articulated ὀψέ in imitation of the Hebrew.

The incense offering," explicative of θυμιάσει ἐπ᾽ αὐτοῦ, is called ἐνδελεχισμοῦ διὰ παντός, a doublet rendering for MT's תמיד . For the daily sacrifice see the discussion at 29:38. The doublet is in reverse order in the Byzantine text whereas an F s x variant omits διὰ παντός; this would equal MT but this may be coincidental since the shorter text is stylistically an improvement in removing the tautology.

This offering is to be "before the Lord[7] throughout their generations." -- The B z text omits the article of τὰς γενεάς, but this is not original.[8] -- Problematic is the third person pronoun both here and in v.10 in the phrase εἰς τὰς γενεὰς αὐτῶν for MT's לדרתיכם. Neither "their" nor "your (plural)" fits into the context. Possibly the translator's awareness that only Moses was being addressed stimulated an indefinite "their" (i.e. the people's), although Exod does not usually avoid changing to the plural along with MT, but cf v.9.

30:9 This verse is paratactically joined (uniquely) to, and is the negative counterpart to the orders concerning Aaron in vv.7 and 8, and is again in second person; over against MT Exod consistently uses the singular verbs;

7. Sperber's edition of Tar[O] leaves out קדם ייי, but the reading of a number of mss containing it is to be preferred, though the text is not fully in order in this verse; the insertion of בוסמין between "incense offering" and "continually" is taken over from v.7 and seems to have no basis in MT, but cf.v.9.
8. See the discussion in THGE VII.D. sub 29:42.

MT continues the second plural throughout the verse from the לדרתיכם of v.8. It should be pointed out that both verbs in this verse are changed to the plural in the majority of witnesses, a case of an early prehexaplaric revision towards MT. That it is not Exod is clear from the use of αὐτῶν in the phrase preceding this verse.

What may not be offered is "a ἕτερον incense," i.e. different from that ordered in v.7; the term is toned down from זרה, "strange" in a pejorative sense. Nor may the sacrifices which properly belong to the altar of burnt offering described in 27:1--8 be offered here, viz. the κάρπωμα and the θυσία. These are listed asyndetically, making the style most abrupt; the other witnesses have "and" before both. For κάρπωμα as a general term for sacrifice see comment at 29:25, and for θυσία as a designation for the cereal offering see note at 29:41. The former occurs here for the first time to translate העלה; see also 40:6,8,26 where τῶν καρπωμάτων is used to describe the altar of העלה. A popular F M reading changed the case of the first ἐπ' αὐτοῦ to the accusative αυτο (αυτω also occurs, but it is homonymous with the accusative), but it is unlikely that the phrase appearing in vv.7,8 and twice in v.9 should in one of these instances suddenly be aberrant. -- A popular F M text has θυσίαν in the plural; in a row of four singular nouns one appearing as plural is odd, and θυσιας is merely the result of a scribal error.

The prohibition against a libation, which also belongs to the rites of the altar of burnt offering (see 29:40), completes makes the list.

30:10 For the annual rite of propitiation in general see Bible Dictionaries. The verb כפר Piel occurs twice in this verse; for the various translations of this root see discussion at 29:31--33. Propitiation in association with the incense altar is ordered only here in the O.T. When this is described as being "on its horns" ἐξιλάσεται is used; i.e. the verb is used absolutely. But when the verb has an object αὐτό, i.e. the altar, καθαριεῖς is used to translate the verb (see also 29:37). ἐξιλάσκομαι can hardly have "altar" as an accusative modifier; one can atone for sin, propitiate the deity, but not an altar. If "altar" is to be the object one needs a verb like καθαρίζω "purify, cleanse (the altar)."[9] Note also Vulg's distinction between *deprecabitur* and

494

placabit; was Jerome here possibly influenced by LXX? -- An M *f* *x* variant has επ αυτο/αυτω/αυτου after ἐξιλάσεται. Since this is immediately followed by "upon its horns" it is a doublet and cannot be original.[10]

The second clause begins with an ἀπό phrase; the preposition is here used to indicate means.[11] For Exod's difficulties with חטאת as sin offering see comment at 29:14. Here it is described as "the purification of sins." Origen had trouble with this and transposed it as των αμαρτιων του καθαρισμου placing του καθαρισμου under the obelus. The phrase is followed by τοῦ ἐξιλασμοῦ which is in apposition to the phrase, though καθαρισμου is really a synonym of ἐξιλασμοῦ. -- For καθαριεῖ αὐτό see 29:37. -- For αὐτῶν see note at v.8. -- And for ἅγιον τῶν ἁγίων see the comment at 29:37. The unstated subject of the final nominal clause is probably the altar; see 29:37.

30:12 Vv.12--16 deal with the poll tax for the sanctuary. V.12 gives the overall rule. The phrase λάβῃς συλλογισμόν "take on a calculation," i.e. compute, refers to a census in which every male is to pass under review, ἐν τῷ ἐπισκοπῇ αὐτῶν.

The apodosis is introduced by an otiose καί in imitation of the Hebrew. The poll tax is called λύτρα τῆς ψυχῆς αὐτοῦ. λύτρα is Exod's translation for כפר.[12] At the end of the clause (after κυρίῳ) MT has בפקד אתם which Exod in view of the fact that ἐν τῷ ἐπισκοπῇ αὐτῶν already occurs twice within the verse had the good sense to omit though hex has inserted it.

The final clause is coordinated with the apodosis though Tar[P] and Pesh with good understanding introduce the clause with דלא, as a purpose or result clause. In any event it must be so understood. The word πτῶσις "accident, calamity," literally "a falling," is a somewhat milder term than נגף.

---

9. See Helbing 215.
10. For an explanation of its probable source in Lev see THGE VII.O.
11. See Bauer s.v. V.2; cf also Helbing 160.
12. Schl defines this word as *placamen, pretium redemtionis s. expiationis*. The later revisers make this ἐξίλασμα.

30:13 MT begins with זה יתנו "this shall they give" and then as explication of "they" a phrase in the singular, "everyone who undergoes the census." Exod amplifies the opening clause by καὶ τοῦτό ἐστιν ὃ δώσουσιν.[13] The explication of the subject in Exod is a relative clause but plural in congruence with δώσουσιν, - ὅσοι ἂν παραπορεύωνται τὴν ἐπίσκεψιν "whoever pass along under review." This is Exod's rendering of כל העבר על הפקדים.[14] The plural passive participle, הפקדים, idiomatically means "those who are numbered, counted in a census," and ἐπίσκεψιν must be understood in the light of it.[15]

The tax imposed on every male was a half didrachma, Exod's rendering of the Hebrew half shekel. The standard coin of Ptolemaic Egypt was the tetradrachma or four drachm coin, of which the didrachma was half; thus the poll tax was one drachm.[16] The standard to be used was the sacred didrachma;[17] this was to guard against a debased currency. Since to later copyists the coin was no longer current the spelling of the word became uncertain and the stem often became διδραγμ-, and even occasionally διδραγχμ-, but only διδραχμον is correct.

A learned note states that a didrachma was equivalent to 20 oboli, which is anomalous since there were six obeli in the drachm. The statement is a translation of the Hebrew"s "twenty gerahs equal the shekel" and presumably reflects the ideal "sacred didrachma." -- This poll tax is called an εἰσφορὰ κυρίῳ. The εἰσφορά renders תרומה for which see note at 25:2. It is only translated thus when it refers to the poll tax.

30:14 The subject in MT is the same as the explicative phrase "everyone who undergoes the census" in v.13, and here Exod uses the participial form

13. The Three all render this literalistically by τοῦτο δώσουσι.
14. Theod retains the verbal root but makes a more literal translation: πᾶς ὁ παραπορευόμενος ἐπὶ τὰς ἐπισκοπάς, whereas Sym made it πᾶς ὁ παρερχόμενος ἐπὶ τὰς ἐπισκοπάς and Aq had πᾶς ὁ παρερχόμενος ἐπὶ τὰς ἐπισκεμμένους.
15. For an analysis of this equation in Numbers see J.W. Wevers, "An Early Revision of the Septuagint of Numbers," ERETZ-ISRAEL: Archaeological, Historical and Geographical Studies, Vol.XVI: H.M.Orlinsky Volume (1982), 235*--239*.
16. Aq and Sym translate שקל 1° by στατῆρος, which was equal to a tetradrachma, according to Bauer, s.v. On this reckoning the half shekel would equal a full didrachma.

(πᾶς) ὁ παραπορευόμενος (comp footnote 14 above), but translates the prepositional phrase by εἰς τὴν ἐπίσκεψιν. πᾶς is, however, limited by the phrase "from twenty years old and above," a term first used here and one that was to become popular in the census accounts in Num 1 and 4.

30:15 The poll tax is a set charge, not graduated according to possession or income, i.e. rich and poor alike pay exactly the same half didrachma. -- Exod's ἐλαττονήσει is based on the stem ελαττον-, but with an -εω ending. The A F *b y* text has the same stem but with an -οω ending, whereas the Byzantine tradition used the root ἐλαττόω. All three mean "reduce, make less." -- For the popular διδραγμου spelling see note on v.13.

The second part of the verse in MT begins with לתת by which the attendant circumstance involved is given as "at the giving of the offering to Yahweh." The construction is unusual and Exod simplifies by using ἐν with a marked infinitive, expressing occasion or time when, "when giving the (sanctuary) tax to the Lord." The Byzantine text has added παρα των υιων ιηλ̅, a gloss taken from the following verse.

The verse ends with an infinitival construction showing the purpose of the tax "to make propitiation for your persons."[18] Exod follows the Hebrew in the plural noun and pronoun ψυχῶν ὑμῶν since πᾶς is involved, not just Moses.

30:16 Moses is to take the money of the tax and disburse it for the work of the sanctuary. The term "tax" is no longer תרומה in MT as in vv.13--15 but כפרים, but Exod sensibly uses εἰσφορᾶς as his technical term for the poll tax.

The money is to be used εἰς κάτεργον of the tent of testimony (cf note at 27:21). The majority tradition has added an article probably as a stylistic improvement. The phrase renders the Hebrew על עבדת. κάτεργον refers to the cost of labor, and thus wages.[19] The reference has to do with the general maintenance of the sanctuary, i.e. the operating expenses.

---

17. Cf SS 129.
18. See Helbing 214.
19. Aq nor Sym was satisfied with Exod, so Aq makes it ἐπὶ τὴν δουλείαν "on behalf of the service," whereas Sym more idiomatically has εἰς τὰ ἔργα.

The last clause states that the Israelites shall have (ἔσται τοῖς ...) "a memorial" before the Lord. In contrast to the usage at 28:12, here the reminder is that propitiation has been made. For ψυχῶν ὑμῶν see note at v.15.

The Byzantine text has added μνημοσυνον γαρ εστιν before the infinitive, a rather verbose attempt to clarify the relationship of the infinitive to what preceded. An n x variant has the present infinitive in place of the aorist, but "to make propitiation" is not a process which continues - it is only the μνημόσυνον which persists. And a C s variant has tried to simplify the text by substituting αυτων (i.e. the Israelites) for ὑμῶν (which also means Israelites but in direct address).

30:18(par 38:26a) Vv.18--21 detail the construction, placement and usage of the laver. MT begins the verse with a conjunction even though it is presented as beginning a new divine message (v.17). Exod with greater logic does not, but is then forced to use an imperative rather than a future indicative; comp 25:2.[20] Both laver and a base for it are to be made of bronze. The z tradition has αυτου instead of a dative and equals MT, but this is hardly recensional. The purpose of the laver was לרחצה or ὥστε νίψεσθαι. What is meant is the ritual washing described in the following verses which Tar translate by *qiddush.*

The second clause details its positioning, whereas the last clause orders Moses to "pour out into it water," an idiomatic translation of MT's נתת שמה מים. A b variant to the verb, εγχεεις "pour in" is an attempt at greater logical felicity but ἐκχεεῖς is clearly original.

30:19(par 38:27b) Exod follows Sam in reading the singular verb (by attraction to the nearer element in a compound subject). They are to wash ἐξ αὐτοῦ, i.e. in the laver, hands and feet. Both nouns have suffixes in MT and a popular hex reading therefore adds αυτων to each.[21] The verse ends with the dative ὕδατι, omitted as unnecessary by the majority text in conformity to MT, probably an early preOrigenian revision towards the Hebrew, although the omission might simply be stylistic.

20. The Three "correct" Exod to καὶ ποιήσεις according to Syh.
21. Cf SS 93.

30:20-21(par 38:27b) The two verses must be read together, at least up to the last clause of v.21, since the repeated pattern of ὅταν + subjunctive + modifier as protasis, and νίψονται + modifier + clause with μὴ ἀποθά-νωσιν as apodosis continues into v.21a. These render MT's double pattern of ב + infinitive with subject suffix + modifiers together with main clauses as "wash" + modifiers + ‏ולא ימתו‎.

The protases are parallel in that for a priest to enter the sanctuary is also to approach the altar to engage in cultic service; compare 28:31,39 29:30. For tent of testimony see note at 27:21. In the second protasis Exod has coordinate purposive infinitives (as does Pesh) λειτουργεῖν καὶ ἀναφέ-ρειν modifying the subjunctive προσπορεύωνται, whereas MT has the second explicating the first one. Exod distinguishes between the two and with fine sensitivity uses present forms since the verbal idea is a process. ἀναφέρειν as a translation of ‏קטר‎ Hiphil also occurs at 29:18,25, and for ‏אשה‎ and its rendering by Exod see note at 29:18. -- Instead of ὁλοκαυτώματα an F *ol C s* variant has the synonym ολοκαρπωματα, while its simplex καρπωμα obtains in *n*. And an A *C d t* variant articulates κυρίῳ. Whenever κυρίῳ stands for the tetragrammaton it is usually not articulated in Exod, though occasionally a τῷ does occur.

The two apodoses differ in that the first one interprets ‏ולא‎ as καὶ οὐ μή but the second as ἵνα μή; the second more accurately expresses the relationship between the two clauses: they must wash lest they die. The second also has accusative modifiers to νίψονται, viz. "hands and feet"; MT has "their hands and their feet," and hex supplies an αυτων for both.[22] An *n s* variant reverses the two to make "feet and hands," as unusual a collocation in Greek as it is in English. A very popular A B M dittograph from v.20 has extended the text of v.21 before ὕδατι as υδατι οταν εισπορευωνται εις την σκηνην του μαρτυριου νιψονται. Actually ὕδατι is not represented in MT but corresponds to its use in v.19.

The last clause decrees this to be "a νόμιμον αἰώνιον for them." -- Instead of the tautological "throughout their generations" of MT Exod simply uses μετ᾽ αὐτόν as part of a well known idiom; this improves the text stylistically.

30:23--24 Vv.23--33 describe the composition of the anointing oil and prescribe its use. In vv.23--24 Moses is ordered to gather the necessary ingredients: σὺ λάβε, and thus wisely fails to represent לֹך, a kind of reflexive pronominal element: "with respect to yourself;[23] hex supplied σεαυτῷ. These ingredients are five; four of these are ἡδύσματα "aromatic spices,"[24] and the fifth is a hin of olive oil; for "hin" see note at 29:40. These spices are: a) τὸ ἄνθος σμύρνης ἐκλεκτῆς "the flower of choice myrrh": 500 shekels. The Hebrew has רֹאשׁ מַר דְּרוֹר "the best of דְּרוֹר-myrrh." Just what דְּרוֹר means here is unknown; Tar[O] and Pesh have דכיא "pure" whereas Tar[P] and Vulg support the ἐκλεκτῆς of Exod. The use of ἄνθος "bloom, flower" in the metaphorical sense of the "finest" is well attested.[25] b) κινναμώμου εὐώδους:[26] half as much, 250 (i.e. shekels). κιννάμωμον (as well as κίνναμον) is a Semitic borrowing into Greek;[27] cf MT. c) καλάμου εὐώδους: 250 (shekels). καλάμου "reed, cane" is an exact rendering of קָנֶה. d) ἴρεως "iris": 500 shekels of the sanctuary (i.e. standard). ἴρεως occurs only here in LXX and is rare in the sense of an aromatic. The genitive form is also rare, ἴριδος being the usual inflection.[28] The word is the rendering for קִדָּה usually translated as "cassia"; cf קְצִיעָ(תָ)א of Tar, followed by Pesh Vulg. An *n* reading actually has κασσιας doubtless an import from one of The Three.

30:25(par 38:25) The verb ποιήσεις has two accusative modifiers: αὐτό and ἔλαιον;[29] the αὐτό has no specific antecedent, but refers to the collection ordered in vv.23--24, so "you shall make of it a holy anointing oil." This oil is then described as "a perfumatory perfume, the craft of a perfumer."

---

22. Cf SS 93.
23. Older grammarians ,e.g. GK 119s, with much learning but little illumination called this *dativus commodi* or *dativus ethicus*.
24. Sym substitutes ἀρώματα, which is a synonym of ἡδύσματα.
25. See LS s.v. II.
26. Cf for this phrase and the next SS 66.
27. Cf E. Boisacq, s.v."avec influence, per étym. pop., de ἄμωμος.
28. Schl distinguishes between ἶρις in the sense of "rainbow" and ἴρις (though he adds *vel potius* ἴρις). He also quotes Hesychius as defining ἴρις inter alia as ἀρωματική τις πόα, a meaning not recognized by LS.
29. Cf Helbing 55.

30:26--28 Moses is ordered to anoint with the oil (ἐξ αὐτοῦ)[30] seven of the things ordered made in the preceding account (but excluding the court and the priestly garments). The list in Exod differs from that of MT in that Exod placed "and the table and all its vessels" in sixth place instead of in third. Three items are accompanied by "and all its vessels," viz. the lampstand, the altar of the holocausts (singular in MT) and the table. This corresponds to MT except that "all" is attested for the phrase accompanying the lampstand in only a few Hebrew mss and in Sam. Some witnesses of *O b* omit that πάν-τα, thereby conforming to MT; this might represent an early revision towards the Hebrew. Hex has attempted to "correct" the order of the items as well, although the evidence is not fully clear. και την τραπεζαν και παντα τα σκευη αυτης was added under the asterisk in third place. Its Exod position in sixth place should then have been put under the obelus, but the *O* witnesses omit it; its omission could, however, have been caused by homoiot and its correspondence to MT a coincidence. Also hex is the order of αὐτοῦ τὰ σκεύη in v.28 reordered to conform to MT.

Striking is the fact that both the tent and the ark have identical modifiers: τοῦ μαρτυρίου, though MT has מועד for the first and העדת for the second. The terms "tent of testimony," for which see note at 27:21, and "ark of testimony," for which see note at 25:9, had become set terms in Exod which only become unsatisfactory when they occur next to each other. A majority A F M variant has added "and all its vessels" after "ark of the testimony," but there is no support for it in any of the old witnesses.

30:29 Though Exod reproduces the paratactic pattern of MT the order to sanctify them is not a second action but rather is involved in the anointing ordered in vv.26--28. One might paraphrase the intent by "and so you shall sanctify them and they will be most holy." -- This state of holiness, of being set aside for sacral purposes, is communicable by touch, so that anyone touching one of the holy objects is thereby also holy; cf comment at 29:37.

30:30 Moses is also ordered to anoint Aaron and his sons and (so) sanctify them. That sanctifying something or someone means a setting aside for sacral purposes is clear from the purposive infinitive ἱερατεύειν (μοι). Here the term does not extend only to the high priestly succession (cf e.g. 29:29--30) but to his sons as ordinary priests as well; since Moses is ordered to do this the term καὶ τοὺς υἱοὺς αὐτοῦ can hardly mean a line of single priests succeeding Aaron.

30:31 The Israelites are warned that "this oil will be a holy oil of anointing." The Greek is somewhat tautologous in that it has a doublet for oil. Literally it says "an oil, even a holy oil of anointing, shall this be." ἄλειμμα, the second word for oil, has been omitted by an *O* text which then equals MT. An *ol C* tradition, also bothered by the doublet, substituted χρισμα, but this is no improvement, since this simply forms a new doublet for "anointing." Then an *n s* variant has omitted χρίσεως, for which cf v.25, whereas the Byzantine text has added αγιων after ἅγιον, probably taken from v.29.

For MT's לי Exod alone has ὑμῖν; Exod has merely smoothed out the text by making the dative pronoun agree with the following prepositional phrase "to your (ὑμῶν) generations."

30:32 The opening statement forbids the use of this oil for ordinary purposes. Anointing was on the head not ἐπὶ σάρκα ἀνθρώπου, and to do so is forbidden. The Hebrew verb is ייסך, a root meaning "to be poured out," occurring only here. Sam has יוסך as though it were a Hophal of סוך which is quite unnecessary, since that would be a hapax legomenon as well.

The second clause forbids the use of this recipe for personal use. MT simply has "you shall not make," which Exod restates as "not shall there be made for you yourselves." The verb has been "corrected" to the active ποιησετε by a popular M variant, but the translator avoids the second active future throughout this section,[31] using when the Israelites are involved in an order dative referents such as ὑμῖν or ὑμιν ἑαυτοῖς, for which both here as well as at v.37 the lectio difficilior is to be preferred.[32] A passive inflection is attested by a B *C f* variant ποιηθησεται. -- The word for recipe in MT is מתכנתו literally "its measure, proportion." Exod uses τὴν σύνθεσιν ταύτην "this compound."[33]

---

30. See SS 122.
31. As THGE VII.M.7. argues.
32. See the discussion of this rare usage in THGE VII.G.10.

The verse concludes with two statements: "it (i.e. the oil) is holy and it shall be a holy matter for you." The point is that the oil is consecrated to sacral use and one must treat it as such. The two statements are co-ordinated as in Sam Pesh Vulg against MT, and the καί is probably textually based.

30:33 MT uses the technical term ירקח for making salve or perfume in the first relative clause (compare v.25), but Exod simply renders by ποιήσῃ; this is fully clear in the context of v.32, i.e. "whoever makes such." The *b* text adds ωστε οσφραινεσθαι, but this is borrowed from v.38, where it belongs.

Not only is making the compound a capital offence, so is the giving of it to an outsider, ἀλλογενεῖ, i.e. a non-Israelite "alien."[34] That these are capital offences is clear from ἐξολοθρευθήσεται ἐκ τοῦ λαοῦ αὐτοῦ. To be cut off in such a fashion is to become clanless, to be an outsider, banished from the cultic community. A *C* variant has τουτου for αὐτοῦ, which A *f* omit. The phrase is, however, a standard item in the Pentateuch, and Exod (as Pesh Vulg) has accordingly disregarded the fact that MT has the plural noun; cf also v.38 where, however, Vulg does have the plural *populis suis*.

30:34 Vv.34--38 concern the ingredients, preparation and use of the incense. Moses is told to take certain spices all in the same proportions.[35] The command in MT is simply קח לך which Exod translates literally by λάβε σεαυτῷ. For its parallel see note at v.23. The *y* text prefixes και συ under the influence of v.23. The spices to be taken are stacta, onycha, sweet odored galbanum and translucent frankincense. For these see Bible Dictionaries. The last two are of Semitic origin; cf MT's חלבנה and לבנה.

As in v.23 these are called ἡδύσματα though the Hebrew distinguishes between בשמים as ingredients for the anointing oil and סמים as spices for the incense. As to the spices to be collected MT and Exod differ on "sweet odored galbanum." In Exod galbanum is modified by ἡδύσμου, but in MT the two words are quite separate. The three spices are all connected by conjunctions (for which hex also supplies και for both), but these are then

---

33. Sym and Theod change this to τὴν σύνταξις ταύτην "this organization, arrangement"; cf Exod's use of σύνταξις at 5:8. Aq renders the word literalistically by τὴν συμμετρίαν αὐτοῦ "its proportion."
34. This usage is not the same as in 29:33 where it simply means "a layman."
35. For ἴσον ἴσῳ cf Lee 35.

followed by סמים ולבנה, "spices and frankincense"; in other words "spices" is in apposition to the list of spices which precede. As to the frankincense MT calls it "pure" but Exod makes it διαφανῆ.

30:35 Exod interrupts the orders to Moses by an indefinite third plural ποιήσουσιν, over against MT; since with v.36 the second singular returns, there seems to be no particular reason for it. The section as a whole has frequent change of subject. V.36 ends with a second plural pronoun which leads to second plural references throughout v.37. Then the section concludes in v.38 with an indefinite third singular subject.

The verb has a double object, αὐτὸ θυμίαμα; this θυμίαμα "incense" is then described in a series of modifiers: perfumatory work of a perfumer, mixed (i.e. compounded), pure, a holy product. Of these modifiers μεμιγ-μένον is an old interpretation of ממלח "salted" in MT, for which compare Lev 2:13. The interpretation of the word as "mixed" is also found in Tar, Pesh and Vulg, and represents an ancient understanding of the word.[36] Nor does the tradition change the word in the direction of "salting"; the only variant of note is the popular συνθεσεως "composition," an inner Greek at tempt at clarification; after all such a recipe is a composition with various ingredients, and as a genitive it would as modify θυμίαμα.

The Byzantine text had great trouble with this verse; after θυμίαμα μυρον is added; μυρεψοῦ μεμιγμένον is transposed and the gloss αγιον συνθεσεως is prefixed to it. This text would then mean "incense, a perfume perfumatory, a holy work of composition, of a perfumer mixed...." Of the other text families only C s agree in adding συνθεσεως after "work," i.e. "a work of composition (of a perfumer)."

30:36 MT has the prepositional phrase ממנה modifying the verbs in the first two clauses; the feminine pronoun refers to לבנה of v.34. The prepositions are to be taken as partitive, i.e. "some of it." Exod has ἐκ τούτων in the first clause and the reference is to the ἡδύσματα of v.34, and means "some of them." The phrase is omitted for the second clause; hex supplies it as ἐξ αυτου, which may conform to MT but does not fit well into its context.

36. Though at Lev 2:13 the interpretation "salted by salt" is assured in all the old witnesses.

So Moses is to grind some of them up into powder and place (it) before the testimonies in the tent of testimony. The term "powder" is a good rendering of the free infinitive הדק which follows a lexically related finite verb: "you shall grind some of it powdering (it)." The term "testimonies" is a rendering for העדת, a term which occurs frequently in the book (19 times) and is usually translated by τοῦ μαρτυρίου when it occurs for the free element of a Hebrew bound phrase (except at v.6 where "ark of testimonies" occurs). But when it stands alone (referring to the Ten Words) it is rendered either by (ἐπὶ) τῆς διαθήκης or by the plural "testimonies" as here (except at 16:34 "before the testimony" where the ark of testimony is obviously understood by the phrase). Furthermore here the number distinction clearly separates the two usages.

For γνωσθήσομαι as an interpretation of אועד see the note at 29:42. -- In the final clause the addressee is no longer Moses but the plural ὑμῖν, i.e. this incense of composition "shall be very holy for you."

30:37 The last statement of v.36 is explicated in a practical sense in vv.37-- 38. Exod simplifies MT by omitting the relative clause אשר תעשה entirely and by substituting ταύτην for the pronominal suffix of במתכנתה, thereby creating a simple prohibition: "an incense according to this composition (or recipe) is not to be made for yourselves." For ποιήσεται rather than the popular F M homophonous ποιησετε see the discussion at v.32.[37]

Hex has not only supplied a version of the missing relative clause by ο ποιησεις but also a conjunction and an article και το before θυμίαμα to conform to והקטרת. A further difference between Exod and MT obtains in the concluding clause; MT's לך is in the singular (as in Tar[O] Pesh), but Exod makes it plural consistent with the context. This also occurs in the Qumran text 4Q 365 as well as in Sam Tar[P], and is probably textual in origin.

30:38 A concluding warning similar to the concluding statement to the section on making anointing oil in v.33. As in v.33 MT's "a man who" is

37. For ἑαυτοῖς in preference to the B *O n* variant αυτοις see THGE VII.G.10 sub 20:23.

changed to "whoever," and hex here adds αυηρ at the beginning to equal MT.[38] The *C* text has secondarily transferred the gloss after ὡσαύτως.[39]

V.33 has a coordinate ὃς ἄν clause, but here a ὥστε clause obtains "so as to make himself smell nicely," which is appropriate in the context of incense.[40] Also different from v.33 is the main verb ἀπολεῖται, whereas v.33 had ἐξολοθρευθήσεται. Both represent the same Hebrew word and are simply stylistic variants. -- For "from his people" see note at v.33.

38. As do Aq and Theod; Sym uses ἄνθρωπος.
39. For εαν instead of ἄν in a relative clause see THGE VII.B.
40. For the Hebraistic ἐν αὐτῷ see Helbing 159.

Chapter 31

*31:2(par 35:30)*The verse begins with ἰδού as verbal clause modifier used in exactly the same sense as רְאֵה in MT. -- The main verb used to translate קָרָאתִי is perfect middle and not active as the *C n s* reading ανακεκληκα would have it. Exod chose the middle since showing action advantageous to or affecting the subject is peculiarly fitting here; what the Lord says is "I have called/summoned for myself (by name)."

The one thus divinely summoned is named τὸν Βεσελεήλ, with his patronymic defined as "τὸν τοῦ Οὐρὶ υἱοῦ Ὥρ of the tribe of Judah," copied almost exactly by Exod B except for τῆς (φυλῆς) being changed to ἐκ. The articulation of Beseleel is unique to Exod (in both A and B); this could hardly be demanded by the Hebrew since the verb קָרָא is normally modified by בְּ not by אֵת. The omission of the article by *n* is unlikely to be recensional. Exod's use of the article is fitting since the name is also followed by τόν which when followed by the genitive denotes "the one of," i.e. "the son of."

In the tradition the name is wrongly spelled as βεσσελεηλ, βεσεηλ, βεσελεην, βεσεβηλον; all are palaeographically inspired, and the spelling in Exod is assured. The spelling of Οὐρί is varied in the tradition; aside from the itacistic spelling ουρει, there are ορι, ωρι with change of the opening vowel; ορειμ, ωρειμ with final mimation as though it were a Hebrew masculine plural noun, and some with final ου added: ουριου, ουρειου, ωριου, οριου, which are due to partial dittography since the next word is υἱοῦ. The variant also makes υἱοῦ likely to be original text rather than υιον, τον, τον υιον, or τον του attested in the tradition.[1]

The last phrase designates the clan by the genitive τῆς φυλῆς Ἰούδα. The *C* tradition prefixes this by τον, assuring that the reference is to Beseleel, not to his forebears. Other traditions add ἐκ either before or in place of τῆς; these have been influenced by the Exod B text.

---

1. For a discussion of Οὐρὶ υἱοῦ as original text see the discussion in THGE VII.K.

31:3(par 35:31) Rather than MT's "spirit of God" Exod has πνεῦμα θεῖον "a divine spirit." That "spirit of God" would be πνεῦμα θεοῦ is clear from Gen 41:38 where Pharaoh refers to Joseph as ὃς ἔχει πνεῦμα θεοῦ ἐν αὐτῷ, and it is obvious that Exod is here avoiding a genitive noun. This must be seen in the light of his translation of the three prepositional phrases which follow: בחכמה ובתבונה ובדעת, which he changes to genitives: σοφίας καὶ συνέσεως καὶ ἐπιστήμης, nouns that characterize the divine spirit. One should also compare 28:3 where God commands Moses to speak to all the wise in understanding οὓς ἐνέπλησα πνεύματος αἰσθήσεως for רוח הכמה. Virtues such as wisdom, intelligence and knowledge are attributes which a divine spirit has. The translation thus far is taken over literally by Exod B.

The final phrase in MT has given rise to different interpretations; the difficulty is created by the conjunction which coordinates it to the above virtues, and so ובכל מלאכה has been translated by "and in all craftmanship." But the noun normally means "work" and Exod, followed by Vulg, has solved the difficulty by disregarding the conjunction; ἐν παντὶ ἔργῳ then modifies ἐπιστήμης, i.e. knowledge about all work; so Beseleel was an expert at any kind of job. Hex has added a καὶ to make up for Exod's neglect.

31:4--5(par 35:32--33) That these skills of v.3 do pertain to παντὶ ἔργῳ is clear from the explication of "in all work" in vv.4--5. Exod expands greatly on v.4 of MT's "to devise skillful designs for working in silver and in bronze." For the cognate structure לחשב מחשבת Exod uses coordinate purposive infinitives διανοεῖσθαι (first used for this root in Gen 6:5, but see also the phrase σοφοῖς τῇ διανοίᾳ in 28:3), and ἀρχιτεκτονεῖν "to design" but also "to supervise," i.e. to act as architect. Beseleel is not only to design the work in accordance with his own skills but also to supervise the entire work. That this role of the architect in supervision is really intended by Exod is clear from the additions which he makes to the vehicles of construction; not just the three metals of MT are part of his responsibility but also the list of fabrics: τὴν ὑάκινθον, τὴν πορφύραν, τὸ κόκκινον τὸ νηστόν, τὴν βύσσον τὴν κεκλωσμένην for which see notes at 25:4.[2] The adjective νηστόν "spun" is a hapax legomenon in LXX but creates no

508

difficulty since the verb νήθω is well known; note particularly the participle νενησμένος occurring in the B account but also in A at 26:31.

In the tradition a B *O n* reading has the aorist infinitive αρχιτεκτονησαι instead of the present; the latter is obviously original being the second of three present infinitives characterizing the task of Beseleel with "be devising, supervising, working" all emphasizing a process rather than a single verbal action. The neutral aorist occurs far more frequently in Exod, and the change by an inattentive copyist is easily understood.[3]

In v.5 Exod also interprets freely. MT divides the labors of 5a into two: "in cutting stones for setting (i.e. a reference to gem cutting) and in the carving of wood," two tasks demanding a great deal of skilled work. Exod thought rather of stone masonry and carpentry. למלאת is not translated since settings with respect to stone masonry is not sensible. Hex supplied it by adding πληρωσεως after λιθουργικά. The second labor, וברחשת עץ, he rendered by καὶ εἰς τὰ ἔργα τὰ τεκτονικὰ τῶν ξύλων. Origen did not realize this, and marked εἰς τὰ ἔργα as a plus, placing it under the obelus. Then since in his view only τὰ τεκτονικά rendered the first noun he placed the καί immediately before it. Because this now places εἰς τὰ ἔργα in the spot where למלאת should have had an equivalent some moderns have reconstructed a parent text with למלאכה which is completely unwarranted.[4]

In the last part of the verse the phrase בכל מלאכה does occur. It had also occurred in v.3 for which see note there, but here it is rendered quite differently since it modifies the infinitive לעשרת, and so Exod takes the phrase to mean the norm for working, κατὰ τὰ ἔργα; the nominal is plural since it refers to the various kinds of works which are to be made, i.e. the things lists in vv.7--11.

31:6 MT begins with an unusual pattern: pronoun + הנה + finite verb; Exod follows a more conventional pattern by omitting הנה, for which hex has duly supplied an ἰδου. The verb used in the pattern is δέδωκα which B + have changed to the aorist εδωκα.[5] The verb recurs in the second clause as well and in both clauses the perfect tense is the more appropriate. The

---

2. See SS 123.
3. See discussion in THGE VII.M.5.
4. Cf also the discussion in THGE VII.F.4.

verb has a double personal object "him and Eliab" and must be taken in the sense of "set," then "appointed." A reading with scattered support, αυτω, changes the sense radically: "I have given to him also Eliab." MT has no καί and the Masoretes have vocalized אתו to mean "with him."

The second appointee is Eliab, the spelling of which has almost unanimous ms support, only ελιαμ, ελιακ, ελιβ occurring with different pronunciation in the tradition. His father's name, ' Αχισαμάχ, has suffered much more; aside from an itacistic αχεισαμαχ, the following variants obtain: αχισαμακ, αχισαμααχ, αχισαμεχ, αχισαμα, αχιαμαχ, αχισαβαχ, and two with an αρχ- spelling: αρχισαμακ and αρχησαμεχ. Thus confusion of palatals κ-χ, dittography, confusion of α-ε, apocopation of final consonant, syncopation of an intervocalic *sigma*, confusion of μ-β, and an infixed *rho* to produce an initial αρχ- syllable are all attested. -- For the pattern: τόν + proper name + τὸν τοῦ see note at v.2. -- In contrast to the simple genitive for the clan designation of v.2, here an ἐκ phrase is used; this differs from the Hebrew construction which in both verses uses the preposition ל, i.e. "belonging to a tribe," rather than "coming from a tribe."

The second clause is a divine assurance which must be read together with the last clause which shows the raison d'etre for clause two, i.e. "I have given ... and they shall do (i.e. that they may do)." MT has a rather verbose prepositional phrase בלב כל חכם לב "in the heart of everyone wise of heart (I have put wisdom)," which Exod simplifies by omitting the first לב, παντὶ συνετῷ καρδίᾳ, i.e. "to everyone intelligent at heart" (i.e. everyone innately intelligent). Hex has added εν καρδια at the beginning to equal MT, but then omitted καρδίᾳ over against the Hebrew. It should be noted that Tar Pesh have rendered חכם by the plural, possibly under the influence of the plural עשו of the last clause, but certainly by a legitimate intuition that the word was collective. -- Not surprising is the change in word order of σοι συνέταξα within the relative clause by the majority hex tradition conforming to MT.

31:7--11(par 35:10--11,14--19) The A and B accounts differ considerably, the latter being far more detailed, and no comparison will be made at this point. The verses constitute an inventory of what is to be made but without mention of courtyard or of curtains. Over against MT Exod does not distinguish between the altar of incense and the altar of burnt offering which in the MT list occur between "the pure lampstand and all its vessels" and "the laver"; Exod coalesces the two into καὶ τὰ θυσιαστήρια and places these in fifth place immediately before "the table."

The order of the items in Exod is as follows: 1 tent of testimony; 2 ark of the covenant; 3 propitiatory; 4 furnishings of the tent; 5 the altars; 6 the table; 7 the pure lampstand; 8 the laver and its base; 9 the liturgical garments of the priests; 10 the anointing oil, and 11 the incense compound. Two of the items, nos. 6 and 7, have added καὶ παντὰ τὰ σκεύη αὐτῆς. The fourth item is unusual as τὴν διασκευὴν τῆς σκηνῆς for the Hebrew את כל כלי האהל "all the vessels of the tent." The term "all the vessels" often occurs in the tabernacle accounts of vessels pertaining to some item; in fact, in this inventory the term occurs both with the table and the lampstand (as well as with the altar of burnt offering which addition is not rendered by Exod), but significantly it is always rendered by τὰ σκεύη. But here the singular collective is used; the reason for the use of this rare compound (in LXX it occurs elsewhere only at 2Macc 11:10 in the phrase προῆγον (of the Maccabees) ἐν διασκευῇ) is probably to designate by this collective the component parts of the tent as a whole, inclusive of such parts as the curtains, pillars, veils, bars and screens, not otherwise in the inventory list. It is then quite intentional that the term renders כל כלי, and the hex prefixing of συμπασαν betrays Origen's failure to understand what Exod intended.

The order of the inventory items is quite at odds with the order of detailed instructions in chh.25--30 where the order is (with the altars separately given, that of burnt offering as 5a, that of incense as 5b): 2 3 6 7 1 4? 5a 9 5b 8 10 11. It must be admitted that this order gives no recognizable rationale, whereas the order of the inventory here starting with the tent as a whole, then the ark and the propitiatory and continuing with the garments, oil and incense seems to order the items so that the most essential items for the meeting of God and people precede those which, though indeed holy, are items used by the priests in their liturgical performances such as laver

---

5. The reading is secondary as is argued in THGE VII.M.5.

for washing, garments for wearing, oil for anointing and incense for purifying.

The characterization "ark of the covenant" occurs here for the first time, though a majority variant in 25:14 also has it. τῆς διαθήκης here translates עדת "testimony," and only here and at 39:15(35) is it so rendered, in both cases modifying the ark. For its use see note at 27:21. In the context of the ark it is usually rendered by τοῦ μαρτυρίου for which see note at 25:9, though once in the plural for which see note at 30:6. For its translation as τὰ μαρτύρια see note at 25:15.

That Origen did not fully understand καὶ τὰ θυσιαστήρια as a legitimate rendering of the Hebrew is clear from the fact that he placed it under the obelus whereas και το θυσιαστηριον του θυμιαματος και το θυσιαστηριον του ολοκαυτωματος is added at the end of v.8 in strict conformity to MT, rather than a simple transposition. -- The *oI C* reading, το θυσιαστηριον, makes unclear which of the two altars the reading intends.

In v.10 MT characterizes the priestly garments doubly as ואת בגדי השרד ואת בגדי הקדש, but Exod economizes by omitting the second as an unnecessary doublet, which omission hex rectified by adding και τα ιματια του αγιου. Also likely to be hex is the majority reading adding εις το before the infinitive ιερατευειν.

V.11 gave rise to a number of variant readings. An *s x* text has changed τοῦ ἁγίου to the plural, i.e. "of the sanctuaries." Then the last statement begins with κατὰ πάντα (for ככל), giving the norm for what "they shall do." A *b d* text has και for κατά, but a paratactic construction after the inventory list is hardly expected and the reading is based on a copyist's error. -- The relative clause has the verb in the aorist, with the pronoun ἐγώ preceding the inflected verb.[6] The popular omission of the pronoun was apparently an early prehexaplaric adaptation to the Hebrew. But the tense of the verb was also changed. An A *oI b* reading, εντεταλμαι, is a pedantic attempt to improve the text to mean that which God had commanded and which is still valid, an unnecessary elaboration of the tense values. More obvious is the origin of the popular reading εντελλομαι, the

6. See SS 74.

512

product of a copyist familiar with Deut where ἐντέλλομαι occurs 38 times, whereas Exod uses this only once (at 7:3 to render the imperfect אָצֵוּן).

31:13 Vv.13--17 enjoin strict observance of God's sabbaths. Moses is told: σὺ σύνταξον the Israelites, but MT has the root דבר. The Greek is stronger than MT. That this is intentional is clear from the actual command; in MT the particle אַךְ introduces the statement "my sabbaths you shall observe." This particle is somewhat difficult to translate; it tends to single out what follows from what precedes and so it is rendered by a contrastive δέ at 12:15 21:21. If more is here intended it would probably be somewhat emphatic "only my sabbaths." But Exod substitutes ὁρᾶτε καί "See to it that even (my sabbaths)." Vulg follows Exod with *videte ut*. An early popular correction of the verb to λαλησον is likely a preOrigenian revision towards MT.

For the term σάββατα see note at 16:23. Only here, however, is the term modified by μου in Exod. The appropriateness of the pronoun is made clear by the γάρ clause - my sabbaths you must observe because it is a sign; the observance of God's sabbaths is to remain a sign between God and Israel. Hex corrected ἔστιν γὰρ σημεῖον to οτι σημειον εστιν to equal MT more precisely.[7]

The sign in turn is meant to evoke among the Israelites the recognition that it is the Lord who is setting them apart as his people; the sabbath is to serve as a perpetual reminder of their God who has made them his special people.

31:14 As in the preceding verse the plural σάββατα is referred to by the singular; there the term is referred to as "a sign"; here it is pronominally referred to as τοῦτο, αὐτό, αὐτῷ. The grammatical incongruity has led to the popular "correction" to το σαββατον for which usage see note at 16:23. Another popular A reading has the aorist imperative φυλαξασθε for φυλάξεσθε, but this is not original. Exod throughout renders the Hebrew contextualized perfects by the future indicative, and the aorist imperative is rare.

7. See discussion in THGE VII.F.2.

The central notion of the verse is the holy character of the sabbath; Exod stresses this by adding a deictic element in the ὅτι clause for which the Hebrew has no equivalent: ἅγιον τοῦτό ἐστιν.[8] An early A O b omission of τοῦτό may well be an early revision towards MT. The tradition has glossed the statement by inserting κ̄ω̄ before ὑμῖν, an awkward construction with a double dative, undoubtedly an intrusion from v.15 (but cf also 16:23,25 20:10). The resultant awkwardness was secondarily relieved by changing the gloss to κ̄ῡ even further removed from Exod where it never occurs in such contexts.[9]

Since the sabbath is holy anyone profaning it will actually be put to death. Exod uses a dative cognate noun to render the intensifying cognate free infinitive of MT, which the Byzantine text omits; the omission was probably a haplograph, the finite verb also beginning with θανατω-. This statement is then further defined by the excommunication formula but with a nominative pendens identifying "that soul" as "everyone who does work in it"; note again the use of the singular αὐτῷ referring to the plural τὰ σάββατα. This then makes clear that "profaning it" in concrete terms means "doing work in it."[10] Though the construction is a hanging one outside the subject - predicate Exod has tied it in grammatically by the concluding αὐτοῦ. This can only refer to the pendent construction πᾶς ὅς, and not as one would normally expect to the named subject ἡ ψυχὴ ἐκείνη which is feminine. It should occasion no surprise that a very popular A F M reading has αυτης rather than αὐτοῦ.

31:15 V.15a is a paraphrase of the Sabbath Word of 20:9--10. MT has יעשה vocalized as a Niphal which creates a grammatical incongruity since the subject is the feminine המלאכה. This same incongruity is perpetuated in Sam Tar. Exod has voided this by levelling to ποιήσεις, and Pesh Vulg, to the plural *facietis*. Presumably יעשה was initially intended as a Qal with indefinite subject: "one shall work." -- The modifier is ἔργα in contrast to the ἔργον of the last clause, even though the same lexeme is employed in MT;

8. Sym and Theod emend by omitting τοῦτό, whereas Aq has ἡγιασμένου ἐστιν, possibly chosen rather than ἅγιον to contrast with the מקדש of v.13.
9. Cf the discussion in THGE VII.O.
10. Cf SS 109.

cf also v.14. But the use of the singular refers to "any instance of work" at all being forbidden, whereas in v.15a "all kinds of work" is enjoined for the six days. The distinction is intentional. A popular reading articulating ἔργα is possible, but is not an improvement.

The contrastive δέ clause identifies the difference for the seventh day over against the six days. Syntactically the clause has σάββατα as subject and "on the seventh day" as predicate, with ἀνάπαυσις ἁγία τῷ κυρίῳ in apposition to the subject. This latter differs from the syntactic patterns of MT where the bound phrase שבת שבתון is subject, קדש ליהוה is predicate, and the prepositional phrase is a temporal construction. In Exod the sabbath is further defined as "a holy rest to the Lord," which is later (in v.17) rooted in the activities of creation week when κύριος rested on the seventh day.

The final statement summarizes v.14b in a single sentence, but with some differences from MT. The Hebrew has "on the day of the sabbath," but Exod has "on the seventh day"; note also Vulg: *in hac die*. An A M *O* variant has του σαββατου for "the seventh" an early revision towards MT, as is the popular των σαββατων. Furthermore in contrast to v.14 Exod here omits θανάτῳ before the cognate verb; compare comment there.[11]

31:16 Two problems with the Hebrew text are dealt with differently in Exod. In MT the infinitive with which v.16b begins is modified by את השבת, i.e. by doing (i.e. observing) the sabbath. This immediately follows "and the Israelites shall guard the sabbath," thus "the sabbath" occurs separately as object of שמר and of לעשות; Exod relieves the tautology by substituting αὐτά in the second case (not αὐτό as v.14), though rendering the infinitive literally by the present infinitive ποιεῖν.

The second problem concerns ברית עולם with which the verse ends. MT, followed by Tar, takes "an eternal covenant" as part of v.16 making it a second modifier of the verb, i.e. "as an eternal covenant," which is possible. But if it were not for the *soph passuq* showing the end of the verse the reader would not readily take the phrase with v.16 but with v.17, i.e. an

11. For the originality of the shorter text rather than the very popular addition of θανατω see discussion in THGE VII.O.

eternal covenant between me and the Israelites. This is how Exod took it and so did Pesh Vulg.

31:17 The verse begins with two בֵּין phrases, which Exod represents differently, the first by ἐν ἐμοί and the second by a simple dative, so that the ἐν could be taken as governing it as well.[12] Hex has added εν before "the Israelites" to show that the preposition occurred in both positions; in contrast to this the *C f s* text has omitted ἐν thereby levelling both parties of the eternal covenant to simple datives.

This eternal covenant is then further defined as an "eternal sign that the Lord made...." This is quite different from MT, where the covenant refers to the demands made upon the people to observe; in Exod it is something that points to God's rest after the six days of creation.

The creation action is also presented somewhat differently in Exod. Both texts are agreed that the Lord/ Yahweh made heaven and earth in six days in accordance with the first creation account in Gen 1:1--2:4, but on the seventh day MT says that שָׁבַת וַיִּנָּפַשׁ "he rested and took a breath." The first verb gave no difficulty and was translated by ἐπαύσατο "he rested," but the second, presumably a denominative verb form from the well known noun נֶפֶשׁ, is vocalized as a Niphal and occurs only three times in the O.T. At 23:12 as well as in 2Kgdm 16:14 the aorist of ἀναψύχω is used, thus "be refreshed, took a breathing spell." But only here is it predicated of deity, and the old versions all avoid making a literal rendering; Tar Pesh use the root נוח "to rest," whereas Vulg combines the two verbs into a single expression: *ab opere cessavit*. Exod also avoids a literal rendering by using κατέπαυσεν "he stopped, left off doing." That this was intentional on Exod's part is clear from the fact that he uses exactly the same word in the next verse to translate the Piel of כלה in the construction "(when) he left off (speaking)." The clause could then be translated "and on the seventh day he rested and left off (the creation work)."[13]

12. The Three according to Syh corrected this individually, Aq by a μετάξυ repeated for both nouns as in MT, whereas Sym used the same word but did not repeat it for the second, and Theod stuck to the common rendering for בֵּין, ἀνὰ μέσον, in both positions.
13. Aq stuck closely to the Hebrew translating the two verbs as διέλιπε καὶ ἀνέψυξεν.

31:18 A transition verse created as a bridge between chh. 25 to 31 and the narratives of chh.32 to 34, which narratives can be read as a continuation of chapter 24.

In its present context the ἡνίκα clause must refer directly to vv.13--17 as introduced by v.12, though one could take the reference to speaking with him as referring to all the instructions of chh.25--31:17 which now indeed do come to an end. -- For κατέπαυσεν see comment on v.17. -- For Σινά see note at 19:1. When it is described as a "mountain" it always follows the noun in Exod and except for 19:16 both "mountain" and "Sina" are always articulated as well in spite of the Hebrew. -- Hex has added αυτος before λαλῶν to equal the subject suffix of the Hebrew infinitive. And a marginal reading in M s gives the variant επαυσατο for κατέπαυσεν, probably under the influence of v.17. A popular A M variant changes αὐτῷ to προς αυτον which means the same; neither exactly equals the אתו of MT.

The subject of the sentence is the Lord; it is he who left off talking; it is he who gave Moses the two stone tablets of the testimony, by which the Ten Words of ch.20 are meant. This is the first reference to the tablets as πλάκας first in articulated form as τάς ... πλάκας τοῦ μαρτυρίου (for "of the testimony" as an oblique reference to τὰ μαρτύρια as the Ten Words see notes at 16:34 and 25:15), and then unarticulated in πλάκας λιθίνας in turn modified by "written by the finger of God"; τῷ δακτύλῳ is here a dative of means. Presumably both descriptive modifiers, λιθίνας and γεγραμμένας..., are intended to convey permanence and authenticity for the tablets of testimony.

Chapter 32

32:1 The chapter narrates the golden calf episode. It (see comment on 31:18) takes up events after 24:18 where Moses had entered the cloud and remained there for 40 days and nights. V.1 details the people's impatient response to the long absence of their leader; they had given him up for lost.

Exod correctly interprets the paratactic construction: "And the people saw that ... and the people gathered themselves together" by a temporal subordinate construction καὶ ἰδὼν ὁ λαός ... συνέστη ὁ λαός. -- The perfect κεχρόνικεν interprets the rare Polel of שׁבֹ, probably rightly; the Polel occurs only once elsewhere (Jdg 5:28) where "delay" also fits the context; all ancient witnesses agree on this understanding here.

ὁ λαός is repeated for the main verb συνέστη as well, though it would have been quite unnecessary; Exod merely follows the parent text. For συνέστη an *O* reading has the plural which is also possible with the collective λαός.[1] -- For Exod's use of λέγουσιν as a historical present and its frequency in chh.32--34 see note at 2:13.

The abruptness of asyndetic imperatives עשׂה קוּם is mitigated in Exod by the insertion of καί. The *C s* text reads αναστα for ἀνάστηθι, the present imperative of the late formation ἀναστάω.[2] The present inflection is not particularly appropriate since the form is simply used as an ejaculation introducing an imperative, a call to action: "Up and." -- The gods which they demand of Aaron are presumably thought of as images to be carried in procession ahead of the people on the move through the desert. The demand rests on an underlying assumption that Israel's God who revealed himself to them through Moses is inextricably tied up with Moses' presence; once Moses is no longer there, the Lord is also absent.

This becomes clear from the γάρ clause giving the reason for the demand on Aaron. It is introduced by a long nominative pendens which the main clause only refers to by the indirect pronoun αὐτῷ. The construction

1. Aq, followed by Theod, uses ἐκκλησιάσθη, a characteristic literalism of Aq, while Sym adopted the Exod text.
2. Aq adopts Exod's ἀνάστηθι, but The Others have ἀνάστα.

introduces ὁ ... Μωυσῆς οὗτος ὁ ἄνθρωπος followed by a relative clause modifying ἄνθρωπος; the construction may then be understood as: "this Moses, the man who"; this is Exod's understanding of the unusual זה משה האיש, and may well be correct.3 Vulg simplifies the difficulty by *Moysi huic viro* changing the pendant construction to a dative modifying *acciderit* with which the verse ends. Within the relative clause a majority B F M reading has εξ instead of ἐκ γῆς but only the latter can be correct for Exod as the pattern of translation for "out of the land (of Egypt)" shows.4

32:2 For the historical present λέγει see note at 2:13. Scattered witnesses have the more usual ειπεν, a contextual adaptation rather than a revision towards MT. -- Aaron responds by telling the people: "strip off the golden earrings," but uniquely omits the second item from MT's list: "your wives, your sons and your daughters." Hex has inserted και (against MT) υιων υμων and added υμων after θυγατέρων so as to correspond to MT. Did the translator find the notion of earrings for Jewish sons outlandish, even though (or possibly because) it was acceptable practice among Egyptian youths of the day?

The last imperative is ἐνέγκατε which though transitive is in imitation of the parent text left without an object, and is in fact quite unambiguous.

32:3 The people did what they were ordered to do, and Exod corresponds exactly to MT. A popular M variant περιειλοντο is a classical second aorist inflection whereas Exod has the Hellenistic. The tradition also shows the influence of v.2 on the text of v.3 where αὐτῶν becomes των γυναικων αυτων και των θυγατερων in the C tradition and is των γυναικων αυτων in the majority A text. But Exod's αὐτῶν is clearly original; its antecedent is "their wives and daughters" of v.2, whereas the suffix in MT, being masculine, must have העם as referent.

32:4 The paratactic constructions of MT are imitated by Exod but there are a few significant differences. The pronominal objects of both ἔπλασεν and

3. Though cf GK 126aa which explains משה האיש as in apposition to זה, thus "this one, even the man Moses," probably because of the ləgarmeh accent.

ἐποίησεν are αὐτά, with the *b* tradition also supplying one for ἐδέξατο. The antecedent is then ἐνώτια of vv.2 and 3, whereas in MT these are singular pronouns referring to הזהב. This would be grammatically incongruous for Exod which rendered "of gold" by the adjective τὰ χρυσᾶ. Both cases of αὐτά are changed to the singular in a popular A F M reading which may well represent an early revision towards MT but without regard to the context. A popular A reading omits the article before γραφίδι, probably because an engraving tool had not been mentioned earlier and the indefinite noun would better fit the context. MT incidentally did vocalize בחרט as articulated. -- Changes to plural verbs, επλασαν in *b* and εποιησαν in *z*, are probably merely copyist errors, whereas the imperfect εποιει in *d* is really only an apocopated form of ἐποίησεν plus an itacistic spelling for *eta.*

Of more consequence is Exod's unique use of the singular εἶπεν for the plural ויאמר of MT. A popular A M reading has revised towards MT by ειπαν, but Exod was clearly censorious of Aaron's actions and attributes to him rather than to the people the statement "These are your gods, o Israel." Whether the singular was in the parent text is of course unknown, but it does make sense, particularly in view of the vocative ישראל, although cf v.8. If the plural be read, the people are speaking to themselves, whereas the context has up to this point been singular and referring to Aaron. In Exod the idolatrous identification is attributed to Aaron, stressing thereby the sin of Moses' priestly brother. All the other ancient witnesses follow the plural of MT.[5]

The statement made not only identifies the μόσχον χωνευτόν as "your gods" but even corrupts the great redemptive act of the Lord, the deliverance from the land of Egypt, by attributing it to these gods. The use of the plural is due to the parent text, but it is inconsistent with the singular μόσχον. -- For the *C n s* reading εξ for Exod's ἐκ γῆς see note at v.1.

32:5 The introductory καὶ ἰδών as well as the וירא of MT bears very little semantic content and is used more or less as a filler in the narrative indicating the next stage in the account. It really means "and then" or "furthermore." Incidentally Pesh understood the Hebrew word as **wayyīraᵓ**,

---

4. Cf the note in THGE VII.O. ad init.
5. As do The Three; in fact Sym according to Syh placed some distance

vocalized to mean "and he was afraid" presumably for his skin, i.e. of the populace making demands. -- The accent then falls on the building of θυσιαστήριον κατέναντι αὐτοῦ (of the μόσχον) and Aaron's proclamation of a feast τοῦ κυρίου for tomorrow; note that Exod does not use βωμον (as in 34:13), since this was not a pagan altar but was to be used at the feast of the Lord.

That Aaron should now proclaim (ἐκήρυξεν) a ἑορτὴ τοῦ κυρίου betrays the syncretistic nature of the event. The golden bull calf is proclaimed as "these are your gods," but this is identified as actually part of the Yahweh (κυρίου) cult, a violation of the Word prohibiting image worship, 20:4--6. What kind of ἑορτή this was to be is not clear; certainly it was not one of the three great annual festivals whose observance was demanded of all male Israelites; cf 23:14--17. An A F b f z reading omits the articulation before κυρίου and the possibility that it could be original Exod must be faced. In fact it occurs but once elsewhere, 9:29, where Moses says to Pharaoh that the plague of hail obtains that Pharaoh may know that τοῦ κυρίου ἡ γῆ. Furthermore the phrase ἑορτὴ κυρίου does occur in Exod at 10:9 and 13:6. On the other hand, here it contrasts with legitimate feasts of the Lord; i.e. the rarely articulated genitive is intentional and the variant text is due to the influence of the usually unarticulated word.

32:6 Exod has a fundamentally different interpretation of v.6a at odds not only with MT but with all other ancient witnesses. In these the actions of rising early, offering up holocausts and presenting peace offerings are put in the plural, i.e. are the actions of the people, but Exod has ὀρθρίσας ... ἀνεβίβασεν ... προσήνεγκεν; here it is Aaron who does these things. Aaron's role in the episode was already shown in the unique εἶπεν of v.4; here it becomes obvious that the chief architect in the scandal of the golden calf episode was throughout Aaron. It was he, as chief priest, who prepared and performed both holocausts and peace offerings, and the weak excuse given by Aaron when confronted by his outraged brother (vv.22--24) only places his position in sharper relief.[6]

---

between Aaron and the people by a contrastive αὐτοὶ δὲ εἶπον.
6. Readings from The Three are in part extant in Syh and witness to the plural as well. For the first verb Aq and Theod reproduce MT literally by

Instead of ἐπαύριον the *n* text has αυριον, but this is secondary. Exod always translates מחר by αὔριον (except at 13:14 where it has no Greek equivalent). On the other hand ממחרת occurs only four times in the book; it is always rendered by ἐπαύριον except at v.30 where μετὰ τὴν αὔριον occurs, i.e. Exod rendered the preposition מן separately in a μετά phrase.

Surprising is the singular θυσίαν σωτηρίου over against the plural ὁλοκαυτώματα. All other witnesses have the plural. The singular also occurs at 24:5 for זבחים שלמים but the use there as a second accusative refers to a class of sacrifice; see its note. Here the phrase renders the single word שלמים uniquely for Exod. In later parts of the Pentateuch and throughout LXX when this phrase occurs as a rendering for the single word it is always in the singular. I suspect that here the phrase also refers to the class of "peace offerings," for which term see comment at 20:24. This seems clear from the second part of the verse where reference is made to the people eating and drinking, which must apply to the שלמים sacrifices since they, but not the holocausts, were communal sacrifices in which the worshippers shared.

In v.6b ἐκάθισεν is modified by two coordinate purposive infinitives, a correct interpretation of לאכל ושתו. The two infinitives are resp. bound and free, but the free infinitive is a contextual one, i.e. it is free to take on the grammatical character of its context, in this case a marked bound infinitive. -- In the last clause the verb changes to the plural; the subject is still ὁ λαός, but after the common eating and drinking in connection with the peace offering they now as individuals stood up παίζειν.

32:7 Moses being up on the mountain is unaware of what is happening in the camp, and the Lord informs him in this and the following verse; Exod designates what is said as quoted speech by the direct speech marker over against MT. Exod has a longer text than MT which simply has "(go) רד," whereas Exod adds τὸ τάχος ἐντεῦθεν after κατάβηθι. Exod's parent text must have read רד מהר מזה as in Deut 9:12 where the Greek is the same as in Exod. In the tradition here as well as there changes in word order

καὶ ὤρθρισεν, whereas Sym keeps the participial construction of Exod by his ὀρθρίσαντες δέ. And instead of the verb ἀνήνεγκεν Aq and Sym have ἀνήνεγκαν and Theod has the simplex ἤνεγκαν, all attesting to the plural.

522

occur, but none of these is original.[7] The two imperatives βάδιζε κατάβηθι are joined by και in the *C b s* text, a gloss probably based on partial dittography before κα-.

The reason for God's ordering Moses to go down to the camp quickly is given in the γάρ clause. The people have acted lawlessly, which is Exod's interpretation of שחת; cf also Deut 9:12. In the story the Lord identifies Israel as "your people whom you brought out of the land of Egypt," as though the rejection of the covenant relation made explicit in v.10 is already implicitly given here, as though he negates the divine redemptive action entirely. For the plural relative pronoun οὕς (referring to λαός as a collective) the B *x z* text has ον, which is in grammatical congruity with λαός. οὕς as lectio difficilior is original Exod text.

32:8--9 The verb παρέβησαν is here used in the literal sense of "deviate, turn aside"; the verb is commonly used in the LXX with the meaning of "transgress" based on such a passage as this one: "turn aside from the way which you/I commanded." The verb in the relative clause is second person ἐνετείλω (as in Vulg) which indeed the consonantal text of MT permits, but the Masoretes vocalized the word as first person; see also Deut 9:12 which has simply taken over the Exod rendering. The *C* text has made the opening clause a γαρ construction, but Exod explicates the ἠνόμησεν of v.7. -- The pronoun ἧς is genitive by attraction to its referent.

The "turning aside" is then explained by four paratactic clauses. In the first clause Exod did not render the second word of the phrase עגל מסכה, which hex supplied as χωνευτον.[8]

The middle two clauses have been put into the perfect: προσκεκυνήκασιν ... τεθύκασιν. These constitute idolatrous cultic acts of worship and sacrifice over against ἐποίησαν ... εἶπαν. All four constitute deviation from the way but the cultic acts have lasting effects and are in the eyes of the Lord particularly heinous promoting a divine intention to destroy them (in v.10). A *b s x* reading changing the former to the aorist προσεκυνησαν but leaving the latter untouched is simply a thoughtless

For these retroversions Field is cited.
7. For a fuller discussion see THGE VII.F.4.
8. As Theod Sym; Aq, however, interpreted the phrase as a bound

mistake. All four verbs are plural as is the opening παρέβησαν, with the collective ὁ λαός σου as subject, including εἶπαν which here places the statement in the mouth of the people; the statement itself is identical to that of v.4 where the verb is singular referring to Aaron, which see.[9]

V.9 of MT is uniquely omitted by Exod. All other witnesses including the parallel in Deut 9:13 have it, and there is no evidence for a possible shorter parent text. The omitted passage has Yahweh saying to Moses: I have seen that this people is (literally "and behold it is") a stiff necked people." If the omission was intentional - and I can see no palaeographic factors which would make such an omission accidental - it may have been to increase the dramatic effect of the narrative. It could be looked at as a kind of an excuse given by God for not wanting to destroy the people: they are stiff necked. But to Exod it is Israel's attribution of the great and central act of redemption by her God to other gods, not the fact that it is stiff necked, that results in God's sudden decision to destroy the people. Hex has added και ειπε(ν) κς προς μωυσην εωρακα τον λαον τουτον και ιδου λαος σκληροτραχηλος εστιν to make up for the absent verse.

32:10 The expressed divine intention to destroy the people and begin anew with Moses. The participial construction, θυμαθεῖς ὀργῇ, sets the condition for ἐκτρίψω, though it is a paratactic clause in Hebrew. Hex adds μου so as to render the suffix of אפי. -- The main verb translates the Piel of כלה not usually rendered by ἐκτρίβω (elsewhere only at Ezek 43:8 in a similar context); in fact in Exod it is rendered by συντέλλω, καταπαύω, ἐξαναλίσκω, all of which (along with παύομαι) also occur in Gen.

The last clause is an exact replica of Gen 12:2a. At the end a few mss have the expansion found in 4QpaleoExodᵐ and Sam: και επι ααρων εθυμωθη σφοδρα του εξολοθρευσαι αυτον και ηυξατο μωυσης περι ααρων. How this gloss came into the Greek tradition remains a mystery.

32:11 ἐδεήθη occurs here for the first time as a rendering for the Piel of חלה and correctly interprets the figure ויחל את פני by ἐδεήθη ... κατέναντι; cf Tar Pesh קדם ... צלי for the same understanding. A

construction and translated the missing word by χωνεύσεως, which the Hebrew certainly allows.

popular B simplex ἐναντι represents change to the more common form; ἔναντι is popular throughout the Pentateuch, whereas κατέναντι obtains only three times in Exod (also at v.5 and 19:2).[10] It serves to place somewhat more distance between Moses and God, stressing a proper relationship; Moses pleads over against the Lord his God.[11]

A B f z reading omits αὐτοῦ in the phrase "his God" but this is not original. Of the 41 times that the collocation "Lord God" occurs only twice (13:8 34:14) is there no accompanying genitive modifying "God," and in both cases the genitive would be inappropriate.

The words of the intercessory prayer continue through to the end of v.13. In the opening "Why, o Lord" clause the collocation of the participial construction of v.10 is used again to render the Hebrew חרה אף but with a finite verb, θυμοῖ (ὀργῇ). The tradition shows a great number of variants, even the late equivalent θυμουσαι as from *θυμο-εσαι, the active θυμοις and the future passive θυμωθησεται. The b text changes the construction into a dative noun plus verb: θυμω οργιζει. As in v.10 hex supplied a σου after ὀργῇ so as to render the suffix of אפך.[12]

The relative clause must be seen in the light of v.7b. Moses is here at his most daring in that he corrects God: it is not I who brought out my people from Egypt, but you, Lord; you brought out your people and that by great strength and a raised arm. As in v.7 the plural pronoun οὕς is used to refer to the people; for the O reading ον, cf note at v.6. ἰσχύι and βραχίονι are both modified in the popular text by σου for which there is no warrant in the Hebrew. Nor is there warrant for articulating the second phrase as τω βραχιονι (σου) τω υψηλω; this is an unusual growth in the tradition which did not affect the coordinate phrase, thereby showing its secondary nature.

32:12 MT begins with another למה which Exod renders by μήποτε, which is intended to tie this to the preceding anacoluthic clause. What the μήποτε presupposes is something like "Let it not be (lest)." Vulg inserts *quaeso* in *ne dicant*, to show the progression from v.11 to v.12. The statement is intended

---

9. For the use of the Hellenistic εἶπαν in Exod rather than the variant ειπον see the discussion in THGE VII.M.9.
10. See Helbing 172.
11. For a fuller discussion see THGE VII.N.
12. Cf SS 95.

to persuade God that his reputation among the heathen (the Egyptians) is at stake.

What the Egyptians might well say or think is given with a direct speech marker λέγοντες. What God did, they would say, was μετὰ πονηρᾶς "with evil intent"; the exodus was to kill and annihilate, not to rescue and save. The two coordinate infinitive phrases have pronominal objects in MT and hex adds αυτους after the first one so as to conform exactly to the Hebrew. The pronoun is not necessary in Greek since it is obvious from the αὐτούς which occurs immediately before the infinitive, and its repetition is stylistically inelegant. The parallelism is reinforced by the parallel prepositional phrases modifying the respective infinitives.

With this expressed motivation given Moses proceeds to the petition itself which is also compound, i.e. παῦσαι and ἵλεως γενοῦ, a negative and a positive form: "stop the anger of your wrath" vs. "be propitious of the evil of your people." The genitive modifier of παῦσαι again renders the Hebrew collocation אפך חרון for which see vv.10 and 11, but here transposing the two synonyms ὀργῆς and θυμοῦ.[13] The change in order was probably made simply to vary the expression. Note how Exod had varied the patterns in vv.10 and 11 from participle + dative noun to finite verb + dative noun. -- In the positive counterpart the Attic ἵλεως is used, i.e. God is asked to be gracious, literally "propitious." The choice of verbal figure should be compared to MT's Niphal of נחם. In Exod God is not urged to repent of the evil towards (your) people, but to be gracious over against τῇ κακίᾳ τοῦ λαοῦ σου. Exod thus avoids any notion of God's repentance, or better said, divine repentance is said really to be ἵλεως. Note also how Moses uses the pronoun to emphasize that the sinning people is τοῦ λαοῦ σου; he thereby insists that they are not so much "my people" as "your people." The omission of the pronoun in the Byzantine text is probably rooted in homoiot and not at all intended.

32:13 Over against MT v.13 is subordinated to v.12, a conditioning factor for the double imperatives of v.12b; i.e. God is reminded of the patriarchal promises of seed and land which reminder should serve as further motivations for God to yield to the prayer of Moses. For MT's imperative זכר,

Exod has a participle, μνησθείς, attributive to the addressee of the previous imperatives.

MT has as prepositional phrase modifiers "Abraham, Isaac and Israel"; Exod joins the first two with "and" as well, and changes the last one to the more usual ' Ιακώβ. This contrasts the ישראל of vv.4 and 8 with the third patriarchal father clearly, and is already present in Sam; it is thus likely to have been textual in origin.

The relative οἷς modifies οἰκετῶν and its verb is in turn modified by κατὰ σεαυτοῦ "you swore by yourself"[14] and fortunately there is no translation for the recapitulative להם; the majority A F M hex text does add an αυτοις. A paratactic clause, which sensibly might have been subordinated to the relative pronoun as well, is loosely added in Hebraic fashion" "and you spoke to them, saying." The direct speech marker λέγων is appropriate but has no counterpart in MT or in the other old witnesses.

The direct quotation in Exod extends only through πλήθει. Over against MT Exod stresses the increase in triple fashion. MT simply has "I will make many" which Exod reproduces by the compound πολυπληθυνῶ "I will much multiply," a verb found only here in LXX, and as though this were not enough τῷ πλήθει is added at the end. -- ὡσεί appears as ως in f +, but this does not change the intent. -- The b text changes ὑμῶν to αυτων, likely under the influence of αὐτῶν in the relative clause later on in the verse.

The syntax of the remainder of the verse is loosely constructed. It is introduced by an accusative which has no verb to modify and serves as an accusative pendens which then serves as an antecedent both for the ἥν clause following as well as for the αὐτήν in the last clause. In MT the syntactic pattern is more usual in that the pendent collocation from "and all the land ... to your seed" serves as the object of the verb ונחלו, and the clause as a whole is still part of the direct speech of God. This is demanded by the relative clause "which I said I would give to your seed." But Exod has changed this into something that Moses on his own says to God: ἥν εἶπας δοῦναι τῷ σπέρματι αὐτῶν "which you said (you) would give their seed"; this then becomes a final reminder to God that he had promised (in Gen 26:4) to give this land to the patriarchal descendants and he could not now in good faith destroy this people.

For the last statement: "and they shall possess it for ever" MT does not have an "it" but 4QpaleoExod^m and Sam (as well as Tar^P Pesh and Vulg) do, and it must be textual in origin.

32:14 Again Exod avoids the crassness of וינחם יהוה by his καὶ ἱλάσθη κύριος (περί) "And the Lord was propitiated about," an idiom already used in v.12, for which see its comment.[15] Tar^O has also softened the verb by his ותב מן רוי; cf also Vulg: *placatusque est*. A Byzantine reading ἱλασθητι as an imperative is not particularly sensible in the context and must simply be adjudged as a copyist's error.

The preposition governs τῆς κακίας characterized by the relative clause "which he had said he would do (to) his people." The genitive pronoun, ἧς, is by attraction to its antecedent. An accusative modifier to ποιῆσαι is highly unusual in the sense of affecting someone with evil, and a popular M variant simplifies by an indirect object αυτω; the lectio difficilior must be original text. The main verb εἶπεν is probably also a simplification (along with Tar^P Pesh) over against the דבר of MT "had spoken (of doing)," since דבר is usually rendered by ἐλάλησεν.

32:15 Vv.15--20 describe Moses' immediate reactions to the incident. The paratactic "and he turned and descended" is rendered by a participle ἀπο-στρέψας plus aorist verb. κατέβη is modified by an ἀπό phrase which a popular F text changes to an ἐκ phrase with no real change in meaning; either preposition is possible in the context (see v.1 and 19:14).

This is followed by a nominal construction with "the two tablets of testimony" as subject, and "in his hands" as predicate; this in turn is followed by an appositional construction which has a parallel verbal clause following it explicating "written on both their sides." For the plural ταῖς χερσίν only Tar^O of the old witnesses agrees; all others have the singular. The plural is an obvious rationalization - two tablets presuppose two hands.

Only Exod describes the tablets as λίθιναι as in 31:18 34:1, 4,4 (but not 34:29) which shows Exod at work levelling the text in accordance with the book as a whole. These tablets were inscribed, γεγραμμέναι, on both sides. An early pedantic B z reading changes it to a κατα- compound. In the

528

verbal statement which follows the same z mss also read the compound.[16] That the statements are parallel is clear not only from the repeated participle (the second time with ἦσαν) but also from the modifiers which mean the same as well; "on both their sides" becomes ἔνθεν καὶ ἔνθεν in the second case, i.e. on one side and on the other side.

32:16 A further description of the tablets stressing their divine source: they were "the work of God" and more specifically the writing is the writing of God engraved on the tablets.[17] The tradition does show some variants of interest. The *C* text has the plural εργα for "the work (of God)," possibly because there were two tablets? -- The odd change of tense from imperfect to present led to the *x* reading, ην for ἐστιν, a levelling with the ἦσαν of the first clause. Copyists had a great deal of trouble as well with κεκολαμμένη (from κολάπτω "to carve"): an *f* spelling from κόπτω, another one from καλύπτω, and some mss with an *upselon* instead of *alpha*. But the חרות of MT proves the Exod reading correct.

32:17 Jesous had gone up the mountain, but only Moses had entered the cloud; cf 24:15--18, and now the two are rejoined on the descent; for the historical present λέγει see the note at 2:13. -- The attributive participle ἀκούσας modifies the subject (MT has an inflected verb in a paratactic clause), whereas the second participle κραζόντων modifies λαοῦ. A few scattered witnesses have the grammatically correct κραζοντος, but Exod here uses as he often does throughout the account the plural in referring to the people. Hebrew has the prepositional phrase ברעה; its noun is related to the root of הריע; cf its usage in Josh 6:16, also in a cultic context. It could here be interpreted as referring to cultic shouting. Exod, however, uses the neutral root κράζω.

32:18 For λέγει see note at 2:13. Exod uses the phrase throughout of φω-νή(ν) ἐξαρχόντων in Moses' response to Jesous' φωνή in v.17. The verb ἐξάρχω also occurred at 15:21 of Mariam singing a song, but it can hardly mean that here. Its interpretation depends on how Exod understood ענות

---

13. See Helbing 169.
14. Cf Helbing 71.

in MT. There the infinitive is used bound with גבורה and חלושה resp. in
the first and second instances, but used absolutely in the last case.
Accordingly the Masoretes vocalized the first two as ᶜănŏt "to answer,
respond," but the third one as ᶜannŏt "to sing"; in other words, it is a pun in
Hebrew. Exod has interpreted גבורה and חלושה resp. by κατ' ἰσχύν and
τροπῆς; these are comments on Jesus' πολέμου, and might be rendered
rather loosely by "winning" and "retreating," or better said "in victory" and
"being routed." The participle ἐξαρχόντων must then refer to the shoutings
accompanying stages in battle, the noise of "those taking part in, taking the
lead in" battle. Then the last line must mean "but the sound of those taking
part in wine (i.e. in feasting) I am hearing."[18] Of course the addition of
οἴνου in Exod also has no textual basis but it is an attempt to differentiate
quite properly between what the φωνή was not and what it was, viz. one of
revelry.[19]

32:19 Vv.19 and 20 describe Moses' reaction to what he found in the camp.
Exod as often omits any rendering for the introductory ויהי simply
starting with ἡνίκα. The temporal clause is taken by the Masoretes as
continuing with the וירא clause, but Exod by translating the word by ὁρᾷ
without a conjunction limits the subordinate construction to the ἤγγιζεν
clause. Exod with real sensitivity begins with a contrastive δέ structure.[20]
The tense pattern of the verse should be looked at closely: ἤγγιζεν, ὁρᾷ,

---

15. Cf also Helbing 214.
16. For a discussion of the variant see THGE VII.N.
17. See SS 76.
18. Unfortunately the evidence for the renderings of The Three is buried in
Syh's translation. I cite Field's retroversions here. Theod's renderings are
clear; he has revised Exod slightly inserting πολέμου after φωνή 1°,
changing the second ἐξαρχόντων to the feminine, and deleting οἴνου as
having no equivalent in MT. Aq rendered literalistically but took all three
cases of ענות in the sense of "response, answer," i.e. καταλεγόντων, resp.
with κατ' ἰσχύν, ἀπὸ τροπῆς and nothing. Sym paraphrases rather than
translate by his "it is not a cry of those ordering courage, nor a cry of those
ordering a rout, but the sound of oppression I am hearing." We also have
the evidence of Samariticon. The first φωνή is ἀποκρίσεως ἀνδρείας "a
response of courage"; the second, ἀποκρίσεως ἥττης "a response of defeat,"
and the last a judgmental ἁμαρτιῶν, which is hardly textual but is rather
homiletical.
19. Schl wants to emend οἴνου to αἴνου having misunderstood the clever
play on the part of Exod, and so renders the collocation by *vocem*

ἔρριψεν, συνέτριψεν, i.e. imperfect, present, aorist and aorist. These represent a perfect and three narrative preterites in MT. But in Exod only the last two are simple past: he threw, he broke, and the first two show a lively sense of what is impending, a dramatic build up to the eventual reaction of throwing and breaking, i.e. "when he was coming near he sees the bull calf ... and Moses becoming furious threw...." For ὁρᾷ as historical present see note at 2:13. A popular A F M reading voids the dramatic build up by its aorist ηγγισεν. -- For χορούς see note at 15:20. For ὀργισθεὶς θυμῷ see note at v.12; Exod's rendering of חרה אף here shows a fourth variation, all of which mean to be furious, literally "being angered with wrath."

Moses' fury resulted in his throwing the two tablets from his hands and breaking them at the base of the mountain, i.e. where the Israelites were encamped. Only Exod has "two" which though not incorrect is otiose. MT has written the singular מידו which Pesh and Vulg follow, but Exod follows the Masoretic Qəre and Sam in their plural, for which see note at v.15.

32:20 Not only were the tablets broken but also the bull calf ὃν ἐποίησαν. The plural verb contrasts with v.4 where it is Aaron who made the cast image, but this was of course at the demands of the people (v.1).

Each of the four verbs that follow and describe Moses' action has the pronominal object expressed over against MT, i.e. κατέκαυσεν αὐτόν, κατήλεσεν αὐτόν, ἔσπειρεν αὐτόν, ἐπότισεν αὐτό (referring to ὕδωρ, whereas the others refer to μόσχον). Pesh also has the first three, and Sam, the first two. In all four cases scattered witnesses omit the pronoun though that this might be based on the Hebrew is doubtful. -- The first of these verbs is modified by πυρί without an εν which is supplied by a popular B (hex?) reading. But Exod only uses ἐν πυρί when it precedes a semantically related verb, and the simple dative when it follows.[21]

The second construction simplifies MT's "he ground (it) until it was powdery," with the verb modified by αὐτὸν λεπτόν, i.e. "he ground it fine."

praecinentium hymnum. There is not an iota of evidence for such an emendation.
20. See the analysis in THGE VII.E.1.

The verb is aorist of καταλέω,[22] but an A F *d f t* spelling has κατηλασεν, as though from an analogous root *καταλαζω.

For the third verb an *O* reading has the compound διεσπειρεν for Exod's simplex but with no change in meaning.

32:21 For the formula: A said to B Exod usually indicates the addressee by πρός + proper noun; thus with Moses it occurs 48 times but only once with a simple dative (4:18). In fact, the only other exceptions are τῷ Φαραώ at 1:19, and τῷ ' Ιησοῦ at 17:9. This also applies to God, either as κύριον or τὸν θεόν. On the other hand with pronouns the dative rather than πρός + accusative pronoun is the more frequent. That πρός rather than the τω of B + is original before ' Ααρών is thus assured.

32:22 Aaron excuses himself over against Moses' accusatory question asking for an explanation. Over against MT Exod names the addressee πρὸς Μωυσῆν (Tar[P] as well). The immediate response is a shortened version for יֹחַר אַף since in contrast to earlier renderings (vv.10,11,12,19) Exod uses a simple verb (μὴ) ὀργίζου. Hex has added θυμω to represent the fuller phrase.

Aaron's lame excuse is put into a γάρ clause (against MT), thereby stressing why Moses ought not to be angry with him; *b* omits γάρ thereby equalling MT. Clearly due to revision towards the Hebrew is hex's addition of μου after κύριε.

What Aaron then says is but a paraphrase of the Hebrew. MT has the unique phrase כִּי בְרַע הוּא modifying אֶת הָעָם: "(you know) the people that it tends to evil." Exod has recast the entire collocation as a single modifier of "you know" as τὸ ὅρμημα τοῦ λαοῦ τούτου. ὅρμημα means "impulse, motive," but in this context it must be understood pejoratively, thus "the (evil) impulse of the people."

32:23 For the historical present see note at 2:13. The words attributed to the people are an exact repetition of what the people said in v.1 except for

---

21. See the discussion in THGE VII.L.1.
22. This form is not recognized by LS s.v. which cites only κατάλασα as aor.I, but cf Dan(LXX) 2:34 with the same form as here, as well as

an opening ἀνάστηθι - קֻם which v.23 does not have. See notes at v.1.

32:24 The excuse gets progressively lamer. Exod prefers εἶπα to the classical second aorist inflection ειπον of *O f n* (the ειπεν of two *n* mss is a subvariant palaeographically inspired).[23] What Aaron reported as having said to the people when they made their idolatrous demands is much shorter than in v.2; in fact it is almost crudely abrupt: "if to someone there is gold, strip it"! χρυσία is a neuter plural (reflecting the ἐνώτια of v.2?), but the singular χρυσιον found in scattered witnesses though theoretically reflecting זהב more closely is not an improvement. An *O* variant smooths out the abruptness of the statement by adding και περιειλαντο after the imperative περιέλεσθε. Aaron's statement to the people begins with the particle εἴ which most witnesses omit; the omission is auditorily conditioned.

What Aaron then did by his own account is to "throw (them) into the fire - and (surprise!) this bull calf emerged." ἔρριψα is used absolutely over against all the other old witnesses, with hex adding αυτα (referring to χρυσία) to conform to MT.

32:25 V.25 is introduced by a participle which makes this verse dependent on v.26, with a parenthetical γάρ clause intervening as a comment on the preceding. The opening statement uses a direct object with a ὅτι clause modifying it, i.e. "the people that it ...," with the verb διεσκέδασται "was dispersed." The verb renders the passive participle פרע "be loosened," here probably from its moorings.[24]

The γάρ clause is a parenthetical statement explaining διεσκέδασται. It uses the same verb but in an active aorist form with Aaron as subject and with a double accusative, i.e. "Aaron dispersed them as an ἐπίχαρμα to those who are over against them (i.e. their enemies)."[25]

καταλέσας at Deut 9:21.
23. Fully discussed in THGE VII.M.9.
24. Aq rendered the participial construction by ἀποπετασμένος (αὐτός) "it was spread out." Sym has γεγύμνωνται "it had been stripped bare," hence "left defenceless," whereas Theod simply revised Exod by a participial construction διεσκεδασμένος ἐστίν. Vulg's *esset nudatus* is a straight borrowing from Sym.
25. Aq and Theod used the aorist active forms of the participles found in

Problematic is לשׁמצה, a hapax legomenon of uncertain meaning. Tar understood the word as שׁם בּריע.[26] Exod renders it by ἐπίχαρμα, a word which means "laughing stock, something one pokes fun at" but in a pejorative sense, thus "an object of gloating." What Exod is saying is clear: Aaron in dispersing the people has made them an object of gloating to their enemies. -- Exod renders the plural participle קם idiomatically by ὑπεναντίοις.[27]

32:26 Though v.25 is subordinate to v.26 and ἰδών has "Moses" as subject, v.26 begins with a δέ construction with Μωυσῆς repeated as subject. The reason for the δέ is undoubtedly the intervening γάρ clause which has "Aaron" as subject and the change in subject indicated is from Aaron to Moses. In the tradition the δέ construction gave much trouble, many omitting the conjunction, others reading καὶ εστη.

Moses issues his call at the gate of the encampment, a call which is most abrupt in MT: "who is to the Lord? - to me"! All the old versions supply a verb "come" for good sense; Exod uses ἴτω, a third singular imperative of εἶμι. An *f* reading has the accusative for the genitive after ἐπί, but this is largely a matter of preference. -- The *C s* text changed εἶπεν to the historical present λεγει under the influence of v.27 where λέγει occurs twice. For Moses' statement the *b* text reads ει τις προς κν εγγισατο προς με, presumably an attempt at better Greek.

The response includes an οὖν showing the logical connection of the call to arms and the coming together of the Levites. A popular A F M text has the Hellenistic form συνηλθοσαν instead of συνῆλθον.[28]

32:27 For καὶ λέγει as historical present see note at 2:13. The majority text reads ειπεν. Moses' instructions to the Levites are introduced by the divine messenger formula, for which see note at 4:22. The formula always has

their ὅτι clauses (thus Theod retained Exod), whereas Sym has προέδωκεν "abandon."
26. Aq's εἰς ὄνομα ῥύπου also follows Tar's interpretation, as does Sym with his εἰς κακωνυμίαν. Theod left well enough alone and kept the Exod text.
27. The Three all render the word literally by ἀνθεστηκόσιν "those standing up against."
28. See the discussion in THGE VII.M.9.

κύριος as subject, except at 5:10 (with Pharaoh). The adverbial use of the demonstrative pronoun τάδε occurs only in this formula except for twice with ἐρεῖς (19:3 20:22), in both cases of the Lord to Moses.

In the first command to the Levites θέσθε as middle imperative obtains, for which the *n* + text substitutes the corresponding active form with little change in meaning. Its object is the ἑαυτοῦ ῥομφαίαν, reordered (but with αυτου) by hex to conform to MT. This noun also occurs at 5:21 and Gen 3:24, whereas μάχαιρα occurs three times in Exod and five times in Gen. It is doubtful that Exod distinguished between the two. The sword is to be put ἐπὶ τὸν μηρόν, without an otiose genitive pronoun.[29] Nonetheless hex has supplied αυτου in view of MT.

The second imperative is διέλθατε, for which the majority of mss have the more classical inflection διελθετε, shared by The Three.[30] The verb is preceded by καί (as in Sam Pesh), the other old witnesses including MT lacking a conjunction. The verb lacks a modifier, but this is clarified by the coordinate clause "and go back and forth from gate to gate through the camp." A change of preposition from ἐπί to εἰς in the phrase "to gate" in *b d t* represents an attempt to get away from the less precise preposition, possibly because of its use early in the verse with a more locative sense "on the thigh."

The final imperative "kill" has a triple ἕκαστος + accusative modifier, again in imitation of the Hebrew. The precise distinctions among the modifiers are not fully certain: ἀδελφόν, πλησίον, ἔγγιστα. The first is clear; the second is usually rendered by "neighbour," but how do these two differ from the third one, literally, "the one nearest"? The Hebrew is no help since קרבו is also "one near to him." Probably it means "his closest relative," but how this then contrasts with ἀδελφόν is not obvious. But it could also be the one physically nearest, i.e. the next door neighbour, but then what about πλησίον?

32:28 Only Exod renders the prepositional phrase כדבר משה by a clause καθὰ ἐλάλησεν αὐτοῖς Μωυσῆς. Exod always rendered the phrase כדבר in

29. Cf SS 93.
30. For Exod's preference in the matter of Hellenistic inflection of this stem see THGE VII.M.9.

this fashion, in contrast to Gen which never does, but regularly uses a κατά phrase; in fact only once, at 44:10, where כדבריהם occurs does Gen use a clause: ὡς λέγετε.

The second clause gives the result of the Levites' action. The verb has the Hellenistic inflection with a popular Byzantine reading having the classical ἐπεσον. MT has the singular verb as do Sam Tar, but Exod has "corrected" to a plural. The verb is modified by an ἐν prepositional phrase showing time when. This usage is not changed by the popular A M omission of ἐν. -- A B oII n z reading changes the order of τῇ ἡμέρᾳ ἐκείνῃ in which the pronoun stands first.[31] -- Instead of "about 3000 men," Vulg has *quasi viginta tria millia hominum*, a reading shared by a few Greek witnesses where, however, it involves the replacement of εἰς by εικοσι, which is probably the origin of the larger number.

32:29 Exod adds the addressee αὐτοῖς, followed by Pesh, over against MT, the reference being thus specifically to the Levites (not the Israelites). Its omission by a few mss is posthexaplaric as is clear from the fact that it is under the obelus.

The statement by Moses in Exod is quite different from that of MT. It begins with an imperative "fill (your hand)," an idiom which usually refers to ordination, though the vocalization by the Masoretes as a Qal imperative is unusual. Exod has an aorist indicative second person plural, and must mean "you have become ordained (i.e. to the priesthood)." Its modifiers, σήμερον κυρίῳ, must then be references to their carrying out the orders to destroy (vv.27--28).

MT follows this by a כי clause: "because each (was) against his son and against his brother," which Sam Tar support, but in Exod as in Pesh Vulg the כי is disregarded and the "each +" construction modifies ἐπλήρωσαν. What Exod means is that the consecration has been validated by the sacrifice of a near of kin; cf v.27. Hex has added an αυτου to both nouns to conform to the Hebrew. It has also supplied a repeated εν before the second one to equal MT. Furthermore for the conjunction ἤ the majority A F M text follows the καί of Aq Sym, following the Hebrew.

31. This is not an Exod order as the discussion in THGE VII.F.3 proves conclusively.

The verse ends with an unmarked purposive infinitive δοθῆναι which is Exod's rendering of ולתת. The omission of the conjunction in Exod is probably based on a shorter parent text; since ובאתי is immediately before it the *waw* of ולתת was either lost by haplography or is itself the product of dittography. The shorter text makes good sense and may be rendered by "that he may put a blessing on you." MT also has הרים, which Exod omits; it is otiose in view of the σήμερον earlier in the verse, but hex repeats it to conform to MT.

32:30 For the pattern: καὶ ἐγένετο + timer + verb see note at 18:13. This was revised by the addition of και before the verb to equal MT in a majority (hex?) A F M reading. For μετὰ τὴν αὔριον see note at v.6. The z variant επαυριον does not change the meaning, but the *b* reading, μετα την πληγην, changes it to a reference to the slaughter of the people by the Levites.

In Moses' first statement the use of the perfect ἡμαρτήκατε is nicely chosen. The people had indeed sinned and its effects (cf v.35) are still about. The second statement ends with a ἵνα clause indicating why Moses intends to go up to God. Exod does not use κυριον here in spite of MT's tetragrammaton. Could this not have been intentional? Israel has broken their covenant; the people must be restored to that relationship again; it is the God-people bond that must now be reestablished.

The ἵνα clause is a reinterpretation, not necessarily incorrect, of an אולי clause; this particle introduces an independent clause with the sense of "perchance, perhaps," and expresses the possible realization of something desirable here expressed by ἐξιλάσκωμαι - אכפרה "make atonement, appeasement."

32:31 Moses' relationship is still intact; he returned to κύριον and addresses him as κύριε (but with no counterpart in MT). The verse begins with a δέ structure which a C s reading changes to και; the δέ structure can be defended since the text changes to a third person verb and the subject is no longer "I" but Moses. The verb used is ἐπέστρεψεν, a common rendering for וישב. A B f z reading has υπεστρεψεν which is probably palaeographically inspired; at least it does not occur elsewhere in Exod, and is unlikely to be original text.[32] Clearly secondary is the passive ἀπεστραφη of the *C s* tradition.

The particle of entreaty אָנָּא is well rendered by the idiomatic δέομαι. The omission of κύριε by *s* + could represent a revision towards MT. -- This is followed not by a prayer but by a confession on behalf of the people, and the "great sin" is specified as their having made θεοὺς χρυσοῦς.

32:32 The actual prayer. A balanced μέν ... δέ construction obtains: if you do ... but if you don't. Exod also makes the prayer fully alike in its two parts adding with Sam an ἄφες as the apodosis of the first half, left unstated in the other witnesses. Exod also adds αὐτοῖς as a dative modifier of ἄφεις over against MT, and does not render the suffix of חַטָּאתָם, which in view of the dative modifier is unnecessary;[33] it is added as αυτων by a popular B hex text. -- ἄφεις is changed to the present subjunctive αφιης in the *b* tradition but the indicative is the expected form. Note also the itacistic aorist subjunctive αφης in many witnesses.

The negative counterpart expresses the condition economically by εἰ δὲ μή. The apodosis implores God to let him, though personally not guilty, share in the punishment of his people; the prayer is made all the stronger by omitting the particle of entreaty, נָא, from the translation. An A *ol b* + variant changes με to καμε which is an epexegetical attempt at a stylistic improvement: "erase me too (from your book)." God's book is the register of living people, and erasure of the name means death as is clear from v.33 where such erasure is effected only if one has sinned against God. Since the noun is modified by a relative clause with a second person verb the σου is unnecessary and a popular variant omits it.

32:33 God's response to Moses' prayer implicitly denies Moses' quixotic request for inclusion in the people's fate. MT begins with מִי אֲשֶׁר, an indefinite relative,[34] correctly interpreted by Exod as εἴ τις. -- חָטָא is often modified by a ל phrase, which is usually rendered either by a dative or by an

32. Aq and Theod both adopted Exod, though Sym has ἀνέστρεψεν.
33. Cf SS 95.
34. For מִי as an indefinite pronoun cf GK 137c.

εἰς phrase, but at times by a phrase introduced by ἐναντίον (at Gen 39:9), ἐνώπιον (only here in the Pentateuch), or ἔναντι (in Num 32:23 Deut 1:41 9:16 20:18, and cf Lev 4:2).[35] The notion of "to sin before God" is regular in Tar, here חב קדמי in Tar[O], and חטא קדמיי in Tar[P].

32:34 God's provisional relenting in response to Moses' prayer. The δέ after νυνί is contrastive to the statement of v.33, as in Vulg: *tu autem vade*. The Lord first orders Moses to continue the desert journey which had been interrupted by the Sina experience of chh.19--20 and now the golden bull calf episode. The command is put in the form of coordinated imperatives βάδιζε καὶ ὁδήγησον; for the former see notes at 6:6 and 19:24. Only Vulg agrees with Exod in attesting to the conjunction. A B M z gloss (καὶ) κατάβηθι (in the *f* text it replaces βάδιζε) is taken from v.7 (cf also 19:24) and is not really appropriate here at all, since Moses is no longer on the mountain.[36]

Exod's addition of a demonstrative pronoun in "this people" is simply good sense, shared by Pesh Vulg. So too is the filling out of אל אשר to εἰς τὸν τόπον ὄν, a need also felt by Tar who add (א)אתר. -- For εἶπα for דברתי see note at 4:15. The classical εἶπον is attested in *n* +.[37]

The middle statement is a divine promise that God's representative will lead the way; because of the idolatrous action of the people the Lord will not himself go with the people as the next section 33:1--6 clearly shows. God only relents partially, and only further intercession (33:12--16) will fullly restore the people to divine favor. -- The B *oI C* variant προπορεύεται, i.e. omitting *sigma* to make a present tense, is a palaeographically inspired error and can hardly be taken seriously.[38]

The final statement is a warning that the punishment of the people is still incomplete. In MT the root of the bound infinitive and that of the finite verb is the same, i.e. "when I visit I will visit." Exod has adopted the common rendering ἐπισκέπτωμαι for the root פקד for the first case but not for the second where he uses ἐπάξω; for the latter note its occurrence in a similar context but with a different subject in v.21. Exod's rendering may be

35. All and only the cases occurring in the Pentateuch are given here.
36. Cf also the discussion in THGE VII.O.
37. See THGE VII.M.9.

translated as "at whatever time (literally "day") I make a visitation I will bring on them their sin."

32:35 MT does present a problem that all the old translations but Tar[P] (which merely copied the Hebrew) found difficult. Yahweh plagued the people על אשר עשו את העגל "because of the fact that they had made the calf," but then the text continues with another relative clause אשר עשה אהרן, "which Aaron made." It would from this seem that both the people as well as Aaron made the image. Tar[O] gets around the seeming contradiction by rendering the first relative clause by דאשתעבדו לעגלא "(because of) that they had subjected themselves to the calf." Pesh choose a root plé which has a wider semantic range including "to serve, worship"; similarly Vulg has pro reatu vituli, which may well have been influenced by Exod's περὶ τῆς ποιήσεως τοῦ μόσχου. -- The B *O f z* text has ου instead of ὅν, by attraction to the case of the antecedent μόσχου.[39]

---

38. See also THGE VII.M.5.
39. See also the discussion in THGE VII.G.8.

Chapter 33

33:1 For εἶπεν for יובר cf note at 4:15. For πορεύου as a rendering for לך see comment at 4:12. The divine orders to go up hence involved Moses "and your people whom you brought out of the land of Egypt," exactly the same statement as found in 32:7; the addition of σου ("your") against MT may be due to levelling on Exod's part; the pronoun is also attested in Pesh Vulg. For the phrase in general see comments at 32:7.

εἰς τὴν γῆν modifies ἀνάβηθι. -- γῆν is modified by a relative clause "which I swore ... I will give it." For "to Abraam ... Jacob" see comment at 6:8. Over against MT "and" occurs before "Isaak" as in 6:8. -- Exod has the plural pronoun ὑμῶν (as does Pesh) in the phrase "your seed" rather than the singular of MT. Exod is plural presumably because three patriarchs are given, whereas MT's singular reflects the three fathers successively.

33:2 For God's promise to send his messenger before them see 32:34. Only Exod of the old witnesses has μου in conformity with 32:34 and Exod has levelled the two. The indefinite מלאך without either suffix or article is odd in the context and Exod's reading is smoother. Exod, followed by Pesh, also has the prepositional phrase "before you" in front of the accusative modifier, which hex has changed to fit MT. B x z have the more common προ προσωπου σου instead of Exod's phrase, and the Byzantine text has added it as a doublet in front of it. That πρότερόν σου is original text seems assured.[1]

In the next clause Exod avoids the Lord's direct involvement in the removal of the Canaanite peoples. The Lord is still angry with the people and so it is his messenger who will drive out the inhabitants of the land of Canaan. ἐκβαλεῖ has ἄγγελον as its subject (so too Pesh), whereas the other old witnesses all have a first person verb (i.e. with the Lord as speaker). Exod is thus consistent with 32:34.

The nations to be driven out includes the Girgashite as in Sam (though after, not before, the Perezite). Exod omits the Canaanite, and hex has supplied it to make the full list of seven; in the *b* tradition it is inserted in second place, and in *C n s*, after the Jebusite, In Exod, along with some Hebrew mss Sam Pesh Vulg all items are connected by conjunctions. In BHS there is no conjunction before nos. 2 and 5, whereas Tar^O also lacks one before no. 2 but has one elsewhere, and Tar^P idiosyncratically joins only the last one. In *C n s* the Girashite is placed at the end of the list (after the Canaanite; cf above), and in *O b f* it comes after the Heuite. -- Over against MT Exod does not articulate the list and hex has tried to "correct" this, though the evidence for it is somewhat spotty.[2]

33:3 MT begins with an ellipsis: "into a land," with no verb expressed. Exod has added καὶ εἰσάξει σε, i.e. continuing the third person reference to the messenger; it is he, not God himself, who will bring the people into the land as a B *n z* tradition would have it; a first person verb could not be intended since that would create a blatant contradiction within the verse.[3] Another error which flatly contradicts the facts is a *C* tradition which has εισαξεις, in which Moses himself is to bring the people into Canaan! -- For "flowing with milk and honey" see note at 3:8.

The reason for God himself not personally bringing the people into the Promised Land is given in the γάρ clause. μετὰ σοῦ accents God's accompaniment, whereas MT has בקרבך, which stresses God's dwelling in the midst of his people; both statements highlight God's unwillingness to associate directly with the people of the golden calf.

The διά collocation has created some difficulty for the tradition because the articulation for the infinitive is separated from it both by modifier and subject, i.e. the τό stands directly before λαόν. An M *b d* + tradition has solved the apparent difficulty of τὸ λαόν by omitting the article; a popular tradition has inserted τον which naturally clarified all the relations. The lectio difficilior is of course original.

The final ἵνα clause is exegetically parallel to the διά structure, both modifying the main οὐ μὴ συναναβῶ clause, i.e. God will not go up with them a) because you are a stiff necked people, and b) lest I should exter-

---

1. Cf the discussion in THGE VII.L.3.
2. For the unarticulated list of nations see the full discussion in THGE VII.D.5.

minate you on the way. A popular variant has omitted σε from the διά structure; the pronoun is strictly speaking expendible, though its presence does make the subject more obvious.

33:4 Exod subordinates the first clause by a participle thereby showing the relationship between the two clauses: "On hearing ... they mourned bitterly." What God had said is called τὸ ῥῆμα τὸ πονηρὸν τοῦτο "this evil statement." The reaction was κατεπένθησαν ἐν πενθικοῖς, although MT only has the finite verb. The Greek text seems to presuppose a cognate free infinitive accompanying the verb as parent text. A number of witnesses join B in reading a grammatically congruent singular verb, but Exod tends throughout to use the plural with λαός.

V.4b of MT reads "and they did not put on each his ornaments upon him." Since this contradicts (or is at best proleptic over against) the order in v.5 to remove them, Exod simply omits it and so makes a consistent account. A popular F hex reading, και ουκ εθηκεν ανηρ κοσμον αυτου επ αυτου, has restored the difficulty of MT.

33:5 Exod begins the verse with a shorter text; omitted from the translation are the words אל משה אמר; since the next word is אל it seems likely that either Exod or his parent text omitted the words because of homoiot. The intervening words are supplied by hex as προς μωυσην ειπον. The shorter text must be Exod since the homoiot is only true of the Hebrew, the second addressee in Exod being rendered by a dative τοῖς υἱοῖς ᾽Ισραήλ.

The first clause of the Lord's statement in Exod reproduces MT, but the rest of the verse is quite different. Exod continues with "watch out lest another plague I should bring upon you (plural)." This warning ties in with 32:35 where the Lord's smiting of the people is mentioned. MT has quite a different text: רגע אחד אעלה בקרבך, the last two words also occurring in v.3, and the opening words creating some difficulty of understanding, literally "one moment," so "an instant," and is usually rendered by "should I for a moment go up among you." Exod seems to have read נגע אחר and then to have understood the verb as Hiphil, with an introductory ὁρᾶτε μή added in order to make good sense. In this way the next clause "and I would exterminate you" becomes parallel to ἐπαγάγω ἐφ᾽ ὑμᾶς. This verb has been misread as επαξω εγω in B f which has in turn led to εγω επαξω in the Byzantine group, and even in an F oI C s reading to εγω επαγαγω.[4]

For the imperative clause Exod not only uses νῦν as equal to MT, but adds οὖν to show that the command ἀφέλεσθε is logically rooted in the fact that the Lord might further punish the people by plague and extermination. The imperative occurs in the active αφελετε in a majority A F M reading, and a C Byzantine gloss has added αφ υμων to it. Over against all other ancient witnesses עֶדְיְךָ "your ornaments" is rendered doubly by τὰς στολὰς τῶν δοξῶν καὶ τὸν κόσμον. Supposedly the glorious robes refer to the festal garments which the Israelites wore when worshipping the gold bull calf, though there is no reference to such in the account in ch.32, but see ἐξαρχόντων οἴνου in v.18. That the doublet is intentional is clear from v.6 where עֶדְיֹם is doubly rendered as well; cf comment there. It will be noted that the suffix of "your ornaments" is not translated by Exod nor is the immediately following מֵעָלֶיךָ, but hex added σου απο σου. Up to this point Exod had used the plural throughout to refer to the people and the singular of the hex expansion disregards the context.

The last clause does use the singular σοι, but this is sensible since God says δείξω σοι (ἃ ποιήσω σοι) referring to λαός as a whole. God will only reveal his intent over against the people once they have removed their paraphanalia. In this collocation Exod shows further independence over against the Hebrew's אֵעֱשֶׂה by making the verbal idea transitive (as though it were a Hiphil plus suffix). -- The σοι of the main clause is omitted by oI f z, though its formal equation with MT is probably merely a coincidence. -- A Byzantine revision has changed the relative clause to α ποιησεις; this relieves the text of the difficulty of the change in reference from second plural to the singular, since the σοι would now refer to Moses.

33:6 Here too MT only has "their ornaments"; the περιστολήν must refer to the "glorious robes" of v.5 though the word is different; περιστολή only occurs once elsewhere in LXX (Sir 45:7). Israel then put away all evidence of festal array, any outward betrayal of their festive activity. The verse ends in strict conformity to MT with "from Mount Horeb" which is no more

544

luminous in Greek than in Hebrew. Does it mean as most modern translations have it "from Mt. Horeb onward" (e.g. RSV, ZürB)? Or does it mean "away from Mt. Horeb? -- In the tradition the verb appears popularly with classical inflection as περιειλοντο, an *f* variant has the simplex στολην, and a popular variant omits the article before Horeb which in view of τοῦ ὄρους is not likely to be original.

33:7 Vv.7--11 deal with the tent of meeting, where God and Moses would meet from time to time. Though it interrupts the sequence of the narrative it does fit as a bridge from vv.1--6 to vv.12--16 where Moses continues to intercede for his people.

Two important differences immediately emerge in v.7. In MT the verb is imperfect showing that Moses customarily took the tent and would pitch it, but Exod has λαβών ... ἔπηξεν, i.e. an aorist. And in Exod it is Moses' own tent (as in Pesh) which is then used as the tent of testimony, for which term see note at 27:21. That this should in origin be Moses' own tent is a surprising notion which some scholars in the past thought to have been original.

The hex tradition has changed the order of λαβὼν Μωυσῆς to correspond to that of MT. The phrase "his tent" appears as την αυτου σκηνην in the *b* text, and the phrase has been transposed after ἔπηξεν in the *C n s* tradition, whereas hex has provided an object by adding αυτην to the verb as in MT, while *t* has added εμπροσθεν; this seems to be rooted in an attempt at giving the tent more prominence.

The second clause identifies the tent. Hex has in view of the Hebrew קרא לו added αυτη unnecessarily after the passive verb ἐκλήθη, but this is a good transform of MT's "one called it." The Byzantine text added η σκηνη as subject, which certainly leaves no doubt as to what was meant.

The last construction combines two finite verbs, an unnecessary ἐγένετο together with an imperfect ἐξεπορεύετο: "it happened ... would be going out." The Hebrew has והיה for the first verb, a construction usually omitted in translation when a temporal clause is intended (e.g. in v.8), but here no temporal indicator is present. The clause then shows customary action, and the sense might be given as "when anyone was seeking (i.e. an oracle from) the Lord he would go out into the tent outside the camp." MT has "tent of meeting which (was) outside the camp," and hex has thus added του μαρτυριου την to conform to the longer text.

33:8 Exod omits ויהי for which see note at v.7. The temporal clause has an imperfect "whenever Moses was entering the tent," the verbal element "entering" being a rationalization for MT's "going out (into the tent)." A popular B M reading added (την) εξω της παρεμβολης, an obvious import from the end of v.7.[5]

The apodosis has "all the people" as subject with a compound clause: εἰστήκει ... σκοπεύοντες ... καὶ κατενοοῦν "stood ... watching ... and were paying attention." The first verb, a third singular pluperfect of ἵστημι is grammatically congruous with λαός, but thereafter plural constructions referring to the people as individuals follow. The first is the present participle σκοπεύοντες together with a ἕκαστος construction; note that the plural extends to τὰς θύρας which is framed by the singular "each ... of his tent."

The second part of the apodosis has κατενοοῦν, an imperfect verb which is followed by a genitive absolute structure: "as Moses was going off (until he had gone into the tent)." The B *b* + text witnesses to the rare Hellenistic κατενοουσαν.[6] Presumably the attention focused on Moses by the people is intended to show the awe in which he was held by the people in the camp, not surprising in view of vv.9--10.

33:9 As in v.8 the ויהי at the beginning is disregarded and Exod starts with a ὡς clause. Only in this clause does Exod use an aorist, the verbs of the three main verbs all being in the imperfect of customary action: the cloud pillar was descending and was standing and (he) was speaking. That the subject of the last verb is the Lord is only clear from good sense. The Masoretes so interpreted it by dividing the verse precisely at this point by an ethnach. It must, however, be understood that neither MT nor Exod give an indication of subject change. The pillar of cloud is then the manifestation of deity and its speaking was the voice of God. This fact should

3. For a discussion of this variant see THGE VII.M.4.
4. For a discussion of this verb cf THGE VII.M.6.
5. Cf also the discussion in THGE VII.D.5.

make one chary of adding "the Lord" as RSV does; better is the translation of the ZürB which has "er (d.h. der Herr) redete."

It was as Moses went into the tent that the symbol of the Lord's presence, the pillar of cloud, would descend and take a stand at the doors of the tent. As in v.10 reference to the doors of the tent of testimony is in the plural; this is always the case in Exod A even though פתח never occurs in the plural throughout the book.[7] The singular of the B *f* + text is not due to the Hebrew singular but rather based on the understanding that tents had only one entrance.

33:10 The verse divides into two parts with πᾶς ὁ λαός in both cases being named as subject. Exod emphasizes this more than MT does by using the imperfect tense for the first, but the aorist for the second, a change not particularly fortunate, since both parts of the verse in MT show what the people would do whenever the events of v.9 took place. Exod shows this by the imperfect ἑώρα with "all the people" taken as a singular collective. For the plural "doors" rather than the singular in B *f* see comment at v.9.

But the second part of the verse is in the aorist. The verb is in the plural with the modifying structure "each from the door of his tent"; cf also v.8. Here "door" is in the singular, thus neatly contrasting with the "doors" of the tent of testimony. Both parts of the verse use participles but in different ways. In the first one ἑστῶτα describes the pillars at the tent doors; in the second στάντες is nominative, referring to the people's posture for worship, i.e. they stood to prostrate themselves.

33:11 Exod continues in the aorist even though an imperfect might have been expected. An *f* ms (246) does have the imperfect ελαλει but this is probably the result of apocopation, i.e. ἐλάλη(σεν) to ελαλει by itacism. The Lord's speaking with Moses is described as ἐνώπιος ἐνωπίῳ, in turn described "as though someone might speak to his own friend." The conditional clause idiomatically has an optative λαλῆσαι. The B *f x* variant future must simply be a mistake.[8] Hex could hardly abide the word order of ἑαυτοῦ φίλον which it revised to φιλον αυτου to equal MT. Most witnesses

---

6. See the discussion in THGE VII.M.9. For sigmatic endings for the imperfect third plural see Mayser I 2.83.

omit the τόν which precedes the phrase, but this is contrary to Exod usage. Whenever a reflexive genitive pronoun obtains before the noun it modifies it is always preceded by an article.

The last two clauses are again in the imperfect, with the second contrasting (note the use of δέ) with the first. It was customary for Moses to leave for the camp, but Jesous, the aide, would not leave the tent. The *f* text glossed ἀπελύετο with a ουτως before it. Its function is not clear, since it can hardly serve as a consequence of the Lord's tete a tete with Moses. Hex has added αυτου after θεράπων in view of MT's משרתו.

In the second clause Jesous has three modifiers: θεράπων, υἱὸς Ναυή and νεός. Ναυή occurs in a number of spellings all due to homophony (except for ναη): ναυι, ναβη, ναβι. Also to be noted is its articulation by του in *b* *s*mg thereby making the genitive relation explicit. The third modifier stands by itself, and the *b* text by adding ων attempts a stylistic improvement. It seems that the young man Jesous' function was to serve as single and constant attendant in the tent of testimony.

33:12 With v.12 the narrative of vv.1--6 is again taken up. Vv. 12--16 are a further intercession for the people. In v.12 Moses first reminds God that he had been ordered to bring up this people (see v.1 and especially 32:34), but had not been shown ὃν συναποστελεῖς μετ᾽ ἐμοῦ, a reference to God's ἄγγελος whom he would send (συναποστελῶ v.2) before him. This was merely a bargaining ploy, since Moses was not really interested in having God's messenger pointed out to him; he wanted God himself to accompany the people, i.e. he wanted full forgiveness for their idolatrous action in connection with the calf episode; cf 32:7--10, 31--35, and 33:3--5. -- Hex has changed the order of μοι λέγεις so as to equal MT.

The second half is adversative to the first, an accusatory "but you said to me." MT has no counterpart to μοι; its omission by the *oI n* text is, however, probably only stylistic, since it is otiose. What God had said according to Moses consisted of two statements: "I have known you beyond all others" and "in favor you are with me." The first of these is a free rendering of MT's "I have known you by name."[9] To know someone by name means to be intimately acquainted with; Exod does make the statement much stronger by παρὰ πάντας, which is in line with the late tradition of Moses being uniquely the man of God, the one in whom God confided.[10] The second statement, χάριν ἔχεις, is an unusual rendering for מצאת חן which is normally rendered by εὑρίσκω χάριν; cf e.g. vv. 13,16,17. Exod probably used this idiom for the first occurrence of the phrase in the account to indicate the state of favor in which God says Moses is, after which Moses asks for practical demonstration, i.e. to find favor. The change in idiom then becomes part of the bargaining process. -- As expected hex has transposed the order to fit MT.

33:13 Exod makes v.13 the logical consequence of v.12 by the οὖν particle. God had said that Moses stood in his favor - then "if I really have found favor with you." MT's apodosis is a rather difficult construction, but probably means "make me know your way and I will (i.e. that I may) know you." Exod interprets this in the light of the wider context (compare especially vv.17--23). What Moses asks of God is that he reveal himself ἐμφάνισόν μοι σεαυτόν.[11] Exod maintains that understanding God's way must be based on his self-manifestation; only then γνωστῶς εἴδω σε "would I know you clearly." A majority itacistic variant reads ιδω, but only εἴδω can be Exod in view of MT's ידע.[12]

The ὅπως clause with its perfect subjunctive seeks assurance "that I might have found favor before you." Moses thus calls into question the original premise of the verse, and even God's own statement (v.12) χάριν ἔχεις παρ᾽ ἐμοί. But it is the conjoined ἵνα clause that is the heart of the prayer. The real point of the intercession is that I may know that λαός σου τὸ ἔθνος τοῦτο. What he is saying to God is: is it really true that this nation is your people? Is the Sina covenant (24:3--8) valid or not? -- A widespread B gloss, το μεγα, modifying ἔθνος has come in from Deut 4:6; the gloss is also found in Tar^P Pesh, but does not belong here.[13]

---

7. See the discussion in THGE VII.H.3.
8. Cf discussion in THGE VII.M.6.
9. Cf SS 50, 127.
10. Aq, followed by Theod, has on the authority of Syh ὀνόματι, while Sym has ὀνομαστί. Retroversion follows that of Field.
11. See Helbing 222.

33:14 For the historical present λέγει see note at 2:13. It is the Lord speaking to Moses, which is made explicit by the Byzantine group's addition of αυτω κ̄ς̄, also supported by Pesh. The Byzantine text added εγω before αὐτός, which is fully otiose, since αὐτός modifies the first person subject of προπορεύσομαί. Exod rightly realizes that פָּנַי is to be understood as surrogate for "I personally." In other words, the Lord now capitulates to Moses' prayer. The *C* variant reading the present tense is a palaeographically inspired copyist's error.

The last clause "and I will settle you" has the verb καταπαύσω for which the comment at 10:14 is relevant. It means "to put a stop to," then "to settle," and it has the same reference as MT's "I will give you rest"; Exod and MT both refer to the promise of settlement in Canaan though using somewhat different figures.

33:15 For λέγει see note at 2:13. The majority A F M text has ειπεν. The addressee αὐτόν is now the Lord: "If you don't go yourself, don't bring me up from here." The protasis reflects the idiom of v.14a, i.e. with αὐτὸς σὺ πορεύῃ to translate פָּנֶיךָ הֹלְכִים; cf note on פָּנַי in v.14.[14] Uncertain is the order of the two pronouns with the majority of witnesses transposing them; the oldest witnesses, B and Phil, have the above order and so can be defended as original text.

The tradition has also affected the verb, συμπορευση as an A *b x* reading, προπορευη in the *C* tradition, and συμπορευη as a popular F M reading. Again the oldest text, cod.B, has πορεύη and probably represents Exod.

Exod has uniquely rendered the apodosis by με ἀναγάγῃς; all the other old witnesses have the plural pronoun. An early preOrigenian revision has added μεθ ημων before the collocation in an attempt to approximate MT somewhat more closely. This was not hex, however, which in more mechanical fashion simply transposed the words as αναγαγης με. Exod's change to the singular pronoun is probably intended. Moses has throughout identified his fortunes with those of the sinning people; cf 32:32;

---

12. As convincingly argued by Walters, 199f. See the discussion in THGE VII.Q.
13. Cf discussion in THGE VII.O.

God had distinguished between the two in 32:10 but Moses would have none of it. Now he puts it quite bluntly: if you won't go along yourself, count me out too.

33:16 Moses' final plea: "How shall it really be known that I found favor with you," with ἀληθῶς much stronger than the enclitic אֵפוֹא of the Hebrew.[15] To this the refusal on Moses' part to divorce himself from the people - ὁ λαός σου is immediately added - i.e. "even I and your people" is apposite to the subject of εὕρισκα. The question finds its real point in the ἀλλ᾽ ἤ structure with its genitive absolute construction συμπορευομένου σου μεθ᾽ ἡμῶν which may be rendered as "except for your going along with us."

The next clause is paratactically expressed in imitation of MT, but shows the anticipated result of the Lord's accompanying his people. Exod has taken MT's נפלינו as נפלאנו as his ἐνδοξασθησόμεθα shows, an interpretation which is also found in Vulg: glorificemur; cf also Tar[O]: פלאי.

The plural verb is preferable to the singular of an M f tradition since it is plural in MT; furthermore the singular was probably due to the influence of the ἐγώ which immediately follows.[16] The subject is here not just "I" as with εὕρισκα but clearly and climactically "even I and your people." The verb is modified by a comparative παρά phrase: "beyond all the nations which are upon the earth."[17]

33:17 Change of subject is shown by a δέ structure which is to be preferred to the B *O n z* καί pattern.[18] The verse opens with a preposed accusative modifier along with a dative σοι within it modifying ποιήσω, i.e. literally "also this thing for you which you said, I will do." The σοι is an epexegetical addition over against MT. It is, however, fitting in view of the γάρ clause which follows: I will do this for you "because you have found favor before me." For μου a popular A F variant has the accented ἐμοῦ instead of the enclitic. But Exod only uses the enclitic forms after ἐνώπιον (as well as after ἐναντίον; ἔναντι is never used with pronouns in Exod).

---

14. The Three according to Syh rendered the Hebrew idiom more literally into Greek. Aq has εἰ πρόσωπά σου μὴ πορεύονται, a word for word rendering. Sym Theod translate similarly but entirely in the singular.
15. Cf SS 126.
16. See the discussion in THGE VII.M.2.

For the translation of "(and I know you) בשם" by παρὰ πάντας see the comment at v.12. The καί introducing the clause makes this a second clause governed by γάρ.

33:18 For λέγει see note at 2:13. The *O* text has the aorist ειπεν. The Byzantine text adds "Moses" as a named subject, and the *b* text also adds an αυτω (i.e. to the Lord). Instead of δεῖξόν μοι τὴν σεαυτοῦ δόξαν a B *x* + text has εμφανισμον μοι σεαυτον , a direct borrowing from v.13. Reference to σεαυτοῦ δόξαν simply means "yourself," since the term δόξα when applied to deity means "his revelatory self"; it means God as he appears to man; this becomes fully clear in v.19.

33:19 God will indeed pass by before Moses with his glory. MT has טובי "my goodness" as object of the transitive אעביר, thus "I will make my goodness pass before you." Exod identifies this as being the same as the כבד of v.18. Showing his glory then means "passing by with his glory"; it thus refers to his appearance. Exod's παρελεύσομαι becomes προπαρελευσομαι in the *C* tradition, a reading blending the Exod text with the προπορευσομαι of the *s* tradition; cf v.14 for the latter verb.

That this is a matter of self-revelation is made clear in the second clause. MT reads וקראתי בשם יהוה לפניך. Usually קרא ב means "to invoke" as in 34:5, but that would be grotesque here, and the clause may well mean "and I will proclaim (my) name Yahweh before you," or possibly "call out my name Yahweh before you." Exod renders this by καὶ καλέσω ἐπὶ τῷ ὀνόματί μου Κύριος ἐναντίον σου. The usage here is unusual, and I would translate: and I shall call out before you by (or through) my name "Lord." There are two difficulties; the first is καλέσω ἐπί. What is meant in the context of God's promise to pass by with his glory is a comment on God's self-revelation to Moses. Moses knew God's name as "Lord," and it was by this name that God would reveal himself now orally in Moses' presence. The ἐπί with the dative here expresses means. The majority text omits ἐπί but this cannot be original. At 34:5 the collocation ἐκάλεσεν τῷ ὀνόματι does occur and clearly means "invoked the name," which is excluded from consideration here; the lectio difficilior must be retained.

Also unusual and creating difficulties both for readers and copyists is κύριος, here used elliptically in the nominative, i.e. as an isolate undeclined form. Because of its rarity two popular readings κ̄ν̄ and κ̄ῡ obtain, the former as an accusative modifier of the verb, the latter as modifying ὀνόματι; the latter reading automatically involves the omission of μου af ter ὀνόματί as well, an omission also popularly supported.

The second half of the verse creates little difficulty. God proclaims his absolute freedom to be gracious, merciful, on whomever he chooses. As the Lord he can indeed relent on his earlier intent to destroy, to punish, to withdraw from, his people. He now signals his sovereign acquiescence in Moses' earlier prayers.

33:20 The verse begins with "and he said"; only the context makes clear that the subject is still the Lord. Moses is unable to see μου τὸ πρόσωπον; most witnesses, however, have the pronoun at the end which corresponds to MT. The γάρ clause gives the reason for Moses' inability: no man can see my face and live. Exod repeats τὸ πρόσωπόν (μου) whereas MT simply has "me"; Exod prefers to level the text, though characteristically he does not repeat exactly; here the μου comes at the end; cf above.

33:21 Again God speaks. ἰδού as sentence modifier introduces a nominal clause with παρ' ἐμοί constituting the predicate: "Behold a place is near me." This is followed by an asyndetic verbal clause; this has been "corrected" by adding και (hex ?) before it by most witnesses to conform to MT. The verb is a future passive of ἵστημι "you shall be set (or "set yourself") on the rock.

33:22--23 The mechanics of Moses' seeing the Lord. As commonly in Exod וְהָיָה when followed by an indicator of time is omitted, and the temporal condition sets the stage: "when my glory passes by." Exod's μου ἡ δόξα is but sparsely supported and most witnesses have μου at the end conforming to MT.

The Lord will then by three successive actions protect Moses from seeing his face but allow him a glimpse of his τὰ ὀπίσω. The first of these is

"I will set you in a hole of the rock."[19] The noun נקרה occurs only once elsewhere in MT (Isa 2:21 where it is translated by τὰς τρώγλας "the holes" in LXX).

The second action is σκεπάσω τῇ χειρί μου ἐπὶ σὲ ἕως ἂν παρέλθω "I will cover you with my hand until I pass by." The Hebrew spelling of the verb is unique; שכתי is otherwise always spelled סכתי, i.e. overshadow, cover, screen, and its translation σκεπάσω is accurate.

The third action is ἀφελῶ τὴν χεῖρα "I will take away (my) hand." Hex has added μου unnecessarily to correspond to MT's כפי; it is otiose in view of the τῇ χειρί μου of the preceding statement (and would not even be required there.)

The desired result is clear: "then you shall see τὰ ὀπίσω μου, but my face shall not appear to you." Exod has added a τότε over against MT to show this to be the consequence of what had been described. What Moses would then see are the traces of the Lord's passing, "those things behind me," as it were the afterglow of his presence. Exod quite properly contrasts this by a δέ structure with the negative "but my face οὐκ ὀφθήσεταί σοι"; MT has no equivalent for σοι but this is contextually demanded. Even Moses will not see the face of God in accordance with the statement of v.20.

---

17. Cf SS 147.
18. Cf the discussion in THGE VII.E.1.
19. The Three witness to ἐν τῷ κοιλάσματι "in the hollow."

Chapter 34

34:1 With v.1 a new narrative begins, one concerned with repairing the damage referred to in 32:19, viz. the breaking of the two tablets. The orders are detailed in vv.1--3. The stony tablets are here πλάκας λιθίνας; at 24:12 they had been called τὰ πυξία τὰ λίθινα; πλάκας is the more usual designation not only throughout this chapter but in ch.32 (and 31:18) as well. -- The reflexive σεαυτῷ is in imitation of MT's לך,[1] and serves no real purpose in Greek. The modifying phrase καθὼς καὶ ἀι πρῶται "as even the first one" represents a prepositional phrase in MT. A popular tradition has καθαπερ as in v.4 for καθὼς but this does not change the sense.

The second order has no counterpart in MT but serves a useful function in the narrative. Since the next clause is God's promise that he will write on the tablets Moses must first bring them, and "come up to me on the mountain" is then appropriate; cf 24:12 where the Lord also orders Moses to come up, and then "I will give you the stony tablets."

The ῥήματα are the Ten Words of 20:2--17 and are here defined by a relative clause "which were ἐν (on) the first tablets which you broke," i.e. this was to be a second copy. The preposition in the majority A F reading is επι the literal equivalent to על of MT, but the locative ἐν is appropriate for designating where the "words" were. Exod uses the grammatically correct ἅς (referring to ταῖς πλαξὶν ταῖς πρώταις) since it is the direct modifier of συνέτριψας. A popular B reading αις obtains by attraction to its antecedent πλαξίν.

34:2 The order "be prepared" usually refers to being in a state of readiness, of purity; cf 19:11,15 and Num 16:16, and so here. Moses is to go up Mt. Sina "in the morning." A B + reading has επι (το ορος), but the εἰς of Exod is original. When אל modifies the verb עלה it is never rendered by επι in Exod.[2] In MT the phrase בבקר intervenes between the verb and

---

1. This use of לך is often called with more learning than light a dativus commodi or a dativus ethicus as e.g. in GK 119s.
2. Cf the discussion in THGE VII.L.3.

preposition and Exod omits it as repetitive. Hex adds το πρωι so as to equal MT.

The last order is appropriately put in the future middle "you shall set yourself (to me)," i.e. present yourself to me, an excellent rendering for the Niphal נצבת.

34:3 The entire mountain as well as the immediate vicinity in front of the mountain (אל מול) is surcharged with deity; only Moses is safe in the presence. Throughout the verse third person imperatives are used: ἀναβήτω, ὀφθήτω, νεμέσθωσαν all in the negative. MT makes a distinction in the verbal inflection for the first verb, i.e. לא plus imperfect over against אל plus the short form of the imperfect for the second and third, but the Greek treats them all alike. The first two clauses appear as μηδείς ... μηδέ in both cases representing the indefinite subject איש with negative particles before the verb. A majority A F M reading has και μηδεις for the second which is close to MT's ואיש אל and might well be an early revision towards the Hebrew.

Moses is to approach God completely alone; not only is no one to accompany him, but no one may even be seen in the entire mountain, a prohibition also extending to grazing cattle. Exod translates אל מול by πλησίον. With the Israelites encamped on the plain κατέναντι τοῦ ὄρους (19:2) the cattle would naturally be in front of the mountain, but Exod extends the possible area of feeding to all directions. -- There is some uncertainty as to the gender of βόες. Exod made it feminine ἀι βόες, but a majority of witnesses follow F M in οι βοες. Since καί precedes the article, one might suggest that ἀι was a dittograph., but the masculine is far more frequent and a change from ἀι to οι is more easily explicable than the reverse.

34:4 Moses carried out the Lord's instructions. For the phrase καθάπερ καὶ ἀι πρῶται see the note at v.1.

The second clause with a subordinate participle plus finite verb represents two paratactic clauses in MT correctly. The B text with scattered support omits τὸ πρωί as modifier of ὀρθρίσας as somewhat tautological but Exod always renders the modifier "morning" of הַשֹּׁכֵם and it must be original text.

In one form or another the clause "as the Lord commanded" occurs 22 times in Exod. Here it occurs with καθότι; more often it occurs with καθά, καθότι, καθά and καθάπερ are used as synonyms in Exod[3] and it seemed sensible throughout to follow cod B as the oldest witness. -- Exod usually follows the pattern: verb + dative pronoun + subject as here, and hex has reordered αὐτῷ κύριος to conform to MT.

The last clause differs from MT in adding Μωυσῆς as subject; the subject of the preceding clause "as the Lord had commanded him" was κύριος, and Exod make clears that a new subject is introduced. It is, however, unnecessary since it is obvious that Moses took the tablets along with himself. MT has בידו after the verb which Exod does not translate as such - it is of course obvious that he took the tablets in his hand(s) - Exod not only has added the named subject but also the phrase μεθ᾽ ἑαυτοῦ, as in Vulg: *secum*. Exod probably meant this as a meaningful interpretation of בידו and its omission by B *n* + could reflect a revision towards MT, though it may simply be a stylistic change.

34:5 Exod's text presents the reader with some uncertainty as to the subject of the second and third clauses. The first clause is unambiguous: "And the Lord came down in a cloud," but what follows is not. What Exod says is: "and he was present (παρέστη) to him there, and he invoked the name (τῷ ὀνόματι) of the Lord." Then v.6 continues with "And the Lord passed by." So it seems clear that somewhere after the first clause the subject changed to Moses. This seems obvious for the last clause since καλέω plus the dative of ὄνομα means "to invoke the name (of deity)." Tar[P] makes this fully clear by choosing צלי. But I suspect that Vulg is correct in making the change of subject take place for the second clause as well: *stetit Moyses cum eo invocans nomen Domini*. The antecedent of αὐτῷ is then the κύριος of the first clause. This also fits in with Exod's understanding of the relationship between the Lord and Moses. It is Moses who was to present himself to God in v.2, not the reverse. So too the theophany of 33:21--23 insists on

3. For the adverb as translation of כַּאֲשֶׁר by καθότι, καθά or καθάπερ see the detailed discussion in THGE VII.Q.

Moses not seeing God, but that the Lord puts him on the hollow of the rock.

34:6--7 The opening clause reflects the description of the promised theophany of 33:20--23. And as in v.5 the passage is difficult to understand. The first clause is straightforward: The Lord passed before his face; the use of the preposition πρό is intentionally chosen to show that the Lord carried out his promise; only this clause constitutes the actual theophany.

The difficulty comes immediately afterwards with καὶ ἐκάλεσεν κύριος κ.τ.λ. Is κύριος the subject? Or is κύριος part of what is called? And what about the long string of nominatives continuing through v.7? Or does the subject change so that Moses becomes the subject, i.e. "And he (Moses) said: o Lord, even the Lord God, merciful and gracious, etc." Tar[P] interpreted in this way with צלי משה ואמר; see also Vulg: *quo transeunte coram eo, ait.* In the light of v.5 (see comment there) it is likely that Exod understood the subject to have changed. But then how can one explain the syntax of what follows? There are at least two possibilities: a) as vocative with a string of modifiers: "o Lord, Lord God, merciful and gracious ...," or b) as a nominal sentence: "The Lord, even the Lord God, is merciful and gracious...." Both are possible and plausible, with the second being somewhat less exotic syntactically.

As might be expected haplography has created a B *d n x* reading with only one κύριος, but there is really no good reason why Exod should have departed from the MT repetition (followed by all the other old witnesses.[4]

V.7 is part of the above pattern. Exod begins with a καί against all the other old witnesses, and its omission by the *b* text equals MT. For the first attribute, נצר חסד , Exod has a doublet rendering: καὶ δικαιοσύνην διατηρῶν with the participle an exact rendering for נצר, and καὶ ποιῶν ἔλεος. The noun ἔλεος renders חסד at 20:6, but it is rendered by δικαιοσύνη at 15:13. The B + text has omitted ποιῶν but this seems to be an attempt at stylistic improvement. The doublet probably originates with the Sabbath commandment in 20:6, but must be original with Exod, the longer text serving the purpose of more fully explaining what נצר חסד means.

The next attribute ἀφαιρῶν has a triple object: "lawless and unright-eous acts and sins" resp. rendering עָוֹן, פֶּשַׁע and חַטָּאָה. The first equation, ἀνομία, renders עָוֹן in Exod twice, but only here; elsewhere ἁμαρτία and ἁμάρτημα occur. And for פֶּשַׁע ἀδικία also occurs only here, though at 22:9 ἀδίκημα is used. The third equation is usual; in fact ἁμαρτία is a particularly apt translation for חַטָּאָה. It must be said, however, that various terms for sin (iniquity, guilt, transgression, etc.) in Hebrew seldom have an exact equivalent in Greek and the Greek renderings are only approximations. Note, however, that Exod quite properly used the plural for all three.

V.7b has two parts, a negative verbal clause, and a positive participial structure parallel to those of 7a. The first one is a familiar pattern in MT: cognate free infinitive + (negative) finite verb. MT has rendered this freely by: (negative) verb + accusative object. A popular A F hex tradition has transposed these formally to approximate MT, but this was not good enough for the Byzantine tradition which added a cognate dative noun καθαρισμω at the beginning (probably from Aq or Theod).

The last attribute is a variant on 20:5b. Instead of ἀνομίας the majority A F M tradition has αμαρτιας under the influence of the Sabbath commandment. In all other respects Exod reproduces MT literally except for the epexegetical addition of γενεάν at the end so as to make good sense, and not repeating επι, which hex then does to equal MT.

34:8 Moses' reaction. The paratactic verbal clauses of the Hebrew are put into the Greek pattern of participles: σπεύσας ... κύψας + finite verb. An *O* *f* tradition has added an unnecessary (τω) κω̄ at the end, but only "the Lord" could here be the object of worship.

34:9 Moses makes his final intercessory plea for his sinning people. A number of text groups have the historical present λεγει instead of εἶπεν under the influence of its frequent use in chh.32--34. For "finding favor before God" as a motivation in bargaining with God see comment at 33:12. Exod has omitted the vocative אֲדֹנָי for which hex has added κ̄ς̄.

The plea is "let my Lord go with us," a plea found in more elaborate form in 33:16 for which see comment.[5] Here, however, MT has אדני, and not יהוה, and Exod shows this by the rendering ὁ κύριός μου. A popular A M reading κυριος is an internal Greek variant, since only acquaintance with the Hebrew could distinguish between κύριος and ὁ κύριός μου as representing different Hebrew designations for God.

The γάρ clause shows why a plea is necessary. The Lord is hesitant because "the people are stiff necked." An *O n* text omits the article thereby changing σκληροτράχηλός from a predicate to an attributive adjective.

The last two clauses are verbal both with future verbs. The two differ, however, in intent. Because of the Hebrew both are introduced by καί but semantically the second is dependent on the first, i.e. "and (if) you will forgive ... (then) we shall be yours." Exod has added a σύ after the first verb (against MT) which reflects the σοί of the second clause, thus creating an inclusive structure in which the two clauses are in a balanced relation. The objects of ἀφελεῖς are the reverse of those in MT's לעוננו ולחטאתנו, viz. τὰς ἁμαρτίας καὶ τὰς ἀνομίας ἡμῶν. The two nouns are transposed and a ημων is secured for both nouns by hex thus equalling MT.[6]

The final clause is a free interpretation of MT's ונחלתנו. To Exod the stress should lie not on the Lord's inheriting us but rather on the result of and the status achieved by such divine action: "that we may be yours."

34:10 Exod makes clear who speaker and addressee are, possibly since a new theme is introduced and there is no obvious connection with the preceding account. MT simply has ויאמר. The ἐγὼ τίθημί pattern of pronoun + present tense is usual for MT's pattern: pronoun + participle. The idiom "cut (a covenant)" in Hebrew is rendered in this chapter by the simplex τίθημι (see also vv.12,15, 27). In Gen the compound διατίθημι is used throughout (15:18 21:27,32 26:28 31:44) and Exod had also used it at 24:8 (compare also συγκαταθήσῃ at 23:32). The use of the simplex may reflect a desire to avoid the repetitiveness of a cognate collocation. Exod also adds a dative pronoun σοι. Its omission in A equals MT, but is more likely an error due to auditory confusion than to the Hebrew.

5. For בקרבנו Aq has ἐντὸς ἡμῶν, and Sym Theod have ἐν μέσῳ ἡμῶν.
6. Cf also the discussion in THGE VII.G.2.

The omission of σου from the preposed prepositional phrase in the next clause by the Byzantine text is probably due to homoiot after λαοῦ. A popular M reading adds a και before the verb by which the prepositional phrase is actually made to modify the verb of the preceding clause, τίθημί. -- The wonders are then described by a relative clause: "which has not happened in all the earth and in any nation." MT's verb is the Niphal of ברא, but Exod tones it down by γέγονεν. Is this because of the locative phrases modifying the verb? The second of these phrases has a singular instead ofהגוים, but this does not really change the sense.

The result is given in the remainder of the verse. Exod reproduces MT exactly except for ποιήσω which translates the Hebrew pattern: pronoun + participle; this is more usually rendered by a present tense of incipient action. Hex has added εν μεσω αυτου after εἶ σύ in imitation of MT's בקרבו, but this makes for Hebraic Greek.

34:11 Only here does the collocation שמר לך occur in Exod and he renders the לך by a nominative σύ[7] which is much better Greek than the more usual LXX literal rendering σοι found in C mss, but cf.v.12. The addition of πάντα to introduce ὅσα, though not in MT, does not change the sense. הירם at the end of the relative clause is not translated by Exod; hex has supplied a σημερον from The Three to make up for it. The *b n x* reading α for ὅσα is a free variant which does not change the meaning. The omission of ἐγώ in the clause by the *f* text must be an error since the pattern ἐγώ + present tense is the normal one.

In fact the pattern is repeated in the ἰδού clause as well: ἐγὼ ἐκβάλλω. This time the B O text wrongly omits the ἐγώ. And a popular variant has the future verb, a simple case of haplography. -- In the phrase ἀπὸ προσώπου ὑμῶν the plural pronoun is unique over against all other witnesses. The σοι of vv.10 and 11 had referred to Moses, but this is not sensible for the throwing out of the tribes "from before you," and Exod neatly changes to ὑμῶν. A popular B reading has προ for ἀπό.[8] -- The list of the nations are seven as opposed to the six of MT, "and Gergeshite" having been added in sixth place, though the *C f s* text has the phrase at the end.

7. Cf Helbing 193.
8. See the discussion in THGE VII.L.3.

Over against MT the tribes are all unarticulated, though a very popular A F M text has added articles in all cases.[9]

34:12 When the Niphal imperative of שמר is modified by ל plus second person pronoun that pronoun is rendered by a reflexive dative pronoun, thus σεαυτῷ also at 10:28 23:21 and the plural ἑαυτοῖς in 19:12. This contrasts with the Qal usage in v.11 above.

Exod has the plural τοῖς ἐγκαθημένοις for MT's singular ליושב but this is of course collective.[10] The verb used is again the simplex θῆς for which see note at v.10. The C reading has the compound διαθῆς, whereas a popular A M reading has διαθῆ, the middle form. The middle form occurs almost exclusively in LXX where it is very popular for the idiom כרת ברית. It would appear then that the C reading is a blend of θῆς and διαθῆ. -- The translator imitated the Hebrew in the relative clause modifying γῆς, viz. "into which you are entering εἰς αὐτήν," which is better Hebrew than Greek. Hex has added συ before the verb to conform to MT.

The last clause is another פן clause modifying the first one. Exod, however, has a μή clause rather than μηποτε as in the first one, probably for variety's sake. The majority text does follow the longer hex compound μηποτε. B + has added σοι which is peculiar in view of the ἐν ὑμῖν in the clause.[11] -- For the term πρόσκομμα as a rendering for מוקש see 23:33. The s reading εγκομμα is a synonym.

34:13 This verse has been fully and exactly reproduced in Deut 7:5. In turn the parent text of Exod must have had something like the ופסיליהם תשרפון באש of Deut for the last clause which is lacking in MT. It is of course possible that Exod has amplified the text to make it correspond to the Hebrew of Deut, but in view of his care in rendering MT this seems less likely.

There are four clauses each one demanding the destruction of some form of idolatrous cult. These are τοὺς βωμούς, τὰς στήλας, τὰ ἄλση and τὰ γλυπτὰ τῶν θεῶν. In each case an αὐτῶν obtains referring to the tribes

9. For a full discussion of the list see THGE VII.D.5.
10. Sym also has a plural but changes the expression to τοῖς ἐνοικοῦσι τὴν γῆν which more closely approximates ליושב הארץ than does Exod.
11. Cf the note in THGE VII.O.

in Canaan of v.11. The first of these means "altars" often used of foreign
altars or altars to foreign deities in distinction from θυσιαστήρια. στήλας
"pillars" stands for מצבה, stone monuments used as objects of worship. The
third one means "sacred areas," often of woody areas; cf Vulg: *lucos*. This
rendering for "Asherim" first occurs here and thereafter became the "standard" translation for אשרים. The Hebrew term was early associated with
"trees" in Jewish thought, for which Exod is the earliest evidence. Most
moderns now associate the Hebrew term with the goddess Asherah but the
masculine plural suffix calls this into question here. Possibly images of
Asherah are intended? In any event Exod did not understand it thus nor did
later translators including The Three (e.g. Isa 27:9 where, however, LXX
has τὰ δένδρα). The last item concerns "cast images of their gods" which are
to be burned πυρί, for which B plus some *n z* mss have εν πυρι. For this
variation see note at 32:20.

34:14 The verse consists of two γάρ clauses, the first presenting the basis for
the command to destroy the various cult objects in v.13, and the second
giving a reason for the first. The first prohibits the worship of another god,
and is a short form of The Word in 20:4--6. For ἑτέρῳ the *b* text has
αλλοτρω, an exegetical attempt at a more exact definition.

This prohibition is rooted in the fact that the Lord God is a jealous
God; cf comment at 20:5. The syntax of the clause is, however, somewhat
unusual. Between the subject κύριος ὁ θεός and θεὸς ζηλωτής ἐστιν is the
collocation ζηλωτὸν ὄνομα, which is in apposition to the subject or to the
predicate. Exod is an attempt to make of the two nominal clauses of MT a
single statement. MT's first clause has יהוה as subject and קנא שמו as its
predicate, i.e. "Yahweh's name is holy," and the second one says "he is a
jealous God."[12] Exod has used the double name as subject, which has not
made the analysis simpler, and has not rendered the suffix of שמו, which
hex has supplied by an αυτου. I would translate the second clause by "for
the Lord God is a jealous name, a jealous God."

34:15 The μήποτε clause is an exact replica of its fellow in v.12; cf the note
there. The verb not only has been changed in the tradition to διαθης and

διαθη as in v.12, but the latter has led to an *oI C s* reading θη as well. An odd gloss in B + is προς αλλοφυλους "to the Philistines" identifying the ἐγκαθημένοις; the gloss is not only not original; it is non-Pentateuchal in origin.[13]

The next four clauses as well as the four clauses of v.16 are all governed by the μήποτε at the beginning of the verse, a series of subjunctive verbs paratactically joined. There is, however, an inner logic among these; the first three are third plural and refer to the inhabitants of the land, whereas the fourth is second singular and is dependent on the first three, but particularly on the third "they invite you and you should eat of their sacrifices."

The first of these verbs is ἐκπορνεύσωσιν. The verb is intransitive but can be transitive if accompanied by an accusative. Exod's is intransitive;[14] it is the inhabitants who go fornicating after their gods. A popular variant has added σε thereby making it transitive, but that is quite wrong as the next clause makes clear.

Along with Tar[P] Pesh, Exod has levelled the third and fourth clauses to the plural of the first two: "they should invite you ... their sacrifices"; these are singular in MT: one invites ... his sacrifice." A B O variant has θυματων instead of "sacrifices," for which see comment at 29:28.

34:16 MT has no equivalent for the second clause: "and of your daughters you should give to their sons,"[15] and of the old witnesses only Pesh agrees with Exod; cf Deut 7:3 for a parallel. The four clauses are also governed by μήποτε of v.15 as the subjunctive inflections show. The first two are still in second singular as is the last one in v.15, and the last two are in third plural with "your daughters" as subject. As in v.15 though the clauses are paratactically strung along the change in subject signals a change in relations to that of further actions. Exod levels out all references to the inhabitant(s) to plural (αὐτῶν) references; MT retains the singular of the final clause of v.15 for the first one in v.16 and then changes to plural suffixes.

---

12. Cf SS 76,94.
13. See the discussion in THGE VII.O.
14. Cf also Helbing 78.

Hex has added an εκ in the first clause before "your daughters" to equal the preposition of the Hebrew, In the second clause an A O z reading has changed the verb to the future δωσεις, thus making the line predictive rather than governed by μήποτε, for which see Deut 7:3. Similarly the b text has changed the last two verbs to future inflections with the same result.

34:17 A prohibition against making molten or cast images. The verb is modified by a dative of personal advantage, σεαυτῷ, which the Byzantine group has changed to εαυτω, with no change in meaning. Exod introduces the order with καί over against MT.

34:18 For a more detailed statement on the feast of ἀζύμων see 13:3--10 and for a parallel version to this verse see 23:15. The initial καί is omitted in the O f tradition and probably represents an early revision towards MT. For ἑορτήν see comment at 13:6. For ἀζύμων see 12:8.

For a variant to the second clause see 23:15 where ἔδεσθε is used and the verb in the καθάπερ clause is aorist, and not perfect, while instead of the two prepositional phrases κατὰ τὸν καιρὸν τοῦ μενὸς τῶν νεῶν obtains. The n text also has the aorist, while the z tradition has the present εντελλομαι. For the "month of new things" see comment at 13:4. Vulg has *mensis novorum* here.

The reason for the observance of the feast is given in the γάρ clause, for which see 23:15 where, however, αὐτῷ substitutes for τῷ μηνὶ τῶν νεῶν. Cod B uniquely omits τῷ probably under the influence of ἐν μηνί in the phrase just preceding the clause.

34:19 For the dedication of the firstborn compare 13:12--13 and its notes. V.19 begins with a nominative pendens "as for anyone opening the womb"; then ἐμοί is the predicate, τὰ ἀρσενικά the subject, and the remainder of the verse is in apposition. Over against Exod MT has וכל מקנך immediately after "to me"; for this hex has supplied και παντων των κτηνων σου. The subject is sensible and also occurs at 13:12, but MT has the difficult תזכר vocalized by the Masoretes as a Niphal. No verb "to be a male" is otherwise known and most moderns in desperation emend to

הזכר. Other ancients also had trouble with the word. Pesh omitted it, and Tar[P] and Vulg both presuppose a noun; cf Vulg: *generis masculini*. Tar[O] recognized the word as verb and paraphrased by תקדיש דכרין, probably on the basis of 13:12.

The apposite phrases read "firstborn of cattle and firstborn of sheep," with the second "firstborn" unique to Exod; its omission by *O b* may be due to Hebrew influence.

34:20 Over against 13:13 Exod renders תפדה literally by λυτρώσῃ throughout; cf comment on ἀλλάξεις at 13:13. -- Here Exod uses ὑποζυγίου rather than ὄνου of 13:13. The obverse situation is put into a future more vivid condition: if you will not redeem it (note that MT alone of the old witnesses omits the "it"). The apodosis has τιμὴν δώσεις "you will pay the price (literally "value"), for which 13:13 has λυτρώσῃ. This is not as brutal as MT's וערפתו "then you shall break its neck";[16] see comment at 13:13. A popular A F M text omits αὐτό which may well be a revision towards the Hebrew. And another popular A F M reading has added αυτου to τιμήν.

The second part of the verse is the command to ransom the firstborn τῶν υἱῶν σου. The parallel in 13:13 has אדם בבניך; Sam has adopted this as well. The final statement is asyndetic over against MT, and hex has added the lacking και. The clause also appears in the same form at 23:15, for which see notes.

34:21 The Sabbath commandment; compare 23:12. The positive injunction to work six days contrasts (note the use of δέ) with "but on the seventh day καταπαύσεις - you shall rest"; at 23:12 ἀναπαύσῃς is used; there is no difference in meaning.[17] The compound at 23:12 has invaded the tradition here as well in the *C n s* texts, either as αναπαυσεις or as αναπαυση. The B *f* text has the itacistic καταπαυσις by which a nominal clause is created: "but on the seventh day there (will be) a rest."

---

14. Cf also Helbing 78.
15. Cf SS 161.
16. Aq translates the apodosis by τενοντοκοπήσεις αὐτό "you shall cut through its tendons," and Sym has τραχηλοκοπήσεις αὐτό "you shall cut its neck," while according to Syh Theod has νωτοκοπήσεις αὐτό, for which see

The last clause specifies the rest with respect to agricultural tasks; it is to be τῷ σπόρῳ καὶ τῷ ἀμήτῳ. MT has בחריש for the first, but Tar^O and Pesh interpret as Exod. Of course plowing time is the season for sowing, and the reading does not presuppose a different parent text. The repeated verb at the end of the verse appears spelled as an itacistic noun in a B F M oI C s text, but MT has a verb; it is omitted by d +.

34:22 Two feasts are commanded, that of weeks and that of the ingathering. The order is ποιήσεις μοι whereas all other old witnesses have a second person pronoun לך. Exod is thus consistent with 23:14 where μοι also modifies the verb. Exod makes the point that these festivals are kept not for one's own sake, but for God's; their observance is an act of obedience to the Lord.

The first feast is identified as the beginning of the wheat harvest, but only here is בכורי "firstfruits" ever rendered by ἀρχήν. Also curious is the accusative which usually means extent of time which is semantically difficult with ἀρχή. It must then, it being a feast of weeks, mean during the time of the beginning days (week) of the wheat harvest. Some mss of the Byzantine text have simplified the text by reading a dative αρχη.

That this is what Exod intended is enhanced by the time designation for the second feast,[18] that of "ingathering" with a genitive absolute μεσούσος τοῦ ἐνιαυτοῦ "at the middle of the year." This is a unique interpretation of תקופת השנה literally "at the circuit of the year," i.e. at year's end. Exod's translation is a rationalization based on the postexilic calendar in which the feast of ingathering was celebrated in the seventh month (Tishri) as in the Babylonian calendar. This contrasts with 23:16 where the time is ἐξόδου - צאת of the year.

34:23 This verse is word for word the same as 23:17 except for ' Ισραήλ appearing as σου; cf notes there particularly for Exod's failure to render הֵאָדוֹן. An M oI C + tradition actually has σου after θεοῦ as in 23:17 but also retains ' Ισραήλ! [19] -- For the three appointed feasts in general see also

---

17. According to Syh Aq and Sym read ἤργησεν; cf the F^b reading at 16:30.
18. This festival was also called a ἑορτήν by Aq and Theod, but according to Syh Sym used another word, probably πανήγυρον as in Lev 23:41.

Deut 16 especially v.16 as well as Lev 23 and Num 28:16--29:38.[20]

34:24 The verse is structured as a γάρ statement, a kind of assurance of safety for those making the festival pilgrimages. Syntactically it begins with a temporal condition having two clauses with first singular subject, and has an apodosis with third singular, οὐθείς, as subject; this is modified in turn by a temporal ἡνίκα ἄν clause with second singular subject. The כי clause of MT is thus doubly interpreted both as a causal and as a temporal particle.

The opening conditional clauses also occur at 23:18 in the same form except that ἔθνη is there unarticulated; the *b* text reads as 23:18. For these clauses in general see comments at 23:18. In the first clause a B + text reads προ instead of ἀπό for which see comment at v.11. In the second clause a B *z* text reads the simplex for ἐμπλατύνω.[21] A C *s* reading has εκπλατυνω which means "level out," which can hardly have been meant here; the compound does not occur anywhere in LXX, and is merely a careless error.

The apodosis is signalized in MT by the conjunction *waw* but only the hex text witnesses to a και. The ὅταν clause has made secure the safety of the land. The subject of the apodosis appears in the later form ουδεις in B *f n* + and occurs occasionally even in Exod.[22]

The final ἡνίκα ἄν clause with a present subjunctive verb renders the Hebrew pattern: ב + bound infinitive with pronominal subject suffix. The present tense is expected for the verb since the verbal notion is a process as the "three times per year" makes certain, and the aorist αναβης of *C s* is clearly secondary.[23] That the three ἐναντίον, εναντι, ενωπιον are synonyms is clear from the variation in the tradition.[24]

34:25 The verse consists of two prohibitions, both of which have parallels in 23:18. For the first one the differences between the two are two: for

---

19. For the popular εναντιον see discussion in THGE VII.L. 3. For the semiprepositions as a whole consult Sollamo.
20. Instead of καιρούς Aq has καθόδους "cycles, recurrences" for פעמים both here and in v.24.
21. As do Aq and Sym; see also the discussion in THGE VII.N.
22. For a discussion of these forms in Exod see THGE VII.Q. sub 5:11.

σφάξεις "slaughter" 23:18 has θύσεις, and θυσιασμάτων is there in the singular. For the content see the discussion at 23:18. The singular noun occurs here as well in a popular variant. Similarly the odd θυμιαματων occurs in B +, for which see 23:18 as well. That these sacrifices were the Lord's is clear from μου, and the σου variant of the C text is simply an error.

The second prohibition differs from that of 23:18 considerably. There it was the fat of my feast which was not to be allowed to remain until morning; here it is the sacrificial animals of the passover feast; compare 12:10. For the rules of the passover observance see 12:3--11. A popular F M variant has the singular for θύματα which happens to equal MT, but this is coincidence; the singular is an easy error to make and is hardly intentional. Nor is the odd reading of A + as θυμιαμα original; an incense offering is not part of the passover feast.[25]

34:26 The text of MT is an exact copy of 23:19 and the Exod text differs only in the translation of the first two words, which in 23:19 is translated by τὰς ἀπαρχὰς τῶν πρωτογενημάτων but here by τὰ πρωτογενήματα.[26] For the analysis of the verse see discussion at 23:19. An odd variant in B + is the substitution of θήσεις for the first verb and of προσοισεις for the second.[27] Also obviously secondary in the tradition is the omission of κυρίου by the C s text.

34:27 In γράψον σεαυτῷ the dative reflexive is a Hebraism for לך and would better have been left untranslated, but all the old witnesses including Vulg represent it. It can best be understood as a dative of advantage, and the clause should be translated simply by "write." What is to be written are "these words," to which the C s tradition added "all" for which there is no basis in the Hebrew. The most obvious reference for the phrase would be the set of instructions just given in vv.11--26, but then v.28 would have to be understood as only vaguely related to v.27 where "these words" are

---

23. For the very popular εαν see THGE VII.B.
24. For a discussion of usage in Exod see THGE VII.L.3. sub 6:12.
25. For the articulation of ἑορτῆς by B + see THGE VII.D.4.
26. The Later Revisers rendered the phrase literally by ἀρχὴ τῶν πρωτογενημάτων.
27. For a plausible explanation of this variant see the discussion in THGE

identified as τοὺς δέκα λόγους by which the Ten Commandments of 20:2--17 are meant; cf note at v.28.

The γάρ clause gives the reason for making a written record of these words, which are the basis, ἐπὶ τῶν λόγων τούτων, for the Lord's covenant with Moses and Israel.[28] This is still in the speech of the Lord with the verb in the perfect passive τέθειμαί; for the collocation τίθημι διαθήκην see comment at v.10. The Byzantine reading of τιθημι comes from v.10.

34:28 The subject Μωυσῆς is named over against all other witnesses, though in view of ἔναντι κυρίου it would have been obvious without. B C s have εναντιον instead of ἔναντι.[29] The tradition of Moses' stay for 40 days and nights also occurs in 24:18 where, however, the text reads ἐν τῷ ὄρει rather than "before the Lord"; the prepositional phrase is also found in Sam Tar, whereas Pesh Vulg follow the יהוה עם of MT. Why abstinence from food and drink should characterize Moses' long stay before the Lord is not stated. Is it presupposed that ordinary human functions and needs are suspended in the presence of deity?

The second part of the verse has him writing "these words upon the tablets of the covenant," and "him" can only refer to Moses. The object is again "these words" and so Exod ties this to v.27 where Moses received the order to write these words. Since "these words" are identified as the Ten Words, "these words" can hardly be the regulations of vv.11--26; cf v.27. Exod's "these words" does not accord with MT which has "the words of the covenant," and has הלחת as an articulated free form, with את דברי הברית following it. In this way Exod makes the two verses fully consistent. The majority A F M hex reordering of "these words" after "tablets" approximates MT; the O n tradition also omitted ταῦτα, thereby equalling MT even more exactly. Exod's harmonization of these two verses still leaves the contradiction with v.1 where the Lord had said that he (the Lord) would write the words on the tablets. But to Exod the promise was presumably changed by the order γράψον σεαυτῷ of v.27.

---

27. For a plausible explanation of this variant see the discussion in THGE VII.Q.
28. For ἐπί with the genitive in the sense of standard employed, on the basis

34:29 This verse begins the account of Moses' glittering face and this is shown by δέ. The initial ויהי when followed by ב + bound infinitive is as usual omitted by Exod; cf comment at 2:11; the verse begins with ὡς δὲ κατέβαινεν, an imperfect verb since he was coming down from the mountain. Exod does not transcribe סיני, which is supplied by a majority A F M hex σινα. Another majority A F M variant has added ιδου in the second clause after καί. The addition has no basis in MT but serves to mark the nominal clause clearly as the apodosis of the temporal ὡς construction. Within the nominal clause hex has added της διαθηκης after tablets to conform to MT. Furthermore an A F M *C s y* tradition has omitted δύο as well.

The next clause begins with a genitive absolute construction modifying the subject Moses. It would ordinarily be understood as a modifier of the preceding Μωυσῆ, but there are two problems with that: a) it would be rank tautology, and b) the δέ seems to indicate a contrast of some kind. Though this usage is not common it is attested, e.g. at 4:21.[30] The Masoretes did take this as modifying the preceding clause by placing ההר under the ethnach. Note also that the next word ומשה is introduced by the conjunction, which is not the case in Exod.

The final clause states that "Moses did not know that the appearance of the skin of his face δεδόξασται." The perfect passive verb is a translation of קרן probably a denominative verb from the word for "horn," but in the Qal apparently meaning "to send out rays," as was understood by Tar. The Qal form occurs only in this section (also vv.30,35), and refers to Moses' facial appearance which happened ἐν τῷ λαλεῖν αὐτὸν αὐτῷ. Exod interpreted this (correctly) as having been charged with glory (i.e. the divine appearance), and thus shining brightly."[31] The subject of the verb is ἡ ὄψις τοῦ χρωτός of his face, whereas MT has just עור פניו "skin of his face." This represents Exod's attempt to make clear that this state of effulgence was how Moses looked. Since only God can be said to be effulgent, Moses'

---

29. See the discussion in THGE VII.L.3. sub 6:12.
30. See Bl-Debr 423.3, and Mayser II (3) 157, especially pp.68--70.
31. Aq according to Jerome understood this crassly as *cornuta erat*, i.e. ἐκερατώ(σ)θη (cf v.35), which interpretation promoted Vulg: (quod) cornuta esset, "that he had been horned," a notion well known from medieval and Renaissance art, e.g. da Vinci's Moses sculpture in the

face could hardly be such; it could only appear to be such. Both here and in v.30 a B + tradition has χρωματος "color" for χρωτός; but it is hardly the appearance of his face's color that is here involved.[32]

34:30 The reaction of the leaders. Exod limits this verse to Aaron and the elders of Israel rather than to Aaron and the Israelites. The majority A F M reading does have οι υιοι instead of "the elders," an excellent example of an early (preOrigen) revision towards the Hebrew.

The second clause is a הנה clause in MT but not in Exod. For both ἦν δεδοξασμένη and the subject see comments at v.29. -- The last clause shows the reaction: "they were afraid to approach him." The final pronoun is αὐτῷ, not αυτου as in B *f* +; the latter is but a scribal error, since ἐγγίζω governs the dative.[33]

34:31 Moses is the subject of the first and last clauses, and Aaron and the leaders, of the middle one. A *b* reading makes the middle one a δέ structure, which unnecessarily shows the subject, since this is already named. -- αὐτούς in the first clause refers to "Aaron and all the elders of Israel" of v.30. Moses summoned them in view of the last clause in v.30. In the second clause they are called "Aaron and all the leaders of the assembly," from which it is clear that πρεσβύτεροι and ἄρχοντες are the same people. The Hebrew text for τῆς συναγωγῆς is בעדה, but the genitive modifier is a good rendering. -- In the last clause αὐτοῖς precedes the subject Moses, though MT has משה אלהם. Most witnesses have the literal equivalent μωυσης προς αυτους, but that this is secondary and probably a revision based on MT is clear from the translation pattern: verb of speaking + dative pronoun + subject which is far and away the dominant order in Exod (44 out of 48 instances).[34]

34:32 The time designation μετὰ ταῦτα reflects the respective positions of elders and people. When Moses descended from the mountain he first met the elders who had come partway up the mountain (see 24:1), whereas the

---

Church of St.Peter in Chains in Rome.
32. See the discussion in THGE VII.Q.
33. Cf also the note in THGE VII.G.8.

people remained in the camp. Now the people approach him. -- πρὸς αὐτόν has no equivalent in MT Tar but is represented in all the other old witnesses. The remainder of the verse is an exact rendering of MT except for πρὸς αὐτόν; in MT this is אתו, also supported by Sam, Tar Pesh. The same pattern of support obtains in v.33 in modification of λαλῶν.

34:33 Exod renders two paratactic clauses with discrimination as a "when ... then" statement. A popular F M tradition has επει for ἐπειδή, but the two are synonymous. Oddly a *C* reading substitutes a Hebraic εγενετο οτε; though this does not change the sense the origin of the variant is puzzling, since this Hebraism has no basis in MT. Exod omits משה as named subject, since it is otiose, but hex supplies μωυσης to conform to MT.

ἐπέθηκεν appears in the simplex form in *C s*, but with no change in meaning. Moses placed a מסוה on his face, a word occurring only in vv.33--35, and κάλυμμα "covering" translates it adequately.

34:34 MT opens with a ב + bound infinitive which Exod renders by ἡνίκα δ' ἄν + an imperfect verb εἰσεπορεύετο; this correctly interprets the collocation as one of customary action, also accented by the imperfect περιηρεῖτο of the apodosis: "whenever he would enter ... he would remove." The ἄν particle used with the imperfect emphasizes iterative action, and its removal by the *C b* tradition is not an improvement. The protasis speaks of Moses entering before the Lord; this refers to entering the tent of 33:7--11 outside the camp. -- The ἕως collocation in the apodosis has an articulated infinitive used absolutely over against MT; Hex added an αυτον to represent the suffix in MT.

The second part of the verse also uses the imperfect of customary action, ἐλάλει. The first clause, ויצא, is as usual subordinated as an attributive participle ἐξελθών. Over against MT Exod has added πᾶσιν to designate "the Israelites," possibly to contrast more clearly with Aaron and the leaders of v.31. -- The object of ἐλάλει is the ὅσα clause which the Byzantine text unnecessarily expanded to παντα οσα. In MT the verb יצוה is vocalized by the Masoretes as Pual, i.e. "he was commanded." Exod put it

---

34. See the discussion in THGE VII.F.3. sub 18:9.

actively, ἐνετείλατο αὐτῷ κύριος; cf Sam's יהוה, though Exod has the subject expressed as well.

34:35 The verse has two parts paratactically joined by "and" though the second part is Moses' reaction to the first. In the first part Exod has a compressed text. The ὅτι clause refers to τὸ πρόσωπον Μωυσῆ of the main clause, but simply has δεδόξασται, for which see comment at v.29. But MT adds the subject as עור פני משה, with which compare v.29. In the context little is lost, although hex does add η οψις του χρωτος του προσωπου αυτου as subject as in vv.29 and 30; see note at v.29.[35]

The second part of the verse contrasts with v.34a; there the verb is περιῃρεῖτο "would remove (the veil)"; here it is περιέθηκεν "put (it) on." Here Exod uses the aorist, not calling attention to the action as customary. Its object is an unarticulated κάλυμμα, but a popular A F M hex reading has added the article to equal MT. The verb is also modified by ἐπὶ τὸ πρόσωπον ἑαυτοῦ. As might be expected the tradition has changed the reflexive pronoun to the ordinary αυτου in a popular A variant, but the rarer pronoun is obviously original.

The clause is modified by a ἕως ἄν clause "until he would go in to converse with him (i.e. with the Lord)." εἰσέλθῃ renders MT's באו, a bound infinitive with a subject suffix. The finite verb is a fully adequate rendering but hex pedantically added an αυτος to represent the suffix.[36] The purposive infinitive chosen by Exod to translate לדבר is particularly fine, the present infinitive συλλαλεῖν. The root itself is unique in the Pentateuch, and it interprets the situation perfectly; the action involved is a talking together, a conversation. The tense is also much better than the *f* *s*[mg] aorist reading, since conversation is indeed a process; compare 33:11.

35. Sym added ὁ χρὼς τοῦ προσώπου Μωσεῖ and Aq the more literal δέρμα προσώπου Μωσεῖ. The two also differ with respect to their understanding of the verb קרן, for which see note at v.29 as well. Sym understood the verb correctly and retained Exod but Aq had κεκεράτωτο; cf Vulg: *esse cornutam.*
36. Cf SS 84.

Chapter 35

For chh.35--40 see chapter VI of THGE which is a discussion of the composition of Exod B, the account of the building of the tabernacle and its accoutrements. For convenience the B account is there dealt with in four sections, and this will be done here as well.

The first section, 35:1--36:7(8a), serves as introduction to the account, detailing the materials needed, the items to be made, the people's generous response, and the appointment of the two architects.

35:1(par 31:12--13) Vv.1--3 deal with the Sabbath commandment with which the A account ended (31:12--18). Exod A is no real parallel; it does order Sabbath observance but in quite different language. Moses assembled (the congregation), συνήθροισεν for the Hiphil of קהל, both occurring only here in the book; this equation is unique in the LXX, though it does occur at Josh 22:12 for the Niphal. The Niphal occurs once in Exodus (32:1) where it is translated by συνέστη. -- A sparsely supported A reading articulates συναγωγήν; this equals MT's את but is probably merely an inner Greek stylistic change. Clearly secondary is the unique omission of πρὸς αὐτούς by cod B.

The rendering of צוה by εἶπεν is unusual, only occurring two other times in the entire LXX, Lev 9:6 and Josh 11:20. The verb refers to λόγοι and is easily understood, particularly when modified by the complementary infinitive ποιῆσαι. The *O b* text read ποιειν.[1] Since the present infinitive involves continuity this might well be an attempt at exegetical improvement; after all the assembly should keep on doing the words which the Lord had said.

35:2(par 31:15) For the distinction ἔργα vs ἔργον as renderings for מלאכה see comment at 31:15. As in the A account Exod B uses the second singular verb ποιήσεις which in the MT of both is vocalized as a passive verb. But taking תעשה as Qal means that the יהיה לכם of the second clause does not fit well; Exod substitutes for the phrase the noun κατάπαυσις which the majority A F M text changes itacistically to the verb καταπαυσεις. That the second clause contrasts with the first statement, δέ makes clear. -- שׁבת שׁבתון is rendered in both A and B by σάββατα ἀνάπαυσις with both terms in the nominative. The addition of κατάπαυσις is not a mere doublet but represents a fuller statement on Exod's part. Not only is the Sabbath an ἀνάπαυσις "a rest;" it is also a "making to rest," i.e. in accordance with the Sabbath command in which not only you, but also your son, daughter, servants male and female, ox, ass, cattle and alien, are to rest as well; see 20:10 and also as κατάπαυσις of 34:21.

The Sabbath is called ἅγιον, singular as though referring to a σάββατον, thus "but on the seventh day a making to rest, a holy (sabbath?), a Sabbath rest." Because of the difficult construction most mss have changed either ἅγιον to αγια or σάββατα to σαββατον, but the more difficult reading must be original. -- This day is κυρίῳ, but a C n s text inflects it in the genitive. A majority A F M text has articulated the noun probably under the influence of τῷ κυρίῳ in 31:15. -- A majority A F hex text changed the word order of ἔργον ἐν αὐτῇ to conform to MT. The translator himself does not seem to have been influenced by Exod A, since he translates MT carefully. Note also that in contrast to 31:15 he renders וימת by τελευτάτω.

35:3 This verse obtains only in the B account. ביום is simply translated by the dative of time when[2] but the majority A F M reading has added the preposition εν to conform to MT.

Only the plural τῶν σαββάτων is ever found in Exod.[3] -- Over against MT Exod uniquely adds the affirmation ἐγὼ κύριος. Since the affirmation formula is common throughout the Pentateuch it is useless to speculate on its source here.[4]

35:4--5a(par 25:1--3a) Dependence on Exod A can hardly be affirmed here. The Hebrew texts are quite disparate but where they relate significantly the

1. As does Sym.
2. Cf SS 109.
3. This contrasts with the singular of Aq Sym.

translations differ. In both cases a תרומה is to be taken; in B this becomes ἀφαίρεμα, whereas it is ἀπαρχάς in A; cf comments at 25:2--3.

For the notion of a "free disposition of the heart," Exod B uses ὁ καταδεχόμενος τῇ καρδίᾳ; the parallel A construction becomes (οἷς ἂν) δόξῃ τῇ καρδίᾳ.[5] Both Exod A and B fail to render the suffix of לבו, which hex makes up for with an added αυτου here,[6] but otherwise there seems to be no demonstrable dependence.

In v.5 the use of the double pronoun ὑμῶν αὐτῶν is a characteristic Hellenistic usage in which an otiose αὐτῶν is added to the second personal pronoun. In translation it may be omitted, though it can be rendered reflexively.[7] -- In both instances of κυρίῳ variant texts add the article. In the first case the τω is hex and represents the preposition ל before the tetragrammaton.

35:5b--8(5b--9; par 25:3b--7) The list of materials are identical in the two Hebrew accounts, except for two *waws* (before "onyx stones" and before "spices"). The two Greek lists are almost the same, and it is clear that the B account has taken over the A list. This is obvious from the fact that both lists omit "oil for the light, and spices for the anointing oil, and for the incense compounds," which hex duly adds.[8] Otherwise the B account has the ("correcting") doublet διανενησμένον after διπλοῦν, and omits some of the "ands" in the list whereas A has many of the items connected by καί even before λίθους σαρδίου where MT lacks a conjunction. The doublet rendering is omitted by an A* F *O* reading which may well be a preOrigenian revision towards MT. In vv.5--6 the conjunctions which are omitted by the translator have all been added by hex so as to equal MT. For the items in

---

4. See BDB sub יהוה II.2.
5. To render נדיב of MT Aq uses ἑκουσιαζόμενος, a denominative from ἑκούσιος "voluntary, freely undertaken"; Sym has αὐθαίρετος "independent, self-generated." Both are attempts are a more literal rendering.
6. Cf SS 93.
7. This has actually led to the use of the reflexive pronoun itself in such a context in the LXX occasionally; cf THGE VII.G.10.
8. Taken over from Theod. The addition in Sym is similar merely substituting φαῦσιν for τὸ φῶς, and τῶν ἡδυσμάτων for τῆς συνθέσεως in the Theod reading.

the list see the comments at 25:3b--7.[9]

35:9(10; par 31:6b) MT begins with a singular subject but follows this with a compound verbal predicate in the plural. Exod, as well as Sam Vulg, makes the verbs singular, whereas Tar^O Pesh make the subject plural. The subject is "everyone wise τῇ διανοίᾳ" though in the tradition a majority A F M reading has τη καρδια. The former is the preferred rendering for the Hebrew לב throughout chh.35 and 36, however, and is probably original.[10] -- The compound predicate "come and do" is rendered by an aorist participle plus a third person present imperative which nicely interprets the intent of the Hebrew as potential rather than as future. -- The object of the verb is turned into a καθα clause by C, probably under the influence of the oft-recurring "as the Lord commanded."

35:10--19(11--19; par 31:7--11) For a discussion of the order of items to be made in the much more compressed parallel account see the comments at 31:7--11.

In the list both Exod and MT begin with the tent and the ark (in both cases with various accoutrements), but afterwards the order of items as well as the items themselves differ considerably. The order in Exod thereafter is 1. hangings of the court; 2. emerald stones; 3. incense; 4. anointing oil; 5. table; 6. lampstand; 7. the altar; 8. priestly vestments; 9. anointing oil; 10. incense compound. Over against this MT has 1. table; 2. lampstand; 3. incense altar; 4. anointing oil; 5. incense compound; 6. door screen; 7. altar of burnt offering; 8. laver; 9. hangings of the court; 10. screen for the gate of the court; 11. pegs and cords for tabernacle and court; 12. priestly garments.

It will be immediately obvious that nos.2--4 in the Greek list are an intrusion; no.2 is simply part of the priestly vestments, whereas nos.3 and 4 also occur as nos. 9 and 10. Since in the parallel A account nos.9 and 10 also come at the end after the priestly vestments, this seems to be the reason for their placement here. But in the nos.3 and 4 spot they are joined to the stones of no. 2. In the list of materials in vv.5b--8, both items occur in MT

9. For the Later Revisers' rendering of the three items in v.8 see the notes at 25:6 which also apply here.
10. Cf also THGE VII.Q.

(v.8) where they are followed in v.9 by אבני שהם; Exod, however, lacks both items and only has καὶ λίθους σαρδίου. But שהם can also be translated by τῆς σμαράγδου (v.27; cf also 28:9 and 36:13), and it seems clear that vv.8--9 of MT are the source for these items, though with "stones of emerald" at the beginning.

For the rest Exod disregards the incense altar entirely simply having τὸ θυσιαστήριον over against the plural of 31:8; this is consistent with Exod B's omission of all reference to the incense altar throughout his account; MT distinguishes the two altars in nos.3 and 7. Furthermore Exod places the hangings of the courtyard in first place, whereas in MT they are no.8. The order: table, lampstand (nos.5 and 6) occurs in the same order as nos.1 and 2 in MT (these are followed by the altar in Exod, but by incense altar in MT), whereas the priestly vestments as no.8 is in last place (no.12) in MT. Nos.6, 8,10 and 11 in MT are details which might well be considered part of the accoutrements of tabernacle and courtyard and their omission is made up for by the details subsumed under the item; cf e.g. on the tabernacle at v.10. Oddly enough Origen was sufficiently confused by the differences between Exod and MT not to try to reorder items in the list, limiting his intervention to placing extras in the Greek text under the obelus, and adding materials under the asterisk where he deemed the Greek text to be shorter than the Hebrew. For details cf comments on individual verses below.

35:10(11) Since both משכן and אהל are translated in Exod by σκηνή with MT having as the first provision for the משכן the item את אהלו, a translation problem had to be faced; cf also the comment at 26:7--13. For the tent of the tabernacle see comment at 26:7. Here it is translated not by σκεπην as at 26:7,[11] but by παραρρύματα "things stretched over," i.e. the curtain-like coverings drawn over the tabernacle sides and top, which is what MT really means as the description in 26:7--14 makes clear. Hex has added for this item as well as for the other items in the verse an αυτης to conform to the suffixed nouns in MT. -- The third item is τὰ καλύμματα "the coverings" which correctly renders מכסהו as a collective. -- The next item, קרסיו, is rendered here uniquely by τὰ διατόνια "hooks." In the A account it was rendered by κρίκους (26:6,11). The Hebrew term for "clasps" can be thought of as "hooks" or "rings," and the rendering here is not incorrect. In the only other occurrence of קרסים in B (39:33) the translator omitted it.[12] -- The next item is always bypassed in the B account; for the meaning and translation of קרשים in Exod A see note at 26:15.[13]

MT ends the list with "its pillars and its bases," whereas Exod only has καὶ τοὺς στύλους.
. Presumably the translator felt it quite superfluous to mention the bases which were after all part of the pillars. Hex added και τας βασεις αυτης.

35:11(12) The ark is designated as being τοῦ μαρτυρίου, a phrase which occurs a number of times elsewhere (25:21 26:33,34 40:3,5,19); it also occurs at 25:9 though unarticulated, and as here without support in MT.[14]

For "the propitiatory" Exod has τὸ ἱλαστήριον αὐτῆς with the pronoun referring to κιβωτόν. The כפרת did lie on top of the ark so that the pronoun is not incorrect. The last item is פרכת המסך "the veil of the screen." The more usual reference is simply הפרכת without המסך; in fact the bound phrase occurs elsewhere in the book only at 39:34 and 40:21; the phrase becomes τῶν λοιπῶν τὰ ἐπικαλύμματα in the former (39:21 in Exod), and in the latter τὸ κατακάλυμμα τοῦ καταπετάσματος (v.19). Exod follows the more usual designation and simply has τὸ καταπέτασμα.

35:12(17--18) Exod's text is shorter than MT, having only "and the hangings of the court and its pillars." The first "and" has no basis in MT. Uniquely lacking in Exod is "and its bases and the screen for the gate of the court" at the end, as well as the entire v.18 of MT, i.e. no.10 in the list; cf comments at vv.10--19.

35:13 For the reference to the emerald stones see comment on vv.10--19. In the tradition a z text has inadvertently added αυτης after λίθους but it

---

11. Which is also used by the Later Revisers here.
12. Aq also has τοὺς κρίκους αὐτῆς here, whereas Sym Theod have τὰς περόνας αὐτῆς "its buckles."
13. The Three have τὰς σανίδας "boards, planks."
14. Since MT has את הארן Sym omits καί, and Aq has the odd σὺν τὸ γλωσσόκομον with the preposition σύν for את. For γλωσσόκομον see

obviously does not belong. More puzzling is the popular A F M text which has repeated the article of λίθους after it as well, i.e. as a relative "the stones those of emerald"; it may have come into the text as a dittograph after -θους.

35:14 For this verse as a displacement from v.8 see comment at vv.10--19. Its omission by A* F M C b s may well represent an early revision towards MT. A popular variant has the plural τα θυμιαματα but the word is always in the singular in Exod. A gloss to θυμίαμα in three mss reading της συνθεσεως και το επισπαστρον της θυρας της σκηνης (from Theod?) is clearly based on the MT of v.15b. Of uncertain origin is an *ol z* gloss at the end of the verse: "and oil for the light and spices for the anointing oil and for the incense compound."

35:15(13a) MT does not begin the verse with a conjunction, and it has "and its poles" after "table," which hex supplies. Also added by hex is και τους αρτους του προσωπου for the missing v.13b of MT. The shorter text, however, omits nothing essential, since the poles and the bread may well be taken as included in the cover term πάντα τὰ σκεύη αὐτῆς.

35:16(14) Again Exod abbreviates, with the cover phrase "all its vessels" meant to include MT's "and its lamps and the oil of the light." The "all" is missing in MT but present in Sam; it is certainly appropriate. Hex has added the lacking text from Theod's καὶ τοὺς λύχνους αὐτῆς καὶ τὸ ἔλαιον τοῦ φωτός. Also added from Theod is the missing text of MT's v.15a: καὶ τὸ θυσιστήριον τοῦ θυμιάματος καὶ τοὺς ἀναφορεῖς αὐτοῦ.

35:17(16) Exod B admits of only one altar, the altar of burnt offering, and thus τὸ θυσιαστήριον is sufficient to designate it. In MT the altar of incense and this altar are distinct (cf the hex plus in the preceding verse). -- Again included in "all its vessels" is "and its bronze lattice work, its poles"; hex supplies the missing terms from Sym Theod: τῆς ὁλοκαυτώσεως καὶ τὸ κοσκίνωμα τὸ χαλκοῦν τὸ αὐτοῦ τοὺς ἀναφορεῖς αὐτοῦ. For κοσκίνωμα see footnote 2 at 27:4.

Hex has also added the missing 16b of MT: "and the laver and its base"; Exod B, except for 38:26--27, omits all reference to the laver over against the A account (cf 30:18,28 31:9).

35:18--19(19) The two parts of v.18 are transposed in MT, and hex duly reorders them to fit the Hebrew. In 31:10 the two parts had been compressed into a single phrase "and the λειτουργικάς garments of Aaron," a version by which "holy garments" had been subsumed under "the garments of השׂרד." The Hebrew word is of uncertain meaning, possibly related to Aram סרדא "lattice work, and thus "plaited, woven." Exod interprets as "service," hence "sacerdotal," but since Sam had השׂרת the rendering may be textually based. Here, however, Exod B does differentiate between the two parts of the verse. The "holy garments of Aaron the priest" is a good rendering of v.18b. The second part renders MT's בגדי השׂרד לשׁרת בקדשׁ by τὰς στολὰς λειτουργήσουσιν ἐν αὐταῖς. The A and B accounts are indeed related in that the λειτουργ- root is common to both, but which influenced which is not clear. If the parent text of A was MT rather than Sam, the Hebrew of the B account must have been used to interpret השׂרד; cf note at 31:10.

The Hebraic ἐν αὐταῖς is hardly explicable on the basis of MT which does not have בהם, but rather בקדשׁ. Hex rightly realized that Exod had no equivalent and so added εν τω αγιω. The translator may well have been influenced by the common Hebrew idiom שׁרת בהם, e.g. Num 3:31 4:9,12.

V.19a distinguishes the garments of Aaron's sons from those of Aaron himself as χιτῶνας instead of στολάς although the A parallel uses στολὰς for both. The translator may have been influenced by the A account at 28:36; in fact in ch.29 the distinction of στολάς for Aaron (v.5) and χιτῶνας for the sons (v.8) actually obtains (though in all these cases כתנת is the Hebrew equivalent for χιτῶνας). The B translator's independence from A is also clear from the rendering of לכהן; in the A account an infinitive ἱερατεύειν (μοι) is used, but here the genitive noun τῆς ἱερατείας "of the priesthood" is found.

V.19b has no counterpart in MT and in contrast to the preceding items is based on the A account though with some variation. In A the oil is called τῆς χρίσεως but here, τοῦ χρίσματος; the two are synonymous. The

582

second item in both is called τὸ θυμίαμα τῆς συνθέσεως but in A it is also designated as being τοῦ ἁγίου. A popular F M preOrigenian revision of Exod towards MT has omitted 19b entirely.

35:20 Moses' address, vv.4-19, was finished, and so the people leave (to carry out his orders). The articulation of συναγωγή in the M C n s tradition is stylistic; after all what is meant is "the entire assembly," not "every assembly." Exod's anarthrous noun imitates the Hebrew.

35:21 This verse well-illustrates how freely the translator worked. The phrase כל איש אשר occurs twice here as well as once in v.22 and v.23; each time Exod uses a different rendition: ἕκαστος ὧν, ὅσοις, πάντες ὅσοι and παρ᾽ ᾧ, and cf v.24 παρ᾽ οἷς for כל אשר.

This same kind of freedom occurs with the phrase בגדי הקדש. Here and at 39:19 τ. στολὰς τοῦ ἁγίου obtains, but he has τ. στολὰς τ. ἁγίας at v.18 and 40:11, but τ. στολὰς τῶν ἁγίων at 36:8. In the A account, however, the translator distinguishes בגדי קדש (28:2,4) where the adjectival phrase is used, and בגדי הקדש (29:29) where the free form is rendered by the nominal τοῦ ἁγίου.

Also typical of the B translator's work is the free use of "all" in connection with such words as "vessels," "works." Admittedly כל occurs almost twice as often in the B account as in A, but Exod often adds "all" where MT has no כל. Thus in this verse both πάντα τὰ ἔργα and πάσας τὰς στολάς obtain over against MT.

The opening verb ויבאו is vocalized by the Masoretes as a Qal, in which only the Tar concur, Sam Pesh Vulg following the simpler transitive of Exod ἤνεγκαν. The common Hebraic pattern "they brought, each one" is, however, mitigated by the use of the plural relative ὧν ... αὐτῶν (ἡ καρδία) for the Hebrew אשר ... לבו. The majority A F M text has the hex order η καρδια αυτων due to the Hebrew. A *b n* variant reading οις is an attempt at stylistic improvement.

The two relative clauses "of those whose heart bore" and "to whose spirit (ψυχῇ) it seemed (good)," are both unusual though adequate renderings of MT; both mean roughly "whose spirit moved them." Unusual is the κάτεργον for נדבה (only elsewhere in LXX at 30:16), and ψυχή for רוח (elsewhere only at Gen 41:8 and Sir 7:17).[15]

An odd scrambled dittograph in the tradition is attested by B ƒ in which ἤνεγκαν has ἀφαίρεμα κυρίῳ after it, but (with a misread ΚΩ as ΚΑΙ) has αφαιρεμα και before it as well. The gloss then provides αφαιρεμα as a subject for ἔδοξεν.

The offering of the people identified as κυρίῳ was for the threefold ends "all the works of the tent of testimony (for which see comment at 27:21), all its services, and all the garments of the sanctuary. Presumably these εἰς phrases are intended as overall designations for all the work that follows in the account.

35:22 As in v.21 the Masoretes vocalized ויבאו as a Qal which only Tar[P] follows, all others agreeing with Exod's ἤνεγκαν. The Hebrew verb has "the men" as subject, and is modified by על הנשים, i.e. "besides the women." But Exod by taking the verb as transitive makes the phrase a παρά one with the genitive; Exod thus interprets as the men bringing objects of adornment "from the women," i.e. their wives.

For the collocation (πᾶς) ᾧ ἔδοξεν τῇ διανοίᾳ see comment at v.21.[16] Syntactically the phrase is then subject of ἤνεγκαν 2°; the lack of number congruity is in imitation of MT and is analogous to the "they perform, each ..." pattern.

The objects brought are five in Exod but only four in Hebrew. Of the four two are clear; the second one, נזם, means "earring" and is well-rendered by ἐνώτια; similarly טבעת, "ring," becomes δακτυλίους. The first one is חח which means "thorn, bramble," but as a piece of female adornment is unknown. Tar[O] has שירין "rings, necklace," whereas Vulg has *armillas* "bracelets." I suspect that all of these are guesses. The fourth one is כומז which occurs only three times in MT and is unknown. Sam adds עגיל "hoop, ring" before it, thereby also making five. In fourth and fifth place

comment at 25:9; it is Aq's rendering for אזן; he reserves κιβωτός for תבה.

15. Aq renders the second clause in literalistic fashion: οὗ ἂν ἐκουσιάσατο πνεῦμα αὐτοῦ.

16. Aq has ἑκούσιος καρδία, a literal translation of נדיב לב ; Sym is also closer to the Hebrew with ὁ αὐθαίρετος τῇ διανοίᾳ "the one who is independent in understanding," i.e. one who does something by conscious

Exod has ἐμπλόκια "plaited clasps" and περιδέξια "armlets (for the right arm)." All are articles of jewelry but it seems useless to try to match them.[17]

For πάντες ὅσοι see comment at v.21. Unique is the rendering ἤνεγκαν ἀφαιρέματα for הֵנִיף תְּנוּפַת; in fact φέρω occurs only once elsewhere (Lev 23:12) as a rendering for this verb but in quite a different context, though ἀφαίρεμα also occurs for תְּנוּפָה at 39:7 (and thrice in Lev). The use of ἤνεγκαν is obviously a mark of this section (vv. 20--29) in which it occurs 11 times; in fact ἤνεγκαν ... ἀφαίρεμα(τα) actually occurs as well in vv.21,24,29. The verb serves as Leitmotif of this section, thereby emphasizing what the people brought. ἀφαιρέματα occurs in the singular in the majority A F M reading, probably under the influence of v.21, but here a number of different objects as offerings is intended and the plural is expected. -- Hex text has articulated κυρίῳ to represent the preposition of לַיהוה.

35:23 For παρ' ᾧ as rendering for כָּל אִישׁ אֲשֶׁר see comment at v.21. A popular A F M variant has πας for παρ', to which hex has added ανηρ to equal MT; the Byzantine text has this as παντι by attraction to ᾧ. That παρ' is original is clear from v.24 where παρ' οἷς occurs for כָּל אֲשֶׁר in a similar context. A popular A F hex reading has added παρ αυτω after εὑρέθη to equal the Hebraic אִתּוֹ.[18]

Exod has omitted "blue and purple and scarlet stuff ... and goats' hair," an intentional omission in view of vv.25--26, where these (as well as βύσσος) are the materials woven by the women. βύσσος occurs in both places; otherwise the skins are only mentioned here. Hex has inserted υα-κινθος και πορφυρα και κοκκινον αλλοιουμενον και.[19] For the untranslated וְעִזִּים hex has added και τριχες αιγιαι after βύσσος.[20]

---

choice.

17. See J. Ziegler, Untersuchungen zur Septuaginta des Buches Isaias, 204ff. for an extensive discussion of lists of female adornments including this list, where he concludes that these lists constitute those "damals in Alexandrien gangbaren Fachausdrücken." (p.211).
18. From Theod Sym; Aq has the literal σὺν αὐτῷ.
19. From Theod; Aq has for the last item σκώληκος διάφορον and Sym has κόκκινον δίβαφον, both of them misunderstanding שׁנִי as the root for "to be double." For these readings see the comment at 25:4.
20. Both Aq and Theod have καὶ αἴγεια, whereas Sym attests to καὶ τρίχες.

For the two kinds of skins see comment at 25:5. The two are given in Exod in an unusual reverse order with the blue skins occurring first. Hex has turned them around to the usual order as in MT.

35:24 An early prehexaplaric A F M *O C s* variant has omitted the opening καί on the basis of the Hebrew. The verse divides into two parts: offerings of metals vs the offerings of ἄσηπτα wood. Exod leaves ἀφαίρεμα unarticulated as MT as might be expected, but B *ol f* add the article, decidedly an inferior reading probably due to the τὰ ἀφαιρέματα modifying the verb.[21] The Byzantine text enlarges to include gold in first place, i.e. the usual triad of gold, silver and bronze. M *C s* articulate κυρίῳ but MT has יהוה as the free element of a bound phrase, and the article is a stylistic gloss.

The second part of the verse is introduced by (καὶ) παρ' οἷς which *O* changes to παντι οσοις.[22] For ξύλα ἄσηπτα see comment at 25:5. For the tautological מלאכת העבדה of MT Exod neatly renders the second word by τῆς κατασκευῆς. Thus the phrase is for works dealing with the construction and/or equipage.

35:25--26 Over against the raw materials brought in v.23, here prepared materials are given by women who were expert at sewing. In v.25 a singular subject "every woman wise in understanding to sew with (her) hands" obtains with a plural predicate ἤνεγκαν, for which see comment on v.22. The "her" is added by hex to conform to MT's בידיה. Exod has removed the difficulty of the Hebrew טוו by using the complementary infinitive νήθειν.[23] Sam has simplified it by טוה, i.e. a singular verb, though continuing with the plural ויביאו.

The term for "scarlet" is κόκκινον without an equivalent for שני, as at 28:5; hex has added το αλλοιουμενον.[24]

---

21. Aq also reads ἀφαίρεμα but according to Syh, Sym Theod read ἀπαρχήν.
22. The Three also have πᾶς to represent Hebrew כל with Aq continuing with ῷ, Sym with παρ' ῷ, and Theod with ὅς. All Three add παρ' αὐτῷ after the verb to equal the אתו of MT.
23. Cf Thack 277.
24. For the renderings of The Three for this word see comment at v.23.

V.26 does not state that the sewn goats' hair was brought - since that is obvious - but merely that well-disposed women sewed goats' hair cloth. For the term see comment at 25:4.

35:27--28 The ruler's contributions. V.27 details the gems brought for the ephod and the oracle as the stones τῆς σμαράγδου and the stones τῆς πληρώσεως. At v.8 the former was rendered by σαρδίου, but see comment at 25:6. πληρώσεως was used by The Three (at 25:6) to render המלאים and must mean for the setting (the filling in) of gems. In the tradition both cases of λίθους have the article not only preceding but also after the noun. For the probable origin of the variants see comment at v.13. For the popular itacistic spelling λογειον see comment at 28:15.

The first term in v.28 is συνθέσεις, unique as a rendering for בשם "spices." Later in the verse the singular occurs as equivalent for הסמים "compounds" for both oil mixtures and incense preparations. Exod has omitted "and the oil for the lamp," which hex supplied by its και το ελαιον εις το φως from Theod. The omission may well have been an intentional one. In fact it is only once translated (39:17), and is otherwise not rendered; cf vv.8,16 and 25:6. It should be noted that the anointing oil and the incense compound are both termed holy (30:32,36), which is never said of the oil for the lamp; it is then by definition not a σύνθεσις, and is here too omitted, not through homoiot but by design.

35:29 Only Sam and a few Hebrew mss of the old witnesses support Exod's opening καί. An A *O d t* variant changes the second καί into the correlative η. Hex has added αυτους after αὐτῶν to modify ἔφερεν, thus conforming to MT's אתם. Exod has a fine rendering in εἰσελθόντας ποιεῖν πάντα τὰ ἔργα for להביא לכל המלאכה. This directly modifies ἔφερεν; thus "whose heart impels (those) entering in to do all the work."[25] An F* *f* variant on the participle has the nominative which leaves the ὧν ἔφερεν construction up in the air. A change to an infinitive in *C s* is a sensible simplification of the

25. The Three by more literal renderings do not yield as good a sense. Aq has a marked infinitive τοῦ ἐνεγκεῖν εἰς πᾶν τὸ ἔργον. Sym has εἰσέγκειν and Theod, τοῦ ἐνέγκαι, both continuing with εἰς πάντα τὰ ἔργα.

more difficult participial structure. These groups also simplify by omitting πάντα.

The preposition in διὰ Μωυσῆ renders בּיד and hex inserts an unnecessary χειρος to equal MT more literally. -- The use of ἀφαίρεμα for נדבה is unique in the LXX but like ἤνεγκαν it is a motif for this section.[26]

35:30(par 31:1--2) That the B account was here strongly influenced by the A narrative is clear from the use of the same verbal stem and tense ἀνακέκλη-κεν - ἀνακέκλημαι and both modified by ἐξ ὀνόματος. Odd, however, is the use of ὁ θεός as subject for the יהוה of MT. Only *C s* change to κυριος.[27] Possibly the reference to the πνεῦμα θεῖον in v.2 and in 31:3 may have impelled the translator; i.e. it was God who filled him with the רוח אלהים.

The spelling of Beseleel's name is assured though some variation, all palaeographically inspired, does occur: βεσσελεηλ, βεσεηλ, βεσεβεηλ. For Οὐρί a number of variant spellings also occur: by itacism ουρει and ουρη, by change of the first vowel ωρι, and by adding a final ου ουριου, ουρειου and also οριου. Ouri is called υἱοῦ "Ωρ. The υἱοῦ has undoubtedly promoted the spellings with -ου. A B+ text has τον for υἱοῦ but this is secondary.[28] A popular A F M variant has articulated φυλῆς, probably under the influence of the parallel account in A.

35:31(par 31:3) This verse relied almost completely on the A account; cf comments at 31:3. The two Hebrew accounts are identical except for the person of the verb, here perforce in third person but in 31:3 in first person. Only for the last phrase, יבכל מלאכה, did Exod B go his own way by adding πάντων rather than ἐν παντὶ ἔργῳ. In B πάντων modifies the last of the three genitives ἐπιστήμης, thus "understanding of all things." Actually this is not all that different from MT in meaning."

35:32(par 31:4) Except for the added opening conjunction (which Exod omits) the B account of MT is an exact copy of A. The Greek, however,

26. According to Syh Aq's ἑκούσιον was followed by Theod, whereas Sym used the adverb ἑκουσίως.
27. As do the Later Revisers.

differs considerably. For the opening infinitival construction Exod B does use ἀρχιτεκτονεῖν (cf comment on ἀρχιτεκτονῆσαι at 31:4), but this is modified by an expanded prepositional phrase κατὰ πάντα τὰ ἔργα τῆς ἀρχιτεκτονίας, which does show the nominal cognate to the verb as in MT, but has an enlarged construction dependent on the וככל מלאכה at the end of v.31. In the tradition hex has taken note of this and has transposed the infinitive after ἔργα thereby approximately MT; cf also comment on πάντων at v.31.

The second infinitival construction reproduces MT exactly in contrast to the parallel which has added (over against MT) the list of textiles to the three metals. Since the verse speaks of the work of Beseleel the limitation to metals here is appropriate. The infinitives are purposive modifying ἐνέπλησεν of v.31.

35:33(par 31:5) The Hebrew of v.33 is a copy of 31:5 except for the addition of מחשבת (= σοφίας) at the end, but Exod B is a much more exact rendering of the Hebrew than is A. That B was acquainted with A is clear from λιθουργῆσαι, which reflects τὰ λιθουργικά, but for the rest has disregarded A. B does use κατεργάζεσθαι (note ἐργάζεσθαι in A), but in B this renders בחרשת, whereas in A the infinitive stands for לעשות.

Since the verse begins with καί the three coordinated infinitives are at the same syntactic level as those of v.32 in modifying the verb of v.31. MT uses בחרשת twice, the first one with אבן למלאת for cutting stones for setting, and the second one with עץ for cutting wood. Exod simplifies the first one by λιθουργῆσαι τὸν λίθον; the infinitive is unique in the LXX and means "to work stone" with no further limitation though this might have been expected from the Hebrew, but it is sufficiently general to fit any kind of stone work.

For the second case Exod chose κατεργάζεσθαι τὰ ξύλα "to work up lumber." The translator had a good contextual sense in matters of construction. A popular variant text has κατεργασασθαι τα ξυλικα. The change to an aorist infinitive was probably conditioned by the tense of λιθουργῆσαι earlier in the verse.

---

28. For the originality of Οὐρὶ υἱοῦ see the discussion in THGE VII.K.

Over against MT Exod has coordinated ποιεῖν with the preceding two infinitives; in MT "to work every skilled craft" defines the work of Beseleel as a whole; in Exod it is another aspect of his labors, "to work at every (or any) job of skill."

35:34(par 31:6a) The preposed purposive infinitive προβιβάσαι occurs only here for the Hiphil of ירה; in fact the verb only occurs once elsewhere in LXX (Deut 6:7). The word means "to instruct" presumably tradesmen in the art of metalwork, work in gems, and weaving various goods for the tabernacle and its contents.[29] The verb is given added stress by the particle γε after it.[30] The infinitive modifies ἔδωκεν which is also modified by αὐτῷ ἐν τῇ διανοίᾳ. In MT נתן is modified by בלבו and hex has added an αυτου to represent the suffix; it seems likely that Origen's text lacked the αὐτῷ, which the majority A F M text including all the hex witnesses does not have.[31] The translator felt that a dative pronoun after ἔδωκεν was more to the point than a genitive one after the noun. For διανοίᾳ as rendering for לב see comment on v.9.

αὐτῷ is then taken up again in αὐτῷ τε καὶ ᾽Ελιάβ. MT has the unusual isolate pronoun הוא form which takes up the suffix of לבו.[32] A popular A tradition has added a dative article before ᾽Ελιάβ, but this is quite unnecessary in view of the τῷ following the name. -- The patronymy of Eliab is classically shown by the use of τοῦ rather than υιω.

᾽Αχισαμάχ is the correct transliteration of אחיסמך rather than the αχισαμακ of B+.[33] Other variants in the tradition include αχεισαμαχ, αχισαμακ, αχισαμααχ, αχισαμεχ, αχισαναχ, αχισαμαν, αχιμασαχ, αρχισαμαχ and αρχισαμακ. See the discussion at 31:6.

A popular F M variant adds an article before φυλῆς as a stylistic improvement. But the unarticulated word is original as in v.30.

---

29. Sym has another infinitive ὑποδεῖξαι, more or less synonymous with προβιβάσαι.
30. See LS s.v. II.1, as well as IV.
31. Cf SS 93.
32. See GK 135g--h.
33. See the discussion in THGE VII.K.

590

35:35 Exod departs considerably from MT, though it has been artistically
constructed to reflect relations to its context. The first collocation: "he filled
them with wisdom and skillful knowledge" has three genitives σοφίας (καὶ)
συνέσεως διανοίας by analogy to v.31 where, however, ἐπιστήμης obtains,
not διανοίας. MT simply has לב חכמת, i.e. καὶ συνέσεως has no
equivalent in Hebrew. An old A O b text has omitted it thereby equalling
MT.

This is followed by πάντα συνιέναι ποιῆσαι τὰ ἔργα τοῦ ἁγίου "to
understand how to do all the works of the sanctuary." But MT has no
equivalent for τοῦ ἁγίου and the two infinitives are an interpretation of
לעשׁות in MT, actually in view of the preceding genitives not bad exegesis,
but cf 36:1 below.

This in turn is followed by a coordinate infinitival construction with
ὑφᾶναι preceded by coordinate accusatives as preposed direct modifiers and
followed by coordinate datives of means;[34] the accusatives ὑφαντά and ποικιλτά represent the undyed or white goods and the dyed or colored goods,
resp., whereas the corresponding goods designating the materials for these
are reversed in chiastic fashion "with scarlet stuff and linen." Thus the
description is limited to the work in textiles since the other crafts were dealt
with in vv.31--33.

The Hebrew is quite different. It begins with ורקם וחשׁב חרשׁ and
ends with וארג. Between these two MT has "with blue and with purple,
with scarlet stuff and with linen." The last two are adequately represented
by the coordinate datives, but Exod substitutes for the first two colored
materials the preposed accusatives as explained above.[35]

The final construction in Exod is also infinitival, paralleling the
syntactic patterns of the entire section, vv.31--35. It is a reformulation of
MT's coordinate structures: "those doing every (kind of) work and those

34. Cf SS 123.
35. For ὑφᾶναι ... βύσσῳ The Three have readings more closely
representing MT. Aq has ἐν ὑακίνθῳ καὶ πορφύρᾳ ἐν σκώληκος τῷ
διαφόρῳ καὶ ἐν βύσσῳ. Theod's text is similar though articulating each
noun, and for "scarlet stuff" substitutes ἐν τῷ κοκκίνῳ τῷ ἀλλοιουμένῳ,
and has ὑφᾶναι at the end (for וארג). Sym has διὰ τῆς ὑακίνθου καὶ τῆς
πορφύρας καὶ τοῦ κοκκίνου τοῦ διβάφου καὶ τῆς βύσσου. Many of these
terms are also witnessed in v.23, which see. Hex substituted the text of
Theod for that of Exod.

designing designs." The words "to do all work" in Exod does reframe the first of these structures, but the two genitives ἀρχιτεκτονίας ποικιλίας interpret מחשבת חשבי as "(the skill involved in) architecture (and) weaving," the twin areas of expertize: work in metals and wood vs work in textiles, a distinction which Exod B makes for the two architects as well; cf ch.38. It might be noted that a C f reading has simplified Exod by adding καὶ between the two words.

Chapter 36

36:1 Vv.1--7 have no parallel in Exod A and the Greek is a careful rendering of the Hebrew. V.1 is rather loosely construed with a number of modifiers strung along in approximation to the Hebrew. The singular verb has a compound subject with three members. The third member, πᾶς σοφός, is modified by hex through the insertion of ανηρ to represent the Hebrew איש; σοφός is in turn modified by a relative clause with a passive verb ἐδόθη used to render יהוה נתן in contrast to the ἔδωκεν ὁ θεός in the same context in v.2. Unusual is the hex attempt to "correct" the Greek by adding an agent παρα κυ after the verb to come closer to MT. The passive rewrite then makes MT's modifiers "wisdom and understanding" the subjects in Greek. A *C s* variant transposes the two and adds και συνεσεως, a gloss based on 35:30,35. -- ἐν αὐτοῖς refers to the ἔργα of the sanctuary of the preceding verse.

The συνιέναι ποιεῖν construction modifies ἐδόθη as a purposive infinitive plus complement. The object of לעשת is all the מלאכת עבדת הקרש. Its first word is a dominant motif of this section occurring nine times, as well as seven times in the preceding section, 35:21--35. But it is bound to the phrase עבדת יהוה. The same collocation occurs in v.3 where Exod simply has τὰ ἔργα τοῦ ἁγίου. Here Exod avoids the tautology by translating the phrase עבדת יהוה by κατὰ τὰ ἄγια καθήκοντα "according to the holy things which are fitting." For καθήκοντα see 5:13. There the reference was to the production quotas appropriate for the day, whereas here all the work is voluntary. A well-supported F M variant introduces the phrase with τα used as a relative after ἔργα. Two *O* variants are probably due to Hebrew influences, the omission of κατά and the transposition of τὰ ἄγια after καθήκοντα.

36:2 The verse in MT has a certain amount of repetitiousness in it: "every man wise of heart in whose heart Yahweh had put wisdom" as well as "(come near) to the work to do it." Exod translates by using other words;

thus for the former Exod has "all those having wisdom for whom God had put knowledge in the heart";[1] i.e. "heart" occurs only once, and instead of "wisdom" he uses ἐπιστήμην. Hex has added εν καρδια after "wisdom." Similarly for the second one Greek has "to the works so as to complete (συντελεῖν) them," which also reminds one of 5:13; see comment at v.1.

As in v.1 the main verb immediately involves a triad, but as object not as subject. Beseleel is articulated so as to differentiate it from the nominative Μωυσῆς preceding it.[2] In contrast to v.1 the third element is plural; the emphasis here is on the crowd of Israelites who were joining in the work. This is clear from a fourth object: πάντας τοὺς ἐκουσίως βουλομέ-νους κ.τ λ. "all those who voluntarily were desirous,"[3] a free though correct interpretation of כל אשר נשאו לבו. On the other hand the singularity of the Hebrew is retained in the relative ᾧ clause. Since the antecedent τοὺς ἔχοντας is plural, one would have expected οἷς and a number of witnesses do have this. -- What is odd is Exod's use of ὁ θεός for the tetragrammaton, for which see comment at 35:30. And since MT has לבו hex has also added αυτων.

36:3 The subject of ἔλαβον is the accusative objects of ἐκάλεσεν in v.2 who now take over the materials brought so as to construct all that God had ordered (in chh.25--31). The Hellenistic form of the verb ελαβοσαν occurs in scattered witnesses. As already noted in v.1 Exod omitted עבדה though he added πάντα before τὰ ἔργα. To make up for this hex has added της δουλειας.[4]

In 3b MT used הם to show change of subject to the Israelites; it is they who continue to bring to him (Moses) voluntary offerings every morning. Exod removed the apparent contradiction with vv.4--5 by having αὐτοί use the subjects of ἔλαβον as referent. Accordingly he restructured the content of the clause; they did not continue to bring, but were receiving (the imperfect προσδέχονται); "to him" was of course omitted, and the source for the offerings was added: παρὰ τῶν φερόντων. -- The change of ἔτι to επι in a b f n reading is a scribal mistake which must have confused its

1. Cf SS 136,185.
2. For the originality of the article see THGE VII.D.1.
3. Cf SS 95.

reader; an ἐπι phrase modifying προσδέχομαι makes very little sense indeed.

The rendering of נדבה by τὰ προσφέροντα stresses the sacrificial rather than the free will character of the things brought. Though προσφέρω does mean "to bring to," it has taken on a sacral sense of "to offer sacrifice";[5] the intention is to characterize these gifts as sacrifices offered up to God.

36:4 Exod uses the imperfect παρεγίνοντο to stress the fact that the workmen were coming from all sides rather than the aorist of the *b n z* tradition; the majority A F M tradition has the aorist participle παραγενομενοι which is puzzling. It may have originated under the influence of ποιοῦντες modifying the subject σοφοί. One would then expect the opening καί of v.5 to be omitted as well, since εἶπαν then becomes the main verb, but only a few mss attest that omission.[6]

The subject is modified first by an attributive participial construction, and then by a ἕκαστος structure modified by κατὰ τὸ αὑτοῦ ἔργον, and ἔργον in turn by a relative clause. In the first of these Exod (and Pesh) does not translate כל of כל מלאכת;[7] hex has added παντα. Also hex is the transposition of αὑτοῦ ἔργον in the second structure to equal MT. -- The distributive איש איש is correctly rendered by a single ἕκαστος.

The relative clause at the end is introduced by the accusative ὅ and contains plural references also referring to the subject σοφοί. Some Byzantine witnesses have made these singular: αυτος ειργαζετο, with ἕκαστος as the antecedent. This is fully possible within the Greek tradition but the parent text has the plural. The Hebrew pattern: pronoun + participle becomes pronoun + imperfect verb in Exod which is contextually exactly right.

36:5 Exod has abbreviated the fullness of MT considerably though not omitting anything essential to what is being said. In each case hex has glossed an equivalent for the presumed omission. a) לאמר as a direct

---

4. From Theod; according to Syh Sym used τῆς λατρείας "of cultic service."
5. Cf especially Bauer s.v. 2.
6. The Three according to Syh had the more common rendering for ויבא

speech marker; Exod uses ὅτι but hex has added λεγοντες; b) ‏מדי‎; Exod has for ‏מדי‎ ... ‏מרבים‎ πλῆθος ... παρά, but hex inserts υπερ το ικανον; c) for ‏העבדה למלאכה‎ Exod has (παρὰ) τὰ ἔργα; hex adds της δουλειας between ικανον and παρά; d) ‏אתה‎; omitted by Exod as otiose after "works which ... to do," but hex adds αυτα. Hex also reorders φέρει ὁ λαός to fit the Hebrew order. None of these glosses and changes is necessary for the sense; Exod may be rendered by: "And they said to Moses: The people are bringing much beyond (i.e. more than is necessary for) the works that the Lord ordered (us) to do."

36:6 The use of ἐκήρυξεν is problematic. It is coordinate with προσέταξεν with Moses as subject, but Moses is hardly the one who did the proclaiming. Either the verb must be interpreted causally as in MT's ‏יעבירו קול‎, or the collocation can be understood zeugmatically as "Moses ordered and (someone) proclaimed." What is clearly meant is that a public announcement was made in the camp.

The announcement is introduced by the direct speech marker λέγων. The proclamation read: "As for any man and woman, let them no more be active in the matter of offerings (presentations) for the sanctuary." Note the clustering of the root ἐργάζομαι to render ‏עשה‎ (also in vv.4,8 and 35:9), otherwise found in the book only at 31:4,5 of the A account, the usual word used being ποιέω. The translation omits any reference to ‏מלאכה‎, and Exod must have intended the verb as sufficient for translating ‏יעשׂו מלאכה‎. -- ἀπαρχάς is more usually used for "firstfruits" but also occurs for ‏תרומה‎ for which see comment at 25:2.[8]

The last clause has added an ἔτι for good sense. Note again the use of προσφέρειν "to present offerings" for the Hiphil of ‏בוא‎ for which compare the note at v.3.

36:7 The Hebrew presents a difficulty in that ‏המלאכה‎ occurs twice and apparently in two senses: "The ‏מלאכה‎ was sufficient for them for all the ‏מלאכה‎ to do it." The second occurrence is something to do, i.e. "work" but the first one can be measured and must mean "materials for work." Exod uses τὰ ἔργα for the first one presumably in the sense of the "things done" by the people, i.e. bringing the construction materials, and for the second he uses τὴν κατασκευήν for which see the note at 35:24.[9]

The ἔργα is characterized as ἦν αὐτοῖς ἱκανά "were sufficient for them"; the antecedent for the pronoun is not fully certain but it is probably the ἔργα which the Lord commanded in v.5. Hex has reordered the structure placing the pronoun at the end to conform to דיר.

The final clause in MT has a Hiphil free infinitive in context, i.e. with a prefixed conjunction; accordingly it takes on the finite verbal character of its context; Exod correctly interprets this by its προσκατέλιπον. An A *oII n y* reading has an ill-fitting imperfect but this is merely an itacistic spelling. It simply means "and there were things (materials) left over."

36:8a Only the subject "every wise one among the workmen" and the verb ἐποίησεν are taken from the Hebrew verse to introduce the next section for which see the discussion on 36:8b below. Exod has σοφός for MT's חכם לב, and hex has added τη καρδια to approximate the Hebrew.

36:8b--39:23 This section represents the largest translation problem in the book. The materials of MT are not only considerably shortened but are also arranged in quite a different order in Exod. The following list will show the differences in order. The order given is that of Exod with the MT equivalent given after the = sign.

36:8--40 = 39:1--31; 37:1--2 = 36:8--9; 37:3--6 = 36:35--38; 37:7--21 = 38:9--23; 38:1--3 = 37:1--3; 38:4--9 = 37:5--11; 38:10 =37:13; 38:11--17 = 37:15--23; 38:18--20 = not in MT; 38:21 = 38:20; 38:22--24 = 38:1--5; 38:25 = 37:29; 38:26 = 38:8; 38:27 = 40:30--32; 39:1--8 = 38:24--30a; 39:9 = 38:31; 39:10--11 = 38:30b,32; 39:12 = not in MT; 39:13 = 39:1; 39:14--15 = 39:33,35; 39:16--17 = 39:38,37; 39:18 = 39:36; 39:19 = 39:41; 39:20--21 = 39:40,34,40; 39:22--23 = 39:42--43.

It will be noted that only 38:18--20 and 39:12 have no equivalents in the Hebrew. For details see comments on individual verses.

A reverse list following the order of MT with the Exod equivalents given after the = sign will demonstrate the compression of the Greek text.

καὶ ἦλθον.
7. Cf SS 64.

36:8--9 = 37:1--2; 36:10--34 = not in Exod; 36:35 --38 = 37:3--6; 37:1--10a
= 38:1--11; 37:10b--15 = not in Exod; 37:16--17a = 38:12--17; 37:17b--28
= not in Exod; 37:29 = 38:25; 38:1--7 = 38:22--24; 38:8 = 38:26; 38:9--23
= 37:7--21; 38:24--31 = 39:1--10a; 39:1 = 39:13; 39:2--31 = 36:9--40;
39:32 = 39:10b--11; 39:33 = 39:14; 39:34 = not in Exod; 39:35 =39:15--
16a; 39:36 = 39:18; 39:37--38 = 39:16a--17; 39:39 = not in Exod; 39:40 =
39:20--21; 39:41 = 39:19; 39:42--43 = 39:22--23.

From this list it is clear that the following verses in MT have no
renderings in Exod: 36:10--34, 37:10b--15, 38:1--7, 39:34 and 39. Within
verses the text has also been considerably shortened, and these have been
filled in by hex throughout; similarly the longer sections not represented in
Exod have been filled in by hex. So too the changes in order have been
"corrected" by hex and in the notes that follow these will not be recorded;
i.e. it can be taken for granted that hex has throughout changed the word
order to conform to MT.

36:8(39:1b; par 28:2) Part 2 begins with the first item in the construction
narrative, the priestly garments, and continues through to the end of
chapter 37 which describes the making of the various curtains of the tabernacle and the requisite pillars (=36:35--38 in MT), followed by an account
of the construction of the court and its parts all of which was under
Beseleel's charge, but more particularly for the textiles, under Eliab; this in
MT is found at 38:9--23.

The accent in Part 2 is on the textiles, though in the nature of the case
the construction of the curtains for tabernacle and court had to involve
pillars on which those had to be hung as well. Part 3 is then intended to
stress the metal work as the specialty of Beseleel.

The translator simply lifted the materials from ch.39 of MT and
placed them here. Since MT's 39:1b starts with ויעשו, it was easy to
continue with the translation of את בגדי הקדש, attaching it as the object
of ἐποίησεν, for which see comments on v.8a above. Since the subject is
πᾶς σοφός the verb is singular. With v.9 the plural takes over, for which see
v.4: πάντες οἱ σοφοί. That the textile work involved more than just Eliab
was clear from 35:25--26. By contrast Part 3 uses the singular verb

throughout with Beseleel as subject, since reference to others involved in metal work (though Beseleel must have had help) is not specifically made in the account. The garments are designated as τῶν ἁγίων; the plural is unique in this context, though it does occur modifying τὴν ἐργασίαν in 39:1. A singular genitive modifying στολάς occurs at 35:21 and 39:19. Since Aaron also served (annually) in the adytum the plural can be justified.

Over against MT Aaron is called "the priest." Though emphasis on his priestly function is common to both accounts the title only occurs in B (also at 35:18 37:19); the translator might well have been influenced by the statement of 35:18.

36:9(39:2; par 28:6) The verb is now changed to the plural ἐποίησαν, as in Sam Pesh. The plural is kept throughout the chapter except for vv.14 and 39, though MT has more verbs in the singular. For the rest Exod renders MT literally except for adding καί before ὑακίνθου. -- Only here does B use the simplex νενησμένου, elsewhere using the δια- compound (vv.10,12 35:6); the latter occurs only with κόκκινος, and renders ש‬נ‬י‬; cf comment at 25:4 on the use of the roots νηθ- and κλωθ-.

36:10(39:3) The two clauses of MT are made into one in Exod by omitting the first verb "they hammered out" and making the second one a passive ἐτμήθη with τὰ πέταλα as subject, and with τρίχες as second nominative modifying πέταλα, thus "the leaves of gold[10] were cut up as threads (hairs)." In Exod B's plan this entire section was to deal with textiles, not with metal work, a plan preserved by avoiding terminology associated with metal work. This is further emphasized by the interpretation of "to work in the midst of" as συνυφᾶναι σύν "to weave with."[11] In MT בתוך is repeated with each of the textiles, and Exod repeats σύν as well except for the second one. A tendency to omit the repeated preposition in the interest of better Greek is seen in the tradition, but the Hebraic trend towards repeating prepositions is original. For the textiles listed see notes at 25:4.

The final clause combines MT's מעשה חשב with the עשה לו of the next verse, thus "a woven work they made it."

---

8. See also SS 64 for αἱ ἀπαρχαὶ τοῦ ἁγίου.
9. The Three according to Syh render the phrase literally by εἰς πᾶν τὸ

36:11--12(39:4--5; par 28:7--8) With עשה לו already used for the preceding clause v.11 had to be made explicative of αὐτό in that clause: "the shoulder straps holding together, from both sides, a woven work, alternatively interwoven by itself." By εἰς ἄλληλα and καθ᾽ ἑαυτό the translator was trying to show that the (two) shoulder straps are mirror images of each other. The Exod text is an attempt to make good sense out of a difficult parent Hebrew. The MT texts of A and B are similar, but the two Greek texts are quite different though the B translator shows some awareness of the A text in that he shared a number of lexical items, particularly ἐπωμίδες for כתפת, and see also the common use of μερός and συνέχω.

With v.12 the relation between Exod and MT becomes clearer. The collocation ממנו הוא כמעשהו is contextualized within Exod by introducing ἐποίησαν;[12] since v.11 had been readapted as explicative of αὐτό, it now became necessary to reintroduce the verb (which had been taken from v.11; cf comment on v.10) to make the concluding statement on the shoulder pieces of the ephod, viz. that they were ἐξ αὐτοῦ "of the same (stuff)" and "made according to its workmanship," this then being further defined by the common list of materials, for which see comment at 25:4.

The *d* text has changed ἐποίησαν to the imperfect εποιει; a singular imperfect is not overly fitting in a context of the oft recurring ἐποίησαν, and it is the product of apocopation, i.e. dropping the -σαν ending. A *C s* variant has changed the pronoun in "its workmanship" to εαυτου, thereby making it refer to ἐξ αὐτοῦ, which must be rooted in a misunderstanding of the idiom "of the same (stuff)."

The καθά clause with which the verse ends is almost a leitmotif for the chapter, recurring in the same or similar form at vv.14,29,34,37 and 40.

36:13--14(39:6--7; par 28:9,11--12) That the translator was influenced by the A account is obvious from his addition of ἀμφοτέρους over against MT; the parallel had τοὺς δύο. But in the main he has gone his own way using technical terms which occur only here in LXX.

For השהם as τῆς σμαράγδου see comment on 35:10--19. Exod uses four terms which have to do with gemmology, whereas MT has only three.

600

The first term in MT is מסבכ, a Hophal participle of סבב, thus "surrounded," which Exod interpreted by a hapax legomenon συμπεπορπημένους; its root is based on πόρπη, "brooch, clasp," and the participle may be rendered by "fastened, held in place." The second is משבצת זהב, for which see comment at 28:13. Exod used another hapax, translating the phrase by περισεσιαλωμένους χρυσίω. The root σιαλόω means "to fatten," so literally "fattened about with gold (thread)," probably then "embroidered about, set around with gold."

The third is מפתחת פתוחי חתם. The first word is vocalized by the Masoretes as a Pual participle, thus "opened up with the opening of a seal"; some form of engraving must be intended. Exod again uses a rare cognate expression ἐκκεκολαμμένους ἐκκόλαμμα; in fact, the noun occurs only here in LXX and the verb occurs elsewhere only three times (3Reg 6:35 Prov 24:52 3Macc 2:27). In the Reg passage it is used to describe the cherubs on the leaves of the door to the *debir*, and means "engraved, embossed."[13] In order to make sure that readers would not be misled Exod added a doublet γεγλυμμένους καί before it, a root well known from the A account. The engraving or sculpting was done ἐκ the name of the Israelites, the proposition being chosen because of the ἐκκόλαμμα which it modifies.

The C text revised the initial verb to the singular, a variant due to the singular verb in v.14. -- The Byzantine text added και between the second and third items, but Exod had two pairs rather than a string of four coordinated terms. A majority A F M reading has omitted καὶ ἐκκεκολαμμένους, possibly as an early revision towards MT. A better revision would have omitted the other member of the doublet, since the cognate construction must be original text in view of the Hebrew cognate expression.

The singular ἐπέθηκεν is puzzling; it is of course due to the Hebrew וישם, but it is no whit clearer in the Hebrew. Is the subject then to be understood as the πᾶς σόφος of v.8, or is it Eliab who was chiefly responsible for textiles (cf 35:34--35)? The compound verb is preferred by B to the simplex of A (28:12). The distribution of the two forms as renderings for

---

ἔργου.
10. For the genitive of material see SS 63.

שׂים or נתן is as follows. In B only the compound obtains in chh.36--39 (nine times), but in ch.40 the compound occurs six times and the simplex nine. In Exod A the choice seems to be a matter of indifference, the compound occurring 21 times, and τίθημι, 12.

36:15--22(39:8--15; par 22:15--22) The construction of the oracle. The translator relied heavily on Exod A, at times departing from his parent text to follow the A account. For the technical terms borrowed from the parallel see the comments on 28:15--22. A detailed comparison follows below.

36:15(39:8; par 28:15) In A the oracle pouch is called חשׁן משׁפט and rendered by λόγιον τῶν κρίσεων, whereas here MT has את החשׁן; i.e. it is already defined in the A account; but Exod renders it by λόγιον, i.e. without an article as in A; hex has of course added an article. In both accounts it is called the work of a designer." In A חשׁב is translated by ποικιλτοῦ, and here, by ὑφάντου ποικιλτοῦ; For its meaning see comment at 28:6. Only close familiarity with Exod A could have led to the choice of such a rendering for חשׁב.

Over against A Exod here retains some individualistic trends. For the phrase "according to the מעשׂה of the ephod" he does not use the unusual ῥυθμόν of A but the common rendering τὸ ἔργον. For the usual list of textiles he does not render שׁ ר by κεκλωσμένου as in A, but by his own preferred δαινευησμένου for which see the comment at 25:4. For λόγιον and its meaning, as well as for the popular M misspelling, see the discussion at 28:15.

A popular A reading of the verb in the singular εποιησεν is an early revision toward MT. Exod followed Sam Pesh in the contextually appropriate plural. Also attested is an A M *b z* reading of the genitive in place of the dative ποικιλίᾳ, an attempt at stylistic betterment.

36:16(39:9; par 28:16) The Hebrew text of 16a is somewhat more expansive than in A which is in turn reflected in Exod, though it does omit an equivalent for היה thereby making the two clauses of MT into a single one: "square, doubled, they made the oracle." Hex has by adding ην after "square" restored the two clauses of MT. An odd *O f* variant has the verb in the singular, ἐποίησεν (as does Sam); this makes Eliab the maker of the oracle, but that can hardly have been intended by Exod.

For 16b Exod B has followed the A account exactly except for the repeated διπλοῦν at the end which equals MT. Its omission by Sam is probably due to 28:16. For the shape and size of the oracle see the comment at 28:16.

36:17a(39:10a; par 28:17a) The opening verb in Hebrew in both accounts is the Piel of מלא, for which see comment on 28:17. Exod makes the verb passive but retains the rest of the A text exactly, with the nominal construction which is the object of καθυφανεῖς in A now becoming the subject of συνυφάνθη, the verb in B.

36:17b--20a(39:10b--13a; par 28:17b--20a) In v.17b MT begins with a simple bound construction טורי אבן; this is rendered by στίχος λίθων which was taken over from Exod A, which had, however, also added an ἔσται; one would have expected a plural στιχοι, and only the A text which in MT had the odd אבן טור, can be taken as the background for στίχος; cf comment at 28:17.

For the twelve stones in the four rows see comments on 28:17b--20a. The two Greek texts are identical except for the first row in which A gives the three stones asyndetically, whereas B joins them with καί throughout. The other three rows are all in the pattern: a + b + c, whereas MT has them in the pattern: a b + c for all four in B, but in A only for the first three rows, but for row four: a + b + c .

36:20b(39:13b; par 28:20b) For a discussion of the different participles and their relations to MT in the two accounts see the discussion in 28:20b. MT has only one זהב but in the two accounts both participles are modified by χρυσίῳ, though in A the second one is introduced by ἐν. It should be noted that for B the text is not fully certain since a majority A F M text also reads εν χρυσω. Since either reading makes good, if not exactly the same, sense

---

11. Cf the note in Helbing 311.
12. See SS 81.

it is probably wise to accept the reading of the oldest Greek witness, cod B, which does not have the preposition.

Both accounts end with (plus "shall be" in A) "in their settings," which neither Greek translation recognizes. Exod A has in its place ἔστωσαν κατὰ στίχον αὐτῶν, whereas B has nothing.

36:21(39:14; par 28:21) V.21a is exactly the same in both Greek accounts except for the forms of the verb "to be"; in A it is present imperative, but in B, perforce in the imperfect. That the two accounts were not independently formed is clear from the ἐκ construction for the first על but κατά for the second in both accounts even though the two phrases are identical in the Hebrew: על שמת. It might be noted that a B + variant text has changed the κατά to an ἐκ phrase.[14]

The second part of the verse begins in MT of both accounts with פתוחי חרתם/חתם, but Exod A and B differ; instead of A's γλυφαὶ σφραγίδων Exod here has a perfect passive participle in ἐγγεγλυμμέναι φραγῖδες "engraved seals"; in v.13 the same phrase had been rendered differently; cf comment at vv.13--14. The B + text has the strange reading εγγεγραμμενα εις σφραγιδας.[15]

The next expression is ἕκαστος ἐκ τοῦ ἑαυτοῦ ὀνόματος for איש על שמו. Here the A account is more idiomatic with its ἕκαστος κατὰ τὸ ὄνομα. Exod B was probably still under the influence of the earlier ἐκ τῶν ὀνομάτων. On the other hand the use of the reflexive ἑαυτοῦ is precise. -- The concluding "for the twelve tribes" also occurs in A.

36:22(39:15; par 28:22) Except for the automatic change in verbal inflection to an aorist (third plural) this verse is an exact copy of A, except that the work of עבת is not rendered by ἀλυσιδωτοῦ but by ἐμπλοκίου, a word used of a female ornament at 35:22; it refers to something twisted like a rope, which is probably what is intended here, i.e. the work of a plaited object; its parallel is something "chainlike."[16]

---

13. Schl renders the verb by *insculpto, caelo*, and the noun as *sculptura, caeletura.*
14. See the discussion in THGE VII.L.3.

36:23--29(39:16--21; par 28:13--14,22,24--25) This section describes how the oracle pouch is to be firmly attached to the ephod, more particularly to the shoulder straps of the ephod. Its parallel in A is much abbreviated and is not overly helpful in understanding the more detailed picture here.

36:23--24(39:16) For the term ἀσπιδίσκας as a translation for מֹשְׁבְצֹת see comment at 28:13.[17] -- The two golden rings were then put on the two corners of the oracle pouch. For ἀρχάς in the sense of "corners" see Act 10:11 11:5. The Hebrew text has קְצֹות. Exod again states that they were "golden" rings, which MT does not repeat, it having already been stated in v.23.

36:25(39:17) On these rings they then put twisted clasps of gold on both sides μερῶν (קְצֹות) of the oracle. The term ἐμπλόκια is the same as that used in 35:22 where they were objects of female adornment, but here they are ties of some kind used to bind the oracle to the ephod. A C s variant has both the verb and the noun in the singular: επεθηκεν το εμπλοκιον, but this is barely sensible.

What follows further defines the placement: "even at the two correspondence points (junctures) the two plaited clasps." This is Exod's rendering of the first part of 39:18 "and the two ends (קְצֹות) of the two cords." In MT this begins a new clause with the verb נָתְנוּ, but Exod transposes the two nominals and makes it define the positioning of the clasps. Note how Exod interprets by taking קְצֹות as a fluid term with different meanings in different contexts; here it is translated by συμβολάς.

The Byzantine text makes the gold καθαρου. Majority A F M readings gloss δακτυλίους by "two," and change the preposition in "ἐπ᾽ both sides of the oracle" to εξ.

36:26(39:18) The verse consists of a καί ... καί construction, i.e. instead of נָתְנוּ, for which see comment at v.25, Exod has καὶ ἐπέθηκαν; this is then repeated for the second clause as well, with both predicates lacking expressed objects. This is done to make the verb define the δύο συμβολάς of

---

15. See the discussion in THGE VII.C.
16. According to Syh Aq had πεπλεγμένον, whereas Theod probably read ἀλυσιδωτόν as rendering for עֲבֹת.

v.25. These junctures, points of correspondence on the ephod, i.e. where the rings belong, are on the two bosses. Then the second clause states that these correspondence points are located on the shoulder (straps) of the ephod over against (each other) in front. These are thus fully visible. This attachment deals with the rings at two corners of the oracle pouch which are attached by plaited clasps of gold to the small bosses (which are presumably sewn, or better still, woven into) the front side of the shoulder straps of the ephod.

The Byzantine text has omitted the first καί thereby equalling MT, though this creates a new problem since now the preceding phrases become part of the first clause. -- Popular hex revisions have added an αυτους in the second clause so as to provide an object to the verb as well as an αυτου after πρόσωπον; both of these are due to the Hebrew.

36:27(39:19) This and the following verse describe the attachment of the other two corners of the oracle to the ephod. Again two more rings are made which were then put on the πτερύγια ἐπ' ἄκρου of the oracle on the ἄκρον τοῦ ὀπισθίου of the ephod ἔσωθεν. By elimination the untranslated words about the oracle must refer to the remaining corners, but why "wings at the edge" is not immediately clear. The Hebrew has "on the two קצות of the oracle על שפתו. Presumably ἄκρου is the rendering for קצה, and "wings" translates "at its lip." But what are the πτερύγια? Did Exod think of some kind of extensions, of loops attached at the corners to which the rings were attached? In any event the rings had to reach around to the shoulder straps at the rear. Exod pictures the lower corners as attached with πτερύγια which reached around (under the arms) to the inside edge of the back shoulder strap. A B *oII z* variant by adding a και before "on the ἄκρου" has clarified this somewhat.

36:28(39:20) Two golden rings are then made for the ephod (the other four were all for the oracle); their placement is defined as on both shoulder straps of the ephod κάτωθεν αὐτοῦ κατὰ πρόσωπον at the juncture above the webbing of the ephod. The first phrase probably means "at its lower part"; this must be the place since it is just above the woven band at the

606

upper part of the garment below the straps, i.e. at the juncture. The rings are again κατὰ πρόσωπον, i.e. from the position of the viewer, in front, though attached according to v.27 to the front side (the inside) of the shoulder at the back.

36:29(39:21) The actual attachment of these lower corners of the oracle to the lower inside edge of the back shoulder straps is now described. But over against MT the verb is in the singular, which is perplexing, since throughout the account the indefinite plural, ἐποίησαν, ἐπέθηκαν, is used. Good sense demands that it be understood indefinitely as well, but it remains puzzling. The tying up is from the rings which were on it (i.e. on the oracle) to the rings of the ephod. These rings were both held together by blue (by a thread; MT defines this as בפתיל תכלת), as well as woven together into the fabric of the ephod, a kind of interweaving into the woven material of the ephod. Syntactically it is the rings which are woven into the fabric, συμπλεγμένους, not the blue (thread) which is in the genitive singular. This careful and firm joining was done so that the oracle pouch could not be loosened, χαλᾶται, from the ephod.

36:30(39:22; par 28:27) The highpriestly robe is delineated in vv.30--34. The verb is plural as in all ancient sources except MT which has ויעש. The "robe of the ephod" is rendered by τὸν ὑποδύτην ὑπὸ τὴν ἐπωμίδα. It is indeed the outer robe but the ephod is worn over it as the Greek makes explicit, though MT does not. The Byzantine text has υποδυτην ποδηρη as a doublet after ὑποδύτην, borrowed from the parallel account in 28:27.[18]

36:31(39:23; par 28:28) The translator opens with a δέ structure, which is rare in Exod B; in fact it occurs elsewhere only at 35:2 39:12 and 40:31, in all cases used in contrastively. -- For the "collar of the robe" cf comment at 28:28. Exod renders בתוכו more closely than does A by ἐν τῷ μέσῳ. The predicate of this nominal construction is διυφασμένον συμπλεκτόν, which

---

17. As at 28:13 Aq translates by σφιγτῆρας. According to Syh Sym reads a compound συσφιγτῆρας, whereas Theod has συσφιγξείς. Retroversions are those of Field.
18. The Three render מעיל האפד more exactly. On the witness of Syh Aq had ἔνδυμα τοῦ ἐπενδύματος which promoted Sym's τὸ ἐπένδυμα τοῦ

might be rendered as "interwoven, plaited together"; obviously it is Exod's rendering for the difficult כפי תחרא for which see comment at 28:28. Also predicative is the next collocation "having a border around the collar" which reflects the A account. The verse ends with ἀδιάλυτον "untearable, unrippable," a smoother though a less literal translation than A's ἵνα μὴ ῥαγῇ.

36:32--33(39:24--25; par 28:29) Of these two verses the first is dependent almost word for word on the A account and the comments on the text there are applicable here as well. The differences between the two accounts except for the necessary one in verbal inflection are τοῦ λώματος instead of the accusative, ὡς for ὡσεί, and the simplex instead of the compound διανενησμένου. Clearly Exod relied heavily on A.

V..33 has no close correspondent in the A account, but is a good rendering of MT except for its omission of טהור and the first occurrence of בתוך הרמנים; the latter is indeed tautologous. Hex has added translations of the omitted text in both cases.

A *C s* text has changed the verb to a different compound ὑπεθηκαν, presumably because of the position of the bells below the hem. But Exod B favors ἐπέθηκαν throughout the account; in fact ὑποτίθημι is used only once in B, 40:18, of placing the poles under (ὑπό) the ark. -- τὸ λῶμα appears in the genitive in a popular variant probably due to v.32. The use of the plural in hex is a revision towards MT.

36:34(39:26; par 28:30--31) MT begins with פעמן ורמן repeated which Exod represents only once but with "bell" characterized as χρυσοῦς. Exod is otherwise a literal rendering of MT. The nominal clause has as predicate the prepositional phrase "upon the hem of the robe round about" with an εἰς plus marked infinitive to show the raison d'etre of these ornaments as "for doing cultic service." By itself the latter statement is cryptic, explicable only from the parallel in 28:31 which see.

36:35--37(39:27--29; par 28:35--36) The A and B accounts are quite disparate and except for vocabulary items little is served by comparing the two.

36:35(39:27) Exod renders MT literally except for leaving χιτῶνας unarticulated. The linen garments are for priests in distinction from the blue robe of the high priest described in vv.30--34.

36:36(39:28) Three further linen accoutrements for the priests coordinate with the χιτῶνας of v.35. These are τὰς κιδάρεις, τὴν μίτραν and τὰ περισκελῆ. The distinction between the first two is unclear. In MT the first is called המצנפת and the second פארי המגבעת, but this is not very helpful since these two are also difficult to define. The first in both cases is "the turban(s)," but μίτραν only translates מצנפת elsewhere. Furthermore it is in the singular, whereas the other two are both plural. It is possible then that the Greek has transposed the two. But it is still difficult to distinguish between the two terms though possibly μίτραν may be a headband as opposed to a turban.[19] -- For the last item, the linen drawers, see comment at 28:38. In MT these are characterized by הבד.[20]

36:37(39:29) A final item in the list is τὰς ζώνας αὐτῶν; the pronoun is added over against MT. These are made not only of linen (MT has שש משזר) but also of blue, purple and scarlet yarn. A popular Byzantine reading has the compound διανενησμενου for Exod's simplex; the two are synonyms. For ποικιλτοῦ see note at 26:36. --The concluding statement "as the Lord commanded Moses" is introduced by ὃν τρόπον rather than the usual καθά, but cf also v.40 below.

36:38--39(39:30; par 28:32) The πέταλον, a thin golden plate, is characterized in MT as a נ זר הקדש, "a holy crown," a phrase which also occurs at 29:6 where it is simply called τὸ ʾΑγίασμα for which see comment at 29:6. Exod's choice here of ἀφόρισμα τοῦ ἁγίου is unique in LXX for rendering this expression.[21] It would not be so unusual if it applied to the priest, but here it refers to the πέταλον.

ἐπενδύματος (cf comment at 28:27), whereas Theod had τὸν ἐπενδύτην τῆς ἐπωμίδος all three using a genitive for the second noun to represent the bound structure of MT.

19. See LS sub μίτρα II, but see also II,4 and 5.

20. Aq and Sym have added τοῦ ἐξαιρέτου, whereas according to Syh Theod transliterated as dbʾd, "of bad."

V.39 again has the puzzling singular verb, though here it might be due to a rationalization of the situation over against the plural of MT; after all, the inscribing of two words on a thin plate could hardly be the work of more than one person.

פתוחי חותם occurs twice elsewhere in this chapter; cf comments at vv.13 and 21, as well as in the A account in ch.28. In 28:21 it is rendered by γλυφαὶ σφραγίδων. Here ἐκτετυπωμένα (σφραγῖδος) is based on the parallel ἐκτύπωμα of 28:32; such a change from a noun to a participle in B was also noted in vv.13 and 21. Exod B here adopts the phrase to fit the γράμματα, and illustrates how well the translator studied the context in each case.

36:40(39:31; par 28:33) But the πέταλον, though made and inscribed, was not yet attached or placed, and so "they placed upon the border (i.e. of the plate) something blue (i.e. a blue cord or thread); the phrase ἐπὶ τὸ λῶμα is a clarification of עליו which without further refinement would refer to the πέταλον itself. Then the phrase תכלת פתיל is simply rendered by ὑακίνθινον "something blue," i.e. with no word for פתיל. This led to some misunderstanding, especially by Origen who thought that the λῶμα must stand for פתיל, and so changed τό to αυτο. This then would mean "he put on it (the plate) a blue hem. Since the plate was made of gold a blue hem is a most unlikely tale indeed. Furthermore λῶμα never renders פתיל but only שול.

The point of putting a blue cord on the border of the plate was to make the plate lie firmly on the headband ἄνωθεν, i.e. at the upper part of it, in the place of prominence. Note that the concluding clause is a ὃν τρόπον one, for which see comment at v.37.

---

21. Aq Sym render נזר at 29:6 by ἀφόρισμα "a dedicated object, something set apart." In fact, Aq usually uses the root ἀφορίζω to translate נזר. It would appear that Aq's understanding rests on an old Jewish tradition already attested in the time of Exod B.

Chapter 37

This chapter concerns the αὐλαῖαι and καταπετάσματα of the tabernacle, and for the courtyard, its ἱστία and/ or αὐλαῖαι together with the pillars and attachments, and the καταπέτασμα τῆς πύλης with its pillars and attachments, as well as the tentpins of the court. It ends with a summation attributing oversight for the cult service of the Levites to Ithamar, and mentioning the two architects with the textile fabrication specifically the responsibility of Eliab. This leads naturally to Part 3 where Beseleel's work is detailed.

MT's account obtains in 36:8b--38 and 38:9--23 and the parallel in Exod A is found at 26:1--37 27:9--19; in other words the order of the A account, with the automatic bypassing of the description of the altar of the holocaust in 27:1--8, is retained.

What is difficult to understand is Exod's omission of the detailed description of the construction of the tabernacle curtains, the קרשׁים pillars and the bars of 36:10--34 in its entirety. This might be defensible for vv.20--34 which have nothing to do with textiles, but vv.10--19 describe the inner ten curtains of colored stuff as well as the eleven outer curtains of goats' hair. Apparently the translator felt reference to the dimensions of the inner ten curtains to be sufficient as far as the tabernacle itself was concerned.

37:1--2(36:8b--9; par 26:1--2) From v.1 it is clear that it is not the tabernacle that "they made" but only the ten curtains for it. This contrasts with the A account which has the accusative τὴν σκηνήν and the ten curtains a s a second accusative. A popular Byzantine variant has changed the dative τῷ σκηνῇ to the accusative; this voids the distinction which B has; in B the statement is not the whole story; the ten curtains are but for (i.e. part of) the tent.

Furthermore all reference to the materials for the curtains in MT is completely omitted. This contrasts with the construction of the καταπετά-σματα of tent and courtyard in vv.3,5 and 16 below.

For verse 2 the Hebrew text of A and B are identical, with Exod A closely following MT. Exod here seems deliberately to distance himself from A by reordering freely over against it and MT. The predicate for the first two statements is preposed, i.e. "28 cubits was the length ... four cubits was the breadth," and the concluding statement that "there was one measure for all the curtains" in MT and Exod A is abbreviated to "the same they were for all" and put between the statements on length and breadth! Note the peculiar statement τὸ αὐτὸ ἦσαν πάσαις in which the unnamed subject must refer to the πήχεων, and πάσαις referring to the αὐλαίαις of v.1 with the accusative τὸ αὐτό serving adverbially.

37:3(36:35; par 26:31) The account is consistently told in the plural as in ch.36 (cf comment at 36:9) in contrast to MT, only Pesh agreeing with Exod. For the materials out of which the καταπέτασμα was made see notes at 25:4.[1]

The work is characterized as an ἔργον ὑφαντὸν χερουβίμ, the last word being a second accusative. A popular B reading has ὑφαντόν in the genitive, an early correction towards MT, but the accusative has become almost a set phrase in Exod.[2] MT has "he made it" before "cherubim," which Exod did not translate as being otiose, but hex in disregard of the context rendered it by εποιησεν αυτο.

37:4(36:36; par 26:32) This verse illustrates how the translator used Exod A in the course of his work. He not only has a parent text, but the Exod A account as well. Here Exod abandons MT entirely in favor of Exod A as source. MT has: "And he made for it (i.e. the veil) four pillars of shittim wood and overlaid them with gold, and their hooks were gold, and he cast for them (the pillars) four bases of silver," but Exod mirrors the pattern account. In fact, except for the change of ἐπιθήσεις to ἐπέθηκεν Exod has taken over the A version changing only the case after ἐπί from the accusative to the genitive, and the simplex participle to the compound κατακεχρυσωμένους.

1. Aq translated פרכת here by παραπέτασμα; the word is a synonym but occurs elsewhere in LXX only once, and is attested only here for Aq.
2. See the discussion in THGE VII.H.3.

612

37:5(36:37; par 26:36) This verse was consciously constructed as parallel to v.3; in fact, except for designating the veil as τῆς θύρας τῆς σκηνῆς τοῦ μαρτυρίου it is an exact copy, in spite of differences in MT where instead of הפרכת את v.5 has מסך and for חשב it has רקם. Nor did Exod base his work on Exod A where the Hebrew distinctions are upheld in the Greek, i.e. ἐπίσπαστρον and ποικιλτοῦ for מסך and רקם resp. That the translator intentionally modelled these two verses as parallels is clear from the addition of χερουβίμ which has no basis in v.5 at all; it has been taken over from v.3.[3]

The designation "door of the tent" is characterized as τοῦ μαρτυρίου over against MT; the expression "door of the tent of testimony" is a favored one in B; cf also 38:26 39:8 40:5,6,10. -- For the genitive ὑφαντου as a popular A variant see comment at v.3.

37:6(36:38; par 26:37) Since the first two nouns are governed by an את preposition but are left hanging in the air, Exod does begin with two accusatives, τοὺς στύλους αὐτοῦ ... τοὺς κρίκους αὐτῶν, but restates and transposes the following וצפה as κατεχρύσωσαν so as to include their κεφαλίδας and their ψαλίδας as well. This removes the ambiguity of the opening words of the verse by making all four nouns the object of the verb. This interpretation shows acquaintance with the A version in that the στύλους are specifically ordered to be gilded with gold. Early errors in the tradition changed αὐτοῦ to the plural and left out the first αὐτῶν.[4]

The verse ends with a nominal clause.[5] A popular A M variant has χαλκας for χαλκαῖ; presumably this must then be understood as a zeugma: "they gilded with gold ... and with bronze."

37:7--18(38:9--20; par 27:9--19) This section is a single unit. It begins with "and they made the court," and then continues with a long series of nominal

3 Aq did not use καταπέτασμα for מסך but rather παρατάνυσμα, for which see comment at 27:16.
4 See the discussion in THGE VII.G.5.
5 Taken over word for word by Theod; in Aq, however, the last word is a genitive noun χαλκοῦ so as to correspond more precisely with MT; Sym, on the other hand, has turned Exod's statement into the accusative, but since

clauses. For the difference in orientation in Exod A see comment at 27:9--15. Here the orientation is eastward both in Exod and MT (as in MT of A). Over against A Exod B shortens the text considerably by omitting all references to העמדים וחשקיהם ווי as well as to the metals with which they were made. Furthermore the term קלעים is inconsistently rendered here both by ἱστία and αὐλαῖαι. In A only ἱστία is used for the curtains of the court, whereas those for the tabernacle, the יריעת, were called αὐλαῖαι for the inner tent, and δέρρεις for the outer curtains made of skins. Exod B makes no reference to the leather outer covering at all, but does make a distinction between the materials for the veils (vv.3,5,16) and those for the curtains (vv. 7,14) the latter consisting only of twisted linen and the former of various colored materials. It will be noted that in v.1 Exod had omitted · all reference to the materials out of which the tabernacle curtains were made.

37:7(38:9; par 27:9) The first nominal clause specifies that the curtains towards the λίβα side of the court were made of twisted linen and their dimensions were ἑκατὸν ἐφ' ἑκατόν. For the latter phrase see comment at 27:18. The odd phrase is probably taken in the same sense as in 27:18; note that there חמשים בחמשים is parent text for πεντήκοντα ἐπὶ πεντήκοντα signifying the broad sides of the court, though the verse also has מאה באמה as here and also rendered it by ἑκατὸν ἐφ' ἑκατόν.[6] It is, however, also possible to understand the phrase "hundred on hundred" as giving a double measure, i.e. the length of the side as well as the length of the curtains; thus here it would mean that the curtains were hundred (cubits) on a hundred (cubit) long side.

A popular reading has νοτον instead of λίβα but the latter is favored throughout Exod; the two words both occur in the sense of "south," and the variant text does not change the sense.

37:8(38:10; par 27:10) For the side the number of pillars and of their bases is given in the pattern: καὶ οἱ στῦλοι ... καὶ αἱ βάσεις, repeated in subsequent verses for all but the west side as well; in MT only the second conjunction occurs. Exod A follows MT exactly in this matter. -- A majority variant adds χαλκοι which conforms to MT, but only the hex witnesses have the full equivalent to the Hebrew, also adding "and the ornaments of the pillars and their bands of silver."[7]

37:9(38:11; par 27:11) For the side towards the north the dimensions, though not the materials, are given. For the dimensions see comment at v.7. The pattern τὸ κλίτος τὸ πρός is used here as well as in vv.10 and 11, but not in v.7, though in all four verses MT has לפאת + a direction. In contrast to v.7 the parent text here does not have קלעי החצר, but see v.10 where the parent text has both לפאת and קלעים but Exod retains the "side" pattern as well as αὐλαῖαι. A B + variant has an odd misplaced doublet: και το κλιτος το προς νοτον εκατον εφ εκατον which might be sensible in v.7 but not here.

37:10(38:12; par 27:12) The west side. Here the curtains are called αὐλαῖαι and the dimensions are simply given as "fifty cubits."[8] A majority A M tradition has changed the preposition of πρὸς θάλασσαν to κατα, which was taken from the par text 27:12.

Instead of the usual καὶ οἱ στῦλοι (cf vv.8,9,12,13) this verse has only στῦλοι. It is obvious that the translator had the text of Exod A before him since the deviation from the usual pattern occurs there for the west side as well (though in subsequent verses there as well). -- For the variant spelling πηχων see comment at 25:16.

37:11--13(38:13--15; par 27:13--15) The east side is simply designated as τὸ πρὸς ἀνατολάς for the double designation in MT: קדמה מזרחה; hex has added πρωτον after τό, which creates a text which must have puzzled the thoughtful reader. The east side, being the front side, is described in much greater detail. Its total length was 50 cubits. -- For the variant πηχων see comment at 25:16. -- These 50 cubits were divided into a 20 cubits wide gate plus two flanking sides of 15 cubits each. The gate itself is not dealt with until v.16, whereas the two sides of the gate, described as ἔνθεν καὶ ἔνθεν

the context for Sym is not extant the syntax cannot be analyzed.
6 Cf SS 128.
7. From Theod; according to Syh Aq had instead καὶ αἱ κεφαλίδες τῶν

κατὰ τὴν πύλην τῆς αὐλῆς, are detailed in vv.12 and 13. These sides, called τὸ κατὰ νώτου and ἐπὶ τοῦ νώτου τοῦ δευτέρου resp. for the Hebrew כתף "shoulder," are each assigned fifteen cubits (a B + variant bizarrely has 150 cubits for the second side!) as well as three pillars and bases," but the curtains are called ἱστία for the first side and αὐλαῖαι for the second; since they are obviously paired it is clear that Exod B uses the two terms as exact synonyms.

The ἔνθεν collocation translated above is unfortunately placed after "on the second side" in imitation of MT. Syntactically it must then be taken as an anacolouthon, a general comment or aside.

As might be expected νώτου is misspelled by many mss as νοτου, a homonym meaning "south" (cf comment on v.7), and must not be taken seriously; it is simply the word for "side" misspelled.

37:14(38:16) This verse is a summary statement reflecting the beginning of this section (v.7). A popular B variant has the summary statement apply to the σκηνης rather than to the αὐλῆς; this was probably based on v.1 where the αὐλαῖαι were made τῇ σκηνῇ, but here that is inappropriate. -- Note that Exod also disregards סביב as being unnecessary.

37:15(38:17) Exod is at best only a paraphrase of MT. It is a statement on the metals used in connection with the pillars and their parts. With MT Exod states that the bases of the pillars were bronze. MT continues with "the ווי of the pillars and חשוקיהם were silver." Exod only has "and their αἱ ἀγκύλαι were silver." ἀγκύλαι is a translation in the B account for ווים; cf v.17 39:6 and also compare 38:18,20, but in Exod A it occurs only for the ללאת of the tabernacle curtains in 26:4--11. In A the word refers to the loops made of dyed cloth material on the edge of the tabernacle curtains; in B they refer to metal hooks on the pillars.[9] -- Both Exod and MT refer to the plating of their capitals with silver, and both texts end with the phrase "all the pillars of the court." But MT has the clause והם מחשקים כסף "and they were banded (or filleted) with silver," which has no counterpart in

---

στύλων καὶ τὰ συγκολλήματα αὐτῶν. Retroversion is according to Field.
8 The Three have, as might be expected, called the curtains ἱστία.
9 According to Syh The Three had τὰ συγκολλήματα "connecting bands or

Exod; except for v.6 Exod never renders the root חשׁק, it being omitted twice in this verse alone. He was, however, faced with a problem. This verse is a summary of metals used in connection with pillars and their parts, but MT says nothing about the pillars themselves, so taking his cue from the clause about their capitals, a clause about οἱ στῦλοι is inserted and are also "plated with silver." That this was important is also clear from v.18a which see.

37:16--18(38:18--20; par 27:16,19) Again Exod uses καταπέτασμα to render מסך rather than the κάλυμμα of par. The reading of Exod A did influence the tradition, however, since the majority A F reading has καλυμμα. The veil of the gate (cf comment on vv.11--13 above) is described quite separately from its flanks (the fifteen cubit sides), since the curtains of the two flanks along with the other three sides of the court were made of twisted linen, but the curtains of the gate were made of colored materials. And these curtains for the gate were the work of ποικιλτοῦ, not as in the case of the other καταπετάσματα an ἔργον ὑφαντόν (vv.3,5).

V.16b gives the size of the veil, but an ambiguity obtains because two measurements are given: twenty cubits and five cubits, but three dimensions: length and height and breadth, to which is appended "corresponding to the curtains of the courtyard." That the dimensions of the curtains were 20 X 5 is clear, but what does "and height" refer to? At 27:15 it was argued that τὸ ὕψος referred to the upright position in the loom, and must then refer to the length. If that is what Exod meant one would render "the length, even the height, and the breadth." This is not what MT has, however, since its text has ארך ורקומה ברחב, i.e. קומה is modified by the prepositional phrase ברחב "height in the matter of breadth." Since the matter is obscure no comma is used in the critical text. But it should be noted that at 27:14--16 τὸ ὕψος had no counterpart in MT. -- For the spelling πηχων see note at 25:16.

V.17a is literally rendered by Exod, but the remainder of the verse is largely borrowed from v.15; in fact all of the verse beginning with καὶ αἱ ἀγκύλαι through the first part of v.18 (through ἀργυρίῳ) is to be found word for word in v.15 except that αὐτοί is substituted for οἱ στῦλοι. When one compares the Hebrew the pattern is all the more striking since the same Hebrew patterns occurred and are here dealt with in the same way, viz. the use of ἀγκύλαι for וו, the rendering of צפוי by περιηργυρωμέναι ἀργυρίῳ, the omission of the last clause, and the addition of "and οἱ στῦλοι (but αὐτοί in v.18) plated with silver." The widespread omission of this addition here in the tradition is probably a recensional.

The last nominal clause in the series beginning at v.7 concerns the tentpins of the court. In MT the tentpins are characterized as "for the tabernacle and for the court," but as in the A account the reference to the משכן is omitted in Exod.

37:19(38:21) In MT this verse along with vv.20--21 introduces the summary statement on the amount of metals used for various parts of the structure (vv.24--31), in turn leading to the textiles (39:1) with which the priestly garments were made. But Exod B has rearranged the materials so that the work with textiles was first described, and only thereafter (ch.38) all the work with metals. Accordingly the statement on the amount of metals used was transferred to the end of the description of the metal work (39:1--12). This then meant that 37:19--21 in Exod serves a different purpose in the account. MT could begin with אלה פקודי and then have אשר פקד על פי משה "these are the reckonings (i.e. the counted amounts) ... which were counted at the behest of Moses," but this would make little sense in Exod. Furthermore this was defined in MT as "the עברת of the Levites by Ithamar," which did not fit well either. Accordingly Exod revised the אשר clause in accordance with one of his favored clauses in connection with divine orders to Moses, as καθὰ συνετάγη Μωυσῆ; he retained the passive tradition of MT's פקד but to mean "as it was ordered to Moses."[10] This in turn gave the clue for the reinterpretation of the initial אלה פקד as (καὶ) αὕτη σύνταξις. Note that Exod introduced a καί at the beginning thereby tying the verse to the preceding, whereas MT uses this clause to introduce new material. The use of σύνταξις ... συνετάγη insured a proper view of things. The verb συντάσσω is used in Exod only with God, and so it is clear

---

rods" instead of αἱ ἀγκύλαι; the index in Syh is on ἀγκύλαι and is probably meant to represent the untranslated חשוקיהם.

that the source is divine. This σύνταξις is then defined as the cultic service under the direction of (διά) Ithamar.

This verse is a pivotal one in Exod B since it defines midway in the construction account what the building of the tabernacle and its furnishings was all about; it was intended for the λειτουργίαν of the Levites under the high priest's direction.

The tradition has on the whole not improved the text. A popular M text supports the articulation of Μωυσῆ; that Moses is in the dative thus becomes doubly clear; it was probably due to v.20. Removal of the introductory καί by *n* + does conform to MT but is not appropriate to Exod's interpretation. And the hex rewriting of "ordered to Moses" as συνεταξε μωυσης is a pseudo-correction but is quite wrong. The active verb always has κύριος/θεός as subject in Exod, as e.g. v.20.

37:20(38:22) This verse and the next in Exod constitute the bridge between Part 2 which it ends and Part 3 which follows. On the one hand, v.20 has Beseleel in charge of the work as a whole which points ahead to ch.38 where his particular specialty, work in metals, is detailed. On the other hand, v.21 looks back to Part 2 as the work of his fellow architect, Eliab, the specialist in ὑφαντά, ῥαφιδευτά and ποικιλτά.

In v.20 Beseleel is characterized as "son of Ouri of the tribe of Judah," i.e. without בֶן חוּר, which hex supplies as υιου ωρ. For variant spellings of Beseleel and Ouri see notes at 35:30. -- A majority F M text has articulated φυλῆς which is fully possible, but the unarticulated φυλῆς is likely original here and in v.21 as well as in the earlier mention of these two in 35:30,34.[11]

A *C s* variant has changed the original ἐποίησεν to the plural, a pedantic "correction" based on the fact that the subject is compound; cf καὶ ' Ελιάβ of v.21. -- What was done was ʰκαθά the Lord had commanded Moses." Exod's clause is his usual one in spite of MT's אֵת כֹּל אֲשֶׁר which would favor a παντα οσα (or α) construction.

37:21(38:23) MT begins with אִתּוֹ, i.e. "and with him (was Eliab)"; by omitting this Exod makes Eliab coordinate with Beseleel; thus the καθά clause of v.20 is also applicable to Eliab. This equal status for Eliab is further emphasized by Exod's rendering of חרש וחשב "craftsman and designer" by a relative clause ὃς ἠρχιτεκτόνησεν τὰ ὑφαντά (and with the remainder of the verse coordinated with τὰ ὑφαντά as well), which serves as a fitting subscription to Part 2.[12] For the meaning of the verb see comment at 31:4. Only here is the verb used primarily with Eliab. -- For the variant spellings of ' Ελιάβ see comment at 31:6; for other spellings of ' Αχισαμάχ see comments at 31:6 and 35:34.

The particular work of Eliab is differently defined in Exod. MT has three nouns describing his vocation as חרש וחשב ורקם; for the first two see comment above. Exod has καὶ τὰ ῥαφιδευτὰ καὶ τὰ ποικιλτά, as a doublet to define what רקם is all about; for the Hebrew term see comment at 26:36. The word is usually rendered by the root ποικιλ-, but ῥαφιδευτά more exactly defines the work as embroidery; see comment on ῥαφιδευτοῦ at 27:16.

MT then continues with the usual list of textiles, for which see notes at 25:4, but Exod rewrites this by a complementary infinitive ὑφᾶναι which has no counterpart in MT; this in turn is simply modified by two datives τῷ κοκκίνῳ καὶ τῇ βύσσῳ.[13] Why Exod should shorten the usual list in this fashion is not clear.

A B M d n t text read ποικιλτικα.[14] -- A majority A F M tradition omitted the article before ῥαφιδευτά, but this can hardly be the translator's intent in view of the two coordinated nominals both of which are articulated in the context.[15]

---

10 Cf Helbing 208.
11 Cf THGE VII.D.4. sub 37:21.
12 This reinterpretation could hardly satisfy The Three, and Aq and Sym added μετ' αὐτοῦ after the opening καί to represent MT's ואתו. Theod, however, made it μετὰ ταῦτα which hex adopted, but this hardly equals MT nor is it sensible in the context.
13 Cf SS 123.
14 For the originality of ποικιλτά see the discussion in THGE VIII.Q.
15 Cf also the discussion in THGE VII.D.6. sub 35:35.

Chapter 38

Since Part 2 had dealt with textiles, the translator now concentrates on what remains with particular emphasis on the metal work as the work of Beseleel alone. Over against Part 2 where Eliab and everyone wise among the workers ἐποίησαν the things made of textiles, here the stress is placed on Beseleel as the one who made, cast, placed, etc.; in fact, ten times in vv.18--26 it is said that οὗτος made, cast, silvered, etc. The translator thus contrasts Beseleel's efforts as climactic over against his (lesser) fellow architect's work.

Since Exod B has radically rearranged the materials so as to contrast textile and metal work he must now gather the materials not dealt with in Part 2 for Part 3. Successively he describes briefly the construction of the ark, propitiatory, the table, the staves for ark and table, the table's vessels, the lampstand, the pillars, golden rings and hooks, the tentpins, the bronze altar and its vessels and staves, the anointing oil, the incense compound, the laver and its base. Except for the oil and the compound, all the work involves either plating or casting of metals. The order, except for vv.18--21 which have no counterpart in MT, is that of MT's 37:1--38:8 with the notable exception of 37:25--28 (but cf also v.29); this deals with the incense altar which Exod B consistently omits; cf comment at 35:17. Since Exod is basically only interested in metal work the construction account is much briefer than in MT; the verbs used to ndicate Beseleel's activity give the picture: made (17 times), gilded (four), cast (four), silvered (two), and placed (one). That the translator was mainly interested in work with metals is clear from the chapter; the three metals, gold, silver and bronze, occur a total of 30 times: gold (19), silver (2), and bronze (9 times). Details extraneous to this central interest in metalwork such as dimensions, or wooden cores, are simply deleted. This occasionally puts the translator into difficulty as the notes below will show.

38:1--4(37:1--5; par 25:9--13) The construction of the ark.[1] The subject of
the entire chapter is immediately given in v.1 as Beseleel. Exod details only
the essentials: he gilded it with pure gold within and without, made a golden
molding for it,[2] and cast for it four golden rings, two each for opposite sides
wide enough for the staves with which it could be carried. Omitted are
references to the acacia wood frame and the ark's dimensions; even the
making of the staves and their gold plating is omitted. Nothing in Exod
contradicts either MT or the A account; it is simply stripped of all non-
essentials. Exod uses διωστῆρες rather than the ἀναφορεῖς of A to designate the staves. Actually except for 35:11 where the ark's staves are called
ἀναφορεῖς Exod B uses only διωστῆρες, whereas Exod A uses (ἀνα)φορεῖς
throughout, except for σκυτάλαις at 30:4.

Striking is the use of εὐρεῖς in the phrase "wide enough for the
staves"; this is a free substitute for MT's "and he brought the staves into the
rings on the side of the ark," but not inappropriate in the context. The word
εὐρεῖς occurs only in this chapter and always in connection with the rings
for staves with which to carry a cultic object, the table in v.10 and the altar
in v.24.

38:5--8(37:6--9; par 25:16--19) The propitiatory is described in much abbreviated form. Both the propitiatory and its two cherubs were made of
(pure) gold, one cherub on its edge and one on its second edge, both
overshadowing the propitiatory with their wings. All the rest of MT or of
the A account is disregarded as not germane to the main theme, that of
Beseleel's work with metals. Exod's freedom over against MT is also
illustrated by the unexpected plus, that of ἄνωθεν τῆς κιβωτοῦ defining the
propitiatory; that it was above the ark was clear from 25:20--21. That this
position was important is clear from what follows, the two cherubs with
wings outspread over the propitiatory as the place where God spoke from;
see 25:21.

Exod's statement, brief though it is, is fully clear, but its text did suffer
considerably in transmission. In v.5 a *C s* reading defined the propitiatory as
being τῆς κιβωτου; since "above the ark" follows immediately this must be a

1 Aq used (τὸ) γλωσσόκομον for "the ark" as at 25:9 which see.
2. For the omission of the reference to the construction of the golden

thoughtless error. Quite uncertain is ἄνωθεν over against a popular B reading of ἐπανωθεν.[3] Another B x variant has omitted καθαροῦ, but χρυσίου without καθαροῦ for זהב טהור is not Exod usage.[4] -- In v.6 the phrase δύο χερουβίμ is unarticulated, but a B n y z variant articulates it. Again the Exod usage is clear. In this chapter nouns are only articulated when not modified by a number.[5] -- And in v.7 comes convincing proof that copyists knew no Hebrew since the words "cherub" 1° 2° specifically designated as ἕνα appear as χερουβειμ or -βειν. -- And finally in v.8 a popular A B variant has σκιαζοντα. But the singular can only be a thoughtless mistake; the word must refer to χερουβίμ since reference is made to ταῖς πτέρυξιν αὐτῶν.[6]

38:9--12(37:10--16; par 25:22--28) The table is called τὴν προκειμένην which has no correspondence in MT but Exod may have been influenced by the שלחן הפנים of Num 4:7 where the phrase is translated as here; literally the phrase means "the table which is set before," by which is meant the table on which there is placed what is set before the presence (of God). Exod's amplification is clarified by 25:29 for which see notes.

The account of the table is as in the case of the propitiatory severely shortened, and is restricted to those elements which involved gold, i.e. the table itself, its four rings, the staves both of ark and table, and its vessels. The account so curtailed that of MT that Origen in despair placed everything from τὴν προκειμένην in v.9 through to the end of v.11 under the obelus and put another translation of that section, [11--15], under the asterisk at the end of v.11. If, however, it is remembered that Exod was basically interested in Beseleel's work in metals the account does make good sense. But even using this interest in gold as a criterion the account is overly brief since the references to moldings of gold in MT are also omitted, probably because Exod considered them subsumed under the table itself.

---

molding in B n + see discussion in THGE VII.P.
3 In THGE VII.N. it is argued that ἄνωθεν as the lectio difficilior is to be preferred over against the compound which is much more common throughout the LXX and is therefore a simplifying variant.
4 See the discussion in THGE VII.P.
5 Cf the statement in THGE VII.D.4.
6 Cf also THGE VII.H.2.

In v.10 a popular A F tradition changed the description of the four golden rings to δυο δακτυλιους επι το κλιτος το εν και δυο δακτυλιους επι το κλιτος το δευτερον obviously under the influence of v.3.

V.12 is clearly a translation of MT in characteristic Exod B style in which the vessels אשר על השלחן become a simple genitive τῆς τραπέζης and the vessels are all rendered without an accompanying αυτης even though three of the four have pronominal suffixes in MT. The last two vessels are transposed in the A account (both in Exod and MT), but Exod follows its parent text in B. For the vessels see comments at 25:28. An A b y reading has σπεισεις instead of σπείσει, based on the par verse 25:28.

38:13--17(37:17--24; par 25:30--39) Exod is hardly a translation of MT, nor does it follow the A account; in fact the two Hebrew accounts are almost word for word the same with only minor differences made necessary by the context, except for 25:37b which is omitted in B. On the other hand, Exod does not contradict the other accounts. It should also be noted that there seems to be an avoidance of many terms found in Exod A. Thus (ἐκ) πλαγίων in A becomes (ἐξ) ἀμφοτέρων τῶν μερῶν αὐτῆς in B; instead of σφαιρωτὴρ καὶ κρίνον B has οἱ βλαστοί; for κρατῆρες it has τὰ λαμπάδια αὐτῶν, and the terms מלקחיה ומחתתיה become τὰς λαβίδας ... τὰς ἐπαρυστρίδας, not τὸν ἐπαρυστῆρα ... τὰ ὑποθέματα as in A (for which see note at 25:38).

The language in later references in Num 4:9 8:4 and Zach 4:2 seems to have been influenced by Exod B rather than by A. Whether these shorter Hebrew accounts, which were certainly known to the translator, influenced Exod's account cannot be determined.

38:13 The lampstand is here characterized by a relative clause ἣ φωτίζει which has no counterpart in MT, but cf 25:37b. Exod in spite of his general compression of the second tabernacle account often tends to pick out some detail of cultic importance which could easily be overlooked in a simple account of metal work; thus in v.5 the place of the propitiatory as ἄνωθεν τῆς κιβωτοῦ is added, and in v.9 the table is called τὴν προκειμένην so as to describe the significance of the table; here too the light-giving function is highlighted in the opening statement; cf also 27:20--21 and מנרת המאור in

Num 4:9. A popular Byzantine variant substitutes την φωτιζουσαν, an intrusion from Num 4:9.

38:14 This verse continues with accusatives governed by ἐποίησεν of v.13, viz. the καυλόν and the καλαμίσκους, for which see comments at 25:30. The word στερεάν is feminine and must modify λυχνίαν of v.13, and not καυλόν as the versification would imply, i.e. "he made the lampstand ... golden, solid, the shaft and the branches." Exod translated מקשה not as a technical term for which see note at 25:17, but etymologically as "hard, solid," an interpretation taken over by Num 8:4 as well, and not by τορευτήν as in 25:30; cf 25:17.

38:15 Syntactically this verse is parenthetical, interrupting the list of components which were begun in v.14 with "the shaft and the branches" and then continuing in vv.16 and 17. It constitutes a description of the branches as "from its (the lampstand's) branches buds were projecting, three on this side and three on the other side, corresponding to each other." The verse is so compressed that only with the help of the A account is it clear what Exod must mean. In 25:30 the branches each had κρατῆρες, σφαιρωτῆρες and κρίνα, for which see comments. In B the last two are compressed into οἱ βλαστοί, whereas the first becomes τὰ λαμπάδια; cf v.16. οἱ βλαστοί does seem to represent פרחיה of the Hebrew 37:17, but here it is used as a cover term for the ornamentation of the lampstand as a whole. But then the τρεῖς can hardly refer to the βλαστοί, but explicates the καλαμίσκους of v.14; this is fully clear from 25:31. With the final modifier, ἐξισούμενοι ἀλλήλοις,[7] this does become clear; the two sets of three branches on either side of the shaft are mirror images of each other.

38:16 This verse gives certain details of the construction of the branches and the shaft. Each branch as well as the central shaft itself had a λαμπά-διον as well as an ἐνθέμιον, i.e. a small cuplike affair (for the oil) and a holder for the actual light, both of which are described as being ἐξ αὐτῶν, which refers to their construction as being of the same piece, molded as part of the branches themselves. The λαμπάδια (αὐτῶν refers to the

7 For its equivalent in למעתה see Helbing 129.

καλαμίσκων) are described as to position and formation. Their position is described by a relative clause, ἅ ἐστιν ἐπὶ τῶν ἄκρων; these were on the ends of the branches, or of the upright shaft ἐπὶ τῆς κορυφῆς ἄνωθεν. As to their formation they are described as καρυωτά, almond-like; this word occurs only here but see comment on καρυΐσκους at 25:32.

The ἐνθέμια were as the word implies the actual holders in which the lamps were placed as the ἵνα clause "that the lamps might be on them" shows. A widespread tradition has ανθεμια, ανθεμιον, probably due to the proximity both of βλαστοί and καρυωτά, both botanical terms, but what is meant here is simply "a holder."

For ἐξ αὐτῶν 2° which describes the holders as being part of the small cups, an O n tradition has εν αυτοις; the statement is correct but trite. -- A majority A F M reading reorders ἐπ' αὐτῶν to the end of the ἵνα clause; this places the subject rather than the modifier immediately after the verb. -- Another very popular A F M variant adds a το after τὸ ἕβδομον; this makes explicit what is already implicit in Exod, viz. that ἀπ' ἄκρου κ.τ.λ. modifies the nominal "the seventh holder."

The verse concludes with στερεὸν ὅλον χρυσοῦν which reflects 37:22b of MT, but in Exod applies only to the seventh holder; in MT כלה "all of it" refers to המנרה "the lampstand."

38:17 The three nouns are all in the accusative and end the row of objects of ἐποίησεν in v.13. Instead of נרתיה Exod has λύχνους ἐπ' αὐτῆς with the pronoun presumably referring to λυχνίαν of v.13. The prepositional phrase is reminiscent of Zach 4:2: נרתיה עליה which may have been in Exod B's mind. The pronoun becomes plural in the C tradition as αυτοις (which is homonymous to αὐτῆς) and αυτους in z; these would then refer to the καλαμίσκους which would be technically correct for six of the seven. Also listed are the snuffers and the oil cans; fittingly in view of Exod's preoccupation in this chapter, all three are individually described as "golden." -- The genitive modifiers to "snuffers" and "oil cans" are changed to the plural; this would make these objects belong to the branches, which can hardly have been intended.[8]

8 Cf also the note in THGE VII.G.7.

38:18--27 This section with its unique and repeated οὗτος referring to Beseleel is a summary list of other objects that involve metal work; in fact these ten verses have six cases of verbs referring to casting or metal plating, five to gold, two to silver, and nine to bronze, a total of 22 references. Particularly vv.18--21 are very compressed and have no counterpart in MT.

38:18 That there is something wrong about vv.18--21 seems obvious. It will be recalled that the construction of the tabernacle had except for the statement of 37:1--2 been omitted and apparently Exod is here trying to make up in part for the deficiency by detailing some of the metal work that was involved, but if that was its purpose it has been badly done since metalwork was also involved in the construction of the courtyard, and the two are not kept apart. Furthermore the translator uses a separate vocabulary of translation throughout the chapter, and one is not always certain as to which detail in the Hebrew account (of either A or B) is actually intended.

The difficulties begin immediately with the opening clause. The verse must be referring to the tent, not to the courtyard, but the pillars of the tent according to MT (26:29 36:34) were plated with gold, yet Exod here has them silverplated; this is actually the case only for the courtyard for which see comment on 27:17 and 37:15.

The next two units can be substantiated from the A account at 26:29, as well as from the Hebrew of 36:34; from these records it is clear that the τοῖς στύλοις of the opening clause must refer to the pillars of the tent. Admittedly a B + variant has this in the singular, but that must be rooted in a careless mistake.[9] Here in contrast to 26:29 ἐχώνευσεν plus the dative is used rather than the verb ποιέω.

The last two units reflect MT of 36:36. For ἀγκύλη as translation in B for ויו see comment at 26:32. Since at 37:4 Exod uses κεφαλίδες to render ויו it appears that his source here is MT, not Exod.

38:19 The first line reflects MT of 36:13, for which cf the par at 26:6. The only oddity of the clause is the καί after ἐποίησεν which must here be intended in the sense of "also" following on the golden ἀγκύλας of v.18. The

9 Cf note in THGE VII.H.2.

majority A F M text actually omits it, but the lectio difficilior must be original.

The second object is peculiar in that no metal is given; it simply reads τοὺς κρίκους τῆς αὐλῆς. According to MT of 38:10 (par 27:10) the ווי of the pillars were silver, whereas the κρίκους of the tent in line one renders קרסים. Why Exod failed to render כסף is obscure, or was the καί after ἐποίησεν intended as part of a καί ... καί construction with χρυσοῦς modifying both cases of κρίκους? But that would be incorrect since the clasps of the courtyard were not golden but silver.

The final κρίκους reflects MT of 36:18 (par 26:11) where the bronze clasps are intended to bind the tent curtains together so that it might be one. The colorful description of the use to which the bronze clasps were to be put, εἰς τὸ ἐκτείνειν τὸ κατακάλυμμα ἄνωθεν, is similar to that of 40:17 which see.

38:20 This verse begins with the statement: "he cast the silver capitals of the tent, and the bronze capitals of the door of the tent, and for the gate of the courtyard"; for the last one "bronze capitals" is not repeated but is certainly intended. But the קרשים of the tent had two bases and no capitals, whereas the capitals of the tent door were gold (37:6), and those of the courtyard gate were silver (37:17).

But κεφαλίδες need not mean "capitals" as its use in 39:4--5 proves. There the term renders אדנים "bases" which is indeed rare. The term can, however, simply mean "extremities," and when it is recalled that Exod interpreted the "two bases under one קרש-pillar" as a pillar with a base on either end, it is clear that one can call such ends either "bases" or "capitals." In any event that is what Exod does here; cf the discussion at 26:19. With this equation in mind the intent of the translator becomes clear. In fact the term βάσεις for pillars does not occur in Part 3 at all, except in 39:8--9. The βάσεις of the tent were indeed silver (26:21); those of the tent door were bronze (26:37) as were those of the courtyard gate (27:17). One could wish that Exod had been less clever in this matter and simply used βάσεις throughout.

The next clause presents no problems; that the hooks for the pillars of the courtyard were silver was stated at 37:15,17, though one should add that the identification of τῶν στύλων as referring to the pillars of the courtyard is not stated; since the phrase immediately before the clause refers to the gate τῆς αὐλῆς one can best take it in this way. This is further made likely by the fact that in 37:15 a coordinate phrase to "their hooks were silver" is "and the pillars were plated with silver," which may well have promoted the final clause of this verse: "he silverplated them (the pillars)."

The tradition had trouble with this verse. A popular A* F text omitted τῆς σκηνῆς after ἀργυρᾶς. Presumably the identification of the silver κεφαλίδας as being of the tent ought not to be necessary, but in view of the special vocabulary is certainly useful. -- Another popular F M variant has τῆς θύρας in the dative; this was probably the result of assimilation to τῇ πύλῃ in the next nominal unit. Instead of τῇ πύλῃ a B z reading has an accusative which is not sensible, while the Byzantine text has the genitive which is possible but secondary.[10]-- A B + variant adds τοις στυλοις after ἐποίησεν; this creates a doublet since "upon the pillars" already occurs in the clause.[11] -- In the final clause the object of "silverplated" is αὐτούς, i.e. referring to pillars. A d t reading has the neuter which must be wrong since there is no neuter antecedent in the context. A B n variant has αυτας probably created by attraction to ἀγκύλας, but this would create an unnecessary doublet with the preceding clause.[12]

38:21 Over against 37:18 and its par 27:19 which refer only to the tentpins of the courtyard, this verse has them for both tent and courtyard, following the Hebrew acounts (27:19 38:20). Later on (39:9) this same information is repeated. It seems likely that it is the Hebrew text, not the Greek, which lies behind this verse. As in v.19 a καί follows ἐποίησεν which a majority A F tradition omits. Here the καί is obviously part of a καί ... καί pattern as is clear from the placement of χαλκοῦς at the end of the verse; the variant is an inferior reading.

38:22(1--2; par 27:1--2) The bronze altar. Over against MT (and par) Exod omits everything but the fact that "he made the bronze altar," i.e. only the opening three words of v.1 and the last word of v.2 are rendered. Instead of

10 See comments in THGE VII.H.3.
11 Cf note in THGE VII.O.

the omitted materials Exod adds a midrash identifying the source as being "from the bronze censers which belonged to the men who rebelled with the assembly of Kore," a reference to Num 16:37--39(MT: 17:2--4). There Eliezar the priest is told to take up τὰ πυρεῖα τὰ χαλκᾶ from among those who were burned ... make them into λεπίδας ἐλατάς περίθεμα τῷ θυσιαστηρίῳ. Obviously Exod was acquainted with this tradition, or rather with the Hebrew where reference to את מחתות הנחשת and to רקעי פחים צפורי תמזבח is made. Since v.24 has τῷ θυσιαστηρίῳ παράθεμα which is hardly a literal translation of צפורי המזבח it seems probable that the Num translator borrowed the phrase from Exod. -- A popular B variant has the plural instead of ἦν. The singular is the classical usage with the neuter plural ἄ and is the earlier form.

38:23(3; par 27:3) The brass vessels of the altar. The list of Exod only partly corresponds to MT. The first two את הסירת ואת היעים are not rendered by Exod. Exod begins his list with τὴν βάσιν which has no counterpart in MT,[13] though "the basin of the altar" is a well known concept; cf e.g. 29:12. This is of course not a vessel. The first vessel listed is τὸ πυρεῖον, the usual equivalent for המחתה, the second is τὰς φιάλας, for המזרקת, and the last one, τὰς κρεάγρας, is the regular rendering of המזלגת. These are also found in par though not in the same order; for these terms see notes at 27:3.

38:24(4--5,7; par 27:4--5,7) Exod B differs considerably from A. Exod here distinguishes the כרכב from the מכבר, but in A both appear as ἔσχαραν; in B the former is rendered by πυρείου and the latter by παράθεμα. Because he took כרכב to be a "fire hearth, fire pan" he would hardly then use ἔσχαραν for מכבר, so he chose the more neutral παράθεμα "something put alongside it, an appendage," which is then defined by ἔργον δικτυωτόν, "a lattice work," for which see notes at 27:4--5. A majority A F reading has περιθεμα under the influence of Num 16:38--39, which would also be sensible, but the less concrete term seems original; see also 39:10. This παράθεμα was placed below τοῦ πυρείου, i.e. the fire hearth - it was thus

---

12 Cf THGE VII.G.7.
13 For the position of τὴν βάσιν in first place, and not in second as in B *f n*

part of the πυρείου constituting the grate - with its placement being further defined as being ὑπὸ αὐτὸ ἕως τοῦ ἡμίσους αὐτοῦ; the antecedent of αὐτοῦ then must be "altar"; cf 27:5 where ἡμίσους is defined as being "of the altar."

MT states: "he cast (four rings at the four sides)," for which Exod has substituted ἐπέθηκεν plus dative which is contextually smoother than ויצק plus ב.[14] Since the placement of the network grate had already been defined, that of the rings is also clear; nor does this conflict with par which defines it as "under the altar's hearth below." Note also that χαλκοῦς occurs at the end of this collocation, and being accusative plural must modify δακτυλίους. Hex changed this to a genitive noun του χαλκου but failed to correct the verb.

The rings are intended as "wide enough for μοχλοῖς so as to carry the altar with them." Why Exod should now use μοχλοῖς rather than διωστῆρσιν, for which see comment at 1--4, is not clear. μοχλός is otherwise reserved for rendering בריח, not only in A and B, but throughout the LXX. Admittedly "bars" are also long (and thin) but only בדים were used to carry the various tabernacle objects. The par account uses φορεῖς, a variant of the more usual ἀναφορεῖς of Exod A. -- For εὑρεῖς see comment at vv.1--4. A weakly supported B variant places the word after μοχλοῖς, which is also possible.[15]

38:25(37:29; par 30:25) Somewhat surprising is the inclusion of this verse in a list otherwise devoted solely to metal work. Since both the holy anointing oil and the incense compound were too important for the cult in which Exod B was obviously interested not to be included some place, a position immediately after the account of the construction of the altar was as good a place as any. Once again it might be parenthetically remarked that the omission of the altar of incense is in this context especially puzzling.

The oil is defined as τῆς χρίσεως, whereas A has χρίσμα. The A account probably led to the majority A F M reading του χρισματος; the terms are synonyms. The second element "the incense compound" is not present in par, though see the inverted phrase τὸ θυμίαμα τῆς συνθέσεως

z, see note in THGE VII.F.4.
14 Cf Helbing 285.

at 31:11 which is there also coordinated with the anointing oil. For the phrase as given here see 35:28.

The Masoretes by their accent intend the masculine טהור to modify קטרת; this gender anomaly probably led to Exod's καθαρόν, a neuter modifying ἔργον; it cannot modify σύνθεσιν which is feminine. The term μυρεψοῦ also occurs in A at 30:25,35.

38:26(8; par 30:18a) The final object in the list of objects made by Beseleel is the laver and its base, both of bronze. This statement renders the Hebrew of v.8a exactly. But the second part of the verse has problems. The laver and its base were made from the mirrors הצבאת אשר צבאו. The במראת is correctly understood as "from the mirrors," the preposition indicating the material out of which something consists of is made,[16] but the participle and cognate verb are difficult. The root in the context of the tent refers (Num 4:23 8:24) to performing service, and is in fact defined as לעבד עבדת or בעבדת for the tent in the Num passages. But here the reference is to women who did not perform cultic service. The Tar (and Pesh) interpreted the phrase as "the women who were coming to prayer" (Tar[P]: "were praying"); Vulg refers to the women *quae excubabant* "who were keeping watch." Exod rather ingeniously has τῶν νηστευσασῶν αἱ ἐνήστευσαν "the women who fasted," fasting being one kind of cultic practice which anyone could perform; the women were thus performing their service by fasting, hardly a translation, but it is an interpretation. That Exod was aware of what he was doing is made doubly clear by his addition at the end of the verse against the other old witnesses ἐν ᾗ ἡμέρᾳ ἔπηξεν αὐτήν. By this gloss Exod makes fully clear that the women were not engaged in cultic duties in the tabernacle; they were near the doors of the tent of testimony at the time of its erection.[17]

38:27(40:30--32; par 30:18a,20--21) The details of the verse are all taken from Part 4, or rather, are transferred to this juncture, since they are

---

15 But see THGE VII.F.4.

16 Cf SS 123.

17 Aq, of course, did not follow such an interpretation, but translates צבאו by its more warlike equivalent στρατευομένων. Aq translates the more common cognate noun צבא usually either by στρατεία or δύναμις; cf

omitted entirely from Part 4. To effect this transference it was imperative to omit the first clause "and he set the laver between the tent of meeting and the altar" entirely and substitute "and he made the laver," repeated from v.26. In fact, the rest of v.30 "and he put water into it for washing" is also disregarded as otiose, and then he rendered v.31 as a ἵνα clause. This transference to Part 3 was generated by the A account where the making of the laver and its base is also connected with its use in similar fashion.

That the Hebrew of 40:30--32 was the parent text for Exod rather than the A account is clear. Exod translates vv.31-32 word for word except for two plusses; neither λειτουργεῖν nor ἐξ αὐτοῦ 2° have a counterpart in MT, but they do not contradict the intent of the Hebrew. The infinitive "to do cultic service" is a purposive infinitive stating the reason why the priests would approach the altar. The prepositional phrase modifying ἐνίπτοντο simply parallels νίπτωνται ἐξ αὐτοῦ earlier in the verse and is stylistically satisfying.

The tradition shows some uncertainty as to αὐτῶν modifying χεῖρες. MT has both "their hands and their feet" consonant with good Hebrew style. Good Greek style might well omit any reference to "their" as being obvious. The Byzantine group has added an αυτων to πόδας as well, and a popular A F M reading has transposed αὐτῶν after πόδας. Since the oldest witness, cod B, has the pronoun only after χεῖρες that is taken as original text.

---

also τοῦ στρατεύεσθαι στρατείαν for Aq at Num 8:24 .

Chapter 39

39:1--13(38:24--31 39:32,1) It is not surprising that Exod in view of his principles of rearrangement should append to ch.38 with its summary of Beseleel's metal work the account of the amount of metals used in the construction from the end of MT's ch.38.

39:1(38:24) The amount of gold used. The gold is defined by a relative clause: "which was worked up for the ἔργα according to all the ἐργασίαν of the holy things."[1] The two cognates are difficult to distinguish semantically: the first being plural must refer to all the works made in gold, whereas the second being singular must be the more abstract "work." Exod uses these two words to render the two cognates מלאכה and מלאכת resp., thereby retaining the flavor of the Hebrew. But MT presents this as a nominal clause with 1b paratactically joined as a verbal clause with ויהי. Exod made this the predicate of 1a with its relative clause, as ἐγένετο plus a genitive of material plus the amount in the nominative, i.e. "all the gold ... was ... of the gold of the offering 29 talents ...." In MT the זהב התנופה is the subject but Exod subordinates it as a modifier of τάλαντα ... σίκλοι.

Unique in LXX is the translation of תנופה by ἀπαρχῆς. It more commonly renders תרומה as at 25:2 and in B at 35:5 and 36:6. But it does agree with 35:5 where bringing τὰς ἀπαρχάς to the Lord is defined in terms of the metals and textiles which were brought by the people. What seems unusual is not Exod's use but rather MT's use of תנופה, for which see comment at 29:24. For the term ἀπαρχῆς see comment at 25:2--3.

The amount given is 29 talents and 730 shekels. A B z reading has εικοσι instead of τριάκοντα, an error due to the influence of εἴκοσι in the preceding phrase; a B + text also omitted the καί before it, but καί joining compounds is characteristic of Exod in this chapter.[2] -- The Greek σίκλος is a word borrowed from the Hebrew שקל.[3] For בשקל הקדש see note at

---

1 See SS 65.
2 For a general discussion involving both variants see THGE VII.I.
3 Instead of σίκλοι ... σίκλου Aq used στατῆρες ... στατῆρα, a standard

30:13.

39:2--3(38:25--26; par 30:13--14) The silver used. Instead of ἀπαρχῆς Exod uses ἀφαίρεμα, a synonym, to define the silver. MT simply has כסף. The source of the offering is the numbered men of the congregation, an offering ordered in 30:13--14. The numbered ones are specifically called ἀνδρῶν over against MT; after all, women were substantial contributors as well according to 35:22, but this silver had a specific source, viz., the poll tax assigned to the adult males of the congregation.

The amount is specified as one hundred talents and 1775 shekels.[4] For "according to the holy shekel," see comment at 30:13. Since the census report summary (Num 1:32) showed 603,550 adult males, the total would be 301,775 shekels; there were 3000 shekels in the talent, and the total collected as 100 talents and 1775 shekels is correct; the tradition supports the amount almost unanimously.[5] For the definition of the count of adult males see comment at 30:14. A B *z* reading has changed both τρισχιλίους and πεντακοσίους into the nominative, but this is a thoughtless error due to v.1 and quite wrong here where the accusative is demanded by εἰς.

39:4--5(38:27) The use to which the one hundred talents of silver was put, viz. for casting the capitals of the tent and of the veil." A B + text has repeated ἑκατον before the two cases of "capitals" but there is no basis for these in MT; they are due to the context in which ἑκατόν occurs three times in vv.4 and 5.[6]

Instead of "the tent" MT has הקרש. To Exod τῆς σκηνῆς was more specific than τον αγιον since that could be understood as including the entire complex: tent and courtyard. The 100 capitals are justified if one consults the A account in ch.26. The two long sides had 20 pillars per side with each pillar having two bases/capitals, thus a total of 80 (26:19,21); the rear or west side, had eight pillars of the same type, making 16 more (26:25), and finally (v.32) for the καταπέτασμα there were four pillars which are specifically said to have had both bases and capitals. Thus 80 plus

---

coin attested in various metals already known from classical times.
4 For the καί joining compound numbers see discussion in THGE VII.I.
5 Instead of drachm Aq has δίδραχμον for which see comment at 30:13.

16 plus 4 equals the 100. The other (east) side had five pillars (v.37) but these were gold plated with gold capitals and bronze bases.

It is clear that Exod calls the אדנים of MT κεφαλίδες throughout these two verses. For this odd equation in Part 3 in which κεφαλίδες and βάσεις are used as synonyms for אדנים see the note at 38:20, but see note at v.6.

39:6(38:28) This clever equation on the part of Exod in vv.4--5 does create a problem in v.6. The first part of the verse is clear enough; of the remaining 1775 shekels of silver the ἀγκύλας of the pillars were made.[7] Exod uses the indefinite plural ἐποίησαν for the Hebrew עשה, which an *O C f* text corrects to the singular. For ἀγκύλας rendering ווים see note at 37:15. But in the second part of the verse, where the verbs are again in the singular and refer to Beseleel as subject, ראשיהם occurs; in other words it is clear that the Hebrew differentiates between capitals and bases for the sanctuary, a distinction which Exod consistently denies for the קרש pillar. Exod understood צפה as meaning "goldplating," and so renders the second part of the verse by "and he gilded their capitals and adorned them." In Exod's view the capitals were made of silver and then goldplated!

The second verb, κατεκόσμησεν, also occurs at Isa 61:10 and 1Macc 4:57 in the sense of "adorn, fashion, ornament," but here it renders the Piel of חשק, a hapax legomenon in MT, though the Pual participle does occur twice (27:17 38:17) in the context of the silver adornment (?) of the pillars of the courtyard.

39:7(38:29) The bronze is also called תנופה as in the case of the gold (cf comment at v.1), but it is here rendered by ἀφαιρέματος for which see comment at 35:22. The total amount listed is 70 talents and 2400 shekels which is the same as in MT.[8] The text tradition had a great deal of trouble with these amounts. The amounts given show the amount of bronze to be considerably less than the more expensive silver, and a popular A M variant has added 400 before "70" making 470 talents, but this is probably due to

---

6 Cf also THGE VII.O.
7. According to Syh Aq Sym have κεφαλίδας for ווים, whereas Theod has κόσμους.The retroversion is that of Field.

the influence of the "400 shekels" later in the verse. An *f s* variant makes it 370 talents, a variant of the more popular "470." -- A B *z* text has χιλιοι for Exod's δισχίλιοι, (possibly reading the αι of the KAI before it as ΔI?) and B *f z* read "500" instead of τετρακόσιοι.⁹

39:8--10(38:30--31 39:32a) In v.8 the term βάσεις is used for the doors of the tabernacle, quite properly made of bronze (ἐξ αὐτοῦ) in accordance with 26:37. The verb ἐποίησεν occurs as plural in a majority A F M tradition for which see note on ἐποίησαν in v.6.

Exod orders the list of things made of bronze in vv.9--10 differently. MT has the bases for the court and its gate and the tentpins for tent and courtyard at the end (v.31), whereas Exod begins with these, though it must be said that except for failing to render כל before "tentpins" it renders the list literally. Exod quite correctly again uses βάσεις to render אדני since for the עמוד pillars of the court and its gate capitals and bases are distinguished. An A F *b y z* text confused the matter by having "bases of the σκηνῆς" instead of the αὐλῆς.

V.10 lists three things: the bronze παράθεμα of the altar, all the vessels of the altar, and all the utensils of the tent of testimony. Over against this MT has (in v.30b): the bronze altar, the bronze grating which belongs to it, and all the vessels of the altar. So Exod omitted the first entirely but then was forced to translate אשר לו by τοῦ θυσιαστηρίου; then he added a third one at the end from MT's 39:32, the rendering of which is continued in v.11; cf note on 39:11 below. For παράθεμα see discussion at 38:24. The omission of the bronze altar from MT's list by Exod was probably occasioned by 38:22 where its bronze is described as coming from a different source. For the last item the translator skipped 39:1--31 of MT (already rendered in 36:8--40) and continued with 39:32, but omitted the verb and adapted it to the new context.

39:11(39:32b) Exod renders MT exactly except for כל אשר as καθά. Exod now obviously places the concluding statement here, thereby both closing off a section of the discourse, and tying it to the closing section by the formulaic "as the Lord commanded Moses (so they did);" see vv.22,23

40:14,17,19, 21,23,24. That it is tied to the earlier part of Part 3 is clear from the οὕτως + ἐποίησαν here reflecting the οὗτος + singular aorist found there ten times.

39:12--13(cf 1,41a) This pair of verses serves as transition between what went before and what follows. That a new subject is introduced is clear from the δέ construction with which it begins; cf note at 36:31. V.12 has no counterpart in MT at all and is composed as a parallel to v.13 which seems to reflect parts of vv.1 and 41a of MT.

It is clear that these verses serve to introduce the next section, vv.14--23, which details the bringing of all the things completed to Moses; then ch.40 is to recount the assemblage of the structure, the arrangement of its contents, and its dedication, after which the divine glory enters the tent and the tent takes up its regular position in the life of the community. Both verses mention the purpose of it all as "λειτουργεῖν with them," i.e. with σκεύη and στολάς. Furthermore that next section begins by stating that they brought the στολάς to Moses as well as the tent and its σκεύη.

But what is puzzling is the reference to the λοιπόν gold in v.12 and the καταλειφθεῖσαν textiles in v.13. λοιπόν cannot refer specifically to vv.1--10/11. First of all the gold is defined as in 35:22 as τοῦ ἀφαιρέματος, but in v.1 the gold is called τοῦ τῆς ἀπαρχῆς, and furthermore nothing in vv.1--10/11 is said about items to be made of gold, in contrast to the descriptions of silver and bronze. The reference makes most sense if it is taken to apply to 38:1--19. Similarly the reference in καταλειφθεῖσαν is also not immediately apparent; in fact it contradicts the ordering of Exod B which starts the textile account in 36:8 with a description of the priestly garments (36:8--40), and only then describes the tent and the courtyard, i.e. "the left over" textiles for στολάς only fits as a reference to 37:1--18. The two verses parallel each other in referring to the end of the construction accounts of metalwork and of textiles resp.

Still unclear is what is meant by σκεύη. After all, gold is the one material common to both the textile and the metalwork accounts, and what is probably intended is a cover term for all items not specifically mentioned in the much abbreviated description of metalwork in ch.38.

What must be clearly understood from these two verses is that cultic service is the central motif in these verses. In v.12 the σκεύη are to be "for cultic service with them before the Lord," i.e. in the sanctuary, whereas in v.13 the garments are described as λειτουργικὰς ʾΑαρών, made "so as to perform cultic service with them in the sanctuary.

39:14--21(33--41) An account of the delivery of all the things made to Moses. There are considerable differences in the lists between those of MT and Exod. In comparing the two lists sub-items such as bars, staves, pillars, etc. are omitted. MT's list is as follows: 1. tent; 2. curtains; 3. ark; 4. table; 5. lampstand; 6. the altar of gold; 7. anointing oil; 8. incense compound; 9. covering for the tent door. 10. the altar of bronze; 11. laver; 12. hangings for the court; 13. covering for the courtyard gate; 14. all the vessels for use in the tent; 15. (woven garments for service in the sanctuary) holy garments for Aaron and his sons.

Over against this Exod has: 1. robes; 2. tent; 3. ark; 4. altar; 5. anointing oil; 6. incense compound; 7. lampstand; 8. table; 9. robes for Aaron and his sons; 10. hangings for the court; 11. covering for the tent door; 12. covering for the courtyard gate; 13. all the vessels and utensils of the tent; 14. curtains; 15. tentpins; 16. all the utensils for use in the tent.

It will be noted that nos. 6 and 11 from MT's list are omitted by Exod, and that Exod has expanded the list by nos. 1, 13 and 15; for no. 1 see v.14 below; no.13 is a doublet for no.16, and no.15, though presented as a separate item, καὶ τοὺς πασσάλους, is merely a sub-item under the court in nos.12 and 13 of MT.

But the order of the items is also considerably different. Exod rearranges MT's items as follows (with X for extra items): X 1 3 10 7 8 5 4 15 12 9 13 X 2 X 14. That Exod should have downgraded both the golden altar and the laver though puzzling is not surprising. The former is completely omitted except for mention in 40:5,24, and the laver occurs only in 38:26--27. And as for the rearrangement of items Exod seems to have arranged the items according to a definite plan. If one takes nos.1 and 2 as introductory cover items, the remainder, except for the unexpected tentpins, are arranged according to the divisions already met in Parts 2 and 3, i.e.

between textiles and metalwork. It will be recalled that the oil and the incense were included in Beseleel's particular tasks, and nos.3--8 are all items mentioned in ch.38, whereas nos.9 --14 involving textiles were the responsibility of Eliab in 36:8--37:18.

Exod in contrast to the Hebrew lists all items syndetically; MT introduces many of the items simply with את instead of ואת; occasionally the conjunction is not supported by Sam Tar^P, and the originality of MT may be questioned.

On the other hand the arrangement of MT's list also follows a plan, since it follows almost exactly the order in which MT had presented the account of the construction except that in that account the covering for the tent door (no.9) followed as no.2, a more logical position than that found here. For details see notes on the individual verses below.

39:14(33) Exod begins with τὰς στολάς rather than MT's את המשכן, and as second item has καὶ τὴν σκηνήν for את אהל. Since Exod uses σκηνή for both nouns, either he had to omit one or substitute something else. The choice of στολάς was probably made to tie the preceding section which ended (v.13) with reference to the στολὰς λειτουργικάς. The consecution "robes" and "tent" serves as a kind of superscription for the materials that follow, i.e. the priestly clothing on the one hand, and the tabernacle and its appurtenances, i.e. tent, courtyard, and all their furnishings, on the other.

MT lists five constituent parts of the tent but Exod omits the first two, קרסיו קרשיו, and changes the order of the three that remain as 3 1 2. στύλους is a term that Exod uses both for קרשים and עמדים but here it is probably the latter which Exod intends since אדניו is rendered by τὰς βάσεις, whereas for קרש pillars (vv.4--6) Exod used κεφαλίδας, not βάσεις. σκηνήν is here a cover term including tent and courtyard (which had עמדים rather than קרשים).

39:15(35) Exod omits ואת הכפרת, probably because the propitiatory lay upon the ark and could be thought of as included in "the ark" viewed as a cover term. Note that the word for staves is διωστῆρας as in 38:4,10,11 and recurring in 40:18; cf comment at 38:1--4.[10]

39:16--17(39,38,37) Since Exod does not designate the altar as being either gold or bronze it would seem likely that Exod intended the latter, and this on two grounds. Exod B has throughout not recognized the golden altar (except for 40:5,24), and furthermore "and all its vessels" finds a counterpart in MT not in v.38 but in v.39. Note also that in ch.38 the construction of the bronze altar is immediately followed by the preparation of the oil and incense. The first of these, τὸ ἔλαιον τῆς χρίσεως is also so called in 38:25 but the second item τὸν θυμίαμα τῆς συνθέσεως is inverted; both in 38:25 and in 35:28 it is called τὴν σύνθεσιν τοῦ θυμιάματος, which is a less exact equivalent to קטרת הסמים.

There follow the "pure lampstand" as in 31:8 and its parts. The first and last parts, its lamps and the oil for the light, are obvious, but the middle one, λύχνους τῆς καύσεως, is puzzling, since in its place MT has "the lamps of המערכה and all its (i.e. the lampstand's) vessels." The Hebrew word refers to the arrangement or setting of the lamps, but occurs only here in the Pentateuch. The synonym מערכת does occur twice (Lev 24:6--7), but for the arrangement of the twelve cakes on the table. That the lamps should be for burning is stated in 27:20--21, and Exod B does at times add the cultic use to which an object is put over against MT.

39:18(36) The table and the show bread. The table is modified by τῆς προθέσεως, i.e. of the presentation; probably what is meant is similar to τὴν προκειμένην of 38:9 which see. What is presented is the ἄρτους τοὺς προκειμένους "the bread which is set before," which can best be understood in the light of the ἄρτους ἐνωπίους ἐναντίον μου of 25:29 which see. πρόθεσιν also occurs as a cognate accusative in 40:4 which explains more fully what the "setting forth" meant; cf note. That προθέσεως and προκειμένους could be used interchangeably is clear from the popular F variant, της προθεσεως, with no change in meaning.

The word order πάντα αὐτῆς τὰ σκεύη is unexpected, and a B *f* variant places αὐτῆς after τά (another variant text placing it after σκεύη is hex). The order of Exod seems preferable to that of the B + order since

8 For the καί joining compound numbers in ch.39 see comment in THGE VII.I.

stylistically τά immediately after πάντα is inelegant; furthermore Exod's order has very strong textual support.[11]

39:19(41b; par 31:10b) For Exod's use of v.41a of MT see comment at vv.12--13. Here only the second part of the verse is rendered. The robes of the sanctuary are specifically identified as "those which belong to Aaron"; they are the high priestly robes, whereas the robes of his sons are simply defined as εἰς τὴν ἱερατείαν. As in the par passage הכהן is not translated, but that passage is rendered quite differently from this one and can hardly be said to have influenced Exod. And elsewhere Exod B does recognize the designation (37:19, and comp 35:19).

39:20--21(40,34) For the court are listed the hangings, the pillars, and its bases. αὐτῆς applies to the court and not to the pillars as might have been expected; cf 37:7--18. That Exod should use βάσεις here accords with his understanding that for the pillars of the court only this term (and not κεφαλίδας) is valid. The B *n* + text omits the reference to βάσεις entirely but this omission is due to homoiot (note the repetition of ואת) and should not be taken seriously.

καταπέτασμα is modified both by "of the tent door" and by "of the gate of the court;" MT only has the latter here, but it had the former separately listed at v.38b; cf discussion at vv.14--21 above.

Verse 21a seems to reflect MT's v.40b, though Exod uses a single σκηνῆς for both tabernacle and tent. But immediately before it MT has את מיתריו ויתדתיו "its cords and its tentpins," which was disregarded here but at the end of the verse "and the tentpins and all the utensils which were for the works of the tent of testimony," occurs as a doublet of v.21a.

But between these doublets Exod has a rendering of v.34 of MT. Exod elsewhere always renders the Hebrew מכסה (26:14 35:10 40:17) by κάλυμμα or by its compound, and he uses this here for the "blue coverings" as well; for the coverings dyed red, however, he has διφθέρας "leather, hide," which is then defined by an appositional modifier δέρματα κριῶν;[12]

---

9 For their secondary nature see the discussion in THGE VII.I.
10 The Later Revisers have ἀναφορεῖς.
11 Cf also the note in THGE VII.F.2.

642

the word occurs only here in LXX.[13] For ὑακίνθινα as a rendering for
תחשים as well as for ἠροθροδανωμένα see note at 25:5. -- The remaining
phrase, καὶ τῶν λοιπῶν τὰ ἐπικαλύμματα, has no equivalent in MT at all,
but is a cover term for all other coverings not specifically included in the
two skin coverings already mentioned. τῶν λοιπῶν was probably triggered
by the otherwise untranslated מיתריו understood as "from the remainders
of it," and τὰ ἐπικαλύμματα was simply supplied from the context.

39:22(42) The introductory ככל אשר is simplified as ὅσα in Exod, and for
the rest Exod follows MT word for word even to the extent of rendering את
before "Moses" by τῷ. Since Μωυσῇ is inflected the article serves no useful
purpose and B + have omitted it. -- What the Israelites did was (τὴν) παρασκευήν which only occurs here in Exod. A popular M variant has the
synonym κατασκευην; this does occur elsewhere in Exod (27:19 35:24 36:7),
but Exod commands strong textual support.[14]

39:23(43) A second concluding statement in part repeating what was said in
v.22, but here in the context of Moses' reception, approval and blessing.
      The syntax of the verse is peculiarly Hebraic. The first clause is clear
enough, but for the paratactic הנה clause of MT which follows Exod has καὶ
ἦσαν πεποιηκότες αὐτά (i.e. the ἔργα); the periphrastic use of the imperfect ἦσαν + perfect participle is very common in Hellenistic Greek as a
substitute for the pluperfect,[15] though infrequent in Exod (12:30 32:15
34:30). In the ὃν τρόπον clause which follows, τῷ Μωυσῇ has no
counterpart in MT, but Exod followed the pattern of v.22. Similarly the unnecessary αὐτά as object of ἐποίησαν is a plus, again following the pattern
of v.22 where πᾶσαν τὴν παρασκευήν occurs as object of (οὕτως
ἐποίησαν).
      The account ends with the fitting benediction: "and Moses blessed
them." The pronoun refers to the Israelites, not as some C mss have it
(αυτα) to the ἔργα.

---

12 Cf SS 67.
13 Though it does occur at Zach 5:1 where Aq and Theod translate מגלה
by διφθέρα. For ἠροθροδανωμένα Aq has πεπυρρωμένα.
14 Cf discussion in THGE VII.Q.
15. See Bl-Debr 352--356, especially 352.2.

Chapter 40

40:2 Exod correctly identifies the dating formula בַיוֹם הַחֹדֶשׁ by ἐν ἡμέρᾳ μιᾷ τοῦ μηνός, i.e. "on day one (of the month)," in turn identified as νουμηνίᾳ which in turn translates בְּאֶחָד לַחֹדֶשׁ;[1] comp v.15. As usual when both מִשְׁכָּן and אֹהֶל occur together only one τὴν σκηνήν is used; cf comments at 26:7--13 35:10. Since these are now divine instructions to Moses the verbs in vv.2--13 are all in the future.

40:3 As the most important piece of furniture the ark is placed in position first, and then as Exod puts it: "you shall cover (or protect) the ark with the veil" (a dative of means). For κιβωτὸν τοῦ μαρτυρίου see note at 25:9. Exod has omitted the Hebrew שָׁם as otiose, but the Later Revisers have added ἐκεῖ after θήσεις.

40:4 The four clauses of this verse divide into two pairs dealing resp. with the bringing in of the table and the lampstand. With respect to the table Moses is ordered προθήσεις τὴν πρόθεσιν αὐτῆς "you shall set forth its presentation." For πρόθεσιν as defining the table see comment at 39:18. To "set forth the presentation" (of the table) means to put the bread of the presence in its place on the table, as v.21 where the order is carried out makes clear.

For the lampstand a special order is also given: "and ἐπιθήσεις its lamps"; the compound verb is used without a prepositional phrase to show where the lamps are to be placed upon. This too is carried out in the same terms in v.23 except for the addition there of "before the Lord.

40:5 The placement of the golden altar for burning incense before the ark. Up to this point Exod B has rigidly excluded all reference to the incense altar, insisting throughout on τὸ θυσιαστήριον only (cf comment at 35:17), but in the assemblage and erection account it is mentioned both here and in v.24. It is golden because it is set before the ark, i.e. in the adyton. Omitted

1. Cf SS 109.

as repetitive of v.3 is the designation of the ark as του μαρτυριου as the majority A F M reading has it.

In the second clause the verb is ἐπιθήσεις (for שמת) though the A F M majority text attests the simplex, which is found in v.24, but here the verb is modified by an ἐπί phrase in contrast to v.24 where an ἐν phrase is used. -- A B f variant has removed both articles from τὸ κάλυμμα τοῦ καταπε- τάσματος, but this is quite at variance with the nature of the account in which all the furnishings of the tent are articulated.[2] The phrase is an amplification of MT's אֵת מסך, and looks like a doublet translation, but this "covering" is also called "the veil," and here it hides both ark and incense altar, and so the double name is used; comp also v.24 where only καταπετάσματος occurs.[3] -- A C s text has εις instead of ἐπί but in view of the verb it modifies being an ἐπί compound it is obviously secondary.

40:6(6,8a) מזבח העלה is rendered by τὸ θυσιαστήριον τῶν καρπωμάτων. κάρπωμα is often used for any kind of sacrifice; see note at 29:25. It is used at 30:9 to designate an עלה over against θυσίαν, i.e. a burnt offering vs a cereal offering. But here it is used in the plural to describe the (bronze) altar in contrast to the golden altar which was for burning incense (v.5). One might have expected ὁλοκαυτωμάτων as at 30:28, but in this chapter "altar of sacrifices" is used; see also vv.8,26. This altar is to be set near or alongside the doors of the tent of testimony. As in v.2 τῆς σκηνῆς suffices for the double מֹשכן אֹהל; see notes at 26:7--13 35:10. The majority A F M reading of the singular την θυραν comes from v.5.

The Hebrew v.7 deals with the laver and is omitted as is all reference to the laver, its placement or use in this chapter; cf comment at 38:27. Exod then translates only v.8a, omitting 8b altogether. The use of περιθήσεις was conditioned by the סביב and presumably it refers to the relation of the court to the tent. In fact, a popular B variant text not only changes αὐλήν to σκηνην but also adds "and all the things of it you shall sanctify"; its source is quite obvious; it comes from v.7.

2. Cf also the comment in THGE VII.D.5.
3. Aq Sym translate the term by τὸ παρατάνυσμα for which see comment at 27:16; Theod has τὸ ἐπίσπαστρον; cf 26:36. For ἐπὶ τὴν θύραν The Three also have different renderings. Theod simply has τῆς θύρας, whereas Aq has τοῦ ἀνοίγματος "opening" and Sym has τῆς πύλης.

40:7(9) Moses is told to take anointing oil and anoint the tent and its contents; this is followed paratactically by "and you shall sanctify it and all its vessels and it shall be holy," in imitation of Hebrew syntax. But anointing and sanctifying are hardly two separate actions; the sanctifying is rather the result of the anointing. This is obviously the case with the final clause as well, i.e. "so that it will be holy."

The oil is defined as τοῦ χρίσματος for which an A *b* reading has της χρισεως, which is a synonym and actually more popular in Exod A (29:21 30:31 31:11 vs 29:7), but in B they occur with equal frequency (see 35:14,19,28 38:25 39:16).

40:8--9(10) Separately mentioned for anointment and sanctification is the altar of offerings, for which see comment on v.6. The verses are constructed as a parallel to v.7 with its χρίσεις ... καὶ ἁγιάσεις ... καὶ ἔσται. In distinction from v.7, however, the resultant holiness of the altar and its vessels is expressed by the superlative expression ἅγιον τῶν ἁγίων. Presumably the altar is to be in that state because it is the central place for cultic service, that of sacrifice. Hex adds a translation of the Hebrew v.11 at the end; it was lacking in Exod since all references to the laver are consistently omitted in Part 4 in Exod.

40:10--13(12--15) Before Aaron and his sons are robed and ordained to service Moses is to wash them; cf also 38:27. This requirement makes the absence of all reference to the laver odd indeed, since it is clearly presupposed.

Aaron is to be clothed with τὰς στολὰς τὰς ἁγίας whose manufacture had been detailed at the beginning of Part 2. MT rather calls them בגדי הקדש "the garments of the sanctuary." These "holy garments" are distinct from the χιτῶνας with which the sons were clothed. Only for Aaron is it said "and you shall sanctify him." In v.13 a different verb for "anoint" is used. In fact ἀλείφω is used to render משח only here and at Gen 31:13 Num 3:3 in LXX. Exod always uses χρίω elsewhere to translate משח. ἀλείφω is a synonym, and is used here simply for variety's sake.

646

The final statement begins with והיתה להית which Exod renders literally by καὶ ἔσται ὥστε εἶναι (αὐτοῖς χρῖσμα) "and it shall happen so that they might have an anointing."[4] The collocation משחתם לכהנת is idiomatically rendered as χρῖσμα ἱερατείας. -- What is expressed is that the anointing to the priesthood is a lifetime consecration and will continue in subsequent generations as well; it is both εἰς τὸν αἰῶνα and εἰς τὰς γενεὰς αὐτῶν.

40:14(16) Most unusual is the use of ἐνετείλατο for צוה in the formulaic clause: as/which + "commanded" + [divine subject + dative of person] or [dative + divine subject]; in fact, it occurs only here in Exod B in contrast with the verb συντάσσω which occurs 23 times. But in Exod 1--34 ἐντέλλομαι occurs in such an environment 17 times, and συντάσσω only eight times. That Exod B must have been influenced here by A seems most likely. -- A majority A F M text actually has συνεταξεν here, but the (for Exod B) unusual verb is to be preferred, since a change to ενετειλατο in the tradition would be difficult to explain. -- As at 39:22 Exod has not translated the preposition in ככל using simply πάντα rather than κατα παντα.

40:15(17) The actual erection of the tabernacle and the placement of its furnishings begin with a date formula based on the Israelites' exodus from Egypt. As in v.2 it is the first day of the new year, though its tautology ἐν ἡμέρᾳ μιᾷ ... νουμηνίᾳ is avoided by using only the latter. V.15, however, adds τῷ δευτέρῳ ἔτει following MT, and with Sam amplifies this by ἐκπορευομένων αὐτῶν ἐξ Αἰγύπτου. The addition of the participial construction is easily comprehensible, since a date "in the second year" inevitably asks: the second year of what? The Byzantine text adds εν before τῷ, and C reads a simplex participle, and along with s has εκ γης for ἐξ, none of these significantly changing the meaning.

The date is that in which "the tabernacle was set up," but it is presupposed that it also governs the actions paratactically presented as the works of Moses through v.27.

40:16(18) Moses is now introduced as the subject and the preceding passive statement is then transformed into its active counterpart; cf comment on v.15. MT continues with four clauses, whereas Exod has only three. MT has: "and he put up (ויתן) its bases, and placed (וישם) its קרשי, and put up its bars, and set up its עמודי." To Exod קרשים and עמודים were both στῦλοι, the former with an ארן on either end and which he translated by κεφαλίς (cf comment at 38:20), and the latter with capital and base, i.e. with κεφαλίς and βάσις. Exod solves the dilemma created by the presence of קרשיו and עמודיו by omitting the clause containing the former but interpreting the ארניו of the first clause as referring to the omitted קרשיו, i.e. he renders it by τὰς κεφαλίδας. He is then free to render עמודיו by τοὺς στύλους. Origen did not understand Exod at all. He thought that the first clause with τὰς κεφαλίδας represented the one with קרשיו, and so he added in first place a translation of the ארניו clause: και εθηκεν τας βασεις αυτης.

The use of verbs is idiomatic. For the κεφαλίδας he used ἐπέθηκεν, but for the μοχλούς he has διενέβαλεν. This shows intimate acquaintance with the function of the bars as described in 26:26--29, especially with the δακτυλίους into which εἰσάξεις the bars in v.29.

40:17(19) Exod neatly dodged the issue of the relation of אהל to משכן in this verse; in MT Moses stretched out the אהל over the tabernacle, but stretching out σκηνήν over σκηνήν would not make much sense, so he uses αὐλαίας instead of אהל. So the picture emerges of Moses taking the sewn-together curtains and stretching them out over the στύλους (i.e. of the קרש type).

The second clause is parallel to the first. What Moses does is to "put the κατακάλυμμα of the tent ἐπ' αὐτὴν ἄνωθεν," i.e. over it above. Since this is the κατακάλυμμα it may well refer to the σκέπην ἐπὶ τῆς σκηνῆς of 26:7, i.e. the outside set of curtains of skins which according to the instructions given in ch.26 was to cover over the inside αὐλαίας. At least that is what συνέταξεν κύριος τῷ Μωυσῇ.

---

4. Cf SS 95.

40:18--19(20--21) The pattern of the subordinate participle λαβών + a finite verb to render וירק + a coordinate verb occurs only here in Exod B, though it was common in chh.1--34, and it is certainly appropriate here. For "the testimonies" as reference to the Ten Words of ch.20 see comment at 25:15.

For the placement of the staves the unusual collocation ὑπέθηκεν ... ὑπὸ (τὴν κιβωτόν) is used, i.e. "he placed them beneath under the ark." It also occurs in Exod at 27:5 (and elsewhere in the Pentateuch only in Gen 47:29). This can make sense in the light of Exod's omission of the third clause and its reference to the propitiatory which lay on top of the ark. The parallel to 27:5 helps to interpret its meaning here. There rings were to be "under the hearth of the altar below"; so here the propitiatory being part of the ark, i.e. lying on top of it, the translator could understand the ὑπό as being not under the ark but under the upper constituent element of the ark; cf comment at 27:5, and for the similar omission of "the propitiatory" see comment at 39:15. The A C text replaces the unusual verb by the more common επεθηκεν but did not revise ὑπό to επι as might then be expected.

V.19 then describes the placement of the ark within the tabernacle in a protected context; cf comment at 26:34. The phrase פרכת המסך "the veil of the covering" also occurs at 35:12 and 38:34; cf comment at 35:11 on τὸ καταπέτασμα. Exod does render both words but apparently has inverted the nouns in his τὸ κατακάλυμμα τοῦ καταπετάσματος. It is this "covering of the veil" which "covered (or protected) the ark of the testimony." It would seem then that "covering of the veil" is simply a fuller version of "the veil," whereas a literal rendering of the Hebrew by which the two nouns would be transposed would be misleading, and is actually never used by Exod. -- The ὃν τρόπον clause is a reference to v.3.

40:20--21(22--23) The table is put inside the tabernacle on the north side in the holy place outside the veil of the tent, i.e. outside the adytum; cf comment on 26:35. MT simply has "outside the veil" and Exod's more careful definition makes it assured that the wrong καταπέτασμα is avoided; the veil of the tent is the one that separates the interior of the adytum from the holy place. A popular A tradition omits the τό introducing "towards the north," but this does not change the sense.

The cognate collocation προέθηκεν ... (ἄρτους) τῆς προθέσεως, "set forth ... bread of the setting forth," is best understood in the light of the ἔναντι κυρίου which follows; the bread is defined as the setting out before the Lord. The term "bread of the presentation" inverts the members of MT's bound phrase הלחם ערך "the arrangement of the bread (before Yahweh)." The accent in Exod is somewhat different in that the cultic nature of the action is more central; the bread is set before the Lord; it is presented as a continual offering to the Lord. All this was in accordance with the Lord's command to Moses in v.3.

A popular A variant has προσεθηκεν, obviously the result of a copyist's error since the noun προθέσεως remains unchanged. In fact that Moses "added" upon it the bread is strange indeed. -- The articulation of ἄρτους by ƒ + is in contrast quite sensible since all the other objects set or placed, etc. in the account are articulated and only the paucity of support deterred one from accepting this variant as original text. -- And a popular A F reading has εναντιον for ἔναντι. But the phrase ἔναντι κυρίου is a favoured phrase in Exod beginning with ch.27. It occurs 20 times whereas ἐναντίον κυρίου occurs only four times.[5]

40:22--23(24--25) The placement of the lampstand and its lamps parallels that of the table, but it is on the south side; that it too was outside the veil of the tent is not stated since that must be obvious in view of the placement of the table in v.20; this would have been ever more obvious if Exod had also rendered השלחן נכח.

V.23 takes up the language of v.4b where Moses is ordered ἐπιθήσεις τοὺς λύχνους αὐτῆς with no indication where they are to be placed. Here the same verb (in the aorist) is used with the same modifier but to it is added ἔναντι κυρίου which gives the "putting up" cultic meaning. For the popular εναντιον κυ see comment on vv.20--21. -- A C ƒ s text reads the simplex form of the verb as e.g. in vv.22 and 24.

---

5. For a fuller discussion see THGE VII.L.3.

40:24--25(26--27) The golden altar is placed ἀπέναντι the veil, which contrasts with the placement of the table in v.20 ἔξωθεν the veil; i.e. the golden altar (along with the ark) was inside the adytum.

The phrase קטרת הסמים when translated always involves the two nominals θυμίαμα and σύνθεσις except for 35:14 where only τὸ θυμίαμα obtains; twice, however, they are in reverse order, τὴν σύνθεσιν τοῦ θυμιάματος (35:28 38:25). More commonly the Hebrew order is followed (30:7 31:11 39:16) as here. The term for "incense" is cognate to the verb "offered" both in MT and in Exod. That Moses did the offering accords with the purposive εἰς τὸ θυμιᾶν ἐναντίον τῆς κιβωτοῦ in the Lord's command to Moses in v.5 to which the καθάπερ clause alludes.

A popular A F M reading omitted the article before θυμίαμα. Wherever the phrase occurs either both nominals are unarticulated as in 30:7 θυμίαμα σύνθετον or (as in all other instances) both elements are articulated. The omission of τό may have been a partial haplography (after αὐτοῦ). Another copyist's error is that of the d text which reads συνεσεως for συνθέσεως; just what the incense of union, understanding or conscience was supposed to mean to a reader is obscure.

40:26(29) Exod has omitted the reference to the setting up the covering of the door of the tabernacle, v.28 in MT, as well as all reference to the placement and use of the laver in vv.30--32 in MT which has been transferred to the end of ch.38; see note at 38:27. Furthermore for v.29 he translated only the first part omitting MT's "and he offered on it (the altar) the holocaust and the cereal offering as the Lord had commanded Moses." All that remains is "and the altar of the offerings he set besides the doors of the tent," also omitting אהל מועד which followed on "tent." This is a carrying out of the order contained in v.6a. For the use of τῶν καρπωμάτων to render העלה see comment at v.6.

40:27(33) The first clause helps to explain the rather cryptic v.6b. Here we are told that the court was set round about the tent (i.e. the משכן) and the altar (i.e. the altar of the offerings). A well-supported d variant omits the "and," and makes the court set round about the tent of the altar. This obviously wrong text changes the reference of θυσιαστηριου, since the "tent" contained the golden altar, not the altar of offerings.

Exod omits MT's middle clause "and he set up the covering of the gate of the court," proceeding immediately to the concluding statement of the account in vv.15--27: "and Moses finished all the works"; MT (along with Tar Pesh) has no "all."

40:28(34) The Lord now takes up his dwelling in the finished tabernacle in fulfillment of his promise in 29:43--46. The cloud as the visible token of his presence covered the tabernacle: "the tent was filled with the glory of the Lord." A popular variant changed the verb to an active one so as to agree with MT. δόξης κυρίου should be taken as a subjective genitive phrase in the sense of the splendor which the deity shows as a revelatory presence; cf comment at 29:43.

40:29(35) For the double augment for the aorist ἠδυνήθη see comment at 12:39; the variant aorist inflection, ηδυνασθη, attested by B +, is equally classically attested.[6] In the presence of the divine glory Moses was unable to enter the tent. In fact, the verse in the ὅτι double clause gives v.28 as the reason, i.e. the cloud overshadowed it[7] and the tent was filled with the divine glory. For the last clause see discussion at v.28, where exactly the same clause also obtains.

40:30--31(36--37) The movement of the cloud as the symbol of the Lord's presence gave notice to the encampment to move. When it would rise (ἀνέβη) from the tent the Israelites would move on; conversely if it failed to rise they would remain. The point of this is fully clear; the Lord himself directed the wilderness journey; his presence alone was to determine Israel's actions.

MT uses a prepositional phrase with a noun cognate to the verb: בכל מסעיהם. Exod uses a good translation for the verb יסע - ἀνεζεύγνυσαν, but instead of using a cognate noun to render the phrase he has σὺν τῇ

6.See note at THGE VII.M.8 for a discussion of the matter. The B inflection was also read by Theod, whereas Sym and Aq have the imperfect ἠδύνατο.

ἀπαρτίᾳ αὐτῶν "with their household goods," and substitutes a contextually suitable noun for מַעַי. That Exod knew perfectly well what he was doing is clear from v.32 where exactly the same phrase occurs but is literally rendered by ἐν πάσαις ταῖς ἀναζυγαῖς αὐτῶν. There the literal rendering was fitting since the cognate verb is lacking.

40:32(38) The pattern of cloud being on the tent by day and fire by night as symbol of the continual divine presence is known elsewhere; cf especially the discussion at 13:21 where the phenomena are used for God to show them the way. The cloud is identified in MT as the ענן יהוה but Exod considered the cloud sufficiently identified and simply has νεφέλη; it is left unarticulated to correspond to πῦρ. Similarly Exod supplies an ἦν to serve as predicate in the first clause to parallel the second, whereas in MT the first clause is a nominal one and the second a verbal one with תהיה, an imperfect to show that this was a regular practice. Exod has ἐπ' αὐτῆς standing before νυκτός as in Sam Pesh, which hex transposes to fit MT. A *C* variant has επ αυτην, which is not as appropriate here since the phrase shows location not movement towards or upon; furthermore in the parallel clause "upon the tent" is also ἐπί with the genitive.

In contrast to v.30 מסעיהם is literally rendered by ταῖς ἀναζυγαῖς αὐτῶν; the symbols of the divine presence were determinative for Israel's journeyings through the desert. It is fitting that the accounts of the tabernacle's construction should end with the symbols of God's presence resting on Israel's cultic center, which after all is what the tabernacle and its furnishings were all about.

---

7. Cf Helbing 284.

Index of Greek Words and Phrases

654

658

660

670

678

ROBERT A. KRAFT (editor)
Septuagintal Lexicography (1975)
Code: 06 04 01
Not Available

ROBERT A KRAFT (editor)
1972 Proceedings: Septuagint and Pseudepigrapha Seminars (1973)
Code: 06 04 02
Not Available

RAYMOND A. MARTIN
Syntactical Evidence of Semitic Studies in Greek Documents (1974)
Code: 06 04 03
Not Available

GEORGE W. E. NICKELSBURG, JR. (editor)
Studies on the *Testament of Moses* (1973)
Code: 06 04 04
Not Available

GEORGE W.E. NICKELSBURG, JR. (editor)
Studies on the *Testament of Joseph* (1975)
Code: 06 04 05
Not Available

GEORGE W.E. NICKELSBURG, JR. (editor)
Studies on the *Testament of Abraham* (1976)
Code: 06 04 06

JAMES H. CHARLESWORTH
Pseudepigrapha and Modern Research (1976)
Code: 06 04 07
Not Available

JAMES H. CHARLESWORTH
Pseudepigrapha and Modern Research with a Supplement (1981)
Code: 06 04 07 S

JOHN W. OLLEY
"Righteousness" in the Septuagint of Isaiah: A Contextual Study (1979)
Code: 06 04 08

MELVIN K. H. PETERS
An Analysis of the Textual Character of the Bohairic of Deuteronomy (1980)
Code: 06 04 09
Not Available

DAVID G. BURKE
The Poetry of Baruch (1982)
Code: 06 04 10

JOSEPH L. TRAFTON
Syriac Version of the Psalms of Solomon (1985)
Code: 06 04 11

JOHN COLLINS, GEORGE NICKELSBURG
Ideal Figures in Ancient Judaism: Profiles and Paradigms (1980)
Code: 06 04 12

ROBERT HANN
The Manuscript History of the Psalms of Solomon (1982)
Code: 06 04 13

J.A.L. LEE
A Lexical Study of the Septuagint Version of the Pentateuch (1983)
Code: 06 04 14

MELVIN K. H. PETERS
A Critical Edition of the Coptic (Bohairic) Pentateuch
Vol. 5: Deuteronomy (1983)
Code: 06 04 15

T. MURAOKA
A Greek-Hebrew/Aramaic Index to I Esdras (1984)
Code: 06 04 16

JOHN RUSSIANO MILES
Retroversion and Text Criticism:
The Predictability of Syntax in An Ancient Translation
from Greek to Ethiopic (1985)
Code: 06 04 17

 LESLIE J. MCGREGOR
The Greek Text of Ezekiel (1985)
Code: 06 04 18

MELVIN K.H. PETERS
A Critical Edition of the Coptic (Bohairic) Pentateuch,
Vol. 1: Genesis (1985)
Code: 06 04 19

ROBERT A. KRAFT AND EMANUEL TOV (project directors)
Computer Assisted Tools for Septuagint Studies
Vol 1: Ruth (1986)
Code: 06 04 20

CLAUDE E. COX
Hexaplaric Materials Preserved in the Armenian Version (1986)
Code: 06 04 21

MELVIN K.H. PETERS
A Critical Edition of the Coptic (Bohairic) Pentateuch
Vol. 2: Exodus (1986)
Code: 06 04 22

(Continued on previous page)

CLAUDE E. COX (editor)
VI Congress of the International Organization for Septuagint
and Cognate Studies: Jerusalem 1986
Code: 06 04 23

JOHN KAMPEN
The Hasideans and the Origin of Pharisaism:
A Study of 1 and 2 Maccabees
Code: 06 04 24

BENJAMIN WRIGHT
No Small Difference:
Sirach's Relationship to Its Hebrew Parent Text
Code: 06 04 26

JOHN WILLIAM WEVERS
Notes on the Greek Text of Exodus
Code: 06 04 30

Order from:

Scholars Press Customer Services
P.O. Box 6525
Ithaca, NY 14851
1-800-666-2211